**41:** *Afro-American Poets Since 1955,* edited by Trudier Harris and Thadious M. Davis (1985)

**42:** *American Writers for Children Before 1900,* edited by Glenn E. Estes (1985)

**43:** *American Newspaper Journalists, 1690-1872,* edited by Perry J. Ashley (1986)

**44:** *American Screenwriters,* Second Series, edited by Randall Clark, Robert E. Morsberger, and Stephen O. Lesser (1986)

**45:** *American Poets, 1880-1945,* First Series, edited by Peter Quartermain (1986)

**46:** *American Literary Publishing Houses, 1900-1980: Trade and Paperback,* edited by Peter Dzwonkoski (1986)

**47:** *American Historians, 1866-1912,* edited by Clyde N. Wilson (1986)

**48:** *American Poets, 1880-1945,* Second Series, edited by Peter Quartermain (1986)

**49:** *American Literary Publishing Houses, 1638-1899,* 2 parts, edited by Peter Dzwonkoski (1986)

**50:** *Afro-American Writers Before the Harlem Renaissance,* edited by Trudier Harris (1986)

**51:** *Afro-American Writers from the Harlem Renaissance to 1940,* edited by Trudier Harris (1987)

**52:** *American Writers for Children Since 1960: Fiction,* edited by Glenn E. Estes (1986)

**53:** *Canadian Writers Since 1960,* First Series, edited by W. H. New (1986)

**54:** *American Poets, 1880-1945,* Third Series, 2 parts, edited by Peter Quartermain (1987)

**55:** *Victorian Prose Writers Before 1867,* edited by William B. Thesing (1987)

**56:** *German Fiction Writers, 1914-1945,* edited by James Hardin (1987)

**57:** *Victorian Prose Writers After 1867,* edited by William B. Thesing (1987)

**58:** *Jacobean and Caroline Dramatists,* edited by Fredson Bowers (1987)

**59:** *American Literary Critics and Scholars, 1800-1850,* edited by John W. Rathbun and Monica M. Grecu (1987)

**60:** *Canadian Writers Since 1960,* Second Series, edited by W. H. New (1987)

**61:** *American Writers for Children Since 1960: Poets, Illustrators, and Nonfiction Authors,* edited by Glenn E. Estes (1987)

**62:** *Elizabethan Dramatists,* edited by Fredson Bowers (1987)

**63:** *Modern American Critics, 1920-1955,* edited by Gregory S. Jay (1988)

**64:** *American Literary Critics and Scholars, 1850-1880,* edited by John W. Rathbun and Monica M. Grecu (1988)

**65:** *French Novelists, 1900-1930,* edited by Catharine Savage Brosman (1988)

**66:** *German Fiction Writers, 1885-1913,* 2 parts, edited by James Hardin (1988)

**67:** *Modern American Critics Since 1955,* edited by Gregory S. Jay (1988)

**68:** *Canadian Writers, 1920-1959,* First Series, edited by W. H. New (1988)

**69:** *Contemporary German Fiction Writers,* First Series, edited by Wolfgang D. Elfe and James Hardin (1988)

**70:** *British Mystery Writers, 1860-1919,* edited by Bernard Benstock and Thomas F. Staley (1988)

**71:** *American Literary Critics and Scholars, 1880-1900,* edited by John W. Rathbun and Monica M. Grecu (1988)

**72:** *French Novelists, 1930-1960,* edited by Catharine Savage Brosman (1988)

**73:** *American Magazine Journalists, 1741-1850,* edited by Sam G. Riley (1988)

**74:** *American Short-Story Writers Before 1880,* edited by Bobby Ellen Kimbel, with the assistance of William E. Grant (1988)

**75:** *Contemporary German Fiction Writers,* Second Series, edited by Wolfgang D. Elfe and James Hardin (1988)

**76:** *Afro-American Writers, 1940-1955,* edited by Trudier Harris (1988)

**77:** *British Mystery Writers, 1920-1939,* edited by Bernard Benstock and Thomas F. Staley (1988)

**78:** *American Short-Story Writers, 1880-1910,* edited by Bobby Ellen Kimbel, with the assistance of William E. Grant (1988)

**79:** *American Magazine Journalists, 1850-1900,* edited by Sam G. Riley (1988)



**(Continued on back endsheets)**

Dictionary of Literary Biography • Volume One Hundred Seven

# British Romantic Prose Writers, 1789-1832

## First Series

Dictionary of Literary Biography • Volume One Hundred Seven

# British Romantic Prose Writers, 1789-1832
## First Series

Edited by
John R. Greenfield
*McKendree College*



A Bruccoli Clark Layman Book
Gale Research Inc.
Detroit, London

Matthew J. Bruccoli and Richard Layman, *Editorial Directors*
C. E. Frazer Clark, Jr., *Managing Editor*

Printed in the United States of America

Published simultaneously in the United Kingdom
by Gale Research International Limited
(An affiliated company of Gale Research Inc.)

The paper used in this publication meets the minimum requirements of American National Standard for Information Sciences—Permanence Paper for Printed Library Materials, ANSI Z39.48-1984. ™



ISBN 0-8103-4587-0
91-1369 CIP

For My Parents with Love

# Contents

# Plan of the Series

*. . . Almost the most prodigious asset of a country, and perhaps its most precious possession, is its native literary product–when that product is fine and noble and enduring.*

Mark Twain*

The advisory board, the editors, and the publisher of the *Dictionary of Literary Biography* are joined in endorsing Mark Twain's declaration. The literature of a nation provides an inexhaustible resource of permanent worth. We intend to make literature and its creators better understood and more accessible to students and the reading public, while satisfying the standards of teachers and scholars.

To meet these requirements, *literary biography* has been construed in terms of the author's achievement. The most important thing about a writer is his writing. Accordingly, the entries in *DLB* are career biographies, tracing the development of the author's canon and the evolution of his reputation.

The purpose of *DLB* is not only to provide reliable information in a convenient format but also to place the figures in the larger perspective of literary history and to offer appraisals of their accomplishments by qualified scholars.

The publication plan for *DLB* resulted from two years of preparation. The project was proposed to Bruccoli Clark by Frederick G. Ruffner, president of the Gale Research Company, in November 1975. After specimen entries were prepared and typeset, an advisory board was formed to refine the entry format and develop the series rationale. In meetings held during 1976, the publisher, series editors, and advisory board approved the scheme for a comprehensive biographical dictionary of persons who contributed to North American literature. Editorial work on the first volume began in January 1977, and it was published in 1978. In order to make *DLB* more than a reference tool and to compile volumes that individually have claim to status as literary history, it was decided to organize volumes by topic, period, or genre. Each of these freestanding volumes provides a biographical-bibliographical guide and overview for a particular area of literature. We are convinced that this organization–as opposed to a single alphabet method–constitutes a valuable innovation in the presentation of reference material. The volume plan necessarily requires many decisions for the placement and treatment of authors who might properly be included in two or three volumes. In some instances a major figure will be included in separate volumes, but with different entries emphasizing the aspect of his career appropriate to each volume. Ernest Hemingway, for example, is represented in *American Writers in Paris, 1920-1939* by an entry focusing on his expatriate apprenticeship; he is also in *American Novelists, 1910-1945* with an entry surveying his entire career. Each volume includes a cumulative index of subject authors and articles. Comprehensive indexes to the entire series are planned.

With volume ten in 1982 it was decided to enlarge the scope of *DLB*. By the end of 1986 twenty-one volumes treating British literature had been published, and volumes for Commonwealth and Modern European literature were in progress. The series has been further augmented by the *DLB Yearbooks* (since 1981) which update published entries and add new entries to keep the *DLB* current with contemporary activity. There have also been *DLB Documentary Series* volumes which provide biographical and critical source materials for figures whose work is judged to have particular interest for students. One of these companion volumes is entirely devoted to Tennessee Williams.

We define literature as the *intellectual commerce of a nation:* not merely as belles lettres but as that ample and complex process by which ideas are generated, shaped, and transmitted. *DLB* entries are not limited to "creative writers" but extend to other figures who in their time and in their way influenced the mind of a people. Thus the series encompasses historians, journalists, publishers, and screenwriters. By this means readers of *DLB* may be aided to perceive litera-

*From an unpublished section of Mark Twain's autobiography, copyright © by the Mark Twain Company.

ture not as cult scripture in the keeping of intellectual high priests but firmly positioned at the center of a nation's life.

*DLB* includes the major writers appropriate to each volume and those standing in the ranks immediately behind them. Scholarly and critical counsel has been sought in deciding which minor figures to include and how full their entries should be. Wherever possible, useful references are made to figures who do not warrant separate entries.

Each *DLB* volume has a volume editor responsible for planning the volume, selecting the figures for inclusion, and assigning the entries. Volume editors are also responsible for preparing, where appropriate, appendices surveying the major periodicals and literary and intellectual movements for their volumes, as well as lists of further readings. Work on the series as a whole is coordinated at the Bruccoli Clark Layman editorial center in Columbia, South Carolina, where the editorial staff is responsible for accuracy of the published volumes.

One feature that distinguishes *DLB* is the illustration policy–its concern with the iconography of literature. Just as an author is influenced by his surroundings, so is the reader's understanding of the author enhanced by a knowledge of his environment. Therefore *DLB* volumes include not only drawings, paintings, and photographs of authors, often depicting them at various stages in their careers, but also illustrations of their families and places where they lived. Title pages are regularly reproduced in facsimile along with dust jackets for modern authors. The dust jackets are a special feature of *DLB* because they often document better than anything else the way in which an author's work was perceived in its own time. Specimens of the writers' manuscripts are included when feasible.

Samuel Johnson rightly decreed that "The chief glory of every people arises from its authors." The purpose of the *Dictionary of Literary Biography* is to compile literary history in the surest way available to us–by accurate and comprehensive treatment of the lives and work of those who contributed to it.

The *DLB* Advisory Board

# Foreword

*Dictionary of Literary Biography*, volume 107: *British Romantic Prose Writers, 1789-1832: First Series* takes as its beginning date not the date of the publication of the *Lyrical Ballads* (1798), important though that event certainly is, but the year in which the French Revolution began and in which William Blake's *Songs of Innocence*, William Bowles's *Sonnets*, and Erasmus Darwin's *The Loves of the Plants* were published. The authors treated in the First Series were all born before 1776. The Second Series will deal with British Romantic prose writers born after that year.

The years between 1789 and 1832 were years of revolution, war, and general political and social change. The ideas and ideals, the promises and disappointments associated with the events and personalities of the French Revolution and the Napoleonic period are so much a part of the Romantic movement in England that most of the writers recognized their importance either for themselves or for society. The writers included in this volume had a profound effect upon both the social and the literary milieu of their time, shaping literary tastes, economic thought, and political ideology.

The philosophical origins of British Romanticism may be found in the empiricism of John Locke, the skepticism of David Hume, the associational psychology of David Hartley, and the political radicalism of William Godwin and Mary Wollstonecraft, among others. These various writers helped to create an atmosphere in which received beliefs about human nature (especially the model of the mind), the natural world, the structure of society, and the place of tradition could be called into question. Jeremy Bentham, James Mill, Thomas Malthus, David Ricardo, Robert Owen, and Samuel Taylor Coleridge all challenged established beliefs, customs, and traditions, helping to shape questions that would be debated during the course of the nineteenth century. Though the first four of these writers could hardly be called "Romantic" in any of the usual senses of the word, their writings certainly helped to shape important questions about society and thought during this period. Moreover, many of the prose writers included herein wrote highly polemical tracts, engaging in the intense fray of their politically charged times. In addition to the writers mentioned above, all of whom confronted political questions in their writings, William Cobbett wrote many polemical pamphlets and actively took part in the political debates of the day. Even writers not normally thought of as political, such as William Wordsworth, Francis Jeffrey, and others, did get involved directly in political issues on occasion.

In addition to addressing the uncertainties of political change, even upheaval, and the challenges of new philosophies, the first generation of British Romantic prose writers was also conscious of developing a new aesthetic of poetry, and they produced seminal prose works to explain and defend their innovations in the practice of poetry. For example, Wordsworth's preface to the 1800 edition of *Lyrical Ballads* is a seminal prose document that explains the poetic experiment of Wordsworth and Coleridge, opposing their views on language and the function of the imagination to eighteenth-century ideas of poetic diction and mimesis. Other important documents that helped to define the new aesthetic include Coleridge's prose writings, such as *Biographia Literaria* (1817), and reviews by influential and respected writers such as Robert Southey; Francis, Lord Jeffrey; and others. The informal literary essay, the biographical and autobiographical essay, and the familiar essay, marked by imaginative vision, reverie, and playful ideas, flourished as a genre in the capable hands of writers such as Charles Lamb, Coleridge, Walter Savage Landor, Henry Crabb Robinson, and later, of course, Thomas De Quincey and William Hazlitt, both of whom will be covered in the second series volume on British Romantic prose writers.

If the British Romantic movement may in one way be viewed as a reaction against the Augustan Age's neoclassical aesthetic premises of imitation, balance, and order, it must also be viewed as a continuation and outgrowth of literary developments that were already under way in the eighteenth century. The literary origins of the Romantic movement may be found in Jean-Jacques Rousseau, especially in *Julie; ou La Nouvelle Heloise* (1761) and *The Confessions* (written 1765-1770); in the young Johann Wolfgang von Goethe, as the author of *The Sorrows of Young Werther* (1774); in so-called pre-Romantic English poets such as James Thomson and William Collins, who began to cultivate an interest in nature and in the feelings; in the cult of sensibility, of which Henry Mackenzie's *Man of Feeling* (1771) is the prime example; in the ballad revival, which was accompanied by an interest in things medieval and primitive in general; and in the popularity of Gothic literature, exemplified by Horace Walpole's *The Castle of Otranto* (1765) and M. G. Lewis's *The Monk* (1795), both of which fostered an interest in the supernatural.

Many of the writers included in this volume wrote reviews (often anonymously) for various periodicals. Though literary magazines undertook to be arbiters of taste, they were also often politically biased and would use reviews to attack authors' politics, or they would simply give writers with opposing political stances bad reviews. The Romantic writers' contemporary critics saw the various poets of both the first and second generations not as a monolithic movement all agreeing upon the basic premises of Romanticism, but as comprising various schools with different orientations concerning taste, religion, and politics. The literary milieu of the time was generally conservative and highly politically conscious, often condemning writers ostensibly for matters of taste but really for matters of politics. The reviewers created various schools of poetry including the following: Joseph Johnson's radical circle in the 1790s which included William Blake, William Godwin, and Mary Wollstonecraft; the Lake Poets, which included William Wordsworth, Samuel Taylor Coleridge, and Robert Southey and which derives its name from the beautiful Lake District in northwest England; the "Cockney School," which included John Keats and Leigh Hunt and refers to certain colloquialisms of style that may be found in their poetry; and the "Satanic School" of Percy Bysshe Shelley and George Gordon, Lord Byron, so called for Byron's reputation for immorality and Shelley's reputation for atheism and radicalism.

Of the twenty writers covered in *British Romantic Prose Writers, 1789-1832: First Series*, three writers—Cobbett, Coleridge, and Lamb—receive extended treatment and eight others—Bentham, Malthus, Ricardo, Owen, Robinson, Landor, Scott, and Southey—receive more attention than minor writers. Yet the essays on the minor writers reveal a rich interplay of personalities, influences, and relationships. The lives and contributions of the minor writers, their voices seldom heard today over the dominant tones of their well-known contemporaries, suggest an active literary milieu within a dynamic social context.

Included at the end of this volume is a selected bibliography that focuses on the most important studies of the historical, social, cultural, aesthetic, psychological, linguistic, and literary dimensions of the British Romantic movement.

The contributors to this volume, some of whom are friends or acquaintances of mine and many others whom I have never met, deserve special gratitude for their promptness in meeting deadlines, their conscientiousness in compiling bibliographies and in checking facts, their efficiency in making revisions, their helpfulness in making suggestions for illustrations, and perhaps most of all, for their cooperation and patience. I would also like to thank a former student of mine, Danyelle Warden, for her editorial assistance performed under the auspices of the internship program at McKendree College. Three secretaries at McKendree, Nancy Ferguson, Ella Doty, and Naomia Severs, deserve thanks for the help they gave me in handling the correspondence associated with this volume. I would especially like to thank Karen Rood and the staff at Bruccoli Clark Layman for their tireless attention to accuracy and detail and their insistence upon high standards. Finally, I would like to thank Judy Durick Greenfield for her patience and understanding during all the time that I spent in editing this project.

*—John R. Greenfield*

# Acknowledgments

This book was produced by Bruccoli Clark Layman, Inc. Karen L. Rood, senior editor for the *Dictionary of Literary Biography* series, was the in-house editor.

Production coordinator is James W. Hipp. Systems manager is Charles D. Brower. Photography editors are Edward Scott and Timothy Lundy. Permissions editor is Jean W. Ross. Layout and graphics supervisor is Penney L. Haughton. Copyediting supervisor is Bill Adams. Typesetting supervisor is Kathleen M. Flanagan. Information systems analyst is George F. Dodge. Charles Lee Egleston is editorial associate. The production staff includes Rowena Betts, Teresa Chaney, Patricia Coate, Gail Crouch, Margaret McGinty Cureton, Sarah A. Estes, Robert Fowler, Mary L. Goodwin, Ellen McCracken, Kathy Lawler Merlette, Laura Garren Moore, John Myrick, Pamela D. Norton, Cathy J. Reese, Laurrè Sinckler-Reeder, Maxine K. Smalls, and Betsy L. Weinberg.

Walter W. Ross and Timothy D. Tebalt did library research. They were assisted by the following librarians at the Thomas Cooper Library of the University of South Carolina: Jens Holley and the interlibrary-loan staff; reference librarians Gwen Baxter, Daniel Boice, Faye Chadwell, Jo Cottingham, Cathy Eckman, Rhonda Felder, Gary Geer, Jackie Kinder, Laurie Preston, Jean Rhyne, Carol Tobin, Virginia Weathers, and Connie Widney; circulation-department head Thomas Marcil; and acquisitions-searching supervisor David Haggard.

Sara Hodson and Kathy Schneberger at the Henry E. Huntington Library provided valuable assistance in illustrating this volume.

Dictionary of Literary Biography • Volume One Hundred Seven

# British Romantic Prose Writers, 1789-1832

## First Series

# Dictionary of Literary Biography

## Anna Laetitia Barbauld

*(20 June 1743 - 9 March 1825)*

Leslie Haynsworth

BOOKS: *Poems* (London: Printed for Joseph Johnson, 1773); enlarged as *Poems. A New Edition, Corrected. To Which is added An Epistle to William Wilberforce, Esq.* (London: Printed for Joseph Johnson, 1792; Boston: Wells & Lilly, 1820);

*Miscellaneous Pieces in Prose, by J. and A. L. Aikin* (London: Printed for J. Johnson, 1773);

*Hymns in Prose For Children* (London: Printed for J. Johnson, 1781; Norwich, Conn.: Printed by John Trumbull, 1786);

*Lessons for Children, from Two to Three Years Old* (London: Printed for J. Johnson, 1787);

*Lessons for Children of Three Years Old. Part I* (London: Printed for J. Johnson, 1788);

*Lessons for Children of Three Years Old. Part II* (London: Printed for J. Johnson, 1788);

*Lessons for Children from Three to Four Years Old* (London: Printed for J. Johnson, 1788);

*An Address to the Opposers of the Repeal of the Corporation and Test Acts* (London: Printed for J. Johnson, 1790);

*Epistle to William Wilberforce, Esq. on the Rejection of the Bill for Abolishing the Slave Trade* (London: Printed for J. Johnson, 1791);

*Evenings At Home, or, The Juvenile Budget Opened*, 6 volumes by Barbauld and John Aikin (London: Printed for J. Johnson, 1792-1796; 1 volume, Philadelphia: Printed by T. Dobson, 1797);

*Civic Sermons to the People. Number I. Nay, Why even of yourselves, judge ye not what is right* (London: Printed for J. Johnson, 1792);

*Civic Sermons to the People. Number II. From mutual wants springs mutual happiness* (London: Printed for J. Johnson, 1792);

*Remarks on Mr. Gilbert Wakefield's Enquiry into the Expediency and Propriety of Public or Social Worship* (London: Printed for J. Johnson, 1792);

*Sins of the Government, Sins of the Nation; or, A Discourse for the Fast, Appointed on April 19, 1793* (London: Printed for J. Johnson, 1793);

*Eighteen Hundred and Eleven* (London: J. Johnson, 1812; Boston: Bradford & Read, 1812; Philadelphia: A. Finley, 1812).

**Editions:** *The Works of Anna Laetitia Barbauld. With a Memoir by Lucy Aikin* (2 volumes, London: Longman, Hurst, Rees, Orme, Brown & Green, 1825; 3 volumes, Boston: David Reed, 1826);

*A Legacy for Young Ladies, Consisting of Miscellaneous Pieces, in Prose and Verse*, edited by Lucy Aikin (London: Printed for Longman, Hurst, Rees, Orme & Green, 1826; Boston: David Reed, 1826);

*Things By Their Right Names, and Other Stories, Fables, and Moral Pieces, in Prose and Verse, Selected and Arranged from the Writing of Mrs. Barbauld. With A Sketch of Her Life by Mrs. S. J. Hale* (Boston: Marsh, Capen, Lyon & Webb, 1840);

*Tales, Poems, and Essays by Anna Laetitia Barbauld, with a Biographical Sketch by Grace A. Oliver* (Boston: Roberts, 1884).

OTHER: *The Correspondence of Samuel Richardson*, edited by Barbauld (London: R. Phillips, 1804);

*Medallion by Wedgwood (from Anna Letitia LeBreton,* Memoir of Mrs. Barbauld, *1874)*

*The British Novelists*, 50 volumes, edited, with an essay and prefaces, by Barbauld (London: Printed for F. C. and J. Rivington, 1810);

*The Female Speaker; Or, Miscellaneous Pieces in Prose and Verse, Selected From the Best Writers*, edited by Barbauld (London: Printed for Baldwin, Cradock & Joy, 1816; Boston: Wells & Lilly, 1824).

Anna Laetitia Barbauld was one of the most prominent literary figures of her time in England. She was a popular poet, a sharp-witted essayist and literary critic, and a much-beloved author of stories and verse for children. She was acquainted with and admired by many of the leading thinkers and writers of her generation, among them Samuel Taylor Coleridge, Joseph Priestley, Elizabeth Montagu, Joanna Baillie, Sir Walter Scott, and William and Dorothy Wordsworth. Coleridge described her as a "great and excellent woman," and in a 1 April 1796 letter, before he had met her, he wrote of Robert Hall, "I think his style the best in the English language—if he have a rival, it is Mrs. Barbauld." On 15 December 1800, when Coleridge and Wordsworth were preparing the second edition (1800) of their *Lyrical Ballads* for publication, Coleridge wrote to publisher Thomas N. Longman urging "that 3 or 4 copies should be sent to different people of eminence," including Mrs. Barbauld.

Unfortunately, however, Barbauld had enemies in literary circles as well. The influential Charles Lamb was scathing in his attacks on her, and the *Quarterly Review* published an unjustly negative review of one of her later poems in 1812. Barbauld was deeply distressed by this response to her work, and, from that point until her death, she retired from literary society and published nothing else. Because her career as a writer ended on a negative note, her reputation

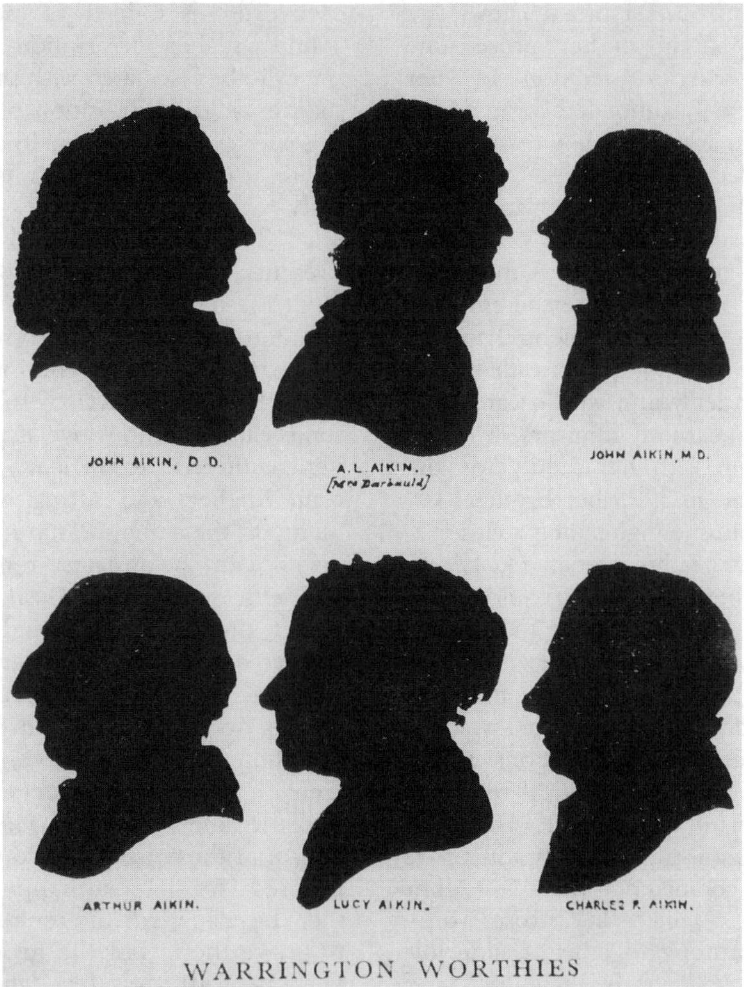


*Silhouettes of Barbauld and her family (from* James Kendrick, Profiles of Warrington Worthies, *1854)*

faded quickly, and, with the exception of the pieces she wrote for young readers, which continued to be staples of the children's canon throughout the nineteenth century, her contributions to literary and political discourse were largely forgotten. Barbauld is, however, a writer worth resurrecting. Her prose is engagingly witty, yet deeply penetrating. Moreover, her style and her perspective offer an interesting contrast to the explicitly Romantic writers whose works have tended to define her age. As Coleridge, perhaps the most fanciful of all the Romantics, put it in his 1 March 1800 letter to John Prior Estlin, "The more I see of Mrs. Barbauld the more I admire her—that wonderful *Propriety* of Mind!—She has great *acuteness*, very great—yet how steadily she keeps it within the bounds of practical Reason. This I almost envy as well as admire—My own Subtleties too often lead me into strange (tho' God be praised) transient Out-of-the-waynesses." Barbauld's prose is at times as rich in fanciful imagery as anything Coleridge wrote, but such fancies are merely the trappings of an underlying insistence upon the value of commonsense practicality, and the popularity of Barbauld's tales and essays among her contemporaries serves to remind us that the ethereal voice of the Romantic poets who tend to define this generation in the twentieth century was not the only influential literary voice of Barbauld's day.

Barbauld was born Anna Laetitia Aikin, in the small, remote village of Kibworth Harcourt, Leicestershire, on 20 June 1743. She was the elder of two children born to Jane Jennings Aikin and John Aikin, D.D., a schoolmaster. She was an extremely precocious child, who read with ease by the time she was three years old. Because her father was a teacher, she was also, at her own request, instructed in Latin and Greek, which were unusual subjects of study for girls in the eighteenth century. Her broad knowledge of the classics is apparent in her prose; one nineteenth-century American edition of her children's pieces is heavily annotated by an editor who clearly assumes that most of her readers will not share such knowledge.

When Barbauld was fifteen, her father accepted a post as a classical tutor at the prominent Dissenting academy at Warrington, Lancashire, which proved to be a much more fertile environment for her intellectual development than her birthplace. Here she met Joseph Priestley, who also taught at the academy and who became one of her warmest and earliest admirers. She remained at Warrington with her family for the next fifteen years, and in 1773 her brother, Dr. John Aikin, with whom she maintained a close relationship throughout her life, persuaded her to collect and publish her poems. Barbauld is reported to have been too modest and too unsure of her abilities to have considered presenting her works to the public, but her brother's confidence in her talents proved justified; that first volume of her poems ran through four editions in the first year of its publication, and critical response to it was almost uniformly enthusiastic.

Having thus demonstrated to his sister that she was a more-than-competent writer, Dr. Aikin next convinced her to collect her prose works and to join him in putting together a slim volume titled *Miscellaneous Pieces in Prose, by J. and A. L. Aikin*, which was also published in 1773 and which, like her volume of poems, was both a popular and a critical success. Because the authors did not sign their names to their respective pieces, there has been some dispute over exactly who wrote what. Those generally attributed to Barbauld are found in most of the posthumous editions of her collected works. Among the essays known to have been written by Barbauld are "The Hill of Science," "Inconsistency in Our Expectations," and "On Romances: An Imitation." "On Romances" is in the style of Samuel Johnson's essays, and Johnson is reported to have said of it, "The imitators of my style have not hit it. Miss Aikin has done it the best, for she has imitated the sentiment as well as the diction." In this essay Barbauld notes that romances are more popular and widely read than learned works, and she argues that their popularity is deserved because "they please the imagination and interest the heart. . . . they ventilate the mind by sudden gusts of passion; and prevent the stagnation of thought by a fresh infusion of dissimilar ideas." Her prose is indeed as lucid and as lively as Johnson's; her description of the human tendency to be fascinated with the stock themes of romance as "the disposition of the mind to riot in this species of intellectual luxury" reveals her ability to use language both precisely and beautifully.

"The Hill of Science" is a witty allegory that presents science as a hill which keeps growing taller the higher one climbs. The road to the top is rough and stony, "and rendered more difficult by heaps of rubbish continually tumbled down from the higher parts of the mountain," so that some climbers soon give up, "while others, having conquered this difficulty, had no spirits to ascend further, and sitting down on some fragment of the rubbish, harangued the multitude below with the greatest remarks of importance and self-complacency." Despite such irreverent remarks, the piece is a thought-provoking allegorical account of human endeavors to acquire higher knowledge. The mountain is surrounded by the Wood of Error and the Fields of Fiction, and those who attempt to ascend it are distracted from their pursuits by personifications of Pride, Pleasure, and Indolence. The last is the most successful of those who seek to impede the climbers' progress, for "Her unhappy captives still turned their faces towards the temple, and always hoped to arrive there; but the ground seemed to slide from beneath their feet, and they found themselves at the bottom before they suspected that they had changed their place." Ultimately, Barbauld concludes, no one will ever succeed in climbing as high up the mountain as he or she wants. Although scientific innovation is a good thing for mankind as a whole, those who manage to find the Mansions of Content in their own daily lives are likely to be the happiest individuals. This essay, then, presents a brief, but penetrating and engaging, metaphorical account of the pitfalls of the quest for the advancement of knowledge. Moreover, its moral lesson exhibits just the sort of practical common sense which Coleridge finds so praiseworthy in Barbauld's approach to life.

In May 1774, when she was just short of thirty-one years old, Barbauld married the Reverend Rochemont Barbauld, a Dissenting minister of French descent who had been a student at Warrington Academy. Shortly thereafter, Reverend Barbauld accepted a position as the head of a Dissenting congregation at Palgrave, Suffolk, where he also founded a boarding school for boys,

*The academy at Warrington, where Barbauld's father became a classical tutor in 1758 and where she spent the next fifteen years of her life (engraving by H. F. Bellars, 1762)*

which he and Mrs. Barbauld ran together for eleven years. The school was quite successful and produced several prominent graduates. Lucy Aikin remarked that this success was "doubtless in great measure owing to the literary celebrity attached to the name of Mrs. Barbauld, and to her active participation with her husband in the task of instruction."

The Barbaulds had no children of their own, but, while at Palgrave, they adopted one of Mrs. Barbauld's brother's sons, Charles, when he was less than two years old. For him and for her other pupils, she composed *Lessons for Children* (1787-1788) and *Hymns in Prose For Children* (1781); both collections remained popular for nearly a hundred years after her death. *Hymns in Prose* was used widely to instruct children in both England and America, and the hymns were also translated into German, French, Italian, Spanish, and Latin. As Jerom Murch observed, "they are poetry in everything but the meter." In the author's preface Barbauld explains that she wrote these pieces in prose because, she felt, small children tend to find poetry difficult and dull, but she wanted young readers to be able to appreciate the sorts of thoughts and sentiments which are normally expressed in verse. Judging by the enduring popularity of this volume, she was quite successful. The hymns celebrate the beauty and bounty of the world, and call upon the reader to praise God for these qualities. They are richly descriptive, but written in language simple enough for young children to understand. Hymn 5, for example, provides lush details of nightfall:

> The glorious sun is set in the west; the night dews fall; and the air, which was sultry, becomes cool.
>
> The flowers fold up their coloured leaves; they fold themselves up, and hang their heads on the slender stalk. . . .
>
> The little birds have ceased their warbling, they are asleep on the boughs, each one has his head behind his wing. . . .
>
> Darkness is spread over the skies, and darkness is upon the ground; every eye is shut and every hand is still.

Barbauld concludes by reminding her readers that God watches over them while they are asleep, and that He made the night for them so that they can sleep.

*"The Nine Living Muses of Great Britain," circa 1775: (seated) Charlotte Lennox, Catherine Macaulay, Hannah More, and Angelica Kauffman; (standing) Elizabeth Montagu, Elizabeth Griffith, Elizabeth Anne Sheridan, Elizabeth Carter, and Anna Laetitia Barbauld (engraving by Page, after Richard Samuel)*

During the years at Palgrave, the Barbaulds frequently vacationed in London, where Barbauld made the acquaintance of many other literary celebrities. In 1785, after eleven successful and prosperous years, stress and ill health caused the Barbaulds to close their school and go abroad. They traveled on the Continent for almost a year, returning to London in 1786. Reverend Barbauld was offered a congregation at Hampstead, where they remained until 1802. He took in a few pupils while Barbauld devoted most of her time to writing. In 1792 she collaborated with her brother on *Evenings at Home, or, The Juvenile Budget Opened*, which became yet another popular book for young readers. Dr. Aikin's contributions compose most of the volume. Barbauld's few selections are, in keeping with the general tone of children's literature of the period, fairly didactic, but Barbauld skillfully diffuses any overt preachiness in them by couching her moral lessons in the forms of beast fables, folktales, or lively dialogues between children and their parents. In "Things By Their Right Names," for example, a child demands that his father tell him a bloody story about murder and mayhem. The father cheerfully complies, but has not gotten far into his narrative when he is interrupted by his son, who complains that he is hearing a tale not of murder but of war. The father concedes that this is indeed the case, but remarks, "I do not know of any *murders* half so bloody" as a battle. In a similar vein many of the other tales and essays in this volume encourage their young audience to examine the world around them closely and to define what they see with care and precision. In this respect most of these tales are characterized less by telling readers what to think as they are by showing them how to think.

Barbauld also urged that things be called by their right names in her *Address to the Opposers of the Repeal of the Corporation and Test Acts* (1790) one of several vehement and forthright political tracts that she wrote. The Test and Corporation Acts denied many privileges to those who did not belong to the Church of England, and Barbauld argues forcefully and persuasively that such politics are outdated: "It is time, so near the end of the eighteenth century, it is surely time to speak with precision and to call things by their proper names. What you call toleration, we call the exercise of a natural and unalienable right. We do not call it toleration first to strip a man of all his dearest rights, and then to give him back a part, or even if it were the whole." Such firm, outspoken language is as characteristic of Barbauld's prose as is her level-headed common sense. Although as a young woman, she was hesitant about her talents, the accolades her early publications received clearly made her sure of her intellect, and in her subsequent works she voiced her opinions confidently and supported them with penetrating logic and perceptive reasoning, nor was she overawed by the reputations of other writers. In a 1791 letter to her brother, for example, she wrote: "We are reading ... Boswell's long-expected Life of Johnson.... Johnson, I think, was far from a great character; he was continually sinning against his conscience and then afraid of going to hell for it. A Christian and man of the town, a philosopher and a bigot, ... acknowledged to be a giant in literature, and yet we do not trace him, as we do Locke, or Rousseau, or Voltaire, in his influences on the opinions of the times.... In short, he seems to be one of those who have shone in the *belles lettres*, rather than, what he is held out by many to be, an original and deep genius in investigation." Barbauld's refusal to let Johnson's high reputation remain unexamined is characteristic of her general approach to all topics. It is akin to her insistence that we look beyond words such as *toleration* and *battle* to the actual facts of which such words are mere shadowy representations.

At her brother's request the Barbaulds moved in 1802 to Stoke Newington, where Dr. Aikin lived, and here Barbauld stayed for the rest of her life. From this point on, much of her work was editorial in nature: in 1804 she collected and edited the letters of Samuel Richardson, and in 1810 she edited a fifty-volume series of British novels, for which she wrote an introductory essay on the art of novel writing, as well as biographical and critical prefaces about the authors whose works were included. Her husband, who suffered from mental illness, died insane in 1808, probably by suicide, and she mourned his loss deeply. In 1812 she published a long and powerful poem, *Eighteen Hundred and Eleven*, which expressed her belief that England's world hegemony was on the wane. It was to this poem that Barbauld's contemporaries reacted with such vehement anger as to discourage her from publishing again. The *Quarterly Review* notice (June 1812) dismissed her pessimism about the nation's future as absurd and chose to overlook the poem's artistic merits. Gloomy in tone, *Eighteen Hundred and Eleven* is an extremely fine poem, which both in theme and in specific imagery is a precursor of *The Waste Land* (1922).

The fact that many of Barbauld's contemporaries scorned one of her later works should not discourage us from recognizing her as one of the most influential writers of the Romantic period. Jerom Murch, who published a biography of Barbauld in 1877, made just such a point when he wrote, "I have chosen this subject because I fear it is either not generally known or not sufficiently remembered how much English literature owes this woman." Murch recalled that Walter Savage Landor once spoke to him of Barbauld "as the first writer of the day," and in so doing Landor was only slightly amplifying the opinions of Barbauld held by Coleridge, Scott, Priestley, and many others. Anna Laetitia Barbauld was a formidably intelligent and articulate writer, and her works clearly deserve more attention than they have received.

**Biographies:**

Anna Letitia LeBreton, *Memoir of Mrs. Barbauld Including Letters and Notices of Her Family and Friends* (London: Bell, 1874);

Jerom Murch, *Mrs. Barbauld and Her Contemporaries; Sketches of Some Eminent Literary and Scientific Englishwomen* (London: Longmans, Green, 1877);

Betsy Rodgers, *Georgian Chronicle: Mrs. Barbauld & her Family* (London: Methuen, 1958).

**References:**

Catherine E. Moore, "Mrs. Barbauld's Criticism of Eighteenth-Century Women Novelists," in *Fetter'd or Free? British Women Novelists, 1670-1815*, edited by Mary Anne Schofield and Cecilia Macheski (Athens: Ohio University Press, 1982), pp. 383-397;

Samuel Pickering, "Mrs. Barbauld's Hymns in Prose: 'An Air-Blown Particle of Romanticism'?," *Southern Humanities Review*, 9 (Summer 1975): 259-268;

Porter Williams, "The Influence of Mrs. Barbauld's *Hymns in Prose for Children* upon Blake's *Songs of Innocence and Experience*, in *A Fair Day for the Affections*, edited by Jack Durant and Thomas Hester (Raleigh, N.C.: Winston Press, 1980), pp. 131-146;

P. M. Zall, "Wordsworth's 'Ode' and Mrs. Barbauld's *Hymns*," *Wordsworth Circle*, 1 (Autumn 1970): 177-179.

# Jeremy Bentham

*(15 February 1748 - 6 June 1832)*

Natalie Bell Cole
*Oakland University*

SELECTED BOOKS: *A Fragment on Government; being an examination of what is delivered, on the subject of Government in General in the introduction of Sir William Blackstone's Commentaries: with a preface, in which is given a critique on the work at large* (London: Printed for T. Payne, P. Elmsly, and E. Brooke, 1776);

*A View of the Hard-Labour Bill; Being an Abstract of a Pamphlet, Intituled, "Draught of a Bill, to Punish by Imprisonment and Hard-Labour, Certain Offenders; and to Establish Proper Places for Their Reception." Interspersed with Observations Relative to the Subject of the Above Draught in Particular, and to Penal Jurisprudence in General* (London: Printed for T. Payne & son, T. Cadell, P. Elmsley, and E. Brooke, 1778);

*Defence of Usury; Shewing the Impolicy of the Present Legal Restraints on the Terms of Pecuniary Bargains. In a Series of Letters to a Friend. To which is added a Letter to Adam Smith, Esq.; LL.D. on the Discouragements Opposed by the Above Restraints to the Progress of Inventive Industry* (London: Printed for T. Payne & son, 1787; Philadelphia: Printed for Mathew Carey by Lang & Ustick, 1796);

*An Introduction to the Principles of Morals and Legislation* (London: Printed for T. Payne & son, 1789);

*Draught of a New Plan for the Organization of the Judicial Establishment in France: Proposed as a succedaneum to the draught presented, for the same purpose, by the Committee of Constitution, to the National Assembly, December 21st, 1789* (London?, 1790);

*'Panopticon': or, the Inspection-House: containing the idea of a new principle of construction applicable to any sort of establishment, in which persons of any description are to be kept under inspection; and in particular to Penitentiary-houses, Prisons, Houses of industry, Workhouses, Poor Houses, Manufactories, Madhouses, Lazarettos, Hospitals, and Schools; with a plan of management adopted to the principle: in a series of letters, written in the year 1787, from Crecheff in White Russia, to a friend in England* (Dublin: Thomas Byrne, 1791; 2 volumes, London: Sold by T. Payne, 1791);

*Panopticon: Postscript; Part I: Containing further particulars and alterations relative to the plan of construction originally proposed; principally adapted to the purpose of a panopticon penitentiary-house* (London: Printed for T. Payne, 1791);

*Panopticon: Postscript; Part II: Containing a plan of management for a panopticon penitentiary-house* (London: Printed for T. Payne, 1791);

*A Protest against Law Taxes* (Dublin, 1793); republished with *Supply Burthen; or Escheat Vice Taxation* (London: Printed for J. Debrett, 1795);

*Traités de legislation civile et pénale*, 3 volumes, translated by Etienne Dumont (Paris: Boussange, Masson et Besson, 1802); first published in English as *Theory of Legislation*, 1 volume, translated by Richard Hildreth (London: Kegan Paul, Trench, Trübner, 1864);

*Scotch Reform; Considered, with reference to the plan, proposed in the late Parliament, for the regulation of the courts, and the administration of justice in Scotland. . . . In a series of Letters, Addressed to the Right Hon. Lord Grenville* (London: Printed by R. Taylor for J. Ridgeway, 1808);

*Théorie des peines et des récompenses*, 2 volumes, translated by Dumont (London: Printed by Vogel & Schulze, sold by B. Dulau, 1811); first published in English as *The Rationale of Reward*, translated and edited by Richard Smith (London: J. & H. L. Hunt, 1825) and *The Rationale of Punishment*, translated and edited by Smith (London: Robert Heward, 1830);

*Panopticon versus New South Wales; or, The Panopticon Penitentiary System and the Penal Colonization System Compared. Containing I. Two Letters to Lord Pelham. 2. Plea for the Constitution, anno 1803, printed, now first published* (London, 1812);

*Pauper Management Improved: Particularly by Means of an Application of the Panopticon Principle of*

*Jeremy Bentham, 1829 (portrait by H. W. Pickersgill; National Portrait Gallery, London)*

*Construction. Anno 1797, first published in Young's Annals of Agriculture; now first published separately* (London: Sold by R. Baldwin & J. Ridgeway, 1812);

*Tactiques des assemblées legislatives, suivi d'un traité des sophismes politiques*, 2 volumes, translated by Dumont (Geneva & Paris: J. J. Paschaud, 1816);

*Chrestomathia, being a collection of papers, explanatory of the design of an institution, proposed to be set on foot, under the name of the Chrestomathic Day School, or Chrestomathic School, for the extension of the new system of instruction to the higher branches of learning, for the use of the middling and higher ranks of life*, 2 parts (London: Printed for Payne & Foss & R. Hunter by J. M'Creery, part 1: 1815 [i.e., 1817], part 2: 1817);

*A Table of the Springs of Action, Shewing the Several Species of Pleasures and Pains, of which Man's Nature is Susceptible* (London: Printed by R. & A. Taylor, 1815 [i.e., 1817]);

*"Swear Not at All": Containing an Exposure of the Needlessness and Mischievousness, as well as Anti-Christianity, of the Ceremony of an Oath* (London: Sold by R. Hunter, 1817);

*Papers relative to Codification and Public Instruction; including correspondence with the Russian Emperor, and divers constituted authorities in the American United States* (London: Printed by J. M'Creary, 1817);

*Supplement to Papers on Codification* (London: Printed by J. M'Creary, 1817);

*Plan of Parliamentary Reform, in the Form of a Catechism, with Reasons for Each Article, with an Introduction, shewing the necessity of radical, and the inadequacy of moderate, reform* (London: Printed for R. Hunter, 1817);

*Church of Englandism and its Catechism Examined* (London: E. Wilson, 1818);

*Bentham's Radical Reform Bill* (London: E. Wilson, 1819);

*The King against Edmonds and Others: Set down for the trial, at Warwick, on the 29th of March, 1820. Brief remarks tending to show the untenability of this indictment* (London: Printed by J. M'Creery, 1820);

*The King against Sir Charles Wolseley, Baronet, and Joseph Harrison, Schoolmaster: Set down for trial at Chester on the 4th of April, 1820. Brief remarks tending to show the untenability of this indictment* (London: Printed by J. M'Creery, 1820);

*Observations on the Restrictive and Prohibitory Commercial System*, edited by John Bowring (London: E. Wilson, 1821);

*The Elements of the Art of Packing, as Applied to Special Juries, particularly in cases of Libel Law* (London: E. Wilson, 1821);

*Three Tracts Relative to Spanish and Portugueze Affairs; With a continual eye to English ones* (London: Printed for W. Hone, 1821);

*On the Liberty of the Press and Public Discussion* (London: W. Hone, 1821);

*An Analysis of the Influence of Natural Religion on the Temporal Happiness of Mankind*, as Philip Beauchamp, edited by George Grote (London: R. Carlile, 1822);

*Codification Proposal, Addressed by Jeremy Bentham to All Nations Professing Liberal Opinions* (London: Printed by J. M'Creery, 1822);

*Leading Principles of a Constitutional Code for Any State* (London: A. Valpy, 1823);

*Traité des preuves judiciares, ouvrage extrait des manuscrits de Jérémie Bentham*, 2 volumes, translated by Dumont (Paris: Bossages frères, 1823); first published in English as *A Treatise on Judicial Evidence, Extracted from the Manuscripts of Jeremy Bentham, Esq., by M. Dumont*, 1 volume (London: Baldwin, Cradock & Joy, 1825);

*Not Paul, but Jesus*, as Gamaliel Smith (London: Printed for John Hunt, 1823);

*The Book of Fallacies: from the unfinished papers of Jeremy Bentham*, edited by Peregrine Bingham (London: J. & H. L. Hunt, 1824);

*Extract from the Proposed Constitutional Code, Entitled Official Aptitude Maximized, Expense Minimized* (London, 1816 [i.e, 1826]);

*The Rationale of Judicial Evidence, Specially Applied to English Practice*, 5 volumes, edited by John Stuart Mill (London: Hunt & Clarke, 1827);

*Constitutional Code: for use of all nations and governments professing Liberal opinions, Vol. I* (London: R. Heward, 1830);

*Official Aptitude Maximized, Expense Minimized, as shown in the several papers in this volume* (London: R. Heward, 1830);

*Emancipate Your Colonies! Addressed to the National Convention of France, 2° 1793* (London: R. Heward, 1830);

*Equity Dispatch Court Proposal* (London: Published by Robert Heward, 1830);

*Jeremy Bentham to his Fellow-Citizens of France on Houses of Peers and Senates* (London: R. Heward, 1830);

*Jeremy Bentham to his Fellow Citizens of France, on Death Punishment* (London: R. Heward, 1831);

*Lord Brougham Displayed: including I. Boa Constrictor.... II. Observations on the Bankruptcy Court Bill, Now ripened into an Act. III. Extracts from Proposed Constitutional Code* (London: R. Heward, 1832);

*Deontology; or, the Science of Morality*, 2 volumes, edited by John Bowring (London: Longman, Rees, Orme, Brown, Green & Longman, 1834);

*The Works of Jeremy Bentham, Published under the Supervision of His Executor, John Bowring*, 11 volumes (Edinburgh: W. Tait, 1838-1843);

*A Comment on the Commentaries: a criticism of William Blackstone's Commentaries on the Laws of England*, edited by Charles Warren Everett (Oxford: Clarendon Press, 1928);

*Bentham's Theory of Fictions*, edited by C. K. Ogden (London: Kegan Paul, Trench, Trübner, 1932);

*The Limits of Jurisprudence Defined*, edited by Everett (New York: Columbia University Press, 1945);

*Jeremy Bentham's Economic Writings*, 3 volumes, edited by W. Stark (London: Published for the Royal Economic Society for Allen & Unwin, 1952);

*A Bentham Reader*, edited by Mary P. Mack (New York: Pegasus, 1969).

**The Collected Works of Jeremy Bentham**, 38 volumes projected:

*The Correspondence of Jeremy Bentham*, 9 volumes to date, general editors J. H. Burns, J. R. Dinwiddy, and F. Rosen (volumes 1-5, London: Athlone Press, 1968-1981; volumes 6- , Oxford Clarendon Press, 1984- );

*Bentham circa 1761, the year after he entered Queen's College, Oxford (portrait by Thomas Frye; National Portrait Gallery, London)*

*An Introduction to the Principles of Morals and Legislation*, edited by Burns and H. L. A. Hart (London: Athlone Press, 1970);

*Of Laws in General*, edited by Hart (London: Athlone Press, 1970);

*A Comment on Commentaries and A Fragment on Government*, edited by Burns and Hart (London: Athlone Press, 1977);

*Chrestomathia*, edited by M. J. Smith and W. H. Burston (Oxford: Clarendon Press, 1983);

*Constitutional Code, Vol. I*, edited by Rosen and Burns (Oxford: Clarendon Press, 1983);

*Deontology, together with A Table of the Springs of Action and The Articles on Utilitarianism*, edited by Amnon Goldworth (Oxford: Clarendon Press, 1983);

*First Principles preparatory to Constitutional Code*, edited by Philip Schofield (Oxford: Clarendon Press, 1989);

*Securities Against Misrule and Other Constitutional Writings for Tripoli and Greece*, edited by Schofield (Oxford: Clarendon Press, 1990).

OTHER: "Bentham on Torture," edited by W. L. Twining and P. E. Twining, in "Bentham on Legal Theory," edited by M. H. James, *Northern Ireland Legal Quarterly*, 24, no. 3 (1973): 39-90;

"Jeremy Bentham's Essay on 'Paederasty,'" 2 parts, edited by L. Crompton, *Journal of Homosexuality*, 3, no. 4 (1978): 383-405; 4, no. 1 (1978): 91-107.

Jeremy Bentham is known as the father of English utilitarianism, the doctrine of using the criterion of "the greatest happiness for the greatest number" to determine the moral value of any given action. Bentham employed utilitarian philosophy to examine governments, law, education, social policies, and individual behavior. Many of Bentham's writings were unpublished in his lifetime, but his "principle of utility," which he later renamed the "greatest happiness principle," was expounded throughout the nineteenth century by Bentham disciples, the Philosophical Radicals, who were to have important roles in the political and administrative reform of Victorian England. The ambitious scope of Bentham's projects, which included an attempt to codify the vast and mazelike constitutional and common law of England, and his confusing prose style made his work inaccessible to many of his peers, causing Edward Bulwer-Lytton to comment: "He acted upon the destinies of his race, by influencing the thoughts of the minute fraction who think" (*England and the English*, 1833). Bentham and his writings remain controversial. His reform efforts, particularly of penal and educational systems, have caused some to see him as a fascistic opponent of liberty while others characterize him as a brilliant and visionary reformer.

Bentham's father, Jeremiah Bentham, was a prosperous London attorney who had married the charming but poor young widow Alicia Grove Whitehorne in 1744. Jeremy Bentham was born 15 February 1748 at Red Lions Street, Houndsditch. He and his brother Samuel, nine years his junior, were the only two of the Benthams' children to survive beyond infancy or early childhood. When Jeremy was ten years old, his mother died, leaving her children to the care of their father and paternal grandmother, Rebecca Tabor Bentham.

The Benthams' elder son proved intellectually precocious, studying Latin at age three and beginning his formal education at Westminster School at age seven. Books that might supply entertainment were forbidden in the Bentham household. At age twelve young Jeremy entered Queen's College, Oxford, where he took a bachelor's degree in 1764. While at Oxford he was required, like all other students, to subscribe to the Thirty-Nine Articles of the Church of England; unlike others, he read all of the articles, had many questions, and, when forced to sign, did so reluctantly. This first major encounter with ambiguous language and entrenched tradition was to resurface in Bentham's later crusade against the "fallacies" of language and the privileges of Church and government establishments. Bentham did not enjoy his days at Oxford, later writing in *Church of Englandism* (1818) that "mendacity and insincerity" are "the sure and only sure effects of an English university education."

In 1763 at age fifteen, Bentham entered Lincoln's Inn and began to attend the Court of King's Bench in preparation for a career as a barrister. For part of 1764 he traveled in France with his father, and, dividing his time between London and Oxford, he took a master's degree at Oxford in 1767. Bentham was admitted to the bar in 1769, but it had already become apparent that he was less interested in the actual practice of law than in a reformed English law, codified (a word Bentham coined) and applied according to the principle of utility.

Bentham's fascination with abuses inherent in the English law and judicial system had actually begun ten years before, when at his grandmother's house he had discovered *An Apology for the Conduct of Mrs. Teresia Constantia Phillips* (1748-1749), a three-volume account of the marital and legal struggles of a prostitute. Mrs. Phillips's sufferings at the hand of the Court of Chancery and unscrupulous lawyers evoked a powerful response in young Bentham, who vowed thereafter to fight "the Daemon of Chicane" in the law.

Combined with this initial perception of injustices inherent in the legal system was Bentham's wish to define himself professionally and intellectually. After reading Claude-Adrien Helvétius's *De l'esprit* (1758) at age twenty-one, he pondered the term *genius*, a name frequently applied to the young Jeremy Bentham, and decided he had "a genius for legislation."

The principle of utility, first articulated in 1776 in *A Fragment on Government*, is the cornerstone of all of Bentham's later thought. He formulated this idea after reading Joseph Priestley's *Essay on the First Principles of Government* (1768), wherein he found the phrase "the greatest good of the greatest number." He was further inspired by David Hume's "Why Utility Pleases" (1751) and Helvétius, whose *De l'esprit* emphasized the importance of jurisprudence as a human endeavor. Bentham's *A Fragment on Government* was written to attack the eminent Sir William Blackstone's *Commentaries on the Laws of England* (1765-1769). Bentham declares that "*It is the greatest happiness of the greatest number that is the measure of right and wrong*" and urges the reclassification of legal of-

*Portrait of Samuel Bentham painted by an unknown artist in St. Petersburg during 1784, the year before his elder brother, Jeremy Bentham, journeyed to Russia for a three-year visit (National Maritime Museum, Greenwich Hospital Collection). Trained as a naval architect, Samuel Bentham later served as the British Inspector-General of Naval Works.*

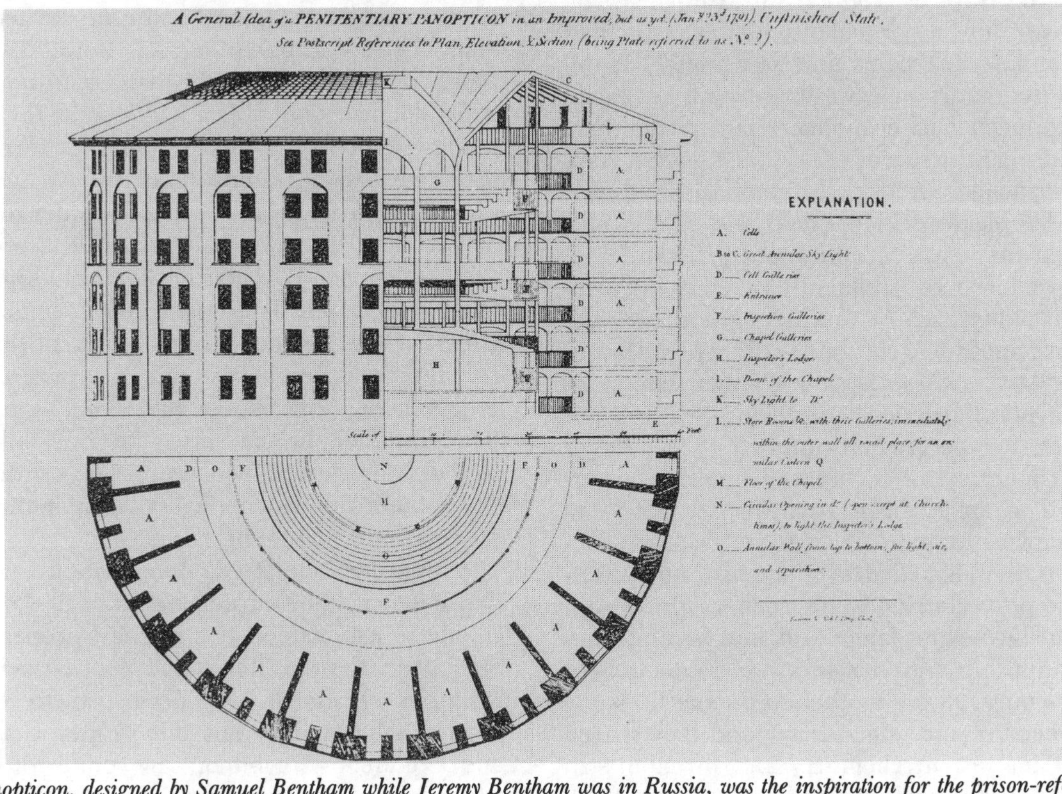


*The Panopticon, designed by Samuel Bentham while Jeremy Bentham was in Russia, was the inspiration for the prison-reform crusade to which the philosopher devoted more than twenty years of his life (from Jeremy Bentham,* 'Panopticon': or, the Inspection-House, *1791).*

fenses with reference to how far they diverge from the "common end" of happiness: "The consequences of any Law, or of any act which is made the object of a Law, the only consequences that men are at all interested in, what are they but *pain* and *pleasure*?" (Bentham's emphasis). Homosexuality is one example of a punishable legal offense which, Bentham believed, does not deleteriously affect the happiness of either the principals or the society at large. According to the principle of utility, homosexuality does not merit the status of a crime. *A Fragment on Government* attacked the "antipathy to reformation" in Blackstone's acceptance of the law as it existed, challenging established powers and special-interest abuses and laying the groundwork for Bentham's later support of democratic reform in the English Parliament. Published anonymously, *A Fragment on Government* garnered considerable attention and was attributed to some of the leading legal minds of the day, but, when a proud Jeremiah Bentham revealed his son's authorship, the work was dismissed as an interesting curiosity.

The principle of utility was an attempt to bring an accurate measure to bear on human actions by classifying pains and pleasures and to use this measure as a guide in creating law on the basis of how a particular action affected individual and social "pains and pleasures." Happiness, in Bentham's view, was largely but not exclusively connected to economic security. Bentham renamed the principle of utility "the Greatest Happiness Principle" in 1822, to emphasize the dual yardsticks, pleasure (happiness) and pain, which governed his vision of ethics and jurisprudence. Two objections most frequently raised to the principle of utility are: 1) the assumption that humans are motivated by only pain and pleasure may be faulty; 2) seeking one's own happiness may not necessarily lead to seeking the "greatest happiness for the greatest number."

Although Bentham has sometimes been characterized as an eccentric bachelor, cut off from commonplace human concerns and lacking emotion, this view is belied by two frustrated courtships, important friendships such as those with Lord Shelburne and James Mill, and his affectionate relationship with his brother, Samuel. Bentham encouraged his brother to pursue his study of architecture and engineering, and they shared an avid interest in chemistry and invention. In 1774-1775 Bentham wanted to marry Mary Dunkley, a surgeon's daughter, but Jeremiah Bentham opposed the match because it would not bring income to his son. Jeremy Bentham reluctantly but obediently ended his engagement. His advice about women in a December 1774 letter to his brother suggests a worldly pragmatism about romantic matters by which Bentham would later painfully live: "But if thou perceivest thyself to feel too much, where it is not convenient, turn aside from that object, and call off thy thoughts from it, to another."

In August 1785 Bentham began a six-month journey to Russia, where his brother was working as an estate manager for Prince Grigory Aleksandrovich Potemkin. He stayed abroad until February 1788, continuing his daily regimen of writing, finishing ten to fifteen folios per day of his *Defence of Usury* (1787) and other works in his house at Zadobrast, near Krichëv. Samuel Bentham provided the architectural design for the Panopticon, the building that inspired the prison-reform project which was to consume Bentham's attention between 1789 and 1812.

In 1781, before his journey to Russia, Bentham had attracted the notice of the illustrious William Petty, Earl of Shelburne, who had been secretary of state for the southern department in 1766-1768 and was to serve briefly as prime minister in 1782-1783. Lord Shelburne invited Bentham to his country estate, Bowood, where Bentham at last enjoyed the aristocratic and influential company his father had sought for him in sending him to Westminster and Oxford. Bentham enjoyed a friendship of twenty-five years with Shelburne (who became marquis of Lansdowne in 1784). Bentham's stay at Bowood in August-October 1781 was important to him in another way as well. It brought him in contact with Lady Shelburne's niece Caroline Fox, at that time only fourteen. Bentham would unsuccessfully propose marriage to Miss Fox in 1805. The pleasure Bentham took in the society at Bowood is recorded in his letters, which produce a vivid sense of Bentham's interest in the ladies and in the political anecdotes that he heard there.

Bentham declared his political independence to Lord Shelburne when they first met, declining to use his pen as a political propagandist. Shelburne showed Bentham's *Introduction to the Principles of Morals and Legislation* to Charles Pratt, Earl Camden, but the former chancellor and exponent of common law could not understand it and thus dismissed it. The friendship with Shelburne never translated into a political or advisory office for Bentham, and he contin-

*Bentham's first mentor, William Petty, Earl of Shelburne (portrait after Sir Joshua Reynolds; National Portrait Gallery, London)*

ued his work on legislative reform without encouragement from political or public sources.

Bentham's next major work, written in 1780 but not published until 1789, *An Introduction to the Principles of Morals and Legislation*, continues to expound the principle of utility and introduces the idea of sanctions, which "give force to any law or rule of conduct." Of the four types of sanctions—physical, political, moral or popular, and religious—Bentham considered the religious sanction the least efficacious in motivating human conduct. An understanding and proper evaluation of sanctions could help to gear the law toward the prevention of crime, which Bentham considered the third age of law (the first being vengeance, the second impartial punishment). Bentham describes punishment as both a "mischief " and an "evil," acceptable according to the principle of utility only "in as far as it promises to exclude some greater evil." In this work Bentham also defines the seven elements of value in assessing pain and pleasure: intensity, duration, certainty or uncertainty, propinquity or remoteness, fecundity, purity, and extent. These elements could be totaled in a "felicific calculus" or "moral arithmetic" to determine if the outcome would be greater pain or greater pleasure. Felicific calculus came to represent to its opponents the worst of utilitarian values: a mechanistic, inhuman approach to human problems, epitomized later in fiction in Charles Dickens's *Hard Times* (1854). *An Introduction to the Principles of Morals and Legislation* had little impact at the time of its publication, due in part to the public's absorption in the political crisis in France.

Bentham's most controversial, and to some most notorious, project was the Panopticon Penitentiary House, which he planned and fought to see implemented in the years 1789-1812. In March 1792 Bentham proposed a contract-management plan, in which the manager would be responsible for the success or failure of his prison. Important elements of Bentham's proposal included "wholesome food," clean and comfortable clothing and bedding, six hours sleep, "spiritual and medical assistance," educational training, profit incentive, life insurance, a resident manager, frequent reports, and open inspection. These goals, modest though they may seem, were a considerable advance over previous eighteenth-century penal policy, which included incarceration in old, abandoned ships, overcrowding, rampant starvation and disease, and no attempt to rehabilitate prisoners.

The design of the Panopticon has aroused a great deal of criticism in twentieth-century evaluations, which typically condemn the plan for denying the basic human need for privacy. The name *Panopticon*, derived from the Greek word for all-seeing, describes a circular building in which all cells and their inhabitants can be seen from a central location, the "inspector's station," without the inspector himself being seen. This system of anonymous surveillance was intended to deprive prisoners of privacy, which might encourage vice. Bentham's Panopticon could house one thousand men, and, he argued, the building design could be adapted for workhouses, factories, madhouses, hospitals, and schools. The prison featured not only invisible surveillance, but constant isolation. Bentham himself tried to resolve objections to his plan:

> [Critics question] Whether the liberal spirit and energy of a free citizen would not be exchanged for the mechanical discipline of a soldier, or the austerity of a monk? And whether the result of this high-wrought contrivance might not be constructing a set of *machines* under the similitude of *men*?. . . Call them soldiers, call them monks, call them machines: so they were but happy ones, I should not care.

Twentieth-century historian Gertrude Himmelfarb traces Bentham's revisions to his original proposal, pointing out that Bentham's concern with saving money and increasing profit might lead to malnourishment and overwork of prisoners, as well as the exploitation of prisoners for public entertainment, as was the custom in some nineteenth-century asylums and hospitals.

In 1794 an act was passed to authorize the implementation of Bentham's plan, but for years obstacles arose to prevent the building of the Panopticon. After repeated frustrations and enormous financial loss by Bentham, a new act was passed in 1811, substituting trust management for contract management and putting an end to all of Bentham's hopes for the Panopticon. In 1813 Parliament awarded Bentham twenty-three thousand pounds in compensation for what he had spent in the last two decades. Bentham's Panopticon failure was yet another element in his later support for democratic reform and his hostility toward corrupt legislative power and an entrenched and powerful aristocracy.

While visiting Bowood, Bentham had met a Swiss writer and clergyman, Etienne Dumont, whose admiration for Bentham's ideas led him to translate some of Bentham's unfinished manuscripts into French, thereby making them available to a larger audience. Bentham's thought had already made an impact in France, where he was awarded the title Citizen of France by the National Assembly on 26 August 1792. Dumont streamlined Bentham's work into condensed, more-readable prose. In 1802 Dumont's translation of Bentham's *Theory of Legislation* was published. Reconsidering what determines fair punishment for a particular offense, the work addressed a timely subject, for in the early nineteenth century the theft of anything valued at forty shillings or more was a capital offense. In 1811 Bentham's *Rationale of Punishment* and *Rationale of Reward* were published in Dumont's two-volume translation. Following Dumont's publications, Bentham's fame spread not only in France, but to Russia, where translations of Dumont's translations appeared in 1806-1811, and to Spain and Latin America, where translations appeared in 1821-1822.

In 1808 the sixty-year-old Bentham met the vigorous, thirty-five-year-old James Mill, who was to disseminate Bentham's work among their fellow Englishmen. The Mills became tenants near Bentham's home at Queen's Square Place, Westminster, inherited from Jeremiah Bentham in 1792. Bentham invited Mill and his family for six-month visits each year to the elegant manor of Ford Abbey, near Chard, which Bentham rented from 1814 to 1818. Mill spent many hours with Bentham discussing utilitarian philosophy and transcribing Bentham's work into publishable

*Bentham circa 1789 (portrait by an unknown artist; University College London)*

form. Mill's recorded impressions of Bentham reveal both affection and admiration. Later, James Mill's nineteen-year-old son, John Stuart Mill, would take on the enormous task of editing Bentham's *Rationale of Judicial Evidence* (1827).

In 1814-1815, at the request of friends concerned with the educational needs of the middle classes, Bentham began to develop a plan for a new kind of educational curriculum and a teaching methodology based on Andrew Bell's and Joseph Lancaster's monitorial systems. His Chrestomathic Day School is described in *Chrestomathia* (1817), its title meaning "conducive to useful learning." Bentham's educational program emphasized "practical" knowledge such as natural history, chemistry, engineering, and medicine; he criticized the priority given Latin and Greek in traditional middle- and upper-class British education, and he advocated the use of visual tables to accelerate learning, scheduling activities for every moment of a pupil's time, the abolition of corporal punishment, and the omission of religious instruction. Francis Place and James Mill raised subscriptions for the building of the school, and together with David Ricardo and William Allen they worked actively to make the Chrestomathic Day School a reality, but plans were eventually abandoned in 1820. Later, Dickens's novel *Hard Times* would portray the apparent obliviousness of utilitarian education to the human needs for amusement and moral and aesthetic enrichment. Dickens's arch-utilitarian Thomas Gradgrind believes in a fact-oriented education and is described as a "cannon loaded to the muzzle with facts, and prepared to blow [the students] clean out of the regions of childhood with one discharge."

Shortly after this venture into educational reform, Bentham turned his attention to religion in *Church of Englandism and its Catechism Examined* (1818), a criticism of the Anglican church's abuses of power; *An Analysis of the Influence of Natu-*

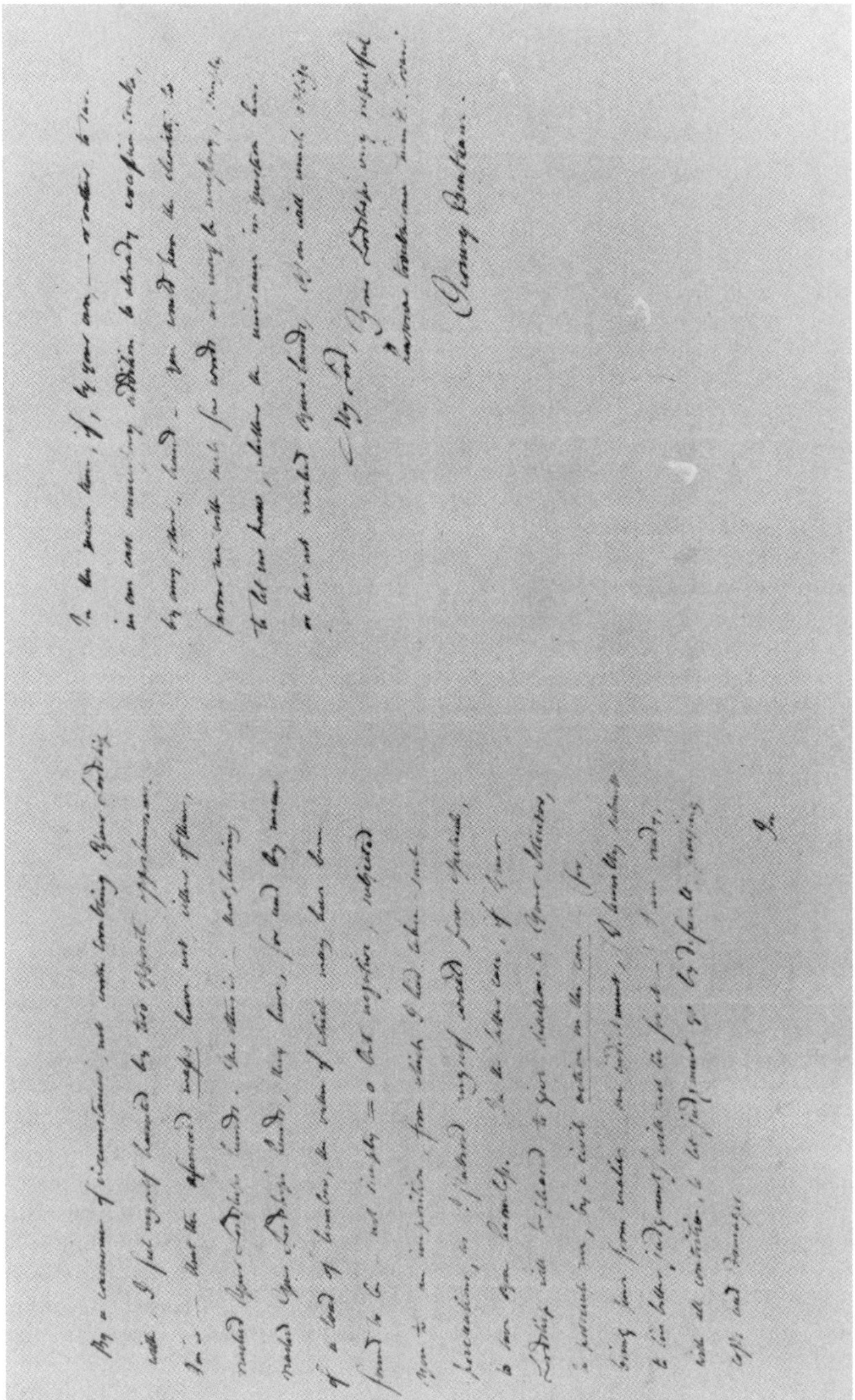

*Pages from Bentham's 8 September 1811 letter to Henry Richard Vassall Fox, Baron Holland (Pierpont Morgan Library, from the Collection of Gordon N. Ray). Bentham was concerned because Lord Holland had not acknowledged receipt of Bentham's proposal, mailed on 27 August, to rename the United Kingdom "Brithibernia." Lord Holland returned the "curious and interesting paper" in December, suggesting that the name was unlikely to be adopted.*

*ral Religion on the Temporal Happiness of Mankind* (1822), his most radical attack on religion; and *Not Paul, but Jesus* (1823), which argues that Paul destroyed the true Christian spirit. Bentham, reared as an Anglican, did not profess any personal religious beliefs but was tolerant of the beliefs of others.

Also at this time Bentham began to advocate the democratic reform of the English Parliament, arguing for the secret ballot, universal manhood suffrage, equal electoral districts, and annual elections. In his *Plan of Parliamentary Reform* (1817) Bentham, who had earlier favored a strong monarchy, described the king and aristocracy as "*C*[orrupto]*r-General & Co.*" formed to drain "the contents of all pockets into its own." Bentham's democratic sympathies can be traced back to 1789-1790 and 1809-1810, but his most vehement writings came later: *Plan of Parliamentary Reform* (1817), *Radical Reform Bill* (1819), and "Securities Against Misrule" (written in 1822-1823 and first published in John Bowring's edition of Bentham's *Works* [1838-1843]).

In 1823 Bentham founded the *Westminster Review*. Featuring articles on utilitarian perspectives, the review, which first appeared in 1824 and continued to be published until 1914, ranked in the top echelon of nineteenth-century intellectual periodicals. A new acquaintance, John Bowring (1792-1872), became political editor and then general editor of the review. Bentham later named him as his literary executor.

Published in 1816 in French and in 1824 in English, *The Book of Fallacies* undertook the reform of language, which—according to Bentham—was used in law and politics to deceive and obfuscate. "Vague generalities" such as "matchless constitution," "balance of power," and "glorious revolution" are analyzed, as well as "question-begging" euphemisms such as the use of the terms *honor* and *glory* in wartime. Bentham's distrust of figurative language and imaginative literature may be traced to Jeremiah Bentham's outlawing of poetry and fiction in the Bentham household and to Jeremy Bentham's early awareness of ambiguous language in English law. He zealously crusaded against legal "fictions" (falsehoods used to incorporate a new kind of case under an old rule; for example, considering husband and wife one person). Bentham called rhetoric and poetry "the two branches of the art of misrepresentation" and seemed numb to the aesthetic pleasure of imaginative literature, although he enjoyed music. In a now-well-known argument against public subsidies for the arts Bentham remarked that "the game of push-pin is of equal value with the arts and sciences of music and poetry" (*The Rationale of Reward* ). Bentham's failure to acknowledge spiritual and aesthetic human needs became a rallying point for anti-utilitarian Victorians.

Bentham's writing poses many challenges. As suggested by Bentham's request in a January 1791 letter to George Wilson for "a receipt for making readable books," he was aware that his writing often confused his readers. Perhaps part of the problem lies in the wide range of his inquiries. Nearly twenty years earlier, in a 14 October 1772 letter to his father, he expressed his inability to examine only a portion of any subject: "I cannot rest till I feel myself every where at the bottom—I cannot go on with what is *before* me, while I have any thing behind me unexplor'd. . . ."

Perhaps the ultimate expression of Bentham's fascination with thorough investigation and analysis of a subject may be seen in his ambition to write a complete and comprehensive code of all English law. He hoped his code would eliminate judicial and legal abuses and make adjudication more fair and efficient. The adoption of his reforms having met with so little success in his own country, Bentham offered his codifying services to President James Madison in the United States and Alexander I of Russia, and probed for opportunities in Portugal, Spain, Turkey, and Colombia. In 1830 the first volume of his massive *Constitutional Code* was published; the remaining two volumes have yet to be published in the form that Bentham intended. Bentham's proposed civil-court reforms of laws pertaining to the admission of certain kinds of evidence, bankruptcy, insolvency, and imprisonment for debt were also valuable contributions to British law.

John Stuart Mill and Thomas Carlyle criticized Bentham for his failure to appreciate private ethics; as Mill wrote in "Bentham" (1838), "Man is never recognised by him as being capable of pursuing spiritual perfection as an end. . . ." But it should be noted that Bentham's primary concern was not with individual morality but with public policy.

Bentham's interest in quantifying pains and pleasures is seen by many historians as "a movement toward the modern social sciences," and Richard Altick calls Bentham the "founder of the science of public administration." Bentham favored government interventionism that would en-

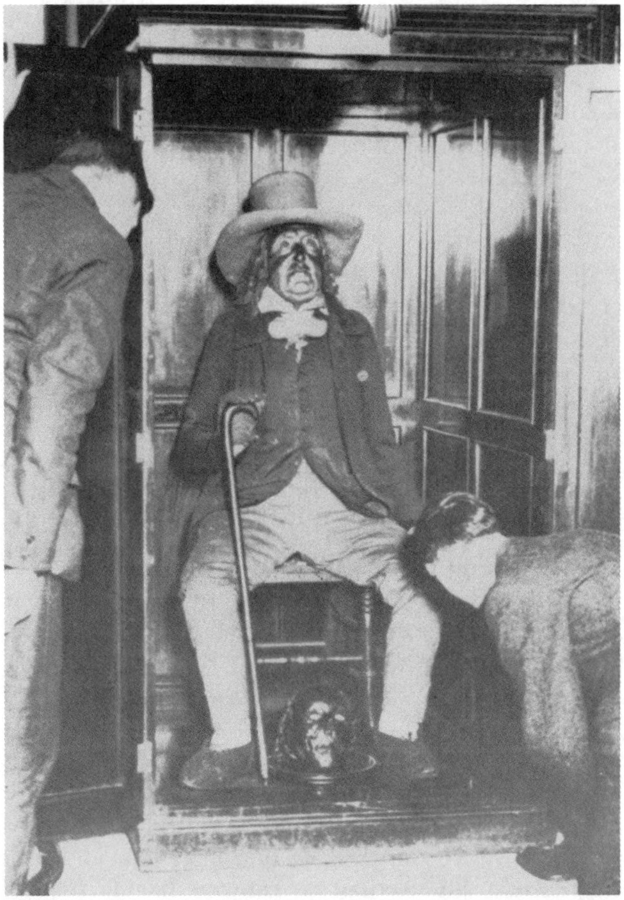

*Bentham's "Auto-icon"—his skeleton, stuffed, dressed, and topped with a wax effigy of his head—in its case at University College London. His skull, which rests at his feet in this photograph, has since been removed from the case.*

hance security; thus he proposed the office of the "Preventative Services Minister," who would oversee crisis management of disasters and safety regulations for bridges, mines, factories, and buildings; and the office of "Indigence Relief Minister," who would oversee poor relief. Bentham inspired reforms of factory legislation, the inadequate Elizabethan poor laws, public-health laws, and the penal code. His ideas about international relations, the rights of women, and the treatment of homosexuals were advanced. He continued work on his codification of British law until his death at the age of eighty-four.

Bentham's best-known eccentricity involves his instructions for the preparation of his own corpse. He willed his body to University College London for medical research and instructed that his remains be publicly displayed in preserved form as an "Auto-icon." Bentham's skeleton, stuffed with straw, dressed in his clothes, and topped with a wax effigy of his head, is on view in a glass case at University College London.

John Stuart Mill's evaluation of Bentham as "a man of both remarkable endowments for philosophy, and of remarkable deficiencies for it" sums up the difficulty of pronouncing a final assessment of Bentham's life and contributions. Whatever Bentham's limitations as human being, ethicist, or social reformer, he was always, in Mill's words, "the great questioner of things established" and a legal reformer whose efforts were of such scope that mythological comparisons are not inappropriate. As Mill wrote, "He found the philosophy of law a chaos, he left it a science: he found the practice of the law an Augean stable, he turned the river into it which is mining and sweeping away mound after mound of its rubbish."

**Letters:**

*The Correspondence of Jeremy Bentham*, 9 volumes to date, general editors J. H. Burns, J. R. Dinwiddy, and F. Rosen (volumes 1-5, London: Athlone Press, 1968-1981; volumes 6- , Oxford: Clarendon Press, 1984- ).

**Bibliographies:**

C. W. Everett, "Bibliography," in *The Growth of Philosophic Radicalism*, by Elie Halévy, translated by Mary Morris (London: Faber & Gwyer, 1928), pp. 522-546;

David Lyons, *In the Interest of the Governed: A Study in Bentham's Philosophy of Utility and Law* (Oxford: Clarendon Press, 1973), pp. 138-143;

James E. Crimmins, *Secular Utilitarianism: Social Science and the Critique of Religion in the Thought of Jeremy Bentham* (Oxford: Clarendon Press, 1990), pp. 317-319.

**Biographies:**

Charles Milner Atkinson, *Jeremy Bentham: His Life and Work* (London: Methuen, 1905);

Charles Warren Everett, *The Education of Jeremy Bentham* (New York: Columbia University Press, 1931);

Mary P. Mack, *Jeremy Bentham: An Odyssey of Ideas, 1748-1792* (New York: Columbia University Press, 1963; London: Heinemann, 1963).

**References:**

Richard D. Altick, *Victorian People and Ideas* (New York & London: Norton, 1971), pp. 114-145;

David Baumgardt, *Bentham and the Ethics of Today* (Princeton: Princeton University Press, 1952);

James E. Crimmins, *Secular Utilitarianism: Social Science and the Critique of Religion in the Thought of Jeremy Bentham* (Oxford: Clarendon Press, 1990).

J. R. Dinwiddy, *Bentham* (Oxford & New York: Oxford University Press, 1989);

Eldon J. Eisenach, "The Dimension of History in Bentham's Theory of Law," *Eighteenth-Century Studies*, 16 (Spring 1983): 290-316;

David A. Funk, "Bentham as Pioneer in Legal Semiotics," in *Semiotics 1984*, edited by John Deely (Lanham, Md.: University Presses of America, 1985), pp. 219-224;

Elie Halévy, *La Formation du radicalisme philosophique*, 3 volumes (Paris: Alcan, 1901-1904); translated by Mary Morris as *The Growth of Philosophic Radicalism* (London: Faber & Gwyer, 1928);

Ross Harrison, *Bentham* (London: Routledge & Kegan Paul, 1983);

Gertrude Himmelfarb, "Bentham Scholarship and the Bentham 'Problem,'" *Journal of Modern History*, 41 (June 1969): 189-206;

Himmelfarb, "The Haunted House of Jeremy Bentham," in her *Victorian Minds* (New York: Knopf, 1968), pp. 32-81;

Richard A. Hixson, "Bentham's *The Rationale of Reward*," *Journal of the Rutgers University Libraries*, 63 (June 1981): 18-24;

Elissa S. Itzkin, "Bentham's *Chrestomathia*: Utilitarian Legacy to English Education," *Journal of the History of Ideas*, 34 (April-June 1978): 303-316;

David Lyons, *In the Interest of the Governed: A Study in Bentham's Philosophy of Utility and Law* (Oxford: Clarendon Press, 1973);

Mary P. Mack, Commentary in *A Bentham Reader*, edited by Mack (New York: Pegasus, 1969);

John Stuart Mill, "Bentham" and "Utilitarianism," in his *Essays on Ethics, Religion and Society*, edited by J. M. Robson, volume 10 of *The Collected Works of John Stuart Mill* (Toronto: University of Toronto Press, 1969), pp. 75-115, 203-259;

Bhikhu Parekh, *Jeremy Bentham: Ten Critical Essays* (London: Frank Cass, 1974);

John Plamenatz, *The English Utilitarians* (Oxford: Blackwell, 1949);

Robert Shackleton, "'The Greatest Happiness for the Greatest Number': The History of Bentham's Phrase," *Studies on Voltaire and the Eighteenth-Century*, 90 (1972): 1461-1482;

James Steintrager, *Bentham* (Ithaca, N.Y.: Cornell University Press, 1977);

Leslie Stephen, *The English Utilitarians*, 3 volumes (London: Duckworth, 1900);

Jeremy Waldron, *'Nonsense upon stilts': Bentham, Burke, and Marx on the rights of man* (London & New York: Methuen, 1987);

Miriam Williford, "Bentham on the Rights of Women," *Journal of the History of Ideas*, 36 (January-March 1975): 167-176.

**Papers:**

There are collections of Bentham's papers at the British Library (Series of Additional Manuscripts) and at University College London, catalogued in D. G. Long's *The Manuscripts of Jeremy Bentham: A Chronological Index to the Collection in the Library of University College London* (London: Printed by the Bentham Committee at University College London, 1982).

# Sir Samuel Egerton Brydges

*(30 November 1762 - 8 September 1837)*

Thomas L. Cooksey
*Armstrong State College*

BOOKS: *Sonnets and other Poems; with a Versification of the Six Bards of Ossian* (London: Printed for G. & T. Wilkie, 1785; enlarged, 1785; enlarged again, London: Printed for B. & J. White, 1795);

*Mary De-Clifford, a Story Interspersed with Many Poems* (London: Printed for H. D. Symonds, 1792);

*Verses on the Late Unanimous Resolutions to Support the Constitution. To which are added some other poems* (Canterbury: Printed by Simmons, Kirkby & Jones, 1794);

*Arthur Fitz-Albini, a Novel*, 2 volumes (London: Printed for J. White, 1798);

*Reflections on the Late Augmentations of the English Peerage* (London: Printed for J. Robson & J. Debrett, 1798);

*Tests of National Wealth and Finances of Great Britain in December 1798* (London: Printed for J. White, 1799);

*Memoirs of the Peers of England During the Reign of James the First* (London: Printed for J. White by Nichols & son, 1802);

*Le Forester, a Novel*, 3 volumes (London: Printed for J. White by T. Bensley, 1802);

*Polyanthea; or, a Collection of Interesting Fragments in Prose and Verse* (London: Budd, 1804);

*Poems* (London: Hurst, Rees & Orme, 1807);

*A Biographical Peerage of the Empire of Great Britain*, 4 volumes (London: Printed for J. Johnson, 1808-1817);

*An Analysis of the Genealogical History of the Family of Howard* (London: Printed & published for the author by H. K. Causton, 1812);

*Letters on the Poor Laws* (London: Longman, Hurst, Rees, Orme & Brown, 1813);

*The Ruminator: Containing a Series of Moral, Critical and Sentimental Essays*, 2 volumes (London: Longman, Hurst, Rees, Orme & Brown, 1813);

*The Sylvan Wanderer; Consisting of a Series of Moral, Sentimental, and Critical Essays*, 4 volumes (Kent: Printed at the Private Press of Lee Priory by Johnson & Warwick, 1813-1821);

*Restituta; or, Titles, Extracts, and Characters of Old Books in English Literature, Revived*, 4 volumes (London: Printed by T. Bensley for Longman, Hurst, Rees, Orme & Brown, 1814-1816);

*Occasional Poems, Written in the Year MDCCCXI* (Kent: Printed at the Private Press of Lee Priory by Johnson & Warwick, 1814); facsimile in *Samuel Egerton Brydges and Edward Quillinan* (New York & London: Garland, 1978);

*Select Poems* (Kent: Printed at the Private Press of Lee Priory by Johnson & Warwick, 1814);

*Bertram, a Poetical Tale* (Kent: Printed at the Private Press of Lee Priory by Johnson & Warwick, 1814); facsimile in *Samuel Egerton Brydges and Edward Quillinan* (1978); revised as *Bertram, A Poetical Tale in Four Cantos* (London: Longman, Hurst, Rees, Orme & Brown, 1816);

*Desultoria: or Comments of a South-Briton on Books and Men* (Kent: Printed at the Private Press of Lee Priory by Johnson & Warwick, 1815);

*Fragment of a Poem, Occasioned by a Visit to the Old Mansion of Denton, July 23, 1815* (Kent: Lee Priory Press, 1815);

*A Brief Character of Matthew, lord Rokeby* (Kent: Printed at the Press of Lee Priory by J. Warwick, 1817);

*Arguments in Favour of the Practicability of Relieving the Able-bodied Poor* (London: Printed by Bensley for Longman, 1817);

*Reasons for a Farther Amendment of the Act 54 Geo. III. c. 156, being an act to amend the Copyright Act of Queen Anne* (London: Printed by Nichols, son & Bentley, 1817); facsimile in *Four Tracts on Copyright, 1817-1818* (New York & London: Garland, 1974);

*A Summary Statement of the Great Grievances imposed on Authors and Publishers; and the Injury done to Literature, by the Late Copyright Act* (London: Printed for Longman, Hurst, Rees, Orme & Brown, 1818); facsimile in *Four Tracts on Copyright, 1817-1818* (1974);

*Frontispiece to volume 1 of Brydges's autobiography*

*A Vindication of the Pending Bill for the Amendment of the Copyright Act, from the Misrepresentations and Unjust Comments of the Syndics of the University Library, at Cambridge* (London: Printed for Longman, Hurst, Rees, Orme & Brown, 1818); facsimile in *Four Tracts on Copyright, 1817-1818* (1974);

*Answer to the Further Statement, ordered by the Syndics of the University of Cambridge to be printed and circulated* (London, 1818); facsimile in *Four Tracts on Copyright, 1817-1818* (1974);

*Five Sonnets, Addressed to Wootton, the Spot of the Author's Nativity* (Kent: Printed at the Private Press of Lee Priory by John Warwick, 1819); facsimile in *Samuel Egerton Brydges and Edward Quillinan* (1978);

*Lord Brokenhurst. Or, a Fragment of Winter Leaves: A Tragic Tale* (Paris & Geneva: J. J. Paschoud / London: R. Triphook, 1819);

*Coningsby, A Tragic Tale* (Paris: J. J. Paschoud / London: R. Triphook, 1819);

*The Population and Riches of Nations* (Paris & Geneva: J. J. Paschoud / London: R. Triphook, 1819);

*Tragic Tales: Coningsby, and Lord Brokenhurst*, 2 volumes (London: Printed for Robert Triphook, 1820);

*Sir Ralph Willoughby: An Historical Tale of the Sixteenth Century* (Florence: I. Magheri, 1820);

*Letters from the Continent*, 2 parts (Kent: Printed at the Private Press of Lee Priory by J. Warwick, 1821);

*What Are Riches? or, An Examination of the Definitions of this Subject Given by Modern Economists* (Geneva: Printed by W. Fick, 1821; Kent: Printed at the Private Press of Lee Priory by John Warwick, 1822);

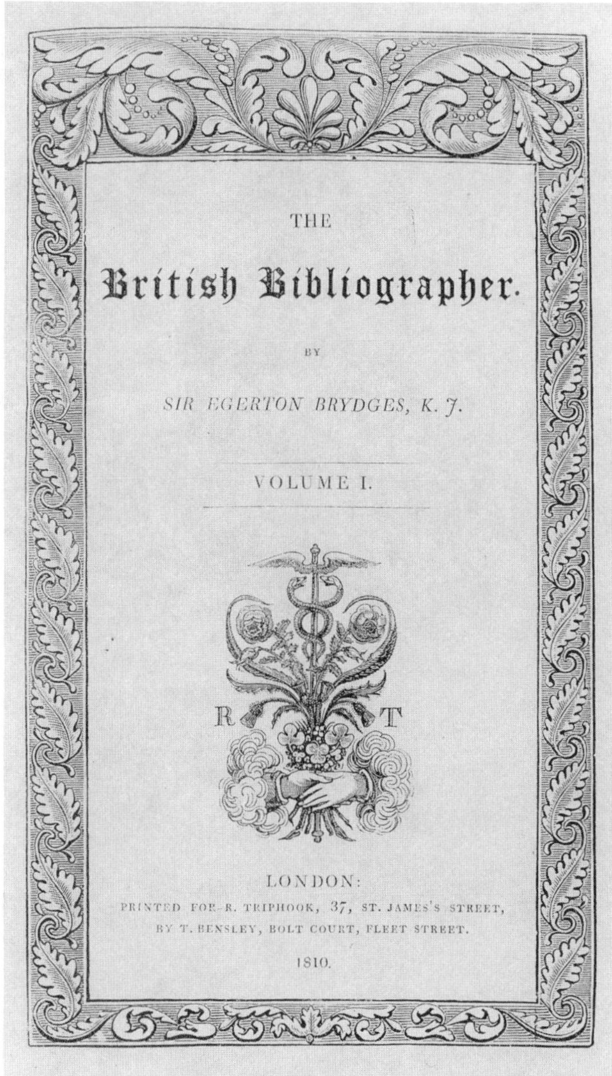

THE

British Bibliographer.

BY

SIR EGERTON BRYDGES, K. J.

VOLUME I.

R T

LONDON:

PRINTED FOR R. TRIPHOOK, 37, ST. JAMES'S STREET,

BY T. BENSLEY, BOLT COURT, FLEET STREET.

1810.

*Title page for one of the collections of British Renaissance works for which Brydges and his friends wrote bibliographical and historical commentaries (Special Collections, Thomas Cooper Library, University of South Carolina)*

*The Hall of Hellingsley: A Tale*, 3 volumes (London: Longman, Hurst, Rees, Orme & Brown, 1821);

*The Anti-Critic for August 1821, and March, 1822. Containing Literary, Not Political, Criticisms, and Opinions* (Geneva: Printed by W. Fick, 1822);

*Odo, Count Lingen: A Poetical Tale in Six Cantos* (Geneva: Printed by W. Fick, 1824; facsimile, New York & London: Garland, 1978);

*Gnomica: Detached Thoughts, Sententious, Axiomatic, Moral and Critical* (Geneva: Printed by W. Fick, 1824);

*Letters on the Character and Poetical Genius of Lord Byron* (London: Longman, Hurst, Rees, Orme, Brown & Green, 1824);

*An Impartial Portrait of Lord Byron* (Paris: Published by A. & W. Galignani, 1825);

*Recollections of Foreign Travel, on Life, Literature, and Self-Knowledge*, 2 volumes (London: Printed for Longman, Hurst, Rees, Orme, Brown & Green, 1825);

*Travels of my Nightcap, or Reveries in Rhyme* (London: G. B. Whittaker, 1825);

*Stemmata Illustria: Præcipue regia* (Paris: Printed by J. Smith, 1825);

*A Note on the Suppression of Memoirs announced by the author in June 1825; containing numerous strictures on contemporary public characters* (Paris: Printed by J. Smith, 1825);

*Who Was Ita, Countess of Hapsburg, Who founded the monastery of Muri in Switzerland, in 1018, and died in 1026?* (Paris: Printed by J. Smith, 1826);

*Lex Terrae. A Discussion of the Law of England, regarding Claims of Inheritable Rights of Peerage* (Geneva: Printed by William Fick, 1831);

*Modern Aristocracy, or, the Bard's Reception: The Fragment of a Poem* (Geneva: Printed by A. L. Vignier, 1831);

*The Lake of Geneva, a Poem, Moral and Descriptive, in Seven Books*, 2 volumes (Geneva: Printed by A. L. Vignier for A. Cherbuliez, 1832);

*The Autobiography, Times, Opinions, and Contemporaries of Sir Egerton Brydges, bart.*, 2 volumes (London: Cochrane & M'Crone, 1834);

*Imaginative Biography*, 2 volumes (London: Saunders & Otley, 1834);

*The Life of John Milton* (London: Printed for John Macrone, 1835);

*Human Fate, and an Address to the Poets Wordsworth & Southey: Poems* (Great Totham: Printed at C. Clark's Private Press, 1846).

OTHER: Edward Phillips, *Theatrum Poetarum Anglicanorum*, edited, with additions, by Brydges (Canterbury: Printed by Simmons & Kirkby for J. White, London, 1800);

*Censura Literaria*, 10 volumes, edited, with contributions, by Brydges (London: Printed by T. Bensley for Longman, Hurst, Rees & Orme, and J. White, 1805-1809; facsimile, New York: AMS Press, 1966);

*The British Bibliographer*, 4 volumes, edited, with contributions, by Brydges (London: Printed for R. Triphook by T. Bensley, 1810-1814; facsimile, New York: AMS Press, 1966);

Richard Edwards, *The Paradise of Dainty Devices*, edited by Brydges (London: Printed for Robert Triphook, 1810);

*England's Helicon: A Collection of Pastoral and Lyric Poems, First Published at the Close of the Reign of Q. Elizabeth*, edited by Brydges (London: Printed by T. Bensley for Robert Triphook, 1812);

Arthur Collins, *Collins's Peerage of England: Genealogical, Biographical, and Historical*, 9 volumes, edited and augmented by Brydges (London: Printed for F. C. & J. Rivington, Otridge & son, 1812);

Robert Greene, *Greene's Groatsworth of Wit*, edited, with a preface, by Brydges (Kent: Printed at the Private Press of Lee Priory by Johnson & Warwick, 1813);

Sir Henry Wotton, *The Characters of Robert Devereux, earl of Essex; and George Villiers, duke of Buckingham*, edited by Brydges (Kent: Printed at the Private Press of Lee Priory by Johnson & Warwick, 1814);

Michael Drayton, *Nymphidia: The Court of Fairy*, edited by Brydges (Kent: Printed at the Private Press of Lee Priory by Johnson & Warwick, 1814);

Thomas Stanley, *Poems by Thomas Stanley*, edited by Brydges (London: Longman, Hurst, Rees, Orme & Brown, 1814);

Margaret Cavendish, Duchess of Newcastle, *A True Relation of the Birth, Breeding, and Life of Margaret Cavendish, Duchess of Newcastle*, edited, with a critical preface, by Brydges (Kent: Printed at the Private Press of Lee Priory by Johnson & Warwick, 1814);

*Excerpta Tudoriana; or, Extracts from Elizabethan Literature*, edited, with a critical preface, by Brydges (Kent: Printed at the Private Press of Lee Priory by Johnson & Warwick, 1814-1818);

*Archaica: Containing a Reprint of Scarce Old English Prose Tracts*, 2 volumes, edited, with critical and biographical prefaces and notes, by Brydges (London: From the Private Press of Longman, Hurst, Rees, Orme & Brown, printed by T. Davison, 1815);

Richard Brathwaite, *Brathwayte's Odes; or, Philomel's Tears*, edited by Brydges (Kent: Printed at the Private Press of Lee Priory by Johnson & Warwick, 1815);

Nicholas Breton, *Breton's Melancholike Humours*, edited, with a critical preface, by Brydges (Kent: Printed at the Private Press of Lee Priory by Johnson & Warwick, 1815);

Breton, *Breton's Praise of Virtuous Ladies*, edited by Brydges (Kent: Printed at the Private Press of Lee Priory by Johnson & Warwick, 1815);

George Wither, *Hymns and Songs of the Church*, edited, with a preface, by Brydges (London: Longman, Hurst, Rees, Orme & Brown, 1815);

William Hammond, *Occasional Poems, by William Hammond, Esq.*, edited by Brydges (London: Printed by T. Bensley & son for Longman, Hurst, Rees, Orme & Brown, 1816);

John Hagthorpe, *Hagthorpe, Revived; or, Select Specimens of a Forgotten Poet*, edited by Brydges (Kent: Printed at the Private Press of Lee Priory by John Warwick, 1817);

William Percy, *Coelia: Containing Twenty Sonnets by W. Percy*, edited by Brydges (Kent: Printed at the Private Press of Lee Priory by J. Warwick, 1818);

Charles Fitz-Geffrey, *The Life and Death of Sir Francis Drake*, edited by Brydges (Kent: Printed at the Private Press of Lee Priory by J. Warwick, 1819);

Edward Quillinan, *Carmina Brugesiana: Domestic Poems by Edward Quillinan*, edited by Brydges (Geneva: Printed by W. Fick, 1822);

*The Green Book; or, Register of the Order of the Emerald Star*, edited by Brydges (Geneva?, 1822).

Jane Austen expected little of Egerton Brydges. In a 25 November 1798 letter to her sister Cassandra, the twenty-three-year-old Austen reported that she and her father had been reading the first volume of Brydges's new novel, *Arthur Fitz-Albini*: "We have neither of us yet finished the first volume. My father is disappointed—*I* am not, for I expected nothing better." She added, "Never did any book carry more internal evidence of its author. Every sentiment is completely Egerton's." Brydges, a brother of Anne Brydges Lefroy (Austen's beloved Madame Lefroy), often seems to resemble one of Austen's villains. He was obsessed with his pedigree and titles, claiming descendency from the extinct house of Chandos, editing Arthur Collins's *Peerage of England* to support his position, and styling himself baron Chandos (*per legem terrae*). He was also a sullen snob who looked upon himself as an unacknowledged genius, the victim of fashion and the vulgarity of the age. A prolific poet and novelist of Gothic and melancholy sensibilities, Brydges did seem to be out of place in his world. As Donald H. Reiman observes, "Brydges had the misfortune of having been born a little too early to have become a Romantic poet, though his ideals are not far from those of Wordsworth, Shelley, and Byron." Brydges was also a passionate antiquarian, compiling, editing, and publishing many volumes of Elizabethan literature, including his multivolumed *Censura Literaria* (1805-1809) and *The British Bibliographer* (1810-1814).

Samuel Egerton Brydges was born on 30 November 1762 in the manor house of Wootton, between Canterbury and Dover. He was the second son of Edward Brydges (or Bridges) of Wootton and Jemima Egerton Brydges, daughter of William Egerton, the prebendary of Canterbury Cathedral and chancellor of Hereford Cathedral. From an early age Brydges showed a taste and sensibility for literature. "Reality never satisfied me," Brydges recollected in his autobiography, "the imaginative commonly did so. The intense delight with which I read romances and fairy tales from the earliest age is indescribable." While largely distant from his son, Edward Brydges gave him his lifelong taste for Elizabethan literature as well as the conviction that he was a genius. "Once, and only once, my father spoke to me in terms of literary encouragement; . . . on some occasion he dropped the words '*your genius*,' and they have ever since hung like a charm upon my ear."

Brydges received his early education at Maidstone School and King's School, Canterbury. In October 1780 he entered Queen's College, Cambridge, where he found the focus on mathematics and the Lockean tradition unsuitable to his temperament. After Christmas 1782 he began legal studies at the Middle Temple in London, but he found this subject uncongenial as well. Thus he turned his attention to poetry, publishing his first volume, *Sonnets and other Poems*, in 1785. The work received modest notice, not the attention that Brydges thought it warranted. He determined to abandon creative literature, marrying Elizabeth Byrche, niece of Thomas Barrett of Lee Priory, in 1786 and settling in Hampshire, near his sister Anne (Mrs. Isaac Peter George Lefroy). Here he entered into the circle of young Jane Austen and her family. Years later, Brydges recalled, "When I knew Jane Austen, I never suspected that she was an authoress; but my eyes told me that she was fair and handsome, slight and elegant, but with cheeks a little too full." She remembered him as moody and distant.

Brydges returned to London in late 1787 and was called to the bar, but he never practiced law. Instead he took a house in London so that he could pursue his literary, genealogical, and antiquarian studies at the British Museum. Brydges also returned to creative literature, publishing his first novel, *Mary De-Clifford*, in 1792. The story, he suggested, "darted" upon him while he walked in the park of Lee Priory one misty morning. In the tradition of Samuel Richardson's *Sir Charles Grandison* (1753-1754) and Charlotte Smith's *Emmeline, or the Orphan of the Castle* (1788), the work is typical of Brydges's novels, with more emphasis on the melancholy romantic setting and sentiment than on plot or character. Indeed, most of Brydges's creative efforts reflect a spontaneous overflow of powerful emotions, but without the mediation of recollection or tranquility, with the result that while they have moments of powerful imagery, the works are limited in structure and logical development. In her 25

November 1798 letter to Cassandra Austen, Jane Austen complained that in *Arthur Fitz-Albini* "There is very little story, and what there is is told in a strange, unconnected way." Brydges himself admitted that *Mary De-Clifford* "is deficient in story, as I believe all my tales are." He added, "Were I to live again, and renew this part of my literary career, I would certainly give more story." *Mary De-Clifford* also anticipates Brydges's recurrent obsession with a parvenu nobility that values wealth over ancient honor and dignity. The work proved to be a moderate success.

In 1792 Brydges retired with his family to Denton Court in Kent, an Elizabethan mansion near Wootton. Always extravagant in his tastes, Brydges entered into several projects, including the restoration of the house and an unsuccessful scheme for farming. Both these projects proved ruinous. During this period he also made an unsuccessful run for Parliament, and became a captain in the fensible cavalry, part of the local militia. In 1796 Brydges's wife died. Left with the responsibility of their two sons and three daughters, he married Mary Robinson, a niece of Lord Rokeby, the following year. Throughout this period, he continued both with his literary and scholarly efforts, editing and contributing to the *Theatrum Poetarum Anglicanorum* and other works.

Brydges's passion for genealogy and antiquarian studies was the source of his most enduring achievements and his deepest frustrations. In 1788 he discovered that he was distantly related to the historian Edward Gibbon and began a brief correspondence that lasted until Gibbon's death in 1794. In 1789 he traced his lineage to the Norman knight Robert de Chandos, concluding that his family had a claim to the title of baron of Chandos of Sudeley, which had fallen extinct that year with the death of the last baron of Chandos. Brydges persuaded his older brother, the Reverend Edward Tymewell Brydges, to assert a claim to the title. The convoluted genealogical and legal investigations lasted for more than a decade until the Committee of Privileges of the House of Lords finally concluded in 1803 that the claim was not convincing. The disappointment deeply humiliated Brydges, who had begun to style himself "Sir" Egerton Brydges. He raged for the rest of his life that he was the victim of a conspiracy. "I frankly confess that I consider the greater part of the modern nobility to be insolent *parvenus*; ... This is one of those confessions which, I am aware, will give great offence; but I have received injuries from them which can never be repaired." In 1807 Brydges was consoled by his election as a knight in the Swedish order of St. Joachim, an honor, as he was fond of mentioning, that had also been awarded to Admiral Horatio Nelson. In 1814 he was made a baronet, becoming, ironically, a member of the parvenu nobility.

Of greater importance were Brydges's antiquarian studies. For years he had contributed articles on various literary and antiquarian matters to several periodicals. A correspondence with Thomas Park in 1798 led to significant contributions to the *Poetical Register and Repository for Fugitive Poetry*. This association grew into Brydges's editorship of the *Censura Literaria*. He was chiefly responsible for the first volume, published in 1805, and edited the contributions of Park, O. Gilchrist, and John Hasleton for the subsequent volumes. After the tenth volume, they initiated a new series known as *The British Bibliographer*. While Brydges was the directing editor, most of the contributions were prepared by Park, Thomas Frognall Dibdin, and Joseph Haslewood.

Both the *Censura Literaria* and *The British Bibliographer* are collections and digests of British Renaissance poetry, romances, biographies, and miscellaneous documents as diverse as "Fitzherbert's husbandry" and Thomas Nash's 1599 comic squib, "A Pill to Purge Melancholie." The digests are accompanied by scholarly commentaries and articles describing the publication history of the documents and explaining their backgrounds. Brydges and his collaborators anticipated the modern scholarly awareness of the value of minor figures and documents in establishing the cultural and historical texture of an age. Both series served a valuable function in preserving many important documents of the Renaissance, and in making them readily available to scholars. As Brydges remarked in the preface to volume 1 of *The British Bibliographer*, "That many of these sunk into oblivion for want of eminent merit, may be admitted; but the progress of time has given them attractions of a different sort from that by which they originally endeavoured to force themselves into notice."

In October 1810 Brydges moved his family, which had grown to fifteen children, from Denton to Lee Priory near Canterbury, the estate of his eldest son, Thomas Barrett Brydges. The location proved satisfactory to Brydges, who established himself as a lavish host. He corresponded with many authors, including Robert Southey and Sir Walter Scott. He was also visited by a se-

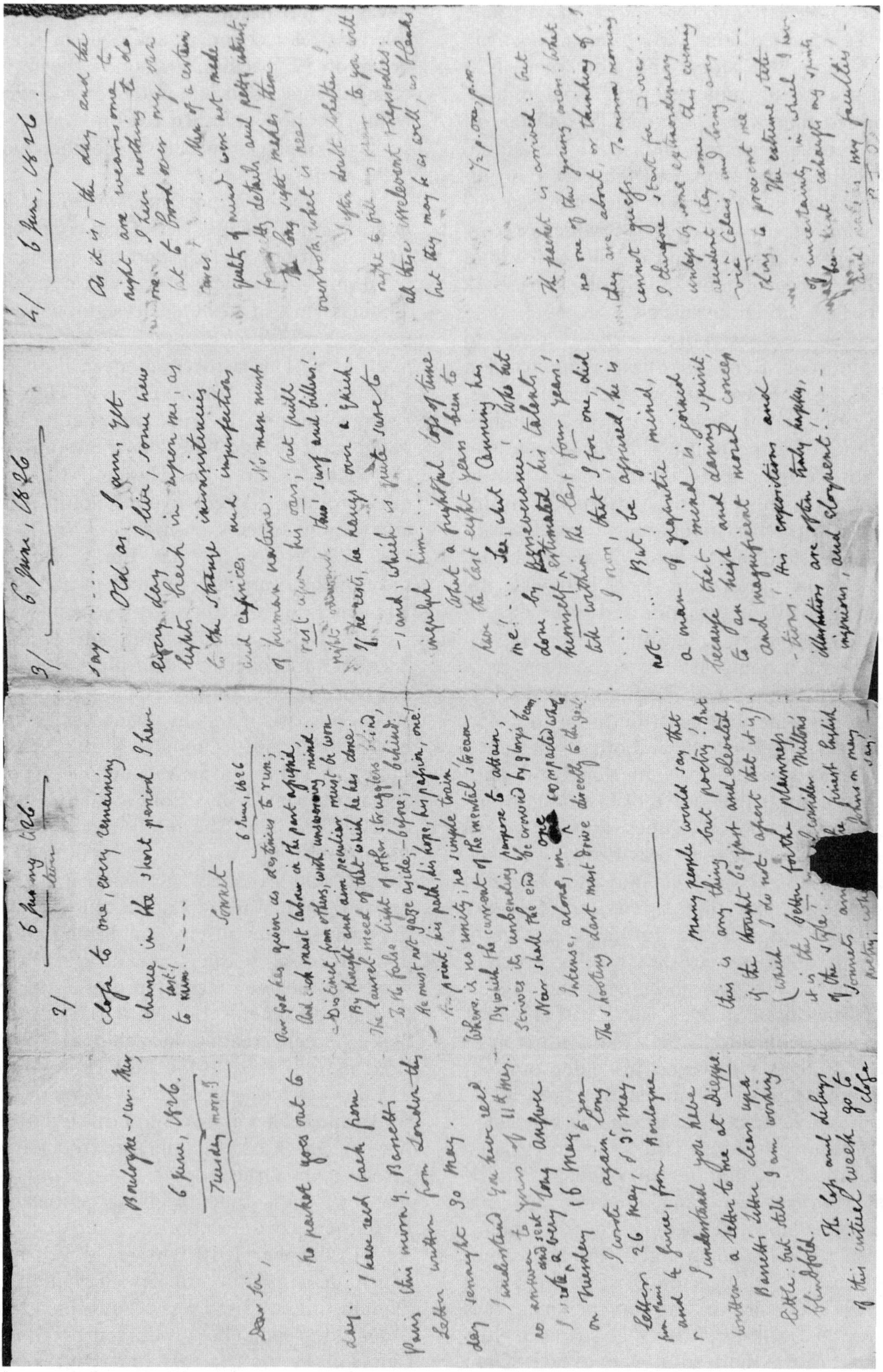

*Letter to J. S. Brooks in London, written from Boulogne on 6 June 1826, just before Brydges returned to England for his only visit after he fled the country in 1818 to escape his creditors (Special Collections, Thomas Cooper Library, University of South Carolina)*

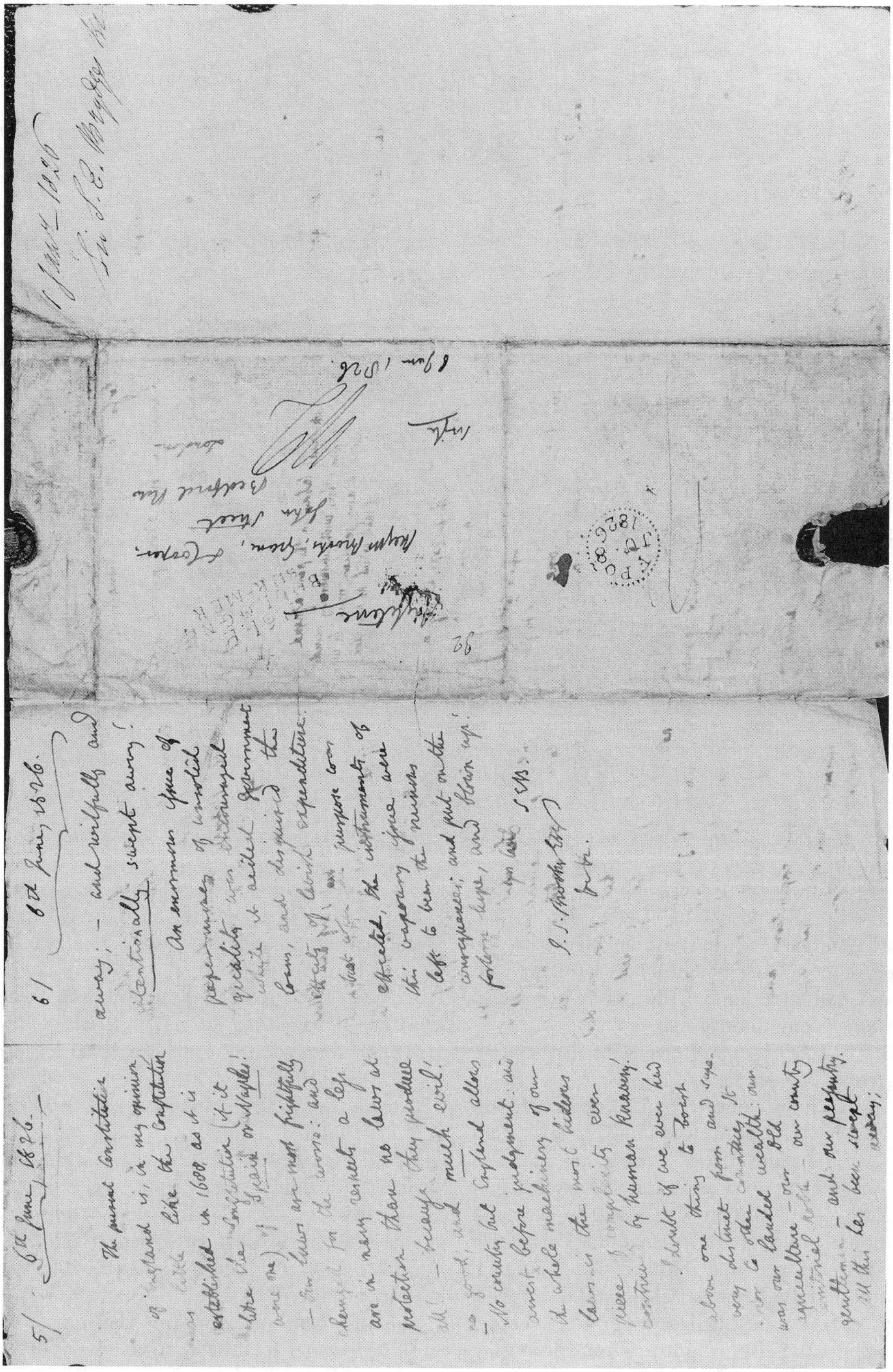

*Portrait by Daniel Maclise in the* Fraser's Magazine *"Gallery of Illustrious Literary Characters" (1830-1838)*

lect court of younger writers, such as R. P. Gillies, Robert Bloomfield, and the Irish poet Edward Quillinan, at the time an officer in the Third Dragoon Guards. Quillinan later married Brydges's daughter Jemima and, after her death, Wordsworth's daughter Dora.

In 1812 Brydges was elected to Parliament, representing Maidstone until 1818. Although he rarely spoke, he became very interested in the reform of the Copyright Act and the Poor Laws, publishing several pamphlets. Turning his attention to the study of political economy, he argued that the wealth of the nation was based on the land and not on commerce and manufacturing. He called for reform that enhanced agricultural labor and decreased industrial labor. Like Wordsworth, Percy Bysshe Shelley, and others, he reacted against the rise of industrialism, proposing a self-sufficient agrarian society as the ideal. Such a society echoes the melancholy nostalgia for a feudal ideal that suffuses Brydges's poetry and novels. It also undergirds his antipathy for the parvenu nobility whose power was not derived from the land.

In 1813 printer John Johnson, who later wrote *Typographia, or The Printer's Instructor* (1824), and compositor John Warwick founded Lee Priory Press, a private press. Brydges was to provide copy, while Johnson and Warwick produced limited editions of high quality which would then be sold at their risk to collectors. The press functioned until 1822, putting out some forty-five books and pamphlets of typographical excellence, especially in the early volumes before Johnson left the project in 1816. The first volume produced by Lee Priory Press was an edition of poems by Margaret Cavendish, Duchess of Newcastle, but the first volume that went on sale was Brydges's *Sylvan Wanderer* (1813), a collection of essays and meditations. The press also be-

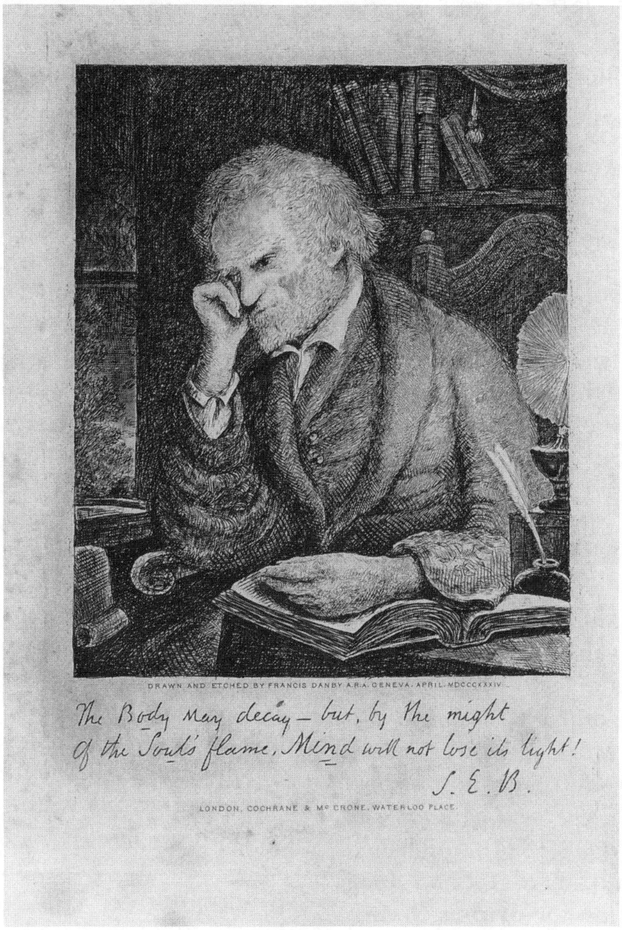

DRAWN AND ETCHED BY FRANCIS DANBY A.R.A. GENEVA. APRIL. MDCCCXXXIV.
The Body may decay—but, by the might
Of the Soul's flame, Mind will not lose its light!
S. E. B.
LONDON, COCHRANE & MC CRONE, WATERLOO PLACE.


*Frontispiece to volume 2 of Brydges's autobiography*

came a vehicle for Brydges's poetry as well as that of Edward Quillinan.

Brydges was a prolific poet, generating odes, verse romances, descriptive lyrics, and numerous sonnets most of his life. As with his novels, his poetry was the product of a spontaneous overflow of emotion with little sense of an overarching theme or a coherent unifying vision. For Brydges, powerful sentiment was the hallmark of genius. "Genuine poetry," he declared, "lies in the thought and sentiment, not in the dress; and these spring from the native powers of the head and heart, which no study or artifice can give." Lines from his "The Poet's Joys and Sorrows" are suggestive of his sensibilities:

O Autumn, thou nursest the spells of the Bard
 He loves thy faint tints, and thy murmuring tones;
He seeks in the visions thou bring'st him his reward;
 And he lists to Love's tales, and to Pity's soft moans.

In a Keatsian mood, he adds,

But the world, the base world calls him back to its cares,
 And the joy of the past each nice sense has refin'd
To the pang, that with torment more sensible tears,
 And outweighs all the bliss of the high-gifted mind!

Throughout he looks upon nature with a melancholy nostalgia for a lost world of grace.

Writing for the *Dictionary of National Biography*, Warwick Wroth dismissed Brydges's poetry as "mediocre description, recalling the dullest efforts of Bowles or Thomas Warton." Donald H. Reiman offers a more favorable assessment, suggesting that "Brydges—like Milton and all the Romantics at their best—strives to remake the world to conform to his personal vision of the Good, the True, and the Beautiful." He goes on to speculate that Coleridge would have found more substance in Brydges's sonnets than he found in those of William Lisle Bowles. Brydges, he concludes, had the misfortune of writing too early to find his true audience among the Romantics.

Throughout his life, Brydges enjoyed a lavish style of life beyond his means of support. With the dissolution of Parliament in 1818, he was no longer protected from his many creditors. Fearing prosecution, Brydges moved his family to the Continent, living principally near Geneva. Except for a stay in England from June 1826 to October 1828, during which Brydges contemplated another run for Parliament, he never returned.

The first years of Brydges's stay on the Continent were spent much as they had been spent in England, balanced between bibliographical and genealogical research, and creative writing. He wrote several more novels, including *Coningsby, A Tragic Tale* (1819) and *Sir Ralph Willoughby: An Historical Tale of the Sixteenth Century* (1820), based loosely on the life of Sir Walter Raleigh. He also produced more poetry—including verse romances, such as *Odo, Count Lingen* (1824); *Modern Aristocracy* (1831), about Byron; and *The Lake of Geneva* (1832), an ambitious work in blank verse—as well as travel books and essays. The most important prose was his *Letters on the Character and Poetical Genius of Lord Byron* (1824), published shortly after Byron's death. Brydges had long been an enthusiastic advocate for Byron's character and genius.

The last part of Brydges's stay on the Continent was devoted to writing his *Autobiography* (1834), in many ways his best book. A work of eccentric and cranky genius, part autobiography, part confession, and part apologia, it provided Brydges with a genre well suited to his genius. As with his novels and poetry, he eschewed the restrictions of chronology or systematic exposition. Rather, the work unfolds by association, moving from one topic to the next as each arises in Brydges's mind: "It is my purpose to communicate my observations and opinions, and I must follow them as the associations of my ideas bring them to my mind." As a result, the work returns again and again to Brydges's obsessions, a series of recurrent themes and variations that reveal his mind more by what they dwell upon than what they say. As one might expect, Brydges works his claims to the Chandos barony and the corollary concerns with the parvenu nobility. He is also concerned with the nature of genius, especially his own, and the role of chance and popular opinion in determining literary fame. In the midst of these themes, he offers interesting evaluations and assessments of the literary figures of the age. Just as Brydges's antiquarian work helped to establish the literary texture of the Renaissance, so his *Autobiography* helps to establish the texture of his own times.

Brydges died at Campagne, Gros Jean, near Geneva, on 8 September 1837, largely forgotten and never truly appreciated. His life was well summarized by poet and translator Edward Fitzgerald. "Do you know anything of poor Sir Egerton Brydges?" he asked Frederick Tennyson in an 1841 letter: "poor fellow, he wrote them [his sonnets] for seventy years, fully convinced of their goodness, and only lamenting that the public were unjust and stupid enough not to admire them also. He lived in haughty seclusion, and at the end of life wrote a doting Autobiography." Despite the general truth of this assessment, Brydges's efforts as a bibliographer and editor are an enduring achievement. Further, while his autobiography may often be "doting," it is always fluent, often interesting, and even occasionally a work of genius.

**Biography:**

Mary Katherine Woodworth, *The Literary Career of Sir Samuel Egerton Brydges* (Oxford: Blackwell, 1935).

**References:**

Roderick Cave, *The Private Press*, revised and enlarged edition (New York: Bowker, 1983), pp. 44-45;

Colin Franklin, *Private Presses* (London: Studio Vista, 1969), pp. 20-21;

William Powell Jones, "Sir Egerton Brydges on Lord Byron," *Huntington Library Quarterly*, 13 (May 1950): 325-337;

Donald H. Reiman, Introduction to works by Brydges, in *Samuel Egerton Brydges and Edward Quillinan* (New York & London: Garland, 1978), pp. v-x.

**Papers:**

A large collection of Brydges's papers is to be found in the Houghton Library at Harvard University.

# William Cobbett

*(1763 - 18 June 1835)*

James Sambrook
*University of Southampton*

and

Elizabeth Thornton

See also the Cobbett entry in *DLB 43: American Newspaper Journalists, 1690-1872.*

BOOKS: *The Soldier's Friend; or, Considerations on the late pretended Augmentation of the Subsistence of the Private Soldier*, possibly by Cobbett (London: J. Ridgeway, 1792);

*Impeachment of Mr. Lafayette: containing his Accusation (Stated in the Report of the Extraordinary Commission to the National Assembly on the 8th of August, 1792) supported by Mr. Brissot of Warville; and his Defence by Mr. Vaublanc: with a Supplement, containing the Letters, and other Authentic Pieces relative thereto*, translated by Cobbett (Philadelphia: Printed by John Parker, 1793);

*Observations on the Emigration of Dr. Joseph Priestley, and on the Several Addresses delivered to him on his Arrival at New York* (Philadelphia: Printed by Thomas Bradford, 1794; London: Printed for John Stockdale, 1794); enlarged edition, adding *A Story of a Farmer's Bull* (Philadelphia: Published by Thomas Bradford, 1795; London: Printed for J. Wright, 1798);

*A Bone to gnaw for the Democrats*, part 1 as Peter Porcupine (Philadelphia: Printed by Thomas Bradford, 1795); part 2 (Philadelphia: Printed & sold by Thomas Bradford, 1795); parts 1 and 2 republished with *A Rod for the Backs of the Critics* by John Giffard, as Humphrey Hedgehog (London: Printed for J. Wright, 1797);

*A Kick for a Bite; or Review upon Review, with a Critical Essay on the Works of Mrs. S. Rowson*, as Peter Porcupine (Philadelphia: Printed by Thomas Bradford, 1795).

*Le Tuteur Anglais, ou Grammaire Regulière de la Langue Anglaise* (Philadelphia: Chez Thomas Bradford, 1795); republished as *Le Mâitre d'Anglais, ou Grammaire Raisonée* (Paris: Warée, 1801);

*A Little Plain English addressed to the People of the United States on the Treaty negotiated with his Britannic Majesty*, as Peter Porcupine (Philadelphia: Published by Thomas Bradford, 1795; London: Printed for F. & C. Rivington, 1795);

*A Summary of the Law of Nations*, by Georg Friedrich von Martens, translated by Cobbett (Philadelphia: Published by Thomas Bradford, 1795); expanded as *A Compendium of the Law of Nations* (London: Cobbett & Morgan, 1802);

*The Works of Peter Porcupine* (Philadelphia: Published by Thomas Bradford, 1795);

*A Topographical and Political Description of the Spanish Part of Saint-Domingo*, 2 volumes, by Médéric Louis Elie Moreau de Saint-Méry, translated by Cobbett (Philadelphia: Printed & sold by the author, printer & bookseller, 1796);

*A New Year's Gift to the Democrats*, as Peter Porcupine (Philadelphia: Published by Thomas Bradford, 1796);

*A Prospect from the Congress-Gallery, during the session, begun December 7, 1795*, as Peter Porcupine (Philadelphia: Published by Thomas Bradford, 1796);

*The Bloody Buoy*, as Peter Porcupine (Philadelphia: Printed for Benjamin Davies, 1796; London: Printed & sold by J. Owen, 1796?); republished as *Annals of Blood* (Cambridge, U.K.: Printed & sold by F. Hodson, sold also by G. & T. Wilkie, London, and by J. Deighton, Cambridge, 1797);

*The Scare-Crow*, as Peter Porcupine (Philadelphia: Printed for & sold by William Cobbett, 1796);

*The Life and Adventures of Peter Porcupine*, as Peter Porcupine (Philadelphia: Printed for & sold by William Cobbett, 1796; London: Sold by J. Wright, 1797); abridged as *The Life of Wil-*

William Cobbett (portrait by an unknown artist; National Portrait Gallery, London)

*liam Cobbett* (London: Printed for W. Hone, 1816);

*An Antidote for Tom Paine's Theological and Political Poison* [*The Political Censor* for September 1796], as Peter Porcupine (Philadelphia: Printed for & sold by William Cobbett, 1796); republished as *The Life of Thomas Paine, interspersed with Remarks and Reflections* (London: Printed for J. Wright, 1797)—based on Henry Mackenzie's abridgement of George Chalmers's *Life of Thomas Pain.*

*The Gros Mousqueton Diplomatique, or Diplomatic Blunderbuss*, by Pierre Auguste Adet, translated and edited by Cobbett (Philadelphia: Printed for & sold by William Cobbett, 1796);

*History of American Jacobins* (Philadelphia: Printed for W. Cobbett, 1796; Edinburgh: Printed for J. G. Henderson, 1797);

*A Letter to the Infamous Tom Paine*, as Peter Porcupine (Philadelphia: Printed for William Cobbett, 1796; London: Printed for David Ogilvy & son, 1797);

*Porcupine's Works*, 2 volumes (Philadelphia: W. Cobbett, 1796-1797);

*Observations on the Debates of the American Congress on the Addresses presented to General Washington*, as Peter Porcupine (London: Printed for David Ogilvy & son, 1797);

*The Democratic Judge or the Equal Liberty of the Press*, as Peter Porcupine (Philadelphia: Published by William Cobbett, 1798); republished as *The Republican Judge, or the American Liberty of the Press* (London: Printed for J. Wright, 1798);

*Detection of a Conspiracy formed by the United Irishmen* (Philadelphia: Published by William Cobbett, 1798; London: Printed for J. Wright, 1799);

*French Arrogance, or 'the Cat let out of the Bag', a Poetical Dialogue between the Envoys of America, and X.Y.Z. and a Lady* (Philadelphia: Published by Peter Porcupine, 1798);

*Remarks on the Insidious Letter of the Gallic Despots* [single sheet], as Peter Porcupine (Philadelphia: Printed by William Cobbett, 1798);

*The Detection of Bache, or French Diplomatic Skill developed* [single sheet] (Philadelphia, 1798);

*Democratic Principles illustrated by Example*, parts 1 and 2 (London: Printed for J. Wright, 1798)—a republication of parts of *A Bone to Gnaw for the Democrats, Part II* (1795) and *The Bloody Buoy* (1796);

*Remarks on the Explanation lately published by Dr. Priestley*, as Peter Porcupine (London: Printed for J. Wright, 1799);

*Cobbett's Advice* [single sheet] (London: Printed by J. F. Dove, 1800);

*The Trial of Republicanism* (London: Printed for Cobbett & Morgan, 1801);

*Porcupine's Works*, 12 volumes (London: Printed for Cobbett & Morgan, 1801);

*A Collection of Facts and Observations relative to the Peace with Bonaparte* (London: Cobbett & Morgan, 1801; Philadelphia; Printed for John Morgan & sold by Benjamin Davis, 1802);

*Letters to the Right Honourable Lord Hawkesbury on the Treaty of Amiens* (London: Cobbett & Morgan, 1802);

*Letters to the Right Honourable Henry Addington, . . . on the Fatal Effects of the Peace with Buonaparté* (London: Cobbett & Morgan, 1802);

*Letter to Lord Aukland on the Abuses in the General Post Office* (London: Cobbett & Morgan, 1802);

*Narrative of the Taking of the Invincible Standard* (London, 1802);

*The Empire of Germany divided*, by Jean Gabriel Peltier, translated by Cobbett (London: Printed by E. Harding, 1803);

*Four Letters to the Chancellor of the Exchequer Exposing the Deception of His Financial Statements* (London: E. Harding, 1803);

*Important Considerations for the People of this Kingdom* (London, 1803);

*The Political Proteus: a View of the Public Character and conduct of R. B. Sheridan* (London: Cox, son & Baylis, 1804; London: Budd, 1804);

*Cobbett's Remarks on Sir F. Burdett's Letter to his Constituents* (London, 1810);

*Three Letters to the Independent Electors of Bristol* (Bath, 1812);

*Letter to the Inhabitants of Southampton on the Corn Bill* (London, 1814);

*Five Letters to Lord Sheffield* (London, 1815);

*Letters on the Late War between the United States and Great Britain* (New York: Published by J. Belden, printed by Van Winkle & Wiley, 1815);

*An Address to the Clergy of Massachusetts* (Boston: Printed at the Yankee Office, 1815);

*The Pride of Britannia humbled* (Philadelphia: William Reynolds / New York: Daniel Griffin / Baltimore: J. Campbell / New Jersey: P. Boyle, 1815);

*Paper against Gold*, 2 volumes (London: Printed by J. M'Creery, 1815; New York: John Doyle, 1834);

*To the Journeymen and Labourers of England, Wales, Scotland, and Ireland* (Manchester: Printed for the Proprietors by J. Molineaux, 1816);

*A Letter Addressed to Mr. Jabet, of Birmingham* (Coventry: Printed & sold by J. Aston, 1816);

*Cobbett's New Year's Gift to Old George Rose* (Nottingham: Printed by Sutton & son, 1817);

*Mr. Cobbett's taking leave of his Countrymen* (London: Printed by Hay & Turner, published by W. Jackson, 1817);

*Cobbett's Address to the Americans* (London: Printed by Hay & Turner, published by J. Duncombe, 1817);

*Mr. Cobbett's Address to his Countrymen* (London: Printed by R. Carlile, 1817).

*A Year's Residence in the United States of America*, 3 parts (London: Sherwood, Neely & Jones, 1818, 1819; New York: Printed for the author by Clayton & Kingsland, 1818-1819);

*A Grammar of the English Language, in a Series of Letters. Intended for the Use of Schools and of Young Persons in General; but more especially for the Use of Soldiers, Sailors, Apprentices, and Plough-boys* (New York: Printed for the author by Clayton & Kingsland, 1818; London: Printed for the author & sold by T. Dolby, 1819 [i.e., 1818]; enlarged edition, adding *Six Lessons intended to prevent Statesmen from using false Grammar* (London: Printed for J. M. Cobbett, 1823);

*Long Island Prophecies* (London: J. M. Cobbett, 1819);

*A Letter from the Queen to the King* (London, 1820);

*An Answer to the Speech of the Attorney-General against her Majesty the Queen* (London: W. Benbow, 1820);

*The Queen's Answer to the Letter from the King to his People* (Philadelphia, 1821);

Cobbett in 1800 (portrait by John Raphael Smith; Collection of Lady Lathbury)

*Cobbett's Monthly Religious Tracts*, nos. 1-3 (London: C. Clement, March - May 1821); nos. 4-12 titled *Cobbett's Monthly Sermons* (London, June 1821 - February 1822); republished with *Good Friday* (1830) as *Thirteen Sermons* (New York: J. Doyle, 1834);

*Preliminary Part of Paper against Gold* (London: J. M. Cobbett, 1821);

*The American Gardener* (London: C. Clement, 1821; Baltimore: J. Robinson, 1823);

*Cottage Economy* (seven monthly parts, London: C. Clement, 1 August 1821 - 1 March 1822; 1 volume, London: C. Clemens, 1822); enlarged edition, adding *Instructions Relative to the Selecting, the Cutting and the Bleaching of the Plants of English Grass and Grain, for the purpose of making Hats and Bonnets* (London: Printed for J. M. Cobbett, 1823; New York: S. Gould & son, 1824);

*The Farmer's Friend, to the Farmers of the Kingdom* (London: Printed & published by C. Clement, 1822);

*Cobbett's Warning to Norfolk Farmers* (London: Printed by C. Clement, 1822);

*The Farmer's Wife's Friend* (London: Printed & published by C. Clement, 1822);

*Reduction no Robbery* (London: C. Clement, 1822);

*Cobbett's Collective Commentaries* (London: Printed for J. M. Cobbett, 1822);

*To Lord Suffield* (London, 1823);

*A French Grammar* (London: C. Clement, 1824; New York: J. Doyle, 1824; Paris, Bossange, 1825);

*A History of the Protestant 'Reformation,' in England and Ireland*, 16 parts (London: Printed & published by Charles Clement, 1824-1826; Baltimore, 1824-1826);

*Gold for Ever* (London: C. Clement, 1825);

*Big O. and Sir Glory: or, "Leisure to Laugh." A Comedy* (London: J. Dean, 1825);

*The Woodlands*, 7 numbers (London, December 1825 - March 1828);

*Cobbett's Poor Man's Friend*, 5 parts (London, 1 August 1826 - 18 October 1827); abridged and revised as *Poor Man's Friend. . . . Addressed to the Working Men of Scotland* (London, 1833);

*Elements of the Roman History*, by Jean Henrique Sievrac, translated by Cobbett (London, 1828);

*Noble Nonsense* (London: Printed & published by W. Cobbett, 1828);

*The English Gardener* (London, 1829 [i.e., 1828]);

*Facts for the Men of Kent* (London: William Cobbett, 1828);

*A Letter to his Holiness the Pope* (London: William Cobbett, 1828);

*A Treatise on Cobbett's Corn* (London: W. Cobbett, 1828);

*The Emigrant's Guide* (London: Published by the author, 1829);

*First [-Fifth] Lecture on the Present Prospects of Merchants, Traders, and Farmers* (London: J. Chappell, 1829, 1830);

*An Abridged History of the Emperors*, by Sievrac, translated by Cobbett (London, 1829);

*Advice to Young Men and (incidentally) to Young Women*, 14 parts (London, June 1829 - September 1830; 1 volume, New York: J. Doyle, 1831);

*An Accurate Report of Mr. Cobbett's Lecture-Speech on the Present Distresses of the Country* (Halifax, 1830);

*Three Lectures on the State of the Country* (Sheffield, 1830);

*Mr. Cobbett's Address to the Tax-Payers of England* (London, 1830);

*Good Friday, or the Murder of Jesus Christ by the Jews* (London: Published for the author, 1830); republished with *Cobbett's Monthly Sermons* (1821) as *Thirteen Sermons* (New York: J. Doyle, 1834);

*Rural Rides in the Counties of Surrey, Kent, Sussex, Hampshire, Wiltshire, Gloucestershire, Herefordshire, Worcestershire, Somersetshire, Oxfordshire, Berkshire, Essex, Suffolk, Norfolk, and Hertfordshire* (London: W. Cobbett, 1830);

*Cobbett's Exposure of the Practice of the Pretended Friends of the Blacks* (London, 1830);

*French Revolution: an Address to the People of Paris* (Birmingham, 1830);

*Tableau de l'Angleterre en 1830* (Paris: Laran, 1830).

*Eleven Lectures on the French and Belgian Revolutions*, 11 parts (London: W. Strange, 1830);

*A Letter to the King* (London, 1830);

*History of the Regency and Reign of George IV*, 2 volumes (London: W. Cobbett, 1830, 1834);

*Cobbett's Plan of Parliamentary Reform* (London: W. Strange, 1830);

*Cobbett' Two-Penny Trash, or Politics for the Poor*, 24 monthly parts (London: Printed for the author, July 1830 - July 1832);

*A Spelling Book* (London, 1831);

*Cobbett's Letter on the Abolition of Tithes* (Dublin, 1831);

*Cobbett's Manchester Lectures* (London, 1832);

*A Geographical Dictionary of England and Wales* (London: William Cobbett, 1832);

*Mr. Cobbett's Answer to Mr. Stanley's Manifesto* (London: William Cobbett, 1832);

*The Speeches of W. Cobbett, M.P. for Oldham*, nos. 1 and 2 (London: William Cobbett, 1833);

*The Flash in the Pan, or Peel in a Passion* (London: William Cobbett, 1833);

*Disgraceful Squandering of the Public Money* (Glasgow, 1833);

*Cobbett's Tour in Scotland, and in the Four Northern Counties of England* (London, 1833);

*A New French and English Dictionary* (London, 1833);

*Popay, the Police Spy* (London: Cleave, 1833);

*Rights of Industry*, by Cobbett and John Fielden (London, 1833);

*Four Letters to the Hon. John Stuart Wortley* (London: William Cobbett, 1834);

*Mr. Cobbett's Speech, and the Other Speeches on his Motion for an Abolition of the Malt Tax* (London, 1834);

*Get Gold! Get Gold!* (London: William Cobbett, 1834);

*To the Earl of Radnor* (London: William Cobbett, 1834);

*Three Lectures on the Political State of Ireland* (Dublin, P. Byrne, 1834);

*Surplus Population and Poor-Law Bill, a Comedy* (London: Published at Cobbett's Register Office, 1835);

*Cobbett's Legacy to Labourers* (London, 1834 [i.e., 1835]); introduction republished as *Mr. Cobbett and the New Poor Law Act. A Letter to Sir Robert Peel* (London, 1836);

*The Malt Tax kept upon the Backs of the People by the Whigs* (London, 1835);

*Cobbett's Legacy to Parsons* (London, 1835; New York: John Doyle, 1835);

*Portrait by Daniel Maclise in the* Fraser's Magazine *"Gallery of Illustrious Literary Characters" (1830-1838)*

*Cobbett's Legacy to Peel* (London: Published at Cobbett's Register Office, 1836).

**Editions:** *Selections from Cobbett's Political Works*, 6 volumes, edited by John M. Cobbett and James P. Cobbett (London: A. Cobbett, 1835-1837);

*Rural Rides* [with "Northern Counties" from *Cobbett's Tour in Scotland*], edited by James Paul Cobbett (London: A. Cobbett, 1853);

*A History of the Last Hundred Days of English Freedom*, with introduction and biographical index by J. L. Hammond (London: Labour Publishing/Allen & Unwin, 1921)—from *Cobbett's Weekly Political Pamphlet [Political Register]*, 26 July - 18 October 1817;

*Rural Rides in the Southern, Western and Eastern Counties of England, Together with Tours in Scotland and in the Northern and Midland Counties of England and Letters from Ireland*, edited by G. D. H. and Margaret Cole (London: Davies, 1930);

*The Progress of a Plough-Boy to a Seat in Parliament*, edited by William Reitzel (London: Faber & Faber, 1933); republished as *The Autobiography of William Cobbett* (London: Faber & Faber, 1947);

*The Opinions of William Cobbett*, edited by G. D. H. and Margaret Cole (London: Cobbett Publishing, 1944)—selections from *Cobbett's Political Register*;

*Cobbett in Ireland: A Warning to England*, edited by Dennis Knight (London: Lawrence & Wishart, 1984).

OTHER: Henry Mackenzie, *An Answer to Paine's Rights of Man. . . . To which is added a Letter by P. Porcupine to Citizen John Swanwick an Englishman, the Son of a British Waggon-master, and Member of Congress for the City of Philadelphia* (Philadelphia: Printed for & sold by William Cobbett, 1796);

William Playfair, *The History of Jacobinism, its Crimes, Cruelties, and Perfidies . . . With an Appendix, by Peter Porcupine, containing a History of the American Jacobins commonly denominated Democrats*, 2 volumes (Philadelphia: Printed for William Cobbett, 1796)—Cobbett's appendix separately published as *History of American Jacobins* (1796);

*A Letter from the Right Honorable Edmund Burke to a Noble Lord*, includes a preface by Cobbett (Philadelphia: Printed for B. Davies, H. & P. Rice, and J. Ormrod, 1796);

Thomas Erskine, *A View of the Causes and Consequences of the Present War with France*, includes a dedication and an appendix by Cobbett (Philadelphia: Printed by William Cobbett, 1797);

Robert Goodloe Harper, *Observations on the Dispute between the United States and France*, edited, and perhaps partly written, by Cobbett (Philadelphia: Printed & sold by Thomas Bradford, 1797; London: Printed, by direction of the editor, at the Philanthropic Press, sold by Stockdale, Debrett, and Wright, Hookham & Carpenter, Egerton, Kearsley, Vernor & Hood, Richardson, 1797);

Anthony Aufrère, *The Cannibals' Progress; or, The Dreadful Horrors of the French Invasion*, edited by Cobbett (Philadelphia: Published by William Cobbett, 1798; London, 1798);

William Forsyth, *A Treatise on the Culture and Management of Fruit Trees. . . . To which are added an introduction and notes, adapting the rules of the Treatise to the Climates and Seasons of the United States of America. By William Cobbett* (Philadelphia: Printed for J. Morgan, 1802);

*Cobbett's Parliamentary Debates*, edited by Cobbett and John Wright (London, 1804-1810);

*Cobbett's Spirit of the Public Journals; volume 1, for the year 1804* [no more published], edited by Cobbett (London: J. Budd, 1805);

*Cobbett's Parliamentary History of England*, volumes 1-12, edited by Cobbett and Wright (volumes 1-7, London: Published by R. Bagshaw; volumes 8-12, London: Published by Longmans, 1806-1812);

*Cobbett's Complete Collection of State Trials*, volumes 1-10, edited by Cobbett, Wright, and T. B. Howell (volumes 1-9 London: Published by R. Bagshaw; volume 10, London: Published by Longman, 1809-1811);

Robert R. Livingston, *An Essay on Sheep*, edited, with a preface and notes, by Cobbett (London: J. Budd, 1811);

*The Trial of Miss Mary Ann Tocker*, edited, with a letter and an address, by Cobbett (New York: Printed for William Cobbett by Clayton & Kingsland, 1818);

Jesse Torrey, *American Slave Trade*, includes a preface by Cobbett (London: Printed by C. Clement & published by J. M. Cobbett, 1822);

Jethro Tull, *The Horse-Hoeing Husbandry*, edited with an introduction, by Cobbett (London: J. M. Cobbett, 1822);

William M. Gouge, *The Curse of Paper-Money and Banking*, edited, with an introduction, by Cobbett (London, 1833);

John Henry Eaton, *Life of Andrew Jackson*, abridged and edited by Cobbett (London, 1834; New York: Harper, 1834).

PERIODICALS: *The Political Censor*, nos. 1-9 (Philadelphia, March 1796 - March 1797);

*Porcupine's Gazette and United States Daily Advertiser* (Philadelphia: Published by William Cobbett, 4 March - 23 April 1797); retitled *Porcupine's Gazette* (Philadelphia: Published by William Cobbett, 24 April 1797 - 26 October 1799; farewell number, New York: Published by William Cobbett, 13 January 1800); republished three times a week as *The Country Porcupine* (Philadelphia: Published by William Cobbett, 5 March 1798 - 28 August 1799);

*The Rush-Light* [fortnightly], nos. 1-7 (New York: Published by William Cobbett, 15 February - 30 April 1800); nos. 1-4 republished as *The American Rush-Light* (London: Published for the author by J. Wright, 1800);

*The Porcupine* [daily] (London, 30 October 1800 - 31 December 1801);

*Cobbett's Political Register* [weekly] (London, 1 January 1802 - 8 August 1835)—also variously titled *Cobbett's Annual Register, Cobbett's Weekly Register, Cobbett's Weekly Political Register* and *Cobbett's Weekly Political Pamphlet*;

*Cobbett's American Political Register* [weekly] (New York, 6 January - 29 June 1816, May 1817 - January 1818);

*Cobbett's Evening Post* [daily], nos. 1-55 (London, 29 January - 1 April 1820);

*Cobbett's Parliamentary Register* [weekly] (London, 6 May - December 1820);

The Life of WILLIAM-COBBETT, – written by himself –
"Now you lying Varlets you shall see how a plain Tale will put you down!"
1st Plate.
Father kept the sign of the Jolly Farmer at Farnham. I was his Pot Boy and thought an Ornament to the profession. – at Seven Years Old my natural genius began to expand and display'd itself in a taste for Plunder and oppression. – I robbed Orchards, set Fathers Bull Dog at the Cats. – quarrelled with all the Poor Boys, and beat all the little Girls of the Town. – to the great admiration of the inhabitants; – who prophecied that my talents (unless the Devil was in it) would one day elevate me to a Post in some publick situation

The Life of WILLIAM-COBBETT, – written by himself.
2d Plate.
– as I shot up into a hobble-dehoy I took to driving the Plow for the benefit of mankind which was always my prime object; – hearing that the Church Wardens were after me, I determined to become a Hero and secretly quitting my agricultural pursuits and Sukey Stubbs, – Volunteerd as a Private – Soldier into the 51st Regiment commanded by that tried Patriot and Martyre Lord Edwd Fitzgerald, and embarked for the Plantations. –

The Life of WILLIAM-COBBETT, – written by himself.
3d Plate.
arrived in safety (according to the proverb), being a Scholard, (for all the world knows that I can Read and Write) I was promoted to the rank of a Corporal, and soon after appointed to teach the Officers their duty. – found them all so damnably stupid, that 'though I took the pains to draw up my instructions on Cards, I could not with all my Caning and Kicking drive one manual movement into their thick heads! –

The Life of WILLIAM-COBBETT, – written by himself.
4th Plate.
– I was now made Sarjeant Major and Clerk to the Regiment, and there being only One Man in it besides myself, who could read or keep him-self sober (viz. – poor little Corporal-Bestland). I constituted him my Deputy; – being intrusted with the care of the Regimental Books, the Corporal and myself (tho' both of us blastedly afraid of a pair of Bloody Shoulders.) – purloined, and Copied by night such Documents as promised to be serviceable in the great National Object which I had in view; – namely, to Disorganize the Army, preparatory to the Revolutionizeng it altogether! –
— Vide – my Own Memoirs in the Political Register of 1809.


*James Gilray's Tory parody of Cobbett's autobiography*

The Life of WILLIAM-COBBETT,_ written by himself.
5th Plate
my next step was to procure a Discharge from my ever lamented associate the Lord Edwd. Fitzgerald,_ with this I returned to England and directly set about writing "the Soldiers Friend"_ which I nightly dropt about the Horse Guards, and drank "Damnation to the House of Brunswick!"_ moreover I wrote 27 Letters to my Royal Master to Mr Pitt and the Judge Advocate against my Officers, 23 of which Letters were stolen by the public Robbers, and never came to hand, so that I had no means of obtaining Credit for my Charges & procuring a Court Martial but by solemnly Pledging my precious Soul to the Devil in the presence of Judge Gould for the Truth of my alegations, and my ability to support them by evidence!!!

The Life of WILLIAM-COBBETT,_ written by himself.
London, Published Septr 29.1809, by H. Humphrey 27. St James's Street
Plate .6th_
_the Court Martial was assembled at Chelsea as I requested, and Captn. Powele and the other accused Persons were placed at the Bar;_ _when_blast-my-Eyes!_I saw, the whole of that damn'd 51st Regiment Drummers, Fifers and all, marching boldly into the Hall to bear Testi-mony against Me!!_ on this, I instantly ran to a boat which I had Providentialy secured, and crossed the Thames._____ _damn'd infernal-Ideots!_ did the Judge-Advocate and his Gang of Publick Robbers think that I would stay to witness my own Exposure and condemnation?
_Vide, my own Memoirs
in the Political Register_1809

The Life of WILLIAM-COBBETT,_ written by himself.
Plate 7th.
I did not look behind me, till I got to St Omers_& thence fled to America;_here I offer'd to become a Spy for the English Government which was scornfully rejected;_ I then turned to Plunder & Libel the Yankees for which I was Fined 5000 Dollars & kicked out of the Country!_ I came back to England (after absconding for Seven years), & set up the Crown & Mitre to establish my Loyalty;_accepted from the Doctor £4000 to print & disperse a pamflet against "the Hell fire yell of Reform"._but applied the Money to purchase an estate at Botley, & left ye Doctor to pay the Paper & Printing!_ being now Lord of the Manor, I began by sowing the Seeds of discontent through Hampshire; I oppressed the Poor, sent the Aged to Hell, & damn'd the Eyes of my Parish Apprentices before they were open'd in the morning!_& being now supported by a band of Reformers, I renewed my old favourite Toast of "Damnation to the House of Brunswick!"_& exalted by the sale of 10000 Political Registers every week, I find myself the greatest Man in the World!_ except that Idol of all my Adorations, his Royal & Imperial Majesty NAPOLEONE!...

The Life of WILLIAM-COBBETT,_written by himself.
Plate 8th.
_but alas, in the midst of my towering prospects, while I was yet hesitating between a Radical Reform and a Revolution, & doubtful whether to assume the Character of Old-Noll or Jack Cade,_down came my Political Register, & the fabrick of my visionary greatness vanished. my Schemes for my Country's good perished by the blaze of my own Candles!_ The Ghost!_ _slid!_Lord forgive me for swearing!_the Ghost of Captn. Powell utter'd a scream of Joy. little Jessy's brandy-faced-bitch of a Mother_Lord pardon me!_called out for Justice!_ the Bats and Harpies of Revolution hid their heads in the gloom of night,_ and to compleat the horrible Scene, the rigid Pawnbroker of Hell, Old-Beelzebub, entered and demanded his property, the Forfiet Soul, which I had pledged!_ Lord have mercy upon me!_ _Our Father!_to the Truth of my accusations! oh! oh!_ oh!___Hell Flames
_Vide, My own Memoirs
in the Political Register. 1809

*The Statesman* [daily evening newspaper], partly owned by Cobbett, who contributed articles (London, March 1822 - May 1823);

*The Norfolk Yeoman's Gazette* [weekly] (Norwich, 8 February - 3 May 1823).

Thomas Carlyle called William Cobbett "The pattern John Bull of his century, strong as the rhinosceros, and with singular humanities and genialities shining through his thick skin" (*Essay on Scott*, 1838). Cobbett was a leading advocate of parliamentary reform in the quarter century before the Reform Act of 1832; his lifelong campaign for social justice made him worthy of the self-awarded title "The Poor Man's Friend"; as a defender of the freedom of the press he became, in William Hazlitt's phrase, "a kind of *fourth estate* in the politics of the country" (*The Spirit of the Age*, 1825).

Nearly the only source of information on Cobbett's early life is Cobbett himself. In *The Life and Adventures of Peter Porcupine* (1796) and in many short passages of autobiography scattered through his later writings, he selected significant reminiscences to indicate stages in his growth and to point the contrast between a golden past and an iron present. There is, however, ample evidence that the countryside around Farnham in Surrey—the place where Cobbett was born in 1763—was as prosperous and lovely as he claimed it to be.

The third of four sons born to George and Anne Vincent Cobbett, William Cobbett was proud of his plebian ancestry. He wrote in his *Life and Adventures of Peter Porcupine*:

> With respect to my ancestors, I shall go no further back than my grandfather, and for this plain reason, that I never heard talk of any prior to him. He was a day-labourer; and I have heard my father say, that he worked for one farmer from the day of his marriage to that of his death, upwards of forty years. He died before I was born, but I have often slept beneath the same roof that sheltered him, and where his widow dwelt for several years after his death. It was a little thatched cottage, with a garden before the door. It had but two windows; a damson tree shaded one, and a clump of filberts the other. Here I and my brothers went every Christmas and Whitsuntide to spend a week or two, and torment the poor old woman with our noise and dilapidations. She used to give us milk and bread for breakfast, an apple pudding for our dinner, and a piece of bread and cheese for supper. Her fire was made of turf, cut from the neighbouring heath, and her evening light was a rush dipped in grease. . . .
>
> My father, when I was born, was a farmer. . . . When a little boy, he drove plough for two pence a-day; and these earnings were appropriated to the expenses of an evening school. What a village school-master could be expected to teach, he had learnt; and had, besides, considerably improved himself, in several branches of the mathematics. He understood land-surveying well, and was often chosen to draw the plans of disputed territory; in short, he had the reputation of possessing experience and understanding, which never fails, in England, to give a man in a country place, some little weight with his neighbours. He was honest, industrious, and frugal.

Turning to himself Cobbett proudly asserted that he was 'bred at the plough-tail':

> I do not remember the time, when I did not earn my living. My first occupation was, driving the small birds from the turnip-seed, and the rooks from the peas. When I first trudged a-field, with my wooden bottle and my satchel swung over my shoulders, I was hardly able to climb the gates and stiles; and, at the close of the day, to reach home, was a task of infinite difficulty. My next employment was weeding wheat, and leading a single horse at harrowing barley. Hoeing peas followed, and hence, I arrived at the honour of joining the reapers in harvest, driving the team, and holding plough.

In spare moments Cobbett's father taught his sons how to read, write, and cipher. At thirteen or fourteen years of age Cobbett was a strong, unruly, inquisitive, intelligent boy, already feeling that hunger of the imagination that would drive him so far.

One youthful episode (recalled in the *Political Register* for 19 February 1820) illustrates that hunger. At the time in question he was a gardener's boy, clipping box edgings and weeding flowerbeds for the bishop of Winchester at Farnham Castle. When he heard a description of the royal gardens at Kew, however, he decided to go to work there and set out the next morning with only thirteen halfpence and the clothes on his back. By afternoon he had reached Richmond, where he bought food and found himself left with only three pence:

> With this for my whole fortune, I was trudging through Richmond, in my blue smock-frock and my red garters tied under my knees, when, staring about me, my eyes fell upon a little book in a

*Silhouettes of Cobbett (circa 1785) and Ann Reid Cobbett (circa 1818), whom Cobbett married in February 1792 (Collection of Lady Lathbury)*

bookseller's window, on the outside of which was written: *"Tale of a Tub,* price *3d."* The title was so odd, that my curiosity was excited. I had the three pence, but, then, I could have no *supper.* In I went, and got the little book, which I was so impatient to read, that I got over into a field, at the upper corner of Kew Gardens, where there stood a *hay-stack.* On the shady side of this, I sat down to read. The book was so different from any thing that I had ever read before: it was something so *new* to my mind, that, though I could not at all understand some of it, it delighted me beyond description; and it produced what I have always considered a sort of birth of intellect. I read on till it was dark, without any thought about supper or bed. When I could see no longer, I put my little book in my pocket, and tumbled down by the side of the stack, where I slept till the birds in Kew Gardens awaked me in the morning; when I started to Kew, reading my little book.

The gardener there gave him work, and Cobbett remembered how the future George IV "and two of his brothers laughed at the oddness of my dress." The gardener lent him some gardening books,

> but these I could not relish after my *Tale of a Tub,* which I carried about with me wherever I went; and when I, at about [twenty-two] years old, lost it in a box that fell overboard in the Bay of Fundy, in North America, the loss gave me greater pain than I have ever felt at losing thousands of pounds.

After this impulsive move to Kew, Cobbett spent little time in Farnham. He worked as a clerk in Guildford and London, joined the army in February 1784, and by 1785 was serving with his infantry regiment in Nova Scotia and New Brunswick. There he was made clerk to the regiment, and in a short time was responsible for all the returns, reports, and other official papers, so that "neither adjutant, pay-master, or quarter-master, could move an inch without my assistance" (*Political Register,* 17 June 1809). Within a year he was promoted over the heads of thirty sergeants to the rank of sergeant major (and earned half-a-crown a day). From his own account he seems to have been a perfect specimen of the higher noncommissioned officer, indispensable to his officers and considerate but firm toward his men. He developed a stubborn passion for good order, discipline, smartness, and early rising which was to remain with him through life.

Cobbett's years as a sergeant major formed his character and perhaps did something as well to shape the brisk, "parade-ground" peremptoriness of his prose style. They also instilled in him a contempt for artificial distinctions. He later told many stories of his officers' incapacity and the extent to which they depended upon him. For example, when a revised drill manual was brought into use:

> I had to give lectures of instruction to the officers themselves, the Colonel not excepted; and, for several of them, I had to make out, upon large cards, which they bought for the purpose, little plans of the position of the regiment, together with lists of the words of command, which they had to give in the field. There was I, at the review, upon the flank of the grenadier company, with my worsted shoulder-knot, and my great high, coarse, hairy cap; confounded in the ranks amongst other men, whilst those who were commanding me to move my hands or my feet, thus or thus, were, in fact, uttering words, which I had taught them; and were, in everything except mere authority, my inferiors; and ought to have been commanded by me. It was impossible for reflections of this sort not to intrude themselves; and, as I advanced in experience, I felt less and less respect for those, whom I was compelled to obey (*Political Register*, 17 June 1809).

Yet he detested the dishonesty of officers more than what he saw as their incompetence, indolence, drunkenness, or swagger. As early as 1787 he began collecting evidence of certain officers' peculations from muster books and accounts with the intention of bringing them to justice.

He was discharged from the army back in England in November 1791. In January 1792 he sent to Sir George Yonge, secretary at war, a series of charges against his former commanding officer, adjutant, and quartermaster, accusing them of making false musters and returns, and of various forms of misappropriation of public money or soldiers' pay. A court-martial, where Cobbett would act as prosecutor, was arranged for March 1792, but a few days before it was convened he and Ann Reid Cobbett, the wife he had married on 5 February 1792, fled secretly to France. The court sat, the charges were read, but none of the witnesses summoned by Cobbett was prepared to speak. In the absence of the prosecutor, the accused were honorably acquitted. Cobbett's charges may have been well founded, but the social position of Cobbett and his witnesses, who were mostly common soldiers still serving in the regiment, relative to that of the accused officers made it virtually certain that Cobbett's prosecution would have failed.

France, during the brief period of liberty between the fall of the Bastille in 1789 and the onset of the Reign of Terror in 1793, was a ready haven for Cobbett, who feared he was suspected of sedition, but his ultimate destination was America. As a boy of thirteen he had seen his father at Weyhill Fair drink to the success of General Washington against George III, and as a soldier serving in the barren wasteland of New Brunswick, he had heard reports of the beautiful, fertile land to the south. While Cobbett studied French, he and his new wife stayed in a small northern village near St. Omer until August, when they set off to spend the winter in Paris. At Abbeville, however, after hearing that Louis XVI was dethroned and a war between England and France was likely, Cobbett changed his plans. They went to Le Havre, where they boarded a ship for an uncomfortable voyage across the Atlantic.

They reached America in October 1792, and, after three months in Wilmington, Delaware, they moved to Philadelphia, then capital of the United States. Cobbett made a living by translating French books and by serving as an English tutor to immigrant Frenchmen who had escaped the Reign of Terror in France or fled from Negro rebellions in the French West Indies. From them he gained a horror of revolutionary excess, and from the lessons he taught them he compiled a highly successful and profitable textbook, *Le Tuteur Anglais* (1795). By August 1794 he had begun to write pamphlets against the pro-French faction, led by Thomas Jefferson and supported by Democratic Clubs and societies of Irish revolutionaries, who wanted the United States and France to go to war against England and the other monarchies. The Federalist government under George Washington's presidency wanted to prevent the spread of revolutionary influences in America and to preserve abroad a neutrality sympathetic to England, her best trading partner. When Cobbett threw himself into controversy with works such as *A Bone to gnaw for the Demo-*

*Cobbett bought Botley House, in Hampshire about five miles east of Southampton, in 1805*

*crats* (January 1795) and *A Kick for a Bite* (March 1795)—under the happy pseudonym Peter Porcupine—he did so both as an American Federalist and as an English patriot.

The political pamphlet of most permanent interest from these years is *The Life and Adventures of Peter Porcupine* (1796), written in a controversial spirit to refute charges that he was an agent for the British government, but relatively free from polemic. In passages where he recreated his honest pride and happy days in Farnham, Cobbett blended his sense of the value of his life into an attractive, idealized vision of Old England. Like his Romantic contemporaries in that age of autobiographies, he found that his own life had a representative significance.

Peter Porcupine continued to shoot his quills against French Jacobins and their friends the American democrats until he brought upon himself a libel action and returned to England, where he founded the weekly *Cobbett's Political Register*, which continued under various titles from January 1802 until after Cobbett's death. Initially Cobbett devoted the *Political Register* and his other pamphleteering to support of the government against "Jacobinism" at home and French imperialism abroad. Gradually, though, as the war progressed, he came to see that the real enemy of the English common people, with whom Cobbett always identified himself, was not France but William Pitt's financial system of paper money, stock jobbing, taxation, placemen, and sinecurists. He discovered that there were no true political parties at Westminster, only coalitions of selfish men bent on plunder and power. Whig and Tory, in office or out of it, were alike "Court" parties according to traditional, seventeenth- and eighteenth-century political nomenclature. Cobbett was the nearest thing to a one-man "country party" on the nineteenth-century political scene: he adapted to the revolutionary world of 1800 many of the notions of a Tory squire of 1700 and in this process, over the ensuing years, became, without any consciousness of inconsistency, a leader of industrial, working-class radicalism.

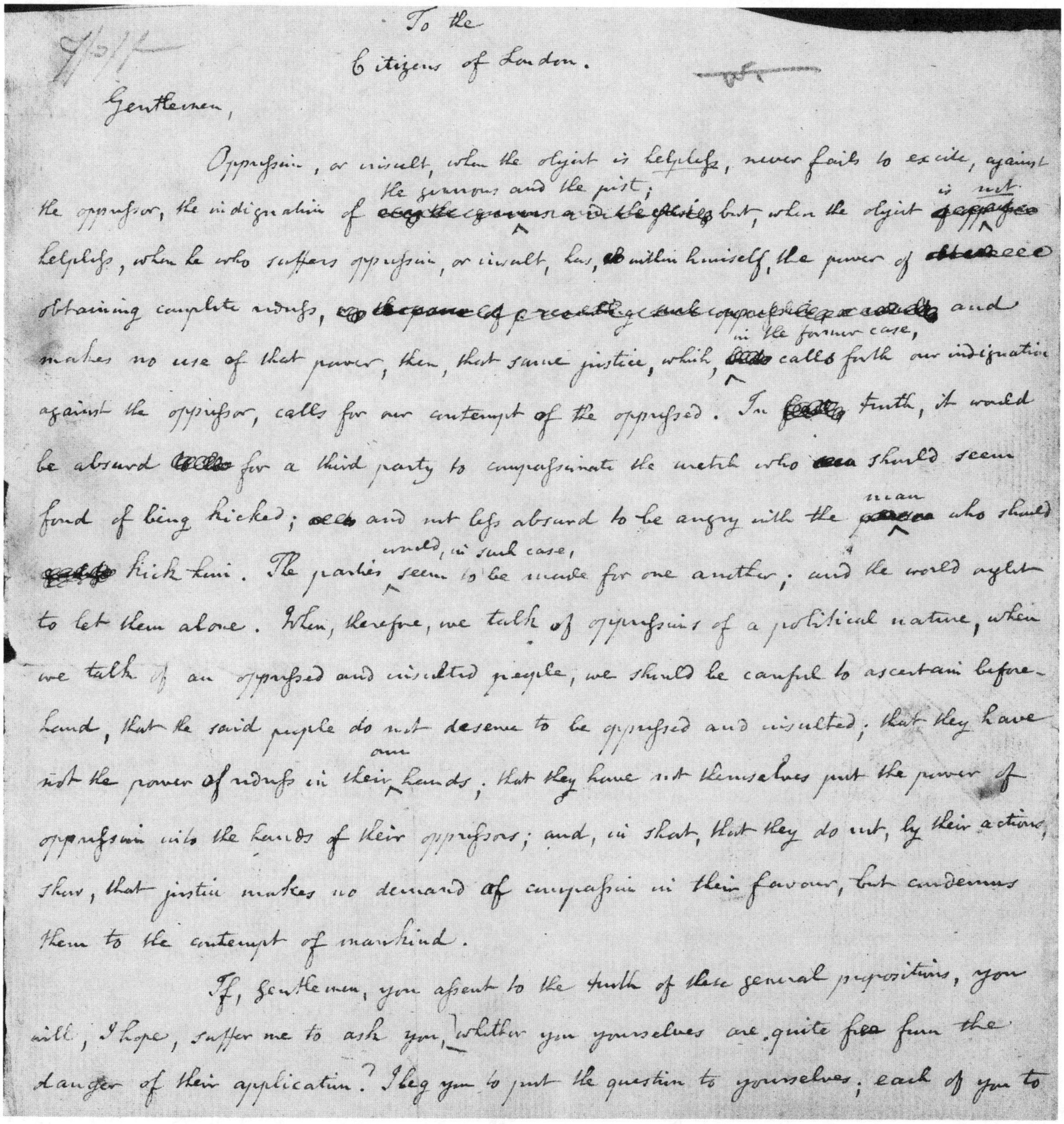

To the
Citizens of London.

Gentlemen,

Oppression, or insult, when the object is helpless, never fails to excite, against the oppressor, the indignation of the generous and the just; but, when the object is not helpless, when he who suffers oppression, or insult, has, within himself, the power of obtaining complete redress, and makes no use of that power, then, that same justice, which, in the former case, calls forth our indignation against the oppressor, calls for our contempt of the oppressed. In truth, it would be absurd for a third party to compassionate the wretch who should seem fond of being kicked; and not less absurd to be angry with the man who should kick him. The parties would, in such case, seem to be made for one another; and the world ought to let them alone. When, therefore, we talk of oppressions of a political nature, when we talk of an oppressed and insulted people, we should be careful to ascertain before-hand, that the said people do not deserve to be oppressed and insulted; that they have not the power of redress in their own hands; that they have not themselves put the power of oppression into the hands of their oppressors; and, in short, that they do not, by their actions, shew, that justice makes no demand of compassion in their favour, but condemns them to the contempt of mankind.

If, Gentlemen, you assent to the truth of these general propositions, you will, I hope, suffer me to ask you, whether you yourselves are quite free from the danger of their application? I beg you to put the question to yourselves; each of you to

*Pages from an address that Cobbett delivered on 9 November 1809 (HM 17026; Henry E. Huntington Library and Art Gallery)*

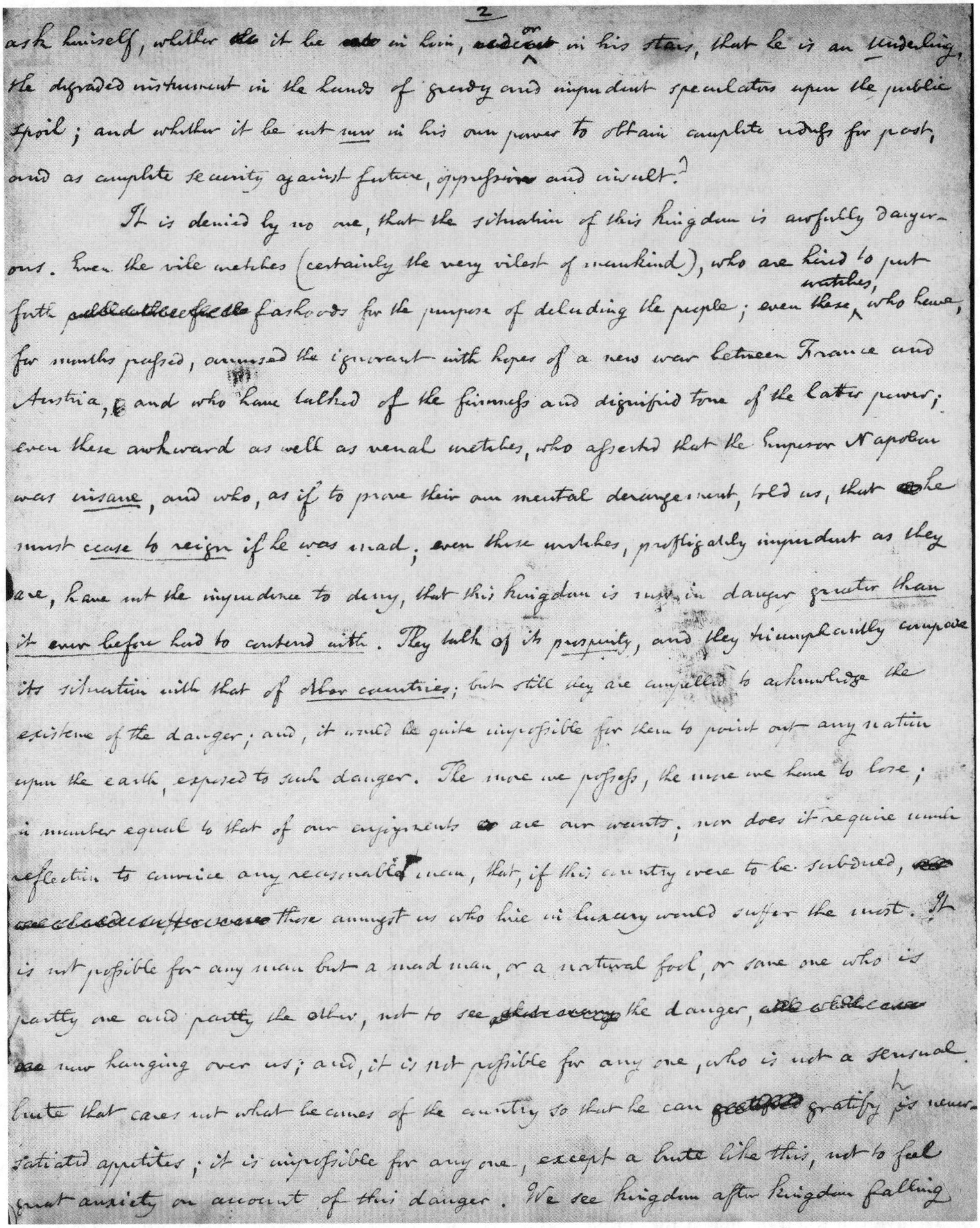

2

ask himself, whether it be in him, or in his stars, that he is an underling, the degraded instrument in the hands of greedy and impudent speculators upon the public spoil; and whether it be not now in his own power to obtain complete redress for past, and as complete security against future, oppression and insult?

It is denied by no one, that the situation of this kingdom is awfully dangerous. Even the vile wretches (certainly the very vilest of mankind), who are hired to put forth falsehoods for the purpose of deluding the people; even these wretches, who have, for months passed, amused the ignorant with hopes of a new war between France and Austria, and who have talked of the firmness and dignified tone of the latter power; even these awkward as well as venal wretches, who asserted that the Emperor Napoleon was insane, and who, as if to prove their own mental derangement, told us, that he must cease to reign if he was mad; even these wretches, profligately impudent as they are, have not the impudence to deny, that this kingdom is now in danger greater than it ever before had to contend with. They talk of its prosperity, and they triumphantly compare its situation with that of other countries; but still they are compelled to acknowledge the existence of the danger; and, it would be quite impossible for them to point out any nation upon the earth, exposed to such danger. The more we possess, the more we have to lose; in number equal to that of our enjoyments are our wants; nor does it require much reflection to convince any reasonable man, that, if this country were to be subdued, those amongst us who live in luxury would suffer the most. It is not possible for any man but a mad man, or a natural fool, or some one who is partly one and partly the other, not to see the danger, now hanging over us; and, it is not possible for any one, who is not a sensual brute that cares not what becomes of the country so that he can gratify his never-satiated appetites; it is impossible for any one, except a brute like this, not to feel great anxiety on account of this danger. We see kingdom after kingdom falling

In 1805 Cobbett acquired a house at Botley in Hampshire, where he practiced advanced farming and old-fashioned hospitality until he went bankrupt in 1820. Botley House and its attendant farms were his havens from the storm of national politics, but they also embodied the values that Cobbett brought into politics. Cobbett shaped a setting at Botley that expressed much of his personality and gave a large measure of reality to an imaginative pastoral world, opposed at every point to Court and City. Cobbett's rural estate earned by profits of the pen became a meeting place for opposition politicians and the moral base for a political stance. The *Political Register* papers written from Botley implicitly and explicitly contrast that scrap of Old England with all the misery and degradation that flowed into the nation from the corruptions of the City and the Pitt system.

Typical of Cobbett's old-fashioned "country" politics is his denunciation of foreign trade in a series of *Political Register* articles in 1807-1808. Cobbett argued that for the most part foreign trade brought only debilitating luxuries, such as tea, tobacco, wines, and spirits, while in exchange England parted with such valuable necessaries as hardware and cloth. All true wealth comes from one's own land, he argued; commerce is merely a diversionary channel through which such wealth can flow for the enrichment of the few and the ultimate impoverishment of the nation: "the great tendency of the commercial system is to draw the real wealth of the whole country towards the metropolis, there, upon the labour of the working classes, to maintain, in idleness and luxury, innumerable swarms of place-men, pensioners, tax-gatherers, jews, jobbers, singers, parasites, and buffoons." In this phrase there is a touch of satirical "yoking" which Cobbett may have learned from Swift, just as his characterization of the typical merchant as "Sir Baalam" a little later is perhaps from Pope. Early-eighteenth-century fears about the growth of London, the distaste with which John Gay, Pope, and others regarded nouveau-riche patronage of Italian opera, and that dread of national "effeminacy" proclaimed in John Brown's *Estimate of the Manners and Principles of the Times* (1757), all blend into Cobbett's simple chauvinism when he attacks the "effeminating luxuries" of the metropolis, such as those "squeaking wretches," the Italian singers and their retinue.

In a series of *Political Register* articles republished as *Paper against Gold* (1815) Cobbett tried to probe to the bottom of the Pitt system of paper money, the national debt, taxation, and tyranny, where the financial power of the City propped up a Court party—whether Whig or Tory, enabling it to divide fat sinecures and pensions among its supporters. This Court party remained permanently in office through its control of rotten boroughs and passed laws to give wealthy men their privileged position while the laboring people were reduced further to pauperism and slavery. Cobbett joined the movement for parliamentary reform, "from the want of which it is my firm opinion, and, I believe, the opinion of a great majority of the nation, that great part of our calamities have arisen."

Constitutional reform was associated in Cobbett's mind with the freedom of the press, which was difficult to practice because the law of seditious libel made it an offense to bring into hatred or contempt, or to create disaffection for, the king, his heirs, his ministers, and the administration of justice. "Vice and folly, of whatever description, hate the light," Cobbett wrote; "publicity is their natural enemy." All that needed to be said in justification of the freedom of the press had been said in Pope's *Epilogue to the Satires* (1738), and Cobbett was the self-proclaimed heir of Swift and Pope. Cobbett's many writings and the large numbers of compilations that he edited or published gave substance to his often-proclaimed goal of making the whole truth available for general political debate. In 1804 Cobbett began *Cobbett's Parliamentary Debates*, a serial publication which became *Hansard's Parliamentary Debates*. However, when he employed his journalistic freedom to condemn violently the flogging of five English militiamen at Ely after they had complained about a stoppage in their pay, the government charged him with seditious libel. In July 1810 he was sentenced to two years' imprisonment and fined a thousand pounds.

After his imprisonment Cobbett continued the radical campaign for parliamentary reform. His cheap reprints of *Political Register* articles, christened "Twopenny Trash" by Robert Stewart, Viscount Castlereagh, achieved such wide circulation in 1816-1817, particularly among working men in the industrial north, that Cobbett became effectively what Hazlitt called him: "a kind of *fourth estate* in the politics of the country." In March 1817, faced with widespread popular discontent, the government passed bills to suspend habeas corpus and to strengthen considerably existing legislation against seditious meetings,

*Cobbett in Newgate Prison, 1810 (portrait by John Raphael Smith; British Museum)*

against tampering with the loyalty of the armed forces of the crown, and against reading rooms keeping literature which any magistrate might consider to be "of an irreligious, immoral, or seditious tendency." In the debates Whigs and Tories in both houses railed against the mischief of a seditious press and of twopenny pamphlets in particular. Cobbett saw dangers to his own liberty in these proceedings and fled to the United States at the end of March.

During his third period in America, Cobbett occupied a farm in Hyde Park (now New Hyde Park), Long Island, and continued to write on the English political scene, though by his flight he had lost his primacy in the radical cause. He kept a farming journal, out of which grew a discursive blend of agricultural treatise, travel book, radical pamphlet, and autobiography which he published in London and New York as *A Year's Residence in the United States of America* (1818-1819). Cobbett praises the United States as a nation of farmers: "Here, Governors, Legislators, Presidents, all are farmers. A farmer here is not the poor dependent wretch that a Yeomanry-Cavalry man is, or that a Treason-Jury man is." He announces his own credentials as a writer upon farming:

> I was bred at the plough-tail, and in the Hop-Gardens of Farnham in Surrey, my native place, and which spot, as it so happened, is the neatest in England, and I believe, in the whole world. All there is a garden. The neat culture of the hop extends its influence to the fields round about. Hedges cut with shears and every other mark of skill and care strike the eye at Farnham, and become fainter and fainter as you go from it in every direction. I have had, besides, great experience in farming for several years of late; for, one man will gain more knowledge in a year than another will in a life . . .

> . . . Time never hangs on the hands of him, who delights in these pursuits, and who has books on the subject to read. Even when shut up within the walls of a prison, for having complained that Englishmen had been flogged in the heart of England under a guard of German Bayonets and Sabres; even then, I found in these pursuits a source of pleasure inexhaustible.

Both national and local, Cobbett's patriotism is allied to family piety. He has to pay tribute to Farnham, alluding to the affectionate bonds of family life in his father's house and in his own, and the healthful pursuits in which those affections were exercised. He wrote directly from his own experience and made himself the measure of all things. His writing flashes upon the reader some awareness of the shining wholeness of his life, as it is contrasted with the shadows—the yeomanry cavalry, the packed jury, the mercenary army—which threatened him and the homeland of which he feels himself to be an embodiment.

Believing that the English poor could better their condition through education, Cobbett published his popular *Grammar of the English Language. . . . for the Use of Soldiers, Sailors, Apprentices, and Plough-boys* (1818). Cobbett's *Grammar* is written in a series of letters to his third son. This form of direct and sometimes intimate address gives a freshness and spontaneity unusual to the subject. Cobbett loses no opportunity to score a political point. For example, in warning the reader to look at his nominative before putting verb to paper, he offers as examples of correct usage:

> 'a soldier *or* sailor, who *has* served his country faithfully, *is* fairly entitled to a pension; but who will say, that a prostituted peer, a pimp, *or* a buffoon, *merits* a similar provision from the public? . . . .
> "The borough-tyranny, with the paper-money makers, *have* produced misery and starvation." And not *has*, for we mean that the two have *co-operated*. . . .

As an example of faulty usage, he offers:

> "Neither the halter *nor* the bayonets *are* sufficient to prevent us from obtaining our rights". . . .
> "The gang of borough-tyrants *is* cruel, and *are* also notoriously as ignorant as brutes;" (using nouns of multitude, such as "*mob, parliament, gang*"). . . .

The *Grammar* as a whole is a political act. By writing it Cobbett hoped to create "numerous formidable assailants of our insolent, high-blooded oppressors." In his own life he had shown dramatically that mastery of language brought political consciousness and power. With radical logic he attempted to make some of that power available to the lower orders.

Cobbett arrived back in England in December 1819. In the winter of 1821-1822 he took the first of his "rural rides" to observe and report on the condition of the poor and to speak on parliamentary reform. The journals of these rides were published serially in the *Political Register* over the following years. Cobbett continued his attack on the government and his political education of the working classes with a series of *Monthly Sermons* (1821-1822) on subjects such as drunkenness (largely an oblique but unmistakable attack upon the new king, George IV), "The Rights of the Poor and the Punishment of Oppressors," "God's Judgement on unjust Judges," "The Sluggard" (who practiced what was, in Cobbett's eyes, one of the worst of vices), "God's Vengeance against Murderers," "The Gamester," "God's Vengeance against Public Robbers," "The Unnatural Mother" (on the virtue of breast feeding), and "The Sin of Forbidding Marriage" (directed against Thomas Malthus). Cobbett's aim is to teach the common people their rights and to strengthen their self-respect. In the fourth sermon, on the rights of the poor, he goes against all the economic orthodoxy of that day (or this) to assert human values in the marketplace:

> labour is not merchandize, except, indeed, it be the labour of a slave. It is altogether personal. It is inseparable from the body of the labourer; and cannot be considered as an article to be cheapened, without any regard being had to the well-being of the person who has to perform it.

Believing that a full belly for the laborer was the only true basis for public morality, Cobbett published another work in monthly parts, *Cottage Economy* (1821-1822), by which he hoped to teach the laborer and his wife how to establish a material basis for that independence of spirit which he had called for in his *Monthly Sermons*. It was difficult to be a militant reformer on a diet of tea, sorrel, and potatoes. Cobbett would show that the laborer, if given a fair wage, could, with careful management and self-help, enjoy the full larder that his class had enjoyed in Cobbett's ideal Old England:

*When Cobbett returned to England in 1819, he brought with him the remains of Thomas Paine, hoping to raise money for a memorial. This plan evoked more humor than any other event in Cobbett's life: at left he is shown leaving Liverpool harbor with Paine's coffin on his back; at right he is "The Hampshire Hog" (a reference to his residence at Botley House) carrying Paine's bones and followed by his friend and political ally Henry Hunt. Cobbett's proposal was unsuccessful and Paine's bones were eventually lost.*

> The people of England have been famed, in all ages, for their *good living*, for the *abundance of their food* and *goodness of their attire*. The old sayings about English roast beef and plumb-pudding, and about English hospitality, had not their foundation in *nothing*. . . . it is *abundant living* amongst the people at large, which is the great test of good government, and the surest basis of national greatness and security.

Cobbett taught such declining arts as home brewing and home baking so that the laboring class could have cheaper and better substitutes for the products of commercial bakers and brewers. He also delivered, in passing, his customary philippics against tea—"a weaker kind of laudanum which . . . communicates no strength to the body" and "wastes time and fuel"—and "Ireland's lazy root"—the unnourishing potato. A laboring family could live well if it practiced small economies; for instance, if, instead of buying candles, it made rushlights, as Cobbett's grandmother used to.

Cobbett also involved himself in the struggle for Roman Catholic emancipation; to that end he wrote *A History of the Protestant 'Reformation,' in England and Ireland, showing how that event has impoverished and degraded the main body of the People in those Countries* (1824-1826). His theme is that the "Reformation" (which henceforth he habitually put within quotation marks) was not an act of purification but one of bloody devastation, a fraud "engendered in lust and brought forth in hypocrisy and perfidy," which had engendered more and more monstrous "reformations" in the shape of the Cromwellian Commonwealth and the "Glorious Revolution," which had brought into being the national debt, the seeds of the Pitt system and all present woe. All the wars against France in the eighteenth century, so expensive to the taxpayer, were kin to this unholy progeny, he argued, because they had been fought to keep an unpopular Protestant dynasty on the English throne.

Throughout *A History of the Protestant 'Reformation'* an ideal pre-Reformation England is contrasted to a miserable present reality. When the medieval church held its property in trust for the poor there were no paupers; only the spoliation of the church by Tudor "reformers" had made a Poor Law necessary. The nation had declined since the days when Plantagenet kings with patriotic levies (not standing armies) had conquered France. Even population had declined, Cobbett argued. England must have been more populous in the Middle Ages; otherwise, Cobbett asked, how

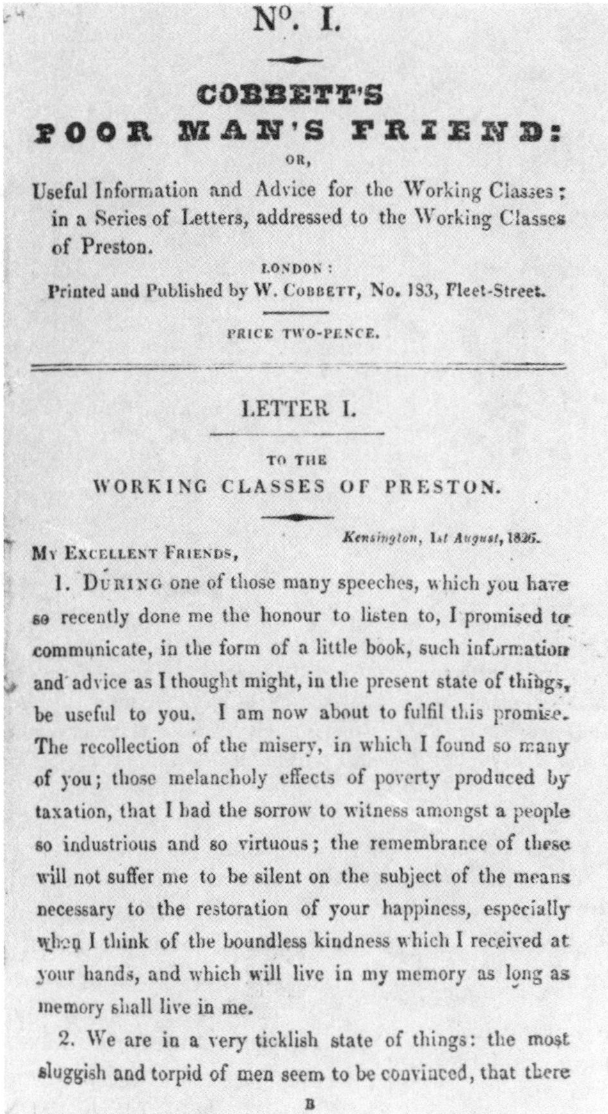

N°. I.

COBBETT'S
POOR MAN'S FRIEND:
OR,
Useful Information and Advice for the Working Classes; in a Series of Letters, addressed to the Working Classes of Preston.

LONDON:
Printed and Published by W. COBBETT, No. 183, Fleet-Street.

PRICE TWO-PENCE.

LETTER I.

TO THE
WORKING CLASSES OF PRESTON.

Kensington, 1st August, 1826.

MY EXCELLENT FRIENDS,

1. DURING one of those many speeches, which you have so recently done me the honour to listen to, I promised to communicate, in the form of a little book, such information and advice as I thought might, in the present state of things, be useful to you. I am now about to fulfil this promise. The recollection of the misery, in which I found so many of you; those melancholy effects of poverty produced by taxation, that I had the sorrow to witness amongst a people so industrious and so virtuous; the remembrance of these will not suffer me to be silent on the subject of the means necessary to the restoration of your happiness, especially when I think of the boundless kindness which I received at your hands, and which will live in my memory as long as memory shall live in me.

2. We are in a very ticklish state of things: the most sluggish and torpid of men seem to be convinced, that there

B

*The first number in the series of five pamphlets that Cobbett called "the most learned book that I ever wrote"*

could men have raised and filled the many great churches now standing in tiny, poverty-stricken villages, or alone on the sites of vanished villages. Cobbett was ridiculed in his own day, and later, for asserting that the national population had decreased. Though his argument was wrong, however, he was right in claiming that many villages had shrunk or disappeared since the Middle Ages. Lamenting lost medieval charity, Cobbett observed that where William of Wykeham spent his income on providing churches, hospitals, and schools, the present bishop of Winchester (Sir George Pretyman Tomline, once Pitt's tutor) had divided "twenty-four livings, five prebends, one chancellorship, one archdeaconship, and one mastership, worth perhaps, altogether more than twenty thousand pounds a year" among ten of his relations, and was supplementing his income by allowing "small beer to be sold out of his episcopal palace at Farnham." In William of Wykeham's day,

> the poor of the parish of Farnham, having [Waverley Abbey] to apply to, and having for their neighbour a Bishop of Winchester, who did not sell small beer out of his palace, stood in no need of poor-rates, and had never heard the horrid word pauper pronounced. Come, my townsmen of Farnham, you, who, as well as I, have, when we were boys, climbed the ivy-covered ruins of this venerable abbey. . . . You know what poor-rates are and you know what church-rates are. Very well, then, there were no poor-rates

> and no church-rates as long as Waverley Abbey existed and as long as Bishops had no wives. . . . The Church shared its property with the poor and the stranger, and left the people at large to possess their own earnings. And, as to matters of faith and worship, look at that immense heap of earth round the church, where your parents and my parents, and where our progenitors, for twelve hundred years, lie buried; then bear in mind, that, for nine hundred years out of the twelve, they were all of the faith and worship of the monks of Waverley; and, with that thought in your mind find if you can, the heart to say, that the monks of Waverley, by whose hospitality your fathers and my fathers were, for so many ages, preserved from bearing the hateful name of pauper, taught an idolatrous and damnable religion.

Here there is a touch of conventionally romantic "Gothic" sentiment, but the reader feels more strongly the sense of place, the sense of history, and the constant pressure of Cobbett's egotism, while an appeal to direct, particular, personal experience is coupled with the widest and wildest generalizations.

Cobbett's *History of the Protestant 'Reformation'* was a best-seller, but his *Rural Rides* (1830) has proved more enduring. This book is a collection of journals written during his tours on horseback between September 1822 and October 1826 in the area south and east of a line from Norwich to Hereford. The "Rides" are republished exactly as they appeared in the *Political Register*, and Cobbett's narrative retains all the freshness and immediacy of its original form: a daybook written in snatches. He rode on horseback, rather than by coach, to see the country and to meet country people of his own choosing. For a man of sixty he displayed (and boasted of ) great hardiness. He was often in the saddle fasting from daybreak to sunset in all weather. On one occasion he rode for two hours wet to the skin in order to rid himself of "hooping cough." He was usually accompanied by one of his sons or a friend, and, whenever he could, he stayed with a farmer or a landowner friend.

Cobbett's objective was to see the condition of the country folk and talk politics to them. He delivered his formal "Rustic Harangues"—on tithes, taxes, corn laws, placemen, paper money and the need for reform—to meetings of farmers and freeholders in market towns, and he talked to the laborers in the fields as he passed, speaking to them of the true causes of their misery. Farmers could not afford to pay living wages to their laborers because they were so heavily taxed to support the "dead-weight" of pensioners, sinecurists, fund holders, and a standing army in time of peace. Loan mongers and stock jobbers became rich and propped up a corrupt government, which protected their interests and retained perpetual power by its control of rotten boroughs. The landed gentry had enough political power to check this corruption, but, in order to share the places and pensions, they had thrown in their lot with the moneyed men.

Consequently, farm workers starved amid plenty, their share of food and raiment taken off to support the debt, the "dead-weight," and the standing army. At Crickdale Cobbett came to a farm near the new canal:

> I saw in *one single farm-yard here* more food than enough for four times the inhabitants of the parish . . . but, while the poor creatures that raise the wheat and the barley and cheese and the mutton and the beef are living upon potatoes, an accursed *Canal* comes kindly through the parish to convey away the wheat and all the *good food* to the tax-eaters and their attendants in the Wen. . . . We have very nearly come to the system of Hindoostan, where the farmer is allowed by the Aumil, or tax-contractor, only *so much* of the produce of his farm to eat in the year! The thing is not done in so undisguised a manner here; here are *assessor, collector, exciseman, supervisor, informer, constable, justice, sheriff, jailor, judge, jury, jack-ketch, barrack-man.* Here is a great deal of *ceremony* about it.

The canal is an unlikely agent of villainy, but it is something new, and that is enough to spur Cobbett to generate a grotesque list of professional oppressors who constitute a kind of Asiatic despotism. The bizarre comparison and the list of assorted professions have in them a hint of Swift.

According to Cobbett, because the countryside has been impoverished to enrich the towns, urban growth is itself a sign of rural decay. Some of his bitterest invectives are reserved for Cheltenham,

> which is what they call a "*watering place*"; that is to say, a place, to which East India plunderers, West Indian floggers, English tax-gorgers, together with gluttons, drunkards, and debauchees of all descriptions, *female* as well as male, resort, at the suggestion of silently laughing quacks, in the hope of getting rid of the bodily consequences of their manifold sins and iniquities. When I enter a place like this, I always feel dis-

*Cobbett circa 1830 (lithograph from a portrait attributed to George Cooke)*

> posed to squeeze up my nose with my fingers. It is nonsense, to be sure; but I conceit that every two-legged creature, that I see coming near me, is about to cover me with the poisonous proceeds of its impurities. To places like this come all that is knavish and all that is foolish and all that is base; gamesters, pick-pockets, and harlots; young wife-hunters in search of rich and ugly and old women, and young husband hunters in search of rich and wrinkled or half-rotten men, the former resolutely bent, be the means what they may, to give the latter heirs to their lands and tenements.

Cobbett is attacking in the conventional way a common eighteenth-century satirical target; he is almost Tobias Smollett's Matthew Bramble to the life. Yet he goes beyond such convention: the physical and moral infirmities of the visitors to this watering place symbolize the diseased condition of the whole corrupt and corrupting carcass of the "Thing," while indicating that the death of the "Thing" cannot be long delayed.

Cobbett's rides took him to many medieval parish churches and all the cathedrals in his area. He comments on them as a politician, not as an antiquarian, but amid his invectives a sense of wonder is faintly discernible. In Salisbury Cathedral he marvels at the men who would represent as ignorant and benighted their medieval forefathers who "conceived the grand design, and who executed the scientific and costly work," who "carried so far towards the skies that beautiful and matchless spire." "These fellows in big white wigs, of the size of half a bushel, have the audacity, even within the walls of the Cathedrals themselves, to rail against those who founded them." Among the few surviving ruins of Malmesbury Abbey,

> there is now a *door-way*, which is the most beautiful thing I ever saw, and which was nevertheless, built in Saxon times, in "the *dark* ages," and was built by men, who were not begotten by Pitt nor by Jubilee-George. What *fools*, as well as ungrateful creatures, we have been, and are! There is a broken arch, standing off from the sound part of the building, at which one cannot look up without feeling shame at the thought of ever having abused the men who made it. No one need *tell* any man of sense; he *feels* our inferiority to our fathers, upon merely beholding the remains of their efforts to ornament their country and elevate the minds of the people.

Everywhere Cobbett observes the situation of the land, the soil, the drainage, the condition of the crops and livestock. Good husbandry is his first concern, and whenever he comes to a new scene he first describes the nature of the soil and says what it will best grow. Thus, between Selborne and Thursley, he notes, "I am here got into some of the very best barley-land in the kingdom; a fine, buttery, stoneless loam, upon a bottom of sand or sand-stone. Finer barley and turnip-land it is impossible to see." In the Vale of Pewsey he says that the trees, "generally *elms*, with some *ashes* . . . delight in the soil that they find here." He senses the wholeness of nature and of man in nature because he is constantly alive to the physical character of the land and the manner in which it shapes, and is shaped by, the husbandmen.

There is no formal unity in *Rural Rides*, but all is connected within Cobbett's consciousness, a characteristic that is especially apparent in those places where the landscape is a landscape of memory. When he shows his son one of his youthful haunts at Farnham, he remembers,

> There is a little hop-garden in which I used to work when from eight to ten years' old; from which I have scores of times run to follow the hounds, leaving the hoe to do the best that it could to destroy the weeds; but the most interesting thing was, a *sand-hill*, which goes from a part of the heath down to the rivulet. As a due mixture of pleasure with toil, I with two brothers, used occasionally to *desport* ourselves, as the lawyers call it, at this sand-hill. Our diversion was this: we used to go to the top of the hill, which was steeper than the roof of a house; one used to draw his arms out of the sleeves of his smock-frock, and lay himself down with his arms by his sides; and then the others, one at head and the other at feet, sent him rolling down the hill like a barrel or a log of wood. By the time he got to the bottom, his hair, eyes, ears, nose and mouth, were all full of this loose sand; then the others took their turn, and at every roll, there was a monstrous spell of laughter. . . . This was the spot where I was receiving my *education*; and this was the sort of education; and I am perfectly satisfied that if I had not received such an education, or something very much like it; that, if I had been brought up a milksop, with a nursery-maid everlastingly at my heels; I should have been at this day as great a fool, as inefficient a mortal, as any of those frivolous idiots that are turned out from Winchester and Westminster School, or from any of those dens of dunces called Colleges and Universities.

This sort of raucousness tends to appear whenever Cobbett admits himself "perfectly satisfied that," but the sandhill also becomes a concrete symbol of his own self-reliance, of permanent characteristics which unite the child and the man, and which, it is implied, have been transmitted to the man's child, who also is to be spared school and university.

The only work that contains as much of Cobbett's personality as *Rural Rides* is his *Advice to Young Men* (published in fourteen sixpenny parts between June 1829 and September 1830). While this work is not primarily political, it is something of a radical's *apologia pro vita sua*. For years government supporters and churchmen had denounced the reformers as examples of every vice; Cobbett replied with a self-portrait demonstrating all the benefits of industry, sobriety, independence, and thrift. He quoted, approvingly, Jean-Jacques Rousseau's observation that men are happy, first, in proportion to their virtue, and next, in proportion to their *independence*, and he illustrated it from his own life. Men must work, he advises, not only because of their duty to their dependents and fellow men, but because useful work is the clue to happiness. He did not doubt that his public success and private happiness were triumphs of will, effort, and character training. He believed that others could achieve similar happiness if they developed their own powers as he had. Entirely by his own exertions, Cobbett had raised himself from common plowboy to one of the most powerful political writers in the land. Even his good health was self-made, for it was at-

*Ann Cobbett circa 1830*

tributable to self-imposed habits of early rising, sobriety and frugality, and love of exercise and fresh air. His physical regimen and love of hard work even gave him a moral advantage over other political writers: as he had never been debased by luxury, he had never become a drone or slave.

For Cobbett the purpose of government was to secure the well-being of the common people, that is, to restore the laborer's life to what it was when Cobbett was a boy. Denunciation and retrospective idyll again play in counterpoint but in *Advice to Young Men* the idyllic tones are dominant:

> Those who have, as I so many hundreds of times have, seen the labourers in the woodland parts of Hampshire and Sussex, coming, at night-fall, towards their cottage-wickets, laden with fuel for a day or two; whoever has seen three or four little creatures looking out for the father's approach, running in to announce the glad tidings, and then scampering out to meet him, clinging round his knees, or hanging on his skirts; whoever has witnessed scenes like this, to witness which has formed one of the greatest delights of my life, will hesitate long before he prefer a life of ease to a life of labour. . . . This used to be the way of life amongst the labouring people; and from this way of life arose the most able and most moral people that the world ever saw, until grinding taxation took from them the means of obtaining a sufficiency of food and of raiment; plunged the whole, good and bad, into one indiscriminate mass, under the degrading and hateful name of paupers.

His retrospective Arcadia is a world of domestic virtues. It is not an utterly lost world, for Cobbett implies that these virtues survive in himself, a living image of Old England.

The dominant theme of *Advice to Young Men* is Cobbett's domestic happiness. He attributes all his public success to the fact that he is happily married, and he writes of a courtship and married

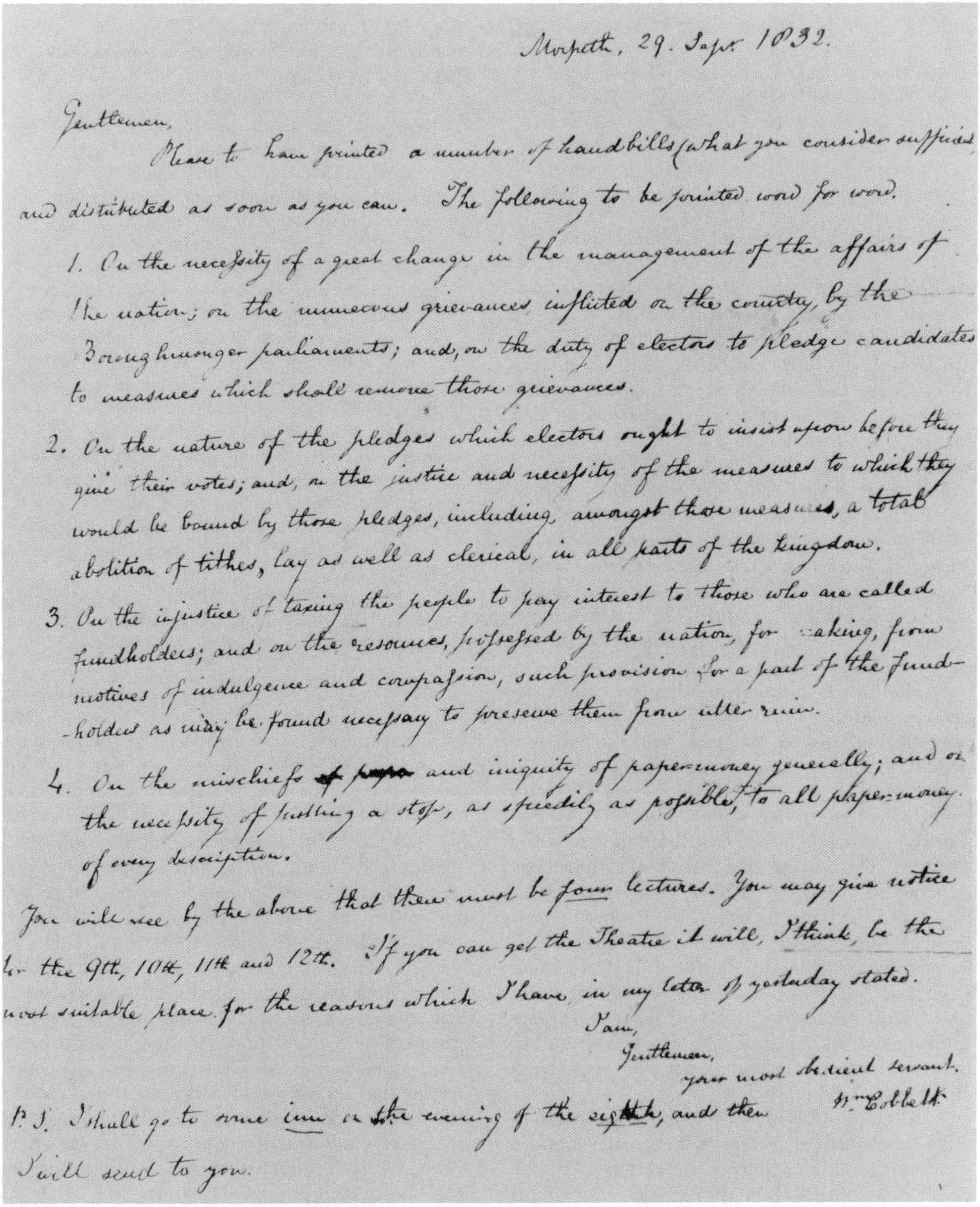

Morpeth, 29. Sept. 1832.

Gentlemen,

Please to have printed a number of handbills (what you consider sufficient) and distributed as soon as you can. The following to be printed word for word.

1. On the necessity of a great change in the management of the affairs of the nation; on the numerous grievances inflicted on the country, by the Boroughmonger parliaments; and, on the duty of electors to pledge candidates to measures which shall remove those grievances.

2. On the nature of the pledges which electors ought to insist upon before they give their votes; and, on the justice and necessity of the measures to which they would be bound by those pledges, including, amongst those measures, a total abolition of tithes, lay as well as clerical, in all parts of the kingdom.

3. On the injustice of taxing the people to pay interest to those who are called fundholders; and on the resources, possessed by the nation, for making, from motives of indulgence and compassion, such provision for a part of the fund-holders as may be found necessary to preserve them from utter ruin.

4. On the mischiefs ~~of paper~~ and iniquity of paper-money generally; and on the necessity of putting a stop, as speedily as possible, to all paper-money of every description.

You will see by the above that there must be <u>four</u> lectures. You may give notice for the 9th, 10th, 11th and 12th. If you can get the Theatre it will, I think, be the most suitable place for the reasons which I have, in my letter of yesterday stated.

I am,
Gentlemen,
your most obedient servant.
Wm Cobbett

P.S. I shall go to some <u>inn</u> on the evening of the eighth, and then I will send to you.

*Order to printers Chadwick and Ireland for handbills to advertise four lectures Cobbett delivered in Edinburgh after the passage of the Reform Bill of 1832 (Pierpont Morgan Library)* life marked throughout by mutual consideration, loyalty, trust, and respect. He writes thus of an episode of his early married life in Philadelphia:

> that famous Grammar for teaching French people English, which has been for thirty years, and still is, the great work of this kind throughout all America, and in every nation in Europe, was written by me, in hours not employed in business, and, in great part, during my share in the night-watchings over a sick, and then only child, who, after lingering many months, died in my arms.

At Botley he wrote his powerful *Political Registers* "amidst the noise of children, and in my whole life never bade them be still. . . . That which you are *pleased with,* however noisy, does not disturb you." Cobbett's tender domestic relations are the obverse of his violent public controversies, and his hatred of his enemies is all the more extreme when they seem to threaten his family. As he would never forget children's tears when imprisoned in 1810, so he rejoiced in the deaths of many of the men then ranged against him: Sir Vicary Gibbs; Edward Law, Baron Ellenborough; Spencer Perceval; Charles Jenkinson, Earl of Liverpool; and George Canning. He hated Malthus because that audacious and merciless parson has declared war on the poor laborer's family.

Malthus is hateful on another score, for Cobbett detested the "filthiness" of birth control. Running through *Advice to Young Men,* indeed, is a prudery which—though some might call it "Victorian"—is, in fact, characteristic of Cobbett's age. Cobbett condemns women who employ man-midwives or use "hireling breasts" to feed their children. The woman who hires a wet nurse does so from the worst of motives, that is, to "*hasten back,* unbridled and undisfigured, to those enjoyments, to have an eagerness for which, a really delicate woman will shudder at the thought of being suspected." He is even offended by the thought of a widow remarrying, for she "has *a second time* undergone that surrender, to which nothing but the most ardent affection, could ever reconcile a chaste and delicate woman."

Although Cobbett was prudish in sexual matters, he shared Jean-Jacques Rousseau's notions concerning the spontaneous development of the child and applied them in the education of his own children. Rousseau had said that the child's natural teachers are his parents and his best environment the countryside; Cobbett's children secured both advantages when the family settled at Botley, and some of the most delightful passages of *Advice to Young Men* are Cobbett's accounts of the way he reared his children there. He pictures a table in the middle of the room, with the children's mother "sitting at her work" and the baby in a high chair:

> Here were ink-stands, pens, pencils, India rubber, and paper, all in abundance, and every one scrabbled about as he or she pleased. There were prints of animals of all sorts; books treating of them: others treating of gardening, of flowers, of husbandry, of hunting, coursing, shooting, fishing, planting, and, in short, of every thing, with regard to which *we had something to do.* One would by trying to imitate a bit of my writing, another *drawing* the pictures of some of our dogs or horses, a third poking over *Bewick's Quadrupeds,* and picking out what he said about them; but our book of never-failing resource was the French *Maison Rustique* or *Farm-House.* . . . I never have been without a copy of this book for forty years, except during the time that I was fleeing from the dungeons of Castlereagh and Sidmouth in 1817; and, when I got to Long Island, the *first book I bought* was another *Maison Rustique.*
>
> What need had we of *schools?* What need of *teachers?* What need of *scolding* and *force,* to induce children to read, write, and love books?

The reference to Robert Stewart, Viscount Castlereagh, and Henry Addington, Viscount Sidmouth, reminds Cobbett's reader of the threatening presences which lay, and in new embodiments still lie, beyond the charmed family circle of health and virtue.

In Cobbett's view formal "education" was a threat to domestic virtue and happiness. It was wrong to gather any human beings into large, systemized masses, and doubly wrong so to gather children. Large schools are like jails, barracks, and factories, which corrupt not "by their walls, but by their condensed numbers." Any scheme of national public education would become the government's tool for indoctrination and intimidation. Cobbett was also wary of Sunday schools (which had spread widely since the foundation of the Sunday School Society in 1785), suggesting that their aim was to make poor children more orderly, tractable, submissive, and dutiful in the factories, workshops, or fields during the other six days of the week. With decent living conditions and freedom from the "comforting" of his so-called betters, any man could establish a happy, virtuous home in which he could create the physical conditions, and set the parental example, by

*After the Reform Bill of 1832 was passed, Cobbett was elected to Parliament. On opening day, 29 January 1833, he sat on the treasury bench, knowing it was reserved for the leader of the house, at that time John Charles Spencer, Viscount Althorp, who is seated on Cobbett's left (sketch by John Doyle; from George Spater,* William Cobbett: The Poor Man's Friend, *1982)*

which his children could healthfully and happily educate themselves.

*Advice to Young Men* is Cobbett's happiest book:

> Born and bred up in the sweet air myself, I was resolved that they should be bred up in it too. Enjoying rural scenes and sports, as I had done, when a boy, as much as any one that ever was born, I was resolved, that they should have the same enjoyments tendered to them. When I was a very little boy, I was, in the barley-sowing season, going along by the side of the field, near Waverley Abbey; the primroses and blue-bells bespangling the banks on both sides of me; a thousand linnets singing in a spreading oak over my head; while the jingling of the traces and the whistling of the ploughboys saluted my ear from over the hedge; and, as it were to snatch me from the enchantment, the hounds, at that instant, having started a hare in the hanger on the other side of the field, came up scampering over it in full cry, taking me after them many a mile. I was not more than eight years old; but this particular scene has presented itself to my mind many times every year from that day to this. I always enjoy it over again; and I was resolved to give, if possible, the same enjoyments to my children.

It is characteristic that Cobbett still enjoyed his experiences, unclouded by the sense of mortality and mutability with which others might recall events of sixty years earlier. Cobbett's joy in life at sixty-six is as fresh and wholehearted as a child's. By recreating a childhood experience in its time, place, and circumstance, he gives a sense of the wholesomeness of work and play in the countryside; and the leaping delight that runs through his recollection is more than sufficient warrant for the rightness of his views on child rearing. The emotions of his youth rush back into his heart and pen at the moment of writing; as in some of the freshest parts of *Rural Rides*, the landscape that Cobbett sees best and loves best of all is the landscape of memory.

In July 1831 Cobbett was tried for a libel published in the *Political Register* of 11 December 1830 "with the intent to raise discontent in the minds of the labourers in husbandry, and to incite them to acts of violence." At his trial Cobbett demonstrated that the indictment quoted only garbled extracts from an article which, as a whole, had a tendency opposed to the one imputed to it. He went on to turn the proceedings into a trial of the government for its callous indifference to the sufferings of laborers. Cobbett had subpoenaed several cabinet ministers, and, after compelling them to listen to his long, blistering denunciation, he called Henry Peter Brougham, Lord Brougham and Vaux, the lord chancellor, to the witness box and forced him to admit that he, in his capacity of president of the Society for the Diffusion of Useful Knowledge, had, only a few days after the publication of the alleged libel, asked Cobbett for permission to republish Cobbett's "Letter to Luddites" (1816), as a dissuasive measure against this most recent wave of machine breaking. "What times are these," declared Cobbett, "when the Lord Chancellor comes to Cobbett's sedition-shop to get something wherewith to quieten the labourers!" The jury failed to agree on a verdict, and the judge discharged him. During the trial the attorney general, prosecuting, had said that the *Political Register* was read by the laboring classes all over the country: "It is taken in many places where the poor are in the habit constantly of resorting." They sat "in great societies" to read it, and it had a prodigious effect. Cobbett retorted, "I hope in God it has."

In his *Grammar of the English Language* Cobbett had written, "Moderate reform—an expression which has been well criticized by asking the gentlemen who use it how they would like to meet *moderate chastity* in a wife," and his own *Plan of Parliamentary Reform* in October 1830 insisted on the full radical program, including annual parliaments, universal male suffrage, and secret ballot. Yet he welcomed the Whigs' moderate Reform Bill, which became law in June 1832. Though this bill broke the power of the boroughmongers by sweeping away the rotten boroughs and giving representation to the growing industrial towns, it made no provision for shortening the duration of parliaments or for the secret ballot; it extended the franchise only to the propertied middle classes. Nevertheless, Cobbett agreed with many other radical leaders that their own movement was not strong or united enough to force radical reform through by constitutional agitation (or, indeed, by armed insurrection), and therefore that it would be expedient to support the bill on the principle that half a loaf is better than no bread. Cobbett, while still expressing distrust of the Whigs, sought to enroll the working classes in support of the bill, even though he realized that they might be resentful.

Cobbett had made several attempts to be elected to the unreformed Parliament under a radical banner and had always failed. He had no difficulty in getting himself elected M.P. for Oldham after the passage of the Reform Act, but he was never an effective parliamentarian. He detested and never mastered the rules of the House of Commons, and was never able to be polite toward his enemies during debates. Above all he hated the parliamentary practice of beginning business after most honest men had finished a day's work and of bringing vital matters up for discussion after midnight. Frustration over his ineffectiveness in Parliament was compounded by financial difficulties and domestic problems. The close-knit, happy family described so idyllically in *Advice to Young Men* was badly split, for obscure reasons, in 1833, after which Cobbett lived most of his life apart from his wife.

Cobbett's audience remained outside Parliament, in the readers of the *Political Register*, which he continued to the end of his life. Declaring that the struggle for the rights of the poor must go on after his death, he published *Cobbett's Legacy to Labourers* (1835) in a "waistcoat pocket" format with a durable limp-leather binding, which gave the book a close (and probably intentional) resemblance to a prayer book. Two companion works, *Cobbett's Legacy to Parsons* (1835) and the posthumously published *Cobbett's Legacy to Peel* (1836), have similar formats, but despite these testamentary dispositions, he regarded himself as still very much alive and active. He planned to write his autobiography under the title "The Progress of a Plough-boy to a seat in Parliament." He would start a newspaper when, perhaps, the *Political Register* could be dropped. His last memorandum book lists titles and chapter headings for the books on which he was at work:

*During the last three years of his life, Cobbett spent much of his time at Normandy Farm, near Ash, Surrey, and only seven or eight miles from his birthplace, Farnham.*

"The Poor Man's Bible, or Selections from the Two Testaments, preceded by an Essay on Infidelity," "Cobbett's Legacy to Dissenters," and a "Legacy to Lords."

As busy and hopeful as ever, Cobbett wrote in the *Political Register* of 18 April 1835 from his last rural property, Normandy Farm in Surrey, to his constituents, the People of Oldham:

> My Friends,
> This morning long before four o'clock, I heard the blackbirds making the fields echo with their whistle, and a few minutes after four I, for the first time this year, heard the *cuckoo*, which I never before heard earlier than *May-day*. And now, this cuckoo will, on Midsummer day, cease to call us up in the morning, and cease its work of sucking the hedge-sparrow's eggs, depositing its own in the nest, making the poor hedge-sparrow bring it up, until it be big enough and strong enough to kill and eat the hedge-sparrow; in all which respects it so exactly resembles the at once lazy and greedy and ungrateful and cruel vagabonds, who devour the fruit of our labour.... But, my friends, I do verily believe that, before we shall hear this harbinger of summer again, the vagabonds, of whom it is the type, will have received a *souse*, such as they never received before.

Cobbett returned to London for another tiring session of a House whose late hours and tobacco smoke he detested so much, but he was on his farm again when he died on 18 June 1835 at the age of seventy-two. A few hours before his death he asked to be carried around the farm to see how the work was going in the fields. The last entry in his diary was on the 12 June; it read: "Ploughing home field."

In his generation Cobbett, Thomas Bewick, and William Wordsworth belong together. The democratic tendencies of their thought and art harmonize with their fundamental conservatism, and their integrity is bound up in a feeling for the land itself. A tradition of poets running from Virgil to Wordsworth would have assented to Cobbett's claim, made in the *Political Register* for 17 March 1821:

> if the cultivators of the land be not, generally speaking, the most virtuous and most *happy* of mankind, there must be something at work in the community to counteract the operations of na-

> ture. This way of life gives the best security for health and strength of body. It does not *teach*, it necessarily produces *early rising*; constant *forethought*; constant *attention*; and constant *care of dumb animals*. The nature and qualities of all living things are known to country boys better than to philosophers.

Cobbett's understanding, and love, of the land and the men who worked upon it is perhaps the only continuous thread in his political opinions during forty years of journalism.

Cobbett's views were not shaped by modern industrialism; yet most of his contemporary readers were members of the nascent working class in the new industrial towns. Despite—or perhaps because of—his industrial leadership his effectiveness lay less in his theories about paper money, electoral reform, or whatever, than in his creation of a mythical, but not insubstantial, lost Eden of old rural England. Cobbett glorified agricultural labor in its hardihood, innocence, and usefulness—and by its associations with patriotism, morality, and the beauties of nature. Like Oliver Goldsmith, he mourned the destruction of a legendary England of happy husbandmen, but his forms, purposes, and experiences are so different from Goldsmith's that the sweet Auburn he creates in the Farnham of his own childhood is altogether less wistful, more workaday, and more substantial than the rural idealizations of any poet. Cobbett exaggerated the material comforts of laborers in Old England, but he did not exaggerate the beauty of the man-made (yet natural) landscape where they worked and the decency of a life regulated by the cycle of the seasons rather than the steam engine. Cobbett's readers may have been mostly in the industrial towns, but many of them had only recently left the land. Cobbett, perhaps more than anyone else, kept alive in the consciousness of urban workers a folk memory of rural beauty and seemliness, and an allied sense of lost rights in the land.

Considered apart from his politics, Cobbett stands with contemporaries such as Gilbert White, John Constable, Bewick, John Crome, William and Dorothy Wordsworth, and Clare, as a teacher who taught Englishman how to see and know their land. He engages the reader in his own delight: for instance in *Rural Rides*:

> The custom is in this part of Hertfordshire.... to leave a *border* round the ploughed part of the fields to bear grass and to make hay from, so that, the grass being now made into hay, every cornfield has a closely mowed grass walk about ten feet wide all round it, between the corn and the hedge. This is most beautiful! The hedges are now full of the shepherd's rose, honeysuckles, and all sorts of wild flowers; so that you are upon a grass walk, with this most beautiful of all flower gardens and shrubberies on your one hand, and with the corn on the other. And thus you go from field to field (on foot or on horseback), the sort of corn, the sort of underwood and timber, the shape and size of the fields, the height of the hedge-rows, the height of the trees, all continually varying. Talk of *pleasure-grounds* indeed! What, that man ever invented, under the name of pleasure-ground, can equal these fields in Hertfordshire?

He may have been blind to new ideas, but Cobbett had a corporeal eye that could not choose but see, and his eye was often caught by natural or man-made beauty. His fresh, unpremeditated georgics and his idyllic "born and bred in the sweet air" recollections are continually springing up out of his polemics like wildflowers among rocks.

Whether he was gathering the impressions of his rural riding or whether he was confidently producing what he claimed to be a definitive history of paper money or Protestantism, Cobbett always wrote rapidly and spontaneously. In his *Grammar of the English Language* his advice on putting sentences together was:

> Use the first words that occur to you, and never attempt to *alter a thought*; for, that which has come of itself into your mind is likely to pass into that of another more readily and with more effect than anything which you can, by reflection, invent.
>
> Never stop to *make a choice of words*. Put down your thoughts in words just as they come. Follow the order which your thought will point out; and it will push you on to get it upon the paper as quickly and as clearly as possible.

Many ideas, puerile or barbarous, sensible or compassionate, came into Cobbett's mind, and his pen would follow whatever should occur to him as he was writing. Whether the theme is paper money or reform, we are likely to find Cobbett talking, inter alia, about Methodism, the plunder of the East, engrossing, tea, William Wilberforce, William Shakespeare, pianos in farmers' parlors, standing armies, John Milton, Cobbett's corn, Malthus, sentimental plays, rural depopulation, Swift, gin, the Italian opera, Pope, blue smock

William Cobbett (portrait by Adam Buck; Collection of Lady Lathbury)

frocks, potatoes, old English hospitality, Sunday schools, thick oak tables, fund-holding widows, tree planting, or Quaker corn factors. Typically, nearly half of his four-thousand-word letter to the editor of the *Agricultural Magazine* (1815) on the subject of potatoes was devoted to attacking the "barbarous trash" of Milton's *Paradise Lost* and Shakespeare's bombast, puns, and obscenities. Such literary opinions, not to mention the style of his political life, might justify the label "Philistine" that Matthew Arnold later attached to him, were it not for Cobbett's enlightened view of Swift and Pope (particularly of Pope's often misjudged character and his feeling for the natural scene, which is quite as sensitive as Arnold's).

Sometimes Cobbett's thoughts push so hard that syntax is forgotten, as in his *Treatise on Cobbett's Corn* (1828):

> Puddings.... must have been of Saxon or British origin; for we not only do not meet with them in France; but Frenchmen who, instead of being the most polite, are, when cookery is talked of, the most rude people in the world; and, while sitting within the smell of one of their own kitchens (for not to smell it, you must get out of the house, be it big as it may); while sitting within the smell of one of these, which is a sort of mixture, between fragrance and a stink; and, while I think of it, there is a place of this sort in Cockspur-street, where the kitchen is under the causeway, having some little gratings in the causeway, for the escape of the fumes; I am sure, that, to fifty different persons, or, at least, fifty different times, in walking over those gratings, I have said to some one or more that were with me, "which of two things that one could name does that smell most like?"

This sentence on, or rather off, puddings is of unusual length and slackness for Cobbett. His syntax and punctuation usually achieve a more staccato effect, as in the sharp main-verbless phrases that open an attack on Wilberforce for alleged indifference to the lot of English laborers: "A very large portion of those who raise all the food, who make all the buildings, who prepare all the fuel, who, in short, by their labour, sustain the community. A very large part of these exist in a state of almost incessant hunger." Cobbett often wrote as if he were physically assaulting his enemies. In the *Political Register* for 18 September 1830 he declared that he would enjoy dealing with the Edinburgh Reviewers exactly as a poacher wires a rabbit. First, he describes in accurate detail how the poacher makes the wire noose and sets it. Then:

> By and by, in the dark, comes the rabbit dancing along, anticipating the clover, as the Edinburgh Reviewers are now anticipating the sweets of the taxes [when the Whigs win the general election in 1830]; his head goes through the noose, down drops the toiler [the stick holding up the noose], he finds himself entangled, pulls to disentangle himself, the harder he pulls the tighter becomes the noose, he dances and pulls in every direction, and at last, down he falls, choked by his own efforts, and in the morning you find him with head doubled in size by his fatal efforts, with eyes forced from their sockets, and, if in a corn or grass field, lying on a circular spot, about four feet in diameter, the grass or corn trampled down as smooth as the turnpike-road. Just in this way I will deal with the Edinburgh Reviewers.

With the demeanor of a poacher picking up a live rabbit and preparing to knock it on the head, Cobbett begins an open letter: "Wilberforce, I have you before me in a canting pamphlet. . . ." Cobbett had no intention, with Jack Ketch and John Dryden, of making a malefactor die sweetly: "Swift has told us not to chop *blocks* with *razors*. any *edge*-tool is too fine for work like this: a pick-axe, that perforates with one end and drags about with the other, is the tool for this sort of business." Cobbett welcomed the charge of "coarseness," often leveled at him by his enemies. He was always a rough fighter and sometimes a dirty fighter, but, like Pope, he received knocks as hard as those he gave.

Like other radical leaders, Cobbett made a great virtue of self-reliance, and elevated his own principles, prejudices, and tastes into moral absolutes. He saw himself as personifying the old rural values, or the ideal family affections, or the spirit of reform; and so he dramatized himself. Planning, toward the end of his life, to write his autobiography, Cobbett presented himself as personifying natural rights:

> my chief object in writing it, or, at least, one of my chief objects, being to assert the natural rights of the working people; to assert the superiority which nature frequently gives them over birth, title, and wealth. I shall entitle my book "The Progress of a Plough-boy to a seat in Parliament, as exemplified in the History of the Life of William Cobbett, Member for Oldham" and, I intend that the frontispiece to the book shall represent me, first in a smock-frock, driving the rooks from the corn; and, in the lower compartment of the picture, standing in the House of Commons, addressing the Speaker.

Cobbett painted himself better than he was; he was sometimes a bully, a liar, and a coward, though perhaps not more so than most men. His financial mismanagement at times verged on dishonesty, but in many respects he justified the admiration which he lavished upon himself. He was manly, shrewd, hardworking, and naively sincere in whatever cause he was, for the moment, embracing, and the enormous self-esteem that enabled him to face and overcome repeated misfortunes seems itself a kind of rectitude. Cobbett's unashamed egotism and constant aggressiveness are those of the ambitious, self-made man who is obstinate, willful, and perhaps insecure. Cobbett made his own private and personal life the measure of all value, and asserted his selfhood against the ills of society. His nostalgia gave him understanding and faith at the same time as it shaped his views on the future, so that his golden age was at once retrospective and prospective.

Cobbett's recollections of oaken tables, bacon, roast beef, plum pudding, pewter plates, sports, and holidays in the 1770s may have helped to form his political blueprints for the 1830s, but the power and urgency of his writing about his childhood suggest that retrospection mattered most to him because it satisfied emotional needs. With Hazlitt he agreed that the past is a "real and substantial part of our being," and "it is the past that gives me most delight and most assurance of reality." The child that Cobbett was is always vividly before him, perhaps trudging afield on his little legs with his bag of bread and cheese and wooden bottle of small beer swung over his shoulders on a little crook, or sitting in his blue smock frock under a haystack at Kew reading *A Tale of a Tub* and experiencing the birth of intellect. In those little retrospective idylls in *Rural Rides* and *Advice to Young Men* Cobbett conveys a sense of personal wholeness within a landscape of memory and expectation that is not dissimilar in effect to Samuel Taylor Coleridge's lovely *Frost at Midnight.* The power, vigor, and beauty of Cobbett's best work, like Wordsworth's, arise from recollected emotion. Cobbett may find a permanent place in political histories, but most people who read Cobbett today will read him in *Rural Rides* and *Advice to Young Men*, as a sensuous egotist who never forgot that his first knowledge grew out of the visible world. He continued to wind his own being around all that he met, and he continually looked back over his existence to suffuse it with "The spirit of pleasure and youth's golden gleam."

**Letters:**

Lewis Melville (Lewis Benjamin), *The Life and Letters of William Cobbett,* 2 volumes (London: John Lane, 1913);

*Letters from William Cobbett to Edward Thornton written in the Years 1797 to 1800*, edited, with an introduction and notes, by G. D. H. Cole (London & New York: Oxford University Press, 1937);

*Letters of William Cobbett*, edited, with an introduction and notes, by Gerald Duff (Salzburg: Institute für englische Sprache und Literatur, 1974).

**Bibliographies:**

M. L. Pearl, *William Cobbett: a Bibliographical Account of his Life and Times* (London: Oxford University Press, 1953);

Pierce W. Gaines, *William Cobbett and the United States, 1792-1835: A Bibliography with Notes and Extracts* (Worcester, Mass.: American Antiquarian Society, 1971);

George Spater, *William Cobbett, the Poor Man's Friend* (Cambridge: Cambridge University Press, 1982), 621-633.

**Biographies:**

Edward Smith, *William Cobbett: a Biography*, 2 volumes (London: Sampson Low, 1878);

E. I. Carlyle, *William Cobbett, a Study of his Life as shown in his Writings* (London: Constable, 1904);

G. D. H. Cole, *The Life of William Cobbett* (London: Collins, 1924); third edition with preface (London: Home & Van Thal, 1947);

G. K. Chesterton, *William Cobbett* (London: Hodder & Stoughton, 1926);

Marjorie Bowen (M. G. Long), *Peter Porcupine, a Study of William Cobbett* (London: Longmans, Green, 1935);

Mary E. Clark, *Peter Porcupine in America: the Career of William Cobbett, 1792-1800* (Gettysburg, Pa.: Times & News Publishing, 1939);

W. Baring Pemberton, *William Cobbett* (Harmondsworth: Penguin, 1949);

James Sambrook, *William Cobbett* (London: Routledge & Kegan Paul, 1973);

George Spater, *William Cobbett, the Poor Man's Friend*, 2 volumes (Cambridge: Cambridge University Press, 1982);

Daniel Green, *Great Cobbett, the Noblest Agitator* (London: Hodder & Stoughton, 1983).

**References:**

*Cobbett's New Register* (Farnham, Surrey: William Cobbett Society, 1977- );

G. D. H. Cole, *Persons and Periods* (Harmondsworth: Penguin, 1945);

W. J. Keith, *The Rural Tradition* (Toronto: University of Toronto Press, 1974);

H. J. Massingham, *The Wisdom of the Fields* (London: Collins, 1945);

J. W. Osborn, *William Cobbett: his Thought and his Times* (New Brunswick, N.J.: Rutgers University Press, 1966);

Roger Sale, *Closer to Home* (Cambridge, Mass.: Harvard University Press, 1986);

E. P. Thompson, *The Making of the English Working Class* (Harmondsworth: Penguin, 1975);

Raymond Williams, *Cobbett* (Oxford: Oxford University Press, 1983).

**Papers:**

George Spater's biography lists more than fifty libraries with holdings of Cobbett manuscripts. The most important of these are the British Library; Nuffield College, Oxford; Cornell University; and the University of Illinois.

# Samuel Taylor Coleridge

*(21 October 1772 - 25 July 1834)*

James C. McKusick
*University of Maryland, Baltimore County*

See also the Coleridge entry in *DLB 93: British Romantic Poets, 1789-1832: First Series.*

BOOKS: *The Fall of Robespierre. An Historic Drama*, act 1 by Coleridge, acts 2 and 3 by Robert Southey (Cambridge: Printed by Benjamin Flower for W. H. Lunn and J. & J. Merrill, sold by J. March, Norwich, 1794);

*A Moral and Political Lecture, Delivered at Bristol* (Bristol: Printed by George Routh, 1795);

*Conciones ad Populum. Or Addresses to the People* (Bristol, 1795);

*The Plot Discovered; Or an Address to the People, against Ministerial Treason* (Bristol, 1795);

*An Answer to "A Letter To Edward Long Fox, M. D."* (Bristol, 1795);

*The Watchman*, nos. 1-10 (Bristol: Published by the author and by Parsons, London, 1 March - 13 May 1796);

*Poems on Various Subjects*, by Coleridge, with four sonnets by Charles Lamb and part of another by Southey (London: C. G. & J. Robinsons / Bristol: J. Cottle, 1796); revised and enlarged as *Poems*, with poems by Lamb and Charles Lloyd (Bristol: Printed by N. Biggs for J. Cottle and Robinsons, London, 1797; third edition, with revisions and deletions, London: Printed by N. Biggs for T. N. Longman & O. Rees, 1803);

*Fears in Solitude, Written in 1798, During the Alarm of an Invasion. To Which are Added, France, an Ode; and Frost at Midnight* (London: Printed for J. Johnson, 1798);

*Lyrical Ballads, with a few Other Poems*, by Coleridge and William Wordsworth (Bristol: Printed by Biggs & Cottle for T. N. Longman, London, 1798; London: Printed for J. & A. Arch, 1798; revised and enlarged edition, 2 volumes, London: Printed for T. N. Longman & O. Rees by Biggs & Co., Bristol, 1800; revised again, London: T. N. Longman & O. Rees, 1802; Philadelphia: Printed & sold by James Humphreys, 1802);

*The Friend; A Literary, Moral, and Political Weekly Paper, Excluding Personal and Party Politics, and the Events of the Day*, 27 parts and one supernumerary (Penrith: Printed & published by J. Brown and sold by Longman & Co. and Clement, London, 1 June 1809 - 15 March 1810); republished with slight revisions as *The Friend; A Series of Essays* (London: Printed for Gale & Curtis, 1812); revised and enlarged as *The Friend: A Series of Essays, In Three Volumes, To Aid in the Formation of Fixed Principles in Politics, Morals, and Religion, with Literary Amusements Interspersed* (London: Rest Fenner, 1818); first American edition, with a preface by James Marsh, 1 volume (Burlington, Vt.: Chauncey Goodrich, 1831);

*Omniana, Or Horae Otiosiores*, 2 volumes by Coleridge and Southey (London: Longman, Hurst, Rees, Orme, & Brown, 1812);

*Remorse. A Tragedy, In Five Acts*, by Coleridge, with a prologue by Lamb (London: Printed for W. Pople, 1813; New York: David Longworth, 1813);

*Christabel: Kubla Khan, A Vision; The Pains of Sleep* (London: Printed for John Murray by William Bulmer, 1816; Boston: Published by Wells & Lilly, sold by Van Winkle & Wiley, New York, and M. Carey, Philadelphia, 1816);

*The Statesman's Manual; or the Bible the Best Guide to Political Skill and Foresight: A Lay Sermon, Addressed to the Higher Classes of Society, With an Appendix, Containing Comments and Essays Connected with the Study of the Inspired Writings* (London: Printed for Gale & Fenner, 1816; Burlington, Vt.: Chauncey Goodrich, 1832);

*A Lay Sermon, Addressed to the Higher and Middle Classes, on the Existing Distresses and Discontents* (London: Printed for Gale & Fenner, J. M. Richardson, and J. Hatchard, 1817; Burlington, Vt.: Chauncey Goodrich, 1832);

*Biographia Literaria; or Biographical Sketches of My Literary Life and Opinions*, 2 volumes (Lon-

Samuel Taylor Coleridge, 1814 (portrait by Washington Allston; National Portrait Gallery, London)

don: Rest Fenner, 1817; New York: Published by Kirk & Mercein, 1817);

*Sibylline Leaves: A Collection of Poems* (London: Rest Fenner, 1817); republished in part as *Selections from the Sibylline Leaves* (Boston: True & Greene, 1827);

*Zapolya: A Christmas Tale, In Two Parts* (London: Printed for Rest Fenner, 1817);

*Remarks on the Objections which Have Been Urged against the Principle of Sir Robert Peel's Bill* (London: Printed by W. Clowes, 1818);

*The Grounds of Sir Robert Peel's Bill Vindicated* (London: Printed by W. Clowes, 1818);

*Aids to Reflection in the Formation of a Manly Character on the Several Grounds of Prudence, Morality, and Religion: Illustrated by Select Passages from Our Elder Divines, Especially from Archbishop Leighton* (London: Printed for Taylor & Hessey, 1825); first American edition with "Preliminary Essay" by James Marsh (Burlington, Vt.: Chauncey Goodrich, 1829);

*The Poetical Works of S. T. Coleridge Including the Dramas of Wallenstein, Remorse, and Zapolya*, 3 volumes (London: William Pickering, 1828; revised, 1829); "deathbed edition," edited by Henry Nelson Coleridge (London: William Pickering, 1834; Boston: Hilliard, Gray & Co., 1835);

*The Devil's Walk; A Poem. By Professor Porson* [pseud.] *Edited with a Biographical Memoir and Notes by H. W. Montagu* [pseud.], by Coleridge and Southey (London: Marsh & Miller / Edinburgh: Constable, 1830);

*On the Constitution of The Church and State, according to the Idea of Each: with Aids toward a Right Judgment on the late Catholic Bill* (London: Hurst, Chance, & Co., 1830; second edition, revised, 1830; New York: Harper, 1853);

*Specimens of the Table Talk of the Late Samuel Taylor Coleridge*, 2 volumes, edited by Henry Nelson Coleridge (London: John Murray, 1835; New York: Harper & Brothers, 1835);

*The Literary Remains of Samuel Taylor Coleridge*, 4 volumes, edited by Henry Nelson Coleridge (London: William Pickering, 1836-1839; New York: Harper, 1853);

*Confessions of An Inquiring Spirit*, edited by Henry Nelson Coleridge (London: Pickering, 1840; Boston: James Munroe, 1841);

*Hints towards the Formation of a More Comprehensive Theory of Life*, edited by Seth B. Watson (London: John Churchill, 1848; Philadelphia: Lea & Blanchard, 1848);

*Notes and Lectures upon Shakespeare and Some of the Old Poets and Dramatists With Other Literary Remains*, edited by Sara Coleridge (London: Pickering, 1849; New York: Harper, 1853);

*Essays on His Own Times; Forming a Second Series of "The Friend,"* 3 volumes, edited by Sara Coleridge (London: Pickering, 1850);

*The Complete Works of Samuel Taylor Coleridge*, 7 volumes, edited by William Greenough Thayer Shedd (New York: Harper & Brothers, 1853);

*Seven Lectures upon Shakespeare and Milton*, edited by John Payne Collier (London: Chapman & Hall, 1856);

*The Complete Poetical Works of Samuel Taylor Coleridge*, 2 volumes, edited by Ernest Hartley Coleridge (Oxford: Clarendon Press, 1912);

*The Philosophical Lectures of Samuel Taylor Coleridge*, edited by Kathleen Coburn (London: Pilot Press, 1949; New York: Philosophical Library, 1949);

*The Notebooks of Samuel Taylor Coleridge*, edited by Coburn, 4 volumes to date (Princeton: Princeton University Press, 1957- );

*The Collected Works of Samuel Taylor Coleridge*, general editors Coburn and Bart Winer, 11 volumes to date (Princeton: Princeton University Press, 1969- ; London: Routledge & Kegan Paul, 1969- ); volume 1: *Lectures 1795: On Politics and Religion*, edited by Lewis Patton and Peter Mann (1971); volume 2: *The Watchman*, edited by Lewis Patton (1970); volume 3: *Essays on His Times*, edited by David V. Erdman, 3 parts (1978); volume 4: *The Friend*, edited by Barbara E. Rooke, 2 parts (1969); volume 5: *Lectures 1808-1819: On Literature*, edited by Reginald A. Foakes, 2 parts (1987); volume 6: *Lay Sermons*, edited by R. J. White (1972); volume 8: *Biographia Literaria*, edited by James Engell and W. Jackson Bate, 2 parts (1983); volume 10: *On The Constitution of Church and State*, edited by John Colmer (1976); volume 12: *Marginalia*, edited by George Whalley, 2 parts to date (1980- ); volume 13: *Logic*, edited by J. R. de J. Jackson (1981); volume 14: *Table Talk*, edited by Carl Woodring, 2 parts (1990);

*Samuel Taylor Coleridge*, The Oxford Authors, edited by H. J. Jackson (Oxford & New York: Oxford University Press, 1985).

OTHER: *The Piccolomini, or the First Part of Wallenstein, A Drama in Five Acts. Translated from the German of Frederick Schiller* (London: T. N. Longman and O. Rees, 1800; New York: David Longworth, 1805);

*The Death of Wallenstein. A Tragedy In Five Acts. Translated from the German of Frederick Schiller* (London: G. Woodfall, for T. N. Longman and O. Rees, 1800);

*General Introduction; Or, Preliminary Treatise on Method*, in volume 1 of *Encyclopedia Metropolitana* (London: Curtis & Fenner, 1818); revised and augmented in *The Friend*, volume 3 (1818).

PERIODICAL PUBLICATIONS: "On the Principles of Genial Criticism Concerning the Fine Arts, More Especially Those of Statuary and Painting, Deduced from the Laws and Impulses which Guide the True Artist in the Production of His Works," *Felix Farley's Bristol Journal* (August and September 1814);

"On the Prometheus of Aeschylus; An Essay, Preparatory to a Series of Disquisitions Respecting the Egyptian in Connection with the Sacerdotal Theology, and in Contrast with the Mysteries of Ancient Greece," lecture delivered 18 May 1825, *Transactions of the Royal Society of Literature*, 2, part 2 (1834): 384-404.

Samuel Taylor Coleridge was a poet, philosopher, and literary critic whose writings have been enormously influential in the development of modern thought. In his own lifetime, Coleridge was renowned throughout Britain and Europe as one of the Lake Poets, a close-knit group of writers including William Wordsworth and Robert Southey, who resided in the English Lake District. Coleridge was also known to many English readers as a talented prose writer, especially as the author of the *Biographia Literaria* (1817), a literary autobiography; *The Friend* (1809-1810), a col-

*The vicarage (left) and church at Ottery St. Mary (engraving based on an eighteenth-century aquatint). The man walking toward his horse is Reverend John Coleridge.*

lection of essays; and *Aids to Reflection* (1825), a series of aphorisms on religious faith. Residents of Bristol might have remembered him as a young radical firebrand who delivered some controversial lectures on politics and religion in 1795, while residents of London would more likely have recalled his lectures on literature (delivered from 1808 to 1819), which first established his public image as a distinguished man of letters endowed with immense cultural authority in matters of aesthetic theory and practical criticism. However, very few of his contemporaries were aware of the wide range of his prose works, which included a large quantity of newspaper articles, occasional pamphlets on politics and religion, and a vast number of letters, notebooks, marginalia, and manuscript treatises on philosophy and theology. Coleridge's prose gradually became better known during the Victorian period, mainly due to the republication of his major works in England and America, which contributed to his growing reputation as a philosopher, theologian, and literary critic.

The sanctimonious and sentimentalizing attitudes of Coleridge's Victorian editors tended to repel readers in the early twentieth century, and his reputation went into temporary eclipse as the English Romantic poets came under attack by Irving Babbitt, T. S. Eliot, and T. E. Hulme. But a Coleridge revival got underway with the publication of John Livingston Lowes's *The Road to Xanadu* (1927), one of the most widely read scholarly books of the twentieth century. This fascinating study of the narrative sources for Coleridge's "Rime of the Ancient Mariner" was sparked by the rediscovery of the "Gutch Memorandum

Book," a manuscript notebook that provided clues to Coleridge's early reading and intellectual development. Thrilled by the prospect of an undiscovered Coleridge lurking in dusty manuscripts, a new generation of scholars began to seek out and publish his widely scattered writings. In 1930 Kathleen Coburn discovered a trove of fifty-five unpublished Coleridge notebooks, which she painstakingly transcribed and annotated in a series of magnificent volumes. Coburn is also serving (with Bart Winer) as general editor of the Princeton University Press edition of Coleridge's *Collected Works*, a landmark of modern textual editing that is finally making available all of Coleridge's unpublished prose.

Readers of Coleridge have always been confronted with a daunting problem in the sheer volume and incredible variety of his writings. His career as an intellectual figure spans several decades and encompasses major works in several discrete fields, including poetry, criticism, philosophy, and theology. The great variety of Coleridge's achievement, and the incomplete or provisional state of most of his writings, poses an enormous obstacle for any reader. Yet the richness and subtlety of his prose style, his startling and often profound insights, and his active, inquiring quality of mind provide ample recompense. Coleridge is now generally regarded as the most profound and significant prose writer of the English Romantic period. No longer dismissed as a mere footnote to his poetry, his prose is coming to be understood as an important achievement in its own right, with continued relevance to the fundamental issues of our own times.

The youngest of ten children, Coleridge was born in the village of Ottery St. Mary, Devonshire, on 21 October 1772. His father, the Reverend John Coleridge, was the local clergyman and master of the grammar school as well as the author of four books, including a Latin grammar and a commentary on the Book of Judges. Coleridge later described his father as an absentminded dreamer, while his mother, Ann Bowdon Coleridge, was more practical and ambitious. He enjoyed an especially close, affectionate relation with his father, who regarded the young Samuel as a highly promising lad destined to follow in his own footsteps as a minister of the Church of England. In a 16 October 1797 letter to Thomas Poole, Coleridge recalled a winter evening when his father took him out stargazing: "he told me the names of the stars—and how Jupiter was a thousand times larger than our world—and that the other twinkling stars were Suns that had worlds rolling round them—& when I came home, he shewed me how they rolled round." This incident remained vividly imprinted in the boy's memory as a moment when he became "habituated *to the Vast*," intensely aware of his imaginative participation in a natural world that enormously overshadowed the self-oriented daily activities of normal human beings. From this childhood episode we can trace the origin of Coleridge's sensitivity to nature and natural objects, so essential to his growth as a poet; his intellectual engagement with the ultimate questions of being and knowledge that he struggled to answer throughout his prose works; and perhaps also his characteristic impatience with the duties and responsibilities of everyday life, which always seemed so petty on the vast scale of the universe.

Coleridge's father died of a sudden illness in 1781, leaving the nine-year-old Samuel and the rest of his siblings to fend for themselves in a bleak, lonely world. The family was soon scattered; Samuel was sent to London and enrolled in 1782 as a "charity boy" at Christ's Hospital, a preparatory school of some intellectual repute, but a cold and inhospitable place for the young and impressionable orphan. The rigors of boarding-school life were mitigated to some extent by the presence in London of his gregarious and alcoholic uncle John Bowdon, who introduced the young Samuel to the delights of London's numerous public houses and encouraged him to drink and carouse like a man. Coleridge also found several close friends among his fellow students at Christ's Hospital, most notably Charles Lamb, who remained a loyal and trusted friend for the rest of his life. Nevertheless, the early years at Christ's Hospital were lonely and difficult ones for Coleridge, who became known to his classmates as an impractical visionary, an incorrigible bookworm, and a precocious classical scholar, deeply learned in the arcane lore of third-century Neoplatonists such as Plotinus and Iamblichus. Coleridge later wrote in a 19 November 1797 letter to John Thelwall: "I am, & ever have been a great reader—& have read almost every thing—a library-cormorant—I am deep in all out of the way books, whether of the monkish times, or of the puritanical aera." On his leave days from school he would wander the streets of London, pondering deep metaphysical questions and accosting clergymen with whom he might discuss theology.

*Coleridge in 1795 (portrait by Pieter van Dyke; National Portrait Gallery, London)*

Coleridge's extraordinary talents were soon noticed by his teachers, who encouraged his reading of classical texts and promoted him to the elite class of "Grecians" destined for the university. James Boyer, the upper grammar master of Christ's Hospital, was remembered by his pupils as a strict disciplinarian, unsparing in his use of flogging and even (in extreme cases) fetters and dungeons, but under his stern tutelage Coleridge flourished in his studies of Latin, Greek, and Hebrew. Coleridge's mathematics teacher was William Wales, a professional astronomer on Capt. James Cook's second voyage, who told his students fascinating tales of his exploits in the Antarctic Ocean, where he encountered icebergs, albatrosses, and strange luminous phenomena. Bernard Smith has suggested that these tales first sparked Coleridge's interest in the history of British maritime exploration, leading him to read voraciously in old travel books, and eventually bearing fruit in his lecture on the slave trade (delivered on 16 June 1795) and his haunting poem of South Sea adventure, "The Rime of the Ancient Mariner" (1798).

In due course Coleridge was awarded the Christ's Hospital Exhibition and a Rustat Scholarship, which provided about £105 per year for his university education, and in October 1791 he enrolled at Jesus College, Cambridge. There he became an academic prodigy, winning the Browne Gold Medal for his Greek sapphic "Ode on the Slave-Trade" in 1792, while at the same time he indulged his newfound sense of intellectual freedom by engaging in radical politics. Coleridge avidly read the "master pamphlets of the day," memorizing entire paragraphs and entertaining eager listeners with his impromptu evening discussions of current events in France. He admired the splendid rhetoric of Edmund Burke's *Reflections on the Revolution in France* (1790), but he responded more sympathetically to Thomas Paine's reply, *The Rights of Man* (1791-1792), which castigated Burke's aristocratic tendencies and sought to vindicate the republican principles of the French Revolution. In May 1793 Coleridge attended the Cambridge trial of William Frend, a fellow of Jesus College whose strong Unitarian beliefs and radical democratic politics were regarded by the authorities as such a dangerous influence that he was dismissed from the college and prosecuted for sedition and defamation of the Church. Coleridge was an ardent defender of Frend, applauding conspicuously at his trial and rallying support for his doomed cause.

Despite his brilliant academic success, Coleridge harbored characteristic feelings of self-doubt that were only confirmed in January 1793 when he failed to win the prestigious Craven Fellowship, an award that would have assured his future as a professional academic. Deeply disappointed, Coleridge neglected his studies and sought to drown his sorrows in a self-destructive cycle of drinking, gambling, and debauchery, running up ever higher debts that he dared not admit to his relatives in Ottery St. Mary. Finally, after fleeing to London, risking his last few shillings in the Irish lottery, and briefly considering suicide, on 2 December 1793 Coleridge enlisted in the Fifteenth Light Dragoons under the assumed name of Silas Tomkyn Comberbache, hoping thereby to escape his debts, evade the reproaches of his family, and begin a new life. Coleridge would later describe this episode in a highly comical way, but such a desperate subterfuge could only have emerged from the depths of a hopeless despair.

Coleridge was physically and temperamentally unsuited to be a cavalryman, a fact which soon became painfully evident to his officers as he stumbled through basic training, always unkempt in personal appearance and repeatedly thrown from his horse. Eventually his brother George discovered his whereabouts and, after weeks of negotiation, obtained his discharge. With diligent effort and suitable contrition, Coleridge was reinstated at Jesus College in April 1794, although he was confined to the college precincts and, as a penance for his transgressions, required to translate the works of Demetrius Phalereus, an exceedingly dull and obscure Greek philosopher. Always eager to make a virtue of necessity, Coleridge was soon declaring his intention to translate a whole series of Latin and Greek poets into modern English verse. He planned to publish a two-volume anthology of choice lyrics, which would provide him with enough income to discharge all of his remaining debts and obligations. This was perhaps the first of Coleridge's many publishing schemes that were never to be realized, owing to his penchant for wishful thinking and his highly developed talent for procrastination.

By June 1794 Coleridge was feeling restless at Cambridge and hungry for new horizons. He set out on a walking tour, rambling from town to town until he reached Oxford, where he met a young radical and fellow poet, Robert Southey. Coleridge remained in Oxford for several weeks, fascinated by his new friend and mentor, finding in him a kindred spirit who shared his relentlessly questioning intellectual outlook and his disaffection with established social and political values. Together they evolved a utopian scheme they called "Pantisocracy," a plan to create an ideal society in an isolated agrarian setting on the banks of the Susquehanna River, in the wilds of northern Pennsylvania. The key elements of Pantisocracy, as it emerged from intense late-night discussions, were the elimination of private property among a small group of emigrant couples and the development of egalitarian values through the sharing of agricultural work and intellectual inquiry. As Southey imagined their daily activities, "When Coleridge and I are sawing down a tree we shall discuss metaphysics; criticise poetry when hunting a buffalo, and write sonnets whilst following the plough" (letter to Horace Walpole Bedford, 22 August 1794).

Since only married couples were expected to embark on the Pantisocratic adventure, Coleridge began casting about for an eligible spouse; and he soon found himself proposing marriage to Sarah Fricker, the attractive and amiable sister of Southey's fiancée, Edith Fricker. Two years older than Coleridge, and the eldest of six children, Sarah was a strong, self-confident, and responsible woman who could offer Coleridge the emotional support and stability that had been lacking since his early childhood. Coleridge became engaged to her in September 1794, finding in "Sara" (as he always spelled her name) not only the ideal Pantisocratic spouse, but an answer to deep emotional needs. Molly Lefebure's biography of Sara Coleridge provides a compelling reassessment of her character, countering the traditional scholarly depiction of her as an insensitive shrew, as well as the claim (advanced by Coleridge himself, jaundiced by later years of marital discord) that he was dragged reluctantly to the altar. During the months following their mar-

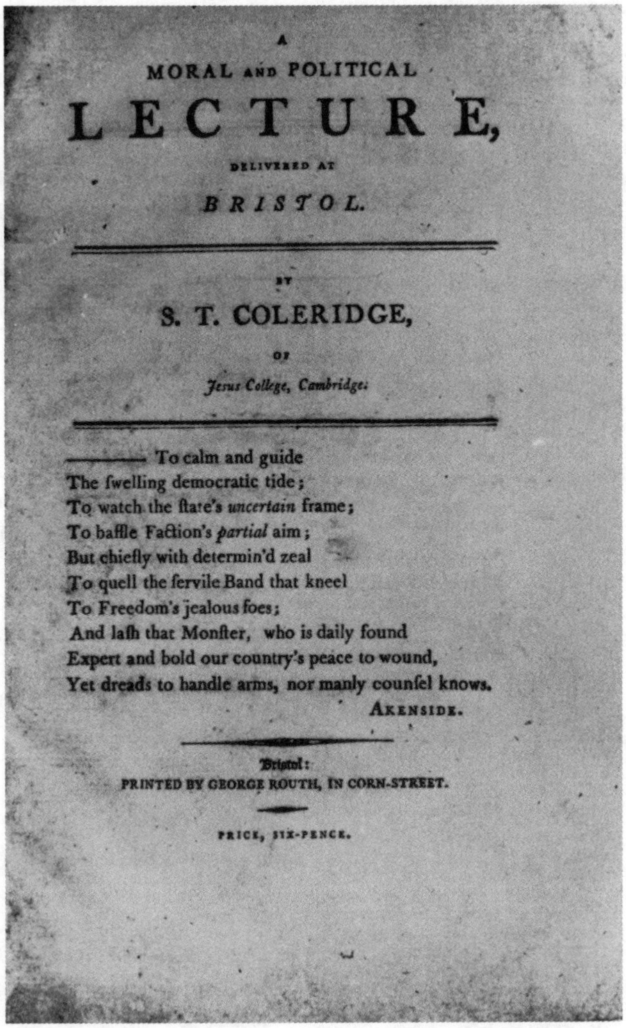

A
MORAL AND POLITICAL
LECTURE,
DELIVERED AT
BRISTOL.

BY
S. T. COLERIDGE,
OF
Jesus College, Cambridge.

——— To calm and guide
The fwelling democratic tide;
To watch the ftate's *uncertain* frame;
To baffle Faction's *partial* aim;
But chiefly with determin'd zeal
To quell the fervile Band that kneel
To Freedom's jealous foes;
And lafh that Monfter, who is daily found
Expert and bold our country's peace to wound,
Yet dreads to handle arms, nor manly counfel knows.
AKENSIDE.

Briftol:
PRINTED BY GEORGE ROUTH, IN CORN-STREET.

PRICE, SIX-PENCE.

*Title page for Coleridge's first political lecture, delivered in early 1795. The* Critical Review *(April 1795) called it "the production of a young man who possesses a poetical imagination" but found it "rather defective in point of precision."*

riage on 4 October 1795, the young couple found deep and abiding happiness together, as Coleridge proudly declared in a 13 November letter to Southey: "I love and I am beloved, and I am happy!"

Meanwhile, Coleridge's friendship with Southey was developing into a close literary collaboration. Together they wrote a play, *The Fall of Robespierre*, in an attempt to earn money for their voyage to America. This "historic drama," published in Cambridge in September 1794, failed to make much impression in the quiet groves of academe. Restless and disaffected with the entrenched conservatism of the university, Coleridge departed from Cambridge in December 1794 and settled in Bristol, a hotbed of radical politics, where he shared lodgings with Southey and continued to collaborate with him on various projects, including a series of lectures on history, politics, and religion. Southey delivered the historical lectures, while Coleridge addressed the other topics. Coleridge's political lectures were immediately published as a series of four pamphlets, but his six "Lectures on Revealed Religion" remained unpublished until 1971, when they appeared in his *Lectures 1795: On Politics and Religion*. Only after the publication of these volumes were scholars finally able to grasp the integrity of Coleridge's early views on civil rights, social justice, and religious dissent.

Coleridge's political lectures attack the British government and its war against France, yet also criticize the violence of the French Revolution, particularly the hideous work of the guillotine during the Terror of 1793-1794. He advocates the moral and political education of the poor and working classes in order to prepare them for full participation in the political process. He calls for parliamentary reform, freedom of speech, and honesty in political debate, criticizing the abuse of language perpetrated by his "aristocratic" opponents, who rely on slogans and catchwords to exercise "almost a mechanical power" over the minds of the common people. Coleridge deplored the plight of his friend and fellow radical, John Horne Tooke, who was imprisoned in the Tower of London and prosecuted for high treason in 1794 because of his writings and speeches in defense of liberty. Horne Tooke, a renowned linguist and etymologist, witnessed the tyranny exerted by the political establishment in its power to alter and misconstrue the meaning of words. The ringleader of this abuse of language, according to Coleridge, was the prime minister, William Pitt, whose false eloquence served to mask the utter vacuity of his public speeches. The windy rhetoric of Pitt's political discourse, Coleridge charged, threatened the English language with a collapse of meaning, a descent into darkness.

Coleridge further developed his critique of established power in his "Lectures on Revealed Religion, Its Corruptions and Its Political Views," attacking the Established Church for its abuse of power, its obscurantist theology, and its betrayal of true primitive Christian values. At the same time, however, he deplored the atheism of many contemporary English radicals, criticizing the mechanistic reasoning of William Godwin, a leading political theorist whose *Enquiry Concerning Political Justice* (1793) outlines a gradual, inevitable evolutionary process toward an ideal society. Although he admired Godwin's utopian vision, Coleridge could not abide his dismissal of Christian fellowship as an agency of social change. As an antidote to Godwin's atheism, Coleridge advocated the ideas of David Hartley, whose philosophical treatise, *Observations on Man, His Frame, His Duties, and His Expectations* (1749), defends the historical truth of Christian revelation, while also explaining all mental activity, including moral judgment, as a product of the "association of ideas." Coleridge's early enthusiasm for Hartley is the result of his synthesis of Christian belief with advanced empirical thought, thus enabling Coleridge to propound his own radical theology, which envisions the elimination of private property, the demise of mercantile capitalism and its endless colonial wars, and the return to a peaceful, agrarian way of life where Christian and democratic values could finally be reconciled.

Coleridge's 1795 lectures show some evidence of hasty and slapdash composition, as well as the vehemence and one-sidedness of his youthful radicalism. They are avowedly polemical and patently unfair to opposing viewpoints. Nevertheless, they are treasured by readers of Coleridge for their forthright adherence to democratic principles, their courageous defense of free speech in the face of censorship, and their refusal to compromise with mere political expedience. The fiery heart of the young Coleridge is fully revealed in these lectures. Moreover, Coleridge's relentless search for absolute principles that would serve as a basis for political action and religious belief, and his rejection of merely utilitarian concerns, would abide throughout his intellectual career, providing a coherent intellectual foundation that endures beneath the often bewildering shifts in his overt ideological allegiances. Unsatisfied with easy answers, Coleridge sometimes seems inconsistent in the development of essential terms and concepts; but his repeated avowal of "the necessity of *bottoming* on fixed Principles" lends rigor and relevance to all of his prose writings, far beyond their immediate context. In "Coleridge" (1840) John Stuart Mill argued that Coleridge's essential contribution to political discourse is precisely this commitment to absolute principle, as opposed to Jeremy Bentham's narrowly utilitarian views. Coleridge's 1795 lectures elucidate the early development of his quest for absolute principles in politics, philosophy, and religion.

Southey's collaboration with Coleridge on the Bristol lectures had disillusioned the future poet laureate about his new friend's capacity for sustained effort; Coleridge had proven unreliable at keeping his speaking engagements and erratic in producing copy for their various publishing schemes. Working closely with Coleridge, Southey had also realized the extent of his opium habit. (Coleridge had started taking opium in adolescence as an antidote for various medical ailments and continued its occasional use during his college years as a recreational drug; by early adulthood he was becoming dependent on regular doses.) Meanwhile, Coleridge found himself disheartened by Southey's dwindling enthusiasm for the Pantisocracy scheme, as well as his seemingly self-interested development of plans for European travel funded by a wealthy uncle. These frictions resulted in an open quarrel in August 1795, which led to the abandonment of Pantisoc-

*Sara Fricker Coleridge, 1809 (engraving based on a miniature by Matilda Betham)*

racy and the end of their collaboration on other literary projects. Southey abruptly departed for Portugal, leaving Coleridge feeling once again alone in the world, abandoned by his closest friend and mentor.

Coleridge responded to this crisis with surprising resilience, discovering new literary interests and developing his contacts with the radical intellectual circles of Bristol. He became a close friend of Dr. Thomas Beddoes, a prominent physician who was an eager advocate of the latest philosophical and scientific thought emanating from Germany. One of the first English proponents of Immanuel Kant's transcendental philosophy, Beddoes stimulated Coleridge's interest in the German language and literature and encouraged his involvement in radical politics. Coleridge was fortunate to find another friend and admirer in the Bristol bookseller Joseph Cottle, who published his political lectures as a series of pamphlets in 1795. With Cottle's almost daily encouragement, advice, and financial assistance, Coleridge published his first volume of poems in April 1796 with a prose preface explaining and justifying his aesthetic principles. This volume received favorable reviews and contributed to his growing reputation as a poet and literary theorist. The preface defends his poetry against charges of egotism and self-indulgence, arguing that "the communicativeness of our nature leads us to describe our own sorrows; . . . and by a benevolent law of our nature from intellectual activity a pleasure results which is gradually associated and mingles as a corrective with the painful subject of the description." Coleridge's terminology here is largely derived from Hartley's theory of association, but his subtle psychological analysis of aesthetic response foreshadows the method of his mature literary criticism.

Coleridge's main energies, however, were focused on a new publishing venture. His 1795 lectures had established him as a leading voice of radical dissent among the people of Bristol. Wishing to capitalize on his newfound popularity, and seeking to reach a larger audience, Coleridge planned a new periodical, *The Watchman*, to appear in regular installments every eight days (thus avoiding the stamp tax on weekly journals). In late 1795, Coleridge published a prospectus outlining his ambitious program of news and political commentary, declaring his intention "to proclaim the State of the Political Atmosphere, and preserve Freedom and her Friends from the attacks of Robbers and Assassins!!" In January 1796 he toured the industrial cities of the Midlands with copies of this prospectus, enrolling almost a thousand subscribers and gauging the tastes and interests of his potential readers.

*The Watchman* began publication in March 1796, and for its brief lifetime it served as a forum for Coleridge's rapidly evolving opinions on politics and religion. Coleridge contributed essays on a wide variety of topics: he defended his own political principles, denounced the fasts ordained by the Anglican church, insisted on the need for belief in God and immortality by modern progressive thinkers, and praised the self-sufficient culture of the ancient Germans. He also contributed reviews of current books and political pamphlets, including a stern critique of Edmund Burke's *Letter to a Noble Lord* and a warm commendation of Thomas Beddoes's *Essay on the Public Merits of Mr. Pitt.* Coleridge reported parliamentary debates and news from the war with France (mostly excerpted from the London journals), taking a critical attitude toward the Pitt ministry but patriotically recounting British naval victories. *The Watchman* printed a few pieces by Beddoes, Charles Lamb, Thomas Poole, William Frend, and John Edwards, but it remained largely a one-man operation. It ceased publication after only ten issues, as Coleridge found himself unable to continue production at such a sustained rate. He was also disheartened by the loss of subscribers who seemed frustrated by the uneven tone and quality of the journal.

Modern readers of Coleridge have also expressed frustration with *The Watchman*, especially with its patchwork texture and its evident slapdash method of composition. Coleridge was never at his best in writing articles against fixed deadlines. But *The Watchman* has lasting value as a record of Coleridge's personal struggle to come to terms with the changing political landscape of Europe after France had lost its allure as a center of advanced social and political experiment and had become just another tyrannical oppressor of its people and a dangerous aggressor against its neighbors. Coleridge's struggle to revise his response to the French Revolution in accord with his own fundamental values can be traced through the pages of *The Watchman*, especially in his "Remonstrance to the French Legislators" (27 April 1796), which censures their arrogant rejection of British peace overtures and their legal restrictions on the right of assembly and the freedom of the press. Coleridge prophetically warns that the curtailment of civil liberties in France could result in the betrayal of revolutionary ideology, the rise of a military dictatorship, and "the slavery of all Europe!" Coleridge's increasing disaffection with the French Revolution would find its climactic statement in "France, an Ode" (1798), which marks his final renunciation of faith in the revolutionary process.

In December 1796 Coleridge and Sara moved into a small cottage at Nether Stowey, a rural village fifty miles southwest of Bristol, where they led a self-sufficient agrarian life, sharing the labor involved in growing vegetables and raising their infant son David Hartley (born 19 September 1796), who was named after Coleridge's favorite philosopher. Their back-door neighbor, Thomas Poole, was a prosperous tanner with a strong commitment to radical democratic principles. A wonderfully warm and accommodating bachelor, Poole temporarily satisfied Coleridge's recurrent need for fatherly advice and support. Coleridge's residence at Nether Stowey was one of his happiest and most productive periods, as he prepared copy for the second edition of his *Poems* (published by Cottle in October 1797), completed his tragedy *Osorio* for submission to Drury Lane Theatre (where it was coolly received), published several articles in the *Morning Post* (a leading London newspaper), and invited John Thelwall (a prominent radical orator) for a brief visit in defiance of a government spy sent to report on their activities.

Coleridge's residence in Nether Stowey also marked the beginning of his collaboration with William Wordsworth. Coleridge had briefly met Wordsworth in Bristol in August 1795, and had been in correspondence with him since then, but their first extended contact came in March 1797, when Wordsworth visited Nether Stowey. The two young poets soon struck up an intimate friendship, finding common ground in their shared experience of radical politics, especially their disillusion with the violence of the French Revolution and their turn to a more inward and domestic way of life. At the time of this visit Coleridge was

*The Coleridges' cottage at Nether Stowey (illustration by Edmund H. New for William Knight's* Coleridge and Wordsworth in the West Country, *1913)*

certainly the more-accomplished author, having already published *The Watchman*, four political pamphlets, and an elegant, well-received volume of poetry. Wordsworth was glad of the advice and assistance of the better-known Coleridge, who already admired Wordsworth's poetry and who eventually came to revere him as the most talented poet of his generation. Two years older than Coleridge, Wordsworth was also educated at Cambridge, and his untroubled self-reliance, his ardent commitment to political justice, and his quiet competence in the craft of poetry must have appealed at a deep level to Coleridge's need for stable companionship with an older, wiser man.

In July 1797 Wordsworth and his sister, Dorothy, moved into Alfoxden House, just three miles away from Coleridge's residence in Nether Stowey. Coleridge soon found himself spending most of his time in their company, often walking out in stormy weather to discuss their ambitious literary projects. Among these was a trip to Germany, where they would study the exciting new developments in literature and philosophy. To finance this venture they arranged to publish a volume of poems together, anonymously, through Joseph Cottle. This volume, *Lyrical Ballads*, appeared in September 1798. Not an instant success, it did receive generally favorable reviews and sold enough copies that a new edition was called for by 1800. From a modern perspective, the *Lyrical Ballads* mark a bold new departure in English verse, signaling the demise of the enervated tradition of Sensibility and the advent of a robust, full-blooded Romanticism.

Immediately following the publication of *Lyrical Ballads*, Coleridge departed for Germany with William and Dorothy Wordsworth. Coleridge had recently received an annuity of £150 from the Wedgwood family, along with a publisher's advance of £100 from Joseph Cottle, freeing him from financial worries and enabling him to broaden his intellectual development through European travel. After arriving in Germany, the Wordsworths settled in Goslar, a remote provincial town where Wordsworth found the solitude he needed to write the long autobiographical poem that eventually became *The Prelude*. Meanwhile, Coleridge went on to Ratzeburg, a small village where he began intensive study of the German language, living in a German household and compiling long lists of German vocabulary in his notebooks. After a few months in Ratzeburg, Coleridge proceeded to the University of Göttingen, which was recognized throughout Europe as a leading center of Germanic philology and biblical exegesis. Many of his later ideas in literature, philosophy, and linguistics grow out of his brief sojourn in the German academy.

Coleridge arrived in Göttingen in January 1799. His declared objective was to prepare a biography of Gotthold Ephraim Lessing, a well-known historian, philologist, and aesthetician whom Coleridge regarded as a kindred spirit in the vast scope of his intellectual activity. It was only as a minor and collateral interest that Coleridge began to study the older Germanic languages; but these soon became a consuming interest to him, no doubt as a result of the inspiring example of the great philologists then at work in Göttingen. Foremost among these was Christian Gottlieb Heyne, an innovative classical scholar who was largely responsible for the "philological explosion" in the German academy. Through Heyne, Coleridge was exposed to the thought of Johann Gottfried von Herder in all of its deep, even mystical historicism and its concern for the remote origins of the Greek and Germanic cultures. Another crucial influence on Coleridge was Johann Gottfried Eichhorn, a controversial figure who was the leading exponent of the Higher Criticism, a new historically oriented textual analysis of the Bible. Coleridge's professors at the University of Göttingen also included Georg Friedrich Benecke, who instructed him in the history of the German language and literature of the Middle Ages, and Thomas Christian Tychsen, a philosophical linguist specializing in the early Germanic dialects.

By the time of his departure from the University of Göttingen in April 1799 Coleridge had gained a keen appreciation for the German language and literature, a basic familiarity with the exciting new discoveries in historical linguistics, and a sense of the boundless enthusiasm that accompanied the early development of Germanic philology. His knowledge of contemporary German literature was broadened by his acquaintance with the poetry of Friedrich Gottlieb Klopstock and Gottfried August Bürger and the plays of Friedrich von Schiller. His wide reading in German would eventually introduce him to the literary criticism of August Wilhelm von Schlegel, who was the first to develop the concept of organic form in Shakespearean drama. He would also encounter the philosophy of Kant and his disciple Friedrich von Schelling, who gave Kant's epistemology an aesthetic turn by elevating the faculty of imagination to a primary generative role within consciousness. These concepts of imagination and organic form would later prove essential to his literary criticism.

Coleridge made a leisurely journey back to England, climbing the Brocken (the highest peak of the Harz Mountains) and wandering through central Germany before finally returning to his family in July 1799. While Coleridge was in Germany, his infant son Berkeley (born 14 May 1798) had died of a long, wasting illness (apparently resulting from complications of smallpox inoculation), and Coleridge seemed reluctant to return home and face the reality of his son's death and his wife's terrible grief and despair. Their little cottage in Nether Stowey, formerly an idyllic abode, now seemed lonely, inhospitable, tainted by the tragic memory of their lost infant son. Unable to provide strength or support for his wife, Coleridge departed on another series of ramblings across the West Country, walking through Devon with his old friend Robert Southey, who had become an accomplished poet, and continuing to Bristol where he met the brilliant young chemist Humphrey Davy. In October and November 1799 he toured the Lake District with Wordsworth, who was planning to purchase a cottage in Grasmere and hoped to entice Coleridge to settle nearby. During this tour Coleridge first met Sara Hutchinson, a short, dark, rather plain, but sprightly and energetic woman who would soon become the object of his hopeless infatuation. Sara was the sister of Mary Hutchinson, Wordsworth's future fiancée, and her presence would become a source of frustrated longing and heartache for Coleridge during his many visits to the Wordsworth household over the next ten years.

During this period of restless wandering, Coleridge received a letter from Daniel Stuart offering him a permanent salaried position as a

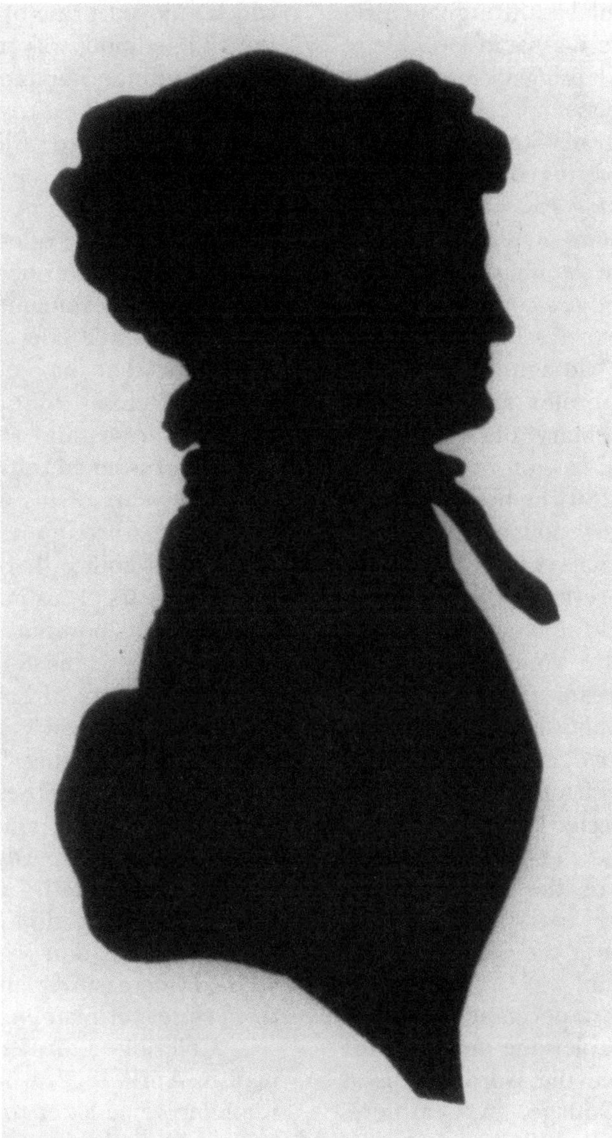

*Silhouette of Sara Hutchinson (Wordsworth Trust, Dove Cottage, Grasmere)*

writer for the *Morning Post.* Coleridge had been contributing poems and articles to this journal since late 1797, and he eagerly accepted the offer of a prominent and lucrative position that would provide him with a headquarters in London and a forum for his views on current affairs. Coleridge hastened to London to accept Stuart's offer, arriving in late November 1799 and getting right to work on a series of articles on the new French constitution. Over the next few months Coleridge was enormously productive; he contributed more than seventy articles to the *Morning Post,* attended sessions of Parliament, and translated Schiller's play *Wallenstein* for the publisher T. N. Longman. Stuart was so pleased with Coleridge's performance that in March 1800 he offered him a proprietary share in the *Morning Post,* an offer that would have assured Coleridge a substantial income and a secure job for the rest of his life. To Stuart's surprise Coleridge declined the offer, citing his reluctance to dedicate his intellect to the ephemeral medium of journalism. Deeper psychological factors may also have influenced his decision, especially his chronic restlessness, his inability to commit himself to a single career or profession, and his recurrent struggles with self-doubt and opium-induced depression. By 1800 Coleridge was fully habituated to heavy doses of opium, normally consumed in the form of laudanum (an alcoholic tincture of opium that was readily available throughout Britain). For the rest of his life he would struggle to control his use of opium, lapsing into extremely heavy usage in times of stress.

Despite his rejection of Stuart's lucrative offer, Coleridge continued to contribute occasional articles to the *Morning Post* over the next few years, amounting to quite a substantial body of journalism that has been republished as *Essays on His Times* (1978). Coleridge's contributions include an obituary of George Washington (1800), a lively satirical "Ode to Addington" (1801), an exposé of the dastardly impostor James Hatfield and his innocent victim, Mary of Buttermere (1802), and an insightful discussion of "The Men and the Times" (1803). In 1804 he began publishing articles on parliamentary politics in the *Courier*, a new London journal edited by Stuart. These newspaper articles reflect Coleridge's engagement in the rough-and-tumble of current affairs in a way that belies the common depiction of him as an indolent dreamer, basking in an opium-clouded haze and wallowing in vain philosophical abstractions. Coleridge is revealed as a much more agile, witty, and topical prose writer than might have been expected by readers of his more formal publications. These articles no doubt convey something of the tone of Coleridge's conversation as he entertained friends and colleagues over drinks at the Salutation and Cat, his favorite London pub.

Following his rejection of permanent employment at the *Morning Post*, Coleridge departed for the Lake District. He visited the Wordsworths at their new home, Dove Cottage, in Grasmere, then (in July 1800) he installed his own family in Greta Hall, Keswick, just thirteen miles away from the Wordsworths, thus seeking to replicate the proximity they had enjoyed two years before in Nether Stowey. Coleridge's domestic life seemed fairly tranquil; on 14 September 1800 Sara gave birth to a son, Derwent. Coleridge and Wordsworth started working on a new edition of *Lyrical Ballads*, although it gradually became apparent that the terms of their creative partnership had subtly altered. Instead of being a truly collaborative venture, the second edition of *Lyrical Ballads* was emerging as a showcase for Wordsworth's poetry, published under Wordsworth's name as sole author. Coleridge's main contribution, the narrative poem "Christabel," was rejected by Wordsworth as unsuitable for the volume, leading Coleridge to abandon it in fragmentary form. "The Rime of the Ancient Mariner," which enjoyed pride of place as the first poem in the 1798 edition, was relegated to the back of the second edition, accompanied by a derogatory note. Despite these overt gestures of rejection, Coleridge labored diligently during the late months of 1800 to see the *Lyrical Ballads* through the press; the volume finally appeared in January 1801 (with the title-page date 1800).

Despite the critical success of the new edition, Coleridge remained deeply uncertain of his own abilities as a poet and tortured by feelings of self-doubt that he sought to allay with ever-increasing doses of opium, which led to prolonged illnesses and a general inability to carry out any sustained efforts at composition. The next few years of his life were passed in restless wandering, through which he sought to rediscover the stability that he had briefly known in the early years of his marriage and in his best moments of collaboration with Southey and Wordsworth. Leaving his family at Greta Hall under the paternal care of Southey, Coleridge returned to London in January 1801. By December of that year he was visiting Thomas Poole at Nether Stowey, returning obsessively to the scenes of his former happiness; and in March 1802 he returned to the Lake District for a stay of several months, marked by frequent visits to Dove Cottage, growing disaffection with his wife, and helpless infatuation with Sara Hutchinson, who seemed increasingly unresponsive to his desire for a close, yet platonic, friendship.

Coleridge's tormented feelings reached a climax in April 1802, when he composed the long, rambling verse-letter to Sara Hutchinson that was first published, in severely edited form, in the *Morning Post* on 4 October 1802 as "Dejection: An Ode." This poem marks a crucial turning point in Coleridge's career as a writer. Lamenting the loss of his poetic talent, his lack of sympathy for natural objects, and his rejection by those closest to him, Coleridge declared his emancipation from "Reality's dark dream" and his reliance on the "shaping spirit of Imagination" as it issues forth from within the self. Henceforth his writing would celebrate the power of the imagination as it seeks to counter the tyranny of objects. This inward turn is also a linguistic turn, since it invokes the power of language to determine our conception of what we perceive. The "Dejection Ode" is the last of Coleridge's great poems, and the end of his long love affair with the beautiful objects of the natural world; yet it also marks a new beginning in his career as a prose writer, as

*Coleridge on 21 March 1804, shortly before his departure for Malta (drawing by George Dance; Wordsworth Trust, Dove Cottage, Grasmere)*

he struggled to discover words adequate to convey the essential meaning of human experience, the ultimate questions of being and knowledge.

As a first step, Coleridge sought to emancipate himself from his uncritical devotion to Wordsworth's poetic career. Responding to the 1802 edition of *Lyrical Ballads*, which contained a revised version of Wordsworth's preface defending his own poetic practice, Coleridge told Southey in a 29 July letter that "there is a radical Difference in our theoretical opinions respecting Poetry—this I shall endeavor to go to the Bottom of." Coleridge's urge to define his own critical distance from Wordsworth, finally achieved in his *Biographia Literaria* (1817), finds its origin here. Coleridge published a new edition of his poems in June 1803, perhaps recognizing that his period of mutually rewarding poetic collaboration with Wordsworth was finished. In September or October of that year he declared in a notebook his intention "to write my metaphysical works, as *my Life*, & *in* my Life," clearly foreshadowing the plan of the *Biographia Literaria* as well as indicating his increasingly philosophical outlook. Meanwhile his wandering way of life continued, marked by such episodes as his solo climb of Scafell Pike (the highest point in England) in August 1802, his journey to South Wales in November 1802, and his tour of Scotland with the Wordsworths in August 1803. Despite the birth of his daughter, Sara, on 23 December 1802, Coleridge still found it impossible to achieve a stable relationship with his wife. Unable to find a resting place at home, and longing for a warmer climate to ease his many illnesses, Coleridge departed for Malta in April 1804. On that remote Mediterranean island he hoped to find the inner peace that seemed unattainable in England.

Coleridge's residence in Malta was formative of his intellect in ways that he could hardly have foreseen; he later called it "the most memorable and instructive period of my life." Shortly after arriving there in July 1804, he found employment as an unofficial private secretary for Alexander Ball, the British high commissioner. In this capacity Coleridge was privy to substantial amounts of fresh information, including some secret documents, on the war in Europe, which was heating up as Napoleon's armies swept across the Continent and the British Navy preyed on enemy shipping. On the basis of this information, Coleridge drafted essential state papers for Ball, while also using his unique knowledge of current events as the basis for articles sent back to the *Courier* in London. In January 1805 Coleridge was appointed acting public secretary in Malta, in recognition of his fine performance as an assistant to Ball, whom Coleridge came to admire as "really the abstract Idea of a wise & good Governor." (Coleridge's "Sketches of the Life of Sir Alexander Ball," depicting his courage and resourcefulness in the Battle of the Nile and the growth of his "practical imagination" in government service, were later published in *The Friend*). Once again Coleridge found himself in a stable situation, providing assistance to an older, wiser man who could fulfill the role of a trusted friend and mentor.

Nevertheless, Coleridge became desperately unhappy in Malta, isolated from his friends and family and often cut off from all outside communication due to the ongoing warfare in the Mediterranean. Many letters to and from Coleridge were lost at sea or delayed for months as a result of naval hostilities. His health continued to deteriorate as a result of the hot weather, unsanitary food and water, and a steady supply of opium. Finally he determined to resign his position and return home. He departed from Malta in September 1805 and arrived in England in August 1806 after an extended journey overland through Sicily, Rome, Florence, and Pisa, and a perilous sea voyage from Leghorn to Portsmouth. To his old friends he appeared to have aged considerably; Dorothy Wordsworth described him as "utterly changed," the shattered hulk of the man she once had known.

Coleridge delayed returning home to his family, remaining in London for several weeks (visiting old friends and looking for employment) and finally reaching Keswick in November 1806. Upon his arrival there, he informed his wife of his determination to separate from her, citing their many episodes of domestic discord and what he regarded as their fundamental incompatibility. Distressed by this prospect, yet unable to alter her husband's fixed determination, Sara Coleridge found herself compelled to remain, with her children, as a permanent houseguest at Keswick, where Southey had established himself with his wife and children. This extended household proved to be a warm and nurturing environment; Southey worked hard to become a professional poet while his numerous children and nephews and nieces roamed playfully in the open air or attended a makeshift schoolroom indoors. In this setting Coleridge's children thrived, particularly his daughter Sara, who later revealed some of her father's precocious talents as a linguist and essayist and who ultimately served, with her husband (and first cousin), Henry Nelson Coleridge, as the editor of her father's posthumously published prose works.

In the years following his return from Malta, Coleridge, unable to lead a settled existence, kept moving between London, where he worked as a reporter for the *Courier*, and Grasmere, where he stayed for long periods with the Wordsworths; he would also occasionally visit his wife in Keswick despite their ostensible separation. Although he found it congenial to work as a roving reporter for the *Courier*, he felt it a waste of his talents to publish his writing in the semi-anonymous form of newspaper articles, and so he evolved a scheme to publish a new periodical as an outlet for his more speculative prose. In November 1808 he published the first prospectus for *The Friend*, a weekly journal dedicated "to uphold those Truths and those Merits, which are founded in the nobler and permanent Parts of our Nature." Ambitiously conceived as a connected series of essays on ethics, aesthetics, linguistics, and politics, with anecdotes and illustrations drawn from the events of the day, *The Friend* aspired to a loftier and more systematic philosophical perspective than Coleridge had ever achieved in his previous periodical writings.

*The Friend* began publication in June 1809, printed at Penrith (a village in the Lake District northeast of Grasmere) and distributed to a list of 632 subscribers. The periodical faced enormous logistical problems: Coleridge sometimes had to walk thirty miles across the fells to deliver copy to the printer, braving winter storms and fording icy streams. There were chronic delays in obtaining suitable types and paper from London,

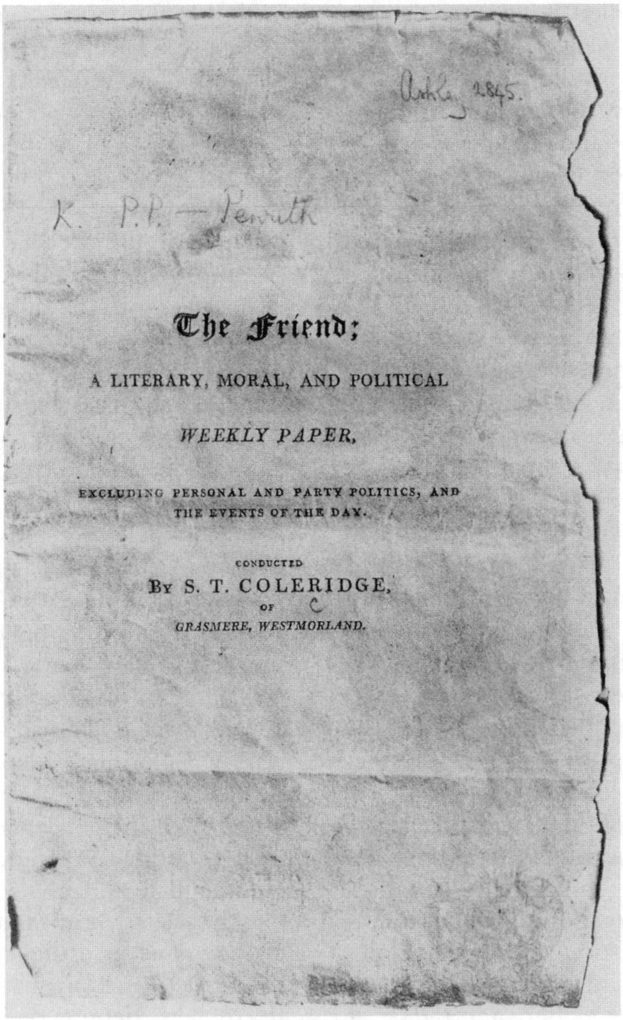

The Friend;

A LITERARY, MORAL, AND POLITICAL

*WEEKLY PAPER,*

EXCLUDING PERSONAL AND PARTY POLITICS, AND THE EVENTS OF THE DAY.

CONDUCTED

BY S. T. COLERIDGE,

OF

*GRASMERE, WESTMORLAND.*

*Cover for the first number of the weekly periodical Coleridge published from 1 June 1809 through 15 March 1810*

and one issue was partially devoured by rats. Despite these obstacles, *The Friend* appeared on a fairly regular weekly basis, running through twenty-eight issues before it finally folded in March 1810. Coleridge's friends were amazed at his ability to accomplish such a consistent schedule of publication; an essential ingredient in his success was the constant presence of Sara Hutchinson, to whom he dictated each number of *The Friend* during his residence with the Wordsworths. It ceased publication only when she left Grasmere and returned to her brother in Wales, unable to endure the relentless, conflicting demands of Coleridge's unrequited passion for her.

Like *The Watchman* a decade earlier, *The Friend* was almost entirely a one-man publication, with only a few items contributed by Wordsworth and Thomas De Quincey. Unlike *The Watchman*, however, it avoided merely topical reporting of current events, seeking to address more fundamental issues of lasting intellectual significance. In the first few essays Coleridge investigated the medium of periodical publication, defending the freedom of the press and denouncing the gossip, libel, and sensationalism typical of ordinary journals. In a series of historical parallels intended to illustrate recurrent tendencies of human nature, Coleridge compared Voltaire with Desiderius Erasmus, and Jean-Jacques Rousseau with Martin Luther, taking Luther's vision of the devil as an occasion for reflection on the psychological basis of supernatural phenomena. Subsequent numbers of *The Friend* addressed issues of more immediate political concern. In a series of "meta-political" essays, Coleridge discussed the causes of the French Revolution and the eventual betrayal of its republican ideology, reexamining his own past political activities and seeking to discover a plausible explanation for the failed hopes and dreams of an entire generation. Coleridge further enlarged the scope of his periodical in later issues, contributing essays on the foundations of international law, morality, and religious faith; "Satyrane's Letters" (written by Coleridge during his travels in Germany); and sketches of the life of Alexander Ball. *The Friend* thus broadened and deepened Coleridge's quest for fixed principles of action and belief in all realms of human endeavor. It contains some of his most lively and characteristic prose, moving easily among diverse fields of thought with a lucidity and accessibility that must be ascribed at least in part to Sara Hutchinson's presence as a sympathetic listener and amanuensis.

Despite its occasional incoherence and obscurity, *The Friend* remains one of Coleridge's most widely read works. Although it failed to reach a large audience as a periodical, *The Friend* was republished as a single volume in 1812, and republished in three volumes, extensively revised and enlarged, in 1818. This 1818 edition eventually reached a wide readership and remains the text normally consulted by Coleridge scholars. It imposes a somewhat more coherent structure upon its enormous variety of materials, organizing the major philosophical essays into three distinct series: an introductory section "on the communication of truth," a middle section "on the principles of political knowledge," and a final section "on the grounds of morals and religion, and the discipline of the mind requisite for a true understanding of the same." Each of these sections is complemented by a "landing-place" comprising a selection of more informal essays on historical, biographical, and literary topics. Founded on the analogy of a "magnificent stair-case, relieved at well proportioned intervals by spacious landing-places," this structure is uniquely Coleridgean in its unsystematic inclusiveness and its exuberant digressiveness, spiraling gradually upward through all realms of human experience to reach an ultimate vantage point. This culminating perspective is provided by the "Essays on the Principles of Method," an essential addition to the 1818 edition of *The Friend.* In these essays Coleridge undertook a comprehensive survey of human knowledge, seeking to discover and exemplify a general principle of "self-organizing purpose" in language, literature, philosophy, and natural science.

*The Friend* is a work of enormous interest and importance for any reader of Coleridge. It is certainly the most informal and accessible of his major prose works, revealing the vast power and scope of his intellect while also providing moments of insight, jocularity, and self-revelation. It contains some of his best thoughts on politics, linguistics, ethics, and religion, as well as his most sustained investigation of the concept of organic development (in the "Essays on the Principles of Method"). Throughout *The Friend,* Coleridge is concerned with the careless, irresponsible, and unexamined use of language that pervades modern society, and he attempts to remedy this abuse of language by reestablishing the proper meaning of words. Coleridge declares the essential purpose of his periodical in an eloquent defense of his "metaphysics," which he uses "to expose the folly and legerdemain of those who have thus abused the blessed machine of language." He proceeds to make a series of precise verbal distinctions, showing that such near-synonymous terms as *genius* and *talent, reason* and *understanding, wisdom* and *prudence, discovery* and *invention* can be unraveled and elucidated by careful linguistic analysis. In Coleridge's view the progress of human understanding requires the precise conformity of words with the concepts they signify.

Coleridge's method of linguistic analysis enables him to distinguish between words that are closely related in meaning and often regarded as synonymous in ordinary usage. This is his technique of "desynonymization," a term he invented in 1803 to denote the act of distinguishing between apparent synonyms. In the *Biographia Literaria* he describes the contribution of this process to the historical evolution of language, arguing that "in all societies there exists an instinct of growth, a certain collective, unconscious good sense working progressively to desynonymize those words originally of the same meaning." He suggests that this gradual process of differentiation can account for the entire formation of a lexicon, from a few simple sounds to an immense nomenclature. Coleridge's critical and philosophical vocabulary derives largely from his own frequent habit of desynonymizing. Several of his most crucial distinctions—between *fancy* and *imagination, symbol* and *allegory, copy* and *imitation*—result from this technique of linguistic analysis. These distinctions play a vital role in the formation of Coleridge's critical discourse in *The Friend,* the *Biographia Literaria,* and his lectures on literature.

After the demise of *The Friend* as a periodical in March 1810, Coleridge remained with the Wordsworths for a few months, unable to write,

*Coleridge in December 1811 (crayon drawing by George Dawe; Collection of Lord Coleridge, Ottery St. Mary)*

numbing his loneliness and frustration with large doses of opium. In October he departed from Grasmere, perhaps sensing that he had worn out his welcome, and traveled to London in the company of Basil Montagu, a newfound friend and admirer. Upon their arrival in London, however, Montagu refused to let Coleridge stay in his home, citing the advice of Wordsworth, who had described Coleridge to Montagu as a habitual drunkard and "an absolute Nuisance in his family." Despite the evident truth of these remarks, Coleridge felt himself betrayed by one of his best and oldest friends and refused to have anything further to do with Wordsworth or Montagu, choosing instead to reside with the Morgan family in Hammersmith. John James Morgan, a prosperous businessman living with his wife, Mary, and her witty and attractive sister Charlotte Brent, provided Coleridge with yet another in a series of cozy domestic situations that seemed essential to the growth of his intellect. The quarrel with Wordsworth, however, marked the decisive break in a relationship that had been going downhill ever since the heady days of revolutionary dreams and shared aspirations that surrounded the publication of *Lyrical Ballads*. Although their quarrel was patched up in May 1812 through the friendly intervention of Charles Lamb and Henry Crabb Robinson, it left deep scars that were never fully healed.

During his residence in London, Coleridge contributed more than a hundred articles to the

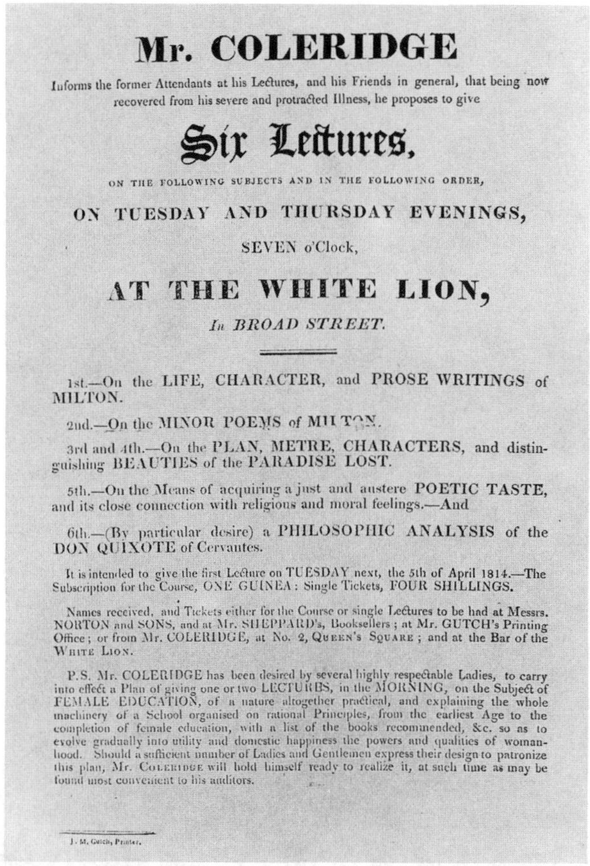

Mr. COLERIDGE

Informs the former Attendants at his Lectures, and his Friends in general, that being now recovered from his severe and protracted Illness, he proposes to give

Six Lectures,

ON THE FOLLOWING SUBJECTS AND IN THE FOLLOWING ORDER,

ON TUESDAY AND THURSDAY EVENINGS,

SEVEN o'Clock,

AT THE WHITE LION,

*In BROAD STREET.*

1st.—On the LIFE, CHARACTER, and PROSE WRITINGS of MILTON.

2nd.—On the MINOR POEMS of MILTON.

3rd and 4th.—On the PLAN, METRE, CHARACTERS, and distinguishing BEAUTIES of the PARADISE LOST.

5th.—On the Means of acquiring a just and austere POETIC TASTE, and its close connection with religious and moral feelings.—And

6th.—(By particular desire) a PHILOSOPHIC ANALYSIS of the DON QUIXOTE of Cervantes.

It is intended to give the first Lecture on TUESDAY next, the 5th of April 1814.—The Subscription for the Course, ONE GUINEA: Single Tickets, FOUR SHILLINGS.

Names received, and Tickets either for the Course or single Lectures to be had at Messrs. NORTON and SONS, and at Mr. SHEPPARD's, Booksellers; at Mr. GUTCH's Printing Office; or from Mr. COLERIDGE, at No. 2, QUEEN'S SQUARE; and at the Bar of the WHITE LION.

P.S. Mr. COLERIDGE has been desired by several highly respectable Ladies, to carry into effect a Plan of giving one or two LECTURES, in the MORNING, on the Subject of FEMALE EDUCATION, of a nature altogether practical, and explaining the whole machinery of a School organised on rational Principles, from the earliest Age to the completion of female education, with a list of the books recommended, &c. so as to evolve gradually into utility and domestic happiness the powers and qualities of womanhood. Should a sufficient number of Ladies and Gentlemen express their design to patronize this plan, Mr. COLERIDGE will hold himself ready to realize it, at such time as may be found most convenient to his auditors.

J. M. Gutch, Printer.

*Prospectus for Coleridge's April 1814 lectures in Bristol (Houghton Library, Harvard University)*

*Willis's Rooms, London (undated watercolor; Museum of London). Coleridge lectured on European drama in the hall behind the six arched windows during May-August 1812.*

*Courier* and delivered a series of literary lectures that raised him to public prominence as a cultural commentator. Always a spellbinding talker, Coleridge used the medium of public lectures to capitalize on his broad familiarity with English literature and the latest methods of textual analysis imported from Germany. His first series of lectures, on "Poetry and the Principles of Taste," was delivered in 1808 at the Royal Institution, where his friend Humphrey Davy was also giving lectures on new discoveries in chemistry. From November 1811 to January 1812, Coleridge delivered another series of lectures on William Shakespeare and John Milton. These were enormously popular, despite Coleridge's usual difficulty in achieving punctuality and adequate preparation; his spontaneity and unexpected insights astonished and delighted his audience, which included such well-known figures as George Gordon, Lord Byron; Samuel Rogers; Charles Lamb; William Hazlitt; Thomas De Quincey; and Henry Crabb Robinson. Shorthand reports of twelve of these lectures were printed in the *Morning Post* and the *Courier*, thus preserving an approximate viva voce record of Coleridge's lecturing style. He delivered a further series of Shakespeare lectures at the Surrey Institution from November 1812 to January 1813. Moving to Bristol once again, Coleridge offered a series of lectures on Shakespeare and education in October-November 1813, followed in April 1814 by further lectures on Milton, Miguel de Cervantes, and the principles of taste. He returned to the London lecture circuit in January 1818 to discuss poetry and drama, followed in early 1819 by two concurrent series of lectures on literature and the history of philosophy.

Shorthand records of varying accuracy and completeness were kept of some of these lectures, while others survive only in the form of fragmentary notes by Coleridge or as vague recollections by his listeners. All of these assorted materials have been assembled in a comprehensive volume, *Lectures 1808-1819: On Literature* (1987). Coleridge's most seminal literary criticism is contained in these lectures, which established his reputation as a profoundly learned and brilliantly insightful reader of English and European literature. Drawing upon his solid education in classical literature, as well as the innovative techniques of the "new philology" that he encountered at the University of Göttingen, Coleridge introduced new methods of close reading and textual analysis to the study of English literature, emphasizing the integral relation of each detail to the larger structure of the work. Coleridge insisted "that in all points from the most important to the most minute, the judgment of Shakespeare is commensurate with his genius," seeking to refute the common eighteenth-century view of Shakespeare as a wild, untutored genius, "fertile in beautiful Monsters." Coleridge stressed the imaginative coherence of Shakespeare's plays, arguing that all aspects of their portrayal of character, theme, and situation are generated by an organic process of growth and development.

Coleridge's reliance on the metaphor of organic development in his Shakespearean criticism is largely indebted to Schlegel, but his use of the concept in the critical analysis of particular plays is highly original, going far beyond Schlegel in elucidating the deep structure of Shakespeare's language and imagery in relation to specific characters. Coleridge is especially remembered for his penetrating psychological analyses of Shakespeare's tragic heroes; he was the first English critic to develop in circumstantial detail the now-familiar conception of Hamlet as an introverted personality, lost in "speculative gloom" and paralyzed by an excess of thought. Hamlet's "aversion to externals, the betrayed Habit of brooding over the world within him," is expressed in a "prodigality of beautiful words, which are as it were the half embodyings of Thought." Coleridge uses this conception to elucidate Hamlet's inscrutable half-madness, which emerges as a psychological defense against adult responsibility and a handy excuse for procrastination. This portrait of Hamlet bears no little resemblance to Coleridge's own personality, as he later acknowledged: "I have a smack of Hamlet myself" (*Table Talk*, 24 June 1827).

Coleridge's Shakespearean criticism has been dismissed as formalistic, pedantic, moralizing, and humorless; he has been accused of engaging in "bardolatry" and the "myth of perfection," even of projecting his own psychopathology onto merely fictional characters. There is some justice in these complaints, which may serve to remind us that Coleridge shared many of the limitations and preconceptions of his own period. Yet he did much to advance the techniques of "practical criticism" (a term he invented), and the endurance of his Shakespearean criticism must be attributed largely to the intelligence and sensitivity of his remarks on individual plays. Coleridge typically focuses on a play's opening scenes, examining the texture of the dialogue in rigorous line-by-line analysis, with penetrating comments on the establishment of dramatic situation and character. He explores the delightful absurdity of the wordplay in *Love's Labour's Lost*, the lively wit combats in *Romeo and Juliet*, the quarrel between Mowbray and Bolingbroke in *Richard II*, and "the wild wayward Lyric of the opening of *Macbeth*." In the first scene of *Hamlet*, Coleridge suggests that the guards' speeches reveal their "imaginative terrors" while also preparing the audience for the advent of the ghost. When Hamlet eventually confronts the ghost, his "impetuous eloquence" reveals his capacity for decisive action at moments of crisis, but he soon lapses back into the "ratiocinative meditativeness" that shields him from the psychological reality of the apparition and the fateful message it bears.

Coleridge's lectures on literature exerted widespread influence in the subsequent development of Shakespearean criticism. Among his contemporaries, Lamb's essays on Shakespeare's tragedies, Hazlitt's lectures on Shakespeare's characters, and De Quincey's essay on the knocking at the gate in *Macbeth*, are all clearly indebted to Coleridge. Throughout the nineteenth century, the discussion of Shakespeare's characters followed along lines laid down by Coleridge, culminating in the work of A. C. Bradley. In the twentieth century Coleridge helped to inspire the development of historical approaches to Shakespeare, calling as he did for a rigorous knowledge of Elizabethan diction, prosody, history, theaters, and minor dramatists. Coleridge also foreshadowed the major doctrines of the New Criticism in his painstaking scrutiny of language and imagery, his careful analysis of puns and wordplay, and his overarching concern for the integrity of the aesthetic object. These contextual methods of criticism, especially as presented by I. A. Richards in *Practical Criticism* (1929) and *Coleridge on Imagination* (1934), contributed directly to the New Critics' use of such concepts as imagination, symbol, and irony, as well as their techniques of close reading. More-recent critics have suggested that Coleridge's model of reading and writing, with its engagement in textuality, its proliferation of marginal commentary, and its recognition of the dialogical nature of linguistic utterance, remains relevant to the postmodern experience of literature. Contemporary criticism, despite its prevailing hostility to "Romantic ideology," remains heavily indebted to Coleridge's bold exploration of the possibilities of critical discourse.

Coleridge's public lectures were a significant source of income to him, especially welcome during these years because half of the Wedgwood annuity had been withdrawn in November 1812, leaving him with a regular annuity of only seventy-five pounds, which was entirely devoted to the support of his wife and children, still living with Southey in Keswick. Casting about for other sources of income, Coleridge dug out the manuscript for his play *Osorio*, revised it, and sent it off to Drury Lane Theatre with the new title *Remorse*; it was accepted for performance and had a successful run of twenty nights in January 1813. The royalties from *Remorse* amounted to four hundred pounds, allowing Coleridge to pay off his accumulated debts, send extra money to his family, and lead an active social life in London, where he was becoming something of a literary celebrity.

In early 1815 Coleridge began to lay plans for a collected edition of his poems, evidently hoping to cash in on the new demand for his work. This edition was to be modeled after the recent edition of Wordsworth's poems, which included a theoretical preface. Coleridge projected a similar preface for his own poems, optimistically informing Wordsworth on 30 May that he planned to write his preface "in two or at farthest three days." He set eagerly to work, dictating his preface in daily installments to John Morgan, with whom he was living at Calne in Wiltshire. Stimulated as always by the presence of a sympathetic listener, Coleridge found the project growing in scope and complexity until by midsummer it had become "an Autobiographia Literaria, or Sketches of my literary Life and opinions, as far as Poetry and *poetical* criticism is concerned" (letter to R. H. Brabant, 29 July 1815). By September 1815 Coleridge had completed a draft of this work, now conceived as a companion volume to the collected poems. By May 1816, however, it was apparent that the manuscript for the *Biographia Literaria* was too long to be published as a single volume; Coleridge was advised by his publisher, John Mathew Gutch, to split it into two volumes, each comparable in size to his collected poems. Coleridge found it difficult to extend his material to the length of two volumes, so the entire project ground to a halt in July 1816. Finding a new publisher in early 1817, Coleridge transferred the printed sheets of the still incomplete *Biographia* from Gutch to the partnership of Gale and Fenner (later Rest Fenner), who had agreed to publish all of his future works. Eager to see the volumes in print, Coleridge padded them out by extending chapter 22, adding "Satyrane's Letters" (that lively description of German life previ-

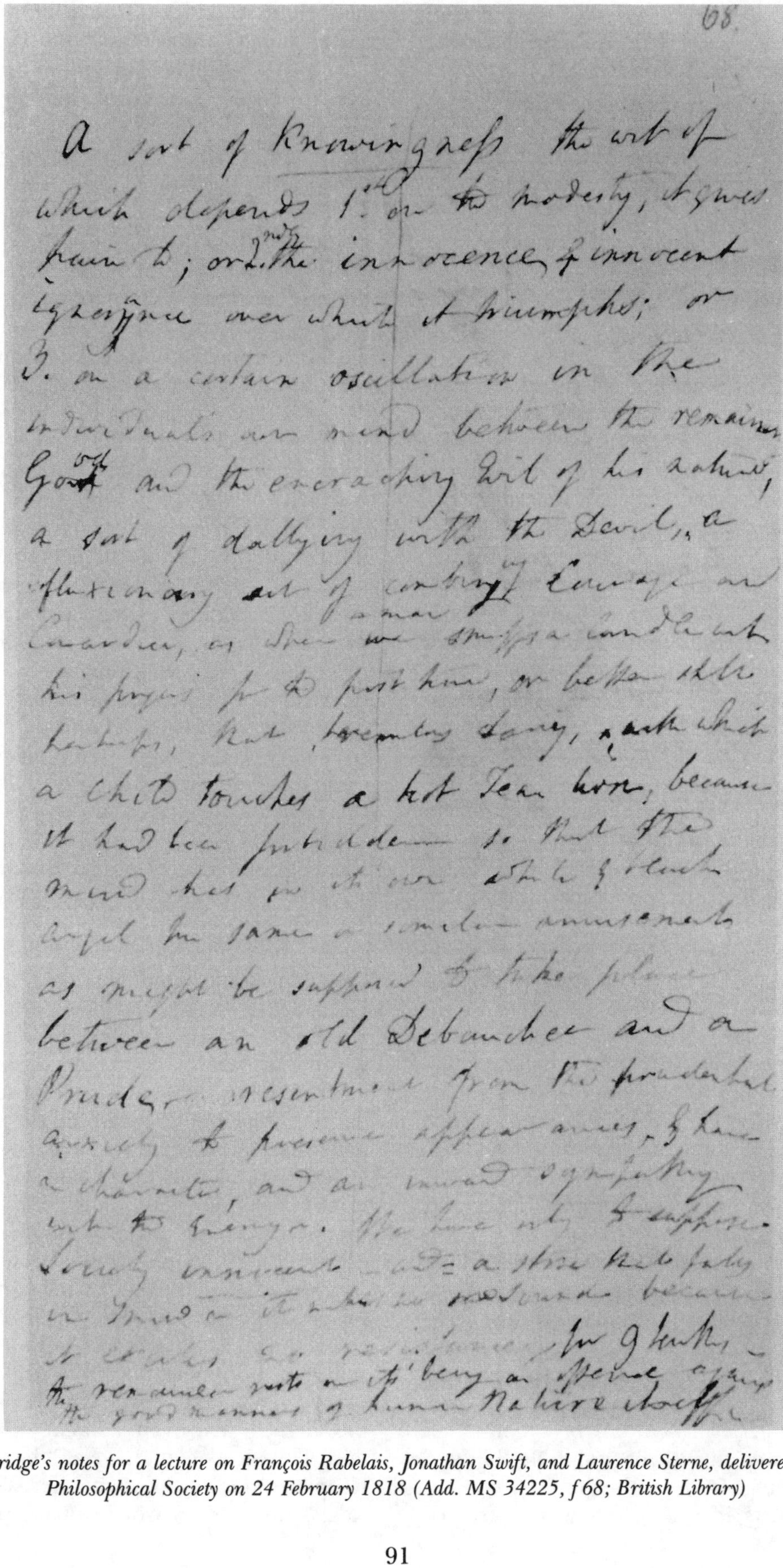

68.

A sort of Knowingness the wit of which depends 1st on the modesty, it gives pain to; or 2ndly the innocence & innocent ignorance over which it triumphs; or 3. on a certain oscillation in the individual's own mind between the remaining Good and the encroaching Evil of his nature, a sort of dallying with the Devil, a fluxionary act of combining Courage and Cowardice, as when a man snuffs a candle with his fingers for the first time, or better still [illegible], that trembling daring, with which a child touches a hot Tea urn, because it had been forbidden — so that the mind has in its own [illegible] [illegible] for same a similar amusement as might be supposed to take place between an old Debauchee and a Prude, — resentment from the prudential anxiety to preserve appearances, & have a character, and an inward sympathy with the Enemy. We have only to suppose Society innocent — and then a stone that falls in snow [illegible] makes no sound — because it excites no resistance; for 9 tenths — the remainder rests on its being an offence against the good manners of human Nature itself.

*Page from Coleridge's notes for a lecture on François Rabelais, Jonathan Swift, and Laurence Sterne, delivered at the London Philosophical Society on 24 February 1818 (Add. MS 34225, f 68; British Library)* ously published in *The Friend*) and a critique of *Bertram* (Charles Robert Maturin's lurid Gothic drama then popular in London). In July 1817 the *Biographia Literaria* was finally published, bulked out to the length of two volumes with these miscellaneous additions, but still consisting essentially of the autobiographical narrative composed in 1815. The companion volume of his collected poems, *Sibylline Leaves*, was published at the same time.

The unconventional structure of the *Biographia Literaria* is partially the result of its odd publication history. Ostensibly an account of Coleridge's "Literary Life and Opinions," it manages only a brief narrative of his early years before digressing into more abstruse topics in the history of philosophy and the theory of imagination. In the first four chapters, Coleridge describes his education at Christ's Hospital, his early admiration for Southey's poetry, and his collaboration with Wordsworth on the *Lyrical Ballads*. In discussing Wordsworth's unique poetic talents, Coleridge introduces his key distinction between *fancy* and *imagination*, an essential basis for much of his literary criticism. Seeking to discover a firm foundation for these terms in the discourse of contemporary philosophy, Coleridge branches off into a detailed exposition of the "law of association" from Aristotle through David Hartley. After demonstrating the inadequacy of Hartley's mechanistic model of the mind, Coleridge traces an alternative philosophical tradition from René Descartes through Benedict Spinoza, Gottfried Wilhelm von Leibniz, Immanuel Kant, Johann Gottlieb Fichte, and Friedrich von Schelling. This philosophical digression reaches its climax in chapter 13, "On the imagination, or esemplastic power," which follows Schelling in establishing the ground of self-consciousness in the synthesizing activity of the imagination. At this point Coleridge abruptly breaks off the exposition, introduces a letter of apology from a fictive correspondent, and proposes complex definitions of *fancy* and *imagination*.

These famous definitions, the result of long meditation on the nature of his own poetic vocation, go to the very heart of human creative activity. *Fancy*, says Coleridge, "is no other than a mode of Memory emancipated from the order of time and space," a playful juxtaposition of preexistent images. *Imagination*, on the other hand, is a creative power, almost magical in its ability to bring forth being from nothingness. This creative power exists in two different aspects, primary and secondary. Coleridge defines the primary imagination as "the living Power and prime Agent of all human Perception, and as a repetition in the finite mind of the eternal act of creation in the infinite I AM." As a faculty of perception, the primary imagination is always unconsciously at work in every human mind, actively projecting a world of external objects. This phenomenal world is not "given" for Coleridge; it must be constructed by the human mind out of the raw material of sensation. Simply in the act of perception, the "finite mind" creates a world, and in this way it repeats the original creation of the universe out of chaos by "the infinite I AM." The secondary imagination is "an echo of the former," a voluntary creative process that can only occur in the self-conscious mind of the poet. According to Coleridge, "it dissolves, diffuses, dissipates, in order to re-create," first breaking the objects of perception into their basic elements, then seeking to recombine these elements in poetic discourse. On a more fully conscious level than the primary imagination, the secondary imagination produces a linguistic analogue of the divine act of creation, using words to shadow forth a microcosm. These gnomic definitions of primary and secondary imagination have been widely discussed and debated ever since their first publication; and they continue to serve as a stimulus for further exploration of the fundamental cognitive and linguistic basis of human creativity.

The remaining chapters of the *Biographia Literaria* are devoted to "practical criticism," the close reading and analysis of literary works for the purposes of understanding and evaluation. Coleridge discusses the original composition of the *Lyrical Ballads*, focusing especially on Wordsworth's preface of 1800 and the critical controversy that arose from its defense of the "language of real life" as a medium for poetry. He suggests that Wordsworth may have been too narrow in his conception of poetic language, restricting it to the rustic language spoken by peasants and shepherds among the unspoiled natural objects of the English countryside. Coleridge, on the other hand, suggests that a truly natural poetic language is neither regional nor specific to any social class; it is the common property of educated speakers, stemming not from any social or geographical context, but from the inner form of the language at a given moment of historical evolution. This view of language as "the product of philosophers, not clowns or shepherds" informs Coleridge's analysis of Wordsworth's poetic practice.

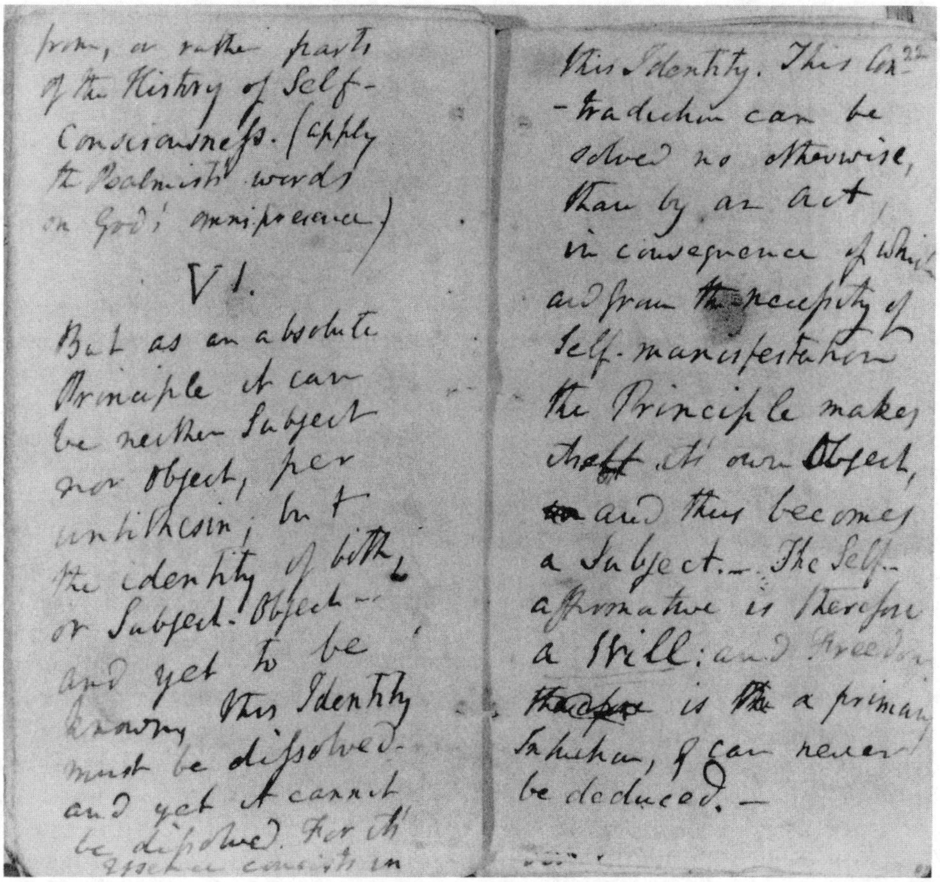
from, or rather parts of the History of Self-Consciousness. (apply the Psalmist's words on God's omnipresence)
VI.
But as an absolute Principle it can be neither Subject nor Object, per antithesin, but the identity of both, or Subject-Object— and yet to be knowing this Identity must be dissolved— and yet it cannot be dissolved. For its essence consists in
this Identity. This contradiction can be solved no otherwise, than by an act in consequence of which and from the necessity of self-manifestation the Principle makes itself its own Object, and thus becomes a Subject.— The Self-affirmative is therefore a Will; and Freedom is a primary Intuition, & can never be deduced.—

*Pages from a draft for the theses in chapter 12 of* Biographia Literaria *(Notebook 61, ff 21$^{v}$ - 22$^{r}$; Victoria College Library, University of Toronto)*

Coleridge argues that Wordsworth's best poetry is not written in rustic dialect, but in standard English informed by his personal sensibility and his enormous powers of imagination. Poetic imagination thus emerges as the essential criterion for Coleridge's evaluation of Wordsworth's poetry.

The *Biographia Literaria* was widely read and reviewed at the time of its original publication and it remains the best known of Coleridge's prose works. It has always been regarded as a great classic of English literary criticism, especially for its brilliant analysis of Wordsworth's preface and its incisive, thoughtful reading of his poems. At the same time, however, its peculiar narrative structure and its extensive reliance on German philosophy have perplexed even its staunchest advocates. The middle section, on the history of philosophy and the concept of imagination, is the most controversial and problematic part of the work, partly because of the inherent difficulty of the conceptual material, and partly because of Coleridge's unacknowledged borrowings from German authors, most notably the intellectual historian Johann Gebhard Ehrenreich Maass and the post-Kantian philosophers Schelling and Friedrich Heinrich Jacobi. Generations of scholars have debated the significance of these unacknowledged borrowings, either condemning Coleridge for his lack of originality and his moral and psychological weakness, or seeking to exonerate him from these charges. Two major contenders in this controversy are René Wellek, who surveys Coleridge's plagiarisms in his *History of Modern Criticism* (1955-1986), and Norman Fruman, whose book *Coleridge: The Damaged Archangel* (1971) presents the most detailed indictment of Coleridge's intellectual dishonesty over the entire course of his career. Thomas McFarland, in *Coleridge and the Pantheist Tradition* (1969), offers a compelling counterargument, describing Coleridge's typical compositional practice as the "reticulation" of varied sources, thus creating an argument of substantial originality in the form of a mosaic.

James Engell and Walter Jackson Bate, in the introduction to their edition of the *Biographia*

*Literaria* (1983), survey the history of this controversy, concluding that the unusual publication history of the *Biographia* may have contributed to its fragmentary structure and its unacknowledged borrowings. They argue that Coleridge, under pressure to produce copy, may have dipped into his favorite works of German philosophy in order to express ideas that were essentially compatible with his own. In defense of this practice Coleridge asserted that "I regard truth as a divine ventriloquist: I care not from whose mouth the sounds are supposed to proceed, if only the words are audible and intelligible." Without resolving the ethical dilemma, this quotation suggests the degree to which Coleridge experienced his own writing as a ventriloquistic process. The *Biographia Literaria*, far from establishing the autonomy of the self-conscious imagination, bears witness to the influx of prior utterance that sweeps aside any attempt at imposing narrative structure or determining the boundaries of discourse. This view of language as undermining authorial intention is implicit in several recent studies of Coleridge's prose, most notably in the work of Jerome Christensen and Jean-Pierre Mileur.

Coleridge's personal life had finally reached a situation of relative stability during the drawn-out process of publishing the *Biographia Literaria*. In April 1816 he found a permanent dwelling place in Highgate (a semirural village north of London) with a loyal friend and admirer, Dr. James Gillman. For the rest of his life Coleridge was to reside with the Gillman family in Highgate, enjoying their hospitality while also relying on them to shield him from unwanted visitors and to control his opium habit. Dr. Gillman was fairly successful in treating his opium addiction, allowing him small maintenance doses while preventing access to larger quantities. Coleridge's lifelong pattern of periodic alcohol and opium binges, followed by illness, depression, and crippling remorse, was ended. Henceforth he is transmuted in historical memory into the Sage of Highgate, ensconced in his hilltop sanctuary overlooking Hampstead Heath. In his *Life of John Sterling* (1851) Thomas Carlyle recorded his personal impression of Coleridge in the late 1820s: "Coleridge sat on the brow of Highgate Hill, in those years, looking down on London and its smoke-tumult, like a sage escaped from the inanity of life's battle; attracting towards him the thoughts of innumerable brave souls still engaged there. . . . He had, especially among young enquiring men, a higher than literary, a kind of prophetic or magician character." Carlyle was just one in a series of distinguished visitors to Highgate that included John Stuart Mill, Ludwig Tieck, Gabriele Rossetti, Harriet Martineau, Richard Chenevix Trench, James Fenimore Cooper, and Ralph Waldo Emerson.

John Keats met Coleridge on a Sunday stroll across Hampstead Heath in April 1819, recording a vivid and sympathetic picture of his prowess as a talker: "I walked with him at his alderman-after-dinner pace for near two miles I suppose. In those two Miles he broached a thousand things—let me see if I can give you a list—Nightingales, Poetry—on Poetical sensation—Metaphysics—Different genera and species of Dreams—Nightmare—a dream accompanied by a sense of touch—single and double touch—A dream related—First and second consciousness—the difference explained between will and Volition—so many metaphysicians from a want of smoking the second consciousness—Monsters—the Kraken—Mermaids—Southey believes in them—Southeys belief too much diluted—A Ghost story—Good morning—I heard his voice as he came toward me—I heard it as he moved away—I had heard it all the interval—if it may be called so." Keats's account suggests the freely associative quality of Coleridge's thought, a quality captured in the dozens of notebooks he kept throughout his life, as well as in the table talk that was recorded by Gillman, Henry Nelson Coleridge, and others. The *Table Talk* volume (published posthumously in 1835) confirms this view of the later Coleridge as a man of diverse intellectual interests and relentlessly probing intelligence: provocative, inquisitive, meditative, sometimes witty, and often profoundly insightful.

During his residence in Highgate, Coleridge rekindled his sense of intellectual vocation, seeking once more to discover an enduring medium of expression for the enormous talents that he felt had been frittered away through so many years of ephemeral journalism, public lectures, and failed periodical publications. The *Biographia Literaria* was a good first step in this direction, offering its readers a systematic approach to the central problems of literary interpretation; but Coleridge still needed to confront those ultimate questions of being and knowledge that had inspired his lifelong quest for fixed principles of action and belief. After the publication of the *Biographia Literaria* he largely abandoned the practice of literary criticism and embarked on a series of works that engage the central issues of epistemology, ontology, theology, and biblical hermeneutics.

In December 1816 Coleridge published *The Statesman's Manual; or the Bible the Best Guide to Political Skill and Foresight*, a work that examines the use and relevance of biblical interpretation in the context of everyday life and political decision making. Coleridge rejects the barren literalism and the moralizing tendencies of many biblical commentators, arguing that the relevance of the Bible to daily life can emerge only through rigorous interpretation informed by the historical circumstances of its composition and sensitive to its variety of generic forms. He makes a crucial distinction between symbol and allegory as modes of discourse, describing *symbol* as "characterized by . . . the translucence of the Eternal through and in the Temporal. It always partakes of the Reality which it renders intelligible; and while it enunciates the whole, abides itself as a living part in that Unity, of which it is the representative." Coleridge regards the symbol as a product of the human imagination that bears witness to the presence of the Eternal (or "the infinite I AM") in the most humble images of everyday life. He stresses the concreteness of symbolic language, its ineluctable grounding in the temporal world. *Allegory*, on the other hand, "is but a translation of abstract notions into a picture-language which is itself nothing but an abstraction from objects of the senses; the principal being more worthless even than its phantom proxy." Allegory is inferior to symbol because it lacks concreteness, drowning the living image in a welter of abstract notions. In Coleridge's view only the symbolic reading of biblical texts can uncover their essential relevance to modern life; allegorical reading tends to reduce these texts to a series of implausible fables and dry moral maxims.

Coleridge's controversial views on biblical hermeneutics were more fully explained in a manuscript published posthumously as *Confessions of An Inquiring Spirit* (1840), which argues forcefully for the critical interpretation of the Bible in light of the entire history of its composition and transmission. His religious views were further developed in his most substantial theological work, *Aids to Reflection* (published May 1825). Written as a commentary on the aphorisms of Archbishop Robert Leighton, a seventeenth-century Anglican divine, this work provided Coleridge with a framework for his own deepest meditations on spiritual growth and the role of religion in everyday life. Like *The Statesman's Manual*, this work failed to arouse much interest at the time of its original publication; but it steadily grew in popularity, reaching a second edition in 1831. Indeed, in the later nineteenth century it proved to be Coleridge's most popular prose work, going through numerous editions in England and America. The first American edition (1829), with its eloquent introduction by James Marsh, was particularly influential among the New England Transcendentalists, who admired its reconciliation of German philosophy with traditional religious faith. Marsh stressed the linguistic dimension of Coleridge's philosophy, particularly his view of etymology as containing deep moral and intellectual truths. In "The Poet" (1844) Ralph Waldo Emerson aptly paraphrased this view of etymology in his remark that "language is fossil poetry."

The immediate public reaction to *The Statesman's Manual* was typical of the response aroused by Coleridge's later works on philosophy and religion. It was greeted by a series of viciously antagonistic reviews by William Hazlitt in the *Examiner* (June, September, and December 1816) and the *Edinburgh Review* (December 1816). Hazlitt attacked the book on the grounds of its obscurity, its excessive reliance on German transcendental philosophy, its alleged unorthodoxy, and its general implausibility. Hazlitt's reviews spoke for a large segment of the British reading public who seemed unwilling to exert themselves sufficiently to fathom Coleridge's argument and may have been reluctant to question their own preconceptions in matters of religion. As a result, *The Statesman's Manual* failed to stir much interest or to sell many copies; and its sequel, a pamphlet titled *A Lay Sermon, Addressed to the Higher and Middle Classes, on the Existing Distresses and Discontents* (published in April 1817) fared even worse. Coleridge's prose works were evidently not much in demand, and for the next few years he would experience great difficulty in getting his work into print. Matters became even worse in March 1819 when his publisher, Rest Fenner, went bankrupt, wiping out large sums in royalties due to Coleridge. Once again, Coleridge found himself without a regular income and in search of a new career. Further disappointment followed in May 1820, when his son Hartley was deprived of his fellowship at Oriel College, Oxford, on the grounds of "sottishness, a love of low company, and general inattention to college rules." Despite Coleridge's best efforts, the authorities were adamant in removing Hartley from the college; he was destined to become a wanderer like his father, writing occasional poems and essays, but lacking a stable career and sinking ever deeper into alcohol and opium addiction.

Coleridge faced these personal crises and setbacks with remarkable fortitude and resilience, finding new intellectual activities and sources of income. In spring 1822 Coleridge began a "Thursday-evening class" for young men aspiring to professional careers. Ostensibly intended to provide instruction in logic, rhetoric, and the history of philosophy, the course became yet another outlet for Coleridge's inexhaustible supply of discourse. In a 15 March letter to Daniel Stuart outlining this class, Coleridge describes its subject matter as comprising "the principles and laws of Language, as the Organ of Thinking, of appropriate Language, and the inherent forms of the Understanding, 1. as the Canon or formal Outline of all *conclusive reasoning*—2. as the Criterion for the detection of error in all the possible species of conscious or unconscious Sophistry—and lastly, the principles of Reason as the Organ of Discovery, whether in Man or in the science of Nature." This subject matter formed the groundwork for a new philosophical treatise, variously titled "Logic" or "Elements of Discourse," which he composed over a span of several years. A partial draft was completed in 1828, but Coleridge was unable to find a publisher. Discouraged by the lack of public interest in his philosophical speculations, he set the manuscript aside; it remained unpublished until 1981, when it was published as *Logic* in *The Collected Works of Samuel Taylor Coleridge*.

*Logic* is not, and does not claim to be, a complete system of philosophy; Coleridge regarded it as an introduction to the main exposition of his "Dynamic or Constructive Philosophy" in the great work that had been promised for many years, wherein he would finally reconcile the conflicting claims of traditional religion and the new German philosophy. However, this *Opus Maximum* (as Coleridge called it) was never completed and exists only in manuscript fragments. *Logic* remains the most substantial discussion of Coleridge's mature philosophy, and it is undoubtedly his most coherent and systematic prose work. As Gian N. G. Orsini points out, "it is more detailed and orderly than any of his published works that deal with philosophy and theology. It is not a miscellany like *The Friend*; it does not break down in the middle, like the *Biographia Literaria*, and then turn in another direction; it does not lose itself in a mass of quotations from another author, like the *Aids to Reflection*; nor does it allow itself any excursions into autobiography, like most of these works; but it proceeds continuously with the main topic from beginning to end."

Perhaps the least known of his major prose works, *Logic* deserves careful attention from all readers of Coleridge, since it contains the fullest articulation of his views on the origin and acquisition of language, the relation between grammar and logic, and the role of language in thought. More than just a paraphrase of Kant's *Critique of Pure Reason* (1781), it enacts a linguistic turn on Kant's philosophy. *Logic* argues that epistemological questions cannot be resolved without a prior analysis of linguistic structures, since language itself constitutes the only possible medium of intellectual inquiry. Coleridge sought to rewrite Kant's philosophy in such a way as to reveal its dependence on lexical and grammatical categories which, as innate modes of conception, determine our perception of reality. The activity of thought, in this view, is wholly constituted by the activity of language, since "what is a fact of all human language is of course a fact of all human consciousness." Considered in relation to Coleridge's earlier works, *Logic* offers a provisional resolution of several key issues concerning the origin of knowledge and the role of language in the formation of human consciousness and social values.

The *Opus Maximum* (soon to be published, as volume 15 of Coleridge's *Collected Works*) pursues this line of thinking into advanced areas of theological speculation. Its alternative title, "Logosophia," provides an indication of its method: Coleridge sees the "Logos" or creative Word of God as a key to the synthesis of all human knowledge, and in this work he attempts to reconcile the totalizing ambition of Schelling's *Naturphilosophie* with the orthodox religious doctrine of the Trinity. Coleridge takes as his fundamental premise that God is "Absolute Will," essential "Causativeness or Act." This "infinite I AM" provides the ontological basis for the finite world of nature, history, and individual identity. However, this finite world is not identical with God; Coleridge insists that our individual self-consciousness must retain its autonomy, its otherness. This otherness or "alterity" is grounded in the Logos, the immanent generative force of divine creation. Thus Coleridge establishes the ontological priority of the "Absolute Will" while maintaining the autonomy of the human will (and avoiding the pitfalls of pantheism). This view of the Logos entails a revision of orthodox theology, since the generation of the Logos out of the primordial "I AM" is conceived as a dynamic process, not a discrete event. Coleridge explains that "I place my first principle, the ground and genesis of my system . . . in an act, in the language of grammarians I begin with the verb, but the act involves its reality—it is an act of being." Rejecting a merely static conception of the Trinity, Coleridge discovers the absolute origin of being, and the ultimate ground of human knowledge, in the eternal self-generation of the Logos out of the "infinite I AM."

Coleridge found it quite difficult to express his "Dynamic or Constructive Philosophy" in a form that would do justice to the complexity and originality of his thought without shocking orthodox sensibilities, and perhaps for this reason his "Logosophia" remained forever unfinished. The lack of any realistic prospect of publication must also have dampened Coleridge's enthusiasm to complete the manuscript. Even in its fragmentary state, however, this work has proven a fruitful source of suggestion to later philosophical inquiry. John H. Muirhead, in his study *Coleridge as a Philosopher* (1930), describes the *Opus Maximum* as an early forerunner of post-Kantian idealistic philosophy in England and America. More generally, John Stuart Mill asserted that nineteenth-century England was indebted to Coleridge "not only for the greater part of the ideas which have been thrown into circulation among its thinking men but for a revolution in its general modes of thought and investigation." Coleridge's theological speculation, with its emphasis on individual struggle to resolve the mysteries of faith in the praxis of everyday life, has also been regarded as prefiguring the existentialist philosophy of Søren Kierkegaard, Martin Heidegger, and Jean-Paul Sartre.

Coleridge's personal fortunes began to improve by the mid 1820s. In November 1822, his wife and his daughter, Sara, came to visit him in Highgate and remained in the neighborhood for four months, marking the return of good feelings and the beginning of an intense intellectual relationship with his charming and accomplished daughter, who had recently made her literary debut by publishing an English translation of a recondite Latin text on the Apibones, an equestrian people of Paraguay. Bradford K. Mudge's biography of Sara Coleridge reveals how deeply enthralled she was by her father's personality and intellect, despite their relatively brief acquaintance. Coleridge found himself increasingly surrounded by younger admirers and disciples, most notably Joseph Henry Green (a brilliant linguist and surgeon who later became his literary executor) and his nephew Henry Nelson Coleridge. Throughout this period, Coleridge worked intensively on his study of the Bible and his reading of seventeenth-century English divines such as Richard Hooker, Jeremy Taylor, and Richard Baxter, filling the margins of their books with copious annotations that include some of his most spontaneous and perceptive thoughts on a great variety of topics. In March 1824 he was named a fellow of the Royal Society of Literature with an annuity of £105 in return for occasional lectures.

In 1825 Coleridge declared that he was about to put to press "a small work on the Church," a promise that was fulfilled in 1830 with the publication of *On the Constitution of The Church and State, according to the Idea of Each: with Aids toward a Right Judgment on the late Catholic Bill.* A revised second edition of this book appeared later that year. The last of Coleridge's prose works to be published in his lifetime, it responds to an immediate political crisis concerning the rights of Catholics in a predominantly Protestant society, arguing cogently in favor of civil rights for religious minorities while also stressing the need for mutual respect and understanding among all social groups. Coleridge takes this current political issue as the occasion for a broader reflection on the institutional structures of the English Constitution and the English church; he critically examines their history and present function, lamenting the decline of the Church of England and the corresponding rise of secular, commercial values. Coleridge declares that the established Church must return to its old values if it is ever to recover its leading role in the intellectual life of the English people. This return to fundamental values is the essential task of the "clerisy," a word that Coleridge invented to describe the elite class of professional men of letters who must provide moral and intellectual leadership in all walks of life.

Coleridge's meditation on the Church and State, despite its conservative political orientation, provoked great discomfort in the contemporary religious establishment because of its frank admission of the increasing marginality of the Church in the public life of the nation. Coleridge's call for reform had little immediate effect, but it exerted a lasting influence in the later years of the nineteenth century, inspiring a grad-

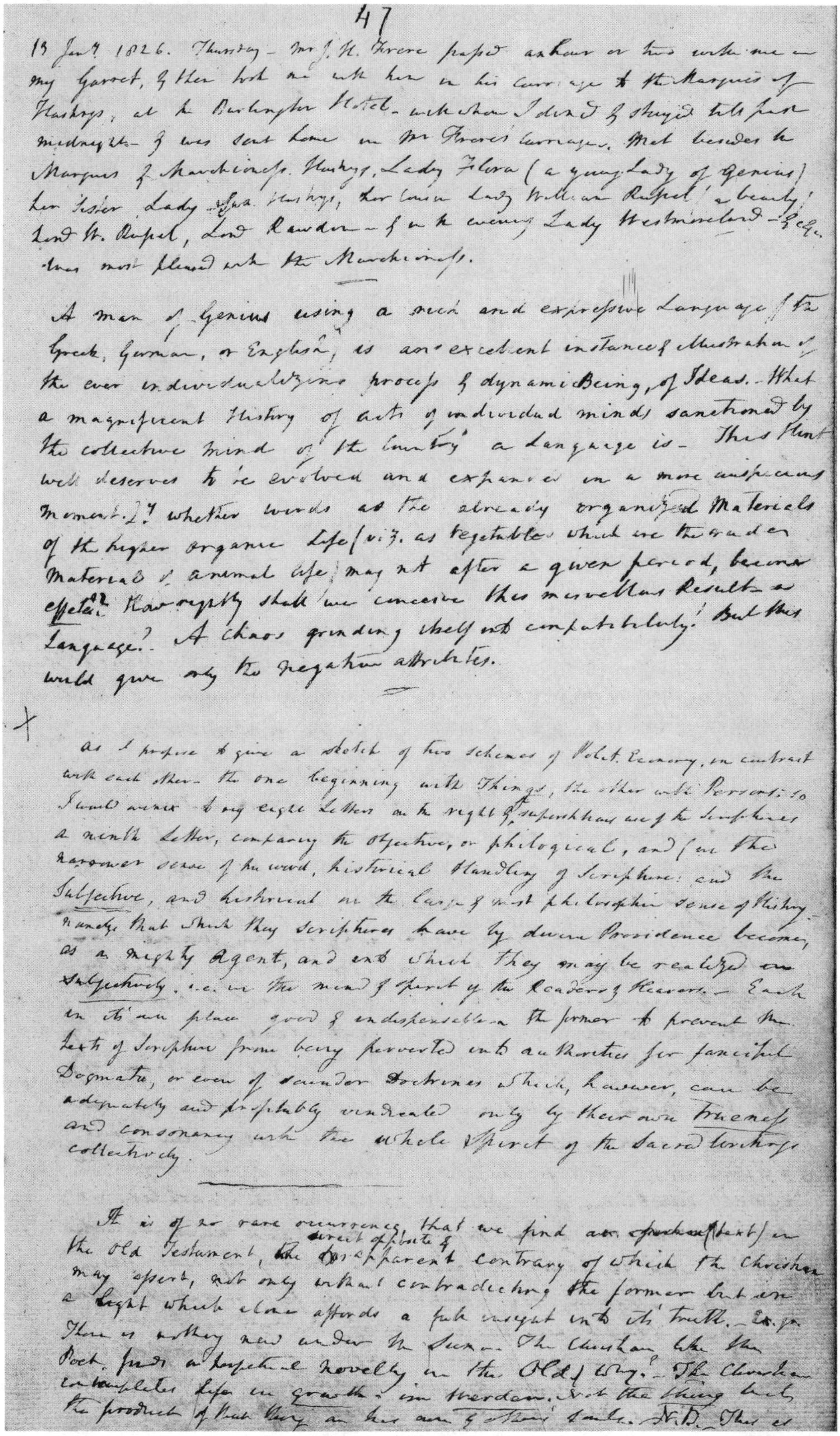

47

13 Jany 1826. Thursday – Mr J. H. Frere passed an hour or two with me in my Garret, & then took me with him in his Carriage to the Marquess of Hastings, at the Burlington Hotel – with whom I dined & stayed till past midnight – & was sent home in Mr Frere's Carriage. Met besides the Marquess & Marchioness Hastings, Lady Flora (a young Lady of Genius) her Sister Lady Sophia Hastings, her Cousin Lady William Russel, a beauty! Lord W. Russel, Lord Rawdon – & in the evening Lady Westmoreland – &c &c. – was most pleased with the Marchioness.

A man of Genius using a rich and expressive Language (the Greek, German, or English) is an excellent instance & illustration of the ever individualizing process & dynamic Being, of Ideas. – What a magnificent History of acts of individual minds sanctioned by the collective mind of the Country a Language is – This Hint well deserves to be evolved and expanded in a more auspicious moment. Qy whether words as the already organized Materials of the higher organic Life (viz. as vegetables which are the crude Materials of animal Life) may not after a given period, become effete? How vividly shall we conceive this marvellous Result – a Language? A Chaos grinding itself into compatibility! But this would give only the negative attributes.

X As I propose to give a sketch of two schemes of Polit. Economy, in contrast with each other – the one beginning with Things, the other with Persons: so I would annex to my eight Letters on the right & superstitious use of the Scriptures a ninth Letter, comparing the Objective, or philological, and (in the narrower sense of the word, historical) Handling of Scripture: and the Subjective, and historical in the largest & most philosophic sense of History, namely, that which the Scriptures have by divine Providence become, as a mighty Agent, and into which they may be realized on Subjectively, i.e. in the mind & spirit of the Readers & Hearers. – Each in its own place good & indispensable – the former to prevent the texts of Scripture from being perverted into authorities for fanciful Dogmata, or even of sounder Doctrines which, however, can be adequately and profitably vindicated only by their own Trueness and consonancy with the whole Spirit of the Sacred Writings collectively.

It is of no rare occurrence that we find an apophthegm (text) in the Old Testament, the direct opposite of the apparent contrary of which the Christian may assert, not only without contradicting the former but in a light which alone affords a full insight into its truth. – Ex. gr. There is nothing new under the Sun. – The Christian like the Poet, finds a perpetual novelty in the Old of Things. – The Christian contemplates Life in growth: in Wisdom. Not the thing but the product of that thing ... N.B. There is

*Notes written in 1826 and 1827 while Coleridge was working on his* Logic *(HM 17299; Henry E. Huntington Library and Art Gallery)*

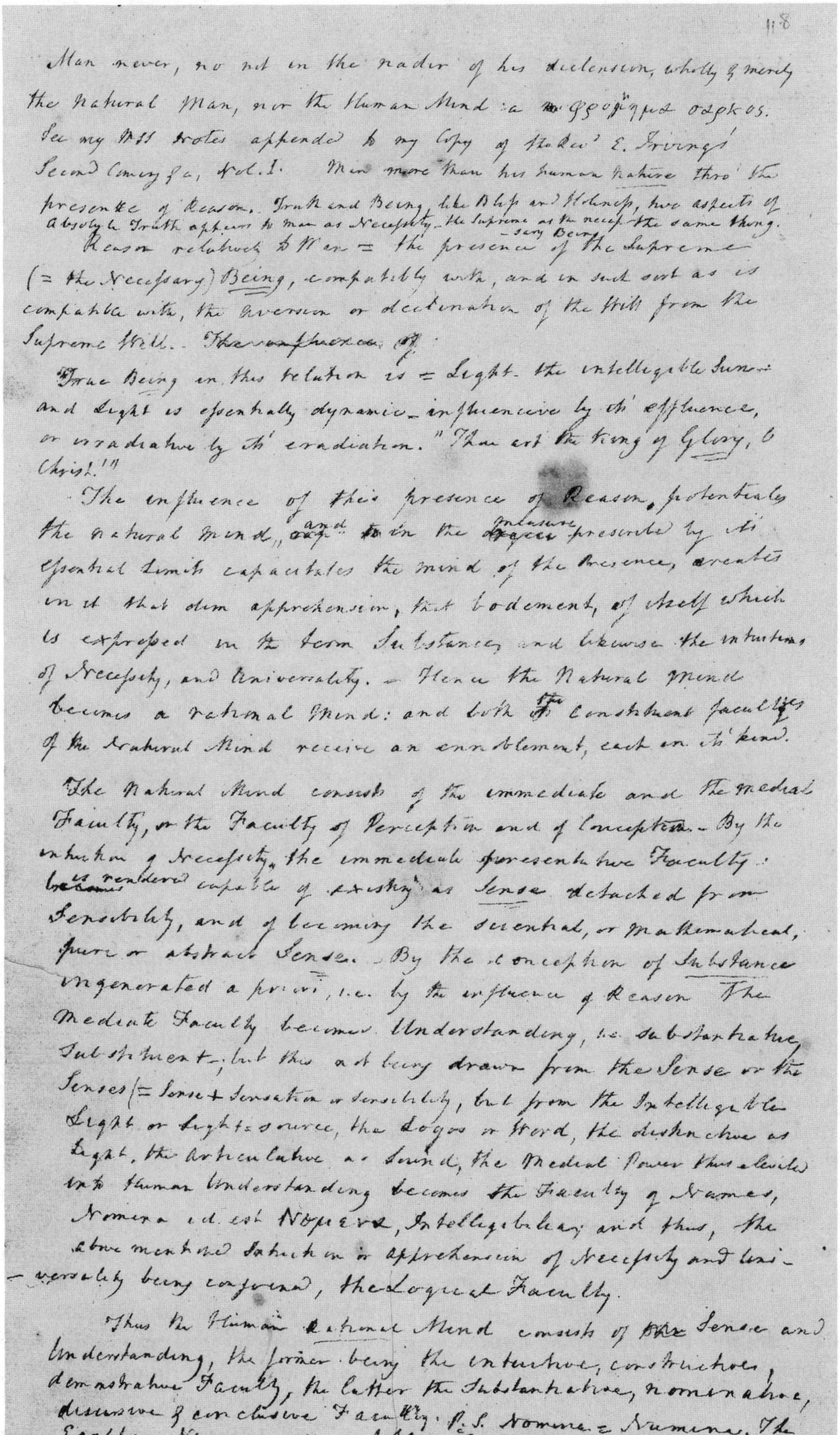

118

Man never, no not in the nadir of his declension, wholly & merely the Natural Man, nor the Human Mind a φρονημα σαρκος. See my MSS notes appended to my Copy of the Rev^d E. Irving's Second Coming &c, Vol. I. Man more than his human Nature thro' the presence of Reason. Truth and Being, like Bliss and Holiness, two aspects of Absolute Truth appears to man as Necessity—the Supreme as the necessary Being—the same thing.

Reason relatively to Man = the presence of the Supreme (= the Necessary) Being, compatibly with, and in such sort as is compatible with, the aversion or declination of the Will from the Supreme Will.

True Being in this relation is = Light—the intelligible Sun—and Light is essentially dynamic—influencive by its effluence, or irradiative by its eradiation. "Thou art the King of Glory, O Christ!"

The influence of this presence of Reason, potentialy the natural Mind, and in the measure prescribed by its essential limits capacitates the mind of the Presence, creates in it that dim apprehension, that bodement, of itself which is expressed in the term Substance and likewise the intuitions of Necessity, and Universality.—Hence the Natural Mind becomes a rational Mind: and both the Constituent faculties of the Natural Mind receive an ennoblement, each in its kind.

The Natural Mind consists of the immediate and the mediate Faculty, or the Faculty of Perception and of Conception.—By the intuition of Necessity, the immediate presentative Faculty is rendered capable of existing as Sense detached from Sensibility, and of becoming the sciental, or mathematical, pure or abstract Sense.—By the conception of Substance ingenerated a priori, i.e. by the influence of Reason The Mediate Faculty becomes Understanding, i.e. substantiative Substitutement, but this not being drawn from the Sense or the Senses (= Sense + Sensation or sensibility), but from the Intelligible Light or Light-source, the Logos or Word, the distinctive as Light, the Articulative as Sound, the Medial Power thus elevated into Human Understanding becomes the Faculty of Names, Nomina id est Νοούμενα, Intelligibilia; and thus, the above mentioned Intuition or Apprehension of Necessity and Universality being conjoined, the Logical Faculty.

Thus the Human Rational Mind consists of the Sense and Understanding, the former being the intuitive, constructive, demonstrative Faculty, the latter the Substantiative, nominative, discursive & conclusive Faculty. P.S. Nomina = Numina. The Egyptian Numina were entities [illegible]

*Sara Coleridge, the poet's daughter, in 1827 (engraving based on a portrait by Charlotte Jones)*

ual reform of the established Church, most notably in the elimination of clerical sinecures and the effort to rediscover the broader role of the Church in society. Such leading intellectual figures as Thomas Arnold, Julius Charles Hare, and Frederick Denison Maurice were profoundly influenced by Coleridge in the development of their religious thought. Maurice, in particular, relied on Coleridge's conception of the "clerisy" in his effort to reawaken the Anglican church to its social and educational responsibilities. John Henry Newman, despite his increasing opposition to the religious establishment, was also deeply influenced by Coleridge in his promulgation of the Tractarian movement. Since the early Victorian period, *On the Constitution of The Church and State* has been regarded as an essential document in the history of religious and political thought.

Coleridge's final years were satisfying and productive despite his increasing illness. Under the competent care of Dr. Gillman and surrounded by his family, friends, and disciples, Coleridge struggled to complete the *Opus Maximum*, while continuing to read and annotate numerous theological works and filling his notebooks with occasional thoughts and reflections. In the summer of 1828 Coleridge went on a tour of the Rhine with Wordsworth and his daughter Dora, immensely enjoying the company of his lifelong friend, their old disputes now forgiven and forgotten. In the last few months of his life, Coleridge worked with his nephew Henry Nelson Coleridge on a collected edition of his poetical works, which appeared shortly after his death. He died on 25 July 1834, leaving behind him a vast and complex assortment of unpublished manuscripts, many in fragmentary states. Some of these manuscripts still remain unpublished, although the steady progress of the Princeton University Press edition of his *Collected Works* has established a more-complete picture of his growth and achievement as a writer.

Coleridge attained only limited professional success in his lifetime. He never reached the enormous popular appeal of Byron or Scott, or the public recognition of Wordsworth or Southey. Yet he always remained in public awareness, and he always found ardent admirers and supporters for his daring aesthetic experiments and his wide-ranging intellectual exploration. As a youthful iconoclast he swayed the hearts and minds of disaffected idealists, holding out the prospect of democratic reform to those weary of censorship and oppression. As a poet he helped inaugurate the English Romantic movement with the publication of *Lyrical Ballads*. In his literary criticism he developed bold insights into the nature of poetic language and the contextual structure of literary works. In his later years as a philosopher and theologian he followed the path of intellectual inquiry into realms unimagined by the prevailing school of British "common-sense" philosophy, once again finding himself surrounded by eager listeners and disciples.

After his death, Coleridge's writings gradually came to have wider influence and readership, as the broad scope of his intellectual accomplishment became more generally known. To the typical Victorian reader, Coleridge was known mainly as a poet and religious thinker, although the *Biographia Literaria* and his lectures on Shakespeare were admired by such prominent literary scholars as Matthew Arnold and George Saintsbury. In America the *Aids to Reflection* and *The Friend* were Coleridge's best-known works throughout the nineteenth century, thanks in part to their eloquent prefaces by James Marsh in the American editions. In a journal entry of 1842, Emerson recorded that "at Andover they sell whole shelvesful of Coleridge's *Aids to Reflection*." In 1853 William Greenough Thayer Shedd (a student of Marsh) published the so-called *Complete Works* of Coleridge, which was the standard American text of his works for almost a century until it was superseded by the *Collected Works*. Although it is far from "complete," Shedd's edition does include most of Coleridge's published prose works and his lectures on literature. Coleridge's prose works have always remained popular in America, where his reputation as a misty-eyed transcendentalist has unfortunately tended to overshadow his concern for linguistic particularity and his alert, questioning mind.

Only in recent decades have Coleridge's informal prose works—his notebooks, letters, and marginalia—become accessible enough to reveal the vast scope of his intellectual endeavor, making it possible to reassess his achievement as a literary critic, philosopher, theologian, and political commentator. These informal prose writings shadow forth a new Coleridge, more intellectually agile and less ponderous and dogmatic than might have been expected. As a prose writer Coleridge lacks the systematic coherence of John Locke, the elegant sententiousness of Samuel Johnson, or the witty informality of Charles Lamb; yet his writing displays a freshness of expression, a richness of insight, a relentless commitment to the discovery of truth, and a magnificent comprehensiveness of vision, that fully compensate for these weaknesses. In many respects his prose style harks back to the qualities that he admired in his favorite writers of the seventeenth century: the architectural intricacy of Richard Hooker, the curious learning of Robert Burton, the "hyperlatinistic" exuberance of Thomas Browne, and the "impetuous, thought-agglomerating flood" of Jeremy Taylor. Coleridge's achievement as a prose writer is well summarized in his description of Shakespeare: in his works "we see a blended multitude of materials; great and little; magnificent and mean: mingled, if we may so say, with a dissatisfying, or falling short of perfection: yet so promising of our progression, that we would not exchange it for that repose of the mind, which dwells on the forms of symmetry in acquiescent admiration of grace." Coleridge will always remain a dynamic presence in the English literary tradition, offering fresh insights and suggestive models of intellectual inquiry.

**Letters:**

*Collected Letters of Samuel Taylor Coleridge*, 6 volumes, edited by Earl L. Griggs (Oxford: Clarendon Press, 1956-1971);

*Selected Letters*, edited by H. J. Jackson (Oxford: Clarendon Press, 1987).

**Bibliographies:**

Thomas J. Wise, *A Bibliography of the Writings in Prose and Verse of Samuel Taylor Coleridge* (London: Bibliographical Society, 1913);

Richard and Josephine Haven and others, *Samuel Taylor Coleridge: An Annotated Bibliography of*

*Coleridge in 1833 (copy of a drawing by J. Kayser; Harry Ransom Humanities Research Center, University of Texas at Austin)*

*Criticism and Scholarship*, 2 volumes to date (Boston: G. K. Hall, 1976- );

Frank Jordan, *The English Romantic Poets: A Review of Research and Criticism*, fourth edition, revised (New York: Modern Language Association, 1985).

**Biographies:**

Thomas Allsop, *Letters, Conversations, and Recollections of S. T. Coleridge*, 2 volumes (London: Moxon, 1836; New York: Harper, 1836);

Joseph Cottle, *Early Recollections; Chiefly Relating to the Late Samuel Taylor Coleridge, during his long residence in Bristol*, 2 volumes (London: Longman, Rees / Hamilton, Adams, 1837); revised as *Reminiscences of Samuel Taylor Coleridge and Robert Southey* (London: Houlston & Stoneman, 1847; New York: Wiley & Putnam, 1848);

James Gillman, *The Life of Samuel Taylor Coleridge*, volume 1 [no more published] (London: Pickering, 1838);

James Dykes Campbell, *Samuel Taylor Coleridge: A Narrative of the Events of His Life* (London & New York: Macmillan, 1894);

E. K. Chambers, *Samuel Taylor Coleridge: A Biographical Study* (Oxford: Clarendon Press, 1938);

Lawrence Hanson, *The Life of Samuel Taylor Coleridge: The Early Years* (London: Allen & Unwin, 1938; New York: Oxford University Press, 1939);

Walter Jackson Bate, *Coleridge* (New York: Macmillan, 1968; London: Weidenfeld & Nicolson, 1969);

Donald E. Sultana, *Samuel Taylor Coleridge in Malta and Italy* (Oxford: Blackwell, 1969);

Basil Willey, *Samuel Taylor Coleridge* (London: Chatto & Windus, 1972; New York: Norton, 1972);

John Cornwell, *Coleridge: Poet and Revolutionary 1772-1804: A Critical Biography* (London: Allen Lane, 1973);

Oswald Doughty, *Perturbed Spirit: The Life and Personality of Samuel Taylor Coleridge* (Rutherford, Madison & Teaneck, N.J.: Fairleigh Dickinson University Press, 1981);

Richard Holmes, *Coleridge: Early Visions* (London: Hodder & Stoughton, 1989);

Stephen M. Weissman, *His Brother's Keeper: A Psychobiography of Samuel Taylor Coleridge* (Madison, Conn.: International Universities Press, 1989).

**References:**


Meyer H. Abrams, *Natural Supernaturalism: Tradition and Revolution in Romantic Literature* (New York: Norton, 1971);

Joseph A. Appleyard, *Coleridge's Philosophy of Literature: The Development of a Concept of Poetry 1791-1819* (Cambridge, Mass.: Harvard University Press, 1965);

Richard W. Armour and Raymond F. Howes, *Coleridge the Talker: A Series of Contemporary Descriptions and Comments* (Ithaca, N.Y.: Cornell University Press, 1940; revised edition, New York: Johnson Reprint Corp., 1969);

Irving Babbitt, "Coleridge and the Moderns," *Bookman*, 70 (October 1929): 113-124;

Babbitt, *Rousseau and Romanticism* (Boston: Houghton Mifflin, 1919);

James V. Baker, *The Sacred River: Coleridge's Theory of Imagination* (Baton Rouge: Louisiana State University Press, 1958);

Owen Barfield, *What Coleridge Thought* (Middletown, Conn.: Wesleyan University Press, 1971; London: Oxford University Press, 1971);

J. Robert Barth, *Coleridge and Christian Doctrine* (Cambridge, Mass.: Harvard University Press, 1969);

Barth, *The Symbolic Imagination: Coleridge and the Romantic Tradition* (Princeton, N.J.: Princeton University Press, 1977);

John B. Beer, *Coleridge the Visionary* (London: Chatto & Windus, 1959);

James D. Boulger, *Coleridge as a Religious Thinker* (New Haven, Conn.: Yale University Press, 1961);

Roberta F. Brinkley, *Coleridge on the Seventeenth Century* (Durham, N.C.: Duke University Press, 1955);

Frederick Burwick, ed., *Coleridge's Biographia Literaria: Text and Meaning* (Columbus: Ohio State University Press, 1989);

Marilyn Butler, "The Rise of the Man of Letters: Coleridge," in her *Romantics, Rebels and Reactionaries: English Literature and its Background 1760-1830* (New York & Oxford: Oxford University Press, 1982), pp. 69-93;

Thomas Carlyle, "Coleridge," in his *Life of John Sterling* (London: Chapman & Hall, 1851; Boston: Phillips, Sampson, 1851), part 1, chapter 8;

Jerome Christensen, *Coleridge's Blessed Machine of Language* (Ithaca, N.Y.: Cornell University Press, 1981);

Kathleen Coburn, *In Pursuit of Coleridge* (London: Bodley Head, 1977);

Ralph J. Coffman, *Coleridge's Library: A Bibliography of Books Owned or Read by Samuel Taylor Coleridge* (Boston: G. K. Hall, 1987);

Dierdre Coleman, *Coleridge and The Friend (1809-1810)* (Oxford: Clarendon Press, 1988);

John A. Colmer, *Coleridge: Critic of Society* (Oxford: Clarendon Press, 1959);

Timothy Corrigan, *Coleridge, Language, and Criticism* (Athens: University of Georgia Press, 1982);

James S. Cutsinger, *The Form of Transformed Vision: Coleridge and the Knowledge of God*, foreword by Owen Barfield (Macon, Ga.: Mercer University Press, 1987);

Graham Davidson, *Coleridge's Career* (New York: St. Martin's Press, 1990);

John Duffy, ed., *Coleridge's American Disciples: The Selected Correspondence of James Marsh* (Amherst: University of Massachusetts Press, 1973);

T. S. Eliot, "Wordsworth and Coleridge," in his *The Use of Poetry and The Use of Criticism* (Cambridge, Mass.: Harvard University Press, 1933), pp. 58-77;

Reginald A. Foakes, *Coleridge's Criticism of Shakespeare* (Detroit: Wayne State University Press, 1989);

Richard H. Fogle, *The Idea of Coleridge's Criticism* (Berkeley: University of California Press, 1962);

Norman Fruman, *Coleridge: The Damaged Archangel* (New York: Braziller, 1971);

A. C. Goodson, *Verbal Imagination: Coleridge and the Language of Modern Criticism* (New York: Oxford University Press, 1988);

Martin Greenburg, *The Hamlet Vocation of Coleridge and Wordsworth* (Iowa City: University of Iowa Press, 1986);

Paul Hamilton, *Coleridge's Poetics* (Stanford, Cal.: Stanford University Press, 1983);

Stephen Happel, *Coleridge's Religious Imagination*, 3 volumes (Salzburg: Institut für Anglistik und Amerikanistik, Universität Salzburg, 1983);

Anthony J. Harding, *Coleridge and the Idea of Love: Aspects of Relationship in Coleridge's Thought and Writing* (Cambridge: Cambridge University Press, 1975);

Harding, *Coleridge and the Inspired Word* (Kingston: McGill-Queens University Press, 1985);

Richard Haven, *Patterns of Consciousness: An Essay on Coleridge* (Amherst: University of Massachusetts Press, 1969);

John A. Hodgson, *Coleridge, Shelley & Transcendental Inquiry: Rhetoric, Argument, Metapsychology* (Lincoln: University of Nebraska Press, 1989);

Richard Holmes, *Coleridge* (Oxford: Oxford University Press, 1982);

Humphrey House, *Coleridge* (London: Hart-Davis, 1953);

J. R. de J. Jackson, *Method and Imagination in Coleridge's Criticism* (London: Routledge & Kegan Paul, 1969);

Jackson, ed., *Coleridge: The Critical Heritage* (London: Routledge & Kegan Paul, 1970);

David Jasper, *The Interpretation of Belief: Coleridge, Schleiermacher and Romanticism* (London: Macmillan, 1986);

Ben Knights, *The Idea of the Clerisy in the Nineteenth Century* (Cambridge: Cambridge University Press, 1978);

Charles Lamb, "Christ's Hospital Five-and-thirty Years Ago," *London Magazine*, 2 (November 1820): 483-490; republished in *Elia and The Last Essays of Elia*, volume 2 of *The Works of Charles and Mary Lamb*, edited by E. V. Lucas (London: Methuen, 1903);

Nigel Leask, *The Politics of Imagination in Coleridge's Critical Thought* (New York: St. Martin's Press, 1988);

Molly Lefebure, *The Bondage of Love: A Life of Mrs. Samuel Taylor Coleridge* (London: Gollancz, 1986; New York: Norton, 1987);

Lefebure, *Samuel Taylor Coleridge: A Bondage of Opium* (New York: Stein & Day, 1975);

Trevor H. Levere, *Poetry Realized in Nature: Samuel Taylor Coleridge and Early Nineteenth-Century Science* (Cambridge: Cambridge University Press, 1981);

John Livingston Lowes, *The Road to Xanadu: A Study in the Ways of the Imagination* (Boston: Houghton Mifflin, 1927);

Paul Magnuson, *Coleridge & Wordsworth: A Lyrical Dialogue* (Princeton: Princeton University Press, 1988);

Emerson R. Marks, "T. S. Eliot and the Ghost of S. T. C.," *Sewanee Review*, 72 (Spring 1964): 262-280;

Thomas McFarland, *Coleridge and the Pantheist Tradition* (Oxford: Clarendon Press, 1969);

McFarland, *Romanticism and the Forms of Ruin: Wordsworth, Coleridge, and the Modalities of Fragmentation* (Princeton, N.J.: Princeton University Press, 1981);

James C. McKusick, *Coleridge's Philosophy of Language* (New Haven, Conn.: Yale University Press, 1986);

Jean-Pierre Mileur, *Vision and Revision: Coleridge's Art of Immanence* (Berkeley: University of California Press, 1982);

John Stuart Mill, "Coleridge," *London and Westminster Review*, 33 (March 1840): 257-302; republished in *Essays on Ethics, Religion and Society*, edited by J. M. Robson, volume 10 of *Collected Works of John Stuart Mill* (Toronto: University of Toronto Press, 1969), pp. 117-163;

John T. Miller, *Ideology and Enlightenment: The Political and Social Thought of Samuel Taylor Coleridge* (New York & London: Garland, 1987);

Raimonda Modiano, *Coleridge and the Concept of Nature* (Tallahassee: Florida State University Press, 1985);

John Morrow, *Coleridge's Political Thought: Property, Moralilty, and the Limits of Traditional Discourse* (New York: St. Martin's Press, 1990);

Bradford K. Mudge, *Sara Coleridge, A Victorian Daughter: Her Life and Essays* (New Haven, Conn.: Yale University Press, 1989);

John H. Muirhead, *Coleridge as a Philosopher* (London: Allen & Unwin, 1930; New York: Macmillan, 1930);

Gian N. G. Orsini, *Coleridge and German Idealism: A Study in the History of Philosophy* (Carbondale: Southern Illinois University Press, 1969);

Walter Pater, "Coleridge," in his *Appreciations* (London & New York: Macmillan, 1889);

Herbert W. Piper, *The Active Universe: Pantheism and the Concept of Imagination in the English Romantic Poets* (London: Athlone Press, 1962);

Stephen Prickett, *Romanticism and Religion: The Tradition of Wordsworth and Coleridge in the Victorian Church* (Cambridge: Cambridge University Press, 1976);

I. A. Richards, *Coleridge on Imagination* (London: Kegan Paul, Trench, Trübner, 1934; New York: Harcourt, Brace, 1935);

Richards, *Practical Criticism: A Study of Literary Judgment* (London: Kegan Paul, Trench, Trübner, 1929; New York: Harcourt, Brace, 1929);

Nicholas Roe, *Wordsworth and Coleridge: The Radical Years* (Oxford: Clarendon Press, 1988);

Charles Richard Sanders, *Coleridge and the Broad Church Movement* (Durham, N.C.: Duke University Press, 1942);

Elinor S. Shaffer, *'Kubla Khan' and the Fall of Jerusalem: The Mythological School in Biblical Criticism and Secular Literature 1770-1880* (Cambridge: Cambridge University Press, 1975);

Bernard Smith, "Coleridge's *Ancient Mariner* and Cook's Second Voyage," *Journal of the Warburg and Courtauld Institutes*, 19 (1956): 117-154;

Anya Taylor, *Coleridge's Defense of the Human* (Columbus: Ohio State University Press, 1986);

Catherine M. Wallace, *The Design of the Biographia Literaria* (London: Allen & Unwin, 1983);

René Wellek, *The Romantic Age*, volume 2 of *A History of Modern Criticism: 1757-1950*, 6 volumes (New Haven: Yale University Press, 1955-1986);

Ian Wylie, *Young Coleridge and the Philosophers of Nature* (Oxford: Oxford University Press, 1988).

**Papers:**

The major manuscript repositories for Coleridge are the British Library in London, the Victoria University Library in Toronto, and the Huntington Library in San Marino, California. The British Library has the most extensive collection of his notebooks, letters, marginalia, and literary manuscripts. The Victoria University Library has numerous Coleridge notebooks, letters, marginalia, and association copies, as well as his manuscript treatise *Opus Maximum*. The Huntington Library holdings include letters, notebooks, his early play *Osorio*, and his late essay "On the Divine Ideas." For a detailed summary of the locations of Coleridge's manuscripts, see Barbara Rosenbaum and Pamela White, *Index of English Literary Manuscripts*, volume 4: *1800-1900, Part 1: Arnold to Gissing* (London: Mansell, 1982; New York: Wilson, 1982).

# Isaac D'Israeli

*(11 May 1766 - 19 January 1848)*

Thomas L. Cooksey
*Armstrong State College*

BOOKS: *A Defence of Poetry. Addressed to Henry James Pye, Esq. To which is added, A Specimen of a New Version of Telemachus* (London: Printed for John Stockdale, 1790); second edition, corrected, *Specimens of a New Version of Telemachus. To which is prefixed, A Defence of Poetry. Address to Henry James Pye, Esq.* (London: Printed for Harrison & Co., 1791);

*Curiosities of Literature* (London: Printed for J. Murray, 1791; facsimile, New York: Garland, 1971; third edition, enlarged, 2 volumes, London: John Murray, 1793; 1 volume, Philadelphia: Printed & sold by William Gibbons, 1793; sixth edition, enlarged, 3 volumes, London: John Murray, 1817);

*A Dissertation on Anecdotes; by the Author of Curiosities of Literature* (London: Printed for C. & G. Kearsley and J. Murray, 1793; facsimile, New York: Garland, 1972);

*Domestic Anecdotes of the French Nation During the Last Thirty Years; Indicative of the French Revolution*, sometimes attributed to D'Israeli (London: Printed for C. & G. Kearsley, 1794);

*An Essay on the Manners and Genius of the Literary Character* (London: Printed for T. Cadell Junr. & W. Davies, 1795; facsimile, New York: Garland, 1970); enlarged as *The Literary Character, illustrated by the History of Men of Genius, Drawn from their Own Feelings and Confessions* (London: John Murray, 1818; New York: Published by James Eastburn & Co., 1818; third edition, enlarged, 2 volumes, London: John Murray, 1823); fourth edition, revised as *The Literary Character; or, The History of Men of Genius, drawn from their Own Feelings and Confessions* (London: Colburn, 1828); revised and republished in *Miscellanies of Literature* (1840);

*Miscellanies; or, Literary Recreations* (London: Printed for T. Cadell & W. Davies, 1796; facsimile, New York: Garland, 1970); enlarged as *Literary Miscellanies: including a Dissertation on Anecdotes* (London: Murray & Highley, 1801); revised and republished in *Miscellanies of Literature* (1840);

*Vaurien: or, Sketches of the Times: Exhibiting Views of the Philosophies, Religions, Politics, Literature, and Manners of the Age* (London: Printed for T. Cadell & W. Davies and J. Murray & S. Highley, 1797);

*Romances* (London: Printed for Cadell & Davies, Murray & Highley, J. Harding, and J. Wright, 1799; New York: Printed & published by D. Longworth, 1803); revised and enlarged as *Romances; Second Edition, Corrected. To which is now added A Modern Romance* (London: Printed for Murray & Highley, 1801; Philadelphia: Printed by Tesson & Lee for Samuel F. Bradford, 1803);

*Narrative Poems* (London: Printed for John Murray, 1803; Philadelphia: Published by J. Conrad, 1803);

*Flim-Flams! or, The Life and Errors of my Uncle and his Friends! With Illustrations and Obscurities by Messieurs Tag, Rag, and Bobtail: A Literary Romance*, 3 volumes (London: John Murray, 1805);

*Despotism: or, The Fall of the Jesuits: A Political Romance, Illustrated by Historical Anecdotes*, 2 volumes (London: John Murray, 1811);

*Calamities of Authors: Including some Inquiries Respecting their Moral and Literary Characters*, 2 volumes (London: John Murray, 1812; New York: J. Eastburn / Philadelphia: E. Earle, 1812); revised and republished in *Miscellanies of Literature* (1840);

*Quarrels of Authors: or, Some Memoirs for our Literary History, Including Specimens of Controversy to the Reign of Elizabeth* (London: John Murray, 1814; New York: Eastburn, Kirk / Boston: Wells & Lilly, 1814); revised and republished in *Miscellanies of Literature* (1840);

*An Inquiry into the Literary and Political Character of James the First* (London: Printed for John Murray by W. Bulmer, 1816); revised and included in *Miscellanies of Literature* (1840);

*Isaac D'Israeli (portrait by Daniel Maclise; Hughenden Manor, National Trust)*

*A Second Series of Curiosities of Literature, Consisting of Researches in Literary, Biographical, and Political History; of Critical and Philosophical Inquiries and of Secret History*, 3 volumes (London: John Murray, 1823; revised and enlarged, London: Bentley, 1838);

*Commentaries on the Life and Reign of Charles the First, King of England*, 5 volumes (London: H. Colburn, 1828-1831);

*The Genius of Judaism* (London: E. Moxon, 1833);

*Curiosities of Literature*, first and second series (6 volumes, London: E. Moxon, 1834; 5 volumes, Boston: Lilly, Wait, Colman & Holden, 1834; revised and enlarged, London: E. Moxon, 1838);

*The Illustrator Illustrated* (London: E. Moxon, 1838);

*Miscellanies of Literature* (London: E. Moxon, 1840; New York: J. & H. G. Langley, 1841);

*Amenities of Literature, Consisting of Sketches and Characters of English Literature*, 3 volumes (London: E. Moxon, 1841; New York: J & H. G. Langley, 1841); revised as *Amenities of Literature: Consisting of Sketches and Characters of English Literature, Illustrating the Literary, Political, and Religious Vicissitudes of the English People*, 2 volumes (London: E. Moxon, 1842).

**Editions:** *The Works of Isaac Disraeli*, 7 volumes, edited, with a memoir and notes, by Benjamin Disraeli (London: Routledge, Warnes & Routledge, 1858-1859).

Balding and bespectacled, genial and good-natured, dressed in the style of an earlier genera-

*D'Israeli's parents, Benjamin and Sarah D'Israeli (left: portrait by an unknown artist; right: portrait by F. Ferrière; both portraits at Hughenden Manor, National Trust)*

tion, Isaac D'Israeli suggests the image of a Jewish Pickwick. Today his fame and reputation have now largely been pushed into the background of that of his famous son, Benjamin Disraeli, first Earl of Beaconsfield (1804-1881), the Victorian prime minister and novelist. In his own day, however, D'Israeli was well regarded in his own right as a scholar, critic, and prolific man of letters. In a 9 October 1821 letter to John Murray, George Gordon, Lord Byron, remarked that D'Israeli "is the Bayle of literary speculation—and puts together more amusing information than anybody." James Ogden, his most recent biographer, notes that he had books in press almost continuously from 1790 to 1840. A sociable man, D'Israeli frequented many literary circles. While conservative in his literary tastes, deeply admiring the poetry of Alexander Pope, he was a vigorous advocate of the genius of Byron, even hiring Tita, Byron's Italian gondolier, as his personal servant after Byron's death. D'Israeli was also an early collector and enthusiast of the work of William Blake. His *Amenities of Literature* (1841) represents one of the first attempts at a comprehensive history of British literature. All his books were widely popular. A review of a late edition of *Curiosities of Literature* in the *Times* (9 January 1849) declared that D'Israeli belonged "to the aristocracy of literature," a view shared by most who knew him.

Benjamin Disraeli liked to romanticize his family origins, suggesting that like Sidonia in his novel *Coningsby* (1844), his roots led back to the Venetian aristocracy. Reality was more mundane. His grandfather Benjamin D'Israeli had immigrated to England in 1748, becoming first a successful merchant, importing Italian manufactured goods, and later a successful stockbroker. The family came not from Venice but Certo, west of Ferrara, where it had been since about the sixteenth century. Settling in London, Benjamin D'Israeli became a member of the Spanish and Portuguese Jewish community around the synagogue of Bevis Marks. Isaac D'Israeli was born in

London on 11 May 1766 to Benjamin D'Israeli and his second wife, Sarah Shiprut de Gabay Villa Real. It was this environment of Jewish émigré businessmen that shaped the young Isaac D'Israeli. Not particularly observant of Jewish customs, he was sometimes at odds with the authorities of the synagogue and eventually had his children baptized into the Anglican church, but he always preserved an affiliation with Judaism, even attending the consecration of the first Reform synagogue in London in 1842.

While Georgian England was relatively tolerant of its Jewish population, D'Israeli's prospects were nevertheless circumscribed. Because he was not an Anglican he had no possibility of university education. The elder D'Israeli saw his son entering business. For his early education the young D'Israeli attended a school in Enfield near his father's country residence. In 1780 the senior D'Israeli sent his son to stay with his business agent in Amsterdam. Here the younger D'Israeli was to complete his education with a tutor and to become familiar with the business world. The tutor, a freethinker, proved inadequate, and Isaac never received a firm knowledge in the Greek and Latin that composed the foundation of a classical education. In the two years that he spent in Amsterdam, he did acquire a knowledge of modern languages and literature, including French, Italian, Spanish, Portuguese, German, and Dutch. He also developed his lifelong taste for the writers of the French Enlightenment, including Voltaire, Rousseau, Montesquieu, and especially Pierre Bayle. Indeed, D'Israeli saw in Bayle a sympathetic model. His article on Bayle in *Curiosities of Literature* was as much a record of his own aspiration as biography: "Amidst the mass of facts which he collected, and the enlarged views of human nature which his philosophical spirit has combined with his researches, Bayle may be called the Shakespeare of dictionary makers; a sort of chimerical being whose existence was not imagined to be possible before the time of Bayle."

D'Israeli returned to England with visions of a literary career. His family, seeing few prospects for poets, objected, initiating a period of tempestuous acrimony between the elder and younger D'Israelis. Benjamin Disraeli offered a fanciful portrait of his father as a sensitive young man, "timid, susceptible, lost in reverie, fond of solitude, or seeking no better company than a book," in conflict with his world. In fact, Isaac was busy at the periphery of several literary circles, currying favor and promoting himself as a poet. He even submitted a collection of his poetry to Samuel Johnson, who, in his final illness, was unable to respond. In December 1786 D'Israeli published his first work, a short essay on Johnson in the *Gentleman's Magazine*.

In 1787 D'Israeli's father sent him on a tour of France, where he spent most of his time among the men of letters in Paris. Like his contemporary William Wordsworth, D'Israeli witnessed the start of the French Revolution in 1789. Returning to England, he took up his literary career, publishing "An Abuse of Satire" in the July 1789 issue of the *Gentleman's Magazine*. The work was an anonymous attack on the satires of Peter Pindar—Dr. John Wolcot. Wolcot, attributing the work to William Hayley, attacked it vigorously. D'Israeli acknowledged his own authorship, which brought him to the attention of the poet Henry James Pye, who became something of a patron for D'Israeli, even convincing the senior D'Israeli of the merits of a literary career.

Most of D'Israeli's poetry is unremarkable, largely heroic couplets in the manner of Alexander Pope, or "Gothick poeticizing" in the manner of Thomas Gray. Indeed, while his early poem "To Laura" was admired by Sir Walter Scott, who included it in *English Minstrelsy* (1810), D'Israeli's admonition in his *Defence of Poetry* (1790) equally applied to himself.

> Thou who behold'st my Muse's rash design,
> Teach me thy Art of Poetry divine;
> Or, since thy cares, alas! on me were vain,
> Teach me that harder talent—to refrain.

*A Defence of Poetry*, published in 1790, was his last serious venture into verse. At this time D'Israeli's true talents as a compiler and literary historian began to emerge.

D'Israeli liked to frequent the reading room of the British Museum, where he began his long friendship with the antiquary Francis Douce, who encouraged his literary efforts. D'Israeli began compiling literary anecdotes from his various readings. By 1791 a volume of these were published by John Murray under the title *Curiosities of Literature*. The compilation of anecdotes was a popular genre at the time, and D'Israeli's compilation proved particularly popular. *Curiosities of Literature* became something of a work in progress, growing with new editions and added volumes. The first volume was little more than a collection of materials that D'Israeli had culled from his

# CONTENTS.

## LITERATURE AND CRITICISM.



CONTENTS.



## HISTORICAL ANECDOTES.



CONTENTS.



## MISCELLANEA.



CONTENTS.



CURI-

*Table of contents for the 1791 edition of* Curiosities of Literature, *the first of D'Israeli's popular compilations of anecdotes he culled from his readings in the library of the British Museum*

*Isaac and Maria D'Israeli in 1805 (portraits by J. Dowman; Hughenden Manor, National Trust)*

*Two of the D'Israelis' children in 1828: Sarah (portrait by Daniel Maclise; Hughenden Manor, National Trust) and Benjamin, the future novelist and prime minister, who changed the spelling of his surname to Disraeli (portrait by Charles Bone; National Portrait Gallery, London)*

readings, an extended book of quotations. In the later volumes D'Israeli began expanding on his topics in the manner of Bayle. *Curiosities of Literature* became a collection of short essays on a wide variety of topics, including "Bibliomania," "Spanish Poetry," "Milton," "Cicero's puns," and even "The History of gloves." The final version contains 276 articles. While D'Israeli was sometimes cavalier with his facts, a matter not lost on early reviewers, *Curiosities of Literature* remains interesting and entertaining reading.

In 1795 D'Israeli turned to a more sustained and ambitious project, *An Essay on the Manners and Genius of the Literary Character*, in which he proposed to explore the psychology of genius. Anticipating the efforts of Wordsworth's *Prelude* (posthumously published in 1850) or Samuel Taylor Coleridge's *Biographia Literaria* (1817), D'Israeli argued for the innate predisposition of genius. Because of this trait, he noted, the man of genius often stood in discord with his world: "He becomes immortal in the language of a people whom he would condemn." In a marginal note that was published in a later edition, Byron concurred with D'Israeli's evaluation. As with *Curiosities of Literature, An Essay on the Manners and Genius of the Literary Character* (later retitled *The Literary Character; or, The History of Men of Genius*) was expanded and illustrated with anecdotes drawn from the autobiographies of men recognized as geniuses.

After the first edition of his essay on genius was published, D'Israeli turned his attention to the composition of fiction, writing several oriental and historical romances and a novel. His most successful romance was *Mejnoun and Leila*, published in *Romances* (1799). He took care with the details of Persian customs, earning the praise of William Beckford, author of the oriental romance *Vathek* (1786). The work was translated into German in 1804, and inspired John Braham's opera *Kais; or, Love in the Desert*, performed at Drury Lane in 1808. The novel *Flim-Flams!* (1805), a cross between *Don Quixote* (1605) and *Tristram Shandy* (1759-1767), satirizes the amateur cognoscenti of the day, including astronomer Caroline Herschel and Edward Cartwright, inventor of the power loom. It is accompanied by an elaborate scholarly apparatus, both real and imaginary, a technique that looks back to Pope's Martinus Scriblerus, and forward to Jorge Luis Borges.

On 10 February 1802, after a period of poor health, D'Israeli married Maria Basevi, like himself from a family of wealthy Jewish merchants of Italian origins. Everything indicates that the D'Israelis enjoyed a happy marriage. Later in 1802 they settled down in a house on Bedford Row, London, not far from the British Museum. Here their five children were born, including Benjamin, their second (21 December 1804). Because they were Jewish, the family was on the edge of respectability, and they often pursued the unconventional. In 1813 Isaac had a falling out with the elders of the Orthodox synagogue that precipitated a full break. In 1817 he had his children baptized in the Anglican church.

D'Israeli's literary reputation grew throughout the first decades of the nineteenth century as he published his *Calamities of Authors* (1812), *Quarrels of Authors* (1814), and *An Inquiry into the Literary and Political Character of James the First* (1816). All these books follow the congenial format of *Curiosities of Literature.*

For many years, D'Israeli frequented the Tory circles around his publisher, John Murray. In 1825, when Murray desired to start a Tory daily paper to oppose the Whig *Times*, young Benjamin Disraeli became involved in planning the project, proposing a title, *The Representative.* Plagued by many problems over the editorship and financial backers, the paper ceased publication in July 1826, after only six months, costing Murray about twenty-six thousand pounds. In Benjamin Disraeli's novel *Vivian Grey*, published in five volumes during 1826 and 1827, Murray was caricatured as the marquess of Carabas. A violent disagreement between Murray and the young novelist eventually engulfed both families, causing a split between D'Israeli and his publisher of many years.

In 1817 the D'Israeli family had moved from their house on Bedford Row to a more fashionable one on Bloomsbury Square. Twelve years later they moved to the country, taking up residence at Brandanham House, Buckinghamshire, where they lived until D'Israeli's death in 1848. Two major works dominate the last part of D'Israeli's life, his five-volume *Commentaries on the Life and Reign of Charles the First* (1828-1831) and his *Amenities of Literature* (1841). A conservative evaluation, *Commentaries on the Life and Reign of Charles the First* has been superseded, but it represented an advance in historical methodology because it is based extensively on manuscript sources in the British Museum. *Amenities of Literature* was the result of D'Israeli's long-planned history of English literature. "It was my design not to furnish an arid narrative of books or of authors," wrote D'Israeli, but to offer the "intellectual history of a people." As with his other books, D'Israeli offered not a unified design, but seventy essays, from "The Druidical institutions" through "The War Against Books"—a history of censorship from William Caxton to John Milton's *Areopagitica* (1644). The essays are roughly chronological in order, though some cover several periods, while others focus on a single author. *Amenities of Literature* was one of the first attempts at a comprehensive history of British literature. Many of D'Israeli's judgments show great insight, often anticipating modern perspectives. He was among the first, for instance, to comment on the role of irony in the works of Geoffrey Chaucer.

In late 1839 D'Israeli, who suffered from what is likely to have been myopic retinal degeneration, became unable to read or write and eventually became entirely blind. In this condition he was helped in his scholarly projects by his daughter Sarah. The last years of his life were spent in relative quiet. Maria D'Israeli died on 24 July 1847, and her husband died early the following year at the age of eighty-one. He had lived an active life as a popular and widely read man of letters. While conservative in his tastes, he possessed an independent mind. Benjamin Disraeli offers a double portrait of his father in the autobiographical *Vivian Grey*: D'Israeli resembles Mr. Sherborne, a man of conservative tastes and little sympathy for contemporary literature, but at the same time he also resembles the character of Horace Grey, Vivian's wise, if bookish father, a man free of prejudice, who taught his son that there were classics other than Greek and Latin.

**Biographies:**

Benjamin Disraeli, "On the Life and Writing of Mr. Disraeli," in volume 1 of *The Works of Isaac Disraeli*, 7 volumes, edited by Benjamin Disraeli (London: Routledge, Warnes & Routledge, 1858-1859);

James Ogden, *Isaac D'Israeli* (Oxford: Clarendon Press, 1969).

**References:**

Martin Fido, "The Key to Vivian Grey of 1827," *Notes and Queries*, new series 12 (November 1965): 418-419;

James S. Malek, "Isaac D'Israeli, William Godwin, and the Eighteenth-Century Controversy over Innate and Acquired Genius," *Mountain Review of Language and Literature*, 34 (1980): 48-64;

James Ogden, "Isaac D'Israeli and Scott," *Notes and Queries*, new series 11 (May 1964): 179-180;

Ogden, "Isaac D'Israeli and Scott," *Notes and Queries*, new series 12 (November 1965): 417-418;

Burton R. Pollin, "Poe's Use of D'Israeli's Curiosities to Belittle Emerson," *Poe Newsletter*, 3 (April 1970): 38;

Richard Tuerk, "Melville's 'Bartleby' and Isaac D'Israeli's Curiosities of Literature, Second Series," *Studies in Short Fiction*, 7 (Fall 1970): 647-649;

Harry C. West, "The Sources for Hawthorne's 'The Artist of the Beautiful,'" *Nineteenth-Century Fiction*, 30 (June 1975): 105-111).

# Francis, Lord Jeffrey

*(23 October 1773 - 26 January 1850)*

Richard D. McGhee
*Arkansas State University*

BOOKS: *Observations on Mr. Thelwall's Letter to the Editor of the Edinburgh Review* (Edinburgh: D. Willison, 1804);

*A Summary View of the Rights and Claims of the Roman Catholics of Ireland* (Edinburgh: Printed by G. Ramsay, 1808);

*The Craniad: or, Spurzheim illustrated. A poem in two parts,* by Jeffrey and John Gordon, M.D. (Edinburgh: Printed for W. Blackwood, 1817);

*Combinations of Workmen. Substance of the Speech of F. Jeffrey Esq. upon Introducing the Toast. . . . At the Public Dinner Given at Edinburgh on Friday the 18th of November 1825* (Edinburgh: Constable, 1825);

*Corrected Report of the Speech of the Right Honourable the Lord Advocate of Scotland upon the Motion of Lord John Russell, in the House of Commons, on the First of March, 1831, for Reform of Parliament* (London: James Ridgway, 1831);

*Contributions to the Edinburgh Review* (4 volumes, London: Longman, Brown, Green & Longmans, 1844; 4 volumes in 1, Philadelphia: Carey & Hart, 1846);

*Samuel Richardson* (London: Longman, Brown, Green & Longmans, 1853);

*Jonathan Swift* (London: Longman, Brown, Green & Longmans, 1853).

**Editions:** *Jeffrey's Literary Criticism,* edited by D. Nichol Smith (London: Frowde, 1910);

*Jeffrey's Criticism: A Selection,* edited by Peter F. Morgan (Edinburgh: Scottish Academic Press, 1983).

OTHER: "Memoir of the Author," in *The Works of John Playfair,* 4 volumes, edited by J. G. Playfair (Edinburgh: Constable, 1822);

"Essay on Beauty," in *Supplement to the Fourth, Fifth, and Sixth Editions of the Encyclopædia Britannica,* 6 volumes, edited by M. Napier (Edinburgh: Constable, 1824);

Inaugural addresses, delivered on 28 December 1820 and 3 January 1822, in *Inaugural Addresses by the Lords Rectors of the University of Glasgow,* edited by John Barras Hay (Glasgow: D. Robertson, 1839);

"Eulogium of James Watt," in *Life of Watt,* by Dominique François Jean Arago (Edinburgh: A. & C. Black, 1839).

William Hazlitt described Francis Jeffrey as "eminently characteristic of the Spirit of the Age," given to "fair and free discussion . . . open to argument and wit," at a time when "every question was tried upon its own ostensible merits, and there was no foul play." Jeffrey was, Hazlitt added, "a person in advance of the age," a man with "a great range of knowledge, an incessant activity of mind," one who "argues well for the future hopes of mankind" (*The Spirit of the Age,* 1825). In his *Life of Lord Jeffrey* (1852), Henry, Lord Cockburn, asserted, "It is impossible, on thus seeing the collected out-pourings of his mind, not to be struck by the variety of his matter. . . . there is scarcely a theme that he has not discussed, with all his fertility of view, and all his beauty of style."

According to Cockburn, "Totally devoid of ill nature, and utterly unconscious of any desire to hurt, he handled the book as a thing to be played with." While George Gordon, Lord Byron, would not have agreed with Cockburn about Jeffrey's motives and methods, he had, in his *English Bards and Scotch Reviewers* (1809), recognized the editor of the *Edinburgh Review* as a powerful person, heir to the "hanging Judge" and Satan himself: "In soul so like, so merciful, yet just, / Some think that Satan has resign'd his trust, / And given the spirit to the world again, / To sentence letters, as he sentenced men."

Francis Jeffrey was a pleasant, social man who subjected literature and ideas to playful, though often painful, analysis. Although he lived a full life as lawyer, judge, and member of Parliament, he is most often remembered as a major contributor to the *Edinburgh Review,* which he and his friends established in 1802 and which he

*Francis, Lord Jeffrey (portrait by Colvin Smith, R.S.A.; Scottish National Portrait Gallery)*

edited from 1803 until 1829. In January 1824 James Mill wrote in the *Edinburgh Review* that its readers were well served by a periodical which, "under the guise of reviewing books," published essays "not only upon the topics of the day, but upon all the important questions of morals and legislation."

When Jeffrey selected essays for inclusion in his *Contributions to the Edinburgh Review* (1844), he chose those "which, by enforcing what appeared to me just principles and useful opinions, I really thought had a tendency to make men happier and better." Jeffrey's analysis of his writing for the *Review* was penetrating and accurate: his work aimed for justice and utility in contributing to the progress of civilization. He carried on the spirit of the Enlightenment from eighteenth-century rationalism to nineteenth-century utilitarianism. The *Edinburgh Review*, under his leadership for twenty-seven years, was a leading intellectual force in nineteenth-century British cultural history. In his *Biographia Literaria* (1817), even Samuel Taylor Coleridge (often a victim of the *Review*) had to commend the "high value" of the services which the *Edinburgh Review* had "rendered to society in the diffusion of knowledge."

Francis Jeffrey was born on 23 October 1773 in Edinburgh, to George Jeffrey, deputy clerk in the Court of Sessions, and Henrietta Jeffrey, daughter of John Louden, a farmer. In 1781 Jeffrey entered the High School of Edinburgh. While there, in winter 1786-1787 he saw Robert Burns passing on the street (he never saw the poet again). Jeffrey's mother died in 1786, and the next year he was sent to Glasgow University (his Tory father wanted him to avoid the liberal views of Dugald Stewart at Edinburgh University). At Glasgow, George Jardine, professor of logic and rhetoric, was a profound influence through his "First Class of Philosophy." Jeffrey

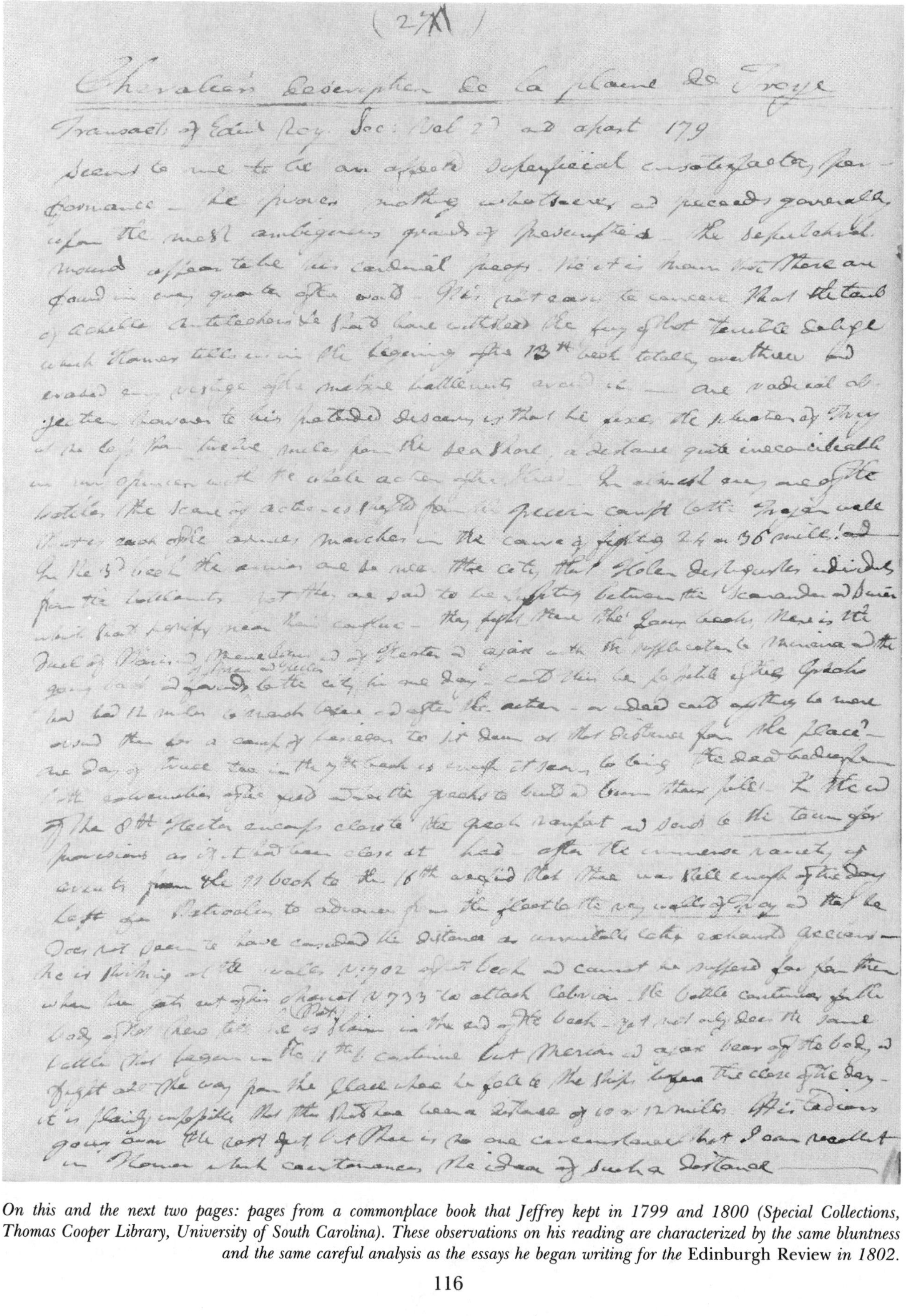

(271)

Chevalier's Description de la plaine de Troye

Transact. of Edin. Roy. Soc: Vol 2d 2d part 179

Seems to me to be an affected superficial unsatisfactory performance — he proves nothing whatsoever and proceeds generally upon the most ambiguous grounds of presumption — the sepulchral mound appear to be his cardinal proofs. No it is known that there are found in every quarter of the world — This (is it easy to conceive that the tomb of Achilles Antilochus &c should have withstood the fury of that terrible deluge which Homer tells us in the beginning of the 12th book totally overthrew and erased every vestige of the mighty battlements around it — one radical objection however to his pretended discovery is that he fixes the situation of Troy at no less than twelve miles from the sea shore, a distance quite irreconcileable in my opinion with the whole action of the Iliad — In almost every one of the battles the scene of action is shifted from the Grecian camp to the Trojan walls & yet each of the armies marches in the course of fighting 24 or 36 miles! and in the 3d book the armies are so near the city that Helen distinguishes individuals from the battlements yet they are said to be fighting between the Scamander and Simois which should signify near their confluence — they fight there tho' [illegible] there is the duel of Paris and Menelaus and of Hector and Ajax with the supplication to Minerva and the going back and forwards to the city in one day of Hector and Helen — could this be possible if the Greeks had had 12 miles to march before and after the action — or could anything be more absurd than for a camp of besiegers to sit down at that distance from the place? — one day of truce too in the 7th book is enough it seems to bring the dead bodies from the extremities of the field and for the Greeks to build a town there [illegible] — In the 8th Hector encamps close to the Greek rampart and sends to the town for provisions as if it had been close at hand — after the immense variety of events from the 11 book to the 16th acquired that there was still enough of the day left for Patroclus to advance from the fleet to the very walls of Troy and that he does not seem to have considered the distance as unsuitable to the exhausted [illegible] — he is thinking of the walls v. 702 of that book and cannot be supposed far from them when he gets out of his chariot v 733 to attack Cebriones. the battle continues for the body of that hero till he is slain [illegible] in the end of the book — yet not only does the same battle that began in the 11th b. continue but Menelaus and Ajax bear off the body and fight all the way from the place where he fell to the ships before the close of the day — it is plainly impossible that there should have been a distance of 10 or 12 miles. this tedious going over the rest of it but there is no one circumstance that I can recollect in Homer which countenances the idea of such a distance —

*On this and the next two pages: pages from a commonplace book that Jeffrey kept in 1799 and 1800 (Special Collections, Thomas Cooper Library, University of South Carolina). These observations on his reading are characterized by the same bluntness and the same careful analysis as the essays he began writing for the* Edinburgh Review *in 1802.*

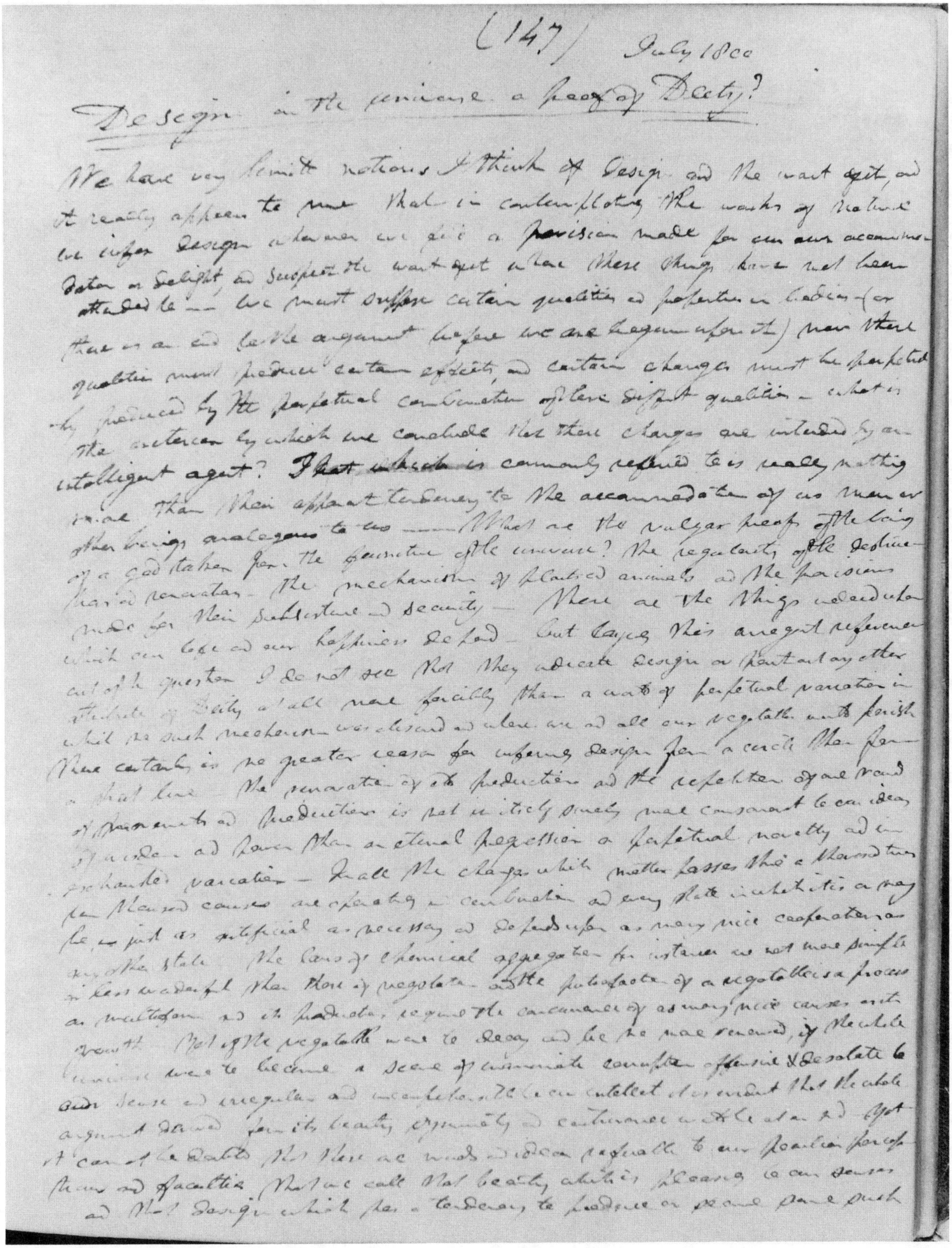
(147) July 1800

Design in the universe a proof of Deity?

We have very limited notions I think of Design and the want of it, and it really appears to me that in contemplating the works of Nature we infer Design wherever we see a provision made for our own accommodation or delight and suspect the want of it where these things have not been attended to — we must suppose certain qualities and properties in bodies (or there is an end to the argument before we are begun upon it) now these qualities must produce certain effects, and certain changes must be perpetually produced by the perpetual combination of these different qualities — what is the criterion by which we conclude that these changes are intended by an intelligent agent? That which is commonly referred to is really nothing more than their apparent tendency to the accommodation of us men or other beings analogous to us — What are the vulgar proofs of the being of a God taken from the structure of the universe? the regularity of the seasons — the renovation — the mechanism of organised animals and the provisions made for their subsistence and security —

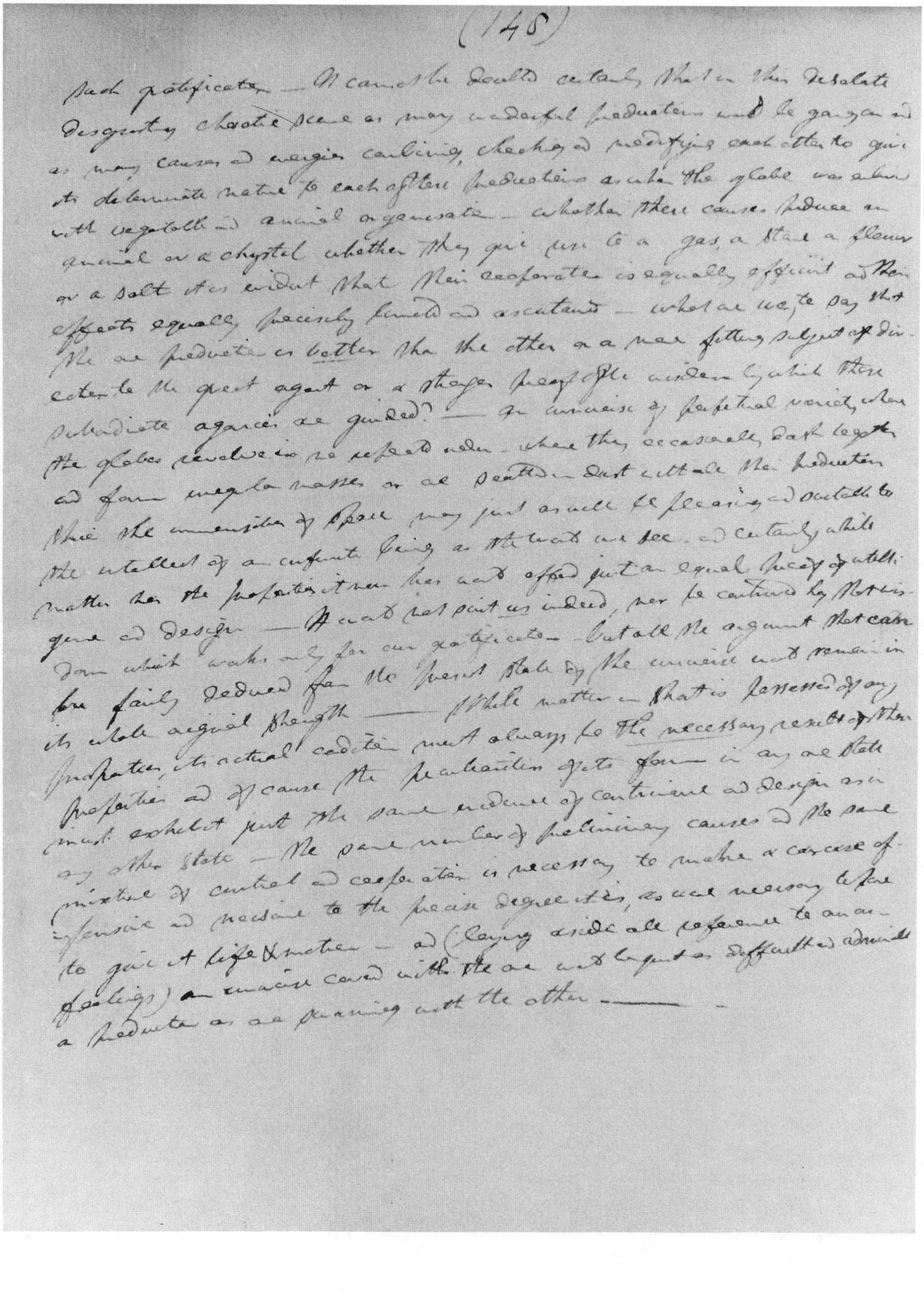

left Glasgow University in May 1789, and until September 1791 he lived at home in Edinburgh, while he attended courses in Scotch and civil law at Edinburgh University. He was then sent to Queen's College, Oxford, which he hated and where he remained only briefly. He wrote his sister Mary on 25 October 1791, "I feel that I shall never become attached to this place," and to his cousin Miss Crockett he wrote on 10 June 1792 of his joy "in the idea of returning among you, because I shall then recover leisure, tranquillity, and content." He returned home in the summer of 1792 and joined the Speculative Society (founded in 1764 by students at Edinburgh University), where he met Walter Scott, Henry Brougham, and Francis Horner.

In 1793 he observed the sedition trial of Thomas Muir, whose calls for parliamentary reform had been interpreted as threats to the government. Jeffrey was disgusted with the injustice of Muir's sentence by the prejudiced court to fourteen years' transportion, and the episode contributed to his liberal political views and Whiggish sympathies. Though Jeffrey was called to the Scottish bar in 1794, he found little legal employment, partly because his Whig politics alienated him from the Tory establishment. Indeed, Tory members of the Speculative Society resigned in 1799 to protest positions taken by Jeffrey on sensitive political issues. In winter of 1801-1802 Jeffrey and other members of the Academy of Physics in Edinburgh decided to start a critical review, choosing as their motto *Judex damnatur cum nocens absolvitur* (The judge is condemned when the guilty is acquitted) from the Roman writer Publius Syrus. The first number of the *Edinburgh Review* appeared in October 1802, with twenty-nine articles in some 250 pages. The lead article was by Jeffrey, a review of Jean Mounier's *De l'influence attribuée aux philosophes . . . sur la révolution de France* (1801). Jeffrey not only analyzed Mounier's argument, but, in a fashion to become his general practice, he enlarged his analysis, using the book as an occasion to consider the causes and effects of the French Revolution in their broadest forms. He showed his preference for moderation in his warnings against the extremism rampant in France and in his call for greater communication between rulers and the ruled.

Jeffrey married Catherine Wilson on 1 November 1801. Their only child, a son, died in October 1802 when only a few weeks old. Because he had so little law work, Jeffrey needed money badly. When he was offered permanent editorship of the *Edinburgh Review* in early 1803, he gladly accepted it, both for the income and for the enlarged opportunity it gave him to carry on with his youthful ambition "to correct the depravity of taste, and to revive the simple and the sublime in all their purity," as he had put it to Miss Crockett in a letter written from Oxford on 9 March 1792. His way of achieving that ambition was to point out intellectual and aesthetic influences for "depravity" or "purity."

In philosophical disputes over priority of mind or matter, he counseled common sense. Reviewing William Drummond's *Academic Questions* in October 1805, Jeffrey wryly confessed that "upon this subject, we entertain an opinion which will not give satisfaction, we are afraid, to either of the contending parties." In his judgment both are right, and both are wrong: "We think that the existence of external objects is not *necessarily* implied in the phenomena of perception; but we think there is no complete proof of their nonexistence." The distinctions are "of as little use in philosophy, as in ordinary life."

Jeffrey required that ideas be useful to "ordinary life." He also required that art satisfy the tastes of ordinary life, a community of shared experience. He objected to eccentricity and peculiarity of aesthetic taste as much as he did to extremism in philosophical and political ideas. Therefore he championed the poetry of George Crabbe in his review of April 1808 and several more times through July 1819 because Crabbe "exhibits the common people of England pretty much as they are" and "shows us something which we have all seen, or may see, in real life." To Crabbe's poetry he contrasted the writings of "the Wordsworths, and the Southeys, and Coleridges," who labor to "bring back our poetry to fantastical oddity and puling childishness."

Jeffrey maintained his test of utility for ordinary life. He elaborated his ideas on taste in his review of Archibald Alison's *Essays on the Nature and Principles of Taste* in May 1811 (revised as an "Essay on Beauty" for the *Encyclopædia Britannica* supplement in 1824). "The best taste," he concluded, "must be that which belongs to the best affections, the most active fancy, and the most attentive habits of observation. . . . all men's perceptions of beauty will be nearly in proportion to the degree of their sensibility and social sympathies." On the other hand "no taste is bad for any other reason than because it is peculiar." It should delight in objects which suggest "common emotions and universal affections." Conse-

*Craigcrook, the house near Edinburgh where Jeffrey and his second wife settled in 1815*

quently, because Wordsworth's poetry showed little good taste, Jeffrey was compelled in his infamous November 1814 review of *The Excursion* to exclaim, "This will never do!" and so Jeffrey had to "give him up as altogether incurable, and beyond the power of criticism." According to Jeffrey, Wordsworth had talent, and his poem showed "heart and fancy," but his taste for peculiar and eccentric experience rendered his art useless for common life.

Catherine Jeffrey died 8 August 1805, leaving Jeffrey miserable long afterward. On 21 January 1806 he wrote to Charles Bell that "home is terrible to me." Although he spent much time in society, he had been unable to sleep "since my angel slept away in my arms." On 9 March he wrote to Francis Horner of his melancholy loneliness, saying he could "taste no substantial happiness." He traveled to relieve his grief, but in London Thomas Moore—who was angry because Jeffrey had denounced Moore's *Epistles, Odes, and Other Poems* as "a public nuisance" and called him "the most licentious of modern versifiers" (*Edinburgh Review*, July 1806)—challenged Jeffrey to a duel in August 1806. The duel was aborted (and satirically depicted in Byron's *English Bards and Scotch Reviewers*). Later Moore became Jeffrey's friend.

By the time his brother, John, sailed to Boston in 1807, Jeffrey was less melancholy but still showed the effects of his grief. His correspondence had taken on an air of bemused disengagement; as he wrote to Horner on 25 November 1806, "The whole game of life appears to me a little childish." His wife's death and his brother's emigration strengthened Jeffrey's personal detachment and professional distance.

The war in Spain threatened to dissolve that detachment, however, for Jeffrey allowed his feelings to rise in the October 1808 review he and Brougham wrote of Don Pedro Cevallos's book on the Spanish war. Jeffrey raised the alarm that British liberties were in danger unless constitutional reforms were undertaken to prevent an outbreak of civil war like that in Spain. Jeffrey had expressed his private belief in his 25 November 1806 letter to Horner: "There is a deplorable want of young senators with zeal for liberty, and liberal and profound views as to the real interests of mankind. The world is going to ruin for want of them." The Tories were indignant over Jeffrey and Brougham's review. In

*Jeffrey in May 1837 (engraving from a drawing by B. W. Crombie)*

1809 Scott and William Gifford began the *Quarterly Review* to counteract the liberal influence of Jeffrey's *Edinburgh Review*, which was well on its way toward a peak circulation of some fourteen thousand by 1818.

Despite political differences with Scott, Jeffrey admired and enjoyed his novels, particularly *Waverley*, which Jeffrey reviewed in November 1814. This story, he said, was "true to Nature throughout," able, "even in the marvellous parts," to copy "from actual existences, rather than from the phantasms of . . . imagination." In this mark of genius, Scott showed the good taste of Crabbe and the gift of Robert Burns for "representing kindness of heart in union with lightness of spirits." Although Scott was a Tory, Jeffrey admired his stories because in them he found what he missed in the poetic tales of Wordsworth: "the representation of rustic and homely characters . . . not as wretches to be pitied and despised—but as human creatures." Storytelling was an art Jeffrey appreciated (not only in Scott; the novels of Charles Dickens were among some of his favorite reading in his last years). Indeed, "the great objection" to novels that he proposed in his review of Scott's *Tales of My Landlord* (March 1817) "is that they are too entertaining." They can be so pleasing they may "produce a disrelish for other kinds of reading."

On 29 August 1813 Jeffrey sailed to America, landing on 7 October. On the fourteenth he married Charlotte Wilkes, to whom he had become engaged during her 1810 visit to England. Before he and his new wife sailed for England, he visited several East Coast cities, including Washington, where he conversed with President James Madison and Secretary of State James Monroe. The Jeffreys landed at Liverpool on 22 February, and in spring 1815 they settled at Craigcrook, northwest of Edinburgh, where Jeffrey indulged his passion for landscape and made his home to the end of his life. He visited the Continent in 1815, when he toured the field of Waterloo some six months after the battle. Jeffrey's review of the third canto of Byron's *Childe Harold* in December 1816 contains reflections derived from meditations of his own at Waterloo. Jeffrey found Byron's apostrophe to Napoleon Bonaparte "splendidly written" but "not true," because tyrants are probably not so noble or unhappy as Byron represents Napoleon. Nor are they, Jeffrey added, "half so much hated as they should be." He had previously expressed his view of Napoleon in his private correspondence: "I hate Bonaparte too, because he makes me more afraid than anybody else, and seems more immediately the cause of my paying income-tax, and having my friends killed with dysenteries and gun-shot wounds. . . ." Jeffrey preferred "a set of tyrants . . . that we can laugh at" (letter to Horner, 9 June 1815).

After some five years of happy marriage, Jeffrey showed in his public and private writing more of his earlier ease and intellectual disinterestedness. On 9 May 1818 he told his father-in-law, Charles Wilkes, "Having long set my standard of human felicity at a very moderate pitch, and persuaded myself that men are *considerably* lower than the angels, I am not much given to discontent. . . . God help us, it is a foolish little thing this human life at the best. . . ." The French Revolution, with the consequence of Napoleon's tyranny, had been instructive to the same end, he believed. Yet it had "laid the foundations, all over Europe, of an inextinguishable and fatal struggle between popular rights and ancient establishments—between democracy and tyranny," and Jeffrey looked for the victory of moderation and "the triumph of reason over prejudice" (letter to Wilkes, 7 August 1818). Nowhere was that triumph more desirable than in Ireland, where British interests had long been a worry to Jeffrey.

Since the Act of Union in 1800, Ireland had given promise of improved relations with England and Scotland, but there were plenty of factions to foment political and religious extremism threatening to ignite the United Kingdom into its own version of a French Revolution or Spanish Civil War. Throughout his career on the *Edinburgh Review*, Jeffrey carefully observed events in Ireland. In his May 1820 review of *The Life of the Right Honorable John Philpot Curran* he praised Curran as a courageous advocate of justice during a period of great injustice for Ireland, despite Curran's defense of such insurrectionists as Wolfe Tone. While Curran deplored the Act of Union, Jeffrey believed it was the salvation of Ireland. This was the point of his review of a *History of Ireland*, by John O'Driscol, in October 1827. At that time of agitation for Catholic Emancipation and fierce reactions by the Orangemen, Jeffrey believed that again religious extremism was threatening civil liberty in the kingdom. He proposed that Ireland should be more completely united with Britain, on the model of Scotland, and by that to hope for political happiness. "The *Union*, in short, must either be made *equal* and *complete* on the part of England—or it will be broken in pieces and thrown in her face by Ireland." When he published this review in his *Contributions to the Edinburgh Review* (1844), Jeffrey added a note to reaffirm this conviction, "now that Catholic emancipation and Parliamentary reform have taken away some, at least, of the motives" for separation or dissolution of the Union.

After Jeffrey was appointed dean of the Scottish Faculty of Advocates on 2 July 1829, he retired as editor of the *Edinburgh Review*; the last of his roughly two hundred articles as a regular contributor was a review of the *Memoirs of Lady Fanshawe*, by Anne Harrison, Lady Fanshawe (October 1829). He wrote only four more for the *Review* during his last twenty-one years of life. In 1844 he collected approximately one hundred of his articles in *Contributions to the Edinburgh Review*, arranging them under seven headings: "General Literature and Literary Biography," "History and Historical Memoirs," "Poetry," "Philosophy of the Mind, Metaphysics, and Jurisprudence," "Novels, Tales, and Prose Works of Fiction," "General Politics," and "Miscellaneous." These rubrics suggest the variety and vigor of his interests over an active writing career of some twenty-seven years.

Jeffrey's career as a writer was mainly ended by 1829. He continued to be active in the law and in the politics of constitutional reform. He was appointed Lord Advocate in 1830 and sent to Parliament in April 1831 for the Borough of Melton. He was reelected in June 1831 and entrusted with leadership in moving the Scottish Reform Bill in 1831 and 1832. He was elected M.P. for Edinburgh on 19 December 1832, after passage of the Reform Bill. On 7 June 1834 he became Lord Jeffrey, as a judge in Court of Session, where he served with distinction. He died on 26 January 1850, leaving a daughter and grand-

*Jeffrey's grave in Dean Cemetery, near Edinburgh*

children as his heirs. Jeffrey was buried in Dean Cemetery, near Edinburgh.

**Letters:**

*Life of Lord Jeffrey, with a Selection from His Correspondence*, volume 2, edited by Henry, Lord Cockburn (Edinburgh: Adam & Charles Black, 1852; Philadelphia: Lippincott, Grambo, 1852);

*The Letters of Francis Jeffrey to Ugo Foscolo*, edited by J. Purves (Edinburgh & London: Oliver & Boyd, 1934).

**Biographies:**

Henry, Lord Cockburn, *Life of Lord Jeffrey, with a Selection from His Correspondence*, volume 1 (Edinburgh: Adam & Charles Black, 1852; Philadelphia: Lippincott, Grambo, 1852);

William Charvat, "Francis Jeffrey in America," *New England Quarterly*, 14 (June 1941): 309-339.

**References:**

David Bromwich, "Romantic Poetry and the *Edinburgh* Ordinances," *Yearbook of English Studies*, 16 (1986): 1-16;

Thomas Carlyle, "Lord Jeffrey," in *Reminiscences by Thomas Carlyle*, edited by James Anthony Froude (2 volumes, London: Longmans, Green, 1881; 1 volume, New York: Scribners, 1881), I: 1-66; also in *Reminiscences*, 2 volumes, edited by Charles Eliot Norton (London & New York: Macmillan, 1887), II: 221-274;

John Clive, *Scotch Reviewers: The Edinburgh Review, 1802-1815* (Cambridge, Mass.: Harvard University Press, 1957);

Raymond J. Derby, "The Paradox of Francis Jeffrey: Reason Versus Sensibility," *Modern Language Quarterly*, 7 (December 1946): 489-500;

David V. Erdman and Paul M. Zall, "Coleridge and Jeffrey in Controversy," *Studies in Romanticism*, 14 (1975): 75-83;

Philip Flynn, *Francis Jeffrey* (Newark: University of Delaware Press, 1978);

J. A. Greig, *Francis Jeffrey of the Edinburgh Review* (Edinburgh & London: Oliver & Boyd, 1948);

Byron Guyer, "The Philosophy of Francis Jeffrey," *Modern Language Quarterly*, 11 (March 1950): 17-26;

William Hazlitt, "Mr. Jeffrey," in his *The Spirit of the Age, or Contemporary Portraits* (London: Printed for Henry Colburn, 1825; facsimile, Menston, U.K.: Scolar Press, 1971), pp. 303-322;

Merritt Y. Hughes, "The Humanism of Francis Jeffrey," *Modern Language Review*, 16 (July-October 1921): 243-251;

Peter F. Morgan, "Francis Jeffrey as Epistolary Critic," *Studies in Scottish Literature*, 17 (1982): 116-134;

Morgan, "Principles and Perspective in Jeffrey's Criticism," *Studies in Scottish Literature*, 4 (1967): 179-193;

W. J. B. Owen, "Wordsworth and Jeffrey in Collaboration," *Review of English Studies*, new series 15 (May 1964): 161-167;

John U. Peters, "Jeffrey's Keats Criticism," *Studies in Scottish Literature*, 10 (1973): 175-185;

David W. Pitre, "Francis Jeffrey and Religion: Excerpts from His 1799-1800 Commonplace Book," *Eighteenth-Century Life*, 8 (October 1982): 95-107;

Pitre, ed., "Francis Jeffrey's Journal: A Critical Edition," Ph.D. dissertation, University of South Carolina, 1980.

**Papers:**

The Jeffrey correspondence is held by the National Library of Scotland. The Horner Collection, held by the British Library of Political and Economic Science, London School of Economics, includes letters from Francis Horner to Jeffrey. A commonplace book kept by Jeffrey in 1799 and1800 is in the Thomas Cooper Library, University of South Carolina.

# Charles Lamb

*(10 February 1775 - 27 December 1834)*

Winifred F. Courtney

See also the Lamb entry in *DLB 93: British Romantic Poets, 1789-1832: First Series.*

BOOKS: *Blank Verse*, by Lamb and Charles Lloyd (London: Printed by T. Bensley for J. & A. Arch, 1798);

*A Tale of Rosamund Gray and Old Blind Margaret* (Birmingham: Printed by Thomas Pearson, 1798; London: Printed for Lee & Hurst, 1798);

*John Woodvil: A Tragedy* (London: Printed by T. Plummer for G. & J. Robinson, 1802);

*The King and Queen of Hearts* (London: Printed for Tho[s] Hodgkins, 1805);

*Tales from Shakespear. Designed for the Use of Young Persons*, 2 volumes, by Charles Lamb and Mary Lamb, attributed to Charles Lamb (London: Printed for Thomas Hodgkins at the Juvenile Library, 1807; Philadelphia: Published by Bradford & Inskeep, and by Inskeep & Bradford, New York, printed by J. Maxwell, 1813);

*The Adventures of Ulysses* (London: Printed by T. Davison for the Juvenile Library, 1808; New York: Harper, 1879);

*Mrs. Leicester's School*, by Charles Lamb and Mary Lamb (London: Printed for M. J. Godwin at the Juvenile Library, 1809; George Town: J. Milligan, 1811);

*Poetry for Children, Entirely Original*, 2 volumes, by Charles Lamb and Mary Lamb (London: Printed for M. J. Godwin at the Juvenile Library, 1809; Boston: West & Richardson, and E. Cotton, 1812);

*Prince Dorus: Or, Flattery Put Out of Countenance. A Poetical Version of an Ancient Tale* (London: Printed for M. J. Godwin at the Juvenile Library, 1811);

*Mr. H., or Beware a Bad Name. A Farce in Two Acts* [pirated edition] (Philadelphia: Published by M. Carey, printed by A. Fagan, 1813);

*The Works of Charles Lamb*, 2 volumes (London: Ollier, 1818);

*Elia: Essays which have appeared under that signature in the London Magazine* (London: Printed for Taylor & Hessey, 1823; [pirated edition] Philadelphia: Carey, Lea & Carey, printed by Mifflin & Parry, 1828);

*Elia: Essays which have appeared under that name in the London Magazine Second Series* [pirated edition] (Philadelphia: Carey, Lea & Carey, printed by J. R. A. Skerret, 1828)—includes three essays not written by Lamb;

*Album Verses, with a Few Others* (London: Moxon, 1830);

*Satan in Search of a Wife* (London: Moxon, 1831);

*The Last Essays of Elia* (London: Moxon, 1833; Philadelphia: T. K. Greenbank, 1833).

**Editions:** *The Works of Charles and Mary Lamb*, 7 volumes, edited by E. V. Lucas (London: Methuen, 1903-1905; New York: Putnam's, 1903-1905);

*Charles Lamb on Shakespeare*, edited by Joan Coldwell (Gerrards Cross: Colin Smythe, 1978);

*Lamb as Critic*, edited by Roy Park (London & Henley: Routledge & Kegan Paul, 1980).

PLAY PRODUCTION: *Mr. H----*, London, Theatre Royal, Drury Lane, 10 December 1806.

OTHER: Samuel Taylor Coleridge, *Poems on Various Subjects*, includes four poems by Lamb (London: C. G. & J. Robinson / Bristol: J. Cottle, 1796); enlarged as *Poems, Second Edition, to which are now added Poems by Charles Lamb, and Charles Lloyd*, includes ten poems by Lamb (Bristol: Printed by N. Biggs for J. Cottle and Robinsons, London, 1797);

Charles Lloyd, *Poems on the Death of Priscilla Farmer*, includes one poem by Lamb (Bristol: Printed by N. Biggs & sold by James Phillips, London, 1796);

*Specimens of English Dramatic Poets, Who Lived About the Time of Shakspeare*, edited, with commentary, by Lamb (London: Printed for Longman, Hurst, Rees & Orme, 1808; New York: Wiley & Putnam, 1845).

With his Elia essays, nearly all written for the *London Magazine* during the years 1820-1826, Charles Lamb, clerk at the East India Company for thirty-three years, achieved a blend of the personal, witty, poetic, and profound in exquisitely subtle short pieces that made him a major Romantic essayist and have been part of the canon of English literature ever since. He was already known to his contemporaries as a novelist, journalist, poet, writer for children, failed dramatist, and fine critic, devoted to "antiquity"—particularly Latin literature and that of Elizabethan and seventeenth-century writers. His popularity extended through the nineteenth century into the twentieth, but waned after 1934, the centenary of his death. Since the 1960s, however, his reputation has risen again with the publication of new biographical and critical works celebrating and analyzing his artistry.

The nineteenth century saw him chiefly as a beloved, even heroic, whimsical, somewhat eccentric figure who, though his life had been darkened by tragedy and sacrifice, managed somehow to be humorous, and whose literary methods defied analysis—a sentimental view which was ultimately resisted by critics such as Graham Greene, F. R. Leavis, and the American New Critics, with the consequent diminution of his reputation, beginning in the decade preceding World War II. Recent scholars, however, have found new qualities in his writings, confirming his strength and steadiness of vision, his compassionate worldview, and his originality. His *Tales from Shakespear* (1807), a children's book written with his sister, Mary Lamb, has never been out of print. In his *Roman-*

*A 1776 engraving of Christ's Hospital, the school Lamb attended from 9 October 1782 until 23 November 1789*

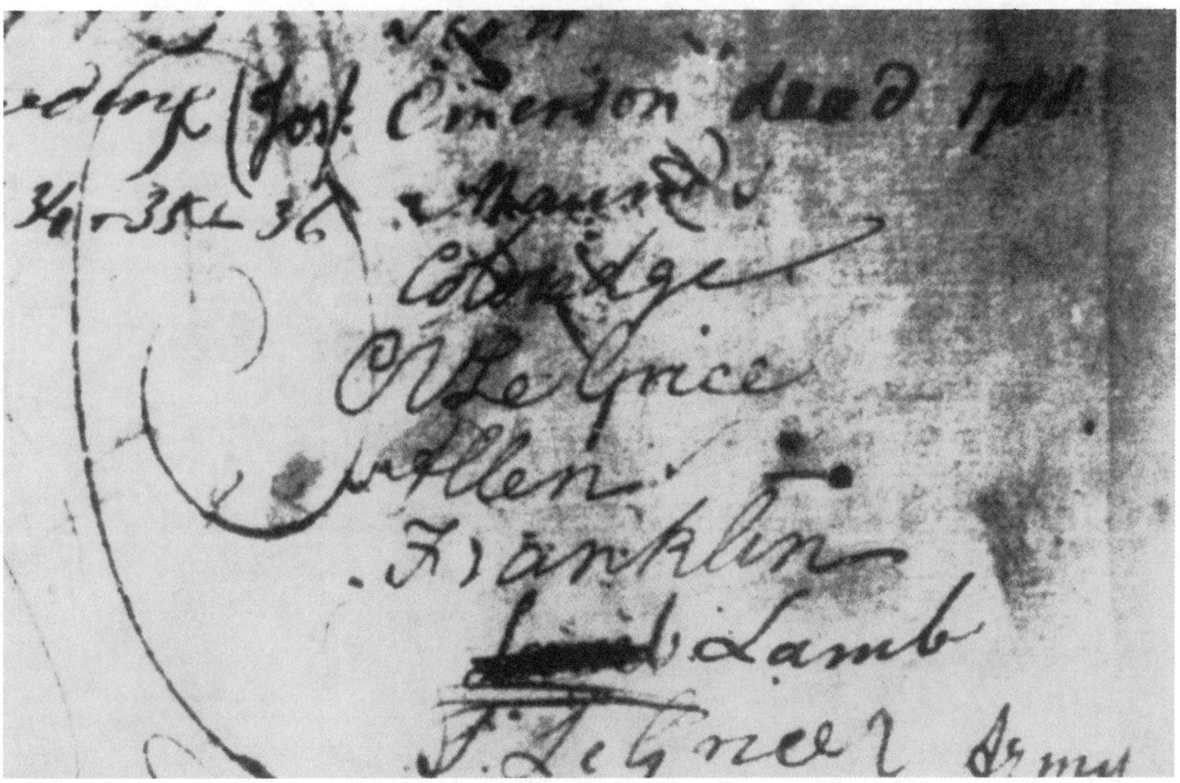


*Signatures in a copy of Homer's* Iliad *shared by Samuel Taylor Coleridge, Charles Valentine Le Grice, Robert Allen, and Lamb at Christ's Hospital (from Richard Holmes,* Coleridge: Early Visions, *1989)*

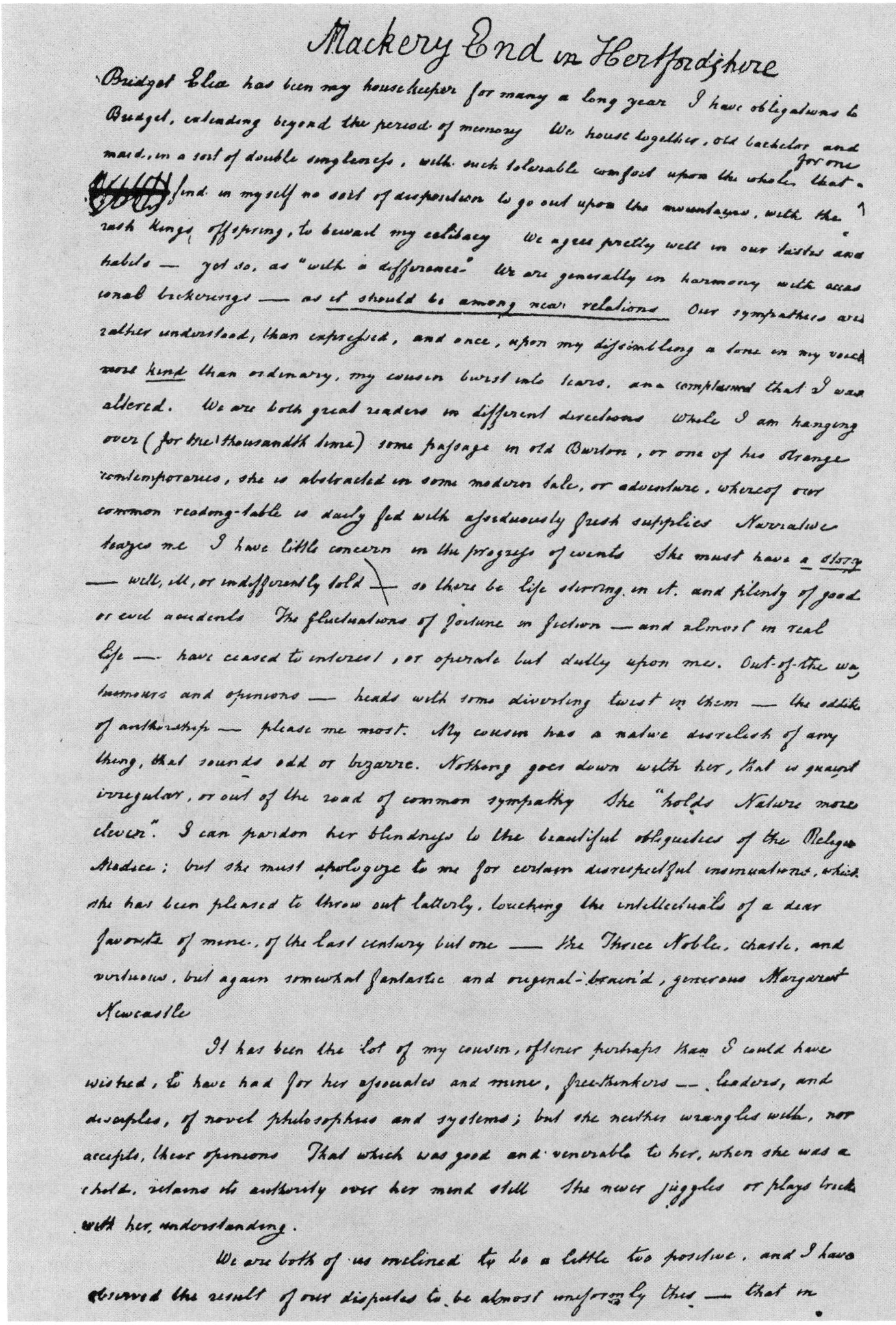

Mackery End in Hertfordshire

Bridget Elia has been my housekeeper for many a long year. I have obligations to Bridget, extending beyond the period of memory. We house together, old bachelor and maid, in a sort of double singleness, with such tolerable comfort upon the whole, that, for one, I find in myself no sort of disposition to go out upon the mountains, with the rash kings offspring, to bewail my celibacy. We agree pretty well in our tastes and habits — yet so, as "with a difference." We are generally in harmony with occasional bickerings — as it should be among near relations. Our sympathies are rather understood, than expressed, and once, upon my dissembling a tone in my voice more kind than ordinary, my cousin burst into tears, and complained that I was altered. We are both great readers in different directions. While I am hanging over (for the thousandth time) some passage in old Burton, or one of his strange contemporaries, she is abstracted in some modern tale, or adventure, whereof our common reading-table is daily fed with assiduously fresh supplies. Narrative teazes me. I have little concern in the progress of events. She must have a story — well, ill, or indifferently told — so there be life stirring in it, and plenty of good or evil accidents. The fluctuations of fortune in fiction — and almost in real life — have ceased to interest, or operate but dully upon me. Out-of-the-way humours and opinions — heads with some diverting twist in them — the oddities of authorship — please me most. My cousin has a native disrelish of any thing, that sounds odd or bizarre. Nothing goes down with her, that is quaint, irregular, or out of the road of common sympathy. She "holds Nature more clever." I can pardon her blindness to the beautiful obliquities of the Religio Medici; but she must apologize to me for certain disrespectful insinuations, which she has been pleased to throw out latterly, touching the intellectuals of a dear favorite of mine, of the last century but one — the Thrice Noble, chaste, and virtuous, but again somewhat fantastic and original-brain'd, generous Margaret Newcastle.

It has been the lot of my cousin, oftener perhaps than I could have wished, to have had for her associates and mine, freethinkers — leaders, and disciples, of novel philosophies and systems; but she neither wrangles with, nor accepts, their opinions. That which was good and venerable to her, when she was a child, retains its authority over her mind still. She never juggles or plays tricks with her understanding.

We are both of us inclined to be a little too positive, and I have observed the result of our disputes to be almost uniformly this — that in

*Page from the manuscript for the Elia essay in which Lamb recalled his childhood visits to a relative's farm in Hertfordshire (from Edmund Gosse,* English Literature: An Illustrated Record, *1904)*

*tic Cruxes* (1987) Thomas McFarland finds that among the Romantics, "Lamb, Hazlitt and De Quincey are very substantial figures, not dizzying elevations like Wordsworth and Coleridge, perhaps, but definitely mountains, not outlying hills." In his introduction to *Lamb as Critic* (1980) Roy Park says Lamb has been perceived as a "cultural teddy-bear in the Victorian Establishment" but goes on to show that Lamb is not only a good critic; he is a great one. Park provides more than three hundred pages of Lamb's criticism to prove his point. According to Park the limited range of Lamb's critical writings "does not entail a corresponding limitation in the range of his critical sensibilities." Park documents the enormous range of Lamb's reading and credits him with "a strong independent mind, contemptuous of critical fashions, and with a penetrating insight into what is of permanent and lasting value in literature." Lamb was among the first to appreciate Samuel Taylor Coleridge's *Ancient Mariner*, and the works of John Clare and William Blake, including Blake's painting. His criticism, mainly in letters, of the work of Coleridge and Wordsworth was sometimes heeded by those poets. A few early assessments share the modern approach to his work, notably those of Walter Pater and George Saintsbury. Charles Dickens and William Makepeace Thackeray were both influenced by Lamb's character studies, as Geoffrey Tillotson observes. The Brontës, Robert Browning, Henry James, and Virginia Woolf praised him. Woolf wrote, "I had no notion what an exquisite writer Lamb is . . . God knows how I shall have the courage to dip my pen tomorrow" (letter to Clive Bell, 1908). John Keats was captivated by a comment of Lamb's on Shakespeare.

Lamb's letters, straightforward and unfailingly entertaining, omit the antiquarian embroideries of many of the Elia essays and are eminently accessible to the modern reader. They record the building of Lamb's interior world and contain the germs—in actual incidents, opinions, observations—of the Elia essays. They are also a record of his many friendships, among which those with Coleridge and Wordsworth are paramount.

Lamb was born in London's Temple district, the parklike home of many lawyers, as it still is today. His father, John Lamb, was general factotum—a combination clerk and servant—to the lawyer Samuel Salt, one of the "Old Benchers of the Inner Temple" in Lamb's Elia essay (*London Magazine*, September 1821). Salt had a library in which Charles and his sister, Mary Anne Lamb (ten years his senior), were free to browse, and Salt sponsored Charles for entrance to Christ's Hospital, a distinguished London charity school for boys. His mother, Elizabeth Field Lamb, served Salt as housekeeper, and much of the care of Charles was left to Mary. Elizabeth Lamb is said to have favored their elder brother, John, who was handsome, athletic, and dashing, while Charles was small, not strong, and bookish, with a hampering stammer. One Elia essay hints that he may have had a serious childhood illness.

Mary and Charles were often able to visit relatives on a farm in Hertfordshire (subject of the essay "Mackery End in H---," *London Magazine*, July 1821), and at Blakesware, a great ancestral home in the same county, where their grandmother Mary Field was housekeeper for the usually absent owners. Sarah Lamb, "Aunt Hetty"—their father's unmarried sister—lived with the Lambs. She adored young Charles and figures in the Elia essays "My Relations" (*London Magazine*, June 1821), "Poor Relations" (*London Magazine*, May 1823), "Christ's Hospital Five and Thirty Years Ago" (*London Magazine*, November 1820) and "A Dissertation upon Roast Pig" (*London Magazine*, September 1822), as well as in "The Witch Aunt," one of Charles Lamb's contributions to the Lambs' children's stories in *Mrs. Leicester's School* (1809). Among Romantics in general and especially in Lamb's work, the interest in childhood was increasingly significant.

The world of Elia began to form in the boy with the lively imagination. After lessons from a governess and time at a small school, he proceeded at age seven to Christ's Hospital, entering on 9 October 1782. He lived at the school and enjoyed much of it—especially his friendships with Coleridge and others, some of whom in time became distinguished in professional fields—though in his second essay on the school, "Christ's Hospital Five and Thirty Years Ago," he portrays some almost medieval hardships suffered by its pupils. (The first, "Recollections of Christ's Hospital," *Gentleman's Magazine*, June 1813, is laudatory.) James Boyer, the principal, was interested in good writing. As a pioneer in encouraging originality and simplicity of style (according to Coleridge), the fierce Dr. Boyer, through Coleridge, Lamb, and Leigh Hunt, may be said to have had a seminal influence on English literature.

Lamb remained at Christ's Hospital—reading voraciously both for school and on his

*East India House, Leadenhall Street, London, as it appeared when Lamb worked there*

*Lamb (gesturing at right) talking to Coleridge (holding glass) in the Salutation and Cat public house (engraving based on the memory of "a frequenter of the house for over forty years")*

own—until 23 November 1789. Of his friendship with Coleridge Lamb said on Coleridge's death in 1834—"I cannot think a thought, I cannot make a criticism on men and books, without an ineffectual turning and reference to him." Coleridge wrote, on his deathbed, next to a copy of his "This Lime-Tree Bower My Prison": "*Ch. and Mary Lamb—dear to my heart, yea, as it were my heart, S. T. C. Aet.*, 63, 1834."

Lamb's stammer prevented his preparation for a university career, which Coleridge undertook, in those days intended to lead to becoming a clergyman in the Church of England. When Lamb was fourteen, his years at Christ's Hospital ended; the prospect of going to work was the next step; again friends of the family assisted. He was employed briefly (circa 1789-1791) in the countinghouse of Joseph Paice, whom he admired and made the subject of "Modern Gallantry" (*London Magazine*, November 1822). Then, with the help of his brother John, who was employed as accountant with the South Sea Company, he proceeded on 1 September 1791 to a clerical position there: the first of the Elia essays describes some of the vagaries of his elder colleagues in "The South-Sea House" (*London Magazine*, August 1820).

Lamb left the South Sea Company on 8 February 1792, and on 5 April 1792 he became clerk to the East India Company in Leadenhall Street. After a three-year period of apprenticeship without salary, he remained there without promotion (though with increased pay) for another thirty years. Samuel Salt died on 27 July 1792, and the family found itself in difficult circumstances, to which brother John appears to have contributed little. The Lambs moved from the Temple to Little Queen Street, in Lincoln's Inn Fields, in 1793. Mary Lamb, already showing signs of manic depression, was working at home as a dressmaker. For a while the family was almost totally dependent on her income, while she took on increasing responsibilities for her parents as her mother became bedridden and her father grew senile.

The period between February and August 1792, when Mary Field died, involved Charles Lamb in some visits to Blakesware to assist his grandmother during her final illness. Here he fell in love with a Hertfordshire girl, Ann Simmons. Ann, or his romantic version of her, became the subject of many of his early sonnets, written on the model of those of poet William Lisle Bowles, to whose sonnets Coleridge had introduced Lamb. Coleridge published these verses together with his own poems in *Poems on Various Subjects* (1796) and *Poems, Second Edition* (1797). (An early sonnet, a tribute to Sarah Siddons, the great actress of the Kemble family, is ascribed to both but is probably mostly Lamb's and testifies to his lifelong interest in the theater, beginning with a visit to the Drury Lane theater at the age of five, which he described in "My First Play" [*London Magazine*, December 1821]).

Ann Simmons—as "Alice W---n," in the Elia essay "Dream Children" (*London Magazine*, January 1822) and as Rosamund Gray in his early novel usually known by that title—became a recurring figure in his work. The actual Ann Simmons soon married another. Mary Field is said to have discouraged Lamb's romantic interest, citing the tinge of insanity in the Lamb family. Lamb pays tribute to his grandmother in "Dream Children," "Blakesmoor, in H——shire" (*London Magazine*, September 1824), and "The Grandame," which the young Quaker poet Charles Lloyd published with verses on his own grandmother in *Poems on the Death of Priscilla Farmer* (1796).

In London during 1794-1795 much of Lamb's spare time was spent discussing love, poetry, and English literature with Coleridge, over a glass of ale and a pipe at the Salutation and Cat public house. In his letters Lamb recalled these sessions—the start of a lifetime love of drink and tobacco, which also figures in his writings. He often stated his intention of giving them up, a goal he never quite achieved. In 1795, through Coleridge, Lamb met young Robert Southey, eventually to become poet laureate of England (1813). After Lamb's love affair with Ann Simmons ended and Coleridge left London in late 1795 Lamb spent six weeks (circa December 1795-January 1796) "very agreeably in a madhouse"—a fact he reported to Coleridge (27 May 1796) in the first of Lamb's letters to survive. The breakdown may have been caused by the loss of his love and his friend both at once, as well as the pressures at home and his new office slavery (for so he regarded it; he felt himself ill-fitted for clerical duties, though they were to prove a harbor of sanity). He was never again to suffer severe mental illness, though he waged a lifelong battle with melancholia. McFarland (with other critics) believes that Lamb's writing, his whimsy, his humor, and the strong expression of feeling so often discernible in his work kept him going—"the politics of survival."

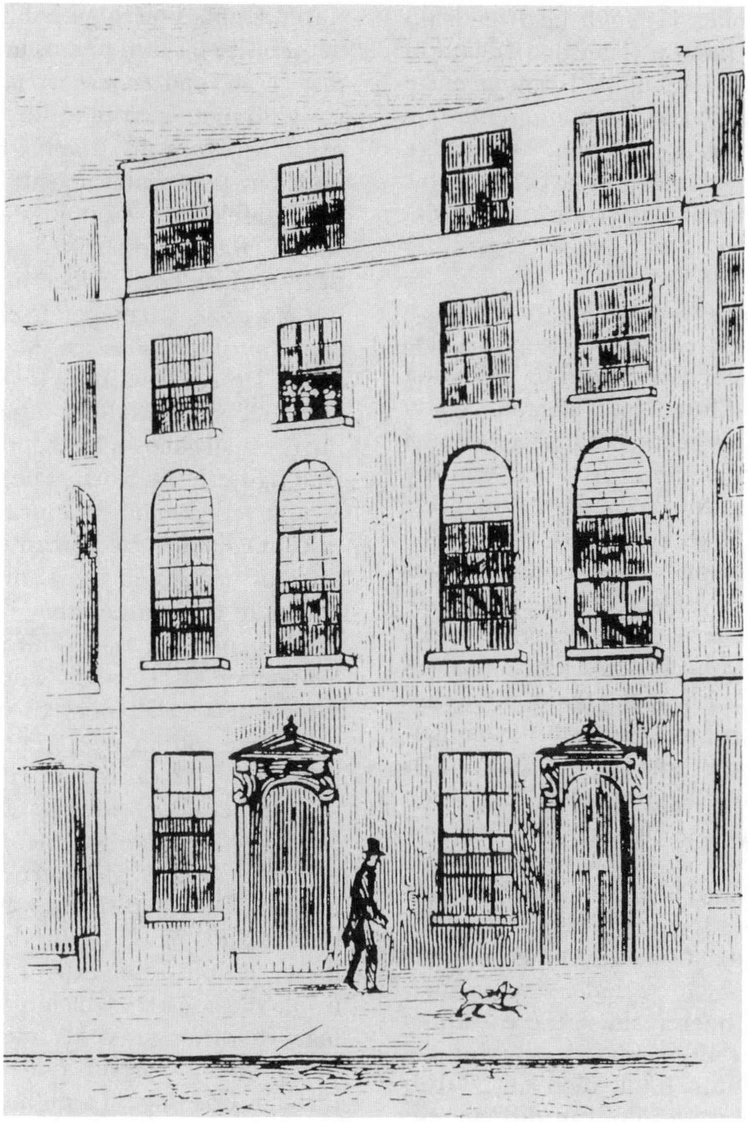

*Number 7 Little Queen Street, where the Lambs were living when Mary Lamb killed her mother in September 1796*

He soon had a bitter family tragedy to survive. On the evening of 22 September 1796, after helping his schoolfellow James White with White's *The Original Letters &c. of Sir John Falstaff and His Friends* (1796), Lamb arrived home to find Mary Lamb with a bloody knife in her hand, his mother dead on a chair, his aging aunt unconscious on the floor, his father incapable of action. Mary, overcome by the pressures of working and caring for her family, had become impatient with a young dressmaking assistant, seized a kitchen knife, and pursued the girl. Elizabeth Lamb had risen from her bed to intervene, and Mary, demented, had turned the knife on her mother. This terrible day was to change the lives and fortunes of Charles and Mary Lamb forever. He found the strength to remove the knife from Mary's hand, and, at age twenty-two, to take charge of her, as the law then allowed, for the rest of her life. She was officially absolved by reason of temporary "Lunacy." Charles's only thought was to keep her from permanent confinement. She recovered, under care in a private asylum, after some six months. Thereafter she was subject to attacks presaging violence, and, as they came on, almost annually, she and Charles would set out sadly, carrying Mary's straitjacket, to kindly caretakers at Hoxton, who would keep Mary for weeks at a time until she recovered. During these periods Lamb himself would be severely depressed, as many of his letters testify. Lamb was ultimately prevented by his lonely responsibility from marrying. Both Charles and Mary Lamb loved children, and they made the heroic best of a difficult situation. Little of the tragedy was known except among the Lambs' few intimates at that time. A "Miss Lamb" had been mentioned in one newspaper account, but it was not until after Mary's death in 1847 that the story was given to the world. In her periods of normalcy Mary was much loved and admired by many friends, and Lamb often praised her good sense as against his own waywardness. In his Elia writings she figured as his "cousin Bridget." William Hazlitt found her the only woman he knew who could *reason*—high praise in those days. But her frequent disappearances into professional care were noticed by neighbors and landlords and were cause for many moves: "We are in a manner *marked*," Lamb wrote to Coleridge on 12 May 1800. As Elia in "New Year's Eve" he says, "My household-gods plant a terrible fixed foot, and are not rooted up without blood. . . . A new state of being staggers me" (*London Magazine*, January 1821).

On recovery Mary went into lodgings during her father's remaining lifetime. Brother John had long had his own apartment in another part of the city, leaving responsibility for their father to Charles and a maid. Charles's lot was not easy: his father demanded many games of cribbage after his tired son's return from work. Aunt Hetty tried living with another relative briefly to relieve the family strain, but soon returned to her beloved Charles, to stay until she died in 1797; John Lamb, Sr., followed her in 1799. Mary was then free to return to Charles's household, which he had moved to 36 Chapel Street. In March 1801 they took an apartment near their former childhood home, in the Inner Temple. With no dependents and Lamb's growing salary (by 1809 it had risen to £160 and in 1815 it was doubled to £480), the two, despite the inevitable intervals, began to know something like peace.

In July 1797 Charles Lamb had managed a visit to Coleridge and his wife in Nether Stowey, Somerset, where Lamb first met William Wordsworth and his sister, Dorothy, who were about to settle at Racedown nearby. Both became Lamb's lifelong friends. While he was there Coleridge wrote one of his great poems, "This Lime-Tree Bower My Prison," addressed to "Charles Lamb, of the India House," in which he refers to Lamb as "gentle-hearted." Lamb resisted this appellation, most strongly in a letter to Coleridge (14 August 1800): "In the next edition . . . please to blot out *gentle hearted*, and substitute drunken dog, ragged-head, seld-shaven, odd-ey'd, stuttering, or any other epithet which truly and properly belongs to the Gentleman in question." With the vigor and lack of inhibition characteristic of his letters to close friends, he also cried "Damn you" and "*You Dog*!" but modified his indignation at being portrayed as a milksop with his leavening, self-deprecating humor. In general, as McFarland observes, Lamb chose humor rather than "confrontation" with his friends, who were most necessary to him, though sometimes too demanding of his time. The tone of Lamb's letters is not often as delicate as that of Elia. Each letter is very much adapted to its recipient.

With all his troubles, Lamb had continued to write when he could (often at his office). *Blank Verse*, published in May 1798 by Lamb and Charles Lloyd, contains several dense, tragic poems by Lamb. "Written a Year After the Events," relates to but does not reveal the family tragedy. Others express his intense sorrow—for his dead aunt and mother, his sick father and sister. Yet another, "Composed at Midnight," touches on his religious doubts. Lamb and Coleridge discussed religion—chiefly Unitarianism, with which Coleridge was then involved—in their letters of these years. Lamb could not believe in Hell, nor in any God not compassionate (but why, he asked, would such a God let such terrible things happen?). He expresses his distrust of atheism, however, in a poem written at the same time, "Living Without God in the World" (first published complete in Robert Southey's *Annual Anthology* for 1799). In his generally melancholy mood of the late 1790s this series expresses his agony with an urgency found nowhere else. "The Old Familiar Faces," a lament for all those he had lost, also appeared in *Blank Verse*. It is still printed in anthologies.

*Blank Verse* had only a mediocre reception: The *Analytical Review* (May 1788) found the "whining monotonous melancholy" of both poets "tiresome," as did the *Monthly Magazine* ( July 1798); and the conservative *Anti-Jacobin Review* (1 August 1798) discovered radicalism in its poems, chiefly in Lloyd's.

Lamb has often been described as apolitical, and so he more or less considered himself. In fact he followed the daily news, and his sympathies remained with his more radical friends, attacked as "Jacobins" in 1793 at the onset of the British war with France in the wake of the

*Cartoon by James Gillray published in the July [i.e., 1 August] 1798 issue of the* Anti-Jacobin Review and Magazine. *Worshiping the French Revolutionary "trinity" are Lamb and Charles Lloyd (frog and toad) holding a copy of their* Blank Verse, *Coleridge (standing ass) just above Robert Southey (kneeling ass), John Thelwall (on the shoulders of the Leviathan), and Charles James Fox (behind Thelwall), leader of the opposition party in the House of Commons. The Leviathan is Francis Russell, fifth Duke of Bedford, Fox's supporter in the House of Lords.*

French Revolution. Coleridge, Wordsworth, and Southey had welcomed the prospect of a new order. They and others of similar views sought a more representative Parliament, the end of slavery, and other British reforms which have since been achieved, but after 1793 most such reformers were considered to be French sympathizers. In the July [i.e., 1 August] 1798 issue of the *Anti-Jacobin* Lamb was lumped with Coleridge, Southey, and others in satirical verses. An accompanying cartoon by James Gillray portrayed Lamb and Lloyd, clutching *Blank Verse*, as a toad and a frog. Lamb's own satirical political verses, composed at intervals throughout his life, and "What Is Jacobinism?"—which he wrote for the *Albion* newspaper, where it appeared on 30 June 1801 (it was first identified by this writer in 1982)—reveal quite clearly that he formed strong political opinions and in general sided with the persecuted would-be reformers, but he seldom discussed politics in conversation—for him the daily news was too evanescent—nor did politics figure in his major work.

*A Tale of Rosamund Gray and Old Blind Margaret* (published in summer 1798), Lamb's only novel, a short one, is based on the Ann Simmons episode and was admired by Percy Bysshe Shelley, among others. At twenty-three Lamb, who is represented in the novel as "Allan Clare," again transmuted the stuff of his own life, and the charming early chapters are bathed in country sunlight. Yet plot was never his forte, and the story falls off with the introduction of a seducing villain and Rosamund's death, as if Lamb did not know what to do with his characters after the touching romantic scenes.

The novel sold well and by 1799 "touched the hearts of reviewers without exception," according to George Barnett—even that of the *Analytical Review* (February 1799).

Lamb was soon working on a Shakespearean tragedy in blank verse, *John Woodvil*, about a courtier during the reign of Charles II. John Woodvil betrays his father, Sir Walter, a former Roundhead who has taken refuge in Sherwood Forest with companions, and becomes progressively more profligate, alienating the good, innocent Margaret, his fiancée. When his father dies of shock at the drunken John's perfidy, John's repentance, reform, and reconciliation with Margaret follow with unbelievable rapidity. Again Lamb contrived a lame ending to a work that has some virtues and a few lovely poetic lines. It was never performed. When Lamb published it himself in 1802, the critics, especially that of the powerful *Edinburgh Review* (April 1803), were uniformly damning.

In 1803 Lamb composed the poem "Hester," about a young Quaker girl who had caught his fancy but had since died. One of his best po-

*Lamb dressed as a Venetian senator, 1804 (portrait by William Hazlitt; National Portrait Gallery, London)*

etic efforts, it remained unpublished until it appeared in his 1818 *Works*. Lamb had come wisely to the realization that the vocation of serious poet was not for him and had better (with occasional exceptions) be left to Wordsworth and Coleridge.

The only break in Lamb's friendship with Coleridge had occurred in 1798, resulting from Coleridge's hasty remark—"Poor Lamb, if he wants any *knowledge*, he may apply to me." This was reported to Lamb by Charles Lloyd, and Lamb wrote Coleridge a rather sharp letter of remonstrance, but after Coleridge's absence in Germany (autumn 1798 - July 1799) the incident was forgotten, and the friendship resumed. Lamb began to make other friends over these years: Thomas Manning, a young mathematics tutor at Cambridge to whom some of Lamb's best letters were written; William Godwin, whose *Political Justice* (1793) had inspired young disciples but who by 1802, when Lamb met him, had fallen from grace and was widely viewed as a most dangerous—and immoral—Jacobin; and William Hazlitt, artist, later journalist and essayist, who painted the finest portrait of the young Lamb (1804). Soon added were a host of other friends, most either eccentric or especially gifted. Thomas De Quincey was both, as was George Dyer—gifted as classicist, political activist, and historian (he was a mediocre poet) but nearsighted and fearfully absentminded. Elia was to write about Dyer's poor eyesight and absentmindedness as he flitted about Cambridge University, which is called "Oxford" in one of the two Dyer essays, "Oxford in the Vacation" (*London Magazine*, October 1820). The other, "Amicus Redevivus" (*London Magazine*, December 1823) describes how Dyer missed a turn by Lamb's house and walked into the New River, where he nearly drowned. Added to these was Wordsworth's friend Thomas Clarkson, whom the Lambs visited in 1802 when in the Lake District. Clarkson was dedicated to ending slavery and had an important role in the ultimate banishing of it throughout all British possessions.

In 1800, in need of money, Lamb decided to "moonlight" as a journalist. His first attempts as contributor were rejected, but in 1801 he joined yet another eccentric friend, John Fenwick, editor of the new radical newspaper the *Albion*, as part-time assistant and writer, an experience he describes most amusingly in "Newspapers Thirty-five Years Ago" (*Englishman's Magazine*, October 1831). Fenwick was the model for Bigod, the arch borrower in "The Two Races of Men" (*London Magazine*, December 1820)—that is, borrowers and lenders. Lamb, always a generous lender, admires (as Elia) the cheerful confidence of the Bigods, though he is mildly caustic on the subject of "Comberbatch" (approximating the name Coleridge took when he briefly served in the army) as borrower of books. Lamb's epigram on James Mackintosh, "one of the last I *did* for the Albion" (he told Manning in his letter of 22 August 1801) and a virulent one, effectively ended that short-lived paper. The respected Mackintosh, once Godwin's friend, had attacked Godwin publicly and aroused Lamb's fierce loyalty to Godwin. In his next letter to Manning (31 August) he wrote, "The Albion is dead, dead as nail in door, and my revenues have died with it." He soon took another newspaper job, with the *Morning Chronicle*, where, however, three-quarters of what he wrote was rejected. Before long he was providing political "paragraphs"—short cynical commentary on public figures—for the *Morning Post*. For two months in early 1802 he also wrote dramatic reviews, published anonymously (as was the custom), of which only a few have been identified. According to E. V. Lucas, Lamb worked again for the *Post* in 1803-1804 before giving up "paragraphs" for good. (Lamb switches the order of his various jobs in "Newspapers Thirty-five Years Ago.")

In the summer of 1802 Charles and Mary Lamb visited the Coleridges, who were living at Keswick in the Lake District, near William and Dorothy Wordsworth at Grasmere. Though Charles Lamb was a city man and never tired of extolling London, the two Lambs, not yet forty, were in high spirits; they reveled in the freedom and fresh air, climbed Helvellyn and Skiddaw. William Wordsworth, about to marry, was away during the Lambs' visit to the Lake District, but they did see him, and often his family, almost every year when he came to London. After the sad death of his brother John Wordsworth, a sea captain for the East India Company who drowned when his ship was wrecked in 1805, Lamb investigated the case, clearing John of negligence in the loss of his ship.

In 1806 Lamb succeeded in having his short comedy, *Mr. H----* (the title character's name, kept secret from the audience until late in the play, is "Hogsflesh"), produced at the Drury Lane theater with Robert William Elliston in the title part. (Lamb celebrates this actor in two Elia essays.) It proved a dismal failure, though it was pirated anonymously in the United States and produced there some fifteen times by 1832—a triumph of which Lamb never knew. In *A History of English Drama, 1660-1900* (volume 4, 1930), Allardyce Nicoll praises the "easy style" of the play and its "two truly excellent scenes," suggesting that *Mr. H----* "might well prove a modern success," especially in an intimate playhouse; he believes that its "finer tone" and humor were too subtle for large London audiences. Henry Crabb Robinson, who first met the Lambs at this time, reported that on the opening (and only) night when the audience began hissing, Lamb hissed as loudly as anyone, for fear of being known as the anonymous playwright. Robinson became one of the Lambs' most devoted friends and makes constant reference to the pair in his diary, from 1811 to well beyond Mary's death in 1847. Together with Lamb's letters, his accounts of his many hours in their company provide a mine of information for the biographer.

Though Lamb wrote two more comedies—neither of which was produced—and prologues and epilogues to friends' plays, he realized after the failure of *Mr. H----* that drama was not likely to be a source of extra income. William Godwin and his second wife, Mary Jane, had set up as children's publishers. Lamb had already written *The King and Queen of Hearts* (1805), an entertaining verse tale, for Godwin, and in 1807 Charles and Mary Lamb produced their enduring *Tales from Shakespear* for Godwin's Juvenile Library. It was warmly welcomed and has never been out of print. The book first appeared under Charles

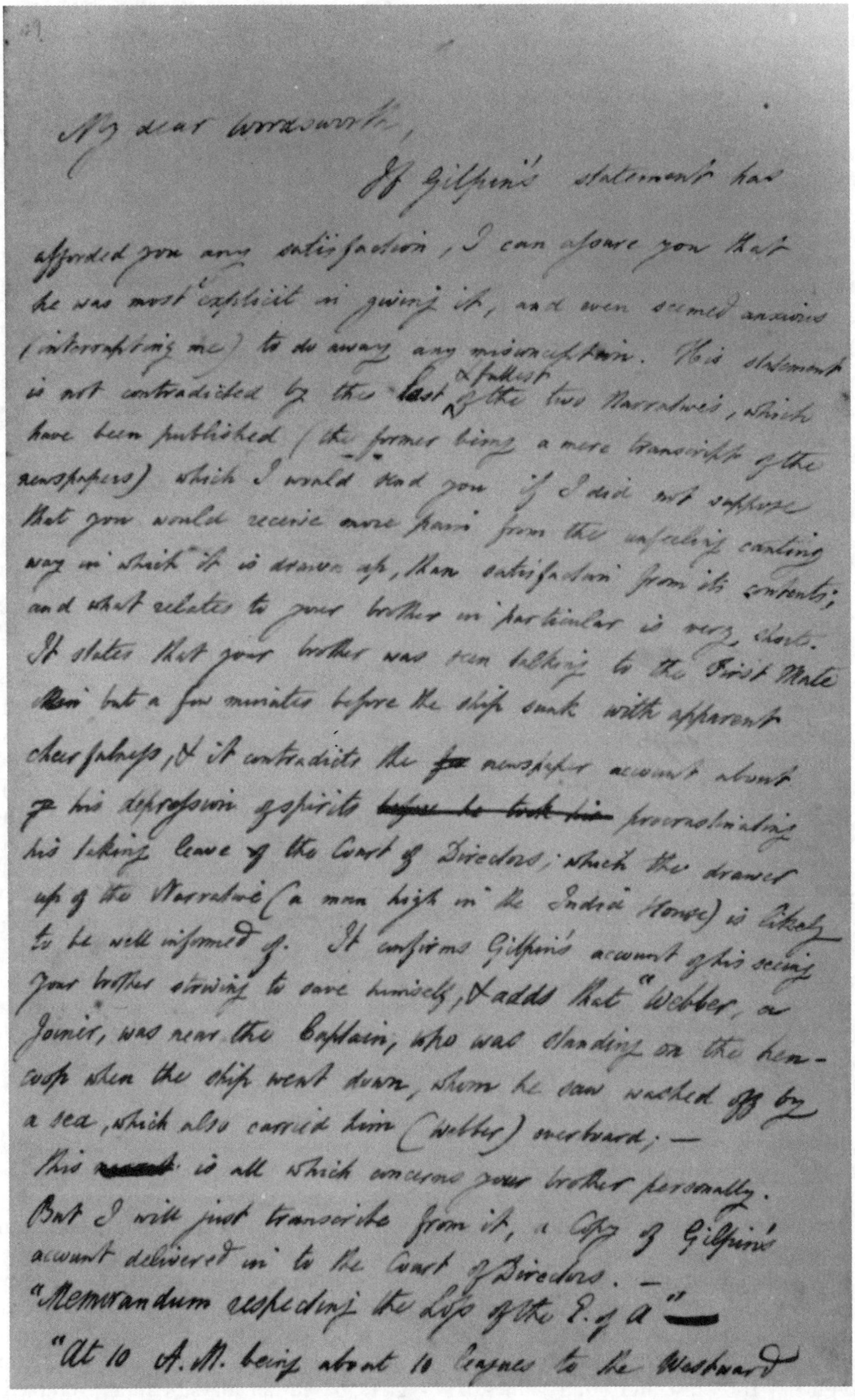

My dear Wordsworth,

If Gilpin's statement has afforded you any satisfaction, I can assure you that he was most explicit in giving it, and even seemed anxious (interrupting me) to do away any misconception. This statement is not contradicted by the last & fullest of the two Narratives, which have been published (the former being a mere transcript of the newspapers) which I would send you if I did not suppose that you would receive more pain from the unfeeling canting way in which it is drawn up, than satisfaction from its contents; and what relates to your brother in particular is very short. It states that your brother was seen talking to the First Mate but a few minutes before the ship sunk with apparent cheerfulness, & it contradicts the newspaper account about his depression of spirits ~~before he took his~~ procrastinating his taking leave of the Court of Directors, which the drawer up of the Narrative (a man high in the India House) is likely to be well informed of. It confirms Gilpin's account of his seeing your brother striving to save himself, & adds that "Webber, a Joiner, was near the Captain, who was standing on the hen-coop when the ship went down, whom he saw washed off by a sea, which also carried him (Webber) overboard; — This is all which concerns your brother personally. But I will just transcribe from it, a Copy of Gilpin's account delivered in to the Court of Directors. — "Memorandum respecting the Loss of the E. of A." —

"At 10 A.M. being about 10 leagues to the Westward

*First page from one of the letters to William Wordsworth (4 March 1805) in which Lamb provided information on the death of Capt. John Wordsworth (Harry Ransom Humanities Research Center, University of Texas at Austin)*

Lamb's name only, though of the twenty plays summarized in the volume Mary had written the paraphrases for the fourteen comedies and Charles for only the six tragedies. *The Adventures of Ulysses* (1808), Charles Lamb's prose version of the *Odyssey*, was less successful (though a school edition was still being published by Ginn in 1886).

In 1809 the Lambs' anonymous *Mrs. Leicester's School* scored another triumph. Again, it was chiefly by Mary, who wrote seven of the ten charming stories for young girls. At a time when fairy tales were decried by certain critics, the Lambs were staunch believers that writing for children should be imaginative, without the moralizing didacticism then becoming mandatory. *Mrs. Leicester's School* is sensitive and accurate in interpreting for young people such common experiences as the losing of a parent or a fortune, the advent of a stepmother, life at a farm (Mary's tale "Louisa Manners" complements Charles's later "Mackery End"), and school life away from home. In "The Witch Aunt" Charles (as the storyteller "Maria Howe") draws the most revealing of his portraits of Aunt Hetty, and of his own childhood fears outside of his Elia essays, wherein witch and aunt never quite coincide. The book was highly successful and went through ten editions by 1847. It can still appeal to children and has been republished in the twentieth century. In his introduction to the 1948 Harvill Press edition, Richard Church praises the "ease of Mary's writing, and the transparency of it" and pays full tribute to her "genius," which here reached its apogee. In contrast, Church considers Charles Lamb's contributions often too complex in style. Walter Savage Landor was a contemporary admirer. There is a record of his only meeting with the Lambs, in September 1832 when Henry Crabb Robinson took Landor to Enfield to visit them.

The Lambs' next offering, *Poetry for Children* (1809), with two-thirds of the verses by Mary, did not reach a second edition. Charles's *Prince Dorus* (1811), a verse tale about a prince with a long nose, was the last of his efforts, as far as is known, for the Juvenile Library.

By 1806 the Lambs had begun their hospitable "evenings," originally on Wednesdays, then Thursdays, when a varied group of their friends gathered regularly for whist and other games, a supper of "heaps of smoking roasted potatoes" and cold meats or veal pie, literary conversation, puns, and drink, often until after midnight. Out of these occasions came Elia's "Mrs. Battle's Opinions on Whist" (*London Magazine*, February 1821) and many descriptions by participants, including William Hazlitt's in his second essay "On the Conversation of Authors" (collected in *The Plain Speaker*, 1826):

> There was L--- himself, the most delightful, the most provoking, the most witty and sensible of men. He always made the best pun, and the best remark in the course of the evening. His serious conversation, like his serious writing, is his best. No one ever stammered out such fine, piquant, deep, eloquent things in half a dozen half sentences as he does. His jests scald like tears; and he probes a question with a play upon words.

T. N. Talfourd, a young admirer and Lamb's first biographer, described the blazing fire, the old-fashioned furniture, and the William Hogarth prints. In the group at one time or another were brother John Lamb; the maid Becky; Capt. James Burney (later admiral), Fanny Burney's brother, who had sailed with Capt. James Cook; Burney's son Martin, an odd but intelligent youth who adored the Lambs; and many actors of the London stage, as well as nearly all the friends previously mentioned. (Politics, as controversial, was usually barred in the talk.) Talfourd noted Lamb's "Quaker primness" (he usually wore black) and "melancholy smile" at the start of an evening; with drink all primness evaporated. These parties continued into the 1820s, and the Lambs often joined other parties at the homes of Leigh Hunt; Capt. Burney; the lawyer Basil Montagu; the first British census taker, John Rickman; and the fine organist and music publisher Vincent Novello. In "A Chapter on Ears" (*London Magazine*, March 1821) Elia declares his hatred of music but exempts Novello and the singer John Braham.

The Lambs sometimes spent his office holidays (at first a week, later a month) at the seaside, which Charles Lamb professed to dislike. (He once told Wordsworth he did not much care if he ever saw a mountain again, but teasing was often his epistolary manner.) As Elia says in "The Old Margate Hoy" (*London Magazine*, July 1823), he despised the stockbrokers who haunted seaside resorts, but he would have enjoyed the smugglers of earlier days. Lamb preferred London, with its teeming life. Praised often in his letters, London had become his subject as early as 1 February 1802, when the *Morning Post* published a

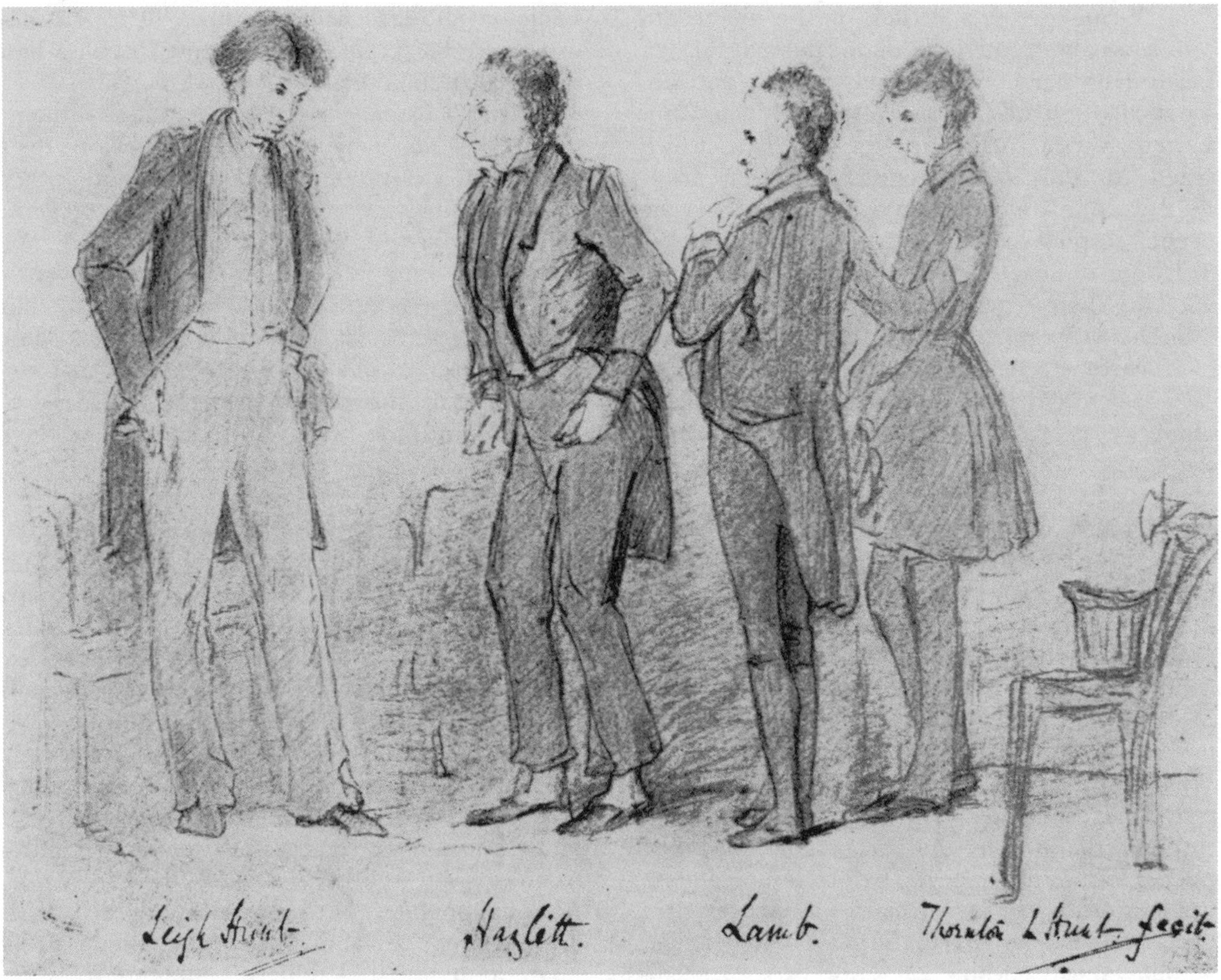


*Thornton Hunt's drawing from memory of a visit from Lamb and William Hazlitt to his father's study (from E. V. Lucas,* The Life of Charles Lamb, *1905)*

short piece called "The Londoner," presaging Elia. Manning encouraged Lamb to write more essays in this vein, as he was to do many years later.

In 1808 he published his first work of extended scholarly criticism—*Specimens of English Dramatic Poets, Who Lived About the Time of Shakspeare*. With no pretense of completeness and with little biographical information or plot summary, Lamb picked his examples for their poetic value, offering as commentary his own acute and highly original perceptions. The book was well received (though sales proved slow), providing him with a new, serious reputation. *Specimens of English Dramatic Poets* was read far into the nineteenth century, and admired by both generations of Romantics. In 1820 John Keats presented it, with his own markings (all favorable) and two handwritten paragraphs of comment, as his last birthday gift to Fanny Brawne, before, mortally ill, he set sail for Italy. In the course of discussing an excerpt from George Chapman, Lamb says, "Shakspeare makes us believe, while we are among his lovely creations, that they are nothing but what we are familiar with, as in dreams new things seem old: but we awake, and sigh for the difference." Keats marked this passage heavily in the margin and underlined it, adding in a handwritten note: "This is the most acute deep sighted and spiritual piece of criticism ever penned. . . . To write a few such things is perhaps as well as shining, a distinguish'd literary Character—." Of this praise Lamb remained forever unaware, but he had already written a favorable review of Keats's *Lamia* (*New Times*, 19 July 1820). He much preferred Keats to Shelley and Byron, in whose verse he found no rewards for himself.

During the first decade of the nineteenth century, Lamb came to know Keats's encourager Leigh Hunt, nine years Lamb's junior and another alumnus of Christ's Hospital. When Hunt started a new magazine, the *Reflector*, which lasted for only four irregular issues in 1811-1812, Lamb was provided with the urging he needed to publish many essays, of which "On the Tragedies of Shakespeare, Considered with Reference to Their Fitness for Stage Representation" (March 1812) and "On the Genius and Character of Hogarth" (October 1811) again proved his critical acumen and remain among his masterpieces. Lamb was perhaps the first to elevate Hogarth to the status of a major artist. His contention that Shakespeare's tragedies were better read than seen proved controversial, though both Hazlitt and Coleridge later agreed. Joseph Addison, indeed, had objected a century earlier (*Spectator* no. 44) to the English propensity for spreading butchered bodies about the stage (one thinks of *Hamlet*), as compared to the practice of Continental playwrights, especially the French, whose character merely reported killings unseen onstage. What Lamb meant, of course, is that Shakespeare transcends the stage and can be appreciated through the eye of the imagination, not that Shakespeare should never be acted: the Lambs went often to see performances of Shakespeare plays. According to Talfourd, Lamb's friend Thomas Barnes, who became the first great editor of the *Times* (London), told Lamb he had "written about Shakespeare, and Shakespeare's own Lear, finer than any one ever did in the world. . . ."

Lamb's many other contributions to the *Reflector*—except for the amusing verses "A Farewell to Tobacco" (March 1812) and comments on the church historian Thomas Fuller (March 1812) —were considerably less remarkable. Among them were "On the Custom of Hissing at Theatres" (October 1811), "On Burial Societies" (October 1811), "Edax on Appetite" (March 1812), "The Good Clerk" (March 1812), "On the Inconvenience Resulting from Being Hanged" (July 1811), and "A Bachelor's Complaint on the Behaviour of Married People" (March 1812). They touch on themes that would occupy Elia, and writing them provided good practice. "A Bachelor's Complaint" and another early piece, "Confessions of a Drunkard" (*The Philanthropist*, no. 9, 1813), are collected in the Elia volumes, where they strike a slightly discordant note, being entirely cynical. The Elia of the 1820s was usually mellower and leavened his ironies. (The "Drunkard" piece later caused Lamb some trouble when it was taken too literally.)

Hunt's *Examiner* was a long-lived and influential weekly newspaper, to which Lamb in 1812 began to contribute "Table-Talk" and other pieces. Hunt was no friend of the regent, George, Prince of Wales (later George IV), nor was Lamb, who satirized him sharply in verses called "The Triumph of the Whale," published in the *Examiner* for 15 March 1812. A week later Hunt himself wrote of the prince (not inaccurately) in terms that the government considered libelous. Hunt was tried in December and ultimately spent two years in prison (1813-1815) in the somewhat easy conditions provided for "gentlemen" in those days. He had his growing family with him, and could entertain friends, including the Lambs, who were constant visitors—perhaps in part because Charles Lamb felt somewhat responsible for Hunt's plight. Hunt later extolled him in a verse epistle referring to those visits (collected in *Foliage*, 1818).

In 1814 Wordsworth asked Lamb to review his new poem, *The Excursion*, for the conservative *Quarterly Review*, edited by William Gifford, who in 1812 had referred in print to some of Lamb's comments in *Specimens of English Dramatic Poets* as "the blasphemies of a maniac" (Gifford then knew nothing of Lamb's history and later made a kind of apology). Lamb was anxious to assist Wordsworth, especially since Hazlitt (who had borrowed Lamb's copy) had just damned *The Excursion* in the *Examiner*. Lamb wrote a positive review, but, much to his distress, he found it heavily mangled by Gifford in the October 1814 issue of the *Quarterly*.

The Lambs left the Temple in 1817 for Great Russell Street (now simply Russell Street) in Covent Garden near their beloved Drury Lane theater. On 28 December of that year Benjamin Robert Haydon gave his "Immortal Dinner" under Haydon's enormous painting *Christ's Triumphant Entry into Jerusalem*, in which Wordsworth, Keats, and Hazlitt (but not Lamb, as has sometimes been said) were depicted among the welcoming crowd. Keats later wrote a brief account of the dinner, and Lamb referred to it in his letters, but Haydon's brilliant account of the evening in his autobiography is one of the most vivid pictures we have of Romantics at play. His guests included a tipsy Lamb, as well as Keats, Wordsworth, and John Kingston, a comptroller at the Stamp Office, for which Wordsworth was now a

*Fanny Kelly, 1819 (engraving by Thompson, after a portrait by Partridge)*

northern distributor of tax stamps, supplementing his meager income to support a large household. Keats and Lamb barely concealed their contempt for the bureaucrat. Lamb made the philistine Kingston butt of his humor, offering to study the unfortunate official's cranium. Wordsworth, who had not met Kingston or recognized his superior's name, was taken aback when, in the midst of Lamb's jollity, Kingston identified himself as comptroller. Finally, as Lamb grew merrier and more insulting, Keats and Haydon managed to shut him in Haydon's painting room. Earlier in the evening more serious conversation ranged from Homer, Shakespeare, and Milton, to African exploration and Isaac Newton, who—Lamb and Keats agreed—destroyed the poetry of the rainbow by breaking it into prismatic colors. Leigh Hunt's *Autobiography* (1850) provides other fascinating anecdotes of the Lamb-Keats-Wordsworth-Coleridge circle.

In 1818 Lamb published most of his *Works* to date in two small volumes, the first dedicated to Coleridge and containing the poetry, *John Woodvil*, *Rosamund Gray*, and "Recollections of Christ's Hospital." The second, all prose and dedicated to Martin Burney, includes the Shakespeare essay, excerpts from *Specimens of English Dramatic Poets*, his critiques of Fuller and George Wither, his essay on Hogarth, "The Londoner," several more *Reflector* essays, and *Mr. H----*. Lamb's *Works* was widely reviewed, in general with the same mixed reception given the individual works when first published. Lamb's prose was admired more than his poetry, and especially the criticism. The previously uncollected *Reflector* pieces, especially the essays on Shakespeare and

Hogarth, and "Recollections of Christ's Hospital," now received attention and praise. In an August 1818 review, *Blackwood's*, which had previously been hard on the "Cockney school" of poets, of which Lamb was considered a member (the *Blackwood's* attack on Keats is notorious), found merit even in Lamb's poetry. The net result was to make the forty-three-year-old author a literary figure to be reckoned with, though his best work was yet to come.

Lamb's 1818 *Works* includes a sonnet, "You are not, Kelly, of the common strain," written in 1813 and addressed to comic actress Frances Maria (Fanny) Kelly (1790-1882). By 1819 he was in love with the woman whose "divine plain face" he had extolled in a letter to Wordsworth's wife (18 February 1818). Fanny Kelly had become the Lambs' friend and in Russell Street their neighbor, to whom Mary Lamb taught Latin. In 1819 Lamb published warm reviews of her acting, including the tribute "What a lass that were to go a gipseying through the world with" (*Examiner*, 4 and 5 July 1819). He proposed to her by letter on 20 July 1819. Miss Kelly, though she claimed another attachment, could not face being tied to a household of three, especially one with Mary's problems, and refused him. Lamb wrote a humorous-sad short note of acquiescence—"I feel myself in a lackadaisical no-how-ish kind of a humour. I believe it is the rain, or something. . . . You will be good friends with us, will you not? . . . N. B. Do not paste that last letter of mine into your Book" (20 July 1819). Miss Kelly did keep the letter and remained a close friend. Later she founded the first dramatic school for girls and assisted Charles Dickens with his amateur theatricals. She never married. Lamb faced the blow with his usual courage, and not long after, as Elia, he worked off some of his unhappiness over never having married or had children in the lovely essay "Dream-Children" (*London Magazine*, January 1822).

On the publication of Keats's *Lamia* (1820) Lamb, who with others had resented the *Blackwood's* attack on the young poet, wrote the very first review of it (*New Times*, 19 July 1820), praising the book as a whole and admiring *Isabella and the Pot of Basil*, in particular "those never-cloying stanzas which we have cited, and which we think should disarm criticism, if it be not in its nature cruel; if it would not deny to honey its sweetness, nor to roses redness, nor light to the stars in Heaven; if it would not bay the moon out of the skies, rather than acknowledge she is fair." This passage ends Lamb's short critique, probably cut by the editor, since Keats's whole ode *To Autumn*, as well as excerpts from *Ode to a Nightingale* and from *Hyperion*, possibly Lamb's choices, removed from his review, appeared in the *New Times* shortly afterward. The passage cited also gracefully damns Keats's *Blackwood's* critics. Lamb praises too the "radiance" of *The Eve of St. Agnes*. He was enchanted by the pictures Keats painted and saw his genius.

A 15 May 1824 letter to his Quaker friend Bernard Barton shows Lamb's similar appreciation of William Blake, then sixty-six and still struggling in relative obscurity to maintain himself in London. The letter expresses Lamb's admiration for Blake's watercolors, his Canterbury pilgrims picture, his visionary genius, and quotes from the poem, "Tyger, tyger, burning bright," which he calls "glorious."

The years 1820-1825 found Lamb at the height of his powers as contributor to the *London Magazine*, founded in 1820 by John Scott, for whose *Champion* Lamb had also written. He is said to have been offered the highest pay rate in what became the distinguished stable of *London Magazine* authors. Scott gradually assembled William Hazlitt, Thomas De Quincey (who contributed *The Confessions of an English Opium-Eater* in September and October 1821), the poets John Clare, Bernard Barton, and Bryan Waller Procter—all of whom became Lamb's friends—as well as the Reverend Henry Francis Cary (translator of Dante), Coleridge, Allan Cunningham, and Thomas Hood. (Contributions by George Borrow, Walter Scott, Godwin's daughter Mary Shelley, Keats, Thomas Carlyle, and Byron were also to be found in its pages.) Lamb's Elia contributions date from August 1820, with the appearance of "The South Sea House." Besides the many Elia essays already mentioned, the following should be noted: "A Quaker's Meeting" (April 1821), "On Some of the Old Actors" and "On the Artificial Comedy of the Last Century" (revised versions—along with "On the Acting of Munden"—of parts of essays published in February, April, and October 1822), "Detached Thoughts on Books and Reading" (July 1822), "Distant Correspondents" (March 1822), and "Barbara S---" (April 1825), a disguised report of an experience of Fanny Kelly, as well as a later Elia essay, "Sanity of True Genius," which Lamb contributed to the May 1826 issue of the *New Monthly Magazine*.

*Lamb circa 1825 (drawing by Thomas Wageman; from E. V. Lucas,* The Life of Charles Lamb, *1905)*

"Imperfect Sympathies" (August 1821) and "The Old and the New Schoolmaster" (May 1821) are significant for Romantic theory in their emphasis on feeling over stark, mundane facts, with which Elia the antihero cannot deal. "I love a *Fool,*" he writes in "All Fool's Day": "he who hath not a dram of folly in his mixture hath pounds of much worse matter in his composition." And so Lamb builds his Elia persona. One of the best definitions of "Imagination" occurs in Lamb's earlier *Reflector* essay on Hogarth: "that power which draws all things to one,—which makes things animate and inanimate, beings with their attributes, subjects and their accessories, take one colour, and serve to one effect." That power is apparent throughout the Elia essays, as in this passage on the actor Joseph Munden, which (as has been observed) may also serve to describe Lamb himself: "A tub of butter, contemplated by him, amounts to a Platonic idea. He understands a leg of mutton in its quiddity. He stands wondering, among the common-place materials of life, like primæval man with the sun and stars about him."

In February 1821 John Scott died as a result of a duel and the magazine went to Taylor and Hessey, Keats's publishers, with Thomas Hood assisting John Taylor as editor. (The same year saw the deaths of John Lamb, Admiral Burney, and Keats.) Under Taylor there were lively monthly dinners for contributors, which Lamb attended. In 1823 Thomas Moore described Lamb in his journal as "the hero, at present, of the 'London Magazine.' "

Lamb's development and artistry in the Elia essays have been much analyzed in recent books and articles, many of the latter in the pages of the new series of the *Charles Lamb Bulletin,* pub-

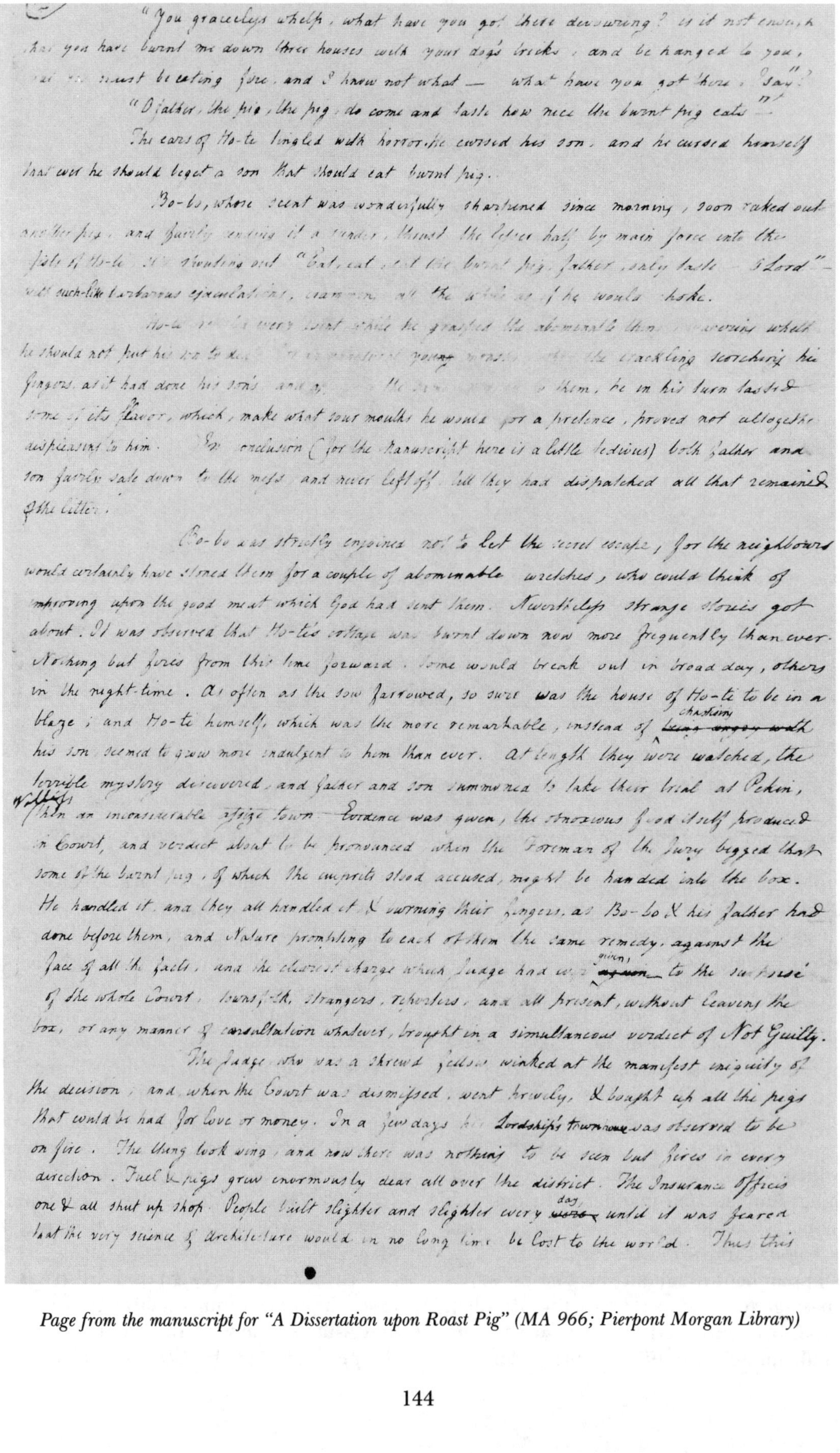

"You graceless whelp, what have you got there devouring? is it not enough that you have burnt me down three houses with your dog's tricks, and be hanged to you, but you must be eating fire, and I know not what — what have you got here, I say?"

"O father, the pig, the pig, do come and taste how nice the burnt pig eats."

The ears of Ho-ti tingled with horror. He cursed his son, and he cursed himself that ever he should beget a son that should eat burnt pig.

Bo-bo, whose scent was wonderfully sharpened since morning, soon raked out another pig, and fairly rending it asunder, thrust the lesser half by main force into the fists of Ho-ti, still shouting out "Eat, eat, eat the burnt pig, father, only taste — O Lord" — with such-like barbarous ejaculations, cramming all the while as if he would choke.

Ho-ti trembled every joint while he grasped the abominable thing, wavering whether he should not put his son to death for an unnatural young monster, when the crackling scorching his fingers, as it had done his son's, and applying the same remedy to them, he in his turn tasted some of its flavor, which, make what sour mouths he would for a pretence, proved not altogether displeasing to him. In conclusion (for the manuscript here is a little tedious) both father and son fairly sate down to the mess, and never left off till they had dispatched all that remained of the litter.

Bo-bo was strictly enjoined not to let the secret escape, for the neighbours would certainly have stoned them for a couple of abominable wretches, who could think of improving upon the good meat which God had sent them. Nevertheless strange stories got about. It was observed that Ho-ti's cottage was burnt down now more frequently than ever. Nothing but fires from this time forward. Some would break out in broad day, others in the night-time. As often as the sow farrowed, so sure was the house of Ho-ti to be in a blaze; and Ho-ti himself, which was the more remarkable, instead of ~~being angry with~~ chastising his son seemed to grow more indulgent to him than ever. At length they were watched, the terrible mystery discovered, and father and son summoned to take their trial at Pekin, then an inconsiderable assize town. Evidence was given, the obnoxious food itself produced in Court, and verdict about to be pronounced when the Foreman of the Jury begged that some of the burnt pig, of which the culprits stood accused, might be handed into the box. He handled it, and they all handled it, & burning their fingers, as Bo-bo & his father had done before them, and Nature prompting to each of them the same remedy, against the face of all the facts, and the clearest charge which Judge had ever ~~again~~ given, to the surprise of the whole Court, townsfolk, strangers, reporters, and all present, without leaving the box, or any manner of consultation whatever, brought in a simultaneous verdict of Not Guilty.

The Judge, who was a shrewd fellow, winked at the manifest iniquity of the decision; and when the Court was dismissed, went privily, & bought up all the pigs that could be had for love or money. In a few days his Lordship's townhouse was observed to be on fire. The thing took wing, and now there was nothing to be seen but fires in every direction. Fuel & pigs grew enormously dear all over the district. The Insurance Offices one & all shut up shop. People built slighter and slighter every ~~week~~ day, until it was feared that the very science of Architecture would in no long time be lost to the world. Thus this

*Page from the manuscript for "A Dissertation upon Roast Pig" (MA 966; Pierpont Morgan Library)*

lished by the Charles Lamb Society in London, which under three excellent successive editors since 1973 has attained a high standard of research and criticism. The origin of the name Elia (pronounced *Ellia*, according to Lamb) has been variously described (or guessed at) by recent scholars. Lamb himself told Taylor that he had stolen it from a deceased colleague at the South Sea Company. Lamb is said to have pointed out elsewhere that *Elia* is the acronym for "a lie," since Elia likes to play tricks with the facts. "Oxford in the Vacation," for example, is really set at Cambridge; the "I" of "Christ's Hospital Five and Thirty Years Ago" is really Coleridge at first; Elia's "cousins" Bridget and James Elia are Mary and John Lamb, Jr.; the old lady whose childhood experience is reported in "Barbara S---" is Fanny Kelly, who was in her early thirties when the essay was first published. Elia delighted in mystification. His style is sometimes almost forbiddingly rich in the seventeenth-century locutions of Sir Thomas Browne and Robert Burton, though Lamb made them his own. He claimed that he read mainly works from the past, though the assertion was not strictly true. After one of his early literary rejections Lamb declared, "Damn the age; I will write for Antiquity!" This tendency has sometimes been found too quaint, with its "peradventures," "marrys," and "haths" or "seemeths." The many classical allusions are often lost on the modern reader. But Lamb's sense is most often clear, with nuances and reverberations; his form is brief, subtle, compact, and alive with wry and witty observations on the human condition—mostly on daily, specific, minutiae as they occur to him, for Lamb is a true Romantic in his rejection of abstraction, rhetorical rules, and broad philosophic systems. He celebrates the "quiddities" of his favorite little-known books, the theater, childhood and youth, the daily round, the daily grind, and most particularly the surprising qualities of some of his friends, for nearly all of his observations are drawn—or transmuted—from life.

His causes can be strong, as in his almost feminist defense of women in "Modern Gallantry" (November 1822), or of the poor in "The Tombs in the Abbey" (October 1823), where the antiquarian mode disappears in firm argument. Lamb's earlier sardonic crudenesses vanish in Elia's mature sympathies—for the young, the helpless, the outcast. As Lamb described Elia in his "Preface, By a Friend of the Late Elia," written for inclusion in *Last Essays* (1833),

> His *Intimados*, to confess a truth, were in the world's eye a ragged regiment. He found them floating on the surface of society; and the colour, or something else, in the weed pleased him. The burrs stuck to him—but they were good and loving burrs for all that. He never greatly cared for the society of what are called good people.

In this amusing autobiographical note Lamb resists the gravity and respectability of age, preferring younger companions, for, like his Elia, he has never really grown up: "He did not conform to the march of time, but was dragged along in the procession." Such immaturity, Lamb concludes, may be a weakness but it is also a "key to explicate some of his writings."

Lamb had occasion to write a serious defense of himself and some of his friends for the October 1823 issue of the *London Magazine*. After the publication of the first volume of Elia essays, Robert Southey, while praising the book, had suggested in "Progress of Infidelity," an article in the January 1823 issue of the *Quarterly Review*, that Lamb's collection "wanted a sounder religious feeling." He deplored what he found in Lamb's "Witches and Other Night-Fears" (first published in *London Magazine*, October 1821), taking Lamb's statement about "Dear little T. H. [Thornton Hunt] who of all children has been brought up with the most scrupulous exclusion of every taint of superstition" to criticize not only Lamb but also the boy's father, Leigh Hunt, for his agnosticism. In reply, Lamb asserted that "religious feeling" was not a sure indicator of character, defending each of his agnostic friends in turn—and rebuked Southey's Church of England for charging admission to the poor people who wanted to visit the tombs in Westminster Abbey. He later used part of this letter—the quarrel with Southey having been patched up—as the Elia essay "The Tombs in the Abbey." By this time Lamb's early religious bent had faded into a distrust of institutional religion, but Coleridge believed him to be always a Christian at heart. He admired the Quakers, though he felt himself too secular in taste and habit to be one of them.

The range of the Elia essays is wide then, within Elian limits, but, despite their artfully managed shifts in mood and style, they are all of a piece, his themes recurring and forming, in the end, a consistent and serious view of the world he often treated so lightly. He proved cheering and inspiring to many readers, a principal cause of his long popularity and the source of the Victorian sentimental estimate of his work. Yet the fact

*Colebrooke Cottage, on the New River at Islington, where the Lambs lived in 1823-1827. This cottage is the setting for "Amicus Redevivus," the Elia essay that describes how Lamb's nearsighted and absentminded friend George Dyer failed to turn on leaving the Lambs' house and walked straight into the river, where he nearly drowned (watercolor by an unknown artist; from E. V. Lucas,* The Life of Charles Lamb, *1905). The cottage still stands, but the river now runs underground.*

that irony was always his weapon may account in part for the resurgence of the Elia essays in the increasingly paradoxical world of the late twentieth century. By July 1825, when he ceased writing for the *London Magazine*, Lamb's reputation was secure. He had by then been invited to a Lord Mayor's dinner (1823) and a meeting with Sir Walter Scott (1821). He continued to contribute to other periodicals as he had been doing throughout his association with the *London Magazine*. In 1821 he had composed a review, probably intended for the *Examiner*, of Hazlitt's first volume of *Table-Talk*. It may have been suppressed by Hunt because of its reference to Hunt's recent quarrel with Hazlitt. Roy Park, who published this review for the first time in *Lamb as Critic* (1980), considers it the most important of Lamb's critiques, not only because of its sensitive and penetrating analysis of his close friend but also for Lamb's estimate of previous essayists in relation to Hazlitt's work and incidentally, therefore, to his own. Lamb points out that the virtues of Plutarch and Montaigne have been lacking in most such writers since, that a series of essays requires, as visible author, a living, breathing human being, with quirks, to hold the reader's interest: "By this balm are [Plutarch and Montaigne] preserved." Hazlitt, he finds, is such a writer—and so, one might add, is Charles Lamb. Hazlitt's discontents, analyses, and praise are of a different order, but

Lamb's generally favorable judgment has stood the test of time and is the twentieth-century view of Hazlitt as he too is reassessed. Lamb found Hazlitt above all honest and acute, with much to contribute to history and letters.

In his Hazlitt review the difference between Lamb and his predecessors—even Joseph Addison and Sir Richard Steele on whose model he and many others had written—is made plain. Elia, no chance arrival, had clearly arisen from Lamb's new and original understanding of what makes lasting literature. The informal, conversational "familiar" essay remains today what Lamb, Hazlitt, De Quincey, and Hunt first made it, and it is enjoying a strong revival, in the pages, for example, of the *New York Times* and even in the popular writings of doctors and scientists such as Lewis Thomas and Stephen Jay Gould.

The Lambs' 1822 journey to Paris to visit the playwright James Kenney and his family at Versailles was their one excursion out of England. Lamb reveled in the beauties of Paris, ate frogs, rejoiced in the bookstalls and their prints, and met François-Joseph Talma, the great French tragic actor. His reports are entirely in letters (Elia did not assimilate France). On his return Lamb found that London looked "mean and new" next to Paris, but Paris had "no St. Paul's or Westminster Abbey." At Amiens Mary Lamb had one of her attacks, and Lamb was forced to return home without her, leaving her in the care of her English nurse (who had accompanied them), the Kenneys, and the ever-attentive Crabb Robinson, who happened to visit Paris at that time. The attack was fortunately a brief one, but the experiment of foreign travel was not repeated.

During this decade the Lambs were becoming acquainted with a young orphan, Emma Isola, granddaughter of Wordsworth's Cambridge tutor in Italian. They met her in 1820 on one of their trips to Cambridge, and in 1823, when she was fourteen, they more or less adopted her. At last Lamb was at least a sort of parent; Emma regarded him and Mary so. Except for intervals away as a governess, Emma lived with them until her 1833 marriage to Edward Moxon, who had become Lamb's publisher three years earlier.

In 1823, too, the Lambs moved to a house with a garden in the Islington suburb of London, near his *London Magazine* colleague Thomas Hood and his family. Mary Shelley, recently returned from Italy, joined the group of friends who visited them there.

By 1825 when Lamb turned fifty, his most fruitful years were nearly over and nagging illness sometimes assailed him. His superiors at the East India House noticed that he looked unwell and, when they commented on his appearance, he replied he might have to resign. The company retired him on 29 March 1825, an experience he describes in the amusing Elia essay "The Superannuated Man" (*London Magazine*, May 1825). His salary had risen by 1825 to £730 annually and his pension was a generous £450 (or £441 after provision for Mary's future was deducted). An artful Elia essay, "Old China" (*London Magazine*, March 1823), which starts from a china teacup and winds back to it, contrasts Elia and Bridget's present affluence with their former poverty—with nostalgia but also with pleasure at no longer having to consider every penny. It is surely a revealing portrait of some of the happiest elements in Charles and Mary Lamb's later life together.

In 1987 Jane Aaron pointed out how mutually interdependent were the two Lambs, citing Gillian Beer's 1984 article as giving Mary Lamb long-overdue credit for providing insights contributing to Charles's unusual understanding of man and woman, child and parent. Aaron cites also Leslie Joan Friedman's recent detailed work on Mary Lamb in a 1976 doctoral dissertation. Modern feminism, Aaron feels, is exploring new territory in reassessing Mary's productive influence on, and support of, her brother, as well as taking a new measure of Mary's own remarkable accomplishment.

With every day a "holyday" (holiday), Charles Lamb sometimes found retirement irksome, and he soon began to haunt the British Museum—where his friend H. F. Cary was assistant keeper of printed books—to make excerpts from David Garrick's collection of old plays. He began publishing these gradually, with pieces of interesting London lore and other oddments, in William Hone's miscellanies—in the 1825 and 1826 volumes of the *Every Day Book*, in the 1827 volume of the *Table Book* and possibly later in Hone's 1832 *Year Book*. All four of these volumes are fascinating fat compendia of what E. V. Lucas calls "folk-lore, antiquarianism, topography, and curious matter," with many admiring references to Lamb's work throughout. Hone had been prosecuted by the government for the unorthodox opinions he had expressed in print. He

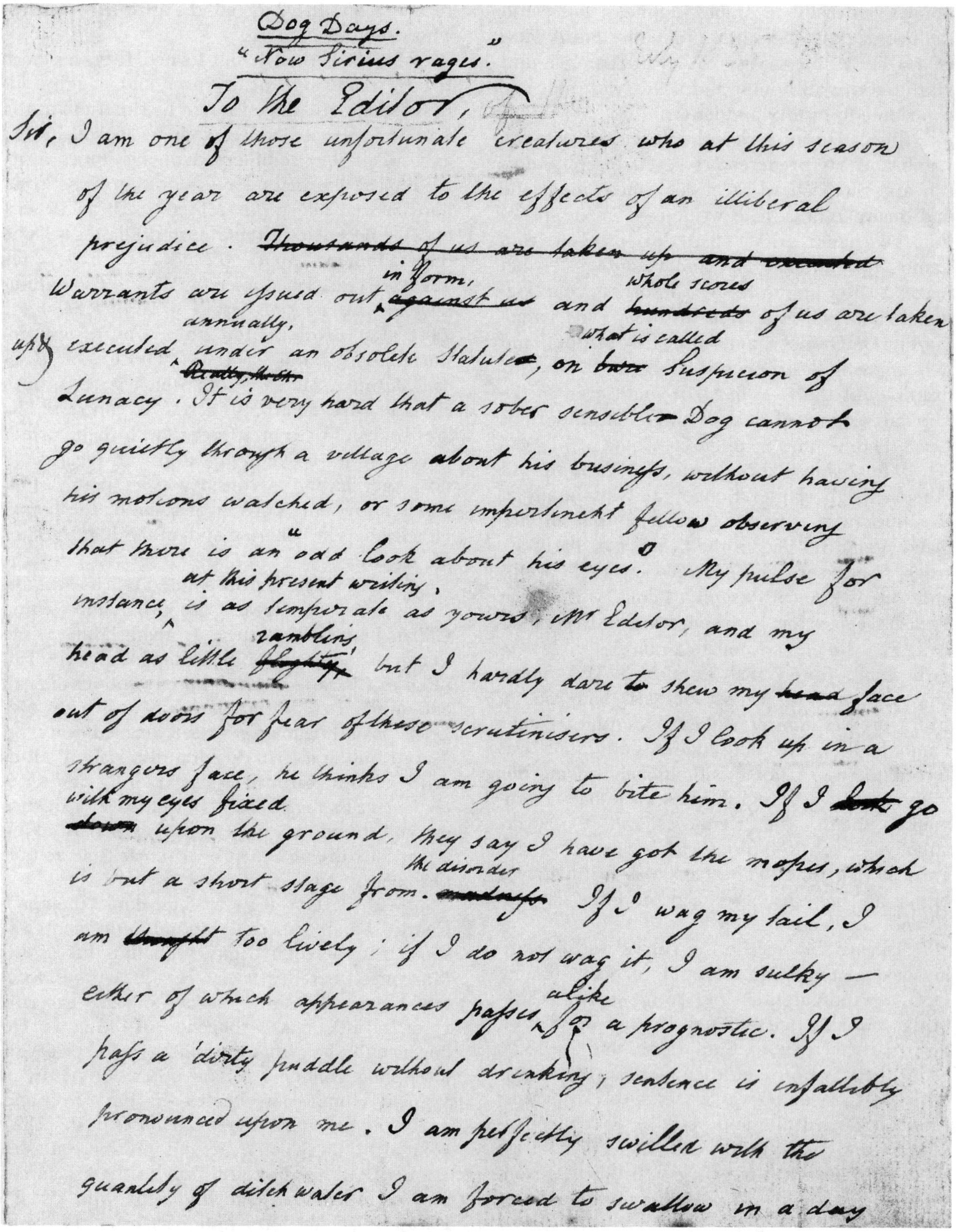
Dog Days.
"Now Sirius rages."
To the Editor,
Sir, I am one of those unfortunate creatures who at this season of the year are exposed to the effects of an illiberal prejudice. ~~Thousands of us are taken up and executed~~ Warrants are issued out, in form, ~~against us~~ and whole scores ~~hundreds~~ of us are taken up & executed annually, ~~Really, Mr.~~ under an obsolete Statute, on what is called ~~bare~~ suspicion of Lunacy. It is very hard that a sober sensible Dog cannot go quietly through a village about his business, without having his motions watched, or some impertinent fellow observing that there is an "odd look about his eyes." My pulse for instance, at this present writing, is as temperate as yours, Mr Editor, and my head as little rambling ~~flighty~~ but I hardly dare ~~to~~ shew my ~~head~~ face out of doors for fear of these scrutinisers. If I look up in a strangers face, he thinks I am going to bite him. If I ~~look~~ go ~~down~~ with my eyes fixed upon the ground, they say I have got the mopes, which is but a short stage from the disorder ~~madness~~. If I wag my tail, I am ~~thought~~ too lively; if I do not wag it, I am sulky — either of which appearances passes alike for a prognostic. If I pass a dirty puddle without drinking, sentence is infallibly pronounced upon me. I am perfectly swilled with the quantity of ditch water I am forced to swallow in a day

*On this and the next two pages: manuscript for "Dog Days," a letter published in William Hone's* Every Day Book *(14 July 1825) after Hone had suggested that dogs should be exterminated (HM 7972; Henry E. Huntington Library and Art Gallery)*

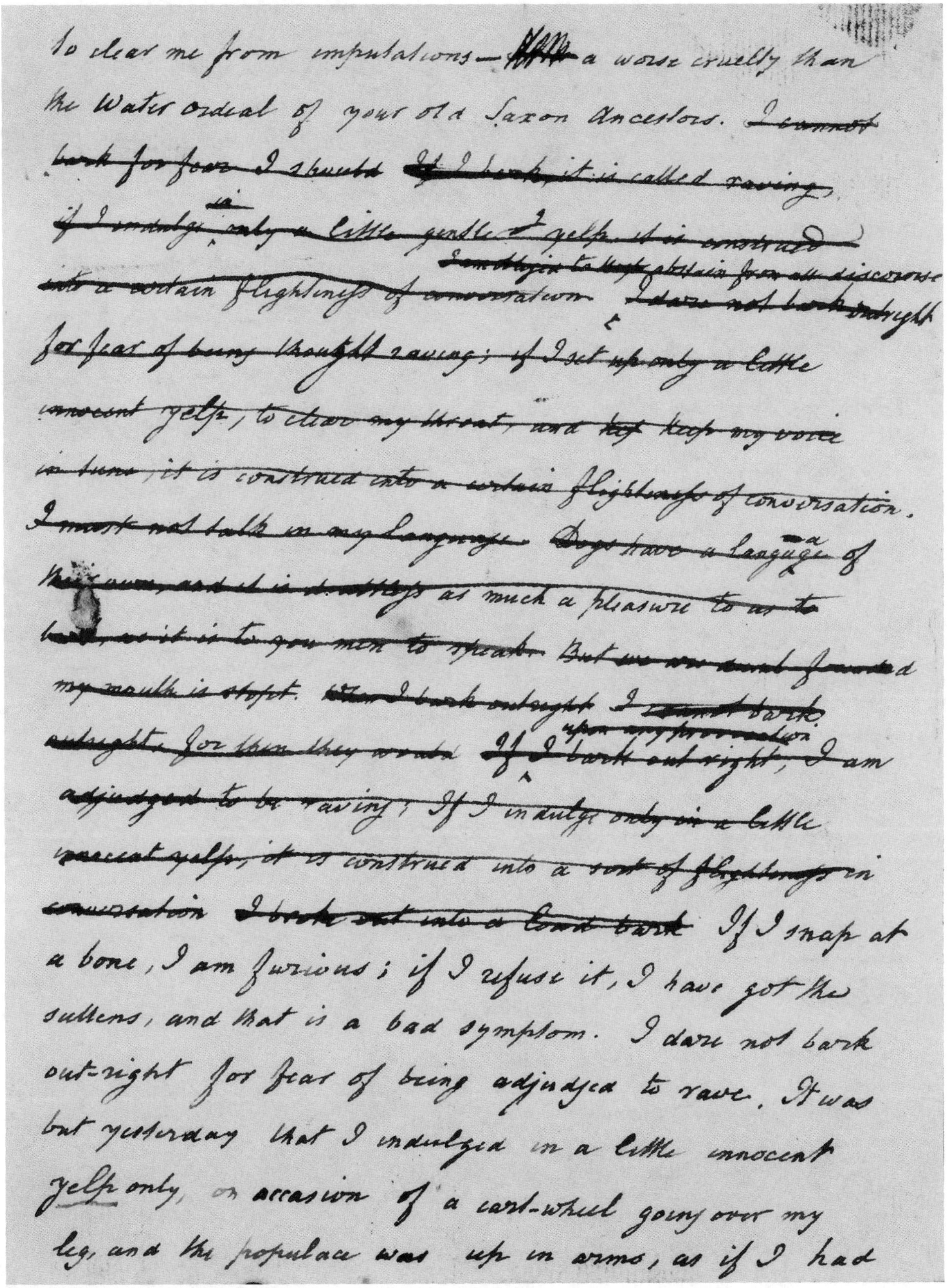

to clear me from imputations — ~~[illegible]~~ a worse cruelty than
the Water ordeal of your old Saxon Ancestors. ~~I cannot~~
~~bark for fear I should~~ ~~If I bark, it is called raving~~
~~if I indulge in only a little gentle yelp, it is construed~~
~~into a certain flightiness of conversation~~ ~~I am obliged to abstain from all discourse~~ ~~I dare not bark outright~~
~~for fear of being thought raving; if I set up only a little~~
~~innocent yelp, to clear my throat, and keep my voice~~
~~in tune, it is construed into a certain flightiness of conversation.~~
~~I must not talk in my Language~~ ~~Dogs have a language of~~
~~their own, and it is doubtless as much a pleasure to us to~~
~~bark as it is to you men to speak.~~ ~~But we are dumb~~
~~my mouth is stopt.~~ ~~When I bark outright~~ ~~I cannot bark~~
~~outright, for then they would~~ ~~If I upon any provocation bark out right, I am~~
~~adjudged to be raving; If I indulge only in a little~~
~~innocent yelp, it is construed into a sort of flightiness in~~
~~conversation~~ ~~I break out into a loud bark~~ If I snap at
a bone, I am furious; if I refuse it, I have got the
sullens, and that is a bad symptom. I dare not bark
out-right for fear of being adjudged to rave. It was
but yesterday that I indulged in a little innocent
yelp only, on occasion of a cart-wheel going over my
leg, and the populace was up in arms, as if I had

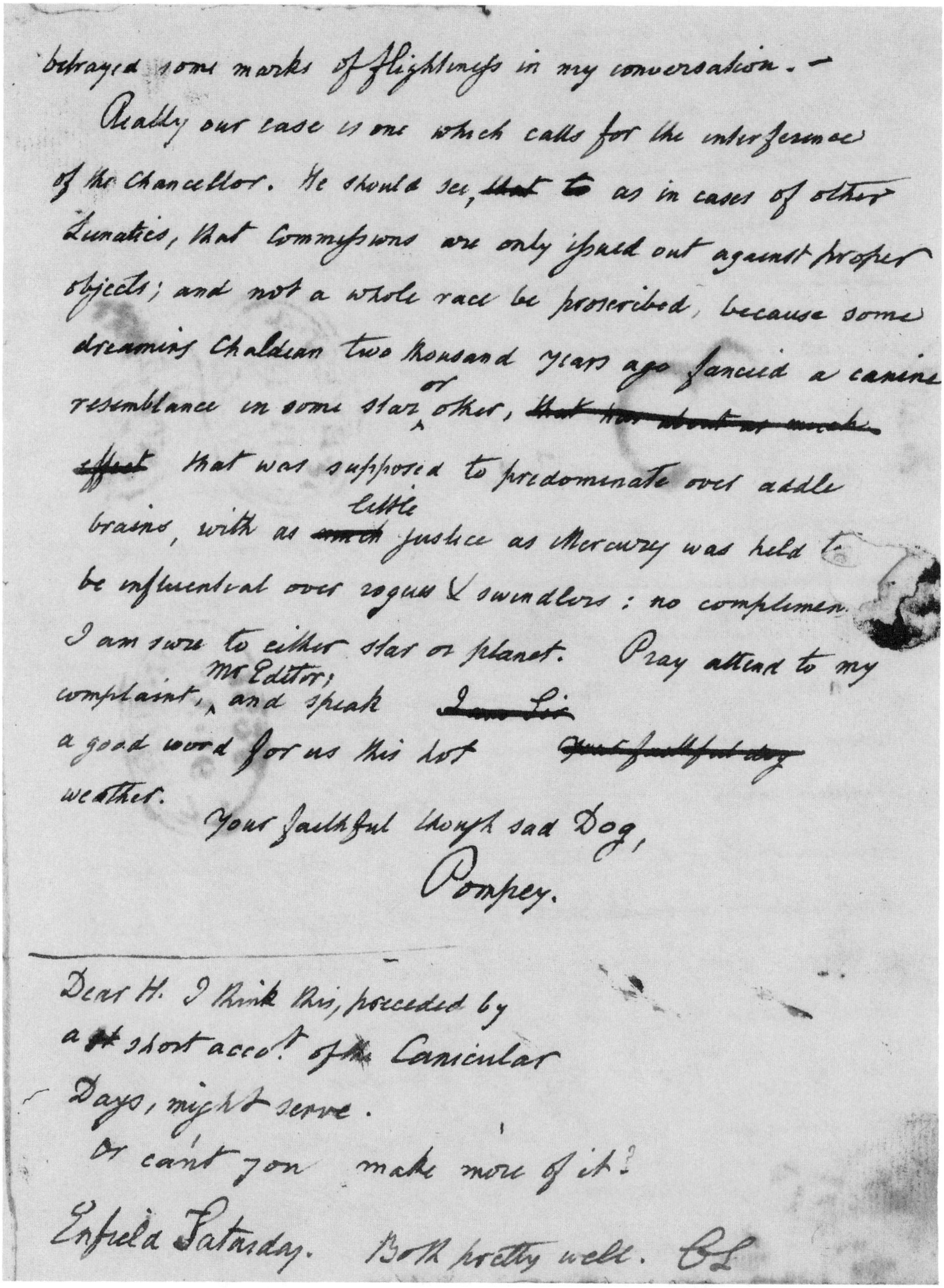

betrayed some marks of flightiness in my conversation. —

Really our case is one which calls for the interference of the Chancellor. He should see, ~~that~~ ~~to~~ as in cases of other Lunatics, that Commissions are only issued out against proper objects; and not a whole race be proscribed, because some dreaming Chaldean two thousand years ago fancied a canine resemblance in some star or other, ~~[illegible]~~ ~~effect~~ that was supposed to predominate over addle brains, with as ~~much~~ little justice as Mercury was held to be influential over rogues & swindlers: no complimen[t] I am sure to either star or planet. Pray attend to my complaint, Mr Editor; and speak ~~I am Sir~~ a good word for us this hot ~~[illegible]~~ weather.

Your faithful though sad Dog,

Pompey.

---

Dear H. I think this, preceded by a ~~[illegible]~~ short acco.t of the Canicular Days, might serve.

Or can't you make more of it?

Enfield Saturday. Both pretty well. CL

was cleared by a jury in 1817, but thereafter he was under a shadow and found himself hard-pressed for funds; much of his work on these volumes was done in debtors' prison. In the May 1825 *London Magazine* Lamb published a verse tribute to the unpopular Hone. Hone was deeply touched by this attention and dedicated his first *Every Day Book* to Lamb, who continued to help Hone in every way he could.

Having ceased to contribute to the *London Magazine*, which had again changed hands and lost its old luster (as well as many of its writers), Lamb continued to write for other publications—*Blackwood's*, the *New Monthly*, the *Spectator*, the *Athenaeum*, and Moxon's short-lived *Englishman's Magazine*, which he acquired in August 1831. The magazine died after Lamb had contributed to the August, September, and October numbers. During its brief run its contributors included not only Lamb but young writers of the future such as Alfred Tennyson and Arthur Henry Hallam. *Blackwood's* published Lamb's last two plays—*The Wife's Trial* (December 1828), a blank-verse drama, and *The Pawnbroker's Daughter* (January, 1830), a prose comedy which concerns the thorny path of true love for two couples including a lover who has been cut down from hanging (for a theft) after a last-minute reprieve—the third time Lamb had introduced this odd theme. Neither play was produced, neither enhanced his reputation, nor did the collection, *Album Verses* (1830) published by Moxon. These poems are verse tributes, written on request for the albums which some of Lamb's young lady friends kept in those days, and are not without charm. *Satan in Search of a Wife* (1831), a humorous ballad, was also negligible.

*Essays of Elia* had not sold well, but Moxon, who was gradually building a distinguished list of authors, including Wordsworth and Coleridge, agreed to publish *Last Essays of Elia* (1833), which also had a slow start. Yet, together with *Essays of Elia*, it was republished in more than a hundred editions and volumes of selections during the next hundred and fifty years. Before its London publication, *Last Essays of Elia*, or most of it, had already been pirated (as *Elia: Essays . . . Second Series*, 1828), in America, where Lamb's popularity became such that in 1892 Brander Matthews called him "one of the foremost American humorists." *Last Essays* was widely reviewed, especially following Lamb's death in 1834, when many tributes to him appeared in the press.

The Lambs left Islington in 1827, after only four years in the charming cottage, which still survives. Thereafter they spent various periods in lodgings and in a house in Enfield, further from the city and less accessible to friends (Lamb felt that too much society affected Mary Lamb adversely). They returned to London briefly in 1830, and in 1833 went to Edmonton, another suburb, to live in the home of the Frederick Waldens—where Mary would be cared for, their final abode. Hazlitt died in 1830 at fifty-two, and Lamb was one of the few mourners at his funeral.

After the loss of Emma Isola to Moxon earlier in 1833, both Lambs' health deteriorated. Charles was sometimes desperate, inclined to drink too much and to appear, when Mary was ill, at the doors of London friends in depressed and miserable condition. The death of Coleridge on 25 July 1834 was a severe blow. Lamb had occasionally visited him in recent years at Highgate, though oppressed by the presence of the host family (not Coleridge's own).

Always a strong walker—Lamb could cover fifteen miles at a stretch almost to the end—he was out one day at Edmonton, when he fell, hitting his face. Erysipelas developed and he died a few days later, on 27 December 1834, at fifty-nine. Mary Lamb lived on, cared for by attendants and watched over by friends. She became increasingly senile, and died in London on 20 May 1847 at eighty-two, having outlived Charles Lamb by more than twelve years. They are buried in the Edmonton churchyard—together, as for so long they had lived.

Jane Aaron's 1987 article, "Charles and Mary Lamb: The Critical Heritage" has provided a close and careful study of Lamb's reputation since 1834, supplementing George L. Barnett's 1976 account of Lamb's critical reception in his lifetime. (Barnett's *Charles Lamb* is invaluable, for scholar and student alike.) Aaron points out that Thomas Carlyle's denigration of Lamb in his *Reminiscences* (1881) and journals is based on few encounters, in particular an 1831 visit in which he found Lamb a poor, rundown creature, suffering from drink and "diluted insanity." Carlyle's report can be contrasted with that of Landor on his visit to the Lambs a year later: Landor was enchanted with the couple. One may point out, as Lamb himself did in his preface to *Last Essays*, that in life he was either loved or hated—and the same is true of his critical reception. A strong and distinct personality such as Lamb's will al-

*Mary and Charles Lamb in 1834 (portrait by F. S. Cary; National Portrait Gallery, London)*

ways conflict with other strong personalities if the mixture is inauspicious.

Wordsworth, who loved him, wrote in an epitaph intended for Lamb's tombstone: "Oh, he was good, if e'er a good Man lived!" The emphasis on Lamb's life of devotion to his sister, after Talfourd's *Final Memorials* (1848) had revealed the events of 22 September 1796, clouded Victorian estimates of his work. "Saint Charles!," the exclamation of William Makepeace Thackeray, provided an E. V. Lucas title, *At the Shrine of St. Charles*, as late as 1934. Thomas Babington Macaulay admired Lamb but took exception to Lamb's happy estimate of Restoration drama in his "On the Artificial Comedy of the Last Century": Macaulay was not the only one to find these comedies immoral. Lamb was almost a lone voice against the moralizing—with evil always punished and good always rewarded—of most of the nineteenth-century plays he saw. He expressed his views particularly in his *Specimens of English Dramatic Poets*, comparing this tendency to the freedom of the Elizabethans. After Macaulay criticized Lamb's view in an 1840 review of Leigh Hunt's edition of plays by Restoration dramatists Lamb was defended in print, probably by George Lewes. The "loving" estimate of Lamb, led by Swinburne, continued to be the prevailing view, reaching its apogee at the centenary of Lamb's death in 1934. Reaction was certain.

It came, says Aaron, most influentially, from F. R. Leavis and his followers, who, in the 1930s, were charting their own reassessment of English literature in the magazine *Scrutiny*, for which Denys Thompson wrote a 1934 article ironically titled "Our Debt to Lamb," which was republished the same year in *Determinations*, edited by Leavis. Its strictures also appeared in

*The grave of Charles and Mary Lamb in the Edmonton churchyard*

Thompson's guide for schools, *Reading and Discrimination* (1934), which went through several editions (including one in 1979, in which Lamb has disappeared altogether). Thompson accused Lamb of having reduced the great tradition of the English essay to charming whimsy and castigated an extract from Lamb's "The Praise of Chimney-Sweepers" as affected, pretentious, and a bad influence. Aaron believes that Thompson's critiques caused the banishment of the study of Lamb from British and American secondary schools, still the situation today. During the mid-twentieth century the "gentlemanly" approach to literature was increasingly rejected. Since the 1970s critics have, Aaron concludes, begun to reassert Lamb's value with new, mature approaches to his work.

Aaron's conclusion is optimistic. She believes that strictly didactic critical judgment is on the wane and is now being regarded as "suspect and lacking in subtlety, while emphatic suggestivity, irony, and a playful ambivalence" in writing are increasingly appreciated. She sees Lamb's reputation, therefore, as likely to "regain all its lost lustre, and to gleam ever more brightly into the twenty-first century."

The Charles Lamb Society in London now attracts a younger generation to its active local membership and international subscribers to its *Charles Lamb Bulletin*. Its officers continue to be distinguished professors, writers on Lamb, and devoted aficionados with long service to the society. It celebrates Lamb's birthday with an annual luncheon, provides lecture series and excursions, and keeps in touch with the present-day Christ's Hospital, now in the countryside south of London. If its new vitality and the new scholarship are any indication, Jane Aaron's happy prediction may not be farfetched.

**Letters:**

*The Letters of Charles Lamb, to Which Are Added Those of His Sister Mary Lamb*, 3 volumes, edited by E. V. Lucas (London: Dent/Methuen 1935; New Haven: Yale University Press, 1935);

*The Letters of Charles and Mary Anne Lamb*, 3 volumes to date, edited by Edwin W. Marrs, Jr. (Ithaca, N.Y., & London: Cornell University Press, 1975- ).

**Bibliographies:**

Luther S. Livingston, *A Bibliography of the First Editions in Book Form of the Writings of Charles and Mary Lamb Published Prior to Charles Lamb's Death in 1834* (New York: Printed for J. A. Spoor, 1903);

Thomas Hutchinson, "Bibliographical List (1794-1834) of the Published Writings of Charles and Mary Lamb," in *The Works of Charles Lamb*, edited by Hutchinson (London & New York: Oxford University Press, 1908), pp. xvii-xlvii;

Joseph C. Thomson, *Bibliography of the Writings of Charles and Mary Lamb* (Hull: Tutin, 1908);

George L. Barnett and Stuart M. Tave, "Charles Lamb," in *The English Romantic Poets & Essayists: A Review of Research and Criticism*, revised edition, edited by Carolyn Washburn Houtchens and Lawrence Huston Houtchens (New York: Published for the Modern Language Association of America by New York University Press, 1966), pp. 37-74.

**Biographies:**

T. N. Talfourd, "Sketch of Lamb's Life" in *The Letters of Charles Lamb, with a Sketch of his Life*, 2 volumes, edited by Talfourd (London: Moxon, 1840); revised version in *Final Memorials of Charles Lamb; consisting chiefly of his Letters not before published, with sketches of some of his Companions*, 2 volumes (London: Moxon, 1848);

Barry Cornwall (Bryan Waller Procter), *Charles Lamb: A Memoir* (London: Moxon, 1866; Boston: Roberts, 1866);

Alfred Ainger, *Charles Lamb*, English Men of Letters Series (London: Macmillan, 1882; New York: Harper, 1882);

Thomas De Quincey, "Recollections of Charles Lamb," in volume 3 of *The Collected Writings of Thomas De Quincey*, 14 volumes, edited by David Masson (Edinburgh: A. & C. Black, 1889-1890);

Benjamin E. Martin, *In the Footprints of Charles Lamb* (New York: Scribners, 1890; London: Bentley, 1891);

E. V. Lucas, *Charles Lamb and the Lloyds* (London: Smith, Elder, 1898);

Jules Derocquigny, *Charles Lamb: sa vie et ses oeuvres* (Lille: Le Bigot, 1904);

Lucas, *The Life of Charles Lamb*, 2 volumes (London: Methuen, 1905); revised edition, 1 volume (London: Methuen, 1921);

Thomas Hood, *Thomas Hood and Charles Lamb: The Story of a Friendship, Being the Literary Reminiscences of Thomas Hood*, edited, "with certain additions," by Walter C. Jerrold (London: Benn, 1930);

Edmund Blunden, comp., *Charles Lamb: His Life Recorded by His Contemporaries* (London: Leonard & Virginia Woolf at the Hogarth Press, 1934);

Henry Crabb Robinson, *Henry Crabb Robinson on Books and Their Writers*, 3 volumes, edited by Edith J. Morley (London: Dent, 1938);

Ernest C. Ross, *The Ordeal of Bridget Elia: A Chronicle of the Lambs* (Norman: University of Oklahoma Press, 1940);

Will D. Howe, *Charles Lamb and His Friends* (New York & Indianapolis: Bobbs-Merrill, 1944);

Winifred F. Courtney, *Young Charles Lamb, 1775-1802* (London: Macmillan, 1982; New York: New York University Press, 1982);

David Cecil, *A Portrait of Charles Lamb* (London: Constable, 1983).

**References:**

Jane Aaron, "Charles and Mary Lamb: The Critical Heritage," *Charles Lamb Bulletin*, new series 59 (July 1987): 73-85;

Aaron, "We Are in a Manner Marked: Images of Damnation in Charles Lamb's Writings," *Charles Lamb Bulletin*, new series 33 (January 1981): 1-10;

John I. Ades, "Charles Lamb—Romantic Criticism and the Aesthetics of Sympathy," *Delta Epsilon Sigma Bulletin*, 6 (December 1961): 106-114;

Ades, "Charles Lamb, Shakespeare, and Early Nineteenth-Century Theater," *PMLA*, 85 (May 1970): 514-526;

R. C. Bald, "Charles Lamb and the Elizabethans," *University of Missouri Studies*, 21 (1946): 169-174;

George L. Barnett, *Charles Lamb* (Boston: Twayne, 1976);

Barnett, *The Evolution of Elia*, Indiana University Humanities Series, no. 53 (Bloomington, 1964);

Barnett, "The History of Charles Lamb's Reputation," *Charles Lamb Bulletin*, new series 10-11 (April-July 1975): 22-33;

Jonathan Bate, "Lamb on Shakespeare," *Charles Lamb Bulletin*, new series 51 (July 1985): 76-85;

Gillian Beer, "Lamb's Women," *Charles Lamb Bulletin*, new series 47-48 (July-October 1984): 138-143;

John Beer, "Did Lamb Understand Coleridge?," *Charles Lamb Bulletin*, new series 56 (October 1986): 232-249;

Ernest Bernbaum, "Charles Lamb," in his *Guide Through the Romantic Movement*, second edition, revised and enlarged, (New York: Ronald Press, 1949);

Edmund Blunden, *Charles Lamb and His Contemporaries* (Cambridge: Cambridge University Press, 1933);

Blunden, "Elia and Christ's Hospital," *Essays and Studies by Members of The English Association*, 22 (1937): 37-60;

F. S. Boas, "Charles Lamb and the Elizabethan Dramatists," *Essays and Studies by Members of The English Association*, 29 (1944): 62-81;

*Charles Lamb Society Bulletin* (1935-1972); new series, *Charles Lamb Bulletin* (1973- );

Winifred F. Courtney, "Charles Lamb and John Keats: The Relationship," *Bulletin of Research in the Humanities*, 87 (1986-1987): 82-100;

Courtney, "*Mrs. Leicester's School* as Children's Literature," *Charles Lamb Bulletin*, new series 47-48 (July-October 1984): 164-169;

Courtney, "New Lamb Texts from *The Albion*?," *Charles Lamb Bulletin*, part 1, new series 17 (January 1977): 1-11; part 2, 18 (April 1977): 28-40; part 3, 20 (October 1977): 73-92;

T. W. Craik, "Charles and Mary Lamb: *Tales from Shakespear*," *Charles Lamb Bulletin*, new series 49 (January 1985): 2-14;

Angus Easson, "The Musician and the Nightingale: Charles Lamb and the Elizabethan Drama," *Charles Lamb Bulletin*, new series 29 (January 1980): 85-99;

Jeremiah S. Finch, "Charles Lamb's Companionship . . . in Almost Solitude," *Princeton University Library Chronicle*, 6 (June 1945): 177-199;

Finch, "The Scribner Lamb Collection," *Princeton University Library Chronicle*, 7 (June 1946): 133-148;

Finch, "The Taylor Lamb Collection," *Charles Lamb Bulletin*, new series 55 (July 1986): 229;

William Flesch, "Friendly and Judicious Reading: Affect and Irony in the Works of Charles Lamb," *Studies in Romanticism*, 23 (Summer 1984): 163-181;

R. A. Foakes, "The Authentic Voice: Lamb and the Familiar Letter," *Charles Lamb Bulletin*, new series 9 (January 1975): 1-10;

Basil Francis, *Fanny Kelly of Drury Lane* (London: Rockliff, 1950);

Robert D. Frank, *Don't Call Me Gentle Charles!* (Corvallis: Oregon State University Press, 1976);

Leslie Joan Friedman, "Mary Lamb: Sister, Seamstress, Murderer, Writer," Ph.D. dissertation, Stanford University, 1976;

Joel Haefner, "Incondite Things: Experimentation and the Romantic Essay," *Prose Studies*, 10 (September 1987): 196-206;

Richard Haven, "The Romantic Art of Charles Lamb," *Journal of English Literary History*, 30 (June 1963): 137-146;

William Hazlitt, *The Complete Works of William Hazlitt*, Centenary Edition, 21 volumes, edited by P. P. Howe (London: Dent, 1930-1934), VIII: 232 ff; XII: 35-38; XVII: 122-134; XVIII: 210-211;

Alan G. Hill, "Lamb and Wordsworth: The Story of a Remarkable Friendship," *Charles Lamb Bulletin*, new series 37 (January 1982): 85-92;

Reginald L. Hine, *Charles Lamb and His Hertfordshire* (London: Dent, 1949);

Walter E. Houghton, Jr., "Lamb's Criticism of Restoration Comedy," *Journal of English Literary History*, 10 (March 1943): 61-72;

Edith C. Johnson, *Lamb Always Elia* (London: Methuen, 1935);

Molly Lefebure, "The Crowning Art of Elia," *Charles Lamb Bulletin*, new series 68 (October 1989): 109-120;

Thomas Manning, *The Letters of Thomas Manning to Charles Lamb*, edited by G. A. Anderson (London: Secker, 1925);

Edwin W. Marrs, Jr., *A Descriptive Catalogue of the Letters of Charles and Mary Lamb in the W. Hugh Peal Collection*, Occasional Paper no. 7, December 1984 (Lexington: University of Kentucky Libraries, 1984);

Brander Matthews, Introduction to *The Dramatic Essays of Charles Lamb*, edited by Matthews (New York: Dodd, Mead, 1892);

Thomas McFarland, "Charles Lamb and the Politics of Survival," in his *Romantic Cruxes: The English Essayists and the Spirit of the Age* (Oxford: Clarendon Press, 1987);

Samuel McKechnie, "Charles Lamb of the India House," *Notes and Queries*, 191 (2 November 1946): 178-180; 191 (16 November 1946): 204-206; 191 (30 November 1946): 225-230; 191 (14 December 1946): 252-256; 191 (28 December 1946): 277-280; 192 (11 January 1947): 9-13; 192 (25 January 1947): 25-29; 192 (8 February 1947): 53-56; 192 (15 February 1947): 72-73; 192 (8 March 1947): 103-106;

Carolyn Misenheimer, "The Pleasures of Early Enlightenment: The Lambs' *Tales from Shakespeare*," *Charles Lamb Bulletin*, new series 67 (July 1989): 69-82;

James B. Misenheimer, Jr., "The Nostalgia of Elia 150 Years After," *Charles Lamb Bulletin*, new series 53 (January 1986): 128-141;

Gerald Monsman, *Confessions of a Prosaic Dreamer: Charles Lamb's Art of Autobiography* (Durham, N.C.: Duke University Press, 1984);

Monsman, "Pater's 'Child in the House' and the Renovation of the Self," *Studies in Literature and Language*, 28 (Fall 1986): 281-295;

Daniel J. Mulcahy, "Charles Lamb: The Antithetical Manner and the Two Planes," *Studies in English Literature*, 3 (Autumn 1963): 517-542;

John R. Nabholtz, "Drama and Rhetoric in Lamb's Essays of the Imagination," *Studies in English Literature*, 12 (1972): 683-703;

Nabholtz, "Elia and the Transformed Reader," in his *My Reader, My Fellow-Labourer: A Study of English Romantic Prose* (Columbia: University of Missouri Press, 1986);

Wallace Nethery, *Charles Lamb in America to 1848* (Worcester, Mass.: St. Onge, 1963);

Nethery, *Eliana Americana: Charles Lamb in the United States 1849-1866* (Los Angeles: Plantin Press, 1971);

Roy Park, Introduction to *Lamb as Critic*, edited by Park (London & Henley: Routledge & Kegan Paul, 1980);

Park, "Lamb, Shakespeare, and the Stage," *Shakespeare Quarterly*, 33 (Summer 1982): 164-177;

Walter Pater, "Charles Lamb," in his *Appreciations* (London & New York: Macmillan, 1889);

P. G. Patmore, "Charles Lamb," *Personal Recollections of Lamb, Hazlitt, and Others*, edited by R. H. Stoddard (New York: Scribner, Armstrong, 1875): 3-47;

Burton R. Pollin, "Charles Lamb and Charles Lloyd as Jacobins and Anti-Jacobins," *Studies in Romanticism*, 12 (Summer 1973): 633-647;

Claude A. Prance, *Companion to Charles Lamb: A Guide to People and Places, 1760-1847* (London: Mansell, 1983);

Fred V. Randel, *The World of Elia* (Port Washington, N.Y.: Kennikat Press, 1975);

Donald H. Reiman, "Thematic Unity in Lamb's Familiar Essays" (1965), Chapter 13, *Romantic Texts and Contexts* (Columbia, Mo.: University of Missouri Press, 1987);

S. M. Rich, comp.: *The Elian Miscellany: A Charles Lamb Anthology* (London: Joseph, 1931);

Joseph E. Riehl, *Charles Lamb's Children's Literature* (Salzburg: Institut für Anglistik und Amerikanistik, 1980);

Riehl, "Charles Lamb's Essays on Education: Christ's Hospital and the Growth of Elia," *Publications of the Arkansas Philological Association*, 8 (Spring 1982): 42-52;

Riehl, "Charles Lamb's *Mrs. Leicester's School* and Elia: The Fearful Imagination," *Charles Lamb Bulletin*, new series 39 (July 1982): 138-143;

Frank P. Riga and Claude A. Prance, *Index to The London Magazine* (New York & London: Garland, 1978);

Mark B. Robson, "Charles Lamb: The Dramatist and Drama Critic," *Publications of the Arkansas Philological Association*, 11 (Fall 1985): 75-89;

Ernest C. Ross, *Charles Lamb and Emma Isola* (London: Charles Lamb Society, 1950);

William Ruddick, "Beautiful Bare Narratives: Charles Lamb's Response to Eighteenth-Century Fiction," *Charles Lamb Bulletin*, new series 47-48 (July-October 1984): 158-164;

Gillian Russell, "Lamb's *Specimens of English Dramatic Poets*: The Publishing Context and the Principles of Selection," *Charles Lamb Bulletin*, new series 65 (January 1989): 1-8;

Thomas B. Stroup, "On Lamb's Style," *English Studies*, 14 (April 1932): 79-81;

Geoffrey Tillotson, "The Historical Importance of Certain 'Essays of Elia,' " in *Some British Romantics*, edited by James Logan and others (Columbus: Ohio State University Press 1966), pp. 89-116;

E. M. W. Tillyard, Introduction to *Lamb's Criticism*, edited by Tillyard (Cambridge: Cambridge University Press, 1923);

A. C. Ward, *The Frolic and the Gentle: A Centenary Study of Charles Lamb* (London: Methuen, 1934);

J. R. Watson, "Lamb and Food," *Charles Lamb Bulletin*, new series 54 (April 1986): 160-175;

Melvin P. Watson, "The *Spectator* Tradition and the Development of the Familiar Essay," *Journal of English Literary History*, 13 (September 1946): 189-215;

Mary R. Wedd, "Charles Lamb: Friend and Critic," *Charles Lamb Bulletin*, new series 51 (July 1985): 61-76;

Wedd, "Lamb as a Critic of Wordsworth," *Charles Lamb Bulletin*, new series 41 (January 1983): 1-16;

Wedd, " 'That Dangerous Figure—Irony,' " *Charles Lamb Bulletin*, new series 73 (January 1991): 1-12;

George Whalley, "Coleridge's Debt to Charles Lamb," *Essays and Studies by Members of the English Association*, new series 11 (1958): 68-85;

George Wherry, ed., *Cambridge and Charles Lamb* (Cambridge: Cambridge University Press, 1925);

Carl R. Woodring, "Charles Lamb in the Harvard Library," *Harvard Library Bulletin*, 10 (Spring 1956): 208-239; 10 (Autumn 1956): 367-402;

Woodring, "Charles Lamb Takes a Holiday," *Harvard Library Bulletin*, 14 (Spring 1960): 253-264.

**Papers:**

There are significant collections in the Henry E. Huntington Library, the New York Public Library, the Pierpont Morgan Library, the British Library, and libraries at Harvard University, Yale University, Princeton University, the University of Texas, and the University of Kentucky. The Charles Lamb Society Library, which holds some autograph items, is now housed in the Guildhall Library, London.

# Walter Savage Landor

*(30 January 1775 - 17 September 1864)*

Keith Hanley
*University of Lancaster*

See also the Landor entry in *DLB 93: British Romantic Poets, 1789-1832: First Series.*

BOOKS: *The Poems of Walter Savage Landor* (London: Printed for T. Cadell & W. Davies, 1795);

*Moral Epistle, Respectfully dedicated to Earl Stanhope* (London: Printed for Cadell & W. Davies, 1795);

*To the Burgesses of Warwick* (Warwick, 1797); edited by R. H. Super (Oxford: Printed for the Luttrell Society by B. Blackwell, 1949);

*Gebir; A Poem in Seven Books* (London: Sold by Rivingtons, 1798; enlarged and corrected edition, Oxford: Printed by & for Slatter & Munday & sold by R. S. Kirby, London, 1803); translated by Landor as *Gebirus, Poema* (Oxford: Printed & sold by Slatter & Munday & sold by R. S. Kirby, London, 1803);

*Poems from the Arabic and Persian* (Warwick: Printed by H. Sharpe & sold by Rivingtons, London, 1800);

*Iambi* (Oxford: Privately printed, circa 1802);

*Poetry by the Author of Gebir* (London: Sold by F. & C. Rivington, 1802);

*Simonidea* (Bath: Printed by W. Meyler & sold by G. Robinson, London, 1806);

*Three Letters, Written in Spain, to D. Francisco Riguelme Commanding the Third Division of the Gallician Army* (Bath: Printed by W. Meyler & sold by J. Robinson and J. Harding, London, 1809);

*Ode ad Gustavum Regem. Ode ad Gustavum Exulem* (London: Printed by A. J. Valpy, 1810);

*Count Julian: A Tragedy* (London: Printed for John Murray by James Moyes, 1812);

*Commentary on Memoirs of Mr. Fox* [printed but suppressed] (London: Printed for the author by T. Davison & sold by J. Murray, 1812); edited by Stephen Wheeler as *Charles James Fox, A Commentary on his Life and Character* (New York: Putnam's, 1907; London: J. Murray, 1907);

*Letter from Mr. Landor to Mr. Jervis* (Bath, 1814);

*Letters addressed to Lord Liverpool, and The Parliament, on the Preliminaries of Peace, by Calvus* (London: Printed for Henry Colburn & sold by George Goldie, Edinburgh, 1814);

*Idyllia Nova Quinque Heroum atque Heroidum* (Oxford: Sold by Slatter & Munday & by Longman, Hurst, Rees, Orme & Brown, London, 1815);

*Sponsalia Polyxenae* (Pistoia, 1819);

*Idyllia Heroica Decem* (Pisa: S. Nistri, 1820);

*Poche Osservazioni* (Naples, 1821);

*Imaginary Conversations of Literary Men and Statesmen,* volumes 1 and 2 (London: Printed for Taylor & Hessey, 1824; corrected and enlarged edition, London: H. Colburn, 1826);

*Imaginary Conversations of Literary Men and Statesmen,* volume 3 (London: Henry Colburn, 1828);

*Imaginary Conversations of Literary Men and Statesmen . . . Second Series,* 2 volumes (London: James Duncan, 1829);

*Gebir, Count Julian, and Other Poems* (London: E. Moxon, 1831);

*Citation and Examination of William Shakspeare* (London: Saunders & Otley, 1834; Boston: Roberts Brothers, 1888);

*Pericles and Aspasia* (2 volumes, London: Saunders & Otley, 1836; abridged, unauthorized edition, Philadelphia: Carey & Hart, 1839; complete edition, 1 volume, Boston: Roberts Brothers, 1871);

*The Letters of a Conservative* (London: Saunders & Otley, 1836);

*A Satire on Satirists, and Admonition to Detractors* (London: Saunders & Otley, 1836);

*Terry Hogan: An Eclogue* (London: Printed by J. Wertheimer, 1836);

*The Pentameron and Pentalogia* (London: Saunders & Otley, 1837); republished in *The Pentameron etc.* (Boston: Roberts Brothers, 1888);

*Andrea of Hungary, and Giovanna of Naples* (London: R. Bentley, 1839);

*Walter Savage Landor, circa 1854 (portrait by Robert Faulkner; National Portrait Gallery, London)*

*Fra Rupert, The last part of a Trilogy* (London: Saunders & Otley, 1840);

*The Works of Walter Savage Landor,* 2 volumes (London: E. Moxon, 1846);

*The Hellenics of Walter Savage Landor. Enlarged and Completed* (London: E. Moxon, 1847); enlarged as *The Hellenics of Walter Savage Landor; comprising Heroic Idyls, &c.* (Edinburgh: J. Nichol / London: R. Griffin, 1859);

*Poemata et Inscriptiones* (London: E. Moxon, 1847);

*The Italics of Walter Savage Landor* (London: Reynell & Weight, 1848);

*Imaginary Conversation of King Carlo-Alberto and the Duchess Belgioioso, on the Affairs and Prospects of Italy* (London: Longman, Brown, Green & Longmans, 1848);

*Statement of Occurrences at Llanbedr* (Bath: Printed by Meyler & Son, 1849);

*Popery: British and Foreign* (London: Chapman & Hall, 1851);

*Tyrannicide* (N.p., 1851);

*Imaginary Conversations of Greeks and Romans* (London: E. Moxon, 1853);

*The Last Fruit off an Old Tree* (London: E. Moxon, 1853);

*Letters of an American, mainly on Russia and Revolution* (London: Chapman & Hall, 1854);

*Antony and Octavius. Scenes for the Study* (London: Bradbury & Evans, 1856);

*Letter from W. S. Landor to R. W. Emerson* (Bath: E. Williams, 1856);

*Selections from the Writings of Walter Savage Landor,* edited by George Stillman Hillard (Boston: Ticknor & Fields, 1856);

*Walter Savage Landor and the Honourable Mrs. Yescombe* (Bath, 1857);

*Mr. Landor Threatened* (Bath, 1857);

*Landor's birthplace, Warwick, in Staffordshire*

*Dry Sticks, Fagoted by Walter Savage Landor* (Edinburgh: J. Nichol / London: J. Nisbet, 1858);

*Mr. Landor's Remarks On a Suit Preferred against him, at the Summer Assizes at Taunton, 1858* (London: Holyoake, 1859);

*Savonarola e il Priore di San Marco* (Florence, 1860);

*Heroic Idyls, with additional poems* (London: T. C. Newby, 1863);

*Imaginary Conversations,* 5 volumes (Boston: Roberts, 1876-1877).

**Editions:** *Imaginary Conversations,* 6 volumes; *Poems, Dialogues in Verse and Epigrams,* 2 volumes; and *The Longer Prose Works,* 2 volumes, edited by Charles G. Crump (London: Dent, 1891-1893);

*The Complete Works of Walter Savage Landor,* 16 volumes: volumes 1-12 [prose] edited by T. Earle Welby, volumes 13-16 edited by Stephen Wheeler (London: Chapman & Hall, 1927-1936); volumes 13-16 republished as *The Poetical Works of Walter Savage Landor,* 3 volumes (Oxford: Clarendon Press, 1937);

*Landor as Critic,* edited by Charles L. Proudfit (London: Routledge & Kegan Paul, 1979);

*Walter Savage Landor. Selected Poetry and Prose,* edited by Keith Hanley (Manchester: Carcanet Press, 1981).

Walter Savage Landor is one of those authors who—like Thomas Hardy, George Meredith, or Rudyard Kipling—is equally known as a prose writer and a poet. He started as a poet and later experimented with verse drama, but, though he continued his efforts in those genres throughout an unusually long and varied career, it was only in middle life that he was to discover the medium through which he finally won a measure of fame: the prose dialogues to which he gave the name *Imaginary Conversations.*

The format for these Conversations, which number more than 150 (and for the other prose works which developed it), derived from the classical tradition of the dialogue. It has been suggested that their concrete settings are associated with the philosophical dialogue introduced by

Plato, that the blending of conversation and didacticism recalls the dialogues of Xenophon (and later Galileo), and that the practice of inserting lengthy poems is comparable to that of Boethius. The greatest classical influence on Landor's discursive Conversations is Cicero, especially in the use of historical characters. Mediating this various classical tradition, however, is the modern one (itself started by Lucian) of "Dialogues of the Dead," popularized by Fénélon, Fontenelle, George, Lord Lyttleton (closest to Landor), and Bishop Richard Hurd, who first applied the term *conversation* to this kind of literature.

Landor's Conversations are notable for the vast range of historical, mythical, and occasionally invented characters he assumes. They are mostly West European, especially English and Italian from all periods down to his own day, though some are Russian, Oriental, and American. Yet his own attitudes (and often his hobbyhorses) preside throughout, and when they are too much to the fore the Conversations become little more than essays. A favored and characteristic alternative kind is the dramatic scene of a heroic, tragic, or pathetic nature. Overall, his originality rests on a fastidious and highly artificial prose style and, often in combination, a succinct portrayal of character.

His chief interests, as the title of the first two series of *Imaginary Conversations* makes plain, were in "Literary Men and Statesmen," though there is also a group of twenty-two dialogues which features famous women. Politically, Landor voiced loudly the Whig side in English politics and took every opportunity to ridicule William Pitt and George Canning, sometimes in classical disguises. He became a leading English proponent of liberal republicanism whose unvarying target was, as he expressed it to a friend, "The conspiracy of kings, first against all republics, now openly against all constitutions."

A recent editor of Landor, Charles L. Proudfit, has illustrated the extent of Landor's interest in a highly individualistic literary criticism of ancient and modern authors, not just in formal reviews and essays, but as a preoccupation throughout all his writings. His favorite topics are Greek dramatists, Greek and Latin poetry, medieval and Renaissance Italian writers (particularly Dante), Chaucer, English Renaissance drama (particularly Shakespeare), and English poetry from Alexander Pope to Landor's contemporaries (particularly Robert Southey and William Wordsworth). His minute textual comments, which specialize in lively responses to concrete details, are spiced and sometimes vitiated by the kind of idiosyncrasy described by Henry Crabb Robinson when he first met him in 1830:

> Of his literary judgments the following are specimens:—Of Dante, about a seventieth part is good; of Ariosto, a tenth; of Tasso, not a line worth anything,—yes, *one* line. He declared almost all Wordsworth to be good. Landor was as dogmatic on paintings as well as on poetry. . . . His judgment was amusingly at variance with popular opinion. He thought nothing of Michael Angelo as a painter; and, as a sculptor, preferred John of Bologna.

Landor's temperament was notoriously impetuous and contradictory. Charles Dickens's portrait of his friend in Lawrence Boythorn in *Bleak House* (1852-1853) is representative of many: "He is always in extremes; perpetually in the superlative degree." William Butler Yeats recognized the creative control that such tumultuousness required and saw in its repression the origin of Landor's classic restraint: "The most violent of men, he uses his intellect to disengage a visionary image of perfect sanity . . . seen always in the most serene and classic art imaginable." Yeats's own motto, "Hammer your thoughts into unity," echoes Landor's imaginary Porson on the struggle between energy and form: "After all our argumentation, we merely estimate poets by their energy, and not extol them for a congeries of piece on piece, sounding of the hammer all day long, but obstinately unmalleable into unity and cohesion."

The kind of "hard" formal organization that in this century has made Landor the object of admiring emulation by modernist poets such as Yeats and Ezra Pound (who attaches that adjective to Landor's style) is most evident in his characteristic epigrams and idylls, but it is equally observable in the taut structures of his dramatic scenes and a corresponding kind of heroic Conversation. Yet what marks off many of Landor's prose works from his poetry is their tendency to relax formal rigidity and emotional restraint. As Pound also wrote of the *Imaginary Conversations*, they embody "all culture of the encyclopedists reduced to manageable size," but they are "full of human life ventilated, given a human body, not merely indexed." Landor told Robert Browning that in his prose works he found "more room" than in his poetry. Indicatively, whereas Landor, who constantly revised his texts throughout life, progres-

*Landor in 1804 (engraving by J. Brown, after a portrait by George Dance)*

sively pared down and reduced his poetic language, he tended rather to expansiveness and the addition of material in his prose. He increasingly allowed his Conversations to sprawl in the manner advocated by his imaginary Milton: "In conversation, as in the country, variety is pleasant and expected." Most interesting, perhaps, is the interplay between Landor's hold on his imaginary speakers and the way in which they enable him to "let himself go," with the result, as he also told Browning, that he became "more a dramatist in prose than in poetry."

Born at Warwick, Walter Savage Landor was the eldest son of Walter Landor, a physician who inherited a large landed estate at Rugeley, Staffordshire, and his second wife, Elizabeth Savage, an heiress from an old Warwickshire family. (One of their younger children was the poet-dramatist Robert Eyres Landor.) He was eventually to inherit the family properties, and, though disastrous mismanagement was to lead to his voluntary exile on an agreed allowance, his independence freed him from the need to make his writing profitable. It also supported his patrician bearing as an English "milord" during his Italian period, when it even financed a pioneering, if sometimes dubious, connoisseurship in Italian primitive painting.

His character problems were deeply ingrained. He was expelled from Rugby School, where he was educated from 1783 to 1791, for insubordination, and sent down from Trinity College, Oxford, where he was a student from 1792 to 1794, over a prankish shooting incident. The crucial role model in his early youth was Samuel Parr, perpetual curate of Hatton near Warwick and noted conversationalist, particularly in his combination of contemporary liberal politics and classical scholarship (more prevalent in the Cambridge than the Oxford of Landor's day) and a cultivation of the Ciceronian style.

After Oxford, Landor quarreled with his father and gave himself to the acquisition of modern languages in London, political controversy, writing poetry, and making love. In 1795 he brought out as his first publications: a book of undergraduate poetry, *The Poems of Walter Savage Landor*, and a satire against Pitt, the *Moral Epistle* in heroic verse, dedicated to the pro-French Charles, Earl Stanhope.

He next moved to South Wales, where he studied Pindar and Milton, and also sired an illegitimate baby, who died in early childhood. It was at Swansea in 1796 that he met Rose Aylmer, whose early death from cholera at Calcutta was to be the origin of one of his best-known epigrams. There too he began his first notable work, the Oriental heroic poem *Gebir*, which he had inconspicuously printed in Warwick in 1798. The most enthusiastic of its few reviewers was Robert Southey in the *Critical Review* for September 1799, thereby laying the ground for what was to become Landor's longest and most significant literary friendship.

The following years, before his father's death in 1805, were desultory. For a while he returned to London to dabble in Whig journalism, writing for the *Courier*, and coming under attack from the *Anti-Jacobin Review and Magazine*. He shared the Whigs' exasperation when, on Pitt's resignation, the Addington ministry was appointed through royal influence in 1801, and, having visited Paris after the Peace of Amiens in 1802 and personally witnessing the acclamation of Napoleon as a new despot, he lamented the ruin of the French Revolution and conceived the hilarious anti-Gallicism that is often evidenced in his works. He recanted his support for Napoleon and the Revolution in the notes to the second edition of *Gebir* in 1803.

His personal life was unsettled. At Bath in 1802 he fell in love with Jane Sophia Swift, his grand passion and the "Ianthe" of his poems. Though she married the following year, they probably remained lovers for some time and were to meet each other occasionally in Italy and England. The main achievement of the next few years was the slender *Simonidea* (1806), containing many of his best-known epigrams. Some are elegiac, but most are love poems to Ianthe and others. The book was produced provincially and anonymously.

At Bristol in 1808 he had the good fortune to meet Southey, who had avoided him as "a mad Jacobin" at Oxford. They were to meet again only rarely, but their mutually supportive correspondence was of importance to both. Landor successfully encouraged Southey to resume writing poetry in 1808 by offering to pay for its publication, while Southey introduced Landor to Wordsworth's poetry and helped preserve his self-esteem in exile. More specifically, it was Southey's example that promoted Landor's efforts at drama in 1812 and at dialogues in 1820.

More generally, however, Landor's thirties were marked by a series of rash undertakings, some of which shaped the rest of his life. At the end of 1807 Landor decided to sell the family estate, together with part of his mother's property, so as to buy Llanthony Abbey, Monmouthshire, a ruined thirteenth-century Austin priory, and the Ewias valley, in which it is located. In August 1808 he impulsively joined in the Spanish revolt against Napoleon. He sailed to Corunna, where he handed over ten thousand reals for the relief of the inhabitants of Venturada, which had been burned by the French, and he raised a body of volunteers with whom he marched to join the Spanish army. With the signing of the Convention of Cintra on 30 August, he returned to England, and the following year he published his violently anti-Napoleonic *Three Letters, Written in Spain* (1809), addressed to the Spanish general Francisco Riguelme.

A more lasting production was his first poetic drama, *Count Julian: A Tragedy* (1812), written at Bath between November 1810 and January 1811. It was probably suggested by Southey's *Roderick, the Last of the Goths* (1814), part of which was sent to Landor in manuscript in July 1810. It is centered on the tragic predicament of a Christian general who can only avenge the dishonoring of his daughter by admitting Moslem arms into the heart of Spain. Like all Landor's "dramatic" efforts in verse and prose, *Count Julian* suffers from a complete lack of action. In the 1846 edition of his *Works*, it was printed together with other pieces, including his later dramas, under the heading "Acts and Scenes" with the following note: "None of these poems of a dramatic form were offered to the stage, being no better than *Imaginary Conversations* in metre." When Landor offered it to Longmans for publication, they declined to print it even at the author's own cost, whereupon Landor burned another unpublished play. It was eventually brought out at Landor's ex-

*Julia Landor with her children Julia and Arnold, circa 1825 (portrait by Trajan Wallis; from Malcolm Elwin,* Landor. A Replevin, *1958)*

pense by John Murray, through Southey's good offices.

With characteristic recklessness, after a courtship of only several months, he married a seventeen-year-old girl, Julia Thuillier, at Bath on 24 May 1811. He took his bride, the daughter of an unwealthy banker, to inhabit part of the ruined abbey while they awaited the building of a new house. It was an uneasy match for a man with an unpredictable disposition. After three years they were to separate temporarily, but they reunited for a period of twenty years during which they had four children.

Over the three years following his marriage, Landor's high-handed experiments in landlordism and overambitious schemes for improvement entangled him in litigation and brought him to the brink of financial ruin. Henceforth, his scorn for the Welsh was second only to that for the French. In May 1814 he retreated to the Continent, leaving the estate in the hands of a family trustee in return for a generous provision for his maintenance.

His mind had been preoccupied throughout this disaster by political and literary affairs. He completed a collection of Latin verse and a comedy, "The Charitable Dowager," supposed to have been written at Bath in 1687 by "Hardcastle." It was never printed. His *Commentary on Memoirs of Mr. Fox* (1812) is a miscellaneous collection of lively opinions on politics and literature, prompted by a review-article in the *Quarterly Review* for December 1811 by Canning and George Ellis on John Bernard Trotter's *Memoirs of Mr. Fox.* It was printed but suppressed by its publisher, John Murray, after his attention had been drawn to its attacks on Canning and its dedication to President James Madison, with whose country England was shortly to be at war.

Landor in 1826 (drawing by William Bewick; British Museum)

After leaving England, the Landors lived for a year at Tours, but with the restoration of the Bourbons after Waterloo they traveled to Como, where they settled for the next three years, until Landor was ordered to leave in the autumn of 1818 after threatening a magistrate with a thrashing. He had been summoned on a charge of libeling an Italian poet in some insulting verses. By the end of the year the family arrived at Pisa, where they stayed until September 1821. There he published a collection of Latin poetry, and pamphlets against the Holy Alliance. He refused to meet Percy Bysshe Shelley, because of rumors of his mistreatment of his first wife, and claimed to have left the city to avoid George Gordon, Lord Byron: "His character in Italy was infamous."

Up to this point Landor was simply a minor poet, deliberately avoiding popularity by composing often in Latin and producing small editions printed in obscure locations. His aspirations were met by a choice circle of admirers in the English Lake District, including Southey, Wordsworth, and Thomas De Quincey. Indeed, he was perhaps to become best known at this time as an associate of Southey through Byron's squib in "The Vision of Judgment" in the *Liberal* for 15 October 1822. But in 1821 in Florence, where the family had moved into a large apartment in a palace belonging to the marchese de' Medici-Tournaquinci, he settled down to the steady composition of his *Imaginary Conversations*, and inaugurated the period that was to be dominated by prose writing, including three other major works, which are all associated particularly with the time he spent in Italy before the breakdown of his marriage in 1835.

Though Landor claimed to have written "two or three" Conversations in 1797, one of which was refused for the *Morning Post*, the impetus toward this form of composition was Southey's announcement in a letter of 14 August 1820 that he was commencing a "series of dialogues" based on those of Boethius. Landor probably started composition soon after in 1820, though the first published, the first of two Conversations titled "Southey and Porson," did not come out (by way of advertisement for the *Imaginary Con-*

*versations of Literary Men and Statesmen*, 1824) until 1823, when it appeared in the July issue of the *London Magazine*.

This first published Conversation stemmed from Landor's decision to withdraw his projected dedication of the first volumes to Wordsworth. He feared Wordsworth would be embarrassed by his own political views as expressed in several of the Conversations, and so he acknowledged him instead by a dialogue largely devoted to a consideration of his poetry. Wordsworth wrote: "I long for the third volume," and heavily corrected his own neoclassical poem, "Laodamia," in accordance with the strictures raised in the Conversation. Landor's admiration for Wordsworth was later substantially qualified. R. H. Super attributes the change to a combination of a chivalric impulse to defend Southey (of whom he believed Wordsworth had remarked "I would not give five shillings for all that [he] has ever written"), resentment at Wordsworth's fancied coolness toward himself, and even jealousy of Wordsworth's reputation. Landor was to attack Wordsworth several times, most notoriously in the second Conversation titled "Southey and Porson" (*Blackwood's*, December 1842), which prompted a spirited defense from Wordsworth's son-in-law, Edward Quillinan.

Of the thirty-six dialogues in the first collection some of the best known are "Lord Brooke and Sir Philip Sidney," "Aeschines and Phocion," "Middleton and Magliabechi," "Lord Chesterfield and Lord Chatham," "Washington and Franklin," and "Marcus Tullius and Quinctus Cicero." Landor experienced difficulties in finding a publisher for the first Conversations. Julius Hare acted as his intermediary with John Taylor, who was, as the history of his relations with John Keats and John Clare further demonstrates, an exceptionally interventionist publisher. He objected to passages not only on political and moral but also on artistic grounds, and he refused to publish without substantial censorship, which Southey was called upon to vet.

When the book came out, the *Quarterly Review* was hostile and William Hazlitt gave a mixed verdict (reworked by Francis Jeffrey) in the *Edinburgh Review*, but generally the book met with a favorable reception and sold well. Visitors from England such as Hazlitt, Leigh Hunt, and Thomas Jefferson Hogg began to seek him out. A new, enlarged edition appeared, from a new publisher, in 1826, and there followed the third volume (dedicated to Simón Bolívar) in 1828 and a second series, comprising two more volumes, from yet another publisher, in 1829. Other well-known dialogues from these subsequent volumes include "Marcellus and Hannibal," "Lucullus and Caesar," "Mr. Pitt and Mr. Canning," "Diogenes and Plato," "Barrow and Newton," "Epicurus, Leontion, and Ternissa," and "Leofric and Godiva."

In 1829, the year of his mother's death, the family moved to the Villa Gherardesca in Fiesole, above Florence, where they remained for six happy years. Enjoying the society of his young family, gardening and cultivating his own orchard—"where," as he told Southey, "Boccaccio led his women to bathe when they had left the first scene of their story-telling"—a generally less-explosive Landor consolidated his reputation in a collection mostly of previously published poetry, *Gebir, Count Julian, and Other Poems* (1831). From May until late October 1832, after an absence of eighteen years, he visited England and was mildly lionized as the author of *Imaginary Conversations*, visiting Crabb Robinson, Charles and Mary Lamb, Samuel Taylor Coleridge, Southey, and for the first time Wordsworth. He returned via Belgium and up the Rhine, meeting, and offending, August Wilhelm Schlegel at Bonn. Back in Fiesole, another pilgrim was Ralph Waldo Emerson, who has left a rich portrait of Landor in his *English Traits* (1865).

In 1834 Landor wrote what is effectively an extended Conversation, *Citation and Examination of William Shakspeare, Euseby Tree, Joseph Carneby, and Silas Gough, before the Worshipful Sir Thomas Lucy, Knight, touching deer-stealing on the 19th day of September in the year of grace 1582, and now published from original papers.* Shakespeare, who is accused of his legendary deer stealing by two of Sir Thomas's keepers and a witness, is tried at Charlecote, Lucy's seat on the road between Warwick and Stratford-upon-Avon. It is full of Warwickshire allusions calling on Landor's local associations.

As Charles Crump noted, the idea may have arisen from Landor's reading of another biographical spoof, James White's *Letters of Falstaff* (1796), which Charles Lamb had loaned to Landor in 1832: "This may have turned his thoughts back to an old subject: in one of the conversations, burned in his quarrel with Mr. Taylor, the speakers were Shakespeare and Sir Thomas Lucy, and doubtless something of the old work survives in the present book."

*Villa Gherardesca, Fiesole, where Landor lived from 1829 until 1835, when he returned to England leaving his family behind in Italy*

The arrangements for publication were made by Marguerite, Countess of Blessington, who was for many years to act as a kind of unofficial literary agent for Landor. It was brought out anonymously and greeted warmly by Lamb, Elizabeth Barrett Browning, and in the *Examiner* for 30 November 1834 by John Forster, the young critic who was to become Landor's most active literary aide, his first editor and biographer. But this book, which is Landor's most sustained attempt at humor, has never attracted significant interest, and Sidney Colvin refers to it as "the nearest approach to an elaborate failure made by Landor in this form of writing."

At Fiesole, too, Landor planned and mostly wrote his epistolary novella in verse and prose set in ancient Athens, *Pericles and Aspasia*, published in 1836 and republished with much additional material in the *Works* of 1846. It was while preparing this book and his *Imaginary Conversations* on classical themes that Landor made his first systematic study of Greek literature. In "The Abbé Delille and Walter Landor" he describes the cultural homogeneity that he found deeply congenial in Periclean Athens: "The temperate greatness and pure eloquence of Pericles formed the moral constitution of Sophocles, who had exercised with him a principal magistracy in the republic: and the demon of Socrates . . . followed Euripides from the school to the theatre."

*Pericles and Aspasia* is an evocation of the greatest period in Greek life, when the powerful character and oratory of Pericles dominated the state. He was on intimate terms with the greatest artists, poets, and philosophers of the day, and his vision was of an Athens embodying the highest attainments of human culture. Landor's book describes the tragic trajectory of his times: from his partial success in making Athens an ideal democracy, leading all Greece, to the Spartan rivalry mounted in the Peloponnesian War, during which he died. His faithful consort (she was not a

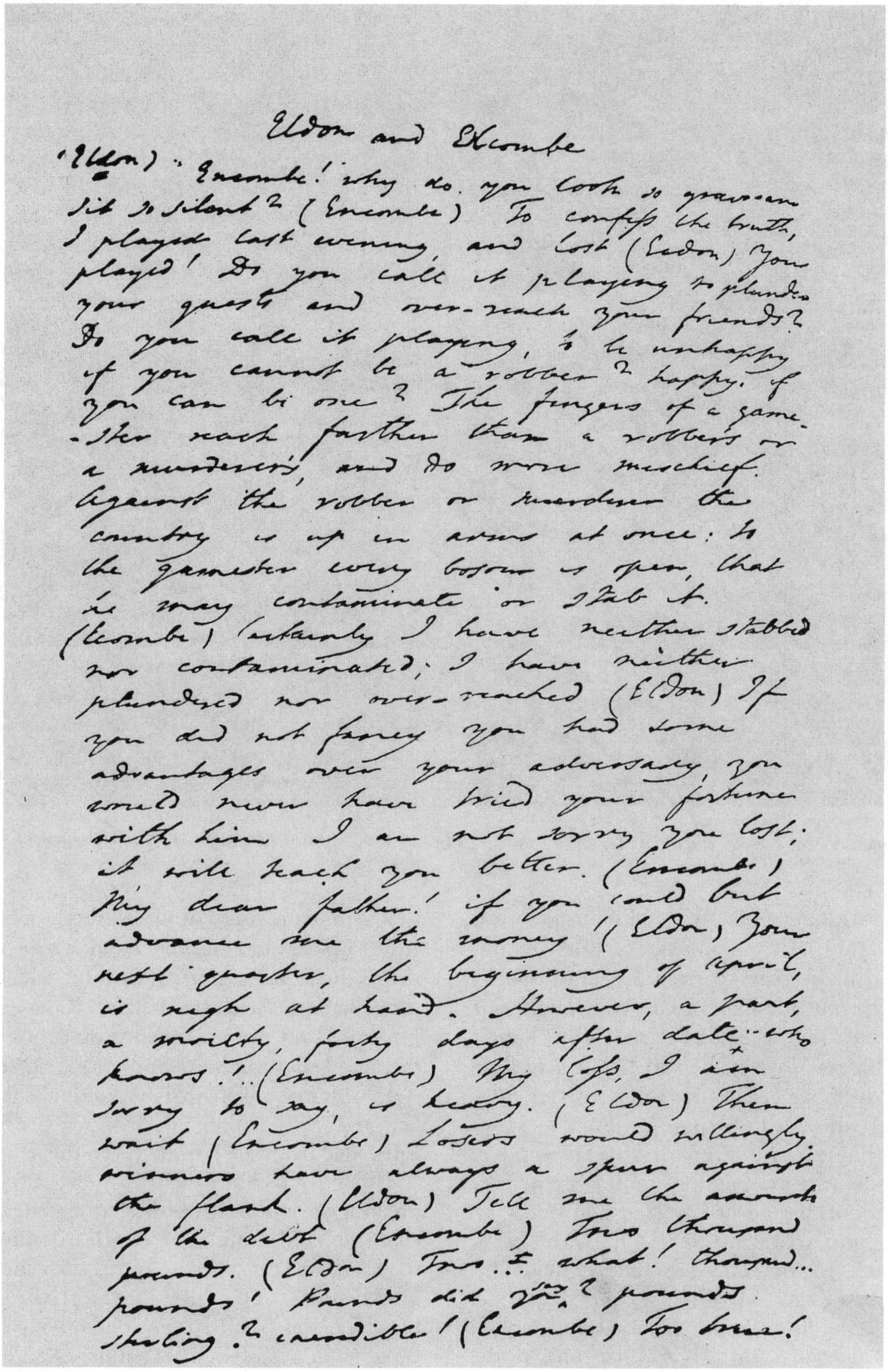

Eldon and Encombe

(Eldon) Encombe! why do you look so grave and sit so silent? (Encombe) To confess the truth, I played last evening, and lost (Eldon) You played! Do you call it playing to plunder your guests and over-reach your friends? Do you call it playing, to be unhappy if you cannot be a robber? happy, if you can be one? The fingers of a gamester reach farther than a robber's or a murderer's, and do more mischief. Against the robber or murderer the country is up in arms at once: to the gamester every bosom is open, that he may contaminate or stab it. (Encombe) Certainly I have neither stabbed nor contaminated; I have neither plundered nor over-reached (Eldon) If you did not fancy you had some advantages over your adversary, you would never have tried your fortune with him I am not sorry you lost; it will teach you better. (Encombe) My dear father! if you could but advance me the money (Eldon) Your next quarter, the beginning of April, is nigh at hand. However, a part, a moiety, forty days after date.. who knows!.. (Encombe) My loss, I am sorry to say, is heavy. (Eldon) Then wait (Encombe) Losers would willingly; winners have always a spur against the flank. (Eldon) Tell me the amount of the debt (Encombe) Two thousand pounds. (Eldon) Two..! what! thousand... pounds! Pounds did you say? pounds sterling? incredible! (Encombe) Too true!

*Page from the manuscript for an "Imaginary Conversation" between John Scott, first Earl of Eldon (lord chancellor, 1801-1827), and his son John Scott, Viscount Encombe, first published in the* Examiner *for 21 August 1836 (from Edmund Gosse,* English Literature: An Illustrated Record, *1904). Landor shared the opinions of William Hazlitt, who accused Eldon of being "against every proposal for the advancement of freedom," and Sydney Smith, who charged that Eldon spent his life "perpetuating all sorts of abuses, and in making money of them."*

native Athenian, so they were unable to marry), and, in Landor's version, his tireless correspondent, was the courtesan Aspasia of Miletus, noted for her intellectual distinction. In their mutual friend, the philosopher and scientist Anaxagoras, Landor is said to have felt that he was in part depicting himself.

Landor indicates the genesis and sources of the work in a letter to Southey: "I began a conversation between Pericles and Aspasia, and thought I could do better by a series of letters between them, not interrupted; for the letters should begin with their first friendship, should give place to their conversations afterwards, and recommence on their supposed separation during the plague of Athens. Few materials are extant: Bayle, Menage, Thucydides, Plutarch, and hardly anything more." This original plan was altered by sustaining the epistolary form almost throughout, and by extending the circle of correspondents, especially by including among them Cleone, an imaginary confidante of Aspasia from Miletus. There are also several speeches and orations attributed to Pericles: for example "to the soldiers round Samos," and one supposedly spoken in 431 B.C. when the Lacedaemonians (Spartans) invaded Attica. The letters and speeches are further diversified by interspersing them with prose fragments and verses supposed to have come from various ancient writers, especially minor Greek poets such as Corinna, Mimnermus, and Myrtis.

The publication of the work was arranged by Landor's novelist neighbor, G. P. R. Graves, and he was paid the single sum of one hundred pounds for it. The book was immediately greeted by several of his friends and the *Examiner* for 27 March 1836 as Landor's masterpiece, and a pirated American edition of selections appeared in 1839.

The Fiesolan idyll came to an end with the breakdown of the Landors' marriage in 1835. Settling his income on his family, left at Fiesole, he drew a modest allowance and returned to Bath, where he remained for more than twenty years, constantly writing and getting to know the young Victorians: Elizabeth Barrett, Thomas Carlyle, Alfred Tennyson, Charles Dickens, and especially Robert Browning, who acknowledged his encouragement in *Sordello* (1840).

In August 1837-April 1838 Hunt printed Landor's series of anecdotal letters, mostly representing English points of view, on *High and Low Life in Italy* in the *Monthly Repository*. Among the letters there is a Conversation, "The Cardinal-Legate Albani and Picture-Dealers." The commentary, which is animated but formless, possibly derived from Tobias Smollett's *Expedition of Humphrey Clinker* (1771), perhaps as mediated in the writings of Pierce Egan. It had been written in 1831, but no publisher would bring it out at the time.

*The Pentameron*, in *The Pentameron and Pentalogia* (the latter work is made up of five scenes in blank verse of crucial moments from Greek myth and European history), was begun during the three months he spent in Germany in 1836, and was first published in 1837. It is made up of a series of five day-long interviews between Giovanni Boccaccio, whose *Decameron* (a collection of tales represented as having been told over ten days) gave Landor the idea for the framework of this work, and Francesco Petrarch. Petrarch is supposed to pay Boccaccio a visit at his villa at Certaldo, between Florence and Siena. Though the two writers had actually met in Florence in 1350—when they became lifelong friends—and Boccaccio was influenced by Petrarch into becoming a Greek scholar and working to reintroduce the influence of Greek literature into Italy, Landor's version of their conversation is imaginary. There are incidental episodes and stories, but their discussions dwell on criticisms of Dante's *Divine Comedy* (rather unsympathetic) and Boccaccio's *Decameron*, and on analysis of the poetry of Virgil and Horace.

Landor's interest in criticism was encouraged by Forster, who, as editor of the *Foreign Quarterly Review*, commissioned him to write two close textual analyses—of Catullus (July 1842) and Theocritus (October 1842)—and a biographical-critical account of Petrarch (July 1843), all of which were republished with alterations in *The Last Fruit off an Old Tree* (1853). His analysis of Theocritus's idylls (which ends with an interesting consideration of the idyll in English poetry) has had some influence. "The perfection of the workmanship," for example, in the "ekphrasis" on the prize cup in the first idyll is considered to achieve the timelessness of great art—"not only what is passing, but also what is past and what is to come"—that Yeats echoes in "Sailing to Byzantium."

The first volume of the collected edition of Landor's *Works* (1846) contains all the Conversations, mostly heavily revised, from the editions of 1826-1829, together with two "second Conversations" between speakers already represented:

*Landor in 1848 (portrait by J. Stewart; from R. H. Super,* Walter Savage Landor: A Biography, *1954)*

"Southey and Porson" and "Demosthenes and Eubulides." The second volume, besides the major prose works, dramas, miscellaneous writings, and a great deal of poetry, old and new, contains twenty-one Conversations collected from periodicals and annuals over the previous fifteen years and twenty-one never previously published, including some of his best-known dialogues, such as "Fra Filippo Lippi and Pope Eugenius the Fourth," and the two Conversations titled "Aesop and Rhodopè."

Landor's creative energy remained unabated, as poetry and prose continued to appear in several periodicals, especially the *Examiner*. He collected his poetry on Latin and Greek themes in *The Hellenics* (1847; enlarged in 1859), and in 1848, the year of European revolutions, he produced as pamphlets a gathering of seven poems, *Italics*, urging the Italians in their struggle, and the *Imaginary Conversation of King Carlo-Alberto and the Duchess Belgioioso, on the Affairs and Prospects of Italy*. The profits from the Conversation were to go to the sufferers in the Sicilian revolt at Messina.

When he collected his Conversations between classical speakers for *Imaginary Conversations of Greeks and Romans* (1853), a volume dedicated to Dickens, Landor composed a few more, and in the miscellaneous collection *The Last Fruit off an Old Tree* (1853) he included eighteen Conversations not published in *Works* (1846), among which are the topical "Louis Philippe and M. Guizot" and "Garibaldi and Mazzini."

Landor's later years were clouded by scandal. He was defrauded by a woman who had a vicious influence over a sixteen-year-old girl whom

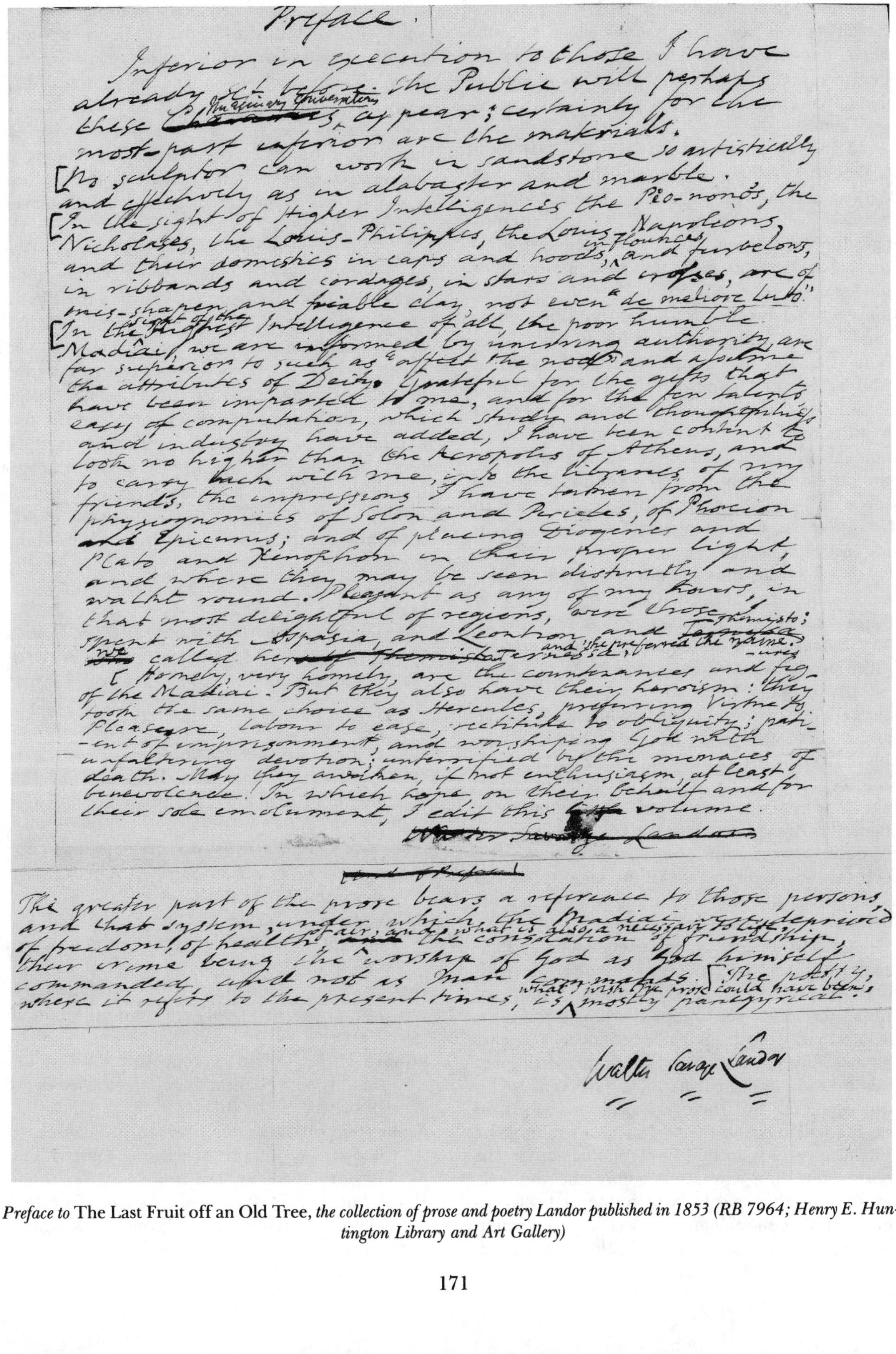

Preface.

Inferior in execution to those I have already set before the Public will perhaps these Imaginary Conversations appear; certainly for the most-part inferior are the materials.

[No sculptor can work in sandstone so artistically and effectively as in alabaster and marble.

[In the sight of Higher Intelligences the Pio-nonos, the Nicholases, the Louis-Philippes, the Louis Napoleons, and their domestics in caps and hoods, and flounces and furbelows, in ribbands and cordages, in stars and crosses, are of mis-shapen and friable clay, not even "de meliore luto."

[In the sight of the Highest Intelligence of all, the poor humble Madiai, we are informed by unerring authority, are far superior to such as "affect the nod" and assume the attributes of Deity. Grateful for the gifts that have been imparted to me, and for the few talents easy of computation, which study and thoughtfulness and industry have added, I have been content to look no higher than the Acropolis of Athens, and to carry back with me, into the libraries of my friends, the impressions I have taken from the physiognomies of Solon and Pericles, of Phocion and Epicurus; and of placing Diogenes and Plato and Xenophon in their proper light, and where they may be seen distinctly and walkt round. Pleasant as any of my hours, in that most delightful of regions, were those spent with Aspasia, and Leontion, and Themisto: we called her Ternissa and she preferred the name.

[Homely, very homely, are the countenances and figures of the Madiai. But they also have their heroism: they took the same choice as Hercules, preferring Virtue to Pleasure, labour to ease, rectitude to obliquity; patient of imprisonment, and worshiping God with unfaltering devotion; unterrified by the menaces of death. May they awaken, if not enthusiasm, at least benevolence! In which hope on their behalf and for their sole emolument, I edit this volume.

The greater part of the prose bears a reference to those persons, and that system, under which the Madiai were deprived of freedom, of health, of air, and of what is also a necessary to life, the consolation of friendship, their crime being the worship of God as God himself commanded, and not as man commands. [The poetry, where it refers to the present times, is what I wish the prose could have been, mostly panegyrical.

Walter Savage Landor

*Preface to* The Last Fruit off an Old Tree, *the collection of prose and poetry Landor published in 1853 (RB 7964; Henry E. Huntington Library and Art Gallery)* he petted. Threatened with libel charges over pamphlets and poetic accusations which he published, he retired once more to Italy, where he spent his final years. He died at the age of eighty-nine at Florence, where he is buried in the Protestant Cemetery.

Landor's prose art particularly lends itself to theoretical analysis from psychoanalytic and Marxist formalist perspectives. Jacques Lacan's definition of the "Imaginary" accounts interestingly for the classical structure of feeling that informs Landor's attempts to arrest moments of timelessness, especially in his heroic Conversations, which revolve around an implicit climax, usually death, which occurs either just before or soon after the dialogue. Conversations such as "Marcellus and Hannibal" seem to be conceived as sculptural tableaux, with the speakers caught in attitudes of heroic assertion or grief. The marmoreal verbal style of conversations such as the two between Aesop and Rhodopè or of Boccaccio's dream in the fifth day's interview in *The Pentameron* similarly aims to fix a language outside historical change.

The extraordinary pull, by which Landor seeks to organize and essentialize a vast diversity of historical experience, is articulated by his imaginary Epicurus: "all history is fabulous." Finding in the preparation for the composition of *Pericles and Aspasia* that "Few materials are extant," he rejoices that he can give full rein to his own imagination: "The coast is clear." Related is the process involved in his dramatic characterization, which Southey referred to as one of "consubstantiating." The tendency toward the incorporation of characters draws them into the kind of frozen stasis desired by Landor's imaginary Dante, who feels that his ability to evoke the same memories as Beatrice, merging her mind with his, gives him a sense of timeless possession.

Certain imaginary characters—such as Phocion, Diogenes, and Anaxagoras—offer straightforward projections of recognizable Landorian traits. Too often in Landor's writings, however, he practices what his imaginary Diogenes, speaking of Plato's use of Socrates in his dialogues, calls a "wide-mouthed mask" to give vent to his own opinions. But there are occasions when, to use Mikhail Bakhtin's terms, Landor's monologic control gives way to other polyphonic voices. His most interesting characters represent the carnivalization that particularly influenced Browning's dramatic monologues, especially in his imitative use of Fra Filippo Lippi. Self-revealing villains such as Pope Leo XII, chatting with his valet, Gigi, or William Pitt the younger, expounding his cynical approach to statecraft, fascinate as they give themselves unblushingly away. Monsters of egotism, such as his Henry VIII, drunkenly abusing the wife he is about to have beheaded, or his Peter the Great, complaining of an empty stomach when he hears of the death of a son he has denounced, unbroach the perversion of absolutism.

The carnivalesque erupts more obviously in his relish for anecdotalism, the curiosity about local color that is evident especially in the *Citation and Examination of William Shakspeare* and *High and Low Life in Italy* and in his enjoyment of sheer gossip in *The Pentameron*. Rather than timelessness, he occasionally captures the Stendhalian tone of the panoptic overview of a specific time and place, as in "General Kleber and French Officers." In such places, he can kick off the traces of his classic restraint and throw away the Holy Book like Shakespeare, the "miscreant knave," who exuberantly gallops away from his examination.

**Letters:**

*The Literary Life and Correspondence of the Countess of Blessington,* 3 volumes, edited by R. R. Madden (London: T. C. Newby, 1855), II: 361-395;

*The Blessington Papers,* in *The Collection of Autograph Letters and Historical Documents Formed by Alfred Morrison,* second series, 1882-1893 (London: Printed for private circulation, 1895);

*Letters and Other Unpublished Writings of Walter Savage Landor,* edited by Stephen Wheeler (London: Bentley, 1897);

*Letters of Walter Savage Landor, Private and Public,* edited by Wheeler (London: Duckworth, 1899);

George Somes Layard, *Mrs. Lynn Linton, Her Life, Letters, and Opinions* (London: Methuen, 1901);

Edward H. R. Tatham, "Some Unpublished Letters of W. S. Landor," *Fortnightly Review,* 93 (February 1910): 361-373;

*Baylor University Browning Interests,* fifth series, edited by A. Joseph Armstrong (Waco, Tex.: Baylor University, 1932);

H. C. Minchin, *Walter Savage Landor: Last Days, Letters and Conversations* (London: Methuen, 1934);

R. H. Super, "Landor's 'Dear Daughter,' Eliza Lynn Linton," *PMLA,* 59 (December 1944): 1059-1085;

Super, "Landor's Letters to Wordsworth and Coleridge," *Modern Philology,* 55 (November 1957): 73-83;

A. Lavonne Ruoff and Edwin Burton Levine, "Landor's Letters to the Reverend Walter Birch," *Bulletin of John Rylands Library,* 51 (1968): 200-261;

Ruoff, "Landor's Letters to his Family: 1802-25," *Bulletin of John Rylands Library,* 53 (1971): 465-500;

Ruoff, "Landor's Letters to his Family: 1826-29," *Bulletin of John Rylands Library,* 54 (1972): 398-433;

John F. Mariani, "The Letters of Walter Savage Landor to Marguerite Countess of Blessington," Ph.D. dissertation, Columbia University, 1973;

Ruoff, "Walter Savage Landor's Letters to His Family, 1830-1832," *Bulletin of John Rylands Library,* 58 (1976): 467-507.

**Bibliographies:**

Thomas James Wise and Stephen Wheeler, *A Bibliography of the Writings in Prose and Verse of Walter Savage Landor* (London: Printed for the Bibliographical Society by Blades, East & Blades, 1919);

Wise, *A Landor Library. A Catalogue of Printed Books, Manuscripts and Autograph Letters* (London: Printed for private circulation, 1928);

R. H. Super, *The Publication of Landor's Works* (London: Bibliographical Society, 1954);

Super, "Walter Savage Landor," in *The English Romantic Poets & Essayists: A Review of Research and Criticism,* revised edition, edited by Carolyn Washburn Houtchens and Lawrence Huston Houtchens (New York: Published for the Modern Language Association of America by New York University Press / London: University of London Press, 1966), pp. 221-253.

**Biographies:**

John Forster, *Walter Savage Landor. A Biography* (2 volumes, London: Chapman & Hall, 1869; 1 volume, Boston: Fields, Osgood, 1869);

Sidney Colvin, *Landor,* English Men of Letters Series (London: Macmillan, 1881; New York: Harper, 1881);

Malcolm Elwin, *Savage Landor* (London: Macdonald, 1941); revised and enlarged as *Landor. A Replevin* (London: Macdonald, 1958);

R. H. Super, *Walter Savage Landor: A Biography* (New York: New York University Press, 1954).

**References:**

Richard Aldington, "Landor's 'Hellenics,' " in his *Literary Studies and Reviews* (London: Allen & Unwin, 1924), pp. 141-154;

William Bradley, *The Early Poems of Walter Savage Landor* (London: Printed by Bradbury, Agnew & Co., 1913);

John Buxton, "Walter Savage Landor," in his *The Grecian Taste. Literature in the Age of Neo-Classicism 1740-1820* (London: Macmillan, 1978), pp. 105-127;

Donald A. Davie, "Attending to Landor," *Ironwood,* 12 (Fall 1984): 103-111;

Davie, "The Shorter Poems of Landor," in *Essays in Criticism,* 1 (1951): 345-355; republished in his *Purity of Diction in English Verse* (London: Chatto & Windus, 1952; New York: Oxford University Press, 1953), pp. 183-196;

Ernest Dilworth, *Walter Savage Landor* (New York: Twayne, 1971);

Felice Elkin, *Walter Savage Landor's Studies of Italian Life and Literature* (Philadelphia: University of Pennsylvania, 1934);

R. W. Emerson, *English Traits* (Boston: Phillips, Sampson, 1856; London: Routledge, 1856);

Edward Waterman Evans, Jr., *Walter Savage Landor. A Critical Study* (New York: Putnam's / London: Knickerbocker, 1892);

Hermann M. Flasdieck, "Walter Savage Landor und seine 'Imaginary Conversations,' " *Englische Studien,* 58 (1924): 390-431;

Guido Fornelli, *W. S. Landor e l'Italia* (Forli: La Poligrafia Romagnola, 1930);

G. Rostrevor Hamilton, *Walter Savage Landor,* Writers and Their Work, no. 126 (London: Published for the British Council & the National Book League by Longmans, Green, 1960);

W. Brooks Drayton Henderson, *Swinburne and Landor* (London: Macmillan, 1918);

Andrea Kelly, "The Latin Poetry of Walter Savage Landor," in *The Latin Poetry of the English Poets,* edited by J. W. Binns (London & Boston: Routledge / Chapman & Hall, 1974);

*Landor in Siena, July 1859 (drawing by William Wetmore Story; from Malcolm Elwin,* Landor. A Replevin, *1958)*

F. R. Leavis, "Landor and the Seasoned Epicure," *Scrutiny,* 11 (December 1942): 148-150;

Vernon Lee, "The Rhetoric of Landor," in her *The Handling of Words and Other Studies in Literary Psychology* (London: John Lane / New York: Dodd, Mead, 1923), pp. 157-174;

A. H. Mason, *Walter Savage Landor, Poète: Lyrique* (Paris: Presses Universitaires de France, 1924);

Jerome J. McGann, *A Critique of Textual Criticism* (Chicago & London: University of Chicago Press, 1983);

Bruce McKinnon, "Three Latin Poems by W. S. Landor," *Durham University Journal,* 72, part 1 (December 1979): 55-59;

Vivian Mercer, "The Future of Landor Criticism," in *Some British Romantics: A Collection of Essays,* edited by J. V. Logan, J. E. Jordan, and Northrop Frye (Columbus: Ohio State University Press, 1966), pp. 43-85;

Richard Monckton Milnes, Lord Houghton, *Monographs Personal and Social* (London: J. Murray, 1873; New York: Holt & Williams, 1873);

Elizabeth Nitchie, "The Classicism of Walter Savage Landor," *Classical Journal,* 14 (December 1918): 147-166;

Robert Pinsky, *Landor's Poetry* (Chicago & London: University of Chicago Press, 1968);

Ezra Pound, *ABC of Reading* (London: Routledge, 1934; New Haven: Yale University Press, 1934);

Pound, "The Case of Landor," *Observer* (London), 14 January 1934, p. 9;

Pound, *Guide to Kulchur* (London: Faber & Faber, 1938); republished as *Culture* (Norfolk, Conn.: New Directions, 1938);

Pound, *How to Read* (London: Harmsworth, 1931);

Ernest de Selincourt, "Classicism and Romanticism in the Poetry of Landor," in *England und die Antike,* edited by F. Saxl (Berlin, 1932);

Leslie Stephen, "Landor's Imaginary Conversations," in his *Hours in a Library,* third series (London: Smith, Elder, 1879);

A. C. Swinburne, *Miscellanies* (London: Chatto & Windus, 1886; New York: Worthington, 1886);

Arthur Symons, "Walter Savage Landor," in his *The Romantic Movement in English Poetry* (London: Constable, 1909; New York: Dutton, 1909);

Francis Thompson, "Landor," *Academy* (27 February 1897): 258-259;

Pierre Vitoux, *L'Oeuvre de Walter Savage Landor* (Paris: Presses Universitaires de France, 1964);

John W. Warren, "A Critic's Defense and Self-Revelation," *Publications of the Mississippi Philological Association* (1988): 162-168;

Hugh Whitemeyer, "Walter Savage Landor and Ezra Pound," in *Romantic and Modern: Revaluations of Literary Tradition,* edited by George Bornstein (Pittsburgh: University of Pittsburgh Press, 1977);

Stanley T. Williams, "Walter Savage Landor as a Critic of Literature," *PMLA,* 38 (December 1923): 906-928;

*Wordsworth Circle,* special Landor issue, edited by Charles L. Proudfit, 7 (Winter 1976).

**Papers:**

Various British and American libraries hold important Landor materials. The only major poetic manuscript to survive—that of "Count Julian"—is in the Forster Collection at the Library of the Victoria and Albert Museum, together with letters from Landor to Forster (mostly published in Forster's *Walter Savage Landor. A Biography*). The British Library has various manuscripts for prose and verse compositions, including the sonnet "To Robert Browning" and *The Pentameron,* and letters to a variety of correspondents, including Charles Lamb, Swinburne, and the countess of Blessington. The Bodleian Library, Oxford; Edinburgh University Library; and John Rylands University Library of Manchester also have significant manuscript collections of correspondence. The Henry E. Huntington Library holds many items, including literary manuscripts, correspondence, and private papers. The Baylor University Browning Collection has many letters from Landor to Browning (unreliable texts of these letters are published in Minchin's *Walter Savage Landor: Last Days, Letters and Conversations*). Arkansas University Library has correspondence with Elizabeth Barrett Browning; the Beinecke Rare Book and Manuscript Library at Yale holds a collection of mostly unpublished letters to Kenneth Robert Henderson Mackenzie and other materials, including the manuscript for an "Imaginary Conversation." The Chicago University Library holds letters, including some to John Forster on literary topics; the Harry Ransom Humanities Research Center at the University of Texas at Austin has correspondence with Dickens. Other items are in the Henry W. and Albert A. Berg Collection, New York Public Library; the Houghton Library, Harvard University; Iowa University Library; Knox College Archives; the Carl H. Pforzheimer Library, New York; the Pierpont Morgan Library, New York; and the University of Virginia Library.

# Thomas Robert Malthus

*(13 February 1766 - 29 December 1834)*

Arthur E. Walzer
*University of Minnesota*

BOOKS: *An Essay on the Principle of Population, as It Affects the Future Improvement of Society. With Remarks on the Speculations of Mr. Godwin, Mr. Condorcet, and Other Writers* (London: Printed for J. Johnson, 1798);

*An Investigation of the Cause of the Present High Price of Provisions, Containing an Illustration of the Nature and Limits of Fair Price in Time of Scarcity, and Its Application to the Particular Circumstances of This Country* (London: Printed for J. Johnson by Davis, Taylor & Wilks, 1800);

*An Essay on the Principle of Population; or, A View of Its Past and Present Effects on Human Happiness; with an Inquiry into Our Prospects Respecting the Future Removal or Mitigation of the Evils which It Occasions* (London: Printed for J. Johnson by T. Bensley, 1803; revised, 2 volumes, 1806; revised again, 1807; first American edition from the 1806 London edition, Washington: R. C. Weightman, 1809; revised again, 3 volumes, London: John Murray, 1817; revised again, 2 volumes, 1826);

*A Letter to Samuel Whitbread, Esq. M.P. on His Proposed Bill for the Amendment of the Poor Laws* (London: Printed for J. Johnson & J. Hatchard, 1807);

*A Letter to the Rt Hon. Lord Grenville, Occasioned by Some Observations of his Lordship on the East India Company's Establishment for the Education of their Civil Servants* (London: Printed for J. Johnson, 1813);

*Observations on the Effects of the Corn Laws, and of a Rise or Fall in the Price of Corn on the Agriculture and General Wealth of the Country* (London: Printed for J. Johnson, 1814);

*An Inquiry into the Nature and Progress of Rent, and the Principles by Which It is Regulated* (London: Printed for John Murray, 1815);

*The Grounds of an Opinion on the Policy of Restricting the Importation of Foreign Corn; Intended as an Appendix to "Observations on the Corn Laws"* (London: Printed for John Murray and J. Johnson, 1815);

*Statements respecting the East-India College, with an Appeal to Facts, in Refutation of Charges Lately Brought against it, in the Court of Proprietors* (London: Printed for John Murray, 1817);

*Principles of Political Economy Considered with a View to their Practical Application* (London: John Murray, 1820; Boston: Wells & Lilly, 1821);

*The Measure of Value Stated and Illustrated, with an Application of It to the Alteration in the Value of the English Currency since 1790* (London: John Murray, 1823);

*Definitions in Political Economy, Preceded by an Inquiry into the Rules Which Ought to Guide Political Economists in the Definition and Use of Their Terms; with Remarks on the Deviation from These Rules in their Writings* (London: John Murray, 1827);

*A Summary View of the Principle of Population* (London: John Murray, 1830);

*The Travel Diaries of Thomas Robert Malthus*, edited by Patricia James (Cambridge: Cambridge University Press for the Royal Economic Society, 1966).

**Edition:** *The Works of Thomas Robert Malthus*, 8 volumes, edited by E. A. Wrigley and David Souden (London: Pickering, 1986).

OTHER: "Population," in volume 6 of *Supplement to Fourth, Fifth and Sixth Editions of the Encyclopædia Britannica*, 6 volumes, edited by M. Napier (Edinburgh: Constable, 1824).

Thomas Robert Malthus, sometimes called "England's first political economist," occupies an important place between the Scottish Adam Smith and David Ricardo in the history of economics, but his claim to a larger fame rests exclusively on his *Essay on Population*, which he first published anonymously in 1798. *An Essay on Population* argued that population tended to increase at a much faster rate than food production and that this tendency would be fatal to proposed utopias that promised to eliminate malnutrition, curtail diseases, and lengthen the average life span.

*Thomas Robert Malthus (engraving by John Linnell, after his own painting)*

It was not a new thesis, having been anticipated by Robert Wallace, among others. But Malthus presented his case dramatically and enshrined his argument with an air of scientific certainty that made it both lively and compelling. It was a stunning rhetorical achievement, perfect in its timing: *An Essay on Population* was most welcome in England during a period when radical social theories similar to those Malthus attacked were seen as laying the groundwork for the Revolution in France that had eventuated in the Terror. But Malthus changed the tone and focus of *An Essay on Population* in the longer version he published in 1803; moreover, the mood in England was quite different, as radical liberal theories on the perfectibility of man were no longer seen as the threat they were earlier. The result was that the essay now seemed to many to say, not merely that utopian schemes were doomed, but that all reform was futile, that collective efforts to alleviate suffering would only make matters worse, that the poor alone were responsible for overcoming the hardships they endured, and that the only way for all to learn this "wisdom" was for the poor to experience more suffering. Thus, *An Essay on Population* became one of the most notorious books of the first half of the nineteenth century, and the mild, scholarly Malthus, who sincerely saw himself as seeking to empower the poor to break the cycle of poverty by limiting the size of their families and thus reducing the supply of labor, was stigmatized as an ogre indifferent to suffering and welcoming the misery and vice whose causes he meant only to trace.

Thomas Robert Malthus, who was known as Robert or Bob throughout his life, was born on 13 February 1766, in Dorking in central Surrey, England, the sixth child and second son of Dan-

*Okewood Chapel, Surrey, where Malthus became perpetual curate in 1793 (photograph by Arthur E. Walzer)*

iel and Henrietta Graham Malthus. Daniel, the only son of a successful lawyer-businessman and heir to modest estates, had pretensions to intellectual interests that were manifest in his assiduous pursuit of an early contact with Jean-Jacques Rousseau, an episode that he wore as the badge of his life. His scholarly bent and attraction to eccentricity were probably behind the unusual education he provided his talented second son. Instead of receiving a standard public-school education, Malthus was enrolled in 1773 at a boarding school in Claverton run by the clergyman and writer Richard Graves. Even more unusual was Daniel's decision to put Robert, who was destined for the ministry in the Church of England, under the tutelage of the Unitarian Gilbert Wakefield, first at the Dissenting Academy at Warrington in 1782 and later, with the closing of the school, in Wakefield's household. In 1784 Malthus enrolled at Wakefield's alma mater, Jesus College, Cambridge, where his tutor was the mathematician and clergyman William Frend, who was to become known as one of the Cambridge Unitarians. Frend publicly renounced the Thirty-Nine Articles and attacked religious tests in resigning his tutorship in 1787, one year before Malthus's graduation. Malthus, who won awards for his declamations in Latin and English, prudently avoided the genuine controversy that surrounded his tutor and distinguished himself by graduating in 1788 as "Ninth Wrangler," an honor bestowed by Cambridge on its best graduates in mathematics. Malthus's contemporaries were fond of remarking that the patient, sensible Robert seemed unaffected by the rebellious heterodoxy of his mentors. But his contact with intelligent, scholarly teachers of unorthodox views may have been behind the pride Malthus always took in assuming the role as an advocate of minority views and the strength he exhibited when these views came under attack.

Malthus took holy orders shortly after his graduation from Cambridge. In 1793 he was named a fellow of Jesus College, which demanded no duties and afforded him a small stipend as long as he remained unmarried. In the same year he was named perpetual curate of Okewood, a small, poor chapel not far from his family home in Surrey. In visiting his parishioners in their mud huts Malthus would have observed rural poverty firsthand, and in baptizing their children he would have witnessed something of the burdens and consolations of large families.

In 1798 Malthus published anonymously *An Essay on the Principle of Population, as It Affects the Future Improvement of Society. With Remarks on the Speculations of Mr. Godwin, Mr. Condorcet, and Other Writers*. The immediate provocation of the essay was a disagreement with his father over William Godwin's "On Avarice and Profusion," which appeared in his *Enquirer* in 1797. But its broader target is Enlightenment optimism and environmentalism, theories of what Malthus calls the "perfectibility of man and society," especially as manifest by Godwin's *Political Justice* (1793) and Antoine-Nicolas, Marquis de Condorcet's *Sketch for a Historical Picture of the Progress of the Human Mind* (1795). Both Condorcet and Godwin imagined a future in which reason reigns and wealth is distributed equally, so that every citizen works moderately and lives well, and where vanity and greed are as forgotten as kings, lords, and priests. Furthermore, impressed by the progress of Enlightenment science, both Godwin and Condorcet speculated on the possibility of improvements in medical science, nutrition, and working conditions such that man's life span might be extended indefinitely.

In the course of inventing arguments against Godwin and Condorcet and defending his own more skeptical, conservative views, Malthus discovered the "principle of population," which is the linchpin of the argument in *An Essay on Population*: the discrepancy between two theoretical rates of increase—the increase in population and the increase in food supply. Assuming that the average family has four children, Malthus argues that population *tends* to increase at a geometric rate by a factor of two every generation; that is, it tends to double every twenty-five years. The actual size of the population does not increase at the rate of its theoretical tendency because, Malthus argues, food production cannot keep pace with it. Food supplies can and do increase but at a much slower, "arithmetic rate," resulting in a lower per capita supply of grain, even as the total amount increases. The discrepancy had been observed by others, but it was never so dramatically expressed as in Malthus's principle of population.

Crucial to Malthus's thesis is his argument that the size of and increase in population is proportioned to food resources by the infamous "Malthusian checks," misery and vice. Malnutrition, disease, and famine are among the species of misery, while war, infanticide, and contraception are among the forms of vice that inevitably follow from the imbalance of the two ratios and limit the actual population to the resources of food. As Malthus sees it, humankind is caught in a cycle in which every increase in food production sets in motion a more rapid increase in population, which eventually outstrips food production and triggers the checks. This cycle has operated in the past, is operating now, and will operate in the future, he insists. Reforms, such as those promoted by Godwin and Condorcet, that would distribute the wealth or guarantee subsistence to children or the aged worsen the problem in the long run because they lessen the fear of poverty and misery that restrains the prudent from having larger families than they can likely support.

The helplessness of man in the face of constant operation of the checks gives *An Essay on Population* a gloomy fatalism—the "melancholy hue" that Malthus acknowledges in the preface. In Malthus's cosmology malnutrition and disease are presented not as inexplicable, but as inevitable, sometimes even as necessary to forestall the still more disruptive forms of misery, such as famine and plagues. Furthermore, in his enthusiasm to defeat Godwin's and Condorcet's facile notions of the perfectibility of man and society, Malthus occasionally seems to reprove all efforts to attenuate the effects of poverty on the grounds that well-meaning efforts to help actually make the problem worse by promoting population growth. The Poor Laws come under particular attack: from Malthus's point of view, they wear away the preventive check of self-restraint by holding out the promise of support to families in poverty, lower the wages of labor by increasing its supply, and raise the price of food by increasing the demand for bread without increasing its supply.

The relevance of *An Essay on Population* assured that it would be noted with interest and respect in the reviews of 1798-1799. It dealt with issues fundamental to the intellectual tenor of the time. It attacked the theories of government that formed the basis for the French Revolution at a time when the Terror and English fear of it were increasing. It criticized the Poor Laws as futile when the costs of implementing them were escalating. In speaking broadly of misery and vice as

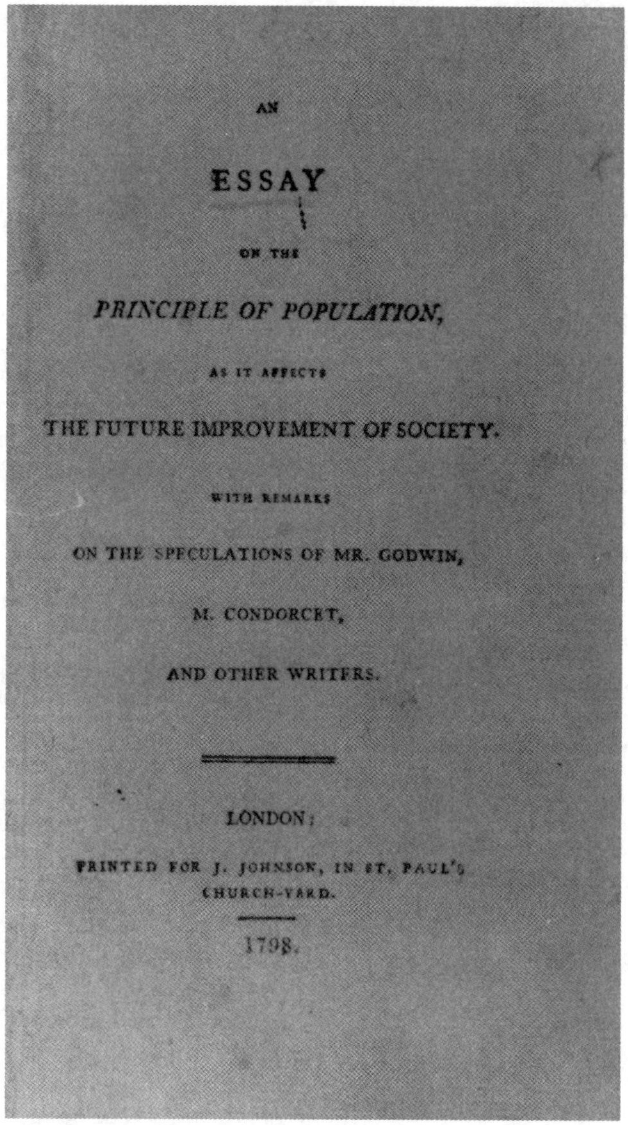
AN

ESSAY

ON THE

PRINCIPLE OF POPULATION,

AS IT AFFECTS

THE FUTURE IMPROVEMENT OF SOCIETY.

WITH REMARKS

ON THE SPECULATIONS OF MR. GODWIN,

M. CONDORCET,

AND OTHER WRITERS.

LONDON:

PRINTED FOR J. JOHNSON, IN ST. PAUL'S CHURCH-YARD.

1798.

*Title page for Malthus's response to William Godwin's belief in the perfectibility of man and society. The second edition (1803), so greatly enlarged that it is virtually a different book, made Malthus one of the most notorious writers of his time.*

resulting from the imbalances of nature, it seemed to call into question conventional versions of that Enlightenment preoccupation, the argument from design. Perhaps above all, the essay seemed to show that the future of man is not only an affair of reason and will. It illustrated in vivid and dramatic ways that biology will have a part to play at a time when England wanted to hear this message. "Mr. Malthus appeared, and we heard no more of Mr. Godwin," was the usual verdict, according to Robert Southey in the *Annual Review* in 1804.

The notice that *An Essay on Population* brought to Malthus spurred him to undertake an extensive program of study and travel to gather more evidence in support of his theory. He read intensely in history and travel literature, and in 1799 he traveled with Cambridge friends, spending most of his time in Sweden and Norway, where he could observe the mores of countries with slower population growth. When he returned, the clamor over sustained high prices for bread prompted him to write a pamphlet, *An Investigation of the Cause of the Present High Price of Provisions* (1800), in which he maintained that the principle of population, specifically the inflationary tendencies of the Poor Laws, was the cause of high food prices. Hanging farmers putatively responsible for the price increase would only make matters worse, Malthus insisted.

The second edition of *An Essay on Population*, published in 1803, reflected the five years of study Malthus had undertaken. It is nearly four times as long as the first essay and might indeed be regarded a "new work," as Malthus recommends in its preface. Godwin and Condorcet and the questions their utopias raised concerning the nature of man have been pushed from center stage to a subordinate place in the third of the four books in this new edition. The "principle of population" is not, as it was in 1798, a crucial piece of evidence in a grand argument over the future of mankind but is itself the subject of a long treatise on the operation of the checks in primitive, ancient, and modern societies (books 1 and 2) and on the ramifications of the principle for contemporary Britain (book 4). Furthermore, Malthus announces in the preface a new check, moral restraint, by which people can slow population growth and avoid misery, without increasing vice, if they choose to live chastely while delaying marriage or if they choose to remain chaste for extended periods within marriage.

The effect of Malthus's changed purposes gives the *Essay on Population* of 1803 a drastically different tone from that of the first. It is not merely that the edition of 1803, heavy with references, is more scholarly. The new emphasis on moral restraint in book 4 introduces a new language to the essay—a language of admonitions, duties, and consequences. The warnings, of the immorality of marrying without a fair prospect of being able to support children and of the evils of the Poor Laws, should issue from the pulpit during the wedding ceremony according to one of Malthus's recommendations. At that point, society's obligation ends, and the worker's duty begins: "This duty is . . . intelligible to the humblest capacity. It is merely that he is not to bring beings into the world for whom he cannot find the means of support. . . . If he cannot support his children, they must starve; and if he marry in the face of a fair probability that he shall not be able to support his children, he is guilty of all the evils which he thus brings upon himself, his wife, and his offspring." In 1798 humankind, sharing universal drives for food and sex, was pitted in common cause against a sparing nature; in 1803 individuals in need and their "redundant" children are pitted against a society from which they are somehow separate and which would do well without them. Malthus's emphasis on moral restraint was no doubt intended to relieve the fatalism of the first *Essay on Population* by showing that human choices can make a difference in alleviating poverty. But while the rhetoric of the first essay may have been gloomy, it was rarely mean. Reading the first essay can be a melancholy experience; reading the 1803 version is depressing.

With the appearance of the 1803 edition, which served as the basis for subsequent editions in 1806, 1807, 1817, and 1826, the criticism of *An Essay on Population* in essays, pamphlets, and books began in earnest. Although longer and more vituperative than many of the attacks, William Hazlitt's comprehensive *Reply to the Essay on Population*, published in its book-length version in 1807, rehearses the themes and suggests something of the flavor of the attacks also levied by Southey and Thomas De Quincey and felt by Samuel Taylor Coleridge and Percy Bysshe Shelley.

The burden of Hazlitt's case is that *An Essay on Population* is illogically pessimistic and dangerous. Hazlitt focuses on Malthus's ratios, which he says are wrong and misleading. Malthus underestimates the increase in food production and overstates the increase in population, he insists. The geometric rate of increase is a fiction. Malthus confuses the *power* of population to increase (its potential to increase at a geometric rate) with its *tendency* (how it tends in fact to operate) because he equates the need for food, which is absolute, with the sex drive, which can be controlled, as the existence of celibates attests. It is symptomatic of Malthus's general confusion, Hazlitt maintains, that he introduces moral restraint as a check in 1803 but does not change the conclusions he advanced in 1798, where the need for food and sex was presented in purely biological terms. Moreover, *An Essay on Population* is dangerous because it is inimical to reform. The idea that a degree of progress is a step toward disaster makes the book "the most effectual recipe for indifference that has yet been found out." It will increase selfishness and promote apathy in the rich and increase despair and promote revolution among the poor. Wondering how "such a miserable reptile performance should ever have crawled to that height of reputation that it has reached," Hazlitt concludes that the answers are to be found in the penchant of English intellectuals to take "what is confused and unintelligible" to be profound and in the upper class who find in Malthus a "convenient doctrine" to justify greed.

With the death of the rector at Walesby in Lincolnshire, Malthus was instituted as rector in November 1803, probably through the office of

*Harriet Malthus, 1833 (portrait by John Linnell; private collection, from Patricia James,* Population Malthus: His Life and Times, *1979)*

his cousin Henry Dalton, the patron of Walesby. This living allowed Malthus to marry Harriet Eckersall, a distant cousin, on 12 April 1804. The thirty-eight-year-old proponent of "moral restraint" must have suffered embarrassment when Harriet gave birth to a son in December, only eight months after the marriage.

Malthus's changed status and the controversy over *An Essay on Population* did not deter him from continuing to take unpopular stands when he thought economic facts supported them. In his *Letter to Samuel Whitbread* (1807) Malthus argues against this M.P.'s proposal to build cottages for impoverished newlyweds on the grounds that the proposal would weaken the check to marriage that the scarcity and high cost of housing provided and that it would depress the wage by enabling employers to depend on the government housing subsidies to bring family income to a subsistence level.

Malthus was appointed the first professor of general history, politics, commerce, and finance of the East India College at Haileybury at the school's founding in 1805. The college was one among many efforts of the British government to professionalize the civil service of the East India Company—by making appointments more dependent on training and achievement than on patronage. Those in the company who regarded appointments as inheritable assets seized the opportunity that periodic, serious disciplinary problems at the school provided to call for Parliament to eliminate the college. Malthus's pamphlets defending the college in 1813 and 1817 may have been crucial to its survival. He remained a professor at the college for all his life, living with his family in a house on the college grounds.

The need to develop lectures in economics at Haileybury directed Malthus to a more comprehensive consideration of questions and texts seminal to classical economics than his focus on the principle of population had permitted. For Malthus economics began with the physiocrats' advocacy of laissez-faire, a tradition which received its paradigmatic statement in Adam Smith's advocacy of "natural liberty" in *The Wealth of Nations* (1776). Smith maintained that if property were secure and if all were free to pursue their self-interests, the "invisible hand" of market forces would assure a productive and harmonious society without the inefficiencies that mercantile or other interventionist systems cause. Practically speaking, these principles favor free trade over tariffs with regard to international economic policies; at home market forces alone determine wages and profit—unions, entitlement programs, and minimum-wage laws being judged as "artificial" restrictions of "natural" liberty.

For the most part Malthus worked within this tradition, accepting the right of property as intrinsic and sharing Smith's lack of confidence in government, but his positions often depart from those of the ideologues who were consciously working to create a science of economics with laissez-faire as the first principle. There were several reasons for Malthus's occasional apostasy. First, as Malthus's attack in *An Essay on Population* on the work of Godwin and Condorcet indicates, he distrusted abstractions and theories, which he associated with the outmoded views of René Descartes. Second, Malthus was willing to compromise laissez-faire and support government intervention into the economy when the result was likely to improve the prospects for English agriculture. For Malthus the agricultural sector was more important than any other, and property rights were prior to all other liberties because he believed that, in the presence of starvation, no liberties would be respected. Government policy favoring agriculture and guaranteeing absolute property rights were means to insure the investment in land necessary to produce sufficient food. Finally, Malthus refused to be wedded to laissez-faire because he developed his ideas in response to particular pressing issues which meant, given his practical bent, that he was always more concerned that his positions met the test of effective policy than the test of theoretical consistency.

Malthus's concentration on exceptions and his penchant for qualifying theory rather than developing it can be seen in the two review articles on the bullion question that he published in the February and August 1811 issues of the *Edinburgh Review*. Malthus essentially agreed with David Ricardo and other bullionists who had written that inflation resulted more from monetary policy than from real changes in the supply of and demand for commodities, but Malthus's more empirical approach leads him to argue that Ricardo, who was willing to put local variables aside in pursuing theoretical clarity and consistency, had overlooked other factors that had also influenced price historically.

Malthus's publication in 1814 and 1815 of three pamphlets dealing directly or indirectly with the controversies over the Corn Law show his willingness to abandon laissez-faire if he thought the effects of tariffs would promote food production and even raise wages, but these pamphlets fueled charges that he was inconsistent. The fall in the price of "corn" (grain) in 1813 prompted British farmers and landowners to complain that they could not recover their costs at current prices. Parliament undertook to investigate the effects of introducing tariffs that would restrict the importation of grain when the domestic price fell below a certain target price. In *Observations on the Effects of the Corn Laws* (1814), Malthus summarizes opposing views with what he regarded as studied neutrality, but in *The Grounds of an Opinion on the Policy of Restricting the Importation of Foreign Corn* (1815) and *An Inquiry into the Nature and Progress of Rent* (1815), Malthus makes his support of the protective legislation and tariffs clear. In *The Grounds of an Opinion on . . . Foreign Corn* he produces evidence to support his view that investment in agriculture follows tariffs and higher prices. He also argues that, contrary to conventional wisdom, a high food price is good for labor because wages increase with rises in the price of bread but do not fall when grain prices stabilize or drop, thus providing higher real wages in the long run. In *An Inquiry into the Nature and Progress of Rent* Malthus defines rents as the result of the difference between the cost of production on a given plot and the cost of food produced from the least productive comparable plot. His analysis may have failed as an effort to defuse arguments against tariffs grounded in resentment of the monopolistic

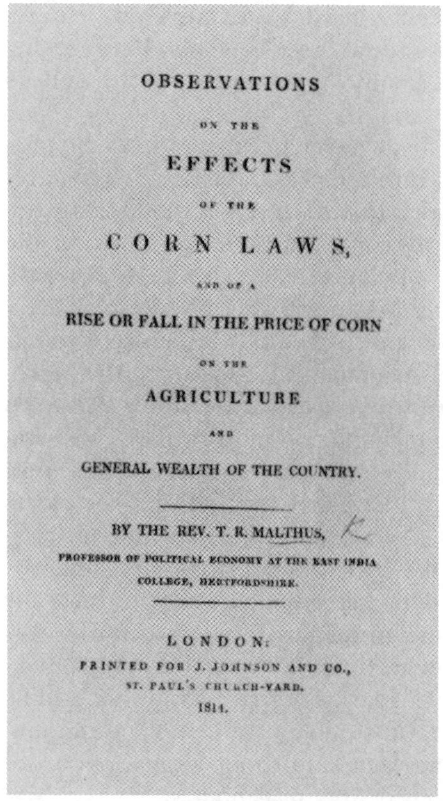

OBSERVATIONS
ON THE
EFFECTS
OF THE
CORN LAWS,
AND OF A
RISE OR FALL IN THE PRICE OF CORN
ON THE
AGRICULTURE
AND
GENERAL WEALTH OF THE COUNTRY.

BY THE REV. T. R. MALTHUS,
PROFESSOR OF POLITICAL ECONOMY AT THE EAST INDIA
COLLEGE, HERTFORDSHIRE.

LONDON:
PRINTED FOR J. JOHNSON AND CO.,
ST. PAUL'S CHURCH-YARD.
1814.

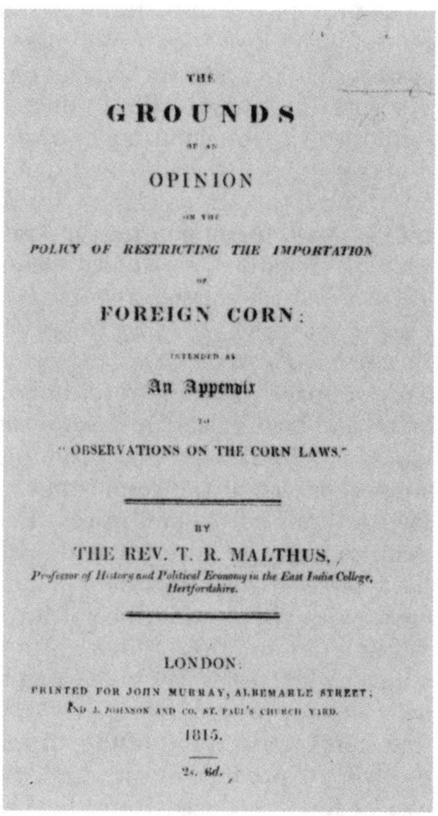

THE
GROUNDS
OF AN
OPINION
ON THE
POLICY OF RESTRICTING THE IMPORTATION
OF
FOREIGN CORN;
INTENDED AS
An Appendix
TO
"OBSERVATIONS ON THE CORN LAWS."

BY
THE REV. T. R. MALTHUS,
Professor of History and Political Economy in the East India College,
Hertfordshire.

LONDON:
PRINTED FOR JOHN MURRAY, ALBEMARLE STREET;
AND J. JOHNSON AND CO. ST. PAUL'S CHURCH YARD.
1815.

2s. 6d.

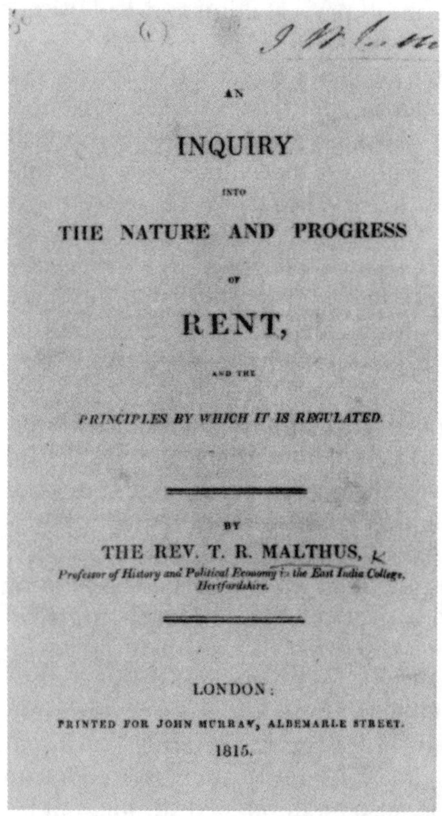

AN
INQUIRY
INTO
THE NATURE AND PROGRESS
OF
RENT,
AND THE
PRINCIPLES BY WHICH IT IS REGULATED.

BY
THE REV. T. R. MALTHUS,
Professor of History and Political Economy in the East India College,
Hertfordshire.

LONDON:
PRINTED FOR JOHN MURRAY, ALBEMARLE STREET.
1815.

*Title pages for the pamphlets in which Malthus supported protective legislation and tariffs on imported grain, prompting some of his critics to charge him with inconsistency for abandoning his advocacy of laissez-faire economics* landed class, but it gained for Malthus a considerable share of credit (with Ricardo and other of his contemporaries) for the discovery of the law of diminishing returns. Regardless of the merits of Malthus's arguments on economic or political grounds, his abandonment of laissez-faire and his shifting views prompted Robert Torrens's remark in his *Essays on the External Corn Trade* (1815) that "Mr. Malthus's scarcely ever embraced a principle which he did not subsequently abandon," not the first or the last time he was accused of inconsistency. His support of protectionism seemed to Whig interests like so much special pleading on behalf of the landed aristocracy; as a result, Whigs saw to it that Malthus's work was at least temporarily no longer welcomed by the *Edinburgh Review.*

By the time Malthus published his most complete statement of his views on economics, his *Principles of Political Economy* (1820), he had become aware of what characterized his approach. Economics, he insists, is not a mathematical science but more like moral or political science: even its most established principles are based on the propensities of human nature, which admit exceptions and which are differently manifest. Economics is a science of "proportions" that involves finding the just means between the tensions inherent in its principles. He faults economists who "simplify and generalize" in an effort to produce elegant theories but at the cost of ignoring significant exceptions and at the sacrifice of workable policy. In these criticisms it is obvious that Malthus has chiefly in mind his friend Ricardo, whose genius was his ability to identify general truths and to follow their implications with a marvelous clarity and logic, while Malthus preferred always to probe the limits of general principles.

In July 1821 Malthus published in the *Edinburgh Review* an unsigned review of William Godwin's *Of Population* (1820), a long answer to the principle of population. The years since Malthus first criticized Godwin's theories in the first *Essay on Population* had not been kind to Godwin, who saw a last chance for immortality in the defeat of Malthus's "accursed apology in favour of vice and misery, of hardheartedness and oppression." In his review Malthus argues that Godwin's book would be undeserving of consideration except for its recent prominent mention in a debate in the House of Commons over the Poor Laws. After offering a detailed critique of Godwin's attack on the estimates in *An Essay on Population* of the rate and cause of rapid population increase in America, Malthus, referring to himself in the third person, argues that Godwin not only misunderstands but intentionally distorts Malthus's views, that indeed Godwin's whole book is founded on the falsehood "that the misery and vice which Mr. Malthus has stated to be the *consequences* of an excessive population, have been proposed by him as its *remedies*, and of representing him, consequently, as a friend to misery and vice; while the letter and spirit of his work clearly show that he is their greatest enemy, and that his whole aim and object is to diminish their amount." Finally, Malthus insists that those who attack his work give a promise to the poor that they cannot keep: "We may *promise* to maintain the poor adequately; but we shall deceive them, and shall not do it. . . ." Better to empower the poor with knowledge that would enable them to direct their own destiny: "If the law of population be such as has been stated, it is a truth which it particularly concerns the poor to know. And, in fact, the general circulation of this truth must be the foundation of all essential improvement in their condition."

During the last ten years of his life, Malthus's voice on questions of political economy was granted less and less authority. Commentators generally judged his pamphlet *The Measure of Value Stated* (1823) as confused. De Quincey, for example, noted in the *London Magazine* (December 1823) that in matters of political economy whoever takes Malthus for a guide must be able to use a compass. Malthus's *Definitions in Political Economy* (1827), which faults Adam Smith, David Ricardo, James Mill, John Ramsay McCulloch, and others for sloppy thinking, was largely ignored. Although his contribution on population for the 1824 supplement to the *Encyclopædia Britannica* is an admirably clear, cogent summary of his principle of population, Malthus must have felt slighted when McCulloch was offered the entry on "political economy" after Ricardo had turned down an invitation to write it.

Malthus's last years were not free from controversy and disappointment, most particularly as a result of the debate over the controversial amendments to the Poor Laws in 1834. The intent of the amendments was to make receiving relief, which was to be provided only in the workhouse, more painful than working and to assure that funds were dispensed efficiently and honestly—in other words, to curtail alleged abuses that Malthus had dismissed in 1798 as irrelevant to what was thought to be the ineffective-

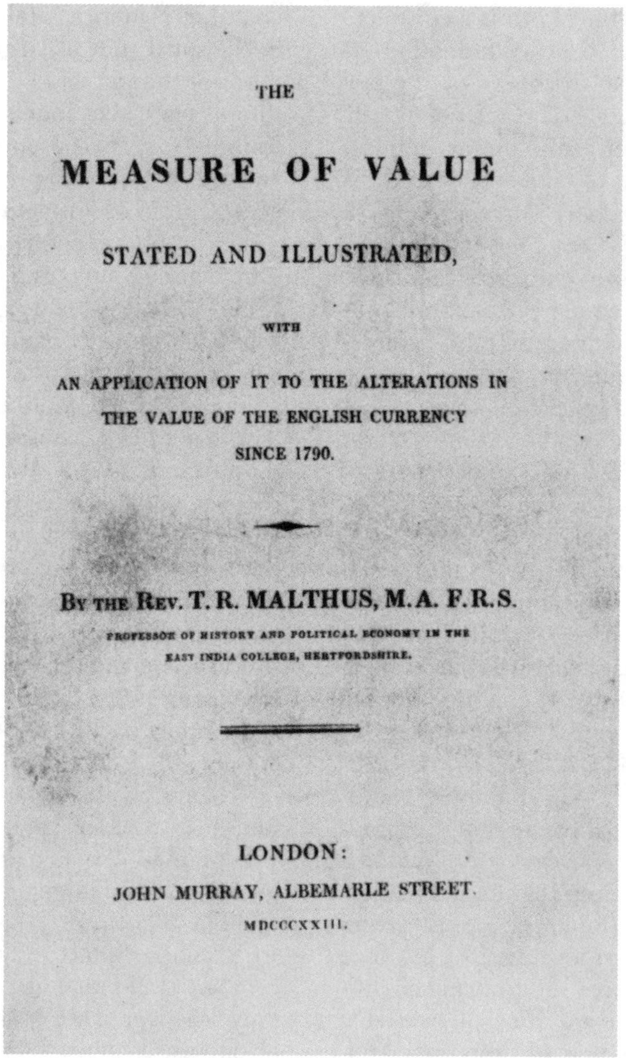
THE

MEASURE OF VALUE

STATED AND ILLUSTRATED,

WITH

AN APPLICATION OF IT TO THE ALTERATIONS IN THE VALUE OF THE ENGLISH CURRENCY SINCE 1790.

BY THE REV. T. R. MALTHUS, M. A. F. R. S.

PROFESSOR OF HISTORY AND POLITICAL ECONOMY IN THE EAST INDIA COLLEGE, HERTFORDSHIRE.

LONDON:

JOHN MURRAY, ALBEMARLE STREET.

MDCCCXXIII.

*Title page for Malthus's 1823 pamphlet, which led Thomas De Quincey to warn that any reader who takes Malthus for a guide should be able to use a compass, "or before he has read ten pages he will find himself . . . disposed to sit down and fall a-crying with his guide at the sad bewilderment into which they have both strayed"*

ness and rising costs of the Poor Laws. Despite this, despite his moderating his opposition to the Poor Laws, despite his insistence throughout his life that his criticism of the Poor Laws was based on their tendency to depress the real wages of labor, Malthus's name was still linked by advocates of relief to callous indifference to suffering. Even those who meant well by him did him no favor, as Malthus learned from the example of an M.P., John Bennett, who, in the course of speaking in favor of the restrictive amendment of 1834, took time to eulogize Malthus, prompting a *Times* editorial (24 July 1834) to suggest sarcastically that Jonathan Swift's *Modest Proposal* (1729) and the "savages' " custom of killing the aged were solutions "more humane than the plan of Mr. Malthus; for starvation must be a painful and lingering death, whereas the tomahawk is as speedy as it is certain in its operation."

Malthus died on 29 December 1834. He was buried in Bath Abbey. A tablet, with a long epitaph written at the time of his burial, has been moved from its original location and today may be seen in the porch of the west end of the church.

Much work has been done on Malthus by scholars of economic history and the history of ideas. In the nineteenth century Malthus was overshadowed as an economist by David Ricardo, who was preferred not only as a superior theorist but also for realizing better than Malthus the significance of the principle of population for classical economic theory. A reevaluation began with John Maynard Keynes's essay on Malthus in

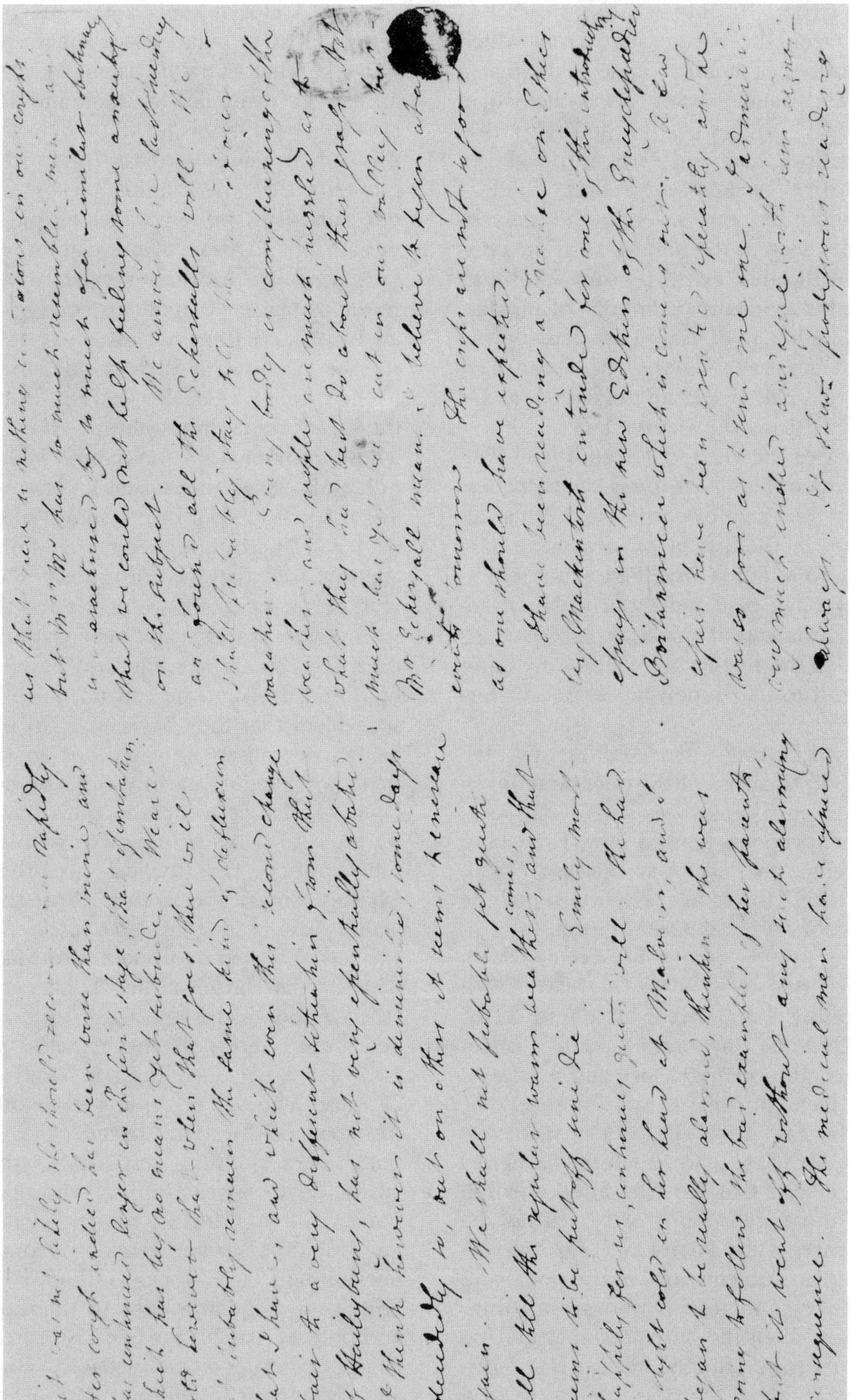

*Pages from Malthus's 22 June 1830 letter to William Otter, one of the friends with whom he traveled through Scandinavia and Russia in 1799 (Pierpont Morgan Library; from the Collection of Gordon N. Ray). In this letter Malthus mentions a trip with his wife and daughter Emily to visit his in-laws, the Eckersalls, and he praises Sir James Mackintosh's "Dissertation on the Progress of Ethical Philosophy," written for the* Encyclopædia Britannica.

1933. Keynes wrote, "If only Malthus, instead of Ricardo, had been the parent stem from which nineteenth-century economics proceeded, what a much wiser and much richer place the world would be to-day!," suggesting the possibility that Malthus's practical, commonsense approach, in comparison to Ricardo's theoretical rigidity, might have modified the severity and detachment sometimes seen as the hallmarks of the "dismal science" in the nineteenth century. Malthus's skepticism of the economic orthodoxy of his day, especially his challenge of Say's Law denying the possibility of a general glut, must have appealed to Keynes as he challenged the orthodoxy of his contemporaries during the Depression.

Both Charles Darwin and Alfred Russel Wallace acknowledged Malthus's *Essay on Population* as the catalyst for their own theories. Thus, although scholars of the history of ideas have paid some attention to Malthus's theological and political ideas, they have paid more particular attention to the relationship of the *Essay on Population* to the genesis of the theory of evolution by natural selection and to its relationship to Social Darwinism.

No comprehensive study of Malthus and Malthusian themes in the work of the poets and novelists of the nineteenth century exists. For the most part the Romantic poets abused him. For example, in his preface to *Prometheus Unbound* (1820) Shelley—referring to what he judged to be Malthus's reactionary, complacent morality—professed that he would "rather be damned with Plato and Lord Bacon, than go to Heaven with Paley and Malthus," and Byron in Canto XI of *Don Juan* (1823) made a hypocritical, selfish, calculating "Malthus" the enemy of love and marriage. A more complex treatment can, however, be found in Thomas Love Peacock's *Melincourt* (1817), where Mr. Fax, who venerates bachelors and spinsters, asserts that the sole cause of evil in the world is "more men than corn," regrets the "baleful influence of the Poor Laws" for destroying the "principle of calculation" in the poor, and admonishes Zukey and Robin, who are on their way to the altar, about the hardships that inevitably follow marriage and family. But Fax is also disturbed (as was Malthus) that less is spent to feed people than pleasure horses ("four-footed sinecurists"), that the children of the poor are used by the state as fodder in war, and that political economists typically withdraw in a protective shell of scientific detachment, rather than face up to the problems confronting society.

In Victorian novels themes related to the principle of population are pervasive, and Malthus-like characters occasionally put in appearances. For example, in Benjamin Disraeli's *Sybil* (1845) Malthusianism, if not exactly Malthus, probably provides the basis for Lord Marney's arguments that the country's economic woes are not caused by the low wages he pays his workers but are "all an affair of population" with the solution lying in lower poor rates, emigration, and fewer cottages: "I build no cottages and destroy all I can; and I am not ashamed or afraid to say so," he announces. Such themes are everywhere in the novels of Charles Dickens, but especially in the Gradgrind philosophy of *Hard Times* (1854), whose founder has a son named Malthus. The angular Mr. Filer in Dickens's New Year's novella *The Chimes* (1845) bears some physical resemblance to Malthus, and some of Malthus's crudest rhetoric reverberates in Filer's philosophy: "a man . . . may labour all his life for the benefit of such people as those; and may heap up facts on figures, facts on figures, facts on figures, mountains high and dry; and he can no more hope to persuade 'em that they have no right or business to be married, than he can hope to persuade 'em that they have no earthly right or business to be born. And *that* we know they haven't. We reduced it to a mathematical certainty long ago!," Filer insists. Less typical are the sentiments Charles Kingsley expresses through the protest leader Crosswaithe in *Alton Locke* (1850). While Crosswaithe claims to reject the "Malthusian doctrines" as an "infernal lie," believing instead that "there's room on English soil for twice the number there is now," he nevertheless vows that he "will never beget children to swell the numbers of those who are trampling each other down in the struggle for daily bread" and recommends that workers and especially their leaders "who have wives be as though they had none. . . ."—Malthus's sentiments exactly.

Malthus was and remains a controversial figure, but he was also a most influential one. The validity and originality, not to mention the moral and political implications, of his principle of population continue to be debated. But opponents and supporters of Malthus can now see, what the novelists also attest to, that *An Essay on Population* drew attention to the conditions of the laboring class. Malthus was a careful, sympathetic observer of the poor: "The sons and daughters of peasants will not be found such rosy cherubs in real life, as they are described to be in romances. . . .

And the lads who drive plough, which must certainly be healthy exercise, are very rarely seen with an appearance of calves to their legs," he noted in the first *Essay on Population*, where he also insisted that we have failed and continue to fail to see the misery that a part of society has always endured because "the histories of mankind that we possess are histories only of the higher classes." It was part of Malthus's intention to change this perspective, to force all to attend, as he did, to the bills of mortality, where the children of the poor were to be found in depressingly large numbers. In "The Claims of Labour," first published in the April 1845 issue of the *Edinburgh Review*, John Stuart Mill, noting that Malthus was the first to insist on the relationship between the number of laborers and the wages of labor, observed, "Though the assertion may be looked upon as a paradox, it is historically true, that only from that time [the publication of Malthus's *Essay on Population*] has the economical condition of the labouring classes been regarded by thoughtful men as susceptible of permanent improvement." We are coming to agree that this attention to the plight of the poor was part, and not an incidental part, of the controversial Malthus's permanent achievement.

**Letters:**

Correspondence with David Ricardo, in volumes 6-9 of *The Works and Correspondence of David Ricardo*, 11 volumes, edited by Piero Sraffa (Cambridge: Cambridge University Press, 1951-1973).

**Bibliographies:**

"Publications of Thomas Robert Malthus" and "Publications about Malthus and his Work," in *The Works of Thomas Robert Malthus*, 8 volumes, edited by E. A. Wrigley and David Souden (London: Pickering, 1986), I: 41-44, 45-52.

**Biographies:**

William Otter, "Memoir of Robert Malthus," in *Principles of Political Economy*, second edition (London: Pickering, 1836);

James Bonar, *Malthus and His Work* (London: Macmillan, 1885; revised edition, London: Allen & Unwin, 1924; New York: Macmillan, 1924);

Patricia James, *Population Malthus: His Life and Times* (London: Routledge & Kegan Paul, 1979);

William Petersen, *Malthus* (London: Heinemann, 1979).

**References:**

William P. Albrecht, "Godwin and Malthus," *PMLA*, 70 (June 1955): 552-556;

Albrecht, *William Hazlitt and the Malthusian Controversy* (Albuquerque: University of New Mexico Press, 1950);

Kenneth Curry, "A Note on Coleridge's Copy of Malthus," *PMLA*, 54 (June 1939): 613-615;

Gertrude Himmelfarb, *The Idea of Poverty: England in the Early Industrial Age* (New York: Knopf, 1984);

John Maynard Keynes, "Robert Malthus: the First of the Cambridge Economists," in his *Essays in Biography* (London: Macmillan, 1933; New York: Harcourt, Brace, 1933; enlarged edition, London: Hart-Davis, 1951; New York: Horizon Press, 1951), pp. 95-149;

*The Malthus Library Catalogue: The Personal Collection of Thomas Robert Malthus at Jesus College, Cambridge*, with contributions by John Harrison and others (New York, Oxford, Toronto, Sydney, Paris, Frankfurt & Tokyo: Pergamon Press, 1983);

George Reuben Potter, "Unpublished Marginalia in Coleridge's Copy of Malthus's *Essay on Population*," *PMLA*, 51 (December 1936): 1061-1068;

C. E. Pulos, "Shelley and Malthus," *PMLA*, 67 (March 1952): 113-124;

Kenneth Smith, *The Malthusian Controversy* (London: Routledge & Kegan Paul, 1951);

Peter Vorzimmer, "Darwin, Malthus, and the Theory of Natural Selection," *Journal of the History of Ideas*, 30 (October-December 1969): 527-542;

Arthur E. Walzer, "Logic and Rhetoric in Malthus's *Essay on the Principle of Population, 1798*," *Quarterly Journal of Speech*, 73 (February 1987): 1-17;

Donald Winch, *Malthus* (Oxford: Oxford University Press, 1987);

E. A. Wrigley and David Souden, Introduction to *The Works of Thomas Robert Malthus*, 8 volumes, edited by Wrigley and Souden (London: Pickering, 1986), I: 7-74.

# James Mill

*(6 April 1773 - 23 June 1836)*

Michael Laine
*Victoria College, University of Toronto*

BOOKS: *An Essay of the Impolicy of a Bounty on the Exportation of Grain; and on the Principles which Ought to Regulate the Commerce of Grain* (London: Printed for C. & R. Baldwin, 1804);

*Commerce Defended: An Answer to the Arguments by Which Mr. Spence, Mr. Cobbett, and Others, Have Attempted to Prove That Commerce is not a Source of National Wealth* (London: C. & R. Baldwin, 1808);

*Schools for All, not Schools for Churchmen Only* (London: Longman & Co., 1812);

*Proposals for Establishing in the Metropolis, A Day School,* by Mill and Francis Place (London: McCreery, 1816);

*The History of British India,* 3 volumes (London: Baldwin, Craddock & Joy, 1817);

*Elements of Political Economy* (London: Printed for Baldwin, Craddock & Joy, 1821);

*Essays on Government, Jurisprudence, Liberty of the Press, and Law of Nations. Written for "The Supplement to the Encyclopædia Britannica"* (London: Printed by J. Innes, 1825);

*Analysis of the Phenomena of the Human Mind,* 2 volumes (London: Baldwin & Craddock, 1829);

*On the Ballot; from the "Westminster Review," for July, 1830* (London: Published by Robert Heward, T. C. Hansard, printer, 1830);

*A Fragment on Mackintosh* (London: Printed for Baldwin & Craddock, 1835);

*The Principles of Toleration* (London: Henry Hooper, 1837).

Much less well-known than his son John Stuart Mill, James Mill nevertheless occupies a position of importance in the history of Western political thought. Rather than a practical politician, Mill was a theorist with a vision of a society improved by its attachment to moral principles. A man possessed of stern moral principles and a highly developed social conscience, James Mill was one of the leading reformers of his day. He became a principal in a group that initially derived its theories from the utilitarianism of Jeremy Bentham but later included a wide spectrum of opinion. To blunt the effect of the term *Utilitarian,* or *Benthamite,* which in the 1830s had become both misleading and unpopular, John Stuart Mill proposed for them the name Philosophic Radicals, by which they are now known. Although James Mill was a leading proponent of Bentham's ideas, they were considerably modified and enhanced in his hands.

Born in Northwater Bridge, Forfarshire, Scotland, Mill was the son of a reasonably prosperous shoemaker, also named James, and Isabel Fenton, the daughter of a farmer. The eldest of three children and encouraged by his mother, he was early destined for a scholar and sent to Montrose Academy. Subsequently, he came to the notice of Sir John and Lady Jane Stuart of Fettercairn, to whose daughter he became tutor and who arranged for him to be sent to Edinburgh University, rather than to Aberdeen as his father intended. He entered in 1790 at the advanced age (for those times) of seventeen. Throughout his student days, Mill was an exceptionally accomplished scholar, particularly distinguishing himself in Greek. Interested in philosophy, he fell under the influence of Dugald Stewart, whose eloquence he placed above that of William Pitt and Charles James Fox. In 1794 he entered the Divinity School at Edinburgh and was licensed to preach in 1798. Apparently he delivered some sermons in his own district but was unable to find a parish and, in 1802, went to London in the company of Sir John Stuart, then the member of the House of Commons for Kincardineshire. Sir John secured him frequent tickets to the gallery of the House of Commons, where he was able to listen to the important debates of the time.

During his first years in London he supported himself as a free-lance journalist writing for the *Anti-Jacobin Review,* subsequently becoming editor of the *Literary Journal* (1802) and the *St. James Chronicle* (1805). He became a volunteer

*James Mill (portrait by an unknown artist; from Alexander Bain,* James Mill: A Biography, *1882)*

soldier for about six months in 1804, and in the same year, having, as Alexander Bain estimates, an income of five hundred pounds a year, he became engaged to Harriet Burrow, daughter of a widow who kept a lunatic asylum. They married on 5 June 1805 and settled in Pentonville, eventually producing nine children, the eldest of whom was John Stuart Mill. The marriage, while perhaps not unhappy, was unequal in terms of temperament and intellectual interests, creating a somewhat strained atmosphere in the home.

The *Literary Journal* ceased publication in 1806, and Mill apparently gave up the editorship of the *St. James Chronicle* two years later; nevertheless his career in journalism continued to the end of his life. He contributed important articles to the *Edinburgh Review*, the *Westminster Review*, the *Philanthropist*, and the *Eclectic Review* as well as other periodicals. In 1804, in answer to William Spence and William Cobbett, Mill published anonymously a pamphlet arguing against the export duty on grain, and in 1808 his *Commerce Defended* advocated the cause of free trade.

In 1808 Mill formed a significant friendship with Jeremy Bentham. Bentham allowed Mill to live in a house that once belonged to John Milton and adjoined Bentham's own. Subsequently, he let him another at a reduced rent until Mill could pay full value. For many years they were close neighbors in town, and the Mills were regular guests, for as long as nine or ten months at a time, at Bentham's summer residence at Ford Abbey. The extent to which James Mill can be seen as a theorist for the new English brand of rad-

*Number 39 Rodney Street, Islington (formerly Number 12 Rodney Terrace, Pentonville), where the Mills were living when their first child, John Stuart Mill, was born in May 1806*

icalism can be seen as a result of his close association with Bentham. It is not to denigrate Mill's accomplishment that he has been described as a disciple of Bentham or as Bentham's lieutenant. There can be no doubt that Mill also had a great influence on David Ricardo, who was shy and unsure of his ability to express his theories clearly. Ricardo became acquainted with Mill in 1807. In 1811 Mill put him in touch with Bentham. Mill persuaded Ricardo to publish in 1816 and in 1819 to enter Parliament. As Bentham said, "I was the spiritual father of Mill and Mill was the spiritual father of Ricardo: so that Ricardo was my spiritual grandson." In his relations with Bentham and with Bentham's work, Mill's contribution was not only to be a theorist and to concentrate on essential matters where Bentham tended to immerse himself in detail, but also to act as a democratizing influence. Moreover, in January 1809, in an article on South American constitutions, "Emancipation of South America," for the *Edinburgh Review*, Mill was the first to base firmly the theory of representative government on strict utilitarian principles.

Along with Bentham and Francis Place, Mill became interested in educational theory. Influenced by the ideas of the Frenchman Claude-Adrien Helvétius, they determined that popular education was the most efficient means to convert the nation to a utilitarian morality. They were impressed with the possibilities of the monitorial system established on the principles of Andrew Bell and Joseph Lancaster. The West London Lancasterian Association was organized, and in 1812 Mill published a pamphlet, *Schools for All, not Schools for Churchmen Only*, that acted as their

*Number 40 Queen Anne's Gate, Westminster (formerly Number 1 Queen's Square), the house where the Mills went to live in 1808*

manifesto. Consistent with his early writing on commerce, it exhibits a strong bias toward the middle classes, whom Mill saw as "the strength of the community [containing] the greatest proportion of the intelligence, industry and wealth of the state." A school for which Bentham was to provide the site was planned but never constructed. In 1816 Mill and Place published *Proposals for Establishing in the Metropolis, A Day School.*

Near the end of 1806 Mill began *The History of British India,* a project which he thought would occupy him for some three or four years; in fact it occupied him for ten. Mill had no direct experience of India and wished for none. Relying almost exclusively on printed sources, selecting from them, judging their value, he produced what he called a "critical history," establishing conclusions by the rules of evidence from fixed principles. Mill had little knowledge of any Indian language and was contemptuous of Hindu society, regarding it as being in a more or less savage state and, accordingly, unaffected or unpolluted by modern ideas of government. Although he disapproved of rule by force, he could see British (that is East India Company) intervention in India as an opportunity to establish a good government informed by utilitarian principles. *The History of British India* displays little sympathy with the attachment of men to the comfort of their own customs and rituals. For Mill, utility was the measure of civilization. India could be enlightened through an understanding of the fundamental laws of human nature applied in accordance with utilitarian principles. Although considered a radical, Mill had a strongly moral cast of mind that made him, in the coming Evangelical temper of the times, eminently eligible for his appointment to the administrative staff of the East India Company. He was appointed assistant to the examiner of India correspondence in 1819 with a salary of eight hundred pounds, rising through East India House until, in 1830, he became chief examiner with a salary of nineteen hundred pounds, responsible to the directors for all departments. He was followed in this career by his son John Stuart Mill.

Between 1816 and 1823 Mill contributed a series of articles to the supplement of the *Encyclopædia Britannica.* Although almost all were republished by 1828, the articles on "Government" and "Education" have survived most securely. "Education," informed by Mill's associationist theories later developed in his *Analysis of the Phenomena of the Human Mind* (1829), appeared in the supplement in December 1819. The article has at its center the principle of utility, and it states unequivocally that the end of education is "to render the individual an instrument of happiness, first to himself and next, to other beings." For Mill, happiness does not come from the gratification of each and every personal desire, but its quantity is increased through the ability to postpone gratification. In the article he suggests, unlike Bentham, that pleasure can be qualified, and that at the root of a utilitarian system of education lie the ancient virtues of temperance and fortitude as well as those of justice and generosity. Then, such a system of education would inform all what the nature of true happiness is and teach each to desire it for himself and for others. In practice Mill's views, although egalitarian, were rigorously intellectual. His eldest child, John Stuart Mill, was not sent to school; at the age of three he began his education with the study of Greek followed by extensive reading in classic texts. Nevertheless, he denied that he had been crammed but insisted, on the contrary, that he had been taught to think for himself. Appropriately, in light of his father's attachment to the monitorial system of Bell and Lancaster, John was set to tutoring his younger brothers and sisters.

James Mill's theory of education, firmly based on utilitarian morality and assuming the perfectibility of mankind, presupposes a connection between education and politics. The encyclopedia article on "Government," in the September 1820 supplement, demonstrates the political application of a utilitarian morality. At first sight the article appears to be highly theoretical, but its true significance is its promotion of representative government. It shows clearly that Mill understood, where Bentham did not, the idea of community of interest. Mill displays a somewhat Hobbesian view; he suggests that if a man obtains power over others, he will use it for an evil purpose. Thus, in any good government, there must be a checking body that will have an identity of interest with the community as a whole. Otherwise it too will abuse its power. Although Mill appears to favor extending the franchise only to the middle class and although much has been made of his apparent exclusion of women and men under forty, the essay actually argues for universal suffrage. But, as both Thomas Babington Macaulay, in his attack on "Government" in the *Edinburgh Review* (March 1829), and J. S. Mill, in his *Autobiography*, have pointed out, Mill's premises were narrow: identity of interest is not the only thing upon which good government depends. Moreover, Macaulay claimed that Mill's laws were merely truisms and that Mill, in his discussion of the franchise, inconsistently held an attachment both to democracy and to elitism. It is, however, necessary to remember that "Government" was designed to promote reform and that James Mill was not a Whig or a liberal, but a Radical.

In *Elements of Political Economy* (1821), strict utilitarian principles are once again applied to the science of government. The book opens with the statement "Political Economy is to the State what domestic economy is to the family." A short defining chapter lays down specific areas of inquiry for determining the laws that regulate the production, distribution, exchange, and consumption of those commodities produced by human labor. Developing his economic views from those of Ricardo, Mill believed in a progressive society dominated by a healthy middle class that would stimulate progressive ideas. Such a view, though assuming inequality of possession of goods and depending upon property rights, did not exclude a desire for a more equal distribution of capital through the application of market forces. The object of an efficient political economy, here as elsewhere in his work, was to produce most efficiently the greatest quantity of happiness. The text, somewhat cryptic and dry in style, was constructed from the outline that his son John, then aged thirteen, made day by day after his father had lectured to him. John Stuart Mill remarked in 1854 that the book, "very useful when written . . . has now for some time finished its work."

In 1822 Mill began work on the *Analysis of the Phenomena of the Human Mind.* Since it required extended periods of concentrated work and Mill could find the time only during his

*Mill in 1831 (drawing by Joseph Slater; from Hugh S. R. Elliot, ed.,* The Letters of John Stuart Mill, *1910)*

monthlong vacations, it was seven years in the making, not to be published until 1829. The argument depends on the theory of association of ideas after John Locke and David Hartley. Although the book is of little interest to modern philosophers, immediately after its publication it became the text for a study group that included Mill's son, John Stuart Mill, who felt that it promoted the cause of the associationists in their quarrel with the institutionalists. He said that the first edition did not achieve the immediate success it deserved and in 1869 edited a new edition with notes by himself, Alexander Bain, George Grote, and the linguist Andrew Findlater. This edition, too, is of limited interest except to students of the younger Mill.

In July 1830 James Mill contributed a long article, "The Ballot," to the *Westminster Review*. A powerful defense of the secret ballot, it reveals a more temperate Mill than "Government." He sees the ballot as the instrument that would free the electoral process from intimidation and corruption and ensure a government directed by those morally and culturally able to provide the best government. Those leaders, though propertied and wealthy, would have interests identical to those of the community at large. He seems willing now to postpone the extension of the franchise and the shortening of the duration of parliaments that he considered essential in "Government." It was not that things could not be altered for the better, but that "the ballot would operate so powerfully as an instrument of good, that the inconveniences which might still arise from these defects, if we had the ballot, would be far less severely felt."

In 1830 Mill produced a violent response to Sir James Mackintosh's article "Ethical Philosophy," written for the *Encyclopædia Britannica*. In attacking the Utilitarians, Mackintosh had criticized, more than somewhat intemperately, the Benthamite slant of Mill's essays on government and education. In *A Fragment on Mackintosh* (1835) Mill sets out a utilitarian ethic in a text that is chiefly an attack on Mackintosh's justification of the "Moral Sense Theory." Mill's antagonism to Mackintosh was no doubt stimulated by his memory of Mackintosh's attack in the *Edinburgh Review* (December 1818) on Bentham's *Plan of Parliamentary Reform* (1817). Among other things, he accuses Mackintosh of perverting Hartley's associationism. William Whewell wrote in a prefatory note to the third edition of Mackintosh's article, published as *Dissertation on the Progress of Ethical Philosophy* (1862), that Mill's remarks not only appeared to him "erroneous in their principles; but more especially worthy of blame as an attempt to lower the reputation of the author by captiousness, contumely, and buffoonery."

Mill's last years were marked by failing health and diminished productivity. Gout, an earlier trouble, had not left him, and he began to suffer from diseases of the lungs. On 23 June 1836 he died peacefully at home. His final article had appeared in the *London and Westminster Review* in April of that year.

Of James Mill's character, his son John wrote in his *Autobiography*: "My father's moral inculcations were at all times mainly those of the 'Socratic viri'; justice, temperance (to which he gave a very extended application), veracity, perseverance, readiness to encounter pain and especially labour; regard for the public good; estimation of persons according to their merits, and of things according to their intrinsic usefulness; a life of exertion, in contradiction to one of self-indulgent sloth. These and other moralities he conveyed in brief sentences, uttered as occasion arose, of grave exhortation, or stern reprobation or contempt." Despite his moralistic nature, he is said to have been a man of charm and of considerable persuasive power.

There has been little recent scholarly work devoted exclusively to James Mill. Although his influence on the practical politics of his own times was slight, and although modern perceptions of nineteenth-century utilitarian ideas seem to remain securely with the writings of his well-known son, it is not possible to understand the contribution of the Philosophical Radicals to contemporary ideas of liberty and democratic government without understanding his work.

**Bibliography:**

Robert A. Fenn, "Concise List of the Works of James Mill," in his *James Mill's Political Thought* (New York & London: Garland, 1987).

**Biography:**

Alexander Bain, *James Mill: A Biography* (London: Longmans, Green, 1882).

**References:**

S. Ambirajan, *Classical Political Economy and British Policy in India* (Cambridge: Cambridge University Press, 1978);

George Spencer Bower, *Hartley and James Mill* (London: Low, 1881);

W. H. Burston, *James Mill on Philosophy and Education* (London: Athlone Press, 1973);

W. R. Carr, "James Mill's Politics Reconsidered: Parliamentary Reform and the Triumph of Truth," *Historical Journal*, 14 (September 1971): 553-580;

William Leslie Davidson, *Political Thought in England: The Utilitarians from Bentham to J. S. Mill* (London: Williams & Norgate, 1915);

Robert A. Fenn, *James Mill's Political Thought* (New York & London: Garland, 1987);

Duncan Forbes, "James Mill and India," *Cambridge Journal*, 5 (October 1951): 19-53;

Elie Halévy, *La Formation Du Radicalisme Philosophique*, 3 volumes (Paris: Alcan, 1901-1904); translated by Mary Morris as *The Growth of Philosophic Radicalism* (London: Faber & Gwyer, 1928);

Joseph Hamburger, *Intellectuals in Politics: John Stuart Mill and the Philosophic Radicals* (New Haven: Yale University Press, 1965);

Hamburger, *James Mill and the Art of Revolution* (New Haven: Yale University Press, 1963);

Hamburger, "James Mill on Universal Suffrage and the Middle Class," *Journal of Politics*, 24 (February 1962): 167-190;

Karl Marx, "Comments on James Mill, *Elémens d' économie politique*," in *Karl Marx and Frederick Engels, Collected Works* (New York: International Publishers, 1975), III: 211-228;

Bruce Mazlish, *James and John Stuart Mill: Father and Son in the Nineteenth Century* (New York: Basic Books, 1951);

John Stuart Mill, *Autobiography* and "A Few Observations on Mr. Mill," in his *Autobiography and Literary Essays*, edited by John M. Robson and Jack Stillinger, volume 1 of *Collected*

*Works of John Stuart Mill* (Toronto: University of Toronto Press, 1981), pp. 1-290, 588-595;

John Morley, "The Life of James Mill," *Fortnightly Review*, new series 31 (April 1882): 476-504;

John Plamenatz, "James Mill," in his *The English Utilitarians* (Oxford: Blackwell, 1958), 97-121;

Theodule Armand Ribot, *English Psychology* (New York: Appleton, 1874);

John M. Robson, "J. S. Mill and Bentham, with Some Observations on James Mill," in *Essays in English Literature from the Renaissance to the Victorian Age Presented to A. S. P. Woodhouse*, edited by Millar MacLure and F. W. Watt (Toronto: University of Toronto Press, 1964), pp. 245-268;

Robson and Michael Laine, eds., *James and John Stuart Mill: Papers of the Centenary Conference* (Toronto & Buffalo: University of Toronto Press, 1976);

William Spence, *Agriculture the Source of Wealth of Britain* (London: Printed by L. Hansard for T. Cadell and W. Davies, 1808);

Leslie Stephen, *The English Utilitarians*, 3 volumes (London: Duckworth, 1900);

Eric Stokes, *The English Utilitarians in India* (Oxford: Clarendon Press, 1959);

William E. S. Thomas, "James Mill's Politics: A Rejoinder," *Historical Journal*, 14 (December 1971): 735-750;

Thomas, "James Mill's Politics: The *Essay on Government* and the Movement for Reform," *Historical Journal*, 12 ( June 1962): 249-284;

Thomas, "James Mill's Science of Politics," in his *The Philosophical Radicals: Nine Studies in Theory and Practice, 1817-1841* (Oxford: Clarendon Press, 1979), pp. 95-146;

William Thompson, *Appeal of One Half the Human Race, Women, Against the Pretensions of the Other Half, Men, to Retain Them in Political, and Thence Civil and Domestic Slavery; in Reply to a Paragraph of Mr. Mill's Celebrated "Article on Government"* (London: Printed for Longman, Hurst, Rees, Orme, Brown & Green, 1825).

**Papers:**

James Mill's commonplace books, four manuscript volumes, are at the London Library.

# Hannah More

*(2 February 1745 - 7 September 1833)*

Nicholas R. Jones
*Oberlin College*

BOOKS: *The Search after Happiness: a pastoral drama* (Bristol: Printed & sold by S. Farley, 1773; Philadelphia: Printed by James Humphreys, Jr., 1774);

*The Inflexible Captive: a tragedy* (Bristol: Printed & sold by S. Farley, 1774; Philadelphia: Printed for John Sparhawk by James Humphreys, Jr., 1774);

*Sir Eldred of the Bower, and the Bleeding rock: two legendary tales* (London: Printed for T. Cadell, 1776);

*Essays on various subjects, principally designed for young ladies* (London: Printed for J. Wilkie & T. Cadell, 1777; Philadelphia: Printed & sold by Young, Stewart & M'Culloch, 1786);

*Ode to Dragon, Mr. Garrick's house-dog, at Hampton* (London: Printed for T. Cadell, 1777);

*Percy, a tragedy* (London: Printed for T. Cadell, 1778);

*The Works of Miss Hannah More in prose and verse* (Cork: Printed by Thomas White, 1778);

*The Fatal Falsehood: a tragedy* (London: Printed for T. Cadell, 1779);

*Sacred Dramas: chiefly intended for young persons: the subjects taken from the Bible. To which is added, Sensibility, a poem* (London: Printed for T. Cadell, 1782; Philadelphia: Printed for Thomas Dobson, 1787);

*Florio: a tale, for fine gentlemen and fine ladies: and, The Bas Bleu; or, Conversation: two poems*, anonymous (London: Printed for T. Cadell, 1786);

*Slavery, a poem* (London: Printed for T. Cadell, 1788; Philadelphia: Printed by Joseph James, 1788; New York: Printed by J. & A. M'Lean, 1788);

*Thoughts on the Importance of the Manners of the Great to General Society* (London: Printed for T. Cadell, 1788; Philadelphia: Printed for Thomas Dobson, 1788);

*Bishop Bonner's Ghost*, as "A good old papist" (Strawberry Hill: Printed by Thomas Kirgate, 1789);

*An Estimate of the Religion of the Fashionable World. By one of the laity* (London: Printed for T. Cadell, 1791; Philadelphia: Printed for & sold by M. L. Weems & H. Willis, 1793);

*Village Politics, addressed to all the mechanics, journeymen, and day labourers in Great Britain*, as "Will Chip, a country carpenter" (London: Printed & sold by F. & C. Rivington, 1792);

*Remarks on the speech of M. Dupont, made in the National Convention of France, on the subjects of religion and public education* (London: Printed for T. Cadell, 1793); republished in *Considerations on Religion and Public Education, with Remarks on the Speech of M. Dupont, Delivered in the National Convention of France* (Boston: Printed by Weld & Greenough, 1794);

*The Cottage Cook; or, Mrs. Jones's Cheap Dishes* (London: Sold by J. Evans & J. Hatchard and S. Hazard, Bath, 1795);

*The Sunday School* (London: Sold by J. Evans & J. Hatchard and S. Hazard, Bath, 1795);

*The Apprentice's Monitor; or Indentures in verse* [single sheet] (Bath: Sold by S. Hazard and J. Marshall & R. White, London, 1795);

*The Carpenter; or, the Danger of evil company* [single sheet] (Bath: Sold by S. Hazard and J. Marshall & R. White, London, 1795);

*The Gin-Shop; or, a Peep into a prison* [single sheet] (Bath: Sold by S. Hazard and J. Marshall & R. White, London, 1795);

*The History of Tom White the Postilion* (Bath: Sold by S. Hazard and J. Marshall & R. White, London, 1795; Philadelphia: Published by B. Johnson, 1798);

*The Market Woman, a true tale, or Honesty is the best policy* [single sheet] (Bath: Sold by S. Hazard and J. Marshall & R. White, London, 1795);

*The Roguish Miller; or, Nothing got by cheating* [single sheet] (Bath: Sold by S. Hazard and J. Marshall & R. White, London, 1795);

*The Shepherd of Salisbury Plain* (Bath: Sold by S. Hazard and J. Marshall & R. White, London, 1795; Philadelphia: Printed by B. & J. Johnson, 1800);

*Hannah More (portrait by Henry Singleton; reproduced from a postcard, Lilly Library, Indiana University)*

*The Two Shoemakers* (Bath: Sold by S. Hazard and J. Marshall & R. White, London, 1795); republished as *The History of the Two Shoemakers. Part I* (Philadelphia: Printed by B. & J. Johnson, 1800);

*The Shepherd of Salisbury Plain. Part II* (Bath: Sold by S. Hazard and J. Marshall & R. White, London, 1795; Philadelphia: Printed by B. & J. Johnson, 1800);

*Patient Joe, or, the Newcastle Collier* [single sheet] (Bath: Sold by S. Hazard and J. Marshall & R. White, London, 1795; Philadelphia: Printed & sold by J. Rakeshaw, 1808);

*The Riot; or, Half a loaf is better than no bread* [single sheet] (London: Sold by J. Marshall & R. White and S. Hazard, Bath, 1795);

*The Way to Plenty: or, the second part of Tom White* (London: Sold by J. Marshall & R. White and S. Hazard, Bath, 1795; Philadelphia: Printed by B. & J. Johnson, 1800);

*The Honest Miller of Glocestershire* [single sheet] (London: Sold by J. Marshall & R. White and S. Hazard, Bath, 1795);

*The Two Wealthy Farmers, or, the History of Mr. Bragwell. Part I* (London: Sold by J. Marshall & R. White and S. Hazard, Bath, 1795; Philadelphia: Printed by B. & J. Johnson, 1800);

*The Two Wealthy Farmers; or, the History of Mr. Bragwell. Part II* (Bath: Sold by S. Hazard and J. Marshall & R. White, London, 1795; Philadelphia: Printed by B. & J. Johnson, 1800);

*Robert and Richard; or the Ghost of poor Molly, who was drowned in Richard's mill pond* (London: Sold by J. Marshall & R. White and S. Hazard, Bath, 1796);

*The Apprentice Turned Master; or, the Second part of the Two Shoemakers* (London: Sold by J. Marshall & R. White and S. Hazard, Bath, 1796); republished as *The History of the Two Shoemakers. Part II* (Philadelphia: Printed by B. & J. Johnson, 1800);

*The History of Idle Jack Brown . . . Being the third part of the Two Shoemakers* (London: Sold by J. Marshall & R. White and S. Hazard, Bath, 1796); republished as *The History of the Two Shoemakers. Part III* (Philadelphia: Printed by B. & J. Johnson, 1800);

*The Shopkeeper Turned Sailor . . . Part I* (London: Sold by J. Marshall & R. White and S. Hazard, Bath, 1796; Philadelphia: Printed by B. & J. Johnson, 1800);

*Jack Brown in Prison . . . Being the fourth part of the History of the Two Shoemakers* (London: Sold by J. Marshall & R. White and S. Hazard, Bath, 1796); republished as *The History of the Two Shoemakers. Part IV* (Philadelphia: Printed by B. & J. Johnson, 1800);

*The Hackney Coachman, or the Way to get a good fare* (London: Sold by J. Marshall & R. White and S. Hazard, Bath, 1796);

*Sunday Reading. On Carrying Religion into the Common Business of Life. A dialogue between James Stock and Will Simpson, the shoemakers* (London: Sold by J. Marshall & R. White, 1796);

*Turn the Carpet; or, the Two weavers: a new song, in a dialogue between Dick and John* (London: Sold by J. Marshall & R. White and S. Hazard, Bath, 1796);

*Betty Brown, the St. Giles's Orange girl* (London: Sold by J. Marshall & R. White and S. Hazard, Bath, 1796; Philadelphia: Printed by B. & J. Johnson, 1800);

*Sunday Reading. The Grand Assizes; or, General gaol delivery* (London: Sold by J. Marshall & R. White and S. Hazard, Bath, 1796);

*The History of Mr. Bragwell; or the Two Wealthy Farmers. Part III* (London: Sold by J. Marshall & R. White; S. Hazard, Bath; J. Elder, Edinburgh, 1796); republished as *The Two Wealthy Farmers or the History of Mr. Bragwell. Part III* (Philadelphia: Printed by B. & J. Johnson, 1800);

*A Hymn of Praise for the Abundant Harvest of 1796* (London: Sold by J. Marshall & R. White and S. Hazard, Bath, 1796);

*Sunday Reading. The History of the Two Wealthy Farmers . . . Part IV* (London: Sold by J. Marshall & R. White and S. Hazard, Bath, 1796); republished as *The Two Wealthy Farmers; or the History of Mr. Bragwell. Part IV* (Philadelphia: Printed by B. & J. Johnson, 1800);

*The Two Wealthy Farmers, with the sad adventures of Miss Bragwell. Part V* (London: Sold by J. Marshall & R. White and S. Hazard, Bath, 1796); republished as *The Two Wealthy Farmers; or, The History of Mr. Bragwell. Part V* (Philadelphia: Printed by B. & J. Johnson, 1800);

*Black Giles the Poacher . . . Part I* (London: Sold by J. Marshall & R. White and S. Hazard, Bath, 1796; Philadelphia: Printed by B. & J. Johnson, 1800);

*Sunday Reading. Bear ye one another's Burthens; or the Valley of tears: a vision* (London: Sold by J. Marshall & R. White; S. Hazard, Bath; and J. Elder, Edinburgh, 1796; Philadelphia: Benjamin Johnson, 1813);

*Black Giles the Poacher. With the history of widow Brown's apple-tree. Part II* (London: Sold by J. Marshall and S. Hazard, Bath, 1796; Philadelphia: Printed by B. & J. Johnson, 1800);

*The Good Militiaman . . . being a new song by Honest Dan the ploughboy turned soldier* (London: Sold by J. Marshall & R. White and S. Hazard, Bath, 1797);

*Tawny Rachel, or, the Fortune teller* (London: Sold by J. Marshall & R. White; S. Hazard, Bath; J. Elder, Edinburgh, 1797); republished as *The Fortune Teller* (Philadelphia: Published by B. Johnson, 1798);

*The Two Gardeners* (London: Sold by J. Marshall & R. White; S. Hazard, Bath; and J. Elder, Edinburgh, 1797);

*The History of Hester Wilmot; or the Second part of the Sunday School* (London: Sold by J. Marshall & R. White; S. Hazard, Bath; and J. Elder, Edinburgh, 1797; Philadelphia: Sunday and Adult School Union, 1818);

*Sunday Reading. The Servant Man turned Soldier; or, the Fair weather Christian* (London: Sold by J. Marshall & R. White; S. Hazard, Bath; J. Elder, Edinburgh, 1797);

*The History of Hester Wilmot; or the New gown. Part II. Being a continuation of the Sunday School* (London: Sold by J. Marshall; S. Hazard, Bath; J. Elder, Edinburgh, 1797);

*The Lady and the Pye; or Know thyself* (London: Sold by J. Marshall & R. White; S. Hazard, Bath; J. Elder, Edinburgh, 1797);

*Sunday Reading. The Strait Gate and the Broad Way, being the second part of the Valley of Tears* (London: Sold by J. Marshall & R. White; S. Hazard, Bath; and J. Elder, Edinburgh, 1797);

*The History of Mr. Fantom, the new fashioned philosopher and his man William* (London: Sold by J. Marshall; S. Hazard, Bath; J. Elder, Edinburgh, 1797; Philadelphia: Printed by B. & J. Johnson, 1800);

*Sunday Reading. The Pilgrims. An allegory* (London: Sold by J. Marshall; S. Hazard, Bath; and J. Elder, Edinburgh, 1797; Philadelphia: Printed & sold by Kimber, Conrad, 1808);

*Dan and Jane; or Faith and works. A tale* (London: Sold by J. Marshall; S. Hazard, Bath; and J. Elder, Edinburgh, 1797);

*The Two Wealthy Farmers; or the Sixth part of the history of Mr. Bragwell and his two daughters* (London: Sold by J. Marshall; S. Hazard, Bath; and J. Elder, Edinburgh, 1797);

*The Two Wealthy Farmers; or, the Seventh and last part of the history of Mr. Bragwell and his two daughters* (London: Sold by J. Marshall; S. Hazard, Bath; and J. Elder, Edinburgh, 1797);

*The Plum-Cakes: or, the Farmer and his three sons* (London: Sold by J. Marshall and S. Hazard, Bath, 1797);

*Strictures on the Modern System of Female Education. With a view of the principles and conduct prevalent among women of rank and fortune*, 2 volumes (London: Printed by A. Strahan for T. Cadell Jun. & W. Davies, 1799; Philadelphia: Printed by Bunn & Bartram for Thomas Dobson, 1800);

*The Works of Hannah More, including several pieces never before published* (8 volumes, London: T. Cadell & W. Davies, 1801; enlarged, 19 volumes, 1818; enlarged, 11 volumes, London: T. Cadell, 1830; enlarged, with a memoir and notes, 6 volumes, London: H. Fisher, R. Fisher & P. Jackson, 1834; 2 volumes, New York: Harper & Brothers, 1837);

*Hints towards forming the Character of a Young Princess*, 2 volumes (London: Printed for T. Cadell & W. Davies, 1805);

*Coelebs in Search of a Wife. Comprehending observations on domestic habits and manners, religion and morals*, as "Coelebs" (2 volumes, London: Printed for T. Cadell and W. Davies, 1808; 1 volume, New York: Published by David Carlisle, 1809);

*Practical Piety; or, The influence of the religion of the heart on the conduct of life*, 2 volumes (London: Printed for T. Cadell, 1811; Albany: Websters & Skinners, 1811; Boston: Munroe & Francis, 1811; Burlington, N.J.: D. Allinson, 1811);

*Christian Morals*, 2 volumes (London: Printed for T. Cadell & W. Davies, 1813; New York: Eastburn, Kirk / Boston: Bradford & Read, 1813; New York: Published by D. Huntington, 1813);

*An Essay on the Character and Practical Writings of Saint Paul*, 2 volumes (London: Printed for T. Cadell & W. Davies, 1815; Boston: Wells, 1815; Philadelphia: Edward Earle / New York: Eastburn, Kirk, 1815);

*Poems* (London: Printed for T. Cadell & W. Davies, 1816; Boston: Wells & Lilly, 1817; enlarged edition, London: Cadell, 1829);

*Moral Sketches of prevailing opinions and manners, foreign and domestic; with reflections on prayer* (London: Cadell & Davies, 1819; Boston: Wells & Lilly, 1819); sixth edition, with a new preface (London: Cadell & Davies, 1820);

*The Twelfth of August: or the Feast of freedom* (London: J. & T. Clarke, 1819); republished as *The Feast of Freedom; or, the abolition of domestic slavery in Ceylon; the vocal parts adapted to music by C. Wesley* (London: T. Cadell, 1827);

*Bible Rhymes on the names of all the books of the Old and New Testament: with allusions to some of the principal incidents and characters* (London: T. Cadell, 1821; Boston: Wells & Lilly, 1821);

*The spirit of prayer. Selected and compiled by herself, from various portions exclusively on that subject, in her published volumes* (London: T. Cadell, 1825; Boston: Cummings, Hilliard, 1826);

*Miscellaneous Works*, 2 volumes (London: Printed for T. Tegg, 1840).

**Collections:** *Cheap Repository*, 3 volumes (London: Sold by J. Marshall and S. Hazard, Bath, 1795-1798);

*The Entertaining, Moral, and Religious Repository*, 2 volumes (Elizabethtown, N.J.: Printed by Shepard Kollock for Cornelius Davis, New York, 1798-1799);

*Cheap Repository*, 3 volumes (Philadelphia: Printed by B. & J. Johnson, 1800-1803).

PLAY PRODUCTIONS: *The Inflexible Captive*, Bath, Theatre Royal, 19 April 1775;

*Percy*, London, Theatre Royal, Covent Garden, 10 December 1777;

*The Fatal Falsehood*, London, Theatre Royal, Covent Garden, 6 May 1779.

OTHER: Ann Yearsley, *Poems, on several occasions*, edited, with a preface, by More (London: Printed for T. Cadell, 1785).

*More in 1787 (portrait by John Opie; from M. G. Jones,* Hannah More, *1952)*

The life and literary achievement of Hannah More are extraordinarily varied: she was a noted conversationalist and poet in the intellectual circles of Elizabeth Montagu and Samuel Johnson; successful dramatist and intimate friend of David Garrick; abolitionist reformer and partner of William Wilberforce; tireless educator in the poverty-stricken villages of western England; principal author, editor, and moving force for an influential series of tracts, circulated in the millions; author of many philosophical works reshaping the education of women, the moral and philanthropic responsibility of the upper classes, and the role of evangelical religion in daily thought and life.

The span of More's life, across four reigns and almost a century, links at least three major and quite distinct literary cultures: the late-eighteenth-century urban Enlightenment, the turn-of-the-century "Romantic" fascination with the life and language of the common person, and the post-Romantic pietizing of literature in the ascendancy of didactic prose. The breadth of change during her life can be seen most vividly when we consider that her own nurse had once worked in the family of a Restoration poet (John Dryden), while More herself was the godmother and childhood mentor of a Victorian sage (Thomas Babington Macaulay). Though few of her substantial literary productions are now read, the best of these, her lively ballads and tracts for distribution to the laboring poor, are beginning to receive critical attention in the light of contemporary interest in issues of class and gender.

Hannah More was born in Stapleton, near Bristol, where her father, Jacob More, was master of a foundation school (a free grammar school for working-class children). The large More family—Hannah was the fourth of five daughters—lived in the school itself; all five daughters were educated by their father, but Hannah was the prodigy. She learned Latin and mathematics with such alarming speed that her father broke off the lessons; Hannah persuaded him to resume Latin but not mathematics. In 1758 the thirteen-year-old Hannah moved to Bristol to join her older sisters at the boarding school they had founded; there she was first a pupil and later, for a few years, a teacher (she was, with short interruptions, to live with her four sisters for the rest of their lives). More expanded her formal education not only with tutorials in Latin but also by plunging into the active cultural life of Bristol—with lectures and meetings (she was well acquainted with Charles Wesley), politics (the sisters supported Edmund Burke's candidacy for Parliament), and plays (Bristol had an active theater and More was a close friend of its finest actor, William Powell).

At about twenty-two, More became engaged to a well-to-do country gentleman, Edward Turner. On the prospect of marrying him, she stopped teaching at the school, but over the next six years, Turner broke three successive engagements to More. When she at last called a halt to the relationship, he settled two hundred pounds a year on her in compensation for breach of promise. This unexpected and at first unwelcome annuity (soon enhanced by substantial profits from her publications) enabled More to spend her professional life in writing and to join the social and literary world of London on lengthy winter visits for more than two decades.

More came to London in 1773, furnished with introductions from her well-connected Bristol friends, allowing her entry to several major intellectual circles of the day. She soon became a close friend of Garrick, and from 1776 on the Garricks' lodgings were her winter home. Through Garrick, More entered the world of the theater. She had already written a play at the age of sixteen: *The Search after Happiness*, a moral pastoral for schoolgirls, was tremendously popular on the school circuit both before and after its publication in 1773. Even in this first work, More allegorizes her lifelong concern that women must improve their status through education, yet at the same time maintain the traditional bounds of decorum, piety, and obedience.

With Garrick's active encouragement and direction, she began to write tragedies for the professional stage. The first of three was *The Inflexible Captive* (1774); though it was well received onstage at Bath in April 1775, the author declined to allow it to be produced at Drury Lane. The play's self-sacrificing Roman actions and grand speeches about glory catch with More's usual fluency the indispensable qualities of the heroic drama of its age. Garrick added an epilogue in which he wittily but problematically defends the notion of a woman as playwright.

Over the summer of 1777 More wrote her second tragedy, on medieval Border material. *Percy* (1778), in a powerful and well-publicized production, took London by storm in December 1777. Theatrically, financially, and critically this play was an unmitigated success, earning More some £750 and an international reputation. The play centers on the dilemma of its heroine, Elwina, acted in its first production by the distinguished Ann Barry. Elwina, though once engaged to Percy (and still in love with him), has been forced by her vengeful father to marry Percy's enemy Douglas; as Percy returns from the crusades—still not knowing of Elwina's marriage—she must deal with the conflicts resulting from his love, her husband's jealousy, and her own emotions of love and duty. Abstract diction, unvaried scene construction, and monolithic characterization make this play difficult to read or to imagine acted today, but it clearly touches on themes of importance to More and her audience—in particular, the role of the privileged woman in a world of powerful and conflicting male demands. A third tragedy, *The Fatal Falsehood* (1779), was interrupted in the writing by the death of Garrick in 1779. Without Garrick's careful management of the production, and with More's own indifference to its fate, the play—though received with great applause—ran only three nights in May 1779.

Cooling to the secular theater as her religious convictions began to take precedence over literary aspirations, More turned to biblical themes, publishing but not producing on stage a series of short *Sacred Dramas* (1782). In her introduction she specifically cites the "moral instruction" of young persons as her goal. In these brief biblical episodes on the lives of Moses (in the bulrushes), David (and Goliath), Belshazzar, and Daniel, precedence in characterization and incident is given to the Old Testament originals, with the poet supplying expansion but relatively little in the way of novelty. The pietizing of More's career was complete by the turn of the century when, in her collected works (1801), she reprinted the secular tragedies, but prefaced them with the disclaimer that there was an "essential radical defect" in the genre. Their dependence on honor, she asserted, must inevitably destroy their Christian quality, and their need to give pleasure to their audiences must conflict with Christian needs for instruction and personal reformation.

In the 1770s and 1780s, however, More balanced her piety and her life in the beau monde, enthusiastically participating in—and working to reform—London theatrical, poetic, and conversational life. She became part of the intellectual circles of Elizabeth Montagu, entering the upper-class women's discussion groups called the "Blue Stockings." She also became a close friend of Samuel Johnson in his old age. He seems to have enjoyed her combination of piety and wit, but she was not a favorite with James Boswell. More wrote several poems imbued with the taste of these fashionable literary environments. Her first poetic publication, *Sir Eldred of the Bower* (1776), is a Gothic-revival ballad, sentimental and tragic; it contains a stanza by Johnson and was given a memorable reading by Garrick. Others are slighter productions—*Ode to Dragon* (1777), addressed to Garrick's dog; *Bishop Bonner's Ghost* (1789), a brief Gothic fantasy given elegant life in print by her friend Horace Walpole at Strawberry Hill. A more ambitious poem, *Florio* (1786), is a witty look at a vapid and frivolous city youth fortunately converted to a taste for the good old pleasures and pieties of the country landowner and his lovely if domestic daughter. This "tale, for fine gentlemen and fine ladies" is an early, upper-class, and consciously clever version of More's cautionary tracts of the 1790s.

In a wholly different mode, *The Bas Bleu*, published with *Florio*, is a clever mock-heroic about the Blue Stockings, in a grand style excoriating the dullness they compete against and praising the brilliance (combined of course with virtue) they represent. Near the end of its five-hundred-odd lines, the poem speaks seriously to the "pure delight / When kindling sympathies unite," the excitement that an intelligence such as More's might have experienced in the conversations of "enlighten'd spirits," the "sparks electric [that] only strike / On souls electrical alike." As M. G. Jones points out, More's poems of this period "advertised" and "popularized" the Blue-Stocking assemblies "in an easy and pleasing manner" that had not been at hand when others (such as Montagu) wrote.

More's major editorial contribution to poetry was her work in support of the impoverished "milkmaid" poet, Ann Yearsley, on behalf of whom More assembled an impressive subscription list, supervised the publication of her poems in 1785, and generally tried to manage her career and life. The patronage ended in a bitter and well-publicized quarrel over the control of the proceeds of the subscription, and a permanent breach between the two poets.

By 1788 More's work had turned away from the aestheticized productions of her early career to take on increasingly serious rhetorical and didactic strategies. Causes for the change may be sought not only in More's age—she was forty in 1785—but also in the political upheaval of the American war; in the deaths of Garrick (1779), of her father (1783), and of Johnson (1784) and, most important, in the rise of evangelical Anglican piety and its corresponding abolitionist fervor. Of tremendous significance in More's life are two charismatic leaders of the Evangelical movement: John Newton, a former atheist and master of a slave ship who had become rector of a fashionable London church and a preacher of a robust and demanding faith, and William Wilberforce, the energetic young reformer, abolitionist, and politician. In January of 1788 as Wilberforce mounted his campaign for a parliamentary bill of abolition, More rapidly composed and published her most significant poem, *Slavery* (later known as *The Slave Trade*), a fierce and energetic plea for British abolition. More had begun to read William Cowper intently, and the compassionate acuity of his vision informs her poem. For More every soul has the same universal religious needs: religious instruction, faith, and consolation. The personal and societal consequences of slavery—"the dire victim torn from social life, / The shrieking babe, the agonizing wife!"—are important, but more so are the effects of the slave trade on the souls of slaver and slave. Both, by this system, are alienated from God: the slaver, and his nation, by "deepest, deadliest guilt"; and the slave by his terrible suffering. In More's Evangelical perspective, that suffering demands a Christian consolation, which, of course, is denied the slave because of the slaver's perversion of Christian life. The fiercest indignation comes when More imagines the slave dying in passage, denied understanding and faith:

When the fierce sun darts vertical his beams,
And thirst and hunger mix their wild extremes;

When the sharp iron wounds his inmost soul,
And his strain'd eyes in burning anguish roll;
Will the parch'd negro own, ere he expire,
No pain in hunger, and no heat in fire?
For him, when agony his frame destroy,
What hope of present fame or future joys?
For *that* have heroes shorten'd nature's date,
For *this* have martyrs gladly met their fate;
But him forlorn, no heroes pride sustains,
No martyr's blissful vision soothe his pains;
Sullen, he mingles with his kindred dust,
For he has learn'd to dread the Christian's trust;
To him what mercy can that God display,
Whose servants murder, and whose sons betray?

By the late 1780s, particularly as the French Revolution focused British attention on social disjunction and upheaval, More's calling as a writer was becoming clearer: to bridge the gap between the classes in order to prevent unrest and possible revolution. She set out to teach a new philanthropy, by educating the fashionable world of Britain, whose language and manners she knew well, about its responsibility toward the unfortunate—slaves abroad and the working poor at home. In an extended literary endeavor that secured the approval if not the direct support of the newly founded Society for the Reformation of Manners, More produced three prose volumes designed to reform the manners and morals of the rich. First, in 1788, she published a loose series of *Thoughts on the Importance of the Manners of the Great to General Society*, which sold out in seven large editions within a few months. Though anonymous, the work's authorship was soon determined, and (despite her fears of being shunned as an "enthusiast" among polite society) More found herself widely celebrated among the rich as a religious and moral adviser. According to the premise of this short book, the lower classes are infected with sins of degeneracy—gambling, loose talk, scorn for moral life, Sabbath-breaking—but these sins are not the book's focus. Rather the book fiercely attacks the hypocrisy of what More ironically labels "the good sort of people," the upper class, whose flagrant disregard for decency, truth, and uprightness sets the example for their servants, tenants, and employees. While the rich believe themselves to be Christian, they are in fact the enemies of religion: "you, like an inadequate and faithless prop, overturn the edifice which you pretend to support."

More's second volume on the fashionable world, *An Estimate of the Religion of the Fashionable World* (1791), is longer and even more critical of the manners of the rich. No longer does More focus on the effect on the poor; the inconsistencies, hypocrisies, and sins of the rich themselves bear the brunt of her examination. The argument is not pragmatic, but pietistic: "Piety is not only necessary as a *means*, but is itself a most important *end*. It is not only the best principle of moral conduct, but is an indispensable and absolute duty in itself." The book, like her earlier treatise, sold in vast quantities, but More—seeing little actual reformation in manners—increasingly grew to distrust the mere success of numbers.

In 1799 she published a third appeal to the upper classes, *Strictures on the Modern System of Female Education*. Like her contemporary Mary Wollstonecraft, from whose Jacobinism More of course carefully distanced herself, More saw the education of women to be a failure, creating vapid, dependent, licentious, and useless members of society. Girls' schools stressed external and decorative acquisitions at the expense of sound foundations for moral decision making and action—in particular, piety and Christian principles. In its rambling way, the book sets out a model for reconstituting female education on useful, moral, and Christian grounds:

> I turn, with an earnest hope, that women thus richly endowed with the bounties of Providence, will not content themselves with polishing when they are able to reform; with entertaining when they may awaken; and with captivating for a day, when they may bring into action powers of which the effects may be commensurate with eternity.

More warns, however, that these "strictures" are far from a call for feminism:

> I am not sounding an alarm to female warriors, or exciting female politicians: I hardly know which of the two is the most disgusting and unnatural character. Propriety is to a woman what the great Roman critic says action is to an orator; it is the first, the second, the third requisite.

The talents of women are to be developed only within the framework of modesty and propriety—the proper duties of the gender. Even so, recent historians such as Mitzi Myers have asserted the need to see the feminist project of More and other conservative Evangelicals as parallel to Wollstonecraft's—essentially critical of social norms, even subversive and "revolutionary."

Arguably the most influential of More's actions and writings was her work in Somerset, founding and maintaining a series of schools for the poor, and her related work with the Cheap Repository Tracts. In 1789 the More sisters had retired from managing their school and moved to Bath; from this time Hannah More began to spend her winters in Bath and her summers in a small cottage at Cowslip Green in Somerset, near the romantically beautiful landscape of Cheddar Gorge. On visiting Cowslip Green, Wilberforce awoke the Mores to the nonromantic ugliness of poverty in the local mine workers—ignorant, blasphemous, and despairing, in a place "where there was not any dawn of comfort, temporal or spiritual."

With extraordinary speed and energy, More activated a plan for establishing schools for the children of these families. By the end of the century, she had a dozen schools operating in the area, all teaching the rudiments of practical and religious education. More speaks for her own class conservatism, and that of much of the English reform movement of her age, when she writes that her plan was "to form the lower class to habits of industry and virtue. . . . To make good members of society (and this can only be done by making good Christians) has been my aim. . . . Principles not opinions are what I labour to give them." The schools achieved amazing success, despite the opposition of local farmers, squires, parents, and curates; despite continual administrative demands on the sisters; and despite one vicious, public, and exhausting controversy over control of teachers and curriculum (the "Blagdon controversy" over alleged Methodist tendencies became a national issue for several years). The schools continued to attract children and patrons and clearly improved the levels of literacy and knowledge in those outlying hill villages.

As she worked with the schools, More saw a vicious circle of lower-class ignorance and moved to break it at two points—with schools for the ignorant children and with Cheap Repository Tracts for the ignorant parents. Her first pamphlet, published separately before the advent of the Cheap Repository, was *Village Politics* (1792), an explicit refutation of Thomas Paine's *Rights of Man*, the second part of which was flooding England with libertarian sentiments in 1792. In More's tract, Tom Hod, a simpleminded mason, has read Paine and is agitating for "liberty and equality, and the rights of man." His friend Jack Anvil, a blacksmith, patiently refutes his feeble notions, until Tom accedes, "I begin to think we're better off as we are."

Swift, direct, lively, this brief dialogue spoke to the potentially seditious in their own language; apparently the many upper-class readers whose reactions are recorded thought nothing amiss with its patronizing tone. Though More herself later declared it "as vulgar as heart can wish . . . the sort of writing repugnant to my nature," she clearly wrote it with enjoyment and verve, and part of the success of this and the many tracts to follow is due to her remarkable ability to write vital fictional prose even while practicing the most class-based propaganda. When Tom complains of the extravagance of the aristocracy, Jack replies without mincing words:

> They do spend too much, to be sure, in feastings and fandangoes; and so far from commending them for it, if I was a parson I'd go to work with 'em, but it should be in another kind of way; but as I am only a poor tradesman, why 'tis but bringing more grist to my mill. Now in this village, what should we do without the castle? Though my lady is too rantipolish, and flies about all summer to hot water and cold water, and fresh water and salt water, when she ought to stay at home with sir John: yet when she does come down, she brings such a deal of gentry that I have more horses than I can shoe, and my wife more linen than she can wash.

Obviously, it is not the responsibility of the poor to correct the morals of the rich.

The style and sentiments of *Village Politics* became the basis for the nearly fifty pamphlets—mostly prose tales, with a sprinkling of ballads—More published in the immensely popular Cheap Repository series of more than one hundred short works by More and her friends, from its inception in late 1794 to its close in 1797. With money raised by a massive subscription effort, the tracts were at first printed and distributed at cost by booksellers in London, Bath, Edinburgh, and Dublin; but More went further and got the work into the hands of the real distributors of literature to the poor, the peddlers and hawkers. A further step was to encourage people of quality to carry tracts with them on philanthropic errands and give them away to the poor. The net effect of such efforts was an amazing circulation of more than two million.

More's tracts, most of them signed "Z," deserve attention—as Myers notes in her 1986 essay—for the insights they can yield to scholars attuned to the interactions of the histories of literature, society, and gender. These simple tales may

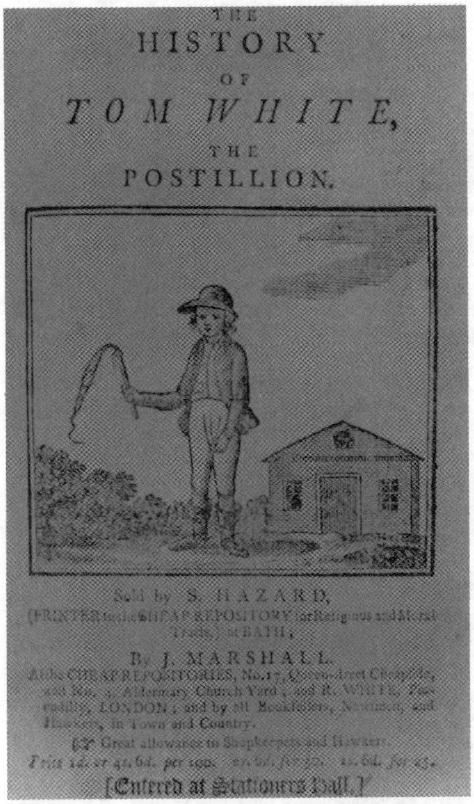
THE
HISTORY
OF
*TOM WHITE*,
THE
POSTILLION.

Sold by S. HAZARD,
(PRINTER to the CHEAP REPOSITORY for Religious and Moral Tracts,) at BATH;

By J. MARSHALL.
At the CHEAP REPOSITORIES, No. 17, Queen-street Cheapside, and No. 4, Aldermary Church Yard; and R. WHITE, Piccadilly, LONDON; and by all Booksellers, Newsmen, and Hawkers, in Town and Country.

☞ Great allowance to Shopkeepers and Hawkers.
*Price 1d. or 4s. 6d. per 100. 2s. 6d. for 50. 1s. 6d. for 25.*

[Entered at Stationers Hall.]

*Title pages for three of More's Cheap Repository Tracts, a series of educational pamphlets that eventually reached a circulation of more than two million*

THE
SHEPHERD
OF
SALISBURY-PLAIN.

Sold by S. HAZARD,
(PRINTER to the CHEAP REPOSITORY for Religious and Moral Tracts,) at BATH;

By J. MARSHALL,
At the CHEAP REPOSITORIES, No. 17, Queen-Street, Cheap-Side, and No. 4, Aldermary Church Yard; and R. WHITE, Piccadilly, LONDON; and by all Booksellers, Newsmen, and Hawkers, in Town and Country.

☞ Great Allowance to Shopkeepers and Hawkers.
*Price 1d. or 4s. 6d. per 100. 2s. 6d. for 50. 1s. 6d. for 25.*

[Entered at Stationers Hall.]

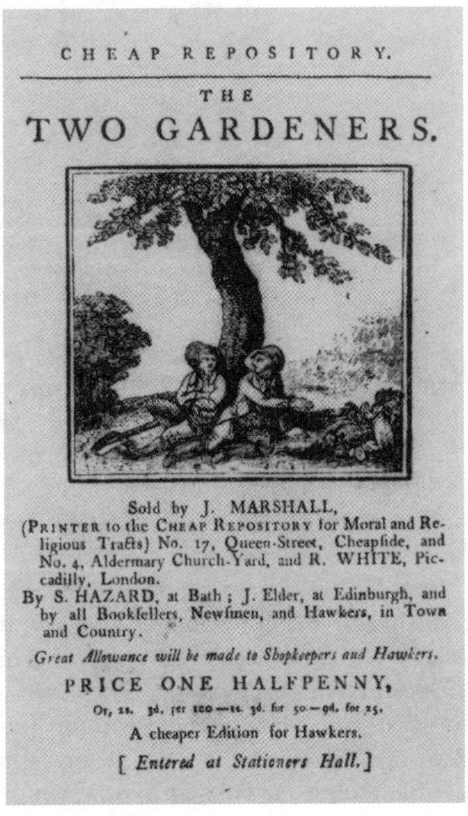
CHEAP REPOSITORY.

THE
TWO GARDENERS.

Sold by J. MARSHALL,
(PRINTER to the CHEAP REPOSITORY for Moral and Religious Tracts) No. 17, Queen-Street, Cheapside, and No. 4, Aldermary Church-Yard, and R. WHITE, Piccadilly, London.
By S. HAZARD, at Bath; J. Elder, at Edinburgh, and by all Booksellers, Newsmen, and Hawkers, in Town and Country.

*Great Allowance will be made to Shopkeepers and Hawkers.*

PRICE ONE HALFPENNY,
Or, 2s. 3d. per 100—1s. 3d. for 50.—9d. for 25.
A cheaper Edition for Hawkers.

[ *Entered at Stationers Hall.* ]

*More in November 1813 at Barley Wood, the house she and her sisters had built in 1801 (drawing by Slater; from M. G. Jones,* Hanna More, *1952)*

be read as fictions inscribing in direct, lively, and skilled forms the intense postrevolution upper-class attitudes toward the working classes. The plots and characterizations reflect the reformers' concern with the connection of civil order with morality. The poor are obsessively categorized: good, like the title character of *The Shepherd of Salisbury Plain* (1795), whose piety and cheerfulness are unshaken by his grinding poverty; or unredeemably bad, like Black Giles the poacher (in the 1796 story of that name), who stoops so low as to steal the whole apple crop of poor Widow Brown. Those who are not firmly good or bad are nonetheless shown to be in uniform motion one way or the other, such as Jack Brown, the idle apprentice in *The Two Shoemakers* (1795), a candidate for the workhouse from the beginning; or Hester Wilmot, daughter of a drunkard father and a violent mother, whose insistence on her right to attend Sunday school leads her to reform her parents and "to grow in grace, and in knowledge" until she herself is headmistress of the school. Even in those stories which show static depravity or inevitable decline, however, the hopefulness of the reform movement comes through strongly in the overall rhetoric: these are clear and accessible models, and those who have ears to hear will lead better lives for the hearing. The possibility of moral and spiritual reformation is always present, not merely as a personal issue for the individuals of the lower class (whom More grants little collective and no legislative interest), but emphatically as a group responsibility for the rich. Such characters and situations, the project implies, would not exist if the upper classes were to take seriously their need to initiate reform for the poor. The rich and educated, like the poor, are subjected to a moral division, between those who carelessly or willfully mislead their servants, such as Mr. Fantom, a foolish Jacobin, whose servant William follows his godlessness into drunkenness, robbery, and the gallows; and those who—such as Mrs. Jones in *The Sunday School* (1795) and its sequel *The History of Hester Wilmot* (1797)—pursue, like More herself, an active, responsible, and unflinching philanthropy.

More's agenda for the tracts was to use an existing literature of the poor in order to change the poor, and she thus appropriated not only the distribution system of existing popular pamphlet literature, but also its general form and unambiguous story lines. It is unclear, even with their tremendous circulation, whether the tracts influenced popular thought or expression. Susan Pedersen points out that More's attempt to pietize popular tract literature did not last significantly past 1797, when the reformers closed the series. Influence in the opposite direction may be more noticeable: if, as Pedersen says, the reformers of the Cheap Repository had entered popular culture only "as crusaders, not participants," the fact of their bridging the long-standing gap between the cultures is significant in itself and parallels other contemporaneous movements by writers of the upper class to assume a language of the lower classes—such as William Blake's *Songs of Innocence* (1789) and *Songs of Experience* (1794) and the *Lyrical Ballads* (1798) of William Wordsworth (who like More was in close touch with the rural poor of Somerset during the time of the Cheap Repository). Myers's recent feminist analysis of the Cheap Repository claims for these tracts a role "as significant channels of female reformist impulse and expressive power."

The turn of the century marked the close of the most active part of More's career: she closed the Cheap Repository in 1797, and, after the exhausting Blagdon controversy wound down in 1802, she took a less active role in the Cheddar schools. In that year she moved into Barley Wood, a pleasant house that she had built not far from her former cottage; in 1804 her sisters gave up residence in Bath and joined her there. At Barley Wood, where she lived until 1827 (she moved back to her birthplace, Stapleton, for the last years of her life), Hannah More received many visitors, kept up a vast correspondence, and maintained an active philanthropy. The literary productions of her final thirty years fill more pages than those from the first part of her life, but are of much less interest, with the possible exception of her only novel, *Coelebs in Search of a Wife* (1808), an anonymous effort in a genre More had earlier deprecated as pernicious or at least frivolous. Given its popularity (twelve editions in the first year in England; thirty editions in More's lifetime in America), *Coelebs in Search of a Wife* deserves historical attention, but is unlikely to get it from many modern readers. As in the tracts, More works to appropriate and reform an unfamiliar genre; but in this case, novelistic expectations of length and upper-class domestic subject matter make for a dull book. In form and theme, it is painfully straightforward: "Coelebs" (Latin for bachelor—a pseudonym of the hero) travels through various genteel homes to find a wife of intelligence and piety; he encounters several obvious rejects before settling on Lucilla Stanley—the woman his late father had already told him to marry. Lucilla is the model of womanly virtue and piety; the search being accomplished, the book ends with their engagement. More tells the story in the voice of Coelebs, who never realizes how monotonous his patronizing seems. Little in incident or verbal texture relieves the steady diet of moral discrimination.

The rest of More's late work comprises four major volumes of didactic prose on familiar themes, with an increasingly Evangelical tone. In 1805 she wrote *Hints towards forming the Character of a Young Princess*, an educational curriculum for the young daughter of the dissolute Prince of Wales. This widely circulated volume was rapidly followed by others: *Coelebs, Practical Piety* (1811), *Christian Morals* (1813), and *An Essay on the Character and Practical Writings of Saint Paul* (1815). The historical criticism of scripture implied in the project of this last volume was perhaps too distant from her skills to prove popular, but the others, encouragements to the Christian life directed toward the religiously inclined readers of the upper classes, were eagerly bought up in edition after edition. To a modern reader they seem disorganized, abstract, and monotonous, but there seems to have been something in their steady language and consistent faith in "the religion of the heart" that met a need in the England of the Napoleonic Wars. In her last years her associations were largely with clerical and Evangelical friends, with few purely literary connections; she largely ignored the Romantic movement, except for Wordsworth, whose poetry she discovered in 1814 and

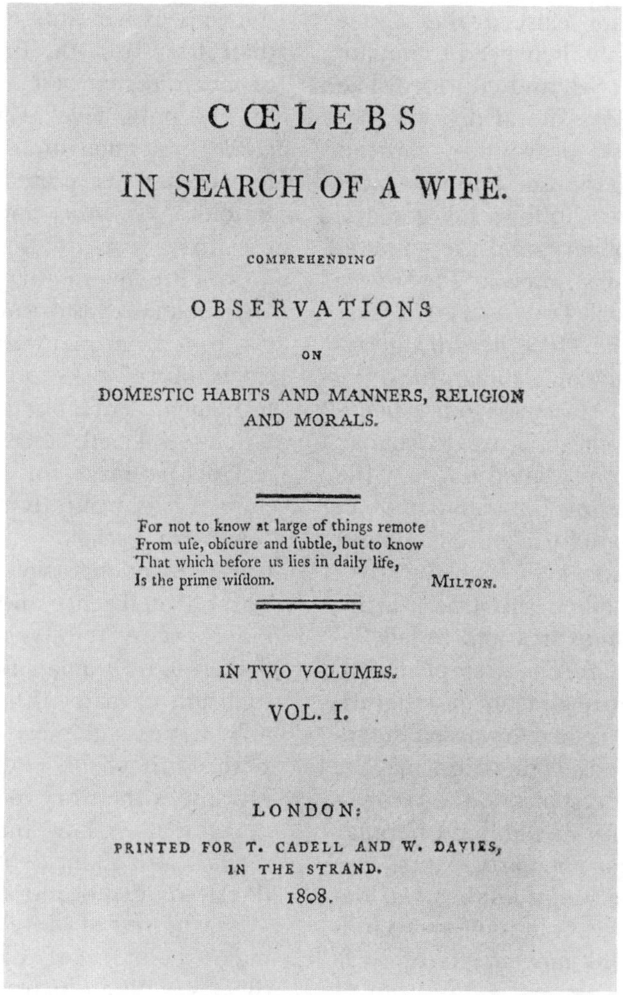

C ŒL E B S

IN SEARCH OF A WIFE.

COMPREHENDING

OBSERVATIONS

ON

DOMESTIC HABITS AND MANNERS, RELIGION AND MORALS.

For not to know at large of things remote
From uſe, obſcure and ſubtle, but to know
That which before us lies in daily life,
Is the prime wiſdom. MILTON.

IN TWO VOLUMES.

VOL. I.

LONDON:

PRINTED FOR T. CADELL AND W. DAVIES, IN THE STRAND.

1808.

*Title page for More's only novel (Special Collections, Thomas Cooper Library, University of South Carolina)*

whose subsequent visit to Barley Wood delighted her.

Still writing (against the orders of her doctors, she would hide inkpot, pen, and paper under her bedclothes) until near her end, More died in 1833 at the age of eighty-eight, leaving a substantial literary achievement from a life of fascinating scope. Her legacy, in its pietistic and conservative texture, is a daunting one to modern readers, but rich in insights into the history of women, reform, evangelical religion, and the relation of popular and high culture.

**Letters:**

*Letters of Hannah More to Zachary Macaulay Esq., containing notices of Lord Macaulay's youth*, edited by Arthur Roberts (London: J. Nisbet, 1860);

*The Letters of Hannah More*, edited by R. Brimley Johnson (London: John Lane, 1925);

Charles H. Bennett, "The text of Horace Walpole's correspondence with Hannah More," *Review of English Studies*, new series 3 (October 1952): 341-345.

**Bibliographies:**

Emanuel Green, *Bibliotheca Somersetensis*, 3 volumes (Taunton: Barnicott & Pearce, 1902);

G. H. Spinney, "Cheap Repository Tracts: Hazard and Marshall Edition," *Library*, fourth series 20 (December 1939): 295-340;

Harry B. Weiss, "Hannah More's Cheap Repository Tracts in America," *Bulletin of the New York Public Library*, 50 (July 1946): 539-549; 50 (August 1946): 634-641.

**Biographies:**

William Roberts, *Memoirs of the Life and Correspondence of Mrs. Hannah More*, 4 volumes (London: R. B. Seeley & Sons, 1834);

*More late in life, at Barley Wood (watercolor by an unknown artist; from M. G. Jones,* Hannah More, *1952)*

Henry Thompson, *Life of Hannah More, with notices of her sisters* (London: Cadell, 1838);

*Mendip annals, or a narrative of the charitable labours of Hannah More and Martha More: being the journal of Martha More,* edited by Arthur Roberts (London: J. Nisbet, 1859);

Helen C. Knight, *Hannah More: or, life in hall and cottage* (New York: American Tract Society, 1862);

Charlotte M. Yonge, *Hannah More* (Boston: Roberts, 1888);

Mary Virginia Hawes Terhune [Marion Harland], *Hannah More* (New York & London: Putnam's, 1900);

Annette M. B. Meakin, *Hannah More, a biographical study* (London: Smith, Elder, 1911);

George Lacey May, *Some eighteenth century churchmen; glimpses of English church life in the eighteenth century* (London: Society for Promoting Christian Knowledge / New York: Macmillan, 1920);

Margaret Emma Tabor, *Pioneer Women,* second series (London: Sheldon Press / New York & Toronto: Macmillan, 1927);

Mary Alden Hopkins, *Hannah More and Her Circle* (New York & Toronto: Longmans, Green, 1947);

M. G. Jones, *Hannah More* (Cambridge: Cambridge University Press, 1952).

**References:**

Betsy Aikin-Sneath, "Hannah More (1745-1833)," *London Mercury,* 28 (October 1933): 528-535;

Alfred Owen Aldridge, "Madame de Staël and Hannah More on society," *Romanic Review,* 38 (December 1947): 330-339;

Thomas Bere, *The Controversy between Mrs. Hannah More, and the curate of Blagdon* (London: W. Hughes for J. S. Jordan, 1801);

Ford K. Brown, *Fathers of the Victorians: The Age of Wilberforce* (Cambridge: Cambridge University Press, 1961);

Philip Child, "Portrait of a woman of affairs—old style," *University of Toronto Quarterly,* 3 (October 1933): 87-102;

Luther Weeks Courtney, *Hannah More's Interest in Education and Government* (Waco, Tex.: Baylor University Press, 1929);

E. M. Forster, "Mrs. Hannah More," *Nation* (London), 2 ( January 1926); republished in his *Abinger Harvest* (New York: Harcourt, Brace, 1936), pp. 241-248;

Gary Kelly, "Revolution, Reaction, and the Expropriation of Popular Culture: Hannah More's *Cheap Repository*," in *Man and Nature / l'Homme et la nature*, Proceedings of the Canadian Society for Eighteenth-Century Studies, edited by Kenneth W. Graham and Neal Johnson (Edmonton: Academic Printing & Publishing, 1987), pp. 147-159;

E. V. Knox, " 'Percy' (The Tale of a Dramatic Success)," *London Mercury*, 13 (March 1926): 509-515;

Beth Kowaleski-Wallace, "Milton's Daughters: The education of eighteenth-century women writers," *Feminist Studies*, 12 (Summer 1986): 275-293;

Eloise Lownsbery, "Hannah More," in her *Saints & Rebels* (New York & Toronto: Longmans, Green, 1937), pp. 171-206;

M. C. Malim, "Hannah More," *Contemporary Review*, 144 (September 1933): 329-336;

Mitzi Myers, "Hannah More's Tracts for the Times: Social fiction and female ideology," in *Fetter'd or free? British women novelists, 1670-1815*, edited by Mary Anne Schofield and Cecilia Macheski (Athens & London: Ohio University Press, 1986), pp. 264-284;

Myers, "Reform or Ruin: 'A Revolution in Female Manners,' " *Studies in Eighteenth-Century Culture*, 11 (1982): 199-216;

Susan Pedersen, "Hannah More meets Simple Simon: Tracts, Chapbooks, and Popular Culture in late Eighteenth-Century England," *Journal of British Studies*, 25 ( January 1986): 84-113;

Paule Penigault-Duhet, "Les femmes et l'église en France et en Angleterre à la fin du 18$^{eme}$ siecle; Actes du colloque tenu à Paris, les 24 et 25 octobre 1975," in *La femme en Angleterre et dans les colonies américaines aux XVII$^{e}$ et XVIII$^{e}$ siècles*, Pub. de l'Universite de Lille III (Lille, 1976), pp. 129-138;

Sam Pickering, "*The Cheap Repository Tracts* and the short story," *Studies in Short Fiction*, 12 (Winter 1975): 15-21;

E. W. Pitcher, Letter to *William and Mary Quarterly: A Magazine of Early American History and Culture*, 43 (April 1986): 327;

James Pitt, "Hannah More and the Blagdon controversy," *Notes and Queries*, third series 8 (26 August 1865): 168-169;

C. L. Shaver, "The publication of Hannah More's first play," *Modern Language Notes*, 62 (May 1947): 343.

**Papers:**

More's correspondence remains largely unpublished, in many private collections as well as at the Folger Shakespeare Library, the Henry E. Huntington Library, the University of Rochester, the Historical Society of Pennsylvania, the Massachusetts Historical Society, Harvard University, Yale University, the Pierpont Morgan Library, the New York Public Library, the John Rylands Library, the Bodleian Library, and the British Library.

# Robert Owen

*(14 May 1771 - 17 November 1858)*

Gregory Claeys
*Washington University*

SELECTED BOOKS: *Observations on the Cotton Trade of Great Britain* (Glasgow: Printed by J. Hedderwick, 1803);

*A Statement Regarding the New Lanark Establishment* (Edinburgh: Printed by John Moir, 1812);

*Essays on the Formation of the Human Character*, 4 essays published in 9 weekly installments (London: W. Strange, 1812); republished as *A New View of Society; or, Essays on the Principle of the Formation of the Human Character* [essays 1 and 2] (London: Printed for Cadell & Davies by R. Taylor, 1813); [essays 3 and 4] (London: Printed by R. & A. Taylor, 1814); [essays 1-4] (New York: E. Bliss & E. White, 1825); published again as *Essays on the Formation of the Human Character* (London: W. Strange, 1834);

*Observations on the Effect of the Manufacturing System* (London: Printed by R. & A. Taylor, 1815);

*Address Delivered to the Inhabitants of New Lanark, on Jan. 1st 1816, at the Opening of the Institute Established for the Formation of Character* (London: Hatchard, 1816);

*Report to the Committee of the Association for the Relief of the Manufacturing and Labouring Poor* (London, 1817);

*New State of Society* (London: Printed by J. Dennett, 1817);

*Peace on Earth—Good Will Towards Men* (London, 1817);

*A Letter Addressed to the Archbishop of Canterbury* (N.p., 1818);

*A Letter to the Earl of Liverpool on the Employment of Children* (N.p., 1818);

*Two Memorials on Behalf of the Working Classes* (Lanark, 1818; London: Printed for Longman, Hurst, Orme & Brown, 1818);

*Adresse aux Souverains à Aix-la-Chapelle et aux Gouvernements Européens* (Paris, 1819);

*An Address to the Master-Manufacturers of Great Britain on the Present Existing Evils in the Manufacturing System* (Bolton, 1819);

*Additional Statements Respecting Mr. Owen's Plan for the Support of the Unemployed Working Classes by their own Labour* (N.p, 1819);

*Report to the County of Lanark, of a Plan for Relieving Public Distress, and Removing Discontent* (Glasgow: Printed at the University Press, 1821);

*Permanent Relief for the British Agricultural and Manufacturing Labourers and the Irish Peasantry* (London, circa 1822);

*An Explanation of the Cause of the Distress Which Pervades the Civilized Parts of the World* (London: Printed by A. Applegath for the British and Foreign Philanthropic Society, 1823);

*A Letter to the Moderator of the General Assembly Upon the Late Attack of the Christian Instructor Upon Mr. Owen* (N.p., 1823);

*Report of the Proceedings at the Several Public Meetings Held in Dublin* (Dublin: Printed by J. Carrick & Son, 1823);

*Letter to the Earl of Lauderdale, May 27th, 1824* (N.p., 1824);

*A Discourse on a New System of Society; As delivered in the Hall of Representatives of the United States . . . on the 7th of March, 1825* (Washington, D.C.: Printed by Gales & Seaton, 1825);

*Discourses on a New System of Society; As delivered in the Hall of Representatives of the United States. . . . On the 25th of February, and 15th March, 1825* (Louisville: Printed by W. Tanner, 1825);

*Speech by Robert Owen at New Harmony* (N.p., 1825?);

*Oration, containing a Declaration of Mental Independence* (New Harmony, Ind., 1826);

*Address Delivered by Robert Owen, at a Public Meeting at the Franklin Institute in the City of Philadelphia . . . June 25th, 1827* (Philadelphia: M. T. C. Gould, 1827);

*An Address to the Agriculturalists, Mechanics, and Manufacturers of Great Britain and Ireland* (Bury: Printed by John Kay, 1827);

*Memorial of Robert Owen to the Mexican Republic*

Robert Owen (engraving after a portrait by W. H. Brooke A.R.H.A)

(Philadelphia, 1827; London: Printed by William Clowes, 1828);

*Robert Owen's Opening Speech and his Reply to the Rev. Alex. Campbell* (Cincinnati: Published for R. Owen, 1829);

*An Address by Robert Owen on His System Delivered at the City of London Tavern, April 12th, 1830* (London, 1830);

*Address to the Operative Manufacturers and Agricultural Labourers in Great Britain and Ireland* (N.p., 1830);

*The Advantages and Disadvantages of Religion* (Glasgow: Printed by R. Harriston, 1830);

*Lectures on an Entire New State of Society* (London: J. Brooks, 1830);

*Outline of the Rational System of Society* (London, 1830);

*The Addresses of Robert Owen as Published in the London Journals* (London: S. Hunt, 1830);

*The New Religion* (London: J. Brooks, 1830);

*Second Lecture on the New Religion* (London: J. Brooks, 1830);

*Address to All Classes in the State* (London, 1832);

*Robert Owen's Reply to the Question What Would You Do If You Were Prime Minister?* (Stockport: Printed by C. Dutton, Jun., 1832);

*Address of Robert Owen, Delivered at the Great Public Meeting Held at the National Equitable Labour Exchange* (London, 1833);

*Institution of the Intelligent and Well-disposed of the Industrious Classes* (London, 1833?);

*Lectures on Charity*, nos. 1-6 (London: B. D. Cousins, *Crisis* Office, 1833-1834);

*Lectures on the Marriages of the Priesthood of the Old*

*Owen circa 1800 (portrait by Mary Ann Knight; Scottish National Portrait Gallery)*

*Immoral World* (Leeds, 1835);

*The Book of the New Moral World* (7 parts, London, 1836-1844; 1 volume, New York: G. Vale, 1845);

*Address to Her Royal Highness the Princess Victoria and to Her Majesty the Queen of Great Britain and Ireland* (London, 1837);

*Public Discussion between Robert Owen, Late of New Lanark, and the Rev. J. H. Roebuck, of Manchester* (Manchester: A. Heywood, 1837);

*Six Lectures Delivered in Manchester Previously to the Discussion between Mr. Robert Owen and the Rev. J. H. Roebuck* (Manchester: Heywood, 1837);

*Exposition of Mr. Owen's Views on the Marriage Question* [broadside] (Coventry: S. Knapp, 1838);

*A Development of the Origin and Effects of Moral Evil* (Manchester: A. Heywood / London: Hetherington, 1838);

*A Dialogue in three Parts Between the Founder of the Association of All Classes of All Nations and a Stranger* (Manchester: A. Heywood, 1838);

*The Catechism of the New Moral World* (Manchester: A. Heywood, 1838);

*The Marriage System of the New Moral World* (Leeds: J. Hobson, 1838);

*Manifesto of Robert Owen* (London: E. Wilson, 1840);

*Socialism or the Rational System of Society* (London: Effingham Wilson, 1840);

*Ten Lectures on the Evils of Indissoluble Marriage* (Leeds, 1840?);
*Statement submitted to the Most Noble Marquis of Normanby* (London, 1840?);
*A Development of the Principles and Plans on which to Establish Self-Supporting Home Colonies* (London: Home Colonization Society, 1841);
*A Lecture Delivered in the Mechanics' Institute, London on the 30th March, 1840* (London: Home Colonization Society, 1841);
*Address to the Tories, Whigs, Radicals* (London: Home Colonization Society, 1841);
*An Address to the Socialists on the Present Position of the Rational System of Society* (London: Home Colonization Society, 1841);
*Lectures on the Rational System of Society* (London: Home Colonization Society, 1841);
*To the Electors of Great Britain and Ireland* [single sheet] (London: Home Colonization Office, 1841);
*The Signs of the Times* (London, 1841);
*Address to the Socialists, Being the Substance of Two Lectures Delivered in London, Previous to the Congress in May 1843* (N.p., 1843);
*Manifesto of Robert Owen, Addressed to All Governments and People Who Desire to Become Civilized* (Washington, D.C.: Printed at the *Globe* Office, 1844);
*Address on Leaving the United States for Europe, June 1st, 1845* [single sheet] (New York, 1845);
*Letter from Mr. Robert Owen to the President and Members of the New York State Convention, Appointed to Revise the Constitution of the State* (Washington, D.C., 1846);
*Reasons for Each Law of the Constitution Proposed to be Introduced first into the State of New York, Afterwards into Each State of the Union, and then from the Universal and Unchanging Truth of the Principles and Innumerable Advantages in Practice to All Other Nations* (Washington, D.C., 1846);
*Manifesto of Robert Owen to the Civilized World* (New York, 1847);
*Adresse à l'Assemblée nationale de France* (Paris: Imprimerie de N. Chaix, 1848);
*Dialogue entre la France, le Monde, et Robert Owen* (Paris: Paulin et Le Chevalier, 1848);
*Dialogue entre les Membres de la Commission Executive, les Ambassadeurs d'Angleterre, de Russie, d'Autriche, de Prusse, de Hollande, des Etats-Unis, et Robert Owen* (Paris: Capelle, 1848);
*On the Employment of Children in Manufactories* (New Lanark, 1848);
*Practical Measures Required to Prevent Greater Political Changes in Great Britain and Ireland* (London, 1848);
*Socialism Misrepresented, and truly Represented* (N.p., 1848);
*The Universal Permanent Government, Constitution, and Code of Laws . . . for the World* (London, 1848?);
*Letters on Education* (London, 1849);
*The Revolution in the Mind and Practice of the Human Race* (London: E. Wilson, 1849);
*A Farewell Address Delivered at the Scientific Institution* (London, 1850);
*Catechism of the Rational System of Society* (London, 1850);
*Addresses to the Delegates of the Human Race at the World's Fair* (London, 1851);
*Calculations showing the Facility With Which the Paupers and Unemployed May be Enabled to Support Themselves* (London, 1851);
*Letters on Government As It Is and As It Ought To Be* (N.p., 1851);
*Robert Owen's Tracts for the World's Fair* (London: Printed by Holyoake Brothers, 1851);
*The Future of the Human Race* (London: E. Wilson, 1853);
*The New Existence of Man upon the Earth*, 8 parts (London: E. Wilson, 1854-1855);
*Robert Owen's Address to the Human Race on His Eighty-Fourth Birthday, May 14th, 1854* (London: E. Wilson, 1854);
*Address on Spiritual Manifestations* (London: J. Clayton & Son, 1855);
*Robert Owen's Address, Delivered at the Meeting in St. Martin's Hall, Long Acre, London; on the First of January, 1855* (London: E. Wilson, 1855);
*The Coming Millennium*, first series, nos. 1-6 (London, 1855); second series, nos. 7-12 (N.p., 1857);
*The Inauguration of the Millennium* (London: J. Clayton & Son, 1855);
*The Millennium in Practice* (London: J. Clayton, 1855);
*Address of Robert Owen to the Profession of Arms, from the Commander in Chief to the Private* [broadside] (N.p., 1857);
*A Letter addressed to the Potentates of the Earth* (N.p., 1857);
*Report of the Meetings of the Advanced Minds of the World* (London: Published by Effingham Wilson, 1857);
*The Life of Robert Owen Written By Himself*, 2 volumes (London: E. Wilson, 1857-1858);
*Address to the National Association for the Promotion of Social Science* (N.p., 1858).

*Nineteenth-century engravings of New Lanark and the school at New Lanark*

**Editions:** *A New View of Society & Other Writings*, edited by G. D. H. Cole (London & Toronto: Dent / New York: Dutton, 1927);

*Robert Owen in the United States*, edited by Oakley C. Johnson (New York: Humanities Press, 1970);

*A New View of Society and Other Writings*, edited by Gregory Claeys (Harmondsworth, U.K.: Penguin, 1991).

OTHER: "An Attempt to Explain the Causes of the Commercial and Other Difficulties Which are now Experienced in the Civilised Parts of the World," in *A Report of the Transactions at the Holkham Sheep-Shearing*, edited by R. N. Bacon (Norwich, 1821), pp. 118-124.

Robert Owen is best known as the founder of British socialism, as an ardent critic of inhumane industrialization, as a pioneering feminist, and as the proponent of just and fulfilling systems of economic organization. He was born in Newtown, Wales, on 14 May 1771, the son of Robert Owen, a saddler, ironmonger, and postmaster. Little is known of the son's early youth, except that he was soon devoted to reading, and devoured all the books a town of a thousand inhabitants could furnish. Religiously inclined, Owen was surprised to find great controversy among the Christian sects, and by the age of ten he had concluded (if we can take his memory seventy years later at face value) that there was something erroneous in all religions as they had been hitherto understood. It was a sentiment which would prove crucial to his later career.

When Owen was ten, his parents consented to allow him to go forth into the world, and he went to London in the care of an elder brother in 1781. Soon after, however, he secured an apprenticeship to a draper in Stamford, Lincolnshire. Treated like a member of the family by James McGuffog, Owen applied himself diligently to selling fabrics to the local gentry and nobility, working long hours while continuing to read and to pore over religious debates in particular. After three years Owen returned to London and continued the same trade. At about the age of seventeen he moved to Manchester, where the cotton-spinning industry was making rapid advances. Owen worked for two years in a shop, but then, with a loan, he set up a spinning shop with a partner. He was soon self-employed and making considerable profits, but, when the opportunity arose, Owen became, at the age of twenty, manager of the largest cotton-spinning factory then operating in Manchester, superintending a work force of five hundred and improving dramatically the quality of the yarn produced. Around 1795 he became a partner in a new enterprise. He soon joined the Manchester Literary and Philosophical Society, where he spoke several times and began to overcome his boyish and provincial awkwardness. While visiting Glasgow he fell in love with the daughter of a wealthy philanthropist and leading Scottish manufacturer, David Dale, who was anxious to divest himself of his spinning mills at New Lanark, on the Clyde south of Glasgow. Owen bought the mills with his partners in summer 1799, married Caroline Dale on 30 September of that year, and moved to become manager at New Lanark on 1 January 1800.

During the next fifteen years Owen made the New Lanark mills world famous for both the quality of thread produced and his humane, caring attitude toward the work force. Dale had already fed, clothed, and educated the five hundred pauper children employed at New Lanark, while employing them for about thirteen hours daily. (Many of them repaired broken threads while the machines were running.) Owen sought to improve the lot of the entire work force of about two thousand and—frequently in opposition to his partners—improved supplies at the village store, established rules for cleanliness and order, and expanded the educational system. In the mill he kept a four-sided, colored "monitor" above the workplace of each employee, rotating it according to performance. By 1816 he was able to reduce hours of labor for children to twelve, and to raise the minimum age of employment to ten years. He also set up a sick fund and savings bank, laid out walks by the river, and planned to establish public kitchens and dining rooms. With these measures, despite initial resistance, Owen won the affection of the work force. He also became exceedingly wealthy, assisted by new partners (who included Jeremy Bentham), and he became anxious to extend his reform proposals to the wider world.

Owen first advertised his ambitions in the *Essays on the Formation of the Human Character*, published in 1812. Here he was centrally concerned to persuade the public that character, rather than being fixed by original sin or any set of overwhelming predispositions, was largely the product of environment and that any character (as he never wearied of repeating) might be given to

*Illustrations of the effects of bad and good environments (engravings from the 1834 edition of* Essays on the Formation of the Human Character*)*

any community given the proper circumstances. (He did not mean, however, that every individual was capable of every task.) Owen had long taken a personal interest in the New Lanark schools, and he insisted that a more flexible, joyous, and spontaneous form of education, which emphasized the promotion of kindness, was possible. He became dominated—his opponents said obsessed—by the ideas that character resulted from circumstances and that the poor could correspondingly be educated to become useful, law-abiding, and productive members of society. He also came to believe that this principle implied that the poor could not be blamed any more than others for their failings, which were not willful misbehavior but merely errors resulting from poor upbringing and ignorance. Anger and all "artificial" punishments had thus to be abandoned, to be replaced by pity, charity, and forgiveness. By all accounts the system of education at New Lanark, which included lectures on natural science, geography, and history as well as singing and dancing lessons, was a considerable success. New Lanark was visited by monarchs and reformers of every variety (nearly twenty thousand people between 1815 and 1825), and Owen's reputation grew steadily.

Having established these principles to his own satisfaction, Owen sought to persuade legislators and his fellow manufacturers to extend them to the laboring population as a whole. He first argued for a national, nonsectarian system of education, while asking the government to take an interest in all who required employment and to provide public works projects if necessary. Owen soon became acquainted with leading politicians, clerics, economists, and philanthropists. He began to write on the effects and implications of the new and rapidly growing factory system, seeking the regulation of child labor in particular, and he gave evidence to various parliamentary committees in the hopes of persuading legislators of his views. Growing postwar distress and unemployment seemed to lend credence to his plans and encouraged him in the view that machinery was transforming the face of society. By 1817, however, he had encountered considerable resistance to his ideas for factory reform, while his philosophic opinions were fortified by a friendship with William Godwin, the author of the *Enquiry Concerning Political Justice* (1793) and one of the most thoroughgoing philosophic reformers of his day. At a series of meetings in August 1817 at the City of London Tavern, Owen denounced all religions as delusive and misguided. Much paternalist philanthropic sympathy for his schemes vanished, and thereafter he rarely received support from the upper classes.

By the spring of 1817 Owen had already decided that the poor and unemployed would be best provided useful labor in communities of five hundred to several thousand people in which agriculture and manufactures were combined. This plan was soon not merely another means of poor-law reform but a proposal to regenerate the entire world both morally and economically. By 1820 he had become convinced that such communities might house the whole population, thus obviating the evils of existing cities. By then too he had come to believe that members of these communities should share goods in common and work cooperatively as one "family," and he condemned "competition" as the key economic and moral evil of society. These proposals were stated most clearly in his *Report to the County of Lanark* (1821), where he asserts that, with the education of a new generation in his principles, the elimination of all punishment and poverty might truly be achieved, while production would be for use rather than profit, labor would be exchanged on the basis of costs of production and labor time rather than profit, with existing forms of money being abolished, and all "unproductive" and superfluous trades and professions would be superseded. Owen's plan was finally fully formed in the late 1830s, with the addition of a scheme for organizing the community according to the principle of age, with all passing through a routine of education, employment, the supervision and assistance of others, and government. Thus Owen felt that all political contests might also be superseded, and a true harmony would pervade the "new moral world" of the future.

Proposals were already afoot by 1820 to establish communities on these principles, and the rest of Owen's career was devoted to this goal. In the early 1820s one of Owen's earliest and most stalwart working-class followers, the Scottish printer George Mudie, helped found (though it was somewhat contrary to Owen's principles) an urban community in London. From 1824 until the end of the decade, Owen himself invested much of his fortune and time in Harmony, a community founded by the German Pietist George Rapp on the banks of the Wabash in Indiana. After buying Harmony from Rapp in 1825, Owen renamed it New Harmony. Another community flourished briefly at Orbiston, not far from New Lanark. These efforts were plagued by poor financing, disagreements about principles, an inability to instill sufficiently a sense of common endeavor, and difficulties in relocating urban dwellers and mechanics onto the land and setting them to rural tasks. Similar causes underlay the failure of the great community attempt at Queenwood, Hampshire, which became the focus of Owen's attention from the late 1830s until its bankruptcy in 1845, when public attention shifted away from Owen's proposals for the last time.

Between the 1820s and the fall of Queenwood, Owen also made several other attempts to introduce his principles. At the Congress of Aix-la-Chapelle in 1818 he approached many of the heads of European states as well as the czar of Russia for support. In 1823 he traveled to Ireland, advertised his views in a much circulated *Report of the Proceedings at the Several Public Meetings Held in Dublin* (1823), and was later gratified by the seeming success of the Ralahine community set up there on his principles. A few years later, following the collapse of New Harmony, Owen endeav-

Owen circa 1823 (engraving based on a portrait by Matilda Heming)

ored unsuccessfully to persuade the Mexican government to grant him a strip of land along the American border, and he began to popularize his ideas partly in terms of a new religious system (see *The New Religion*, 1830).

During the mid 1830s he first founded labor exchanges in London and Birmingham, hoping to eliminate retail profit and commence a system of exclusive buying which would enable the working classes to overturn eventually the existing system based on profit. In 1833-1834 he became extraordinarily popular for a brief time when the first attempt to found a union of all trades, the Grand National Consolidated Trades' Union, accepted him as a leader and took his advice on many matters. For a short time, at least, Owen believed that mass organizations might provide the leverage for introducing the new world, but he was soon again persuaded that a model community offered the best example for the operation of his principles. In the late 1830s in particular he moved substantially toward refining his system, publishing the impressive *Book of the New Moral World* in seven parts between 1836 and 1844, and clarifying his views on marriage in the *Lectures on the Marriages of the Priesthood of the Old Immoral World* (1835). During the 1840s Owenism reached what is often termed its "sectarian" phase, when Owen as the head of an extensive network of local branches attempted to instill a quasi-religious spirit of harmony and mutual endeavor (much indebted to his understanding of Quakerism) in his followers, who numbered in the thousands. There was a brief revival of such efforts in 1848, when revolutions shook Europe and momentarily popularized the socialist ideal much more widely. But Owen's appeal otherwise had been dissipated by the failure of his community experiments, his reluctance to compromise with working-class associates (and to reach any agreement with the much larger Chartist movement during the 1840s), and the considerable opposition his liberal views on marriage and religion aroused. Even Owen's remaining few stalwart followers were startled by his conversion to spiritualism in the early 1850s, though for Owen himself the appeal to the authority and support of the spirit world was sensible given the reluctance of material circumstances to bend to his will. When Owen died in 1858 he was remembered for having long championed the cause of the poor. When the Fabians and others began to revive his memory at the end of the nineteenth century he was seen as among the chief founders of modern non-Marxist socialism and social democracy.

Many of Owen's voluminous writings repetitiously insist upon the principle of the formation of the human character by the external world. This insistence must be understood in terms of existing Christian discussions about free will versus necessity, and the willingness of many to blame social ills, and particularly poverty, upon original sin and the moral evil of the poor, rather than social and political institutions. Nonetheless Owen was also at the forefront of many other social movements, including feminism and the reform of marriage laws, trade unionism, cooperation, ecological reform, religious toleration, and industrial reorganization. His quintessentially rationalist approach to social questions, his unwillingness to accept the finality of Malthusian objections to genuine improvement in the condition of the poor, and his unrelenting faith in the malleability of the personality and improvability of society generally, all place him at a considerable distance from those English Romantics, such as William Wordsworth, Robert Southey, and Samuel Taylor Coleridge, for whom the rationalist ideals of the French Revolution and of Godwinian perfectibility were anathema by the late 1790s. Owen's dismissal of Christianity also divided him from Southey and others.

Nonetheless Owen shared with the leading Romantic poets, as well as radical Romantics such as William Cobbett, a deep love of nature and distrust of cities and industrial life. He saw in the excesses of commercial life the degradation of all that was best in human existence, indeed the destruction of the sociable basis of society itself. Unlike Cobbett, however, Owen disliked and mistrusted popular political activity, and he remained closer to the ideal of reform by a clerisy, an ideal which Coleridge did much to popularize in Victorian England. But unlike all the Romantics, indeed even his chief mentor, Godwin, Owen had no cult of the individual, of genius and creativity, upon which to fall back, and to serve as the basis for a larger social ideal, although his system of education did encourage spontaneity and the all-rounded formation of the personality and he found much to admire in the inhabitants of more primitive societies, such as the North American natives. Instead he sought to reconcile competing individual wills through a more harmonious social life in which labor was more justly rewarded and all treated one another with charity—perhaps the key word in Owen's vocabulary—justice, and tolerance, and in which—to paraphrase one of his favorite sayings—all hearts would be united even if all opinions could not be. Unlike most of his contemporaries, Owen believed poverty could be abolished and the moral world remade, with the benefits of progress shared in common. His was the untainted perfectibilism of the Enlightenment, wedded to a vision of rural harmony in which the benefits of preindustrial life were to be joined with the advantages of modern machinery. In "community" philosopher and cotton spinner were thus to join hands, indeed finally to supersede the fragmentation of the division of labor, to become one amid the ideal reconciliation of nature and industry.

**Biographies:**

William Sargant, *Robert Owen and his Social Philosophy* (1860);

Lloyd Jones, *The Life, Times, and Labours of Robert Owen* (London: Swan Sonnenschein, 1890);

Frank Podmore, *Robert Owen* (London: Allen & Unwin, 1923);

G. D. H. Cole, *The Life of Robert Owen* (London: Macmillan, 1925; revised, 1930);

R. H. Harvey, *Robert Owen: Social Idealist* (Berkeley: University of California Press, 1949).

**References:**

A. E. Bestor, *Backwoods Utopias. The Sectarian Origins and the Owenite Phase of Communitarian Socialism in America, 1663-1829* (Philadelphia: University of Pennsylvania Press, 1950);

*A nineteenth-century engraving of New Harmony, Indiana, and a photograph of the New Harmony Town Hall*

John Butt, ed., *Robert Owen: Prince of the Cotton Spinners* (Newton Abbott, U.K.: David & Charles, 1971);

Gregory Claeys, *Citizens and Saints. Politics and Anti-Politics in Early British Socialism* (Cambridge: Cambridge University Press, 1989);

Claeys, Introduction to *A New View of Society and Other Writings*, edited by Claeys (Harmondsworth: Penguin, 1991);

Claeys, *Machinery, Money and the Millennium: From Moral Economy to Socialism, 1815-1860* (Princeton: Princeton University Press, 1987);

Alexander Cullen, *Adventures in Socialism* (Glasgow: John Smith, 1910);

R. G. Garnett, *Co-operation and the Owenite Socialist Communities in Britain 1825-45* (Manchester: Manchester University Press, 1972);

J. F. C. Harrison, *Quest for the New Moral World: Robert Owen and the Owenites in Britain and America* (London: Routledge & Kegan Paul, 1969);

Sidney Pollard and John Salt, eds., *Robert Owen: Prophet of the Poor* (London: Macmillan, 1971);

Edward Royle, *Victorian Infidels. The Origins of the British Secularist Movement 1791-1886* (Manchester: Manchester University Press, 1974);

Harold Silver, *The Concept of Popular Education: A Study of Ideas and Social Movements in the Early Nineteenth Century* (London: MacGibbon & Kee, 1965).

**Papers:**

Most of Owen's remaining papers are in the Co-operative Library, Manchester. Some manuscript material is also available in the best collection of Owenite primary literature, at the Goldsmith's Library, University of London.

# David Ricardo

*(18 April 1772 - 11 September 1823)*

Ronald J. Hunt
*Ohio University*

BOOKS: *The high price of bullion, a proof of the depreciation of bank notes* (London: J. Murray, 1810; corrected, 1810; enlarged, 1810; enlarged again, 1811);

*Reply to Mr. Bosanquet's practical observations on the Report of the Bullion Committee* (London: Printed for J. Murray, 1811);

*An essay on the influence of a low price of corn on the profits of stock; shewing the inexpediency of restrictions on importation: with remarks on Mr. Malthus' two last publications: "A inquiry into the nature and progress of rent"; and "The grounds of an opinion on the policy restricting the importation of foreign corn"* (London: J. Murray, 1815);

*Proposals for an economical and secure currency; with observations on the profits of the Bank of England, as they regard the public and the proprietors of bank stocks* (London: J. Murray, 1816);

*On the Principles of Political Economy and Taxation* (London: J. Murray, 1817; Georgetown, D.C.: J. Milligan, printed by J. Gideon, Junior, Washington City, 1819);

*On Protection to Agriculture* (London: J. Murray, 1822);

*Plan for the establishment of a National Bank* (London: J. Murray, 1824);

*The Works of David Ricardo*, edited by J. R. McCulloch (London: J. Murray, 1846);

*The first six chapters of the Principles of Political Economy and Taxation of David Ricardo, 1817* (New York & London: Macmillan, 1895);

*David Ricardo on the price of gold* (Baltimore: Johns Hopkins University, 1903);

*Economic essays by David Ricardo*, edited by E. C. K. Gonner (London: Bell, 1923);

*Notes on Malthus' "Principles of political economy,"* edited by Jacob H. Hollander and T. E. Gregory (Baltimore: Johns Hopkins Press / London: Oxford University Press, 1928);

*Minor papers on the currency question*, edited by Hollander (Baltimore: Johns Hopkins Press, 1932);

*The Works and Correspondence of David Ricardo*, 11 volumes, edited by Piero Sraffa (Cambridge: Cambridge University Press for the Royal Economic Society, 1951-1973);

*Notes on Malthus' Measure of Value* (Cambridge: Cambridge University Press, 1991).

David Ricardo had a rich and varied career. He was a successful broker on the London Stock Exchange, an M.P. in the House of Commons, and one of the most highly respected political economists of the nineteenth century. It is chiefly due to his reputation as a political economist, however, that Ricardo is remembered today.

The significance of David Ricardo for the discipline of economics still remains a hotly debated topic more than 165 years after his death. A scholarly consensus concerning the validity of his economic analyses has never emerged. There has never even been a scholarly consensus concerning the correct interpretation of Ricardian economics. As one recent commentator, Mark Blaug, has put it: "On every question, there were at least two, if not three, Ricardo's." Nor is Ricardo's controversiality limited to his theories of capitalist economics. As Blaug says, "that most bourgeois of all bourgeois economists, stands before us as the unwitting founding father of Marxian economics."

David Ricardo was born in London, the third son of Abraham and Abigail Ricardo, in a prosperous Jewish family. Abraham and Abigail had met in London shortly after Abraham's emigration from Amsterdam. Abraham's father, Joseph Israel Ricardo, was a Dutch businessman with substantial sums invested in British funds, and Abraham had moved to London to manage these investments for his father. By all accounts Abraham was a successful businessman. One measure of his success was his induction, in 1793, into a select group of "Jew Brokers," a rare privilege limited to a dozen Jewish businessmen in the City of London. Except for these select brokerships, the licensing of brokers was limited

*Daivd Ricardo (engraving by T. Hodgetts, after a portrait by Thomas Phillips, R.A.)*

to "freemen," precluding Jews on the grounds that they lacked qualifications for citizenship. That David Ricardo's father was one of the rare exceptions to this rule reflected his reputation in the London business community.

David, it seems, was destined to follow in his father's footsteps. Maria Edgeworth, a writer and an acquaintance of David Ricardo, recalled a conversation in which Ricardo remarked: "We were fifteen children—my father gave me but little education—he thought reading and writing and arithmetic were sufficient because he doomed me to be nothing but a man of business. . . ." By the age of fourteen, after a brief sojourn to Amsterdam to further his education, David was employed by his father in the family business.

Moses Ricardo, David's brother and biographer, recalled that, despite his lack of a classical education, David Ricardo demonstrated a high degree of curiosity and independent thinking from an early age. One mark of his independent nature became evident after only six years of employment with his father: he married outside the faith and against the wishes of his family. His marriage to Priscilla Wilkinson occurred on 20 December 1793, creating a breach with his family that resulted in his quitting the employment of his father and going into business for himself. The London *Times* obituary on Ricardo stated that, within a very few years of his resignation from the family business, David had become more successful than his father on the London Stock Exchange.

*The house in Grosvenor Square, London, where Ricardo lived from 1812 until his death*

The key to David Ricardo's meteoric career seems to have been a series of loans to the British government, which relied heavily on borrowed money to finance its war with Napoleon. Ricardo, as a loan contractor, became a principal in sizable loans to the government between 1807 and 1815. It was on the loan of 1815, the so-called Waterloo loan, however, that Ricardo made his single greatest profit, estimated at £1 million.

Concurrent with his activities on the stock exchange, Ricardo maintained an active career as a writer. Ricardo wrote extensively on political economy, a subject directly related to his lucrative career as a loan contractor. His interest seems to have been awakened as a result of his introduction to Adam Smith's *The Wealth of Nations* (1776), which he apparently read along with other works by Adam Smith during a 1799 stay at Bath, where Mrs. Ricardo was recuperating from an illness. Roughly ten years passed before Ricardo's own initial publications, his series of letters to the *Morning Chronicle* in 1809 and 1810, on the subject of the bullion controversies.

The bullion controversies, or "Paper against Gold," as they were more commonly known, were occasioned by the depreciation in the value of paper notes. It was Ricardo's contention that this depreciation was the result of the order in council of February 1897 suspending the redemption of bank notes in specie. This edict came after the Bank of England requested that the government protect the bank's dwindling reserves of gold and silver, which were under considerable pressure due to the public's growing lack of confidence in the value of paper and to the government's demands for bullion to finance the war with Napoleon. Paper money was issued by the Bank of England as well as by country banks, and it was the widespread failure of these country banks, in addition to the financial demands on the Bank of England by the government, that caused a run on the reserves of the Bank of England.

In what was to become his consistent theme over the next ten years, Ricardo contended in his initial letters to the *Morning Chronicle* that the depreciation in the value of paper was a direct result of the suspension of the convertibility of paper and specie. From Ricardo's point of view, the suspension of convertibility had removed the only check on the oversupply of paper notes, thus inducing the depreciation in the value of paper. Only the reintroduction of convertibility could restore a sound monetary policy.

In addition to his letters to the *Morning Chronicle*, Ricardo published several book-length treatises on his theory of monetary policy. *The high price of bullion, a proof of the depreciation of bank notes*, published in 1810, is an in-depth exposition of his fragmentary views on the currency question found in the pages of the *Morning Chronicle*. This work, published in four editions, quite probably influenced the appointment of a select committee of the House of Commons to investigate the depreciation of paper currency. This committee subsequently became known as the Bullion Committee.

*Reply to Mr. Bosanquet's practical observations on the Report of the Bullion Committee* (1811) is, as implied by the title, a rejoinder to Charles Bosanquet's unfavorable views on the recommendations of the Bullion Committee to restore the convertibility of specie and notes. Bosanquet had asserted in his *Practical observations on the Report of the Bullion Committee* (1810) that the depreciation of paper notes was the result of factors other than the inconvertibility of paper and specie, principally a succession of tax increases which, he contended, had raised prices and lowered the value of the circulating medium. Ricardo's polemical rejoinder is an attack on the factual basis of Bosanquet's inferences as well as a spirited defense of the Bullion Committee.

Ricardo's first plan to rectify the mismanagement of the currency was published as the appendix to the fourth edition of *The high price of bullion* in 1811. He further developed his ideas on the subject of what came to be known as "Mr. Ricardo's plan" in his *Proposals for an economical and secure currency* (1816). Ricardo seems to have written this pamphlet, which puts forward the case for a gradual reinstatement of convertibility, at the behest of Pascoe Grenfell, M.P., a proponent of the Bullion Report, to influence the ongoing debates in the House of Commons concerning the recommendations of the Bullion Committee.

If Ricardo's ideas on currency questions were occasioned by the government's suspension of the convertibility of paper notes, his general theory of economics, including his labor theory of value, were inspired by another economic policy to which he took exception, the tariffs on the importation of small grains collectively known as the Corn Laws. Restrictions on the importation of small grains had existed since the fourteenth century, but they had become increasingly controversial. Some believed that they amounted to little more than a subsidy to the landed classes. The Corn Laws had been defended during the Napoleonic Wars because of the perceived need for England to remain self-sufficient in foodstuffs, but they once again became an object of disputation in 1815, after the cessation of hostilities.

A public debate concerning the utility of protectionism ensued, and Thomas Robert Malthus and David Ricardo became two of the most prominent figures in the dispute. The Corn Laws became the occasion for a vigorous exchange of ideas between the two men. Ricardo and Malthus were not unknown to one another, as they had exchanged correspondence on the currency question, but their respective publications on the Corn Laws generated an exchange of ideas on economic theory as well as the more narrow issue of public policy. Although Ricardo was heavily indebted to Malthus for many of his own economic ideas, they clashed over fundamental economic principles as well as the issue of protectionism.

Malthus argued the case for protectionism in *The Grounds of an Opinion on the Policy of Restricting the Importation of Foreign Corn* (1815). Ricardo opposed him in *An essay on the influence of a low price of corn on the profits of stock* (1815). The differences between Malthus and Ricardo concerning this issue were many and varied, but the principal theoretical dispute revolved around their respective explanations of the rate of profits.

Ricardo endeavored to demonstrate that the general rate of profits for all trades was a function of the profits on agricultural stock. His argument was derived from the assumption of "diminishing returns," an argument—central to Malthus's *Inquiry in to the Nature and Progress of Rent* (1815)—that, as agricultural costs increased, food prices would increase. This would force wages to rise to compensate for the higher costs of food. The general rate of profits would fall, according to Ricardo, due to the inability of the entrepreneur fully to offset increased wage costs with higher prices for finished goods. From Ricardo's

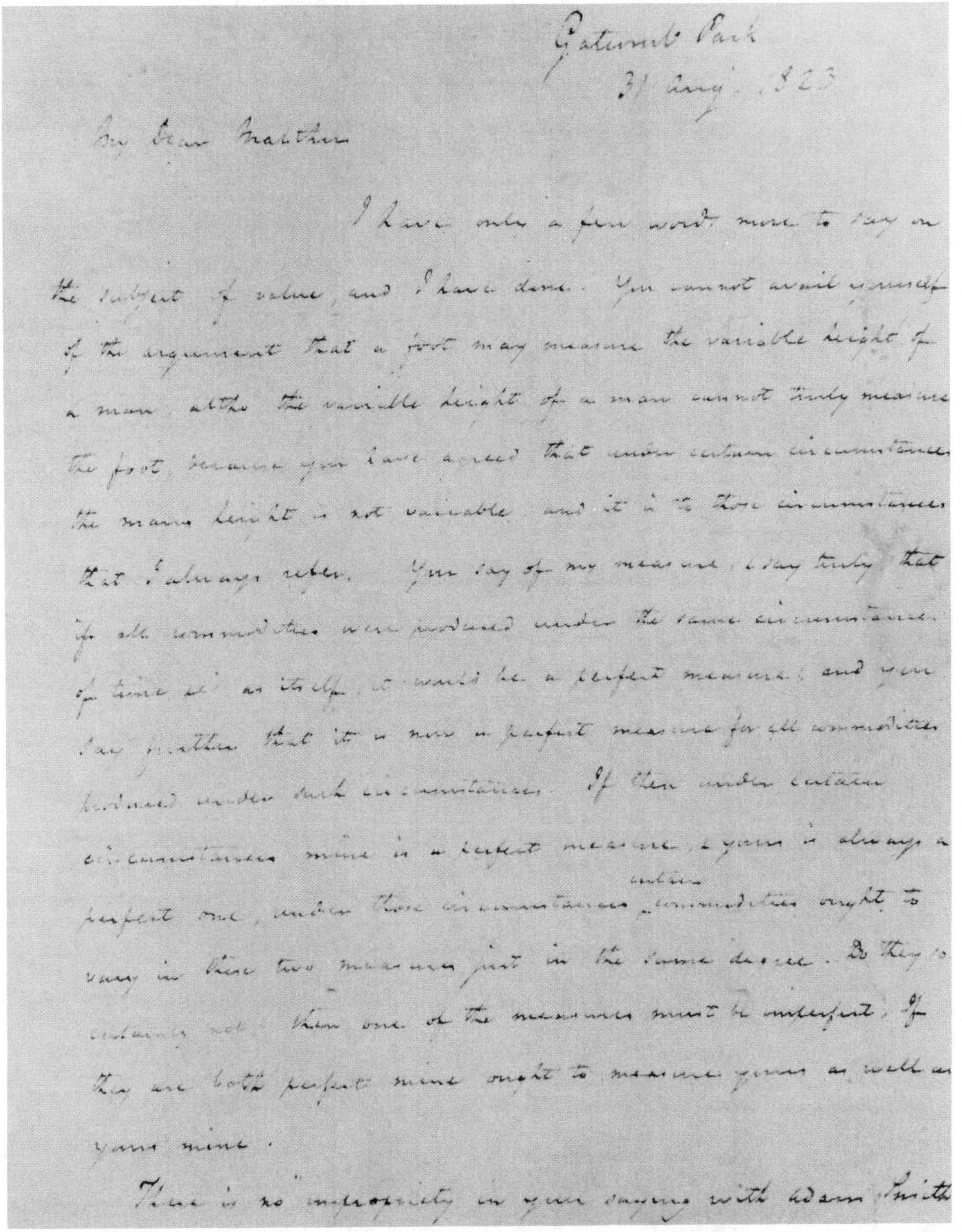

Gatcomb Park
31 Augt. 1823

My Dear Malthus

I have only a few words more to say on the subject of value, and I have done. You cannot avail yourself of the argument that a foot may measure the variable height of a man altho' the variable height of a man cannot truly measure the foot, because you have agreed that under certain circumstances the man's height is not variable, and it is to those circumstances that I always refer. You say of my measure, I say truly, that if all commodities were produced under the same circumstances of time &c. as itself, it would be a perfect measure; and you say further that it is now a perfect measure for all commodities produced under such circumstances. If then under certain circumstances mine is a perfect measure, & yours is always a perfect one, under those circumstances certain commodities ought to vary in these two measures just in the same degree. Do they so? Certainly not. Then one of the measures must be imperfect. If they are both perfect mine ought to measure yours as well as yours mine.

There is no impropriety in your saying with Adam Smith

*On this and the next two pages: Ricardo's 31 August 1823 letter to Thomas Robert Malthus, part of an extended correspondence in which the two men argued their opposing economic theories (from Piero Sraffa, ed.,* The Works and Correspondence of David Ricardo, *volume 9, 1952)*

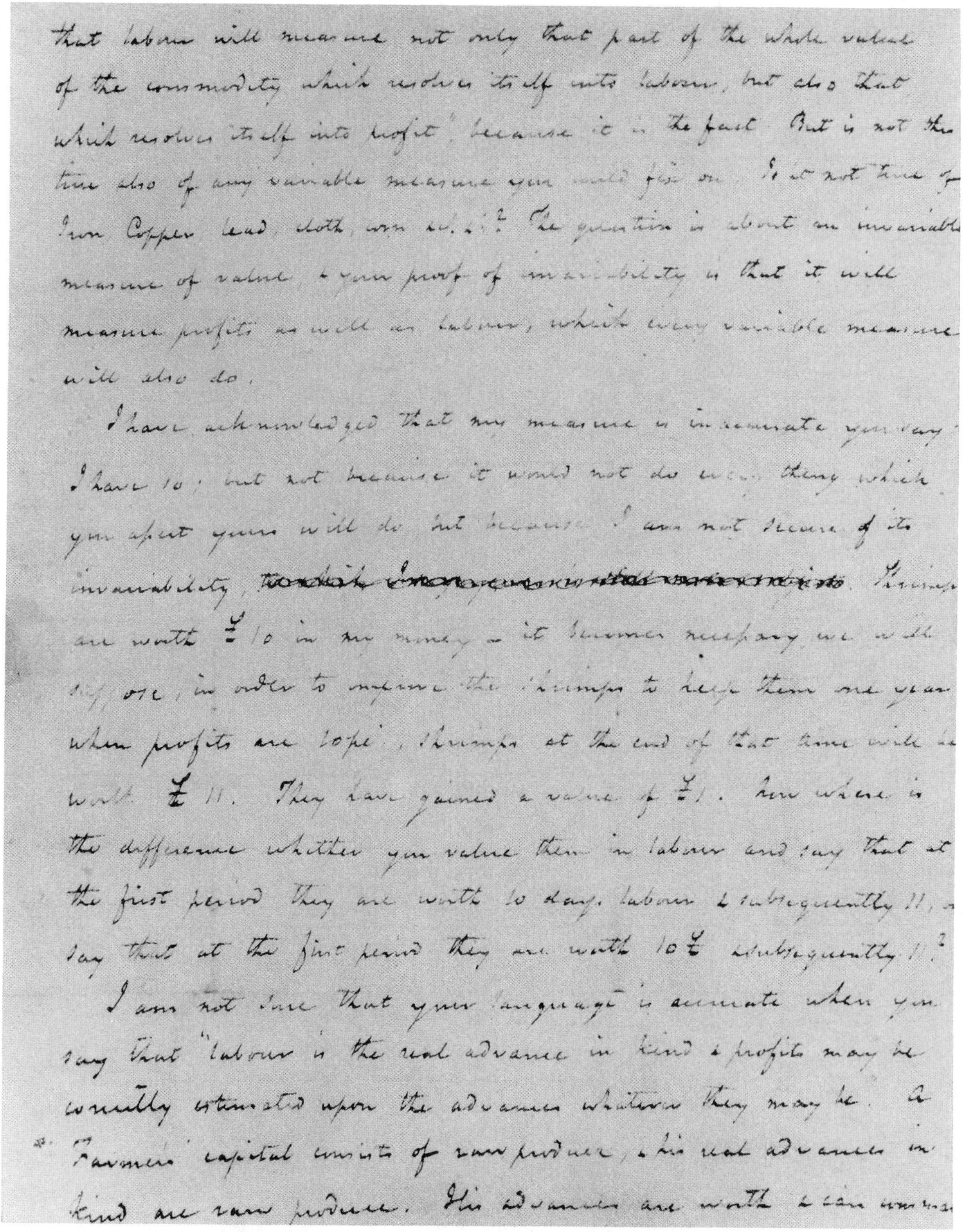

that labour will measure not only that part of the whole value of the commodity which resolves itself into labour, but also that which resolves itself into profit", because it is the fact. But is not this true also of any variable measure you could fix on. Is it not true of Iron Copper lead, cloth, corn &c. &c.? The question is about an invariable measure of value, & your proof of invariability is that it will measure profits as well as labour, which every variable measure will also do.

I have acknowledged that my measure is inaccurate you say. I have so; but not because it would not do every thing which you expect yours will do but because I am not secure of its invariability. ~~[illegible]~~ Shrimps are worth £10 in my money — it becomes necessary, we will suppose, in order to improve the shrimps to keep them one year when profits are 10 pc., shrimps at the end of that time will be worth £11. They have gained a value of £1. Now where is the difference whether you value them in labour and say that at the first period they are worth 10 days labour & subsequently 11, or say that at the first period they are worth 10£ & subsequently 11?

I am not sure that your language is accurate when you say that "labour is the real advance in kind & profits may be correctly estimated upon the advances whatever they may be." A Farmer's capital consists of raw produce, & his real advances in kind are raw produce. His advances are worth & can command

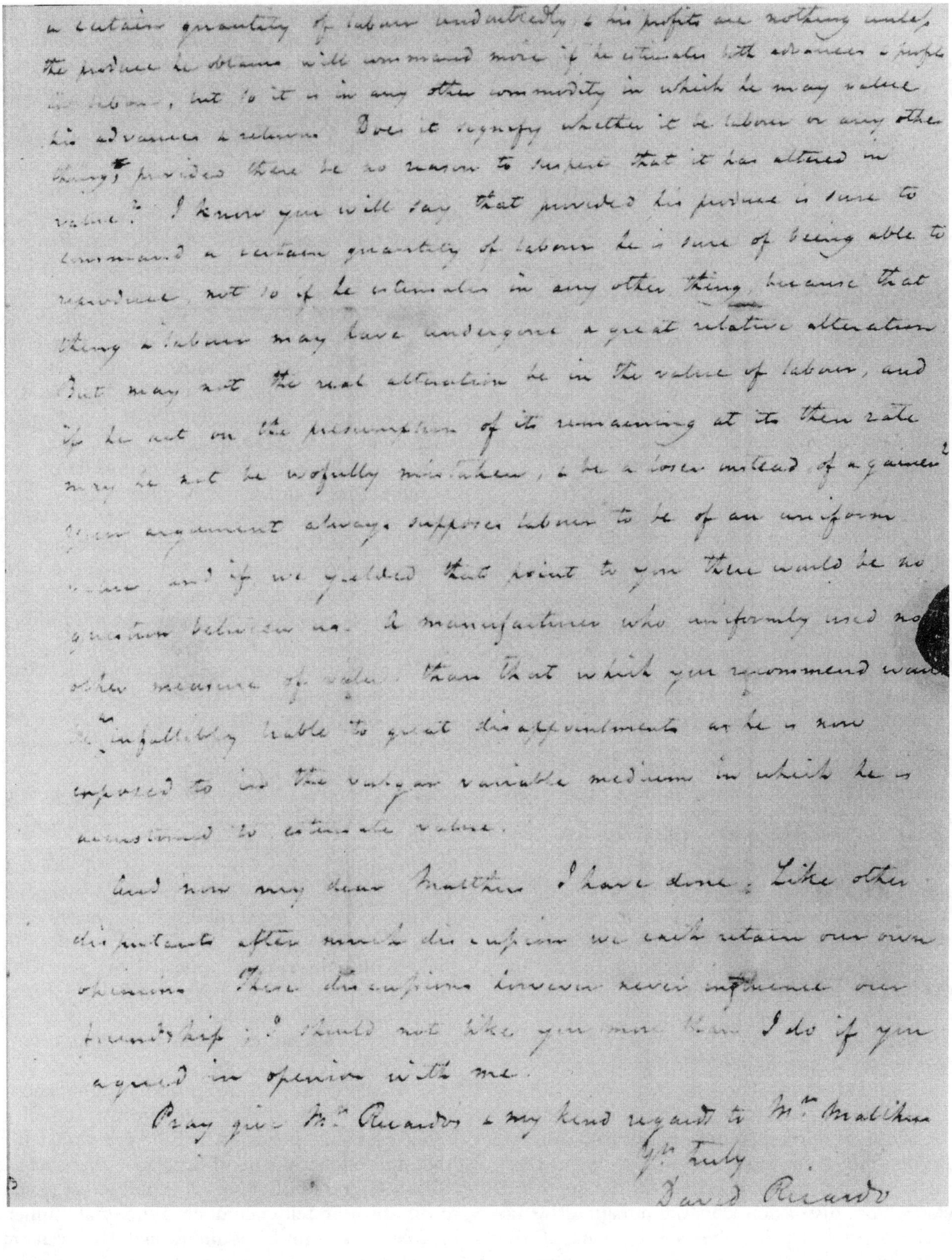

a certain quantity of labour undoubtedly, & his profits are nothing unless the produce he obtains will command more if he estimates both advances & profits in labour, but so it is in any other commodity in which he may value his advances & returns. Does it signify whether it be labour or any other thing* provided there be no reason to suspect that it has altered in value? I know you will say that provided his produce is sure to command a certain quantity of labour he is sure of being able to reproduce, not so if he estimates in any other thing, because that thing & labour may have undergone a great relative alteration. But may not the real alteration be in the value of labour, and if he act on the presumption of its remaining at its then rate may he not be wofully mistaken, & be a loser instead of a gainer? Your argument always supposes labour to be of an uniform value, and if we yielded that point to you there would be no question between us. A manufacturer who uniformly used no other measure of value than that which you recommend would be infallibly liable to great disappointments as he is now exposed to in the vulgar variable medium in which he is accustomed to estimate value.

And now my dear Malthus I have done. Like other disputants after much discussion we each retain our own opinions. These discussions however never influence our friendship; I should not like you more than I do if you agreed in opinion with me.

Pray give Mrs. Ricardo's & my kind regards to Mrs. Malthus

Yrs. truly

David Ricardo

point of view, therefore, because the free importation of corn would presumably act to hold down the costs of agricultural production, it would similarly reduce the costs of production in all trades, increasing the general rate of profits.

Malthus argued that the profits of the farmer no more determined the profits of the manufacturing and commercial sectors than the profits of those sectors determined the profits of the farmer. It now seems clear, regardless of the merits of the respective arguments, that it was Malthus's repeated objections to Ricardo's theory of profits that induced Ricardo to develop the more general theory of value contained in *On the Principles of Political Economy and Taxation*, published in 1817. Ricardo asserted with singular clarity the controversial principle with which he is now most often associated, the labor theory of value:

> That this [the labor realized in commodities] is really the foundation of the exchangeable value of all things, excepting those which cannot be increased by human industry, is a doctrine of the utmost importance in political economy. . . .
>
> If the quantity of labor realized in commodities, regulate their exchangeable value, every increase of the quantity of labor must augment the value of that commodity on which it is exercised, as every diminution must lower it.

The labor theory of value as set forth in Ricardo's classic work provided much of the theoretical bulwark for Karl Marx's critique of capitalist property relations in *Capital* (1867-1894), as did Ricardo's repeated arguments that the interests of the landlord, the manufacturer, and the laborer were inimical. The great favor bestowed upon the labor theory of value by generations of socialists, however, has not been matched by the opinion of subsequent generations of capitalist economists. The advent of marginal utility theory in the latter half of the nineteenth century proved to be the undoing of the popularity of the labor theory of value.

Managing his dual careers as loan contractor and as writer began to cause Ricardo distress. Despite his great financial success, he increasingly referred to his activities on the stock exchange as a distraction from the pursuit of his favorite science. During the closing years of the Napoleonic Wars, Ricardo began making preparations for his retirement from the exchange. His unsuccessful bid on a loan to the British government in 1819 was the closing act of his career on the London Stock Exchange, but Ricardo's interests were apparently more diverse than his intellectual interests. Shortly after his retirement from the exchange he entered Parliament as the representative of Portarlington.

There is ample evidence that his interest in a seat in Parliament preceded his retirement from the exchange. His extensive correspondence with James Mill and Thomas Malthus, among others, reveals that Ricardo had discussed the possibility of a parliamentary career at least five years before he quit the exchange. In November of 1816 he formally declined an invitation to stand for election for a vacant seat at Worcester, but in 1817 negotiations began for the seat at Portarlington, a typical rotten borough in Ireland. Acting on behalf of Ricardo was Edward Wakefield (a mutual acquaintance of James Mill and David Ricardo). John Dawson, Earl of Portarlington, was interested in borrowing a large sum on money to repay previous loans. Wakefield proposed to lend the earl between ten and twenty thousand pounds in return for the privilege of nominating a person for the vacant seat. After an exceedingly difficult and protracted period of negotiations, Ricardo eventually assumed the Portarlington seat in Parliament in February 1819 thanks in no small part to the efforts of Henry Brougham, who interceded on Ricardo's behalf in negotiations with the earl. For his part, Ricardo paid four thousand pounds for the privilege of occupying the seat, in addition to providing the earl a loan of twenty-five thousand pounds at 6 percent interest.

During his brief tenure as an M.P. Ricardo spoke often of his opposition to the government's restriction on the convertibility of paper currency and of his opposition to the Corn Laws. Although the government repealed the restriction on the convertibility of paper on 2 July 1819, a short time after Ricardo assumed his seat, the Corn Laws were not rescinded until 1846, twenty-three years after his death.

In Parliament Ricardo also became known for his advocacy of electoral reform, as well as other economic policies which he felt would further the establishment of free markets, such as his opposition to the Poor Laws and to usury statutes, which he felt encumbered the establishment of free markets for labor and capital. He is remembered as a reformer, one of the growing number of Radicals in the House of Commons who, in his many speeches and recorded votes, articulated the principles of nineteenth-century British

*The country house Ricardo bought in 1814*

liberalism. He spoke often of his advocacy of an extended franchise, of the need for a secret ballot, and of his opposition to laws which restricted the freedom of speech and press.

His death, not long after returning home from an extended tour of Europe, came suddenly in September 1823. He was buried shortly thereafter at Hardenhuish. Summing up his feelings for his brother, Moses Ricardo concluded: "Such was Mr. Ricardo:—as a private character unexcelled; preeminent as a philosopher; and in his public-capacity a model of what a legislator ought to be."

**Letters:**

*Letters of David Ricardo to Thomas Robert Malthus, 1810-1823*, edited by James Bonar (Oxford: Clarendon Press, 1887);

*Letters written by David Ricardo during a tour on the continent* (Gloucester: J Bellows, 1891);

*Letters of David Ricardo to John Ramsay McCulloch, 1816-1823*, edited by J. H. Hollander (New York: Published for the American Economic Association by Macmillan, 1895);

*Letters of David Ricardo to Hutches Trower and others, 1811-1823*, edited by Bonar and Hollander (Oxford: Clarendon Press, 1899).

**Biographies:**

A. Heertje, "On David Ricardo: 1772-1823," *Transactions of the Jewish Historical Society of England*, 24 (1975): 73-81;

David Weatherall, *David Ricardo: A Biography* (The Hague: Martinus Nijhoff, 1976).

**References:**

Mark Blaug, *Ricardian Economics: A Historical Study* (Westport, Conn.: Greenwood Press, 1973);

Giovanni A. Caravale, ed., *The Legacy of Ricardo* (Oxford: Blackwell, 1985);

Caravale and Domenico A. Tostato, *Ricardo and the Theory of Value, Distribution and Growth* (London & Boston: Routledge & Kegan Paul, 1980);

Paul Fabra, *The Exchange of Capital for Future Profit: The Triumph of Ricardian Political Economy over Marx and the Neo-classical* (Totowa, N.J. & London: Rowman & Littlefield, 1990);

Ben Fine, ed., *The Value Dimension: Marx versus Ricardo and Sraffa* (London & New York: Routledge & Kegan Paul, 1986);

Michael J. Gootzeit, *David Ricardo* (New York: Columbia University Press, 1975);

Jacob Harry Hollander, *David Ricardo, a Centenary Estimate* (Baltimore: Johns Hopkins Press, 1910);

Samuel Hollander, *The Economics of David Ricardo* (Toronto & Buffalo: University of Toronto Press, 1979);

Esther Lowenthal, *The Ricardian Socialists* (New York: Columbia University, 1911);

Ernest Mandel and Alan Freeman, eds., *Ricardo, Marx, Sraffa: The Langston Memorial Volume* (London: Verso, 1984);

Maria Cristina Marcuzzo and Annalisa Rosselli, *Ricardo and the Gold Standard: The Foundations of the International Monetary Order*, translated by Joan Hall (New York: St. Martin's Press, 1990);

Michio Morishima, *Ricardo's Economics: A General Theory of Distribution and Growth* (Cambridge: Cambridge University Press, 1989);

Cecil Clare North, *The Sociological Implications of Ricardo's Economics* (Chicago: University of Chicago Press, 1915);

Oswald St. Clair, *A Key to Ricardo* (New York: Kelley & Millman, 1957);

John Roscoe Turner, *The Ricardian Rent Theory in Early American Economics* (New York: New York University Press, 1921);

John Cunningham Wood, ed., *David Ricardo: Critical Assessments* (London: Croom Helm, 1984).

# Henry Crabb Robinson

*(13 May 1775 - 5 February 1867)*

John R. Holmes
*Franciscan University of Steubenville*

BOOKS: *Some account of Dr. Gall's New Theory of Physiognomy, founded on the Anatomy and Physiology of the Brain, and the form of the Skull. With the Critical Strictures of C. W. Hufeland, M.D.* (London: Longman, Hurst, Rees & Orme, 1807);

*Amatonda. A tale from the German of Anton Wall*, translated by Robinson (London: Printed for Longman, Hurst, Rees, Orme & Brown, 1811);

*Exposure of misrepresentations contained in the preface to The correspondence of William Wilberforce* (London: E. Moxon, 1840);

*Diary, Reminiscences, and Correspondence of Henry Crabb Robinson*, 3 volumes, edited by Thomas Sadler (London: Macmillan, 1869; Boston: Fields, Osgood, 1870);

*Blake, Coleridge, Wordsworth, Lamb, etc., being selections from the remains of Henry Crabb Robinson*, edited by Edith J. Morley (Manchester: Manchester University Press / London & New York: Longmans, Green, 1922).

OTHER: Thomas Clarkson, *Strictures on a Life of William Wilberforce*, edited by Robinson (London: Longman, Orme, Brown, Green & Longmans, 1838).

Henry Crabb Robinson, known in his day as a London barrister and journalist—the first foreign correspondent for the London *Times*—is now known primarily as, in Marilyn Gaull's words, "the unofficial diarist of his generation." He was the only writer intimate with the major literary figures of both England and the Continent (especially Germany), and his diary remains a valuable resource for students of European Romanticism. It can even be argued that Robinson was an important catalyst in the interreaction of German and British Romanticism—perhaps more important even than Samuel Taylor Coleridge or Thomas Carlyle, since Robinson was acquainted socially with the writers and thinkers he wrote about.

Henry Crabb Robinson was born on 13 May 1775 in the town of Bury St. Edmunds, the youngest of three sons of Henry Robinson, a tanner, and Jemima Crabb Robinson. Two other children died in infancy. The Robinsons were Dissenters, and Jemima Robinson's Calvinist piety was an important early influence on her son: as a child he had "a great horror of Popery" though religious tolerance characterized his adult life. Crabb Robinson's early education was at several boarding schools, including two run by uncles, both Dissenting ministers. During his last year in his Uncle Crabb's school Robinson heard the news of the French Revolution, at which he and his schoolfellows rejoiced.

The following year, 1790, Robinson was sent to Colchester to study law, as a clerk in the law office of a Mr. Francis. While there he heard John Wesley preach one of his last sermons. On 8 January 1793 Jemima Robinson died. The next year, at the age of nineteen, her son published his first article, a treatise on spies and informers in the liberal journal the *Cabinet*. Like many of his generation, Robinson was inspired by the liberal political theories of William Godwin, whose *Political Justice* (1793) he defended in a 1795 article in the *Cambridge Intelligencer*. Fifteen years later he would become intimate with Godwin, establishing a pattern of hobnobbing with the best minds of his age and recording their conversations in his diary.

On 20 April 1796 Robinson took rooms in Drury Lane, London, in hopes of pursuing a legal career. During the next eighteen months he was a clerk in three different London law offices, until the death of his uncle in January of 1798 gave him an inheritance which freed him from what he considered a drudgery.

A major source of amusement in his brief period as a law clerk, however, was the theater. The first mention of the London stage in Robinson's diary, which he began in 1811, is an account of a production of George Coleman the Elder's adaptation of George Lillo's *The Fatal Curios-*

*Henry Crabb Robinson (drawing by Masquerier; from Edith J. Morley, ed.,* Henry Crabb Robinson on Books and Their Writers, *1938)*

*ity*, starring Sarah Kemble Siddons. His accounts of the plays he saw over the next sixty years form a valuable history of British theater in the first half of the nineteenth century, as well as competent and readable dramatic criticism.

In 1799 Robinson met William Hazlitt, who was then only beginning to find himself as a critic; Robinson prided himself in being one of the first to find promise in Hazlitt as a writer. Hazlitt introduced Robinson to the poetry of the "Lake School," including Wordsworth and Coleridge's *Lyrical Ballads* (1798). All the poets he read at this time—Samuel Taylor Coleridge, William Wordsworth, Robert Southey, and Charles Lamb—were to become close friends and frequent dinner companions with Robinson.

Robinson followed a walking tour of Wales in the summer of 1799 with a tour of Germany in April of 1800, which turned into a five-year residence. He was delighted to discover himself a celebrity for the simple novelty of being an Englishman. Napoleon's soldiers were all over the German state. Because England was at war with France, British subjects were not common or welcome by the French there, and the Germans loved Robinson all the more for being in their country.

Robinson immersed himself in German literature and began introducing himself to the Romantic writers—first Clemens Brentano, whose brother Christian convinced Robinson to study and tour the Swiss Alps with him in the summer of 1801. By the end of the year they reached Weimar, where Robinson was introduced to Friedrich von Schiller and Johann Wolfgang von Goethe—at first only as a formality though his intimacy with both great poets would soon increase. Robinson attended the great theater at Weimar and visited two of the aging dramatists of the

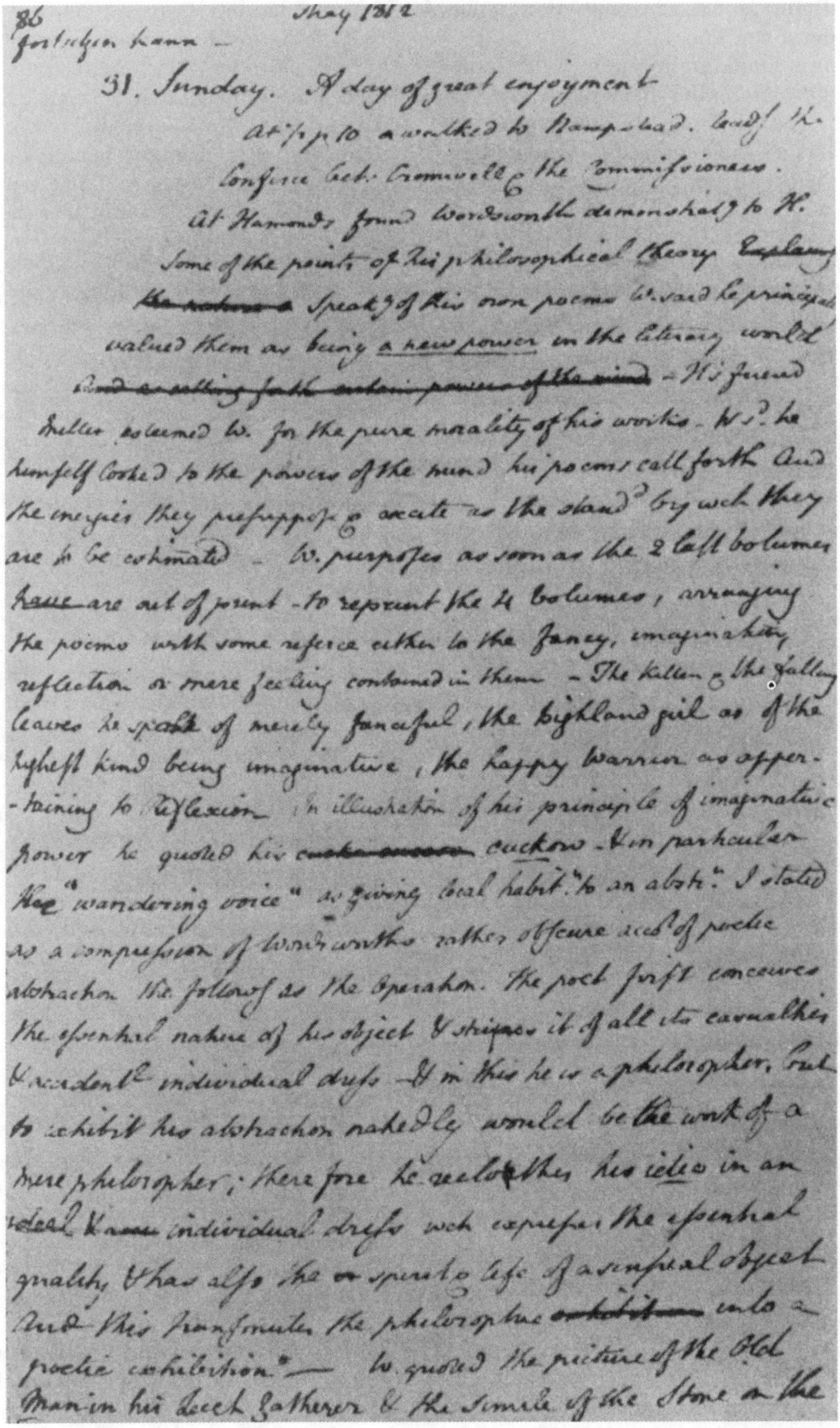
86 May 1812
fortsetzen kann —
31. Sunday. A day of great enjoyment
At ½ p. 10 a walked to Hampstead. Read of the
conference betw. Cromwell & the Commissioners.
At Hamonds found Wordsworth demonstrat^g to H.
Some of the points of his philosophical theory ~~Explaining~~
~~the nature~~ Speak^g of his own poems W. said he principally
valued them as being a new power in the literary world
~~and calling forth certain powers of the mind~~ — H's friend
Miller esteemed W. for the pure morality of his works. W. s^d he
himself looked to the powers of the mind his poems call forth And
the energies they presuppose & excite as the stand^d by wch they
are to be estimated — W. purposes as soon as the 2 last volumes
~~have~~ are out of print - to reprint the 4 volumes, arranging
the poems with some reference either to the fancy, imaginatn,
reflection or mere feeling contained in them — The Kitten & the falling
leaves he spoke of merely fanciful, the highland girl as of the
highest kind being imaginative, the happy warrior as apper-
-taining to reflexion. In illustration of his principle of imaginative
power he quoted his ~~cuckoo~~ cuckoo - In particular
the "wandering voice" as giving local habit.ⁿ to an abstr.ⁿ I stated
as a compression of Wordsworths rather obscure acct of poetic
abstraction the following as the operation. The poet first conceives
the essential nature of his object & strips it of all its casualties
& accident^l individual dress - & in this he is a philosopher, but
to exhibit his abstraction nakedly would be the work of a
mere philosopher; therefore he reclothes his ideas in an
~~ideal dress~~ individual dress wch expresses the essential
quality & has also the ~~—~~ spirit of life of a sensual object
And this transmutes the philosophic ~~exhibition~~ into a
poetic exhibition.* — W. quoted the picture of the Old
Man in his Leech Gatherer & the simile of the Stone on the

*Diary page on which Robinson recorded a conversation with William Wordsworth (from Edith J. Morley,* The Life and Times of Henry Crabb Robinson, *1935)*

Sturm-und-Drang period, Christoph Martin Wieland and August von Kotzebue.

Arriving at Frankfurt in June of 1802, Robinson held lengthy discussions on literature and philosophy with Friedrich von Schlegel, one of the leading writers of the German Romantic movement. The intellectual center of the movement at this time was the University of Jena; Robinson matriculated there on 20 October 1802, and spent the next three years as an undergraduate there. He studied aesthetics and metaphysics with F. W. J. von Schelling, encountering firsthand the post-Kantian idealism that was only slowly and imperfectly trickling into England through Coleridge. Robinson improved the flow by contributing lucid, popularized accounts of German literature and philosophy to the *Monthly Register* in England.

The Weimar theater being fewer than ten miles from Jena, Robinson saw as many productions as his studies allowed. He attended the premier performance of Schiller's *Die Braut von Messina* (20 March 1803), as well as productions of Goethe's *Die Naturliche Tochter* and Gotthold Ephraim Lessing's *Nathan der Weise*. On his trips to Weimar Robinson met with the anti-Kantian philosopher and theologian Johann Gottfried von Herder, then in the last year of his life.

After she was exiled by Napoleon in 1803, Madame Germaine de Staël visited Weimar in 1804, and Robinson became a frequent guest at her table. She sought his advice on which German writers to read, and her understanding of German philosophy, which made her *De l'Allemagne* (1813) the carrier of Romanticism to the rest of the Continent, owed much to Robinson. Exiled along with de Staël was Benjamin Constant, who was to become one of the leading Romantic novelists in France. Constant shared Robinson's admiration for Godwin, and they exchanged ideas on literature and politics.

Madame de Staël was not Robinson's only host at this time. Beginning in March of 1804, he was often invited to Goethe's home, where he met the second Schlegel brother, August Wilhelm. He was also entertained by the Brentanos again (including Christian's sister Bettina), and by several of the aristocratic families of Weimar, particularly Anna Amalia, Duchess of Saxe-Weimar. At the duchess's parties Robinson met a Dr. Gall whose new theory of craniology made such an impression on Robinson that he published a book on it in 1807.

On leaving Germany in late August of 1805, Robinson had to pass through the northern principalities, which were controlled by the French army. Even with a Saxon passport and a flawless German accent, Robinson was almost taken by the French; the kindness of a German innkeeper helped him avoid detection.

Robinson's new Continental perspective on politics made him much in demand by the periodical publishers in London, and the literati sought him as much as he had once sought them. Anna Laetitia Aiken Barbauld and Charles and Mary Lamb were his most frequent hosts in 1806; he was with Charles Lamb on 10 December at the opening of Lamb's play *Mr. H----*. He also made an important and long-lasting connection with John Walter, then a junior editor of the London *Times*. Walter made Robinson the very first foreign correspondent for the *Times* by sending him back to Germany in March of 1807 to report on Napoleon's war.

Though the mail to England was stopped by the Danish fleet, Robinson was able to get his "Letters from the banks of the Elbe" through to the *Times* in diplomatic pouches. When British parliamentarians later criticized their navy's seizure of the supposedly neutral Danish ships, Robinson's evidence of Danish belligerence was instrumental in defending his country's action. After the authorities at Altona were issued orders to arrest all Englishmen, Robinson fled to Hamburg and then to neutral Sweden, where he was able to obtain passage home to London.

On this second return, Robinson found himself lionized by London society. Southey, Coleridge, and Wordsworth all sought his company, and Robinson became lifelong friends with all three Lake Poets. He was retained by the *Times* as foreign editor and sent to Spain in the summer of 1808 to monitor European affairs from another front. Robinson stayed at Corunna until the French army arrived in mid January 1809; as he boarded a ship for London he could hear the first shots of the Battle of Corunna.

On his return, Robinson received his first byline—not in the *Times*, but in the new *London Review*, which originated the practice of signing articles. He also wrote at this time his essay on William Blake, which appeared in the German *Vaterländische Annalen* for January 1811. Robinson became interested in the artist when he attended Blake's exhibition on 23 April 1810. Returning on 10 June with Charles and Mary Lamb and prob-

*Robinson during his 1829 visit to Germany (drawing by Johann Joseph Schmeller; Goethe-Nationalmuseum)*

ably once more with Southey, he bought four copies of the *Descriptive Catalogue* (1809).

Robinson did not meet Blake at this time, but he did become close to Blake's friend and colleague the sculptor John Flaxman, and he discussed Blake with Southey, who was much taken with the "mad" poet/painter/engraver and spoke admiringly of his poem *Jerusalem* (1804-1820). Flaxman became a sounding board for Robinson's aesthetics for the next decade and a half, until the sculptor's death on 7 December 1826.

We know the progress of Robinson's opinions and activities in much more detail at this point, for he began his diary with the new year of 1811. In that year Robinson's translation of Anton Wall's fairy tale *Amatonda* appeared. It did not sell. Though Coleridge and Lamb praised it in literary circles, it was never reviewed in print. The slight volume was fleshed out with other short translations, including the very first English version of works by Jean Paul Richter.

Besides continuing his frequent visits with Coleridge, Southey, Wordsworth, and Lamb, Robinson got to know Dr. Alexander Wolcott (Peter Pindar) and William Hazlitt, although Hazlitt's criticism of Wordsworth kept Robinson from growing too close to him. Robinson cut all ties with Hazlitt in 1816 after he wrote a particularly scathing attack on Wordsworth for the *Examiner* of 24 December 1815. Robinson did, however, attend Hazlitt's lecture series in January and February of 1818.

In 1812 Robinson resumed his law studies, this time with an aim to the bar. It was also a banner year for literary acquaintances. In January Robinson met Leigh Hunt, Samuel Rogers, and

*Robinson at the Athenæum Club, 4 September 1860 (engraving after a sketch by G. Scharf, F.S.A.)*

Lord Byron, at Coleridge's lectures. Robinson did not engage Byron in conversation, and would not see him again. In June he met the "opium-eating" essayist Thomas De Quincey, and on 12 August he viewed the Elgin marbles as they were being uncrated at Burlington House. Five years later (19 May 1817) he would see them fully displayed at the British Museum.

On 7 May 1813 Robinson learned that he was called to the bar, and he took his oaths the following afternoon at four o'clock. A friend gave him his first case that very day, and on 20 August Robinson pleaded for the defendant in his first murder trial. In his brief career as a barrister Robinson established a practice of traveling outside of England each summer: in August of 1814, excited by the abdication of Napoleon, Robinson visited France; the following summer he would tour the battlefield at Waterloo, soon enough after the battle for him to find evidence of the fighting still remaining.

On 22 April 1815 Robinson's father died. Though he corresponded regularly with his older brothers, Habakkuk and Thomas, Robinson had not kept contact with his father and recorded in his diary his lack of love for the man, as well as a bit of guilt for that lack.

Robinson's 1816 excursion kept him in England: he toured the Lake Country at the invitation of Wordsworth, enjoying also the company of De Quincey and Southey, by then the poet laureate. The following June he met one of the few German Romantics he had not known in Germany: Ludwig Tieck, who had been living in Italy during Robinson's last years at Jena. In November of 1817 he met Percy and Mary Shelley at Godwin's house and was not overly impressed: he found the poet's conversation "vehement, arrogant, and intolerant," drenched in "the usual

*Henry Crabb Robinson (portrait by Henry Dawall; National Portrait Gallery, London)*

party slang" of romantic liberals. This was Robinson's only meeting with Percy Shelley, who died five years later.

Robinson's 1818 excursion was a return to Germany, looking up old school friends. The crown prince of Weimar, having heard of Robinson from virtually every writer in his kingdom, invited him to a royal dinner. He did no traveling in 1819, but the following summer he toured Switzerland with the Wordsworths (William, his wife, and his sister), as Wordsworth records in his poetic *Memorials of a Tour on the Continent, 1820* (1822). In 1821 Robinson traveled alone through Scotland, in 1822 through southern France, in 1823 back to Germany and Switzerland, and to Normandy in 1824. Robinson's trip to Ireland in 1826 was marked by his horror of the poverty he found there and by the chance meeting of an old school friend, who had become undersheriff of Cork.

Meeting Blake at a dinner party on 10 December 1825 produced some of the most vivid and valuable contemporary accounts of the visionary poet. Robinson called on Blake at his home a week later and again a week after that, recording as much of these meetings as he could recall. He met with Blake off and on for the next two years, until Blake's death in 1827. Blake's well-known annotations to Wordsworth were made in a copy Robinson loaned him.

At the end of the London court's summer circuit in 1828 Robinson retired from the bar. He began his career later and finished it earlier than most, but he looked back on going to the bar and quitting it as two of his wisest acts. He spent the next year studying Italian in preparation for a trip to Italy. He left England in June of 1829 and toured Germany—renewing old contacts with Goethe, Tieck, and his old professor Schelling before entering Italy from the north, through Switzerland, and reaching Rome in mid November. After touring the Italian peninsula, Robinson returned to Rome, where, on the Feast of Corpus Christi in June, he attended a papal mass. It was the last Corpus Christi mass for Pius VIII, who died the following November. Though frankly suspicious of Roman Catholic pomp in his religious conversations, Robinson recorded an aesthetic admiration for the splendid high mass. He expressed similar admiration, mixed with amusement, at witnessing the coronation of Pope Gregory XVI in January of 1831.

In Florence during August of 1830 Robinson met the only living British Romantic of any note who yet escaped his acquaintance—Walter Savage Landor. He also met the most notable Italian poet of the day, Giacomo Leopardi, shortly after the appearance of the first edition of Leopardi's *Canti* (1831).

On returning to England, Robinson found the nation caught in popular agitation for democratic reform, resulting in the landmark Reform Bill of 1832, bringing England from an absolute to a constitutional monarchy. Ironically, three of Robinson's new acquaintances of this time were major voices in the new struggle for democracy: Thomas Carlyle, a detractor, and Jeremy Bentham and his disciple John Stuart Mill, both supporters of democracy.

Just before passage of the Reform Bill, Robinson received word of the death of Goethe. When William J. Fox, editor of the *Monthly Repository*, heard the news, Robinson was of course the first Englishman he thought of to write a memorial. Robinson responded to Fox's request enthusiastically: his summary of Goethe's works ran for almost a year in the *Repository*, from May 1832 to April 1833.

On 7 March 1833 Robinson was invited by the Society of Antiquaries, of which he was a member, to speak on the origin of the word *mass* in its ecclesiastical sense; his paper was published in the scholarly journal *Archaeologia*. On 10 June Robinson took his first train ride, from Liverpool to Manchester, marveling at the speed of twenty miles per hour. From Manchester he proceeded to Rydal Mount to visit Wordsworth and Southey and then left with Wordsworth for a tour of Scotland. The next summer (1834) Robinson again visited Germany, where he renewed acquaintance with the poets E. M. Arndt and Tieck, and met another Romantic poet, J. J. Goerres, then professor of history at Munich. He also was introduced to one of the Grimm brothers, to whom he contributed a fairy tale he had heard during his visits to Germany.

At this time Robinson suffered the loss of two close friends and celebrated poets: Coleridge and Lamb died in 1834. Robinson consoled Lamb's sister, Mary, with "To the Sister of Charles Lamb," the only scrap of his own poetry that he recorded in the diary:

> Comfort thee, O thou mourner! yet awhile
> Again shall Elia's smile
> Refresh thy heart, whose heart can ache no more.
> What is it we deplore?
> He leaves behind him, freed from griefs and years,
> Far worthier things than tears.
> The love of friends, without a single foe;
> Unequalled lot below!
> His gentle soul, his genius, these are thine;
> Shalt thou for these repine?
> He may have left the lowly walks of men;
> Left them he has: what then?
> Are not his footsteps followed by the eyes
> Of all the good and wise?
> Though the warm day is over, yet they seek,
> Upon the lofty peak
> Of his pure mind, the roseate light, that glows
> O'er Death's perennial snows.
> Behold him! From the Spirits of the Blest
> He speaks; he bids thee rest.

Perhaps the loss of his illustrious friends caused him to tighten his hold on his remaining ones in the following years: introduced to Francis Jeffrey, the influential editor of the *Edinburgh Review*, Robinson snubbed him for his attacks on Wordsworth. Also, at Christmas of 1835 there was established a new tradition: Robinson spent the holidays at Rydal Mount with the Wordsworths, as he would every year until Wordsworth's death in 1850. Wordsworth's sister, Dorothy, attributed a good part of the yule festivity to Robinson's presence, and her aphorism "No Crabb, no Christmas" was echoed by many of Wordsworth's friends.

At that first Christmas celebration Robinson formed an important new friendship with Dr. Thomas Arnold, the revolutionary educator (headmaster of Rugby School), theologian (author of *Principles of Church Reform*, 1833), and father of the poet Matthew Arnold. Robinson continued to attend Arnold's sermons and to correspond with him on theological topics, until the minister's death in 1842.

In the mid 1830s Robinson became more and more involved with efforts to establish a new college in the still-new (1828) University of London. Robinson contributed funds and became a trustee and vice-president of University Hall.

With the Reform Bill of 1832, and the coronation of Victoria in 1837, English politics and literature entered a new era, and Robinson's letters and diaries of this period show him conscious of the change. He joined in the excitement of the new queen's entry into London on 9 November 1837. His new acquaintances now would tend to be the luminaries of the Victorian rather than the Romantic age—Benjamin Disraeli; Felix Mendelssohn; Thomas Babington Macaulay; Alfred Tennyson; Robert and Elizabeth Barrett Browning; Charles Dickens; Arthur Hugh Clough; John Ruskin; Annabella, Lady Byron; and several Americans: Ralph Waldo Emerson, Harriet Beecher Stowe, and Daniel Webster. The one acquaintance of this period who wrote during an earlier age was the Irish Romantic Thomas Moore.

In the spring of 1837 Robinson took a tour of Italy with Wordsworth, recorded in the poet's *Memorials of a Tour in Italy* (published in his *Poems*, 1842), dedicated to Robinson. The tour included a visit to St. Peter's and the Vatican, Assisi, and several monasteries. The next summer's trip was to Paris with Southey; it was his last excursion with a poetic companion, for the deaths of Southey in 1843, Wordsworth in 1850, and Samuel Rogers in 1855 left no poetic friends of his generation alive. Robinson's Continental excursions would become understandably less frequent in the last two decades of his life: back to Rome in 1843; to Germany in 1846, 1851, and (at the age of eighty-eight) 1863; to France in 1850 and 1855.

In 1838 Robinson published, though not in his name, his vindication of the abolitionist William Wilberforce. The work had been undertaken by Wilberforce's colleague in the abolitionist movement, Thomas Clarkson, whose infirmities made it impossible for him to prepare it for publication. Robinson completed the work, mostly editorial, and published his own comments in a separate volume in 1840. The essence of both works was a refutation of spurious charges that Wilberforce and Clarkson campaigned against the slave trade out of impure motives, profiting personally from the money raised to fight it.

During the 1840s Robinson spent most of his time in the company of Wordsworth (poet laureate after 1843) and Rogers. His 1843 Christmas visit to Rydal Mount was marred by an accident: he fell downstairs on his first night there and had to be nursed through the holidays by Wordsworth's servant James. In 1844 Robinson involved himself in the controversy about the "Dissenters' Chapels Bill," an attempt in Parliament to deny property to Unitarian churches on the basis that property was limited, after the Reformation in England, to subscribers to the Anglican articles of faith. Robinson defended his fellow Dissenters, one of the few times he identified himself publicly with any creed.

Robinson began work in 1847 to establish a gallery of his late friend Flaxman's works at the new college; in 1848 University Hall, as it was then named, was inaugurated, and the Flaxman Gallery incorporated there. Robinson was in the gallery as a college representative when Prince Albert visited it in 1851.

In the 1850s Robinson struck up an enduring friendship with Lady Byron. Their many discussions, in letters and table conversations recorded in Robinson's diaries from 1853 to 1860, reveal a more sympathetic attitude toward Lord Byron than seen in Harriet Beecher Stowe's notorious biography of Lady Byron (1870).

The diary entries of the 1860s are full of Robinson's consciousness of old age and approaching death. He knew his 1863 trip to Germany would be his last voyage (though he wrongly suspected the same of his 1850 trip to Paris); he resolved after seeing Shakespeare's *King John* and *Comedy of Errors* at Drury Lane in October of 1866 to see no more plays; he resigned all offices at the college on 11 March 1866. His final diary entry, written on 31 January 1867, ends: "I feel incapable to go on." On 2 February he took to his bed, and on 5 February he died. His elaborate tombstone at Highgate Cemetery, London, is inscribed with the names of his many illustrious friends.

It is appropriate that Henry Crabb Robinson is known as a friend of the great writers, rather than for his own writing, limited mostly to his posthumously published memoirs. For it was as a friend, bringing other friends together, that he most influenced the Romantic age. Though not an original genius, Robinson was a catalyst, uniting not only the German and British Romantics (M. H. Abrams called him "that great popularizer of German ideas"), but also the British Romantics to each other. He patched up a quarrel between Wordsworth and Coleridge in the spring of 1812; he read Blake's poems to Wordsworth and attempted to counter Blake's objections to Wordsworth's "errors."

Robinson's friendships with the giants of his day were no fawning attempts to be all things to all people. He loyally and publicly defended Wordsworth against attacks by Hazlitt, Landor,

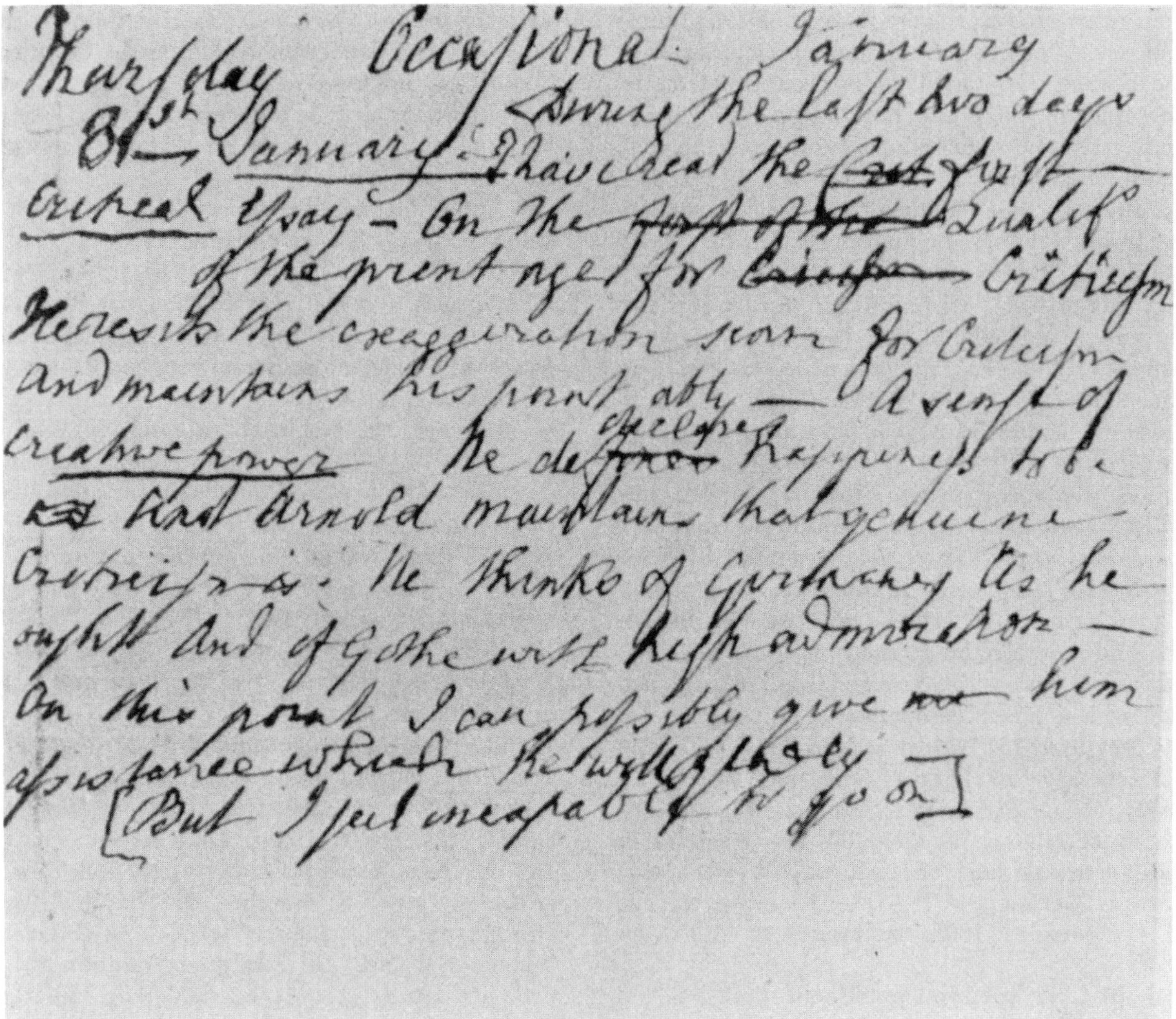

Thursday Occasional January
31st January During the last two days I have read the first Critical Essay — On the Qualif[ications] of the present age for Criticism
He resists the exaggeration scorn for Criticism and maintains his point ably — A sense of creative power He declares happiness to be
And Arnold maintains that genuine Criticism is. He thinks of Germany as he ought And of Goethe with high admiration —
On this point I can possibly give him assistance which he will gladly
[But I feel incapable to go on]

*Robinson's last diary entry, 31 January 1867 (from Edith J. Morley,* The Life and Times of Henry Crabb Robinson, *1935)*

and Jeffrey; yet he felt free himself to criticize Wordsworth where he found his friend wanting. Madame de Staël wrote that her initial interest in Robinson stemmed from the fact that he was the only guest at her table who was not afraid to disagree with her. It is precisely Robinson's conversational counters and probes that sharpen the expression of the ideas he recorded of Goethe, Wordsworth, Coleridge, and Blake. When Blake charged Dante and John Locke with "atheism," for example, Robinson struggled to show him how imprecisely he used the term:

> I tried to ascertain from Blake whether this charge of Atheism was not to be understood in a different sense from that which would be given to it according to the popular use of the word. But he would not admit this. Yet when he in like manner charged Locke with Atheism, and I remarked that Locke wrote on the evidences of Christianity and lived a virtuous life, Blake had nothing to say in reply. Nor did he make the charge of wilful deception. I admitted that Locke's doctrine leads to Atheism, and with this view Blake seemed to be satisfied.

Here Robinson insisted on precision, yet looked for a way to reconcile Blake's views with his understanding, even when Blake was silent.

Though Robinson's diaries and memoirs record his own views and experiences, the focus is overwhelmingly on other people. Through his whole career as a barrister, Robinson wrote little about his court experiences: if a case is mentioned, it is invariably because of the fascinating character of someone in the court. His diary for

*Fresco painted by Edward Armitage on the walls of University College London, depicting Robinson (portrait over mantle) and his friends: (top) Maj. C. W. von Knebel; Ludwig Tieck; Johann Wolfgang von Goethe; Ernst Moritz Arndt; Friedrich von Schiller; Johann Gottfried Herder; Christoph Martin Wieland; Samuel Taylor Coleridge; Mary Lamb; Charles Lamb; Robert Southey; William Wordsworth; William Blake; and John Flaxman; (bottom) William Hazlitt; William Godwin; Thomas Clarkson; Anna Laetitia Barbauld; Walter Savage Landor; Gilbert Wakefield; August Wilhelm von Schlegel; Madame Germaine de Staël; Anna Amalia, Duchess of Saxe-Weimar; Friedrich Karl von Savigny; Edward Irving; Samuel Rogers; Edward Quillinan; Robert Monsey Rolfe, Baron Cranworth; Sir Thomas Noon Talfourd; Augusta, Lady Byron; Reverend F. W. Robertson; Dr. Thomas Arnold; Thomas Paynter; and Christian Karl Josias, Freiherr von Bunsen (from Edith J. Morley,* The Life and Times of Henry Crabb Robinson, *1935)*

1816, however, is filled with references to cases involving the agricultural riots, for he seemed to know intuitively their historical importance.

Robinson's knack for judging the historical value of his experiences (though somewhat exaggerated by the editorial exclusion of many insignificant items from the published versions of his journals) is another reason students of Romanticism are drawn to his work—the primary reason being the intimate portraits of the major Romantic writers. Robinson shows us how the average Britisher reacted to the major events of his time: the French Revolution, the Napoleonic Wars, the battles of Trafalgar and Waterloo, the Convention of Cintra (Robinson reviewed Wordsworth's 1809 pamphlet on the subject for the *London Review*), the Reform Bill, the abolition of slavery, the coronation of Victoria, and even, in the last year of Robinson's life, the assassination of Abraham Lincoln. It is surprising how often one encounters in the diaries what are now commonplace observations about the revolutionary nature of the railroad, the rise of the middle class, or the advent of democracy in England; it must be remembered that Robinson made them without benefit of hindsight.

The same anticipation of posterity's consensus is found in Robinson's literary judgment in the diaries. Like many of his generation, he experienced a revolution in his literary taste upon reading *Lyrical Ballads*. He read the book a year after it appeared, when he was twenty-four. Of John Keats, the only major Romantic he never met, Robinson wrote in 1820: "I am greatly mistaken if Keats do [*sic*] not very soon take a high place among our poets." Hazlitt once told Mary Lamb, "Robinson cuts me, but I shall never cease to have a regard for him, for he was the first person who ever found out that there was anything in me." On the other hand Robinson never made extravagant claims for the poetry of Southey or Rogers, though both were close friends of his and both were offered the post of poet laureate (Rogers declined the honor).

Robinson's style in his memoirs is simple and direct, although it must be remembered that all published versions are compilations by other editors. Robinson donated his diaries, letters, and papers to University Hall (now part of the University of London), and was preparing them for publication when he died in 1867. Thomas Sadler completed the work and published it in three volumes in 1869. Sadler's edition was necessarily incomplete; too many people named in the diaries and letters were still alive, resulting in many blanks for decorum's sake. Edith J. Morley's work fifty years later—selections in 1922 and a fuller edition of letters in 1927—must therefore be considered independently from Sadler's, which it greatly augmented.

Though he will be most likely remembered as the Boswell of the Romantic age, Henry Crabb Robinson is probably more important as the man who introduced German Romanticism, both literature and philosophy, to the rest of Europe. He also created the profession of foreign correspondent and set the standard for foreign reporting in the first era of international journalism. Third, though he never wrote a drama review for the journals, his diary observations on the London theater over half a century, collected in 1966, form one of the most complete records of the drama of that period (1811-1866). Finally, he was a true and loyal friend to the major poets of the first half of the nineteenth century, and for that alone he deserves to be remembered.

**Letters:**

*The Correspondence of Henry Crabb Robinson with the Wordsworth Circle (1808-1866) the greater part now for the first time printed from the originals in Dr. Williams's library*, 2 volumes, edited by Edith J. Morley (Oxford: Clarendon Press, 1927).

**Biography:**

Edith J. Morley, *The Life and Times of Henry Crabb Robinson* (London: Dent, 1935).

**References:**

John M. Baker, "Henry Crabb Robinson in the Light of Unpublished Material and Contributions to Periodicals and the Press," Ph.D. dissertation, Harvard University, 1931;

Diana Behler, "Henry Crabb Robinson as a Mediator of Early German Romanticism to England," *Arcadia*, 12, no. 2 (1977): 117-155;

Marilyn Gaull, *English Romanticism* (New York: Norton, 1988);

Hertha Marquardt, *Henry Crabb Robinson und seine deutschen Freunde: Brücke zwischen England und Deutschland im Zeitalter der Romantik* (Göttingen: Vanderhoeck & Ruprecht, 1964);

Oskar Wellens, "Henry Crabb Robinson, Reviewer of Wordsworth, Coleridge, and Byron in the *Critical Review*: Some New Attributions," *Bulletin of Research in the Humanities*, 84 (Spring 1981): 98-120.

**Papers:**

Robinson's letters, diaries, and reminiscences, many yet unpublished, are at the University of London.

# Sir Walter Scott

*(15 August 1771 - 21 September 1832)*

Richard D. McGhee
*Arkansas State University*

See also the Scott entry in *DLB 93: British Romantic Poets, 1789-1832: First Series.*

BOOKS: *The Eve of Saint John. A Border Ballad* (Kelso: Printed by James Ballantyne, 1800);

*The Lay of the Last Minstrel* (London: Printed for Longman, Hurst, Rees & Orme, and A. Constable, Edinburgh, by James Ballantyne, Edinburgh, 1805; Philadelphia: Printed for I. Riley, New York, 1806);

*Ballads and Lyrical Pieces* (Edinburgh: Printed by James Ballantyne for Longman, Rees & Orme, London, and Archibald Constable, Edinburgh, 1806; Boston: Published & sold by Etheridge & Bliss and by B. & B. Hopkins, Philadelphia, 1807);

*Marmion: A Tale of Flodden Field* (Edinburgh: Printed by J. Ballantyne for Archibald Constable, Edinburgh, and William Miller & John Murray, London, 1808; Philadelphia: Hopkins & Earle, 1808);

*The Lady of the Lake; A Poem* (Edinburgh: Printed for John Ballantyne, Edinburgh, and Longman, Hurst, Rees & Orme and William Miller, London, by James Ballantyne, 1810; Boston: Published by W. Wells & T. B. Wait, printed by T. B. Wait, 1810; New York: E. Sargeant, 1810; Philadelphia: E. Earle, 1810);

*The Vision of Don Roderick: A Poem* (Edinburgh: Printed by James Ballantyne for John Ballantyne, Edinburgh, and Longman, Hurst, Rees, Orme & Brown, London, 1811; Boston: Published by T. B. Wait, 1811);

*Rokeby; A Poem* (Edinburgh: Printed for John Ballantyne, Edinburgh, and Longman, Hurst, Rees, Orme & Brown, London, by James Ballantyne, Edinburgh, 1813; Baltimore: J. Cushing, 1813);

*The Bridal of Triermain, or The Vale of St John. In Three Cantos* (Edinburgh: Printed by James Ballantyne for John Ballantyne and for Longman, Hurst, Rees, Orme & Brown and Gale, Curtis & Fenner, London, 1813; Philadelphia: Published by M. Thomas, printed by W. Fry, 1813);

*Waverley; or, 'Tis Sixty Years Since* (3 volumes, Edinburgh: Printed by James Ballantyne for Archibald Constable, Edinburgh, and Longman, Hurst, Rees, Orme & Brown, London, 1814; 1 volume, Boston: Published by Wells & Lilly and Bradford & Read, 1815; 2 volumes, New York: Van Winkle & Wiley, 1815);

*Guy Mannering; or, The Astrologer. By the Author of "Waverley"* (3 volumes, Edinburgh: Printed by James Ballantyne for Longman, Hurst, Rees, Orme & Brown, London, and Archibald Constable, Edinburgh, 1815; 2 volumes, Boston: Published by West & Richardson and Eastburn, Kirk, New York, printed by T. W. White, 1815);

*The Lord of the Isles, A Poem* (Edinburgh: Printed for Archibald Constable, Edinburgh, and Longman, Hurst, Rees, Orme & Brown, London, by James Ballantyne, 1815; New York: R. Scott, 1815; Philadelphia: Published by Moses Thomas, 1815);

*The Field of Waterloo; A Poem* (Edinburgh: Printed by James Ballantyne for Archibald Constable, Edinburgh, and Longman, Hurst, Rees, Orme & Brown, and John Murray, London, 1815; Boston: T. B. Wait, 1815; New York: Van Winkle & Wiley, 1815; Philadelphia: Published by Moses Thomas, printed by Van Winkle & Wiley, 1815);

*The Ettricke Garland; Being Two Excellent New Songs on The Lifting of the Banner of the House of Buccleuch, At the Great Foot-Ball Match on Carterhaugh, Dec. 4, 1815,* by Scott and James Hogg (Edinburgh: Printed by James Ballantyne, 1815);

*Paul's Letters To His Kinsfolk* (Edinburgh: Printed by James Ballantyne for Archibald Constable, Edinburgh, and Longman, Hurst, Rees, Orme & Brown, and John Murray, London,

Sir Walter Scott, 1822 (portrait by Sir Henry Raeburn; Scottish National Portrait Gallery)

1816; Philadelphia: Republished by M. Thomas, 1816);

*The Antiquary. By the Author of "Waverley" and "Guy Mannering"* (3 volumes, Edinburgh: Printed by James Ballantyne for Archibald Constable, Edinburgh, and Longman, Hurst, Rees, Orme & Brown, London, 1816; 2 volumes, New York: Van Winkle & Wiley, 1816);

*Tales of My Landlord, Collected and Arranged by Jedediah Cleishbotham, Schoolmaster and Parish-Clerk of Gandercleugh [The Black Dwarf* and *Old Mortality]* (4 volumes, Edinburgh: Printed for William Blackwood and John Murray, London, 1816; 1 volume, Philadelphia: Published by M. Thomas, 1817);

*Harold the Dauntless; A Poem* (Edinburgh: Printed by James Ballantyne for Longman, Hurst, Rees, Orme & Brown, London, and Archibald Constable, Edinburgh, 1817; New York: Published by James Eastburn, printed by Van Winkle Wiley, 1817);

*Rob Roy, by the Author of "Waverley," "Guy Mannering," and "The Antiquary"* (3 volumes, Edinburgh: Printed by James Ballantyne for Archibald Constable, Edinburgh, and Longman, Hurst, Rees, Orme & Brown, London, 1818; 2 volumes, New York: J. Eastburn, 1818; New York: Published by Kirk & Mercein, printed by E. & E. Hosford, Albany, 1818; Philadelphia: Published by M. Thomas, printed by J. Maxwell, 1818);

*Tales of My Landlord, Second Series, Collected and Arranged by Jedediah Cleishbotham, Schoolmaster and Parish-Clerk of Gandercleugh [The Heart of*

*Scott's parents, Walter and Anne Rutherford Scott, at the time of their marriage in 1758 (portraits attributed to Robert Harvie; Collection of Mrs. Maxwell-Scott of Abbotsford)*

*Mid-Lothian]*, 4 volumes (Edinburgh: Printed for Archibald Constable, 1818; Philadelphia: M. Carey & Son, 1818);

*Tales of My Landlord, Third Series, Collected and Arranged by Jedediah Cleishbotham, Schoolmaster and Parish-Clerk of Gandercleugh [The Bride of Lammermoor* and *A Legend of Montrose]*, 4 volumes (Edinburgh: Printed for Archibald Constable, Edinburgh, and Longman, Hurst, Rees, Orme & Brown and Hurst, Robinson, London, 1819; New York: Published by Charles Wiley, W. B. Gilley and A. T. Goodrich, printed by Clayton & Kingsland, 1819; Philadelphia: M. Thomas, 1819);

*Provincial Antiquities and Picturesque Scenery of Scotland*, text by Scott with plates by J. M. W. Turner and others (10 parts, Edinburgh: Printed by James Ballantyne, 1819-1826; 2 volumes, London: J. & A. Arch, 1826);

*Miscellaneous Poems* (Edinburgh: Printed for Archibald Constable, Edinburgh, and Hurst, Robinson, London, 1820);

*Ivanhoe; A Romance, by "the Author of Waverley" &c.* (3 volumes, Edinburgh: Printed for Archibald Constable, Edinburgh, and Hurst, Robinson, London, 1820 [i.e., 1819]; 2 volumes, Philadelphia: M. Carey & Son, 1820);

*The Monastery. A Romance. By the Author of "Waverley"* (3 volumes, Edinburgh: Printed for Longman, Hurst, Rees, Orme & Brown, London, and for Archibald Constable and John Ballantyne, Edinburgh, 1820; 1 volume, Philadelphia: Published by M. Carey & Son, 1820);

*The Abbot. by the Author of "Waverley"* (3 volumes, Edinburgh: Printed for Longman, Hurst, Rees, Orme & Brown, London, and for Archibald Constable and John Ballantyne, Edinburgh, 1820; 2 volumes, New York: J. & J. Harper, 1820; 1 volume, Philadelphia: M. Carey & Son, 1820);

*Kenilworth; A Romance. By the Author of "Waverley," "Ivanhoe," &c.* (3 volumes, Edinburgh: Printed for Archibald Constable and John Ballantyne, Edinburgh, and Hurst, Robinson, London, 1821; Hartford: S. G. Goodrich, 1821; Philadelphia: M. Carey & Son, 1821);

*The Pirate. By the Author of "Waverley," "Kenilworth," &c.* (3 volumes, Edinburgh: Printed for Archibald Constable, and Hurst, Robinson, London, 1822 [i.e., 1821]; 2 volumes, Boston: Wells & Lilly, 1822; 1 volume, Hartford: S. G. Goodrich and Huntington & Hopkins, 1822; 2 volumes, New York: E.

Duyckinck, 1822; 1 volume, Philadelphia: H. C. Carey & I. Lea, 1822);

*The Fortunes of Nigel. By the Author of "Waverley," "Kenilworth," &c.* (3 volumes, Edinburgh: Printed for Archibald Constable, Edinburgh, and Hurst, Robinson, London, 1822; 2 volumes, New York: T. Longworth, 1822; Philadelphia: Carey & Lea, 1822;

*Halidon Hill: A Dramatic Sketch* (Edinburgh: Printed for Archibald Constable, and Hurst, Robinson, London, 1822; New York: S. Campbell, printed by E. B. Clayton, 1822; Philadelphia: H. C. Carey & I. Lea, 1822);

*Peveril of the Peak. By the Author of "Waverley, Kenilworth," &c.* (4 volumes, Edinburgh: Printed for Archibald Constable, Edinburgh, and Hurst, Robinson, London, 1822 [i.e., 1823]; 3 volumes, Philadelphia: H. C. Carey & I. Lea, 1823);

*Quentin Durward. By the Author of "Waverley, Peveril of the Peak," &c.* (3 volumes, Edinburgh: Printed for Archibald Constable, Edinburgh, and Hurst, Robinson, London, 1823; 1 volume, Philadelphia: H. C. Carey & I. Lea, 1823);

*St Ronan's Well. By the Author of "Waverley, Quentin Durward," &c.* (3 volumes, Edinburgh: Printed for Archibald Constable, Edinburgh, and Hurst, Robinson, London, 1824 [i.e., 1823]; Philadelphia: H. C. Carey & I. Lea, 1824);

*Redgauntlet. A Tale of the Eighteenth Century. By the Author of "Waverley"* (3 volumes, Edinburgh: Printed for Archibald Constable, Edinburgh, and Hurst, Robinson, London, 1824; 2 volumes, Philadelphia: H. C. Carey & I. Lea, 1824);

*Tales of the Crusaders, by the Author of Waverley [The Betrothed* and *The Talisman]* (4 volumes, Edinburgh: Printed for Archibald Constable, Edinburgh, and Hurst, Robinson, London, 1825; New York: Published by E. Duyckinck, Collins & Hannay, Collins, E. Bliss & E. White, and W. B. Gilley, printed by J. & J. Harper, 1825; 2 volumes, Philadelphia: H. C. Carey & I. Lea, 1825);

*Letter to the Editor of the Edinburgh Weekly Journal from Malachi Malagrowther, Esq. on the Proposed Change of Currency and Other Late Alterations, As They Affect, or Are Intended to Affect, the Kingdom of Scotland* (Edinburgh: Printed by James Ballantyne for William Blackwood, 1826);

*A Second Letter to the Editor of the Edinburgh Weekly Journal, from Malachi Malagrowther, Esq.: On the Proposed Change of Currency, and Other Late Alterations, As They Affect, or Are Intended to Affect, the Kingdom of Scotland* (Edinburgh: Printed by James Ballantyne for William Blackwood, 1826);

*A Third Letter to the Editor of the Edinburgh Weekly Journal, from Malachi Malagrowther, Esq.: On the Proposed Change of Currency, and Other Late Alterations, As They Affect, or Are Intended to Affect, the Kingdom of Scotland* (Edinburgh: Printed by James Ballantyne for William Blackwood, Edinburgh, and T. Cadell, London, 1826);

*Woodstock; or, the Cavalier. A Tale of the Year Sixteen Hundred and Fifty-One. By the Author of "Waverley, Tales of the Crusaders," &c.* (3 volumes, Edinburgh: Printed for Archibald Constable, Edinburgh, and Longman, Rees, Orme, Brown & Green, London, 1826; 2 volumes, Philadelphia: H. C. Carey & I. Lea, 1826);

*The Life of Napoleon Buonaparte,* 9 volumes (Edinburgh: Printed by Ballantyne, for Longman, Rees, Orme, Brown & Green, London, 1827; Philadelphia: Carey, Lea & Carey, 1827);

*The Miscellaneous Prose Works of Sir Walter Scott, Bart.,* 6 volumes (Edinburgh: Cadell, 1827; Boston: Wells & Lilly, 1829);

*Chronicles of the Canongate; By the Author of "Waverley," &c. [The Highland Widow; The Two Drovers; The Surgeon's Daughter]* (2 volumes, Edinburgh: Printed for Cadell, Edinburgh, and Simpkin & Marshall, London, 1827; 1 volume, Philadelphia: Carey, Lea & Carey, 1827);

*Religious Discourses. By a Layman* (London: Henry Colburn, 1828; New York: Printed by J. & J. Harper, sold by Collins & Hannay, 1828);

*Chronicles of the Canongate. Second Series. By the Author of "Waverley" &c. [The Fair Maid of Perth]* (3 volumes, Edinburgh: Printed by Cadell, Edinburgh, and Simpkin & Marshall, London, 1828; 1 volume, Philadelphia: Carey, Lea & Carey, 1828);

*Tales of a Grandfather; Being Stories Taken from Scottish History,* first-third series (9 volumes, Edinburgh: Printed for Cadell, 1828-1830; 8 volumes, Philadelphia: Carey, Lea & Carey, 1828-1830);

*Anne of Geierstein; or The Maiden in the Mist. By the Author of "Waverley," &c.* (3 volumes, Edin-

*Scott's birthplace, the College Wynd, one of the steep, narrow lanes in the Old Town section of Edinburgh (New York Public Library)*

*George Square, Edinburgh (Scottish National Portrait Gallery). Scott lived with his family at number 95 George Square from 1775 until his marriage in 1797.*

burgh: Printed for Cadell, Edinburgh, and Simpkin & Marshall, London, 1829; 2 volumes, Philadelphia: Carey, Lea & Carey, 1829);

*The History of Scotland*, 2 volumes, in *The Cabinet Cyclopædia, Conducted by Rev. Dionysis Lardner* (London: Printed for Longman, Rees, Orme, Brown & Green and John Taylor, 1830);

*The Doom of Devorgoil, A Melo-drama. Auchindrane; or, the Ayrshire Tragedy* (Edinburgh: Printed for Cadell, Edinburgh, and Simpkin & Marshall, London, 1830; New York: Printed by J. & J. Harper, 1830);

*Letters on Demonology and Witchcraft* (London: J. Murray, 1830; New York: J. & J. Harper, 1830);

*Tales of a Grandfather; Being Stories Taken from the History of France* (3 volumes, Edinburgh: Cadell, 1831; 2 volumes, Philadelphia: Carey & Lea, 1831);

*Tales of My Landlord, Fourth and Last Series Collected and Arranged by Jedediah Cleishbotham, Schoolmaster and Parish-Clerk of Gandercleugh [Count Robert of Paris* and *Castle Dangerous]* (4 volumes, Edinburgh: Printed for Robert Cadell, Edinburgh, and Whitaker, London, 1832; 3 volumes, Philadelphia: Carey & Lea, 1832);

*The Journal of Sir Walter Scott*, 3 volumes, edited by John Guthrie Tait and W. M. Parker (Edinburgh: Oliver & Boyd, 1939-1949).

**Editions:** *Waverley Novels*, 48 volumes, with Scott's prefaces and final revisions (Edinburgh: Cadell, 1829-1833);

*Miscellaneous Prose Works*, 30 volumes, edited by John Gibson Lockhart (Edinburgh: R. Cadell, 1834-1846);

*The Miscellaneous Works of Sir Walter Scott*, 30 volumes (Edinburgh: A. & C. Black, 1870-1871);

*The Waverley Novels*, Border Edition, 48 volumes, edited by Andrew Lang (London: J. C. Nimmo, 1892-1894; Boston: Estes & Lauriat, 1893-1894);

*The Poetical Works of Sir Walter Scott, With the Author's Introductions and Notes*, edited by J. Logie Robertson (London: H. Frowde, 1894);

*Lives of the Novelists* (London, New York & Toronto: Oxford University Press, 1906);

*Minstrelsy of the Scottish Border*, edited by Thomas Henderson (London: Harrap, 1931);

*Private Letters of the Seventeenth Century*, edited by Douglas Grant (Oxford: Clarendon Press, 1947);

*The Life of John Dryden*, edited by Bernard Kreissman (Lincoln: University of Nebraska Press, 1963);

*The Journal of Sir Walter Scott*, edited by W. E. K. Anderson (Oxford: Clarendon Press, 1972);

*The Prefaces to the Waverley Novels*, edited by Mark A. Weinstein (Lincoln: University of Nebraska Press, 1978);

*The Letters of Malachi Malagrowther*, edited by P. H. Scott (Edinburgh: Blackwood, 1981);

*Scott on Himself: A Collection of the Autobiographical Writings of Sir Walter Scott*, edited by David Hewitt (Edinburgh: Scottish Academic Press, 1981).

OTHER: *The Chase, and William and Helen: Two Ballads from the German of Gottfried Augustus Bürger*, translated by Scott (Edinburgh: Printed by Mundell & Son for Manners & Miller and sold by T. Cadell, Jun. & W. Davies, 1796);

*Goetz of Berlichingen, With the Iron Hand: A Tragedy. Translated from the German of Goethe*, translated by Scott (London: Printed for J. Bell, 1799);

"The Fire King," "Glenfinlas," "The Eve of Saint John," "Frederick and Alice," and "The Wild Huntsmen," in *Tales of Wonder; Written and Collected by M. G. Lewis, Esq. M.P.*, 2 volumes (London: Printed by W. Bulmer for the author & sold by J. Bell, 1801), I: 62-69, 122-136, 137-147, 148-152, 153-163;

*Minstrelsy of the Scottish Border*, 2 volumes, edited by Scott (Kelso: Printed by James Ballantyne for T. Cadell, Jun. & W. Davies, London, and sold by Manners & Miller and A. Constable, Edinburgh, 1802); enlarged edition, 3 volumes (Edinburgh: Printed by James Ballantyne for Longman & Rees, London, and sold by Manners & Miller and A. Constable, Edinburgh, 1803; revised, 1810; Philadelphia: Carey, 1813);

*Sir Tristrem; A Metrical Romance of the Thirteenth Century; by Thomas of Ercildoune*, edited and completed by Scott (Edinburgh: Printed by James Ballantyne for Archibald Constable, Edinburgh, and Longman & Rees, London, 1804);

*Original Memoirs, Written during the Great Civil War; Being the Life of Sir Henry Slingsby, and Memoirs of Capt. Hodgson*, edited by Scott

*Scott at age six (portrait by an unknown artist; Scottish National Portrait Gallery)*

(Edinburgh: Printed by J. Ballantyne for A. Constable, 1806);

*The Works of John Dryden*, 18 volumes, edited, with a biography, by Scott (London: Miller, 1808);

Joseph Strutt, *Queenhoo-Hall, A Romance; and Ancient Times, A Drama*, 4 volumes, edited by Scott (Edinburgh: Printed by J. Ballantyne for J. Murray, London, and A. Constable, Edinburgh, 1808);

*Memoirs of Capt. George Carleton, An English Officer. . . . Written by Himself*, edited by Scott (Edinburgh: Printed by J. Ballantyne for A. Constable and J. Murray, London, 1808);

*Memoirs of Robert Carey, Earl of Monmouth*, edited by Scott (Edinburgh: A. Constable, 1808);

*The State Papers and Letters of Sir Ralph Sadler, Knight-Banneret*, edited, with an introductory essay, by Scott (Edinburgh: Printed for Archibald Constable and for T. Cadell & W. Davies, William Miller, and John Murray, London, 1809);

*A Collection of Scarce and Valuable Tracts* [The Somers Tracts], second edition, 13 volumes, edited by Scott (London: Printed for T. Cadell & W. Davies, 1809-1815);

*English Minstrelsy. Being a Selection of Fugitive Poetry from the Best English Authors*, 2 volumes, edited by Scott (Edinburgh: J. Ballantyne, 1810);

*The Poetical Works of Anna Seward; with Extracts from Her Literary Correspondence*, 3 volumes,

*Scott and Charlotte Carpenter circa 1797, the year of their marriage (miniatures by unknown artists; Collection of Mrs. Maxwell-Scott of Abbotsford). Scott is wearing the uniform of the Royal Edinburgh Volunteer Light Dragoons, the cavalry unit he had recently joined.*

edited by Scott (Edinburgh: J. Ballantyne, 1810);

*Secret History of the Court of James the First*, 2 volumes, edited by Scott (Edinburgh: Printed for J. Ballantyne, 1811);

*The Works of Jonathan Swift*, 19 volumes, edited, with a biography and notes, by Scott (Edinburgh: Constable, 1814);

*The Border Antiquities of England and Scotland*, 2 volumes, includes an introduction by Scott (London: Printed for Longman, Hurst, Rees, Orme & Brown, 1814-1817);

James, eleventh Baron Somerville, *Memorie of the Somervilles*, 2 volumes, edited by Scott (Edinburgh: Constable, 1815);

*Ballantyne's Novelist's Library*, 10 volumes, edited, with biographical prefaces, by Scott (London: Hurst, Robinson, 1821-1824);

*Memorials of the Haliburtons*, edited by Scott (Edinburgh: Printed by J. Ballantyne, 1824).

At the end of *The Antiquary* (1816) the heroine receives a ring inscribed "*Kunst macht gunst.*" This Teutonic phrase is the family motto of the Antiquary, Jonathan Oldbuck, who explains its meaning as "skill, or prudence, . . . will compel favour and patronage." This motto describes Walter Scott's own life and career. He lived by it, wrote by it, and illustrated it in his themes. Scott's great skill as lawyer, scholar, critic, poet, and novelist brought him fame, favors, some power, and great success. He recalled for his son-in-law and biographer John Gibson Lockhart that, as a youngster at the Edinburgh High School, he was involved in a school-yard dispute with a fellow who initially refused to fight him because "there was no use to harglebargle with a cripple." Young Scott, whose right leg had been lamed by infantile paralysis, bristled and said he would fight anyone his own height, "if he might fight *mounted.*" He and his adversary were both "lashed front to front upon a deal board," whereupon Scott received his first bloody nose but demonstrated his skill at making honor from adversity.

Scott's novels, as well as his narrative poems, were wildly popular, though his characters often spoke a Scots-English which tried the patience of non-Scots readers. Comedy and romance served as convenient forms to shape a rich and complex analysis of history, through which Scott imagined the fate of humankind in the light of its past. Scott's nonfiction prose, of which there is a great deal, is devoted to his vocation as a man of letters. The move from a respect for the power of law embodied in the written word to a practice of scholarship, literary commentary, and historiography was a natural and fulfilling sequence in Scott's career. At the center of his achievement in nonfiction prose is his grand history of the life of Napoleon Bonaparte, which occupied him from 1825 to 1827.

Walter Scott was born in Edinburgh, Scotland, on 15 August 1771, to Walter Scott, a solicitor and son of a sheep farmer, and Anne Rutherford Scott, daughter of a professor of medicine. Scott was crippled by infantile paralysis when he was eighteen months old, and in spring 1773 he was sent to the home of his paternal grandfather, Robert Scott, at Sandyknowe with the hope that exercise and fresh air would cure his malady. He stayed there for extended periods of time until 1778, but neither farm life nor a year spent taking the waters at Bath (summer 1775 - summer 1776) cured his lameness. Scott compensated with athletic prowess. He entered Edinburgh High School in October 1779, and in November 1783 he enrolled in Edinburgh College. He was indentured with his father to begin study of the law in March 1786, joining the Faculty of Advocates in July 1792. In 1796 the woman he loved, Williamina Belsches, became engaged to another. In 1797 he joined a cavalry unit, the Royal Edinburgh Volunteer Light Dragoons, and soon after, on 27 December, he married Charlotte Carpenter after a brief courtship. In 1799 he became sheriff of Selkirkshire (a county judge). The first of his four surviving children, Walter, was born in 1801. Scott's legal practice and earnings grew steadily. Throughout his young adulthood he also showed enthusiasm for literature and laid the foundation for a career in poetry.

In 1790-1791, while preparing for the bar, Scott had formed a Poetry Society, and he was admitted in 1791 to the Speculative Society, where he was known as "Duns Scotus" by the time Francis Jeffrey joined it in 1792. Caught in the enthusiasm for Gottfried Augustus Bürger's ballad "Lenore," in 1795 he translated it as "William and Helen." It was published with "The Chase," his translation of Bürger's "Der Wilde Jäger" in 1796. He also translated poems by Johann Wolfgang von Goethe and began translating German drama. Matthew Gregory Lewis published some of Scott's poems in *Tales of Wonder* (1801). In 1805 Scott's *Lay of the Last Minstrel* was an overwhelming success. His interests in history and literature motivated him to embark on prose and literary scholarship, as well as writing original verse.

In 1801 he wrote "On the Fairies of Popular Superstition," published "Introduction to the Tale of Tamlane" in *Minstrelsy of the Scottish Border*, the collection he produced in 1802. The following year he reviewed Robert Southey's and William Stewart Rose's translations of *Amadis of Gaul*, one of his first contributions to Francis Jeffrey's *Edinburgh Review*, which published two reviews by Scott in the October 1803 issue. His edition of the medieval romance *Sir Tristrem* appeared in 1804. About the same time, he began a prose romance but put aside what later became *Waverley* (1814). By 1806 he was also working on a scholarly edition of the works of Dryden. Poetry, however, was Scott's first love, and his poems made him the most popular writer in Britain until George Gordon, Lord Byron. In 1806 he began his long poem *Marmion* (1808), for which he was paid a thousand guineas sight unseen. Its title character anticipated the gloomy villain/heroes of Byron as well as some in Scott's novels. The enormous success of *The Lady of the Lake*, published in 1810, inspired hordes of tourists to visit Loch Katrine, which is vividly portrayed in the poem.

As his fame grew, Scott found enthusiasts to sponsor his applications for legal positions. In 1806 he received appointment as a clerk of the Court of Session. A social lion when he visited London in February, he met Caroline, Princess of Wales. Increasingly influential as a spokesman for Tory government policies, he was forceful in opposition to the changes in Scotland's legal structure that the Whig government unsuccessfully proposed in 1807. In 1812, having acquired financial resources to become a great landowner, Scott moved to Abbotsford, an estate he had bought the previous year, and began to transform the main house into a romantic castle. There he lived for part of each year, a country gentleman, writing his poems and novels, in alternation with periods when he discharged his legal duties in Edinburgh.

British victories in Spain inspired Scott to compose a poem, *The Vision of Don Roderick* (1811), and to donate the profits from its publication to victims of the war in Portugal. Scott was

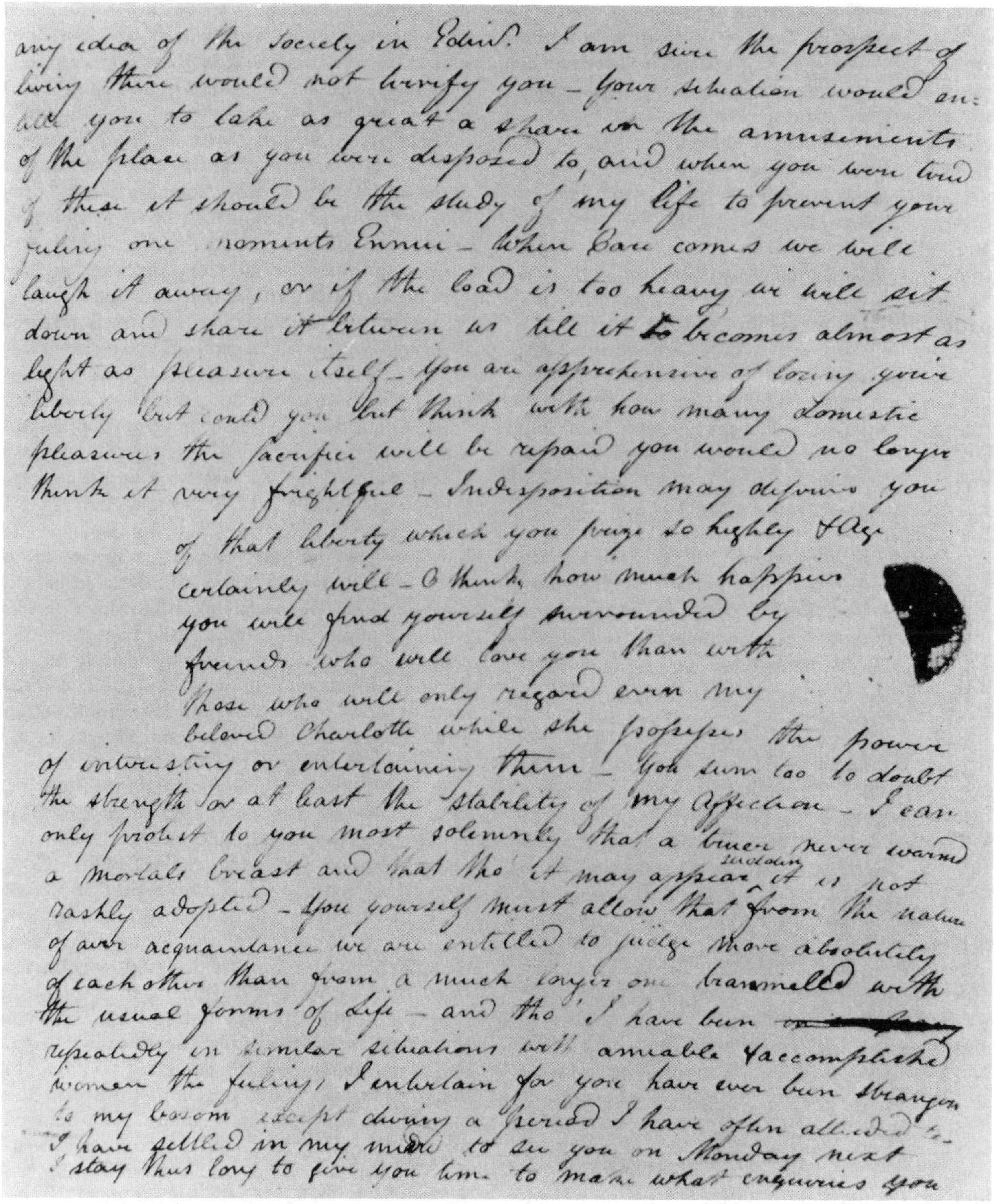

any idea of the Society in Edinr. I am sure the prospect of
living there would not terrify you— Your situation would enable you to take as great a share in the amusements
of the place as you were disposed to, and when you were tired
of these it should be the study of my life to prevent your
feeling one moments Ennui— When Care comes we will
laugh it away, or if the load is too heavy we will sit
down and share it between us till it ~~to~~ becomes almost as
light as pleasure itself— You are apprehensive of losing your
liberty but could you but think with how many domestic
pleasures the sacrifice will be repaid you would no longer
think it very frightful— Indisposition may deprive you
of that liberty which you prize so highly & Age
certainly will— O think how much happier
you will find yourself surrounded by
friends who will love you than with
those who will only regard even my
beloved Charlotte while she possesses the power
of interesting or entertaining them— You seem too to doubt
the strength or at least the stability of my Affection— I can
only protest to you most solemnly that a truer never warmd
a mortals breast and that tho' it may appear sudden it is not
rashly adopted— You yourself must allow that from the nature
of our acquaintance we are entitled to judge more absolutely
of each other than from a much longer one trammelled with
the usual forms of Life— and tho' I have been ~~[illegible]~~
repeatedly in similar situations with amiable & accomplishd
women the feelings I entertain for you have ever been strangers
to my bosom except during a period I have often alluded to—
I have settled in my mind to see you on Monday next
I stay thus long to give you time to make what enquiries you

*Page from Scott's 22 November 1797 letter to Charlotte Carpenter; written about a month before their marriage (MS. 138, no. 16, f. 3; National Library of Scotland)* offered the poet laureateship in 1813, but he declined. Although he gave various reasons, including a desire to help Robert Southey, who was awarded the post, Scott seems to have believed the laureateship would embarrass him with his friends, who were inclined to laugh at it; he also did not want to appear greedy for public honors.

Even as his fame as a poet grew, Scott maintained a vigorous study of history and literature, and he published works which established him as a leading scholar. He edited and wrote a biographical introduction for a volume of British civil war memoirs (1806). He prepared historical notes and an introductory essay for an 1809 edition of the state papers of Sir Ralph Sadler, a diplomat during the reigns of Henry VIII, Edward VI, and Elizabeth I. The biography which he prepared for his edition of Dryden (1808) was a product of painstaking scholarship, building upon Samuel Johnson's criticism and Edmond Malone's edition of 1800. While Scott's biography of Dryden is not authoritative, it is still valuable as a strongly drawn picture of the Restoration period with Dryden at its center. Scott's achievement was to add historical depth to Malone's biography, and, particularly with his annotations to Dryden's works, Scott deepened the critical understanding of Dryden which Johnson had begun.

In 1808, angry with Jeffrey and Henry Brougham's article, "Don Cevallos on the Usurpation in Spain," in the *Edinburgh Review* (October 1808), Scott canceled his subscription to the magazine and supported a new Tory review. He wrote reviews of books on Robert Burns, Southey's translation of *The Cid,* and an essay on Jonathan Swift for the first issue of the *Quarterly Review* in March 1809. In the same year he and James Ballantyne launched the *Edinburgh Annual Register,* to which Scott contributed an anonymous article on "The Living Poets of Great Britain" for the first volume (for the year 1808, published in 1810). Scott's essay focused on Southey, Thomas Campbell, William Wordsworth, and himself. He referred to some thirty poets writing at the time, but, in singling out especially Campbell, Scott showed his preference for poetry which followed classical rules of construction. He criticized his own poetry for failing to satisfy the rules, and he praised Southey's work despite its flights of fancy. Although he liked Wordsworth's poetry, he disputed Wordsworth's claim that good poetry derives from the language of common life. Among the many other poets he mentioned, including Samuel Taylor Coleridge briefly, Scott surprisingly omitted Byron, whose *English Bards, and Scotch Reviewers* (1809) had received much publicity. Also for the same first volume of the *Register,* Scott wrote a long essay entitled "Views of the Changes Proposed and Adopted in the Administration of Justice in Scotland." This pair of essays illustrates how Scott could adapt his talent to a variety of subjects and produce forceful, insightful analyses in expository prose written for the moment and worthy of remembrance. Scott continued to write for the *Register* through volume 7 for 1814 (1816) and volume 8 for 1815 (1817), which contain his long, rigorous essays on the history of 1814-1815, from which Scott later drew material for his *Life of Napoleon Buonaparte* (1827).

On 7 July 1814 Scott's first novel, *Waverley,* was published anonymously, at the same time as his edition of *The Works of Jonathan Swift,* a product of Scott's longtime devotion to that great author. *Waverley* is centered on the Jacobite uprising of 1745, exhibiting for the first time in prose fiction Scott's lifelong interest in the history of his native country, and in particular its military and political trials with England. At the end of July Scott sailed as the guest of a committee charged with surveying Scottish lighthouses and suggesting sites for new ones. Their voyage through the northern isles proved dangerous because of bad weather and American warships. He returned home in early September to learn that the anonymous author of *Waverley* was famous. It sold in huge numbers. Jeffrey praised the novel, hinting that Scott was the author. In London for nine weeks during the spring of 1815 Scott was at the center of social life, dining with the Prince Regent and Lord Byron. Touring Brussels, Waterloo, and Paris in August and early September, he began a journal, published in 1816 as *Paul's Letters To His Kinsfolk.* He also composed a poem, *The Field of Waterloo* (1815), with profits for families of soldiers slain at the Battle of Waterloo (18 June 1815). In May 1816 he published his second novel, *The Antiquary,* again anonymously and again to popular acclaim. Scott showed wit for his own prudent purposes in *Tales of My Landlord,* published a few months later, creating "Jedediah Cleishbotham, Schoolmaster and Parish-Clerk of Gandercleugh," as a pseudonymous rival to the anonymous author of *Waverley* (the name means "Jedediah Thwackass of Gander's Hollow").

Despite pain from gallstones in 1817, Scott finished *Rob Roy* (1818), a novel that, like *The Heart of Mid-Lothian* to follow in the second series

*Three of Scott's four children: Walter (top), who served as an officer in the Eighteenth Hussars (portrait by Sir William Allan); Sophia (bottom left), who married John Gibson Lockhart (portrait by William Nicholson); and Anne (bottom right), who never married and cared for her father during his last years (portrait by William Nicholson; all portraits: Collection of Mrs. Maxwell-Scott of Abbotsford)*

of *Tales of My Landlord* (1818), divides its action, to explore true relationships of romance and reality in the interdependence of Scotland and England during the 1715 Rising. Though not well, Scott was writing *A Legend of Montrose* while finishing *The Bride of Lammermoor.* They were published as *Tales of My Landlord, Third Series* in June 1819 when many in Edinburgh thought Scott was dying. These novels express a darkening vision, which, though it may have arisen from Scott's worsening health, challenged and complicated his fundamentally optimistic themes. Yet by the time they were published Scott had begun work on *Ivanhoe,* which came out at the end of that year though dated 1820 on its title page. In 1820 he also published *The Monastery,* set in the Reformation during the sixteenth century. Scott increasingly examined religious issues in the background to a secular and commercial culture—leading eventually to the Holy Land itself, from *Ivanhoe* to *The Betrothed* and *The Talisman* in *Tales of the Crusaders* (1825) and *Count Robert of Paris* in the fourth series of *Tales of My Landlord* (1832). In March 1820 Scott went to London to receive a baronetcy from the new king, George IV, and in his next novels, beginning with *The Abbot* (1820), he examined more closely the history that made possible the Protestant monarchy of his own time. *Kenilworth,* moving as with Mary to the court of Elizabeth, was published in 1821. Royal romance turned into deathly reality for Scott's heroes, and especially for his heroines. All these novels reinforced his popularity with the critics as well as with the general reading public.

In 1819 Scott's son Walter received an army commission as a cornet and was stationed in Cork, Ireland. His father's fictional heroes and heroines, who usually have to prove themselves to their fathers, increasingly reflected Scott's relationships with his own children, two sons and two daughters. Scott announced the engagement of his daughter Sophia to John Gibson Lockhart in 1820. In 1824 his son Charles, who had been away at schools in London and Wales, entered Brasenose College, Oxford. In 1822 Scott completed *The Fortunes of Nigel,* and he began *Peveril of the Peak,* both with hero-sons who leave home to restore family honor. In 1823 James Ballantyne was alarmed by a seduction scene in *St Ronan's Well,* so Scott reluctantly revised it, obscuring some of the sexual "improprieties." Set at a nineteenth-century health resort, the novel, with its social satire and tragedy of sexual passions, deepened the shadows of Scott's romances. In *Redgauntlet. A Tale of the Eighteenth Century* (1824) there is much of Scott himself in the character of Alan Fairford, the young lawyer-hero of the story, as there is of his father in Saunders Fairford. Sexual passion ends a rebellion and restores order to a chaotic kingdom as well as in the chaotic lives of the two young lawyers. Scott subjected sexual passion of old and young to further testing in *The Betrothed,* set on the Welsh border in the twelfth century. Published in *Tales of the Crusaders* (1825), it expressed Scott's increasing interest in characters who develop moral strength through sacrifices. In February 1825 Scott's son Walter married Jane Jobson after a courtship arranged by Scott, making romance serve reason in real life. In July Scott visited them in Dublin, where Walter was stationed as a captain of Hussars. Scott was much acclaimed and received an LL.D. from Trinity College. Back home in late August, he began work on his life of Napoleon, and on Sunday, 20 November 1825, he started keeping a journal, noting in his first entry, "I have all my life regretted that I did not keep a regular [journal]. I have myself lost recollection of much that was interesting and I have deprived my family and the public of some curious information by not carrying this resolution into effect." Scott's last entry was made at Rome, on 14 April 1832, after a tour from Naples to Rome. Although Scott began his journal late in his career (he was fifty-four), he provided posterity with information of considerable value: from insights into the characters of people to details of political and social affairs. The journal is also a wonderful literary achievement in itself, as an informal, personal autobiography of a man of genius.

In January 1826 his publisher Archibald Constable went bankrupt, and Scott, caught in the financial chaos, dedicated himself to paying off his debts. His concern that he might lose Abbotsford is reflected in Sir Henry Lee's predicament in *Woodstock* (1826). No wonder that in early 1826 he wrote a series of essays attacking the English plan for reorganizing the Scottish banking system. Modeling them upon Swift's *Drapier's Letters* (1724), he called them *Letters of Malachi Malagrowther* (1826), and they had an immediate success in forcing modification of the reforms. Scott had even more painful setbacks in his life; his wife, Charlotte, died in May 1826.

By June, Scott had resumed work on his life of Napoleon. In July Charles Scott, who had left Oxford without taking a degree, came home to

*Edinburgh publisher Archibald Constable, whose declaration of bankruptcy in 1826 nearly brought financial ruin for Scott (portrait by Andrew Geddes; Scottish National Portrait Gallery)*

study languages in preparation for a diplomatic career. In October, to collect information for his life of Napoleon, Scott went to London and Paris, taking his daughter Anne with him. *The Life of Napoleon Buonaparte* was published in the summer of 1827, amid great enthusiasm; though John Stuart Mill criticized it in the *Westminster Review* (April 1828) for lack of scholarship, he admitted it was a strong narrative. According to Lockhart, Johann Wolfgang von Goethe praised Scott's work, which presents Napoleon as a military genius who brought order to the Continent, built a modern system of transportation, and inspired the reform of law. For Scott, Napoleon was a patriot who fell victim to his egotism as he sought to extend his power over the world. As Scott narrates the exciting events of Napoleon's escape from Elba, the Battle of Waterloo, and Napoleon's final years as a prisoner at St. Helena, his absorption in Napoleon's career expresses his self-analysis. He could sympathize with Napoleon's ambition, success, and fall.

The opening sections of *The Life of Napoleon Buonaparte* are devoted to a reconstruction of the events leading to the crisis of affairs which brought Napoleon to the leadership of France. In his view of the French Revolution Scott recalled how the excitement of the time had been a mixture of hopes and fears and how little it was anticipated that the Revolution would end as it did.

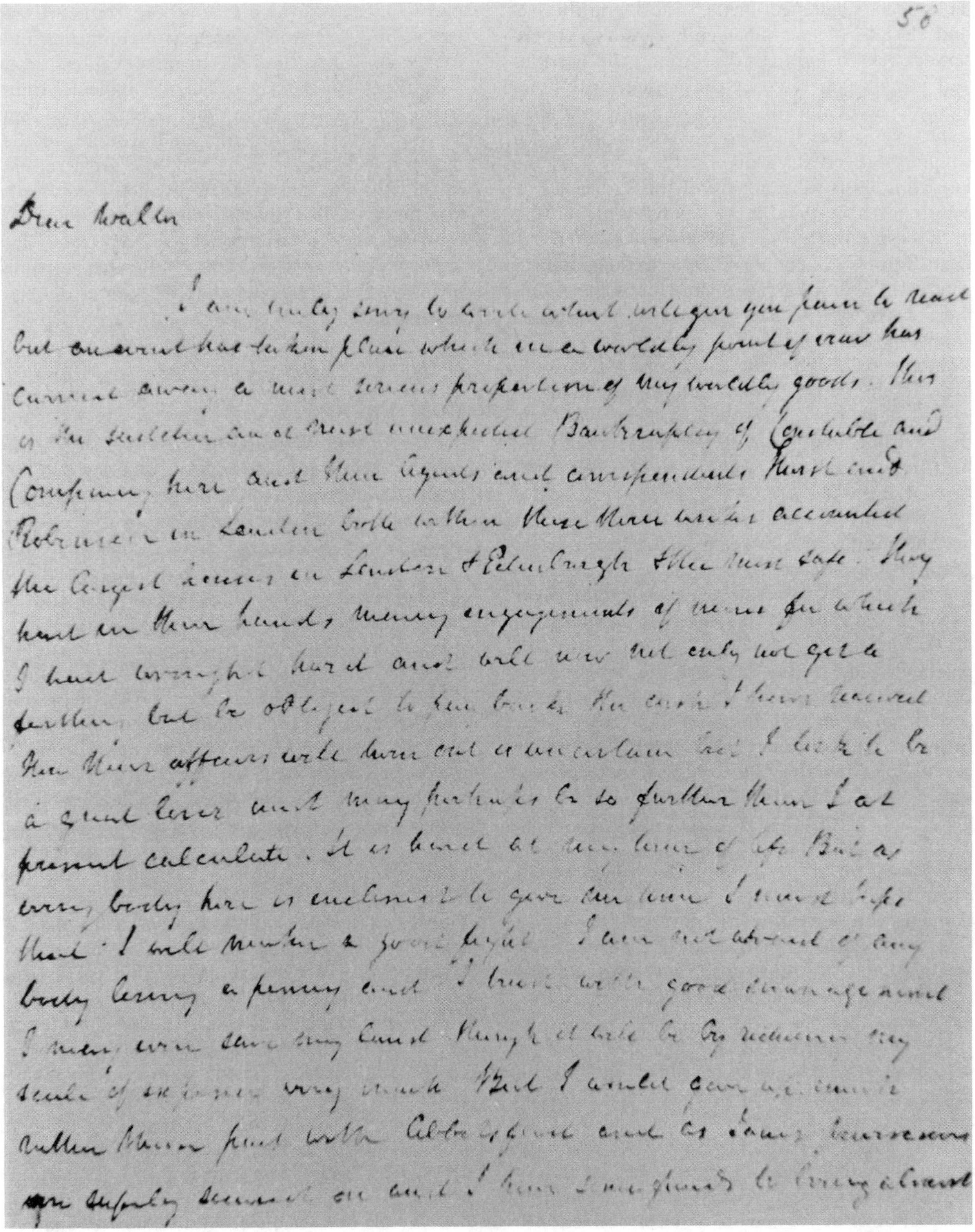
58

Dear Walter

I am truly sorry to write what will give you pain to read but an event has taken place which in a worldly point of view has carried away a most serious proportion of my worldly goods. This is the sudden and most unexpected Bankruptcy of Constable and Company here and their agents and correspondents Hurst and Robinson in London both which were accounted the largest houses in London & Edinburgh & the most safe. They had in their hands many engagements of mine for which I had wrought hard and will now not only not get a farthing but be obliged to pay back the cash I have received. How these affairs will turn out is uncertain but I think to be a great loser and may perhaps be so further than I at present calculate. It is hard at my time of life But as every body here is inclined to give me time I must hope that I will make a good fight. I am not afraid of any body losing a penny and I trust with good management I may even save my land though it will be by retrenching my scale of expence very much. But I would [illegible] rather than part with Abbotsford and as [illegible] [illegible] supply [illegible] [illegible] [illegible] [illegible] to bring about

*Page from Scott's 26 June 1826 letter to his son Walter, informing him of Constable's bankruptcy (MS. 139, no. 58, f. 1; National Library of Scotland)*

The special challenge for the historian in the second decade of the nineteenth century, he observed, was to look clearly through the passions and powers generated by the presence of Napoleon, to see behind this giant man and to understand events which led to his rise to power. In chapter 18 Scott wryly observed how by 1794 the French atheists were apparently being blessed by priests in their military campaigns. With the fall of Robespierre, however, a new phase of European history was about to begin, and chapter 18 concludes with a barrage of questions, heightening the style of the history to re-create the heightened tone of anxiety which attended the fall of Robespierre. Would France return to the old order of monarchy for its rule, or would providence allow radical revolutionaries to continue the bloody course set by Robespierre? Would the next stage be taken by a tyrant and overwhelmed by anarchy?

The answer is in the many chapters which follow, beginning with a sketch of the family background of Bonaparte in Corsica. In twenty chapters of strong, forceful prose narration Scott followed the career of Napoleon from the Siege of Toulon, through the fall of Robespierre, campaigns in Italy, on the Rhine, at the Battle of the Pyramids, to Napoleon's rise to political supremacy which began with the revolution of the 18th Brumaire and concluded with his appointment as consul for life after the Treaty of Amiens was signed on 27 March 1802. This pause in history marks the end of the first third of *The Life of Napoleon Buonaparte,* which then plunges into Napoleon's career of imperial ambition, which began when he invaded Switzerland. While many exclaimed with horror at the invasion, Scott was able to maintain scholarly distance; he was even at times able to represent Napoleon's motives and methods in an understanding if not sympathetic way.

The middle third of *The Life of Napoleon Buonaparte* survey in detailed, reflective, but exciting prose, the conflicts of Napoleon's France with Britain, which began in May 1803, moved through the campaigns in Spain, Holland, and Sweden, to the point of Napoleon's greatest hold on power in 1810. Scott shows, however, that this point was the beginning of the end of Napoleon's career, because his empire was too large to govern. Scott compares Napoleon's European empire to a corpulent body sapping the strength of the mind, wasting the wealth of the person, and silently weakening the spirit of the time. Scott also compares the empire to a tree whose roots are attacked by cankerworms even as its branches and foliage appear to flourish. In nine chapters Scott recounts the disastrous events of Napoleon's campaign in Russia, from the Treaty of Tilsit, through the French victory at Borodino, to the march into Moscow, and finally the great retreat in the Russian winter, during which the French lost nearly a half million men. Scott does not raise his voice in triumph at this spectacle; instead, he renders it as a tragic fall, when fortune turned against the hero whose career it had seemed to favor.

In presenting the terrible, somber episode of Napoleon's retreat from Moscow as a moving spectacle of tragic failure, Scott anticipated the greater, fictional account by Leo Tolstoy. But quickly, at the beginning of the last third of *The Life of Napoleon Buonaparte,* Scott gets down to the reality of the events which occurred when Napoleon returned to Paris. Challenged by the conspiracy of Malet, Napoleon had to reconsolidate his power and regroup his army as he suppressed political enemies to prepare for defense against Britain and its allies. Beginning with the Battle of Leipzig, Napoleon's "imperturbable calmness" (a quality Scott admired in his character) was much tested, until the allies attacked Paris and Napoleon surrendered for exile to Elba in May 1814. In a retrospective (which is a common rhetorical pause for reflection in the book), Scott considers the situation in Europe when Napoleon escaped from Elba in February 1815: for Scott the restoration of the Bourbons upon the throne of France was a mixed blessing because the soldiers were unhappy and the royalists were few and distrusted. France was unstable, and, like inflammable materials, it wanted only a spark to ignite it into yet another episode of political chaos. That spark was, of course, the return of Napoleon from Elba, which ignited another brief, intense period of war, until the decisive battle at Waterloo in June 1815. The British exiled Napoleon to Saint Helena, despite the fallen emperor's protests. Scott narrates Napoleon's life there with moving detail, from his arrival on the island in October 1815 to his death from cancer of the stomach in May 1821.

In his conclusion Scott assesses the character of Napoleon, beginning with a description of his physical appearance. But the exterior man did not interest Scott much. More important was Napoleon's personality, which Scott found to be amiable, though temperamental. Most important,

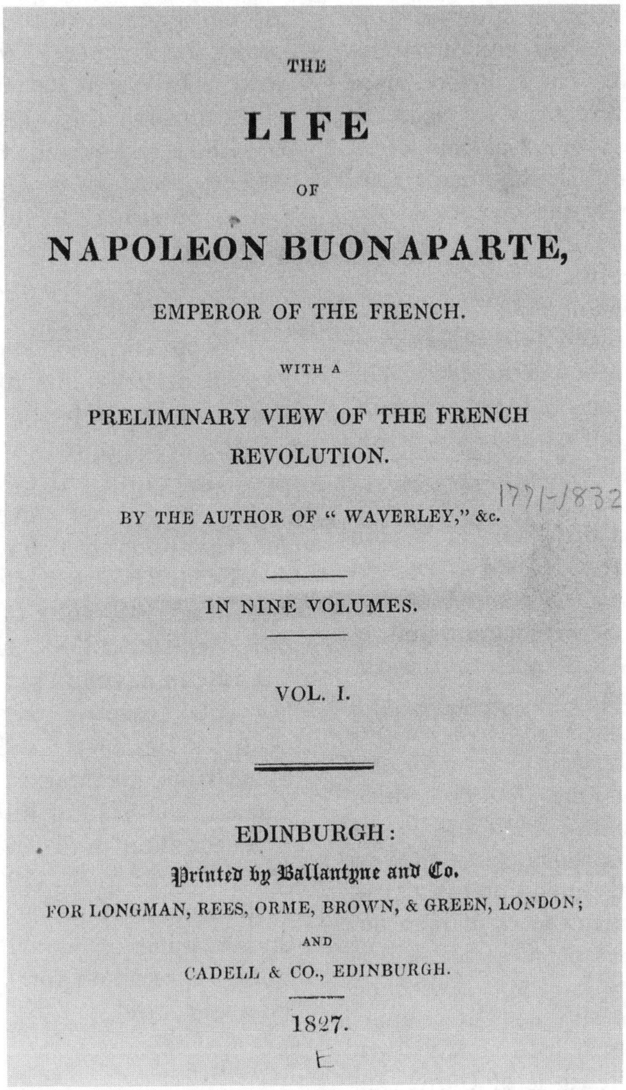

THE

LIFE

OF

NAPOLEON BUONAPARTE,

EMPEROR OF THE FRENCH.

WITH A

PRELIMINARY VIEW OF THE FRENCH REVOLUTION.

BY THE AUTHOR OF "WAVERLEY," &c. 1771-1832

IN NINE VOLUMES.

VOL. I.

EDINBURGH:

Printed by Ballantyne and Co.

FOR LONGMAN, REES, ORME, BROWN, & GREEN, LONDON;

AND

CADELL & CO., EDINBURGH.

1827.

*Title page for Scott's biography of the man he considered a military genius whose faults "were rather those of the sovereign and politician, than of the individual" (Special Collections, Thomas Cooper Library, University of South Carolina)*

however, was Napoleon's genius for war, which raised him to heights of glory. Scott found Napoleon to be "an improver, an innovator, and an inventor" of military strategy and tactics. At the peak of his power, "Napoleon seemed only to occupy the station for which he was born," observed a not altogether unsympathetic Scott, who went on to add, somewhat sadly, that Napoleon allowed his pride to blind him to his larger calling of responsibility to his people's welfare. "Napoleon loved France, for France was his own"; his egotism drove him down pathways of tyranny and defeat because it led him into proud self-deception. Still, Scott believed, "the faults of Buonaparte . . . were rather those of the sovereign and politician, than of the individual." His life was the high heroic drama of "a man tried in the two extremities of the most exalted power and the most ineffable calamity." With few exceptions (which included the young John Stuart Mill), critics and general readers alike applauded this long book (first published in nine volumes), purchasing it in such numbers that it went into a second edition within weeks of its publication.

After *The Miscellaneous Prose Works* and the first series of *Chronicles of the Canongate*, both published in November 1827, Scott produced one of his strongest novels, *The Fair Maid of Perth* (published in *Chronicles of the Canongate, Second Series*, 1828), in which he examines the chaos produced when weak rulers are confronted by strong citizens with violent methods. At this time he wrote introductions and notes for what he referred to as the *Magnum Opus*, the collected edition of his *Waverley Novels* (1829-1833). These introductions constituted a new level of creativity for Scott. In them he invented two new editorial characters, to compete with Jedediah Cleishbotham: Paul Pattieson, who is supposedly the brother of the author of *Count Robert of Paris*, and Crystal Croftangry, editor for the first series to be published under Scott's own name, *The Chronicles of Canongate*. Although he disliked *Anne of Geierstein*, Scott finished it and published it in 1829. The novel, which sold well, narrates how honor diminishes, kingdoms fall, and the natural skill of heroes is insufficient for survival.

Scott suffered a paralytic stroke in February 1830, and he retired from the Court of Session near the end of that year. He had recovered enough, however, to write *Letters on Demonology and Witchcraft*, published in September and well received, though Scott did not care much for this collection of demonic and supernatural tales. The book drew upon his lifelong interest in legends and folklore. Addressing himself to John Gibson Lockhart, Scott wrote ten long "letters," which begin with speculation on the origin of beliefs about demons and the immortality of the soul, to which Scott made several philosophical objections. Describing numerous instances of such beliefs, Scott cited many cases of supposed witchcraft including one as late as 1800, before he concluded in his last letter with a personal anecdote of searching for ghosts in 1814 on the north coast of Scotland, under the castle of Dunvegan. He says that ghost stories are out of date in 1830, when "the present fashion of the world seems to be ill suited for studies of this fantastic nature" and "the sense of humanity is too universally spread to permit them to think of tormenting wretches till they confess what is impossible, and then burning them for their pains."

In 1831 Scott was drawn into debates over the Reform Bill, which he opposed. Attempting to speak in a public meeting, he was hooted down, and later his carriage was stoned by crowds of hostile laborers. Scott's last completed novel, *Castle Dangerous*, published in the fourth series of *Tales of My Landlord* (1832), is a tale of defeat with honor.

The government gave permission for Scott and his daughter Anne to sail on the frigate *Barham* to Malta in October 1831. After arriving he received the painful news he feared, that his beloved grandson John Hugh Lockhart was dead. He burned most of the manuscript he had completed for *The Siege of Malta*, and he began to rewrite it. In May he started home from Venice, traveling through the Alps to Germany and down the Rhine to England. By June he was hopelessly ill and *The Siege of Malta* remained unfinished and unpublished. In July 1832 Scott was at home in Abbotsford, and he died there on 21 September 1832, barely sixty-one. He was buried beside his wife at Dryburgh Abbey, near the Tweed.

Scott earned his fame, but his reputation steadily declined after his death, until the publication of Edgar Johnson's biography in 1970 signaled a new appreciation of his writings. Severe as Whig Francis Jeffrey could be in the *Edinburgh Review*, he did not make Tory Scott the target of his critical power. The turn against Scott came instead with Thomas Carlyle's assault in a review of Lockhart's biography (*London and Westminster Review*, January 1838). The attacks intensified in the twentieth century, typified in 1927 by E. M. Forster's *Aspects of the Novel*, which condemns Scott for lack of art and intelligence. Since then, apart from the Marxist appreciation by George Lukács (1947), most influential critics gave Scott little attention until Alexander Welsh's *The Hero of the Waverley Novels* (1963), which promised a return toward respectability for the intelligence and learning of Scott the Romantic scholar, toward appreciation for the art of Scott the great poet and novelist.

**Letters:**

*The Letters of Sir Walter Scott*, 12 volumes, edited by Sir Herbert J. C. Grierson, assisted by Davidson Cook, W. M. Parker, and others (London: Constable, 1932-1937).

**Bibliographies:**

Greville Worthington, *A Bibliography of the Waverley Novels* (London: Constable, 1931);

William Ruff, *A Bibliography of the Poetical Works of Sir Walter Scott, 1796-1832* (Edinburgh: Edinburgh Bibliographical Society, 1938);

James Clarkson Corson, *A Bibliography of Sir Walter Scott: A Classified and Annotated List of Books and Articles Relating to His Life and Works, 1797-1940* (Edinburgh & London: Oliver & Boyd, 1943);

Jill Rubenstein, *Sir Walter Scott: A Reference Guide* (Boston: G. K. Hall, 1978).

*Scott at work as a clerk of the court of Sessions, 1829 (drawing by Mark Napier; National Library of Scotland)*

## Biographies:

John Gibson Lockhart, *Memoirs of the Life of Sir Walter Scott, Bart.* (7 volumes, Edinburgh: Cadell, 1837-1838; revised, 10 volumes, 1839);

Sir Herbert Grierson, *Sir Walter Scott, Bart.: A New Life Supplementary to and Corrective of Lockhart's Biography* (London: Constable, 1938);

Hesketh Pearson, *Sir Walter Scott: His Life and Personality* (New York: Harper, 1955);

Edgar Johnson, *Sir Walter Scott: The Great Unknown*, 2 volumes (New York: Macmillan, 1970).

## References:

James Anderson, "Sir Walter Scott as Historical Novelist: Scott's Opinions on Historical Fiction," *Studies in Scottish Literature*, 4 (July 1966): 29-41; 4 (October 1966): 63-78; 4 (January 1967): 155-178; 5 (July 1967): 14-27; 5 (October 1967): 83-97; 5 (January 1968): 143-166;

Kenneth Curry, *Sir Walter Scott's Edinburgh Annual Register* (Knoxville: University of Tennessee Press, 1977);

David Daiches, "Scott's Achievement as a Novelist," *Nineteenth-Century Fiction*, 6 (September 1951): 80-95; 6 (December 1951): 153-173;

P. D. Garside, "Scott and the 'Philosophical' Historians," *Journal of the History of Ideas*, 36 (July 1975): 497-512;

A. Norman Jeffares, ed., *Scott's Mind and Art*

(Edinburgh: Oliver & Boyd, 1969);

James Kerr, *Fiction Against History: Scott as Storyteller* (Cambridge: Cambridge University Press, 1989);

John Lauber, *Sir Walter Scott*, revised edition (Boston: Twayne, 1989);

George Lukács, *Tortenelmi regeny* (Budapest, 1947); translated by Hannah Mitchell and Stanley Mitchell as *The Historical Novel* (London: Merlin Press, 1962);

Graham McMaster, *Scott and Society* (Cambridge: Cambridge University Press, 1981);

Jane Millgate, *Walter Scott: The Making of the Novelist* (Toronto: University of Toronto Press, 1984);

Susan Morgan, "Old Heroes and a New Heroine in the Waverley Novels," *English Literary History*, 50 (Fall 1983): 559-587;

Harry E. Shaw, *The Forms of Historical Fiction: Sir Walter Scott and His Successors* (Ithaca, N.Y.: Cornell University Press, 1983);

Donald E. Sultana, *The Siege of Malta Rediscovered* (Edinburgh: Scottish Academic Press, 1977);

Alexander Welsh, *The Hero of the Waverley Novels* (New Haven: Yale University Press, 1963);

Judith Wilt, *Secret Leaves: The Novels of Sir Walter Scott* (Chicago: University of Chicago Press, 1985).

**Papers:**

Collections of manuscripts, letters, documents, and memorabilia are held by the Henry W. and Albert A. Berg Collection and the manuscript division of the New York Public Library, the Boston Public Library, the British Museum, the Folger Shakespeare Library in Washington, D.C., the Foster Collection in the Victoria and Albert Museum, the Houghton Library and the Widener Library of Harvard University, the Henry E. Huntington Library, the Pierpont Morgan Library, the National Library of Scotland, the Carl Pforzheimer Library, the library of Princeton University, and the library of the University of Rochester.

# Sydney Smith

*(3 June 1771 - 22 February 1845)*

Martin A. Cavanaugh
*Washington University*

BOOKS: *Six Sermons, preached in Charlotte Chapel, Edinburgh* (Edinburgh, 1800); enlarged as *Sermons*, 2 volumes (London: Printed for Longman & Rees, 1801);

*A Sermon preached at the Temple May 31st, and at Berkeley Chapel, Berkeley Square, June 28th, upon the conduct to be observed by the Established Church towards the Catholics and other Dissenters* (London: Printed for J. Carpenter and Longman, Hurst, Rees & Orme, 1807);

*Two Letters on the Subject of the Catholics, to My Brother Abraham, Who Lives in the Country*, as Peter Plymley (London: Printed for J. Budd, 1807); *Three More Letters on the Subject of the Catholics, to My Brother Abraham, Who Lives in the Country*, as Peter Plymley (London: Printed for J. Budd, 1807); *Two More Letters (Being the 6th and 7th) on the Subject of the Catholics, to My Brother Abraham, Who Lives in the Country*, as Peter Plymley (London: Printed for J. Budd, 1808); *The Eighth, Ninth, and Last Letter on the Subject of the Catholics, to My Brother Abraham, Who Lives in the Country*, as Peter Plymley (London: Printed for J. Budd, 1808); ten letters collected as *Letters on the subject of the Catholics, to my brother Abraham, who lives in the Country* (London: J. Budd, 1808);

*Sermon preached before his Grace the Archbishop of York, and the Clergy of Malton, at the Visitation, August 1809* (London: Carpenter, 1809);

*The Lawyer That Tempted Christ* (York: Printed by T. Wilson, 1824);

*Catholic Claims* (London: A. Cuddon, 1825);

*A Sermon on Religious Charity* (York: T. Wilson & Sons, 1825);

*A Letter to the Electors, upon the Catholic question* (York: Printed by T. Wilson & Sons, 1826);

*Mr. Dyson's Speech to the Freeholders on Reform* (London: J. Ridgway, 1831);

*Speech at the Taunton Reform Meeting* (London, 1831);

*The New Reign: the Duties of Queen Victoria* (London: Longman, Orme, Brown, Green & Longmans, 1837);

*A Letter to Archdeacon Singleton, on the Ecclesiastical Commission* (London: Longman, 1837);

*Second Letter to Archdeacon Singleton* (London: Longman, Orme, Brown, Green & Longmans, 1838);

*A Letter to Lord John Russell . . . on the Church Bills* (London: J. Mitchell, 1838);

*Third Letter to Archdeacon Singleton* (London: Longman, Orme, Brown, Green & Longmans, 1839);

*Ballot* (London: Longman, Orme, Brown, Green & Longmans, 1839);

*The Works of the Rev. Sydney Smith* (4 volumes, London: Longman, Orme, Brown, Green & Longmans, 1839-1840; 3 volumes, Philadelphia: Carey & Hart, 1844);

*Letters on American Debts* (London: Longman, Brown, Green & Longmans, 1843; New York: J. Winchester, New World Press, 1844);

*A Fragment on the Irish Roman Catholic Church* (London: Longman, Brown, Green & Longmans, 1845; Boston: Redding & Co., 1845);

*Sermons preached at St. Paul's Cathedral, the Foundling Hospital, and several churches in London, together with others addressed to a Country Congregation* (London: Longman, Brown, Green & Longmans, 1846);

*Miscellaneous Sermons* (Philadelphia: Carey & Hart, 1846);

*Elementary Sketches of Moral Philosophy, delivered at the Royal Institution in the years 1804, 1805, and 1806* (London: Privately printed, 1849; London: Longman, Brown, Green & Longmans, 1850; New York: Harper, 1850).

**Editions:** *Selections from the Writings of Sydney Smith*, 2 volumes (London: Longman, 1854);

*Wit and Wisdom of the Rev. Sydney Smith, being selections from his writings and passages of his letters and tabletalk*, with a biographical memoir

*Portrait by Henry Perronet Briggs, 1840; National Portrait Gallery, London*

and notes by Evert A. Duyckinck (New York: Redfield, 1856);

*The Wit and Wisdom of the Rev. Sydney Smith, a selection of the most memorable passages in his writings and conversation* (London: Longman, Green, Longman & Roberts, 1860);

*Essays* (London: Longman, Green, 1873);

*Essays* (London: Routledge, 1880);

*Peter Plymley's Letters, and Selected Essays*, introduction by H. Morley (London: Cassell, 1886);

*Selections*, edited, with an introduction, by Ernest Rhys (London: Walter Scott, 1892);

*Bon-mots of Sydney Smith and R. Brinsley Sheridan*, edited by Walter Jerrold (London: Dent, 1893);

*The Letters of Peter Plymley to his brother Abraham Who lives in the Country, Together with Selected Writings, Sermons, and Speeches*, introduction by G. C. Heseltine (London & Toronto: Dent / New York: Dutton, 1929);

*The Selected Writings of Sydney Smith*, edited by W. H. Auden (New York: Farrar, Straus & Cudahy, 1956).

Sydney Smith, Canon of St. Paul's Cathedral from 1831 to his death in 1845, achieved much of his literary reputation as a founder of and longtime contributor to the *Edinburgh Review*. A Church of England clergyman who supported the liberal Whig ideals of the period, he was known for writings in the *Review* that were

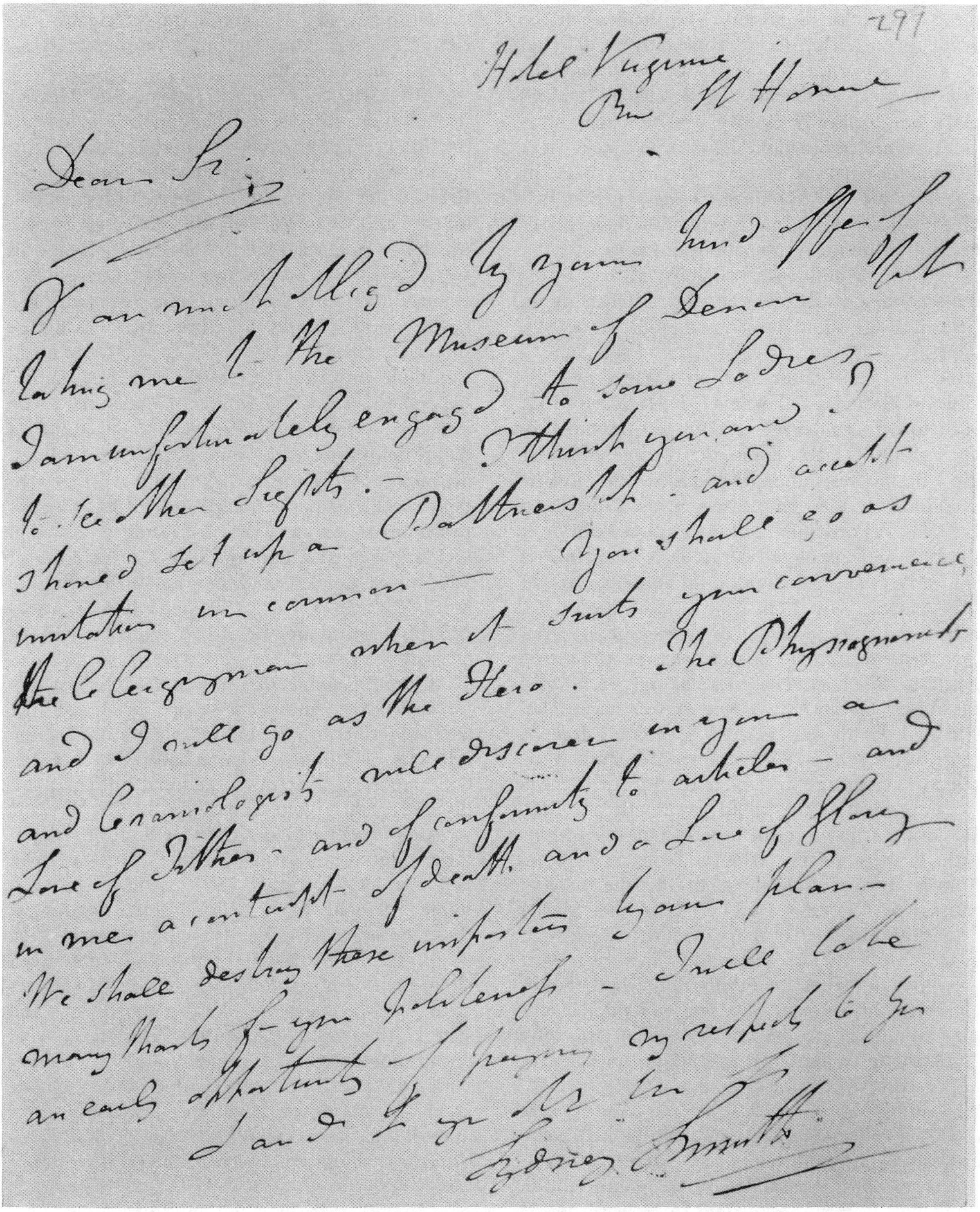

291

Hotel Virginie
Rue St Honore

Dear Sir

I am much obliged by your kind offer of taking me to the Museum of Denon. I am unfortunately engaged to some Ladies to see other sights. I think you and I should set up a Partnership and accept invitations in common — You shall go as the Clergyman when it suits your convenience, and I will go as the Hero. The Physiognomists and Craniologists will discover in you a Love of Tithes and of conformity to articles — and in me a contempt of death and a Love of Glory. We shall destroy these impostors by our plan — many thanks for your politeness — I will take an early opportunity of paying my respects to you and am Sir yr obt Sert

Sydney Smith

*Smith's April 1826 letter to Adm. Sir Sidney Smith, who had served with honor during the Napoleonic Wars (Pierpont Morgan Library). The two men often received one another's mail.*

laced with wit and sarcasm, often directed at the political leaders of the day but always focusing on the issues under discussion. As a member of the Whig social circle, he was constantly in demand as a dinner guest for the wit and humor he brought to a gathering. In describing Smith's mark on English Whig society of the early nineteenth century, Sheldon Halpern, in *Sydney Smith* (1966), says that "almost every memoir, diary, or collection of correspondence from the first half of the nineteenth century contains descriptions of Smith's humor or quotations of his wit."

Sydney Smith was born at Woodford, Essex, the second son of Robert and Maria Olier Smith. After distinguishing himself as a public-school student at Winchester from 1782 to 1789, he entered New College, Oxford, on 5 February 1789, and was elected a fellow in 1791. He received his bachelor of arts degree in 1792, but remained in Oxford until 1794. Smith desired to study for the bar, but his father discouraged him, and he eventually decided on a career in the Church. In 1794 he was ordained a deacon in the Church of England and appointed curate at Netheravon on Salisbury Plain, Wiltshire, at an annual salary of fifty pounds. In 1796 Smith was ordained a priest and also received his master of art's degree, but he still held no permanent ecclesiastical position. Michael Hicks-Beach, an M.P. and the major landowner in Netheravon parish, befriended Smith and offered to employ him as tutor to his son. In 1798 teacher and student arrived in Edinburgh, where Smith's future as essayist and social critic would eventually develop. While in Edinburgh he established friendships with Francis Jeffrey, Henry Peter Brougham, Francis Horner, and others. In 1800 he traveled to England to marry a friend of his sister Maria: Catherine Amelia Pybus, to whom he had been engaged for two years. After their marriage on 2 July they returned to Edinburgh, where Smith continued his tutoring with two new pupils, supplementing his income with occasional preaching at Charlotte Chapel, and embarking on his writing career.

Smith's first publication was *Six Sermons* (1800), a collection of sermons that he had delivered at Charlotte Chapel in Edinburgh. Additional sermons were added for a second edition the following year. According to Howard Mackey, writing in *Wit and Whiggery: The Rev. Sydney Smith, 1771-1845* (1979), these published sermons "helped to establish his reputation as a preacher and writer." While in Edinburgh Smith took the opportunity to attend lectures at the University of Edinburgh and to join two intellectual clubs, the Academy of Physics and the Speculative Society. Through these groups he met Jeffrey, Horner, and Brougham.

In early 1802 Smith, Jeffrey, and Horner proposed a quarterly journal for the purpose of providing lengthy reviews of a limited number of books with special significance or worth in all fields of interest. Smith became the informal editor for the first issue of the *Edinburgh Review*, which was published on 10 October 1802, but his suggested motto, *Tenui musam meditamur avena* (We cultivate literature upon a little oatmeal), was never adopted. Smith is credited with making the financial arrangements with bookseller Archibald Constable, ensuring the contributors' financial independence from the whims of booksellers who might be offended by the journal's contents, a major innovation at the time. Reviewers espoused liberal and Whig ideals, commenting on current social problems and calling for reforms. The appearance of this new review created a sensation in Edinburgh and London. The first printing of 750 copies quickly sold out and, according to Mackey, within a year 2,150 copies had been sold in Edinburgh alone. By 1814 circulation had increased to 13,000.

The *Edinburgh Review* was Smith's first major outlet for writing about the social, cultural, and political issues of the day, such as education, religious toleration, and game laws, and his contribution to the *Review* was exceptional, both in quantity and quality. Volume 5 of the *Wellesley Index to Victorian Periodicals 1824-1900* attributes to him at least eighty-seven articles from 1802 to 1828. Halpern suggests that "the brilliant wit and humor of Smith was a major factor in making it [the *Edinburgh Review*] amusing and readable." In the preface to his *Works* (1839), Smith reminisced about the role of the *Edinburgh Review*: "To appreciate the value of the Edinburgh Review, the state of England at the period when the journal began should be had in remembrance. . . . a thousand evils were in existence, which the talents of good and able men have since lessened or removed; and these effects have been not a little assisted by the honest boldness of the Edinburgh Review."

In 1803, with one child and his wife expecting a second, Smith moved with his family to London in search of a permanent ecclesiastical appointment, supporting himself with occasional preaching. In February 1805 through the influ-

*Portrait by Daniel Maclise in the* Fraser's Magazine *"Gallery of Illustrious Literary Characters" (1830-1838)*

ence of Sir Thomas Bernard, he was offered a post as alternate evening preacher at the Foundling Hospital, which he gratefully accepted and kept until November 1808. During this same period he was also preaching at Fitzroy Chapel and Berkeley Chapel. His sermons were practical, not deeply theological, infused with his trademark wit and humor, and attracting fairly large and attentive audiences.

Through Bernard's influence also, Smith was invited to lecture on moral philosophy at the Royal Institution. These lectures, presented during the years 1804 to 1806, were privately printed in 1849 and commercially published in 1850 as *Elementary Sketches of Moral Philosophy*. They were a rousing success for Smith, with nearly eight hundred people in attendance at any one lecture. The substance was Smith's practical distillation of the major philosophical thought of the day. He continually proclaimed his ignorance of philosophy while popularizing the subject for the nonacademic assemblies.

Also while in London, Smith frequented the house of Henry Richard Vassall Fox, Baron Holland, and his wife, Elizabeth, Lady Holland, a social center for the Whigs. There Smith made several key friendships, including those of the Hollands, who used their influence with Lord Chancellor Thomas Erskine to have Smith appointed rector at Foston, Yorkshire, at an annual salary of five hundred pounds, in 1806. At the time it was not necessary for him to reside at Foston, and he continued living in London.

He also continued his contributions to the *Edinburgh Review*, and in October 1806 he took up the issue of popular education. In 1798 Joseph Lancaster, a Quaker, had established an innovative school in the London slums for poor children who would not otherwise have been educated. Lancaster's methods were criticized by many in England, and one of his major critics,

*Editorial cartoon (published 24 October 1831) by H B (John Doyle) illustrating lines Smith used in his 11 October speech at Taunton, where he compared the efforts of the House of Lords to block reform of Parliament to the labors of a Mrs. Partington, who during a great storm in 1824 was seen at the door of her seaside house "trundling her mop, squeezing out the sea-water, and vigorously pushing away the Atlantic Ocean. . . . She was excellent with a slop or a puddle, but she should not have meddled with a tempest."*

Sarah Trimmer, published a pamphlet maligning his methods and motives in 1805. Smith's response focused on Trimmer's anxiety that anything done by a member of a dissenting sect should be feared, praising any Dissenter who would fill the gap that the Church of England had left in the education of the poor. In an article published in October 1807, Smith proceeded to explain Lancaster's methods, detailing the way the school operated, especially its discipline without flogging, and applauding him for educating the poor.

Smith also criticized the limited focus of British schools. In discussing Lancaster he had advocated extending education to the populace. He also saw a need for changing what was taught. In an October 1809 review of Richard Edgeworth's *Professional Education*, Smith argued for a broadening of the subject base of English education from the traditional instruction in classical Latin and Greek to studies in the natural and social sciences. The study of classics was important, but once students had mastered the languages they should advance to subjects that would have more practical benefit in solving society's problems, such as economics, agriculture, politics, and geography.

During this period Smith also wrote the essays for which he is, perhaps, best remembered. From the summer of 1807 through the spring of 1808, he published a series of pseudonymous pamphlets collectively titled *Letters on the subject of the Catholics, to my brother Abraham, who lives in the Country*, by Peter Plymley. These became known as the Peter Plymley letters, and were first collected in one volume in 1808. The letters, addressed to Peter Plymley's fictitious brother Abraham, a rural clergyman, consider the subject of Catholic emancipation, that is, the removal of legal restrictions on Catholics in Great Britain. Smith argued that England could not continue persecuting the Catholic majority of Ireland and expect their support in a possible war with France. He suggested, in fact, that the Irish might welcome an invasion by Napoleon. While the government protected itself from an internal Catholic element, he pointed out, it might well be destroyed by an external one. He also maintained that England's continuing persecution of the Catholic minority was an infringement of individual liberty that should not be part of a great nation or national church.

Smith's arguments took on a political tone that was infused with some of his most biting wit and sarcasm, much of which was directed against Spencer Perceval, Chancellor of the Exchequer, and a major government voice against emancipation. In the first letter to Abraham, Smith attacks Perceval's irrational fear of Catholic emancipation: "In the first place, my sweet Abraham, the Pope is not landed—nor are there any curates sent out after him—nor has he been hid at St. Alban's by the Dowager Lady Spencer—nor dined privately at Holland House—nor been seen near Dropmore. If these fears exist (which I do not believe), they exist only in the mind of the Chancellor of the Exchequer; they emanate from his zeal for the Protestant interest; and, though they reflect the highest honour upon the delicate irritability of his faith, must certainly be considered as more ambiguous proofs of the sanity and vigour of his understanding." While the Plymley letters gained great popularity (sixteen editions were printed by the end of 1808), they did not have an immediate effect on government policy. However, they did serve as a public discussion of Catholic emancipation, and Smith revisited this theme several times in his writings and sermons over the next twenty years. When the issue resurfaced in government debate in 1825, Smith spoke at several meetings of Anglican clergymen in support of Catholic emancipation. Several pamphlets from this period that recall the themes of the Plymley letters are *Catholic Claims* (1825), *A Sermon on Religious Charity* (1825), and *A Letter to the Electors, upon the Catholic question* (1826). The emancipation for which he began arguing in 1807 finally became a reality in 1829 with the passage of the Roman Catholic Relief Act.

In 1809 Edward Vernon (later Harcourt), the new archbishop of York, citing the Clergy Residence Act, compelled Smith to either reside in the Foston parish or resign the appointment. No clergyman had lived in the Foston parsonage for 150 years, and the rectory was uninhabitable. Smith and family, therefore, moved to Heslington, about twelve miles from Foston, close enough for him to attend personally to the parish. In the meantime he sought an exchange of parishes, but, when he found none by 1813, he decided to build a new rectory in Foston, and he and his family moved there in 1814.

Smith missed the society of London, but settled into the life of a country parson. He was not an exile, however. He continued contributing to the *Edinburgh Review*. In a January 1810 article he argued for broadening the education of women beyond domestic responsibilities, reassuring his readers that educated women would still make suitable wives and mothers. Society in general would benefit if all its members were educated; education should be the right of everyone, not just the ruling-class men.

In August of the same year he again raised the subject of British education, specifically the public-school environment. He criticized the system of fagging that encouraged the older boys to tyrannize the younger ones. He believed that athletics were of little use and that they discouraged scholarship. Supervision by the masters was inadequate because of the size of the schools, leading to laziness in most of the students. He advocated smaller schools, where the master would have more direct involvement with each student, but large enough for the students to come into contact with a wide range of personalities.

Living in Yorkshire introduced Smith to problems encountered by the rural poor. In addition to being the village parson, he was also the village magistrate and, as such, had firsthand experience with administering the Game Laws. The Game Laws were an attempt by the wealthy landowners to prevent the depletion of game on their lands. Poaching was criminalized, and convicted poachers were given harsh sentences. The poor rural renters, who needed game to subsist, continued harvesting game on the rented lands. Many were prosecuted and sent to prison for poaching. In a March 1819 article he attacked the tyranny established by the laws and called for their repeal.

Two years later he wrote about the outrageous practice by the landowners of using spring guns and man traps to discourage poachers. He equated the traps and spring guns to premeditated murder, simply to protect the landowners' property. Smith argued vehemently that no property rights could justify killing a person for simple trespassing. In 1823 a parliamentary committee began investigating the Game Laws, and Smith repeated his arguments in the October issue of the *Edinburgh Review*. In 1827 spring guns were made illegal, and in 1831 the Game Laws were revised.

*Editorial cartoon (published 7 October 1840) by H B (John Doyle) commenting on Smith's opposition to reforms that would equalize incomes of churches. Smith is shown receiving crumbs from the table of Charles James Blomfield, Bishop of London, and William Howley, Archbishop of Canterbury.*

Smith's chances of receiving a more attractive appointment in the Church improved in 1827, with the formation of a Whig government, but the anticipated position never materialized. However, in January 1828, when the Tories had regained the government leadership, Lord Chancellor John Singleton Copley, Lord Lyndhurst, who was also a personal friend, appointed him a prebendary of Bristol Cathedral. Smith at this time ceased contributing to the *Edinburgh Review*, because he did not think it appropriate to his new position in the Church.

With the appointment as a prebendary of Bristol Cathedral, Smith was in need of a parish assignment closer to Bristol. He was able to exchange the parish living at Foston for the one at Combe Florey, Somerset, to which he moved in July 1829. In September 1831 Charles, Lord Grey, prime minister of a new Whig government, appointed him canon-residentiary of St. Paul's. He held this post until his death, never achieving his goal of a bishopric.

The new Whig government put parliamentary reform on its legislative agenda. In his *Speech at the Taunton Reform Meeting* (1831) and *Mr. Dyson's Speech to the Freeholders on Reform* (1831), Smith supported the Whig design for reform. In the Taunton speech he chided the House of Lords for obstructing the passage of reform bills. In an amusing performance he compared the House's resistance to a woman, Mrs. Partington, attempting to withstand the stormy onslaught of the Atlantic Ocean with a mop and bucket.

With his appointment to St. Paul's, Smith became less outspoken in regard to social reforms, and many of his later writings reflect the attitude of a member of the Church establishment. In 1836 the Ecclesiastical Commission was established to study reforms in the Church of England. The proposed changes consisted of redistributing much of the cathedrals' wealth and patronage to smaller parishes. In *A Letter to Archdeacon Singleton, on the Ecclesiastical Commission*

(1837), *Second Letter to Archdeacon Singleton* (1838), *A Letter to Lord John Russell* (1838), and *Third Letter to Archdeacon Singleton* (1839) Smith argued against the intended reforms, especially those that would equalize church incomes. He believed that if large church incomes no longer existed as goals for the clergy, competent men would be discouraged from becoming clergymen.

Two writings of minor importance are Smith's *Ballot* (1839), arguing against the Radical proposal for using the secret ballot in elections, and his *Letters on American Debts* (1843), arguing for the Commonwealth of Pennsylvania to repay on defaulted bond dividends.

Sydney Smith's lasting contributions to British prose literature are his practical expressions of the reform movement's ideals and his role in the establishment of the *Edinburgh Review*. Smith, in addressing such issues as Catholic emancipation, education, and the Game Laws, was able to express his views with wit and humor, making them appealing to a wide range of readers. While his ideas did not always have an immediate or significant effect on government policy, much of his thought was reflected in later reforms.

Smith's role in the formation of the *Edinburgh Review* must also be considered part of his legacy. The *Review* was one of the most influential journals of the nineteenth century, and he played a major part in its establishment and its early literary content. Ian Jack, in volume 10 of the *Oxford History of English Literature* (1963), acknowledges Jeffrey's editorial leadership of the *Edinburgh Review* in the early nineteenth century but indicates that "it was Sydney Smith who had been its 'original projector.' "

Smith's continuing popularity is evident in the number of editions of his works. His collected works were published in four editions from 1839 through 1848. Numerous editions of his selected writings were published between 1854 and 1956. Writers of each generation since his death have done biographical or critical work on him. Both through his writings and his part in the *Edinburgh Review*, Sydney Smith made an enduring contribution to British prose writing of the early nineteenth century.

**Letters:**

*Letters of the Rev. Sydney Smith*, edited by Mrs. Austin, volume 2 of *A Memoir of the Reverend Sydney Smith*, by Saba Holland (London: Longman, Brown, Green & Longmans, 1855; New York: Harper, 1855);

G. C. Heseltine, "Five Letters of Sydney Smith," *London Mercury*, 21 (April 1930): 512-517;

*The Letters of Sydney Smith*, 2 volumes, edited by Nowell C. Smith (Oxford: Clarendon Press, 1953);

David B. Green, "Letters to Samuel Rogers from Tom Moore and Sydney Smith," *Notes and Queries*, new series 2 (December 1955): 542-543;

William G. Lane, "Additional Letters of Sydney Smith," *Harvard Library Bulletin*, 9 (Autumn 1955): 397-402;

*Selected Letters of Sydney Smith*, edited by Nowell C. Smith (London: Oxford University Press, 1956); republished, with an introduction by Auberon Waugh (Oxford & New York: Oxford University Press, 1981);

Ernest Dilworth, "Letters of Sydney Smith," *Notes and Queries*, new series 11 (November 1964): 419-421;

Duane B. Schneider, "Daniel Webster Visits Sydney Smith," *Notes and Queries*, new series 14 (October 1967): 366-367;

Schneider, "Unpublished Letters of Sydney Smith," *Notes and Queries*, new series 14 (August 1967): 307-308;

Alan Bell, "The Letters of Sydney Smith," *Bulletin of the John Rylands University Library*, 59 (Autumn 1976): 13-39.

**Bibliographies:**

Sheldon Halpern, "Sydney Smith in the *Edinburgh Review*: A New List," *Bulletin of the New York Public Library*, 66 (November 1962): 589-602;

Duane B. Schneider, "Sydney Smith in America to 1900: Two Checklists," *Bulletin of the New York Public Library*, 70 (November 1966): 538-543.

**Biographies:**

Saba Smith Holland, Lady Holland, *A Memoir of the Reverend Sydney Smith*, 2 volumes (London: Longman, Brown, Green & Longmans, 1855; New York: Harper, 1855);

Richard Monckton Milnes, Lord Houghton, "The Rev. Sydney Smith," in his *Monographs: Personal and Social* (London: John Murray, 1873; New York: Holt & Williams, 1873), pp. 257-292;

Stuart J. Reid, *A Sketch of the Life and Times of the Rev. Sydney Smith* (London: Sampson Low, 1884; New York: Harper, 1885);

André Chevrillon, *Sydney Smith et la Renaissance des Idées libérales en Angleterre au XIXe siècle* (Paris: Hachette, 1894);

George W. E. Russell, *Sydney Smith* (London: Macmillan, 1905; New York: Macmillan, 1905);

Oswald Saint Clair, *Sydney Smith: a biographical sketch* (London: Francis Griffiths, 1913);

Osbert Burdett, *The Rev. Smith, Sydney* (London: Chapman & Hall, 1934);

Hesketh Pearson, *The Smith of Smiths: Being the Life, Wit and Humour of Sydney Smith*, with an introduction by G. K. Chesterton (London: Hamilton, 1934; New York: Harper, 1934); republished, with an introduction, by Malcolm Muggeridge (London: Folio Society, 1977); Hamish Hamilton edition (1934), with additions and corrections and a new introduction by Richard Ingrams (London: Hogarth Press, 1984);

Gerald Bullett, *Sydney Smith: A Biography & a Selection* (London: Joseph, 1951);

Pearson, "Sydney Smith," chapter 4 in his *The Lives of the Wits* (London: Heinemann, 1962; New York: Harper & Row, 1962), pp. 124-142;

Alan Bell, *Sydney Smith, Rector of Foston, 1806-29* (York: St. Anthony's Press, 1972);

Bell, *Sydney Smith* (Oxford: Clarendon Press, 1980).

**References:**

W. H. Auden, "Portrait of a Whig," *English Miscellany*, 3 (1952): 141-158;

John L. Clive, *Scotch Reviewers: The Edinburgh Review 1802-1815* (Cambridge, Mass.: Harvard University Press, 1957);

Joseph Epstein, "The Mere Common Sense of Sydney Smith," *New Criterion*, 8 (November 1989): 9-20;

Sheldon Halpern, "Coming Up Stairs: The Literary Career of Sydney Smith," Ph.D. dissertation, Columbia University, 1963;

Halpern, *Sydney Smith* (New York: Twayne, 1966);

Charles Kingsley, "Sydney Smith," *Fraser's Magazine*, 52 (1855): 84-91;

William Kirkland, "Character and Opinions of the Late Rev. Sydney Smith," *Godey's Ladies Book*, 33 (1846): 35-39;

Howard Mackey, "Verse and Nonsense: The Rhymes of Sydney Smith," *Research Studies*, 39 (March 1971): 68-82;

Mackey, *Wit and Whiggery: The Rev. Sydney Smith, 1771-1845* (Washington, D.C.: University Press of America, 1979);

Lawrence Patrick Mannion, "Sydney Smith: A Study of His Writings On Education," Ph.D. dissertation, State University of New York at Albany, 1976;

Robert S. McLean, "Tory Noodles in Sydney Smith and Charles Dickens: An Unnoticed Parallel," *Victorian Newsletter*, 38 (Spring 1970): 24-25;

James Murphy, "Some Plagiarisms of Sydney Smith," *Review of English Studies*, 14 (April 1938): 199-205;

Samuel Francis Pickering, "Sydney Smith: A Whig Divine, a Study of His Early Writings, 1800-1814," Ph.D. dissertation, Princeton University, 1970;

Joanna Richardson, "The Smith of Smiths," *History Today*, 21 (June 1971): 433-439;

George Saintsbury, "Sydney Smith," in his *Essays in English Literature 1780-1860* (London: Percival, 1890);

Duane Bernard Schneider, "Sydney Smith's Reputation in America to 1900," Ph.D. dissertation, University of Colorado, 1965;

Alden Clarke Smith, "The Reverend Sydney Smith's Theory of Wit and Humor: Origin, Elements, and Applications To His Rhetorical Practice," Ph.D. dissertation, University of Illinois, 1969;

"Sydney Smith as a Minister of Religion," *Biblical Repertory and Princeton Review*, 28 (1856): 418-443;

Stanley T. Williams, "The Literary Criticism of Sydney Smith," *Modern Language Notes*, 38 (November 1923): 416-419;

"Works of the Rev. Sydney Smith," *Christian Observer*, 50 (1850): 388-400.

**Papers:**

About 650 items of collected correspondence and miscellaneous papers, mainly letters from Smith (1798-1844), are located in the library of New College, Oxford. Several miscellaneous papers and letters, including correspondence with Sir Robert Peel, are in the British Library. Alan Bell, in his *Sydney Smith* (1980), lists forty-seven other institutions and individuals who possess manuscript sources.

# Robert Southey

*(12 August 1774 - 21 March 1843)*

Ernest Bernhardt-Kabisch
*Indiana University*

See also the Southey entry in *DLB 93: British Romantic Poets, 1789-1832: First Series.*

BOOKS: *The Fall of Robespierre. An Historic Drama*, act 1 by Samuel Taylor Coleridge, acts 2 and 3 by Southey (Cambridge: Printed by Benjamin Flower for W. H. Lunn and J. & J. Merrill, sold by J. March, Norwich, 1794);

*Poems: Containing The Retrospect, Odes, Elegies, Sonnets, etc.*, by Southey and Robert Lovell (Bath: Printed by R. Cruttwell, 1795);

*Joan of Arc, an Epic Poem* (1 volume, Bristol: Printed by Bulgin & Rosser for Joseph Cottle, Bristol, and Cadell & Davies and G. G. & J. Robinson, London, 1796; revised edition, 2 volumes, Bristol: Printed by N. Biggs for T. N. Longman and J. Cottle, 1798; Boston: Printed by Manning & Loring for J. Nancrede, 1798);

*Letters Written During a Short Residence in Spain and Portugal. With some Account of Spanish and Portugueze Poetry* (Bristol: Printed by Bulgin & Rosser for J. Cottle, Bristol, and G. G. & J. Robinson, and Cadell & Davies, London, 1797; revised edition, Bristol: Printed by Biggs & Cottle for T. N. Longman & O. Rees, London, 1799); third edition revised as *Letters Written during a Journey in Spain, and a Short Residence in Portugal*, 2 volumes (London: Printed for Longman, Hurst, Rees & Orme, 1808);

*Poems*, 2 volumes (Bristol: Printed by N. Biggs for Joseph Cottle and G. G. & J. Robinson, London, 1797, 1799; volume 1, Boston: Printed by Manning & Loring for Joseph Nancrede, 1799);

*The Annual Anthology*, 2 volumes, by Southey and others (Bristol: Printed for T. N. Longman & O. Rees, London, 1799, 1800);

*Thalaba the Destroyer*, 2 volumes (London: Printed for T. N. Longman & O. Rees by Biggs & Cottle, Bristol, 1801; Boston: Published by T. B. Wait & Charles Williams, 1812);

*Madoc*, 2 volumes (London: Longman, Hurst, Rees & Orme, 1805; Boston: Printed by Munroe & Francis, 1806);

*Metrical Tales, and Other Poems* (London: Longman, Hurst, Rees & Orme, 1805; Boston: C. Williams, 1811);

*Letters from England: By Don Manuel Alvarez Espriella. Translated from the Spanish* (3 volumes, London: Printed for Longman, Hurst, Rees & Orme, 1807; 1 volume, Boston: Printed by Munroe, Francis & Parker, 1808; New York: Ezra Sargent, 1808);

*The Curse of Kehama* (London: Printed for Longman, Hurst, Rees, Orme & Brown by J. Ballantyne, 1810; New York: Published by David Longworth, 1811);

*History of Brazil*, 3 volumes (London: Longman, Hurst, Rees, Orme & Brown, 1810, 1817, 1819; volume 1 revised, 1822);

*Omniana, or Horae Otiosiores*, 2 volumes (London: Longman, Hurst, Rees, Orme & Brown, 1812)—also includes contributions by Coleridge;

*The Origin, Nature, and Object of the New System of Education* (London: Printed for J. Murray, 1812);

*The Life of Nelson*, 2 volumes (London: Printed for John Murray, 1813; New York: Eastburn, Kirk / Boston: W. Wells, 1813);

*Roderick, the Last of the Goths* (London: Printed for Longman, Hurst, Rees, Orme & Brown by James Ballantyne, Edinburgh, 1814; Philadelphia: E. Earle / New York: Eastburn, Kirk, printed by W. Fry, 1815);

*Odes to His Royal Highness The Prince Regent, His Imperial Majesty The Emperor of Russia, and His Majesty the King of Prussia* (London: Longman, Hurst, Rees, Orme & Brown, 1814); republished as *Carmen Triumphale, for the Commencement of the Year 1814. Carmina Aulica. Written in 1814 on the Arrival of the Allied Sovereigns in England* (London: Printed for Longman, Hurst, Rees, Orme & Brown, 1821);

*Robert Southey (portrait attributed to Edward Nash; from Jack Simmons,* Southey, *1945)*

*The Minor Poems of Robert Southey*, 3 volumes (London: Printed for Longman, Hurst, Rees, Orme & Brown, 1815);

*The Poet's Pilgrimage to Waterloo* (London: Longman, Hurst, Rees, Orme & Brown, 1816; New York: W. B. Gilley and Van Winkle & Wiley, printed by T. & W. Mercein, 1816; Boston: Published by Wells & Lilly, 1816);

*The Lay of the Laureate. Carmen Nuptiale* (London: Printed for Longman, Hurst, Rees, Orme & Brown, 1816);

*Wat Tyler. A Dramatic Poem* (London: Printed for Sherwood, Neely & Jones, 1817; Boston: J. P. Mendum, 1850);

*A Letter to William Smith, Esq., M.P.* (London: J. Murray, 1817);

*The Life of Wesley; and the Rise and Progress of Methodism*, 2 volumes (London: Printed for Longman, Hurst, Rees, Orme & Brown, 1820; New York: Published by Evert Duyckinck & George Long, printed by Clayton & Kingsland, 1820; New York: Wm. B. Gilley, 1820);

*A Vision of Judgement* (London: Longman, Hurst, Rees, Orme & Brown, 1821); republished in *The Two Visions; or, Byron v. Southey* (London: W. Dugdale, 1822; New York: W. Borradaile, 1823);

*The Expedition of Orsua; and the Crimes of Aguirre* (London: Longman, Hurst, Rees, Orme & Brown, 1821; Philadelphia: Hickman & Hazard, 1821);

*History of the Peninsular War*, 3 volumes (London: J. Murray, 1823, 1827, 1832);

*The Book of the Church*, 2 volumes (London: J. Murray, 1824; Boston: Wells & Lilly, 1825);

*A Tale of Paraguay* (London: Longman, Hurst, Rees, Orme, Brown & Green, 1825; Boston: S. G. Goodrich, 1827);

*Vindiciæ Ecclesiæ Anglicanæ* (London: J. Murray, 1826);

*All for Love; and the Pilgrim to Compostella* (London: J. Murray, 1829);

*Sir Thomas More; or, Colloquies on the Progress and Prospects of Society*, 2 volumes (London: J. Murray, 1829);

*The Devil's Walk; A Poem. By Professor Porson* [pseud.]. *Edited with a biographical memoir and notes by H. W. Montagu* [pseud.], by Southey and Coleridge (London: Marsh & Miller / Edinburgh: Constable, 1830);

*Essays, Moral and Political*, 2 volumes (London: J. Murray, 1832);

*Lives of the British Admirals, with an Introductory View of the Naval History of England*, 5 volumes, volume 5 by Robert Bell (London: Longman, Rees, Orme, Brown, Green & Longmans, 1833, 1834, 1837, 1840);

*The Doctor, &c.*, 7 volumes, volumes 6 and 7 edited by J. W. Warter (London: Longman, Rees, Orme, Brown, Green & Longmans, 1834-1847; volumes 1-3 republished in 1 volume, New York: Harper, 1836);

*The Poetical Works* (10 volumes, London: Printed for Longman, Orme, Brown, Green & Longmans, 1837, 1838; 1 volume, New York: D. Appleton, 1839);

*The Life of the Rev. Andrew Bell. . . . Comprising the History of the Rise and Progress of the System of Mutual Tuition*, volume 1 (London: Murray / Edinburgh: Blackwood, 1844 [volumes 2 and 3 by Charles Cuthbert Southey]);

*Oliver Newman: A New-England Tale (Unfinished): With Other Poetical Remains*, edited by Herbert Hill (London: Longman, Brown, Green & Longmans, 1845);

*Robin Hood: A Fragment. By the Late Robert Southey and Caroline Southey. With Other Fragments and Poems by R. S. & C. S.* (Edinburgh & London: Blackwood, 1847);

*Southey's Common-Place Book*, edited by John Wood Warter, 4 series (London: Longman, Brown, Green & Longmans, 1849-1851);

*Journal of a Tour in the Netherlands in the Autumn of 1815*, edited by W. Robertson Nicoll (Boston & New York: Houghton, Mifflin, 1902; London: Heinemann, 1903);

*Journal of a Tour in Scotland in 1819*, edited by C. H. Herford (London: Murray, 1929);

*Journal of a Residence in Portugal 1800-1801 and a Visit to France in 1838*, edited by Adolfo Cabral (Oxford: Clarendon Press, 1960);

*The Contributions of Robert Southey to the Morning Post*, edited by Kenneth Curry (University: University of Alabama Press, 1984).

OTHER: *On the French Revolution, by Mr. Necker*, 2 volumes, volume 2 translated by Southey (London: Printed for T. Cadell & T. Davies, Jun., 1797);

*The Works of Thomas Chatterton*, 3 volumes, edited by Southey and Joseph Cottle (London: T. N. Longman & O. Rees, 1803);

Vasco Lobeira, *Amadis of Gaul*, 4 volumes, translated by Southey (London: Printed by N. Biggs for T. N. Longman & O. Rees, 1803);

Francisco de Moraes, *Palmerin of England*, 4 volumes, translated by Southey (London: Printed for Longman, Hurst, Rees & Orme, 1807);

*Specimens of the Later English Poets*, 3 volumes, edited, with notes, by Southey and Grosvenor Bedford (London: Longman, Hurst, Rees & Orme, 1807);

*The Remains of Henry Kirke White, of Nottingham, late of St. John's College, Cambridge; With an Account of His Life*, 3 volumes, edited, with a biography, by Southey (volumes 1 and 2: London: Printed by W. Wilson for Vernor, Hood & Sharp; Longman, Hurst, Rees & Orme; J. Dighton, T. Barret & J. Nicholson, Cambridge; W. Dunn & S. Tupman, Nottingham, 1807; Philadelphia: Printed & sold by J. & A. Y. Humphreys, 1811; volume 3: London: Printed for Longman, Hurst, Rees, Orme & Brown, 1822; Boston: Wells & Lilly, 1822);

*Chronicle of the Cid*, translated by Southey (London: Longman, Hurst, Rees & Orme, 1808; Lowell, Mass.: Bixby, 1846);

*The Byrth, Lyf, and Actes of King Arthur*, 2 volumes, edited by Southey (London: Printed for Longman, Hurst, Rees, Orme & Brown by T. Davison, 1817);

John Bunyan, *The Pilgrim's Progress. With a Life of John Bunyan*, edited, with a biography, by Southey (London: John Murray and John Major, 1830; Boston: Crocker & Brewster / New York: Jonathan Leavitt, 1832);

*Select Works of the British Poets, from Chaucer to Jonson*, edited, with biographical sketches, by Southey (London: Longman, Rees, Orme, Brown & Green, 1831);

*Southey in 1795 (portrait by James Sharples; City Art Gallery, Bristol)*

*Attempts in Verse, by John Jones, an Old Servant; with Some Account of the Writer, Written by Himself: and an Introductory Essay on the Lives and Works of the Uneducated Poets*, introduction by Southey (London: J. Murray, 1831); republished as *Lives of the Uneducated Poets, to Which Are Added Attempts in Verse by John Jones, an Old Servant* (London: H. G. Bohn, 1836);

Isaac Watts, *Horae Lyricae. Poems, Chiefly of the Lyric Kind, in Three Books*, edited, with a memoir, by Southey (London: J. Hatchard & Son, 1834);

*The Works of William Cowper, Esq., Comprising His Poems, Correspondence, and Translations. With a Life of the Author*, 15 volumes, edited, with a biography, by Southey (London: Baldwin & Craddock, 1835-1837).

SELECTED PERIODICAL PUBLICATIONS—UNCOLLECTED: Review of *Lyrical Ballads, Critical Review*, second series 24 (October 1798): 197-204;

Review of *Gebir*, by Walter Savage Landor, *Critical Review*, second series 27 (September 1799): 29-39;

"Malthus's Essay on the Principles of Population," *Annual Review*, 2 (1804): 292-301;

"Ritsons Ancient English Romances," *Annual Review*, 2 (1804): 515-533;

"Thomas Clarkson's History of the Abolition of the African Slave Trade," *Annual Review*, 7 (1809): 127-148;

"The State of Public Affairs," by Southey and R. Grant, *Quarterly Review*, 22 (January 1820): 492-560;

"The Life of Cromwell," *Quarterly Review*, 25 (July 1821): 279-347;

"Superstition and Knowledge," by Southey and F. Cohen, *Quarterly Review*, 29 (July 1823): 440-475;

"Dr. [Frank] Sayers's Work," *Quarterly Review*, 35 (January 1827): 175-220;

"History of the Dominion of the Arabs and Moors in Spain," *Foreign Quarterly Review*, 1 (July 1827): 1-60;

"On the Corn-Laws," *Quarterly Review*, 51 (March 1834): 228-283.

Unlike most of the English Romantics, who wrote predominantly either in verse or in prose, Robert Southey—like his friend and brother-in-law Samuel Taylor Coleridge and, to some extent, Walter Scott—was both poet and prose writer and one as fully as the other. Of his fellow Romantics he was perhaps the most versatile, as well as one of the most prolific. As poet—and eventually poet laureate—he produced epics, romances, and metrical tales, ballads, plays, monodramas, odes, eclogues, sonnets, and miscellaneous lyrics. His prose works include histories, biographies, essays, reviews, translations, travelogues, semifictional journalism, polemical dialogues, and a farraginous work of fiction, autobiography, anecdote, and omnium-gatherum that defies classification. His bent was inherently encyclopedic; and, while his writings lack both moral profundity (as distinct from moral fervor) and "natural magic," they compensate by their vigor and abundance for their dearth of genius. Coleridge rightly called him the complete man of letters.

By common consent, however, Southey's prose is superior to his verse and has proved more durable. His ambitious epic projects were largely dead ends of a moribund tradition. His prose works, on the contrary, did for English prose what William Wordsworth and Coleridge's *Lyrical Ballads* (1798) did for verse: they opposed to the orotund solemnity of the Johnsonian style a new model of republican plainness, perspicuity, and respect for empirical facts. At its worst such a style can be pedestrian and nondescript; at its best it is precise, vigorous, down-to-earth, seemingly effortless, and disarmingly unpretentious. The *sermo pedestris*, often the bane of Southey's poetry, is the chief virtue of his prose and one that can still engage the reader in what might otherwise appear a mere mass of exploded ideas and superseded learning.

Although Southey began to write journalism early and continued to compose verse in later years, his literary career, like those of Coleridge and Scott, is roughly divisible into two phases: an early poetic vein, followed by a midlife shift to prose discourse. His early life is thus bound up mainly with his development as a poet.

Robert Southey was born in Bristol on 12 August 1774 as the oldest surviving son of a feckless and finally bankrupt tradesman of the same name and his wife, Margaret Hill Southey. During much of his childhood he was forced to live away from home, under the stifling and unaffectionate tutelage of an eccentric and domineering aunt, Elizabeth Tyler, at fashionable Bath and at boarding schools with their dreary curricula, lack of nurture, and petty tyranny. From these early experiences Southey developed his lifelong habit of suppressing his intense emotions under a reserved exterior of steely cheerfulness and somewhat frosty amiability and of taking refuge from a bleak and loveless existence in the world of literature. He read William Shakespeare and Francis Beaumont and John Fletcher as soon as he could read and the Renaissance epics of Torquato Tasso, Ludovico Ariosto, John Milton, Luiz de Camões, and especially Edmund Spenser soon thereafter. In his adolescence he read Voltaire, Jean-Jacques Rousseau, Edward Gibbon, Thomas Paine, William Godwin, and other spokesmen for Enlightenment and human emancipation. Moreover, he early tried his hand at writing plays, epics, and incidental verse. While at Westminster public school in London (1788-1792), he offended the school authorities by publishing a "contumacious" satire against corporal punishment —his first prose effort—in the school newspaper and was summarily expelled. The expulsion, along with the bankruptcy and death (possibly by suicide) of his father, produced an emotional crisis, which he sought to overcome by reading Epictetus: the Stoic philosopher remained his vade mecum ever after.

Early in 1793 Southey entered Balliol College at Oxford University to study for holy orders in compliance with the wishes of his maternal uncle, the Reverend Herbert Hill. But he was by now, like many young intellectuals of his time, a fervent republican, deist, and sympathizer with the French Revolution. At odds with Church dogma and the Establishment, incensed by the soulless pedantry and regimentation of the masters and by the snobbery and licentiousness of the scholars, he left the university after only two terms. During this period of ferment and uncertainty, he made two momentous acquaintances.

*Edith Fricker Southey at thirty-five (portrait by Matilda Betham; Fitz Park Museum, Keswick)*

One was a young seamstress, Edith Fricker, whom he met in the fall of 1793 and married two years later (14 November 1795): she proved to be a devoted, though intellectually inert, helpmate and mother of his children for more than forty years, until her mind failed and she died in 1837. The other was Samuel Taylor Coleridge, then of Cambridge, two years Southey's senior and, like him, a budding poet and enthusiastic republican and revolutionary fellow traveler. When the two met in June 1794 an intense friendship developed rapidly, and the two young radicals, in concert with some of their respective college friends, concocted a plan to establish, in the Susquehanna Valley, an egalitarian community, a "Pantisocracy" (meaning "equal rule of all") based on communal property and the fusion of physical and intellectual labor. The scheme eventually failed for lack of sufficient funds and because ideological and personal rifts developed between the idealistic but dilatory Coleridge and his more practical revisionist friend and housemate. When Southey decided to abandon the cause by accepting an invitation to Portugal from his uncle Hill—and a stipend from his school friend Charles Wynn enabling him to switch from divinity to the study of law—Coleridge, who had been persuaded, for the good of Pantisocracy, to become engaged and married to Edith Fricker's sister Sarah, felt trapped and betrayed. For the moment the friendship was over.

Southey's five-month sojourn on the Iberian Peninsula during the first half of 1796 resulted in his first published prose work, *Letters Written During a Short Residence in Spain and Portugal* (1797). By then he had already published, with his friend and fellow Pantisocrat Robert Lovell, a volume of *Poems* (1795)—reflective pieces, "odes, elegies, sonnets, etc.," in the manner of eighteenth-century Sensibility—and had acquired a reputation as the author of an epic with revolutionary overtones, *Joan of Arc* (1796; revised, 1798); he had also written two plays, including a piece of hackwork with Coleridge, *The Fall of Robespierre* (1794), and the notorious *Wat Tyler* (which remained in manuscript until 1817, when it was unearthed and published surreptitiously by political enemies to compromise the "renegade" laureate with a Jacobinical skeleton in his closet). The *Letters* are hardly literature in the sense in which the later *Letters from England* are, but they are an early example of Southey's knack for turning chance occasions to journalistic account. Together with Edith, Southey returned to the Peninsula in 1800-1801 for a second, more extended visit (his *Portuguese Journal* from that year was unearthed and published by Adolfo Cabral in 1960). The two sojourns turned him into a lifelong student of Spanish and Portuguese history and ethnography.

Upon his return to England—and to Edith—in summer 1796, Southey and his wife spent several years in a state of virtual transiency, partly in London, where he desultorily read for the law at Gray's Inn as stipulated by Wynn's annuity, and then at various localities in the south of England after it became clear to him that the law was not for him. There followed the second, year-long stay in Portugal and then eight more months in London and Dublin in an abortive attempt at a civil-service career as private secretary to Isaac Corry, the Irish chancellor of the Exchequer. During these years, Southey produced a large amount of lyrical verse—odes, sonnets, inscriptions, emblematic poems, monodramas, eclogues, and especially ballads dealing with social injustice, crime, guilt, and the supernatural and demonic. He also wrote the first of a planned series of mythological romances, *Thalaba the Destroyer* (1801), illustrating the religion of Islam through the exotic story of a pious young Moslem champion's struggle against a college of malignant sorcerers.

The decisive turning point in Southey's biography occurred in September of 1803, when the successive shocks of the deaths of his mother, a beloved cousin, and his first, infant daughter prompted the Southeys to visit Coleridge at his new domicile, Greta Hall, in Keswick in the English Lake District. The visit turned into a life-long stay. Coleridge, who had repeatedly urged his brother-in-law and ci-devant fellow Pantisocrat to come live with, or at least visit, him in Keswick, ironically promptly departed in search of health and then separated from his wife and family, leaving Southey in charge as chief provider at Greta Hall, a post the scrupulous Southey dutifully kept until his death forty years later. Except for periodic travel abroad (in Scotland, in the Netherlands, in France), visits, and business trips (such as his trip to Oxford to obtain an honorary LL.D. in 1820), Southey never left the Lake District again.

In 1803 he still thought of himself primarily as a poet and continued to do so for another decade or so. During the first years at Keswick, he gave final shape to a project that had occupied him intermittently since his Westminster days, his second, two-part epic, *Madoc* (1805)—"Madoc in Wales" and "Madoc at Aztlan"—about the legendary twelfth-century Welsh prince who supposedly discovered the New World and settled in Aztec country, fighting wars against barbarism, superstition, and priestcraft and establishing a bridgehead for a humane, Christian civilization—Southey's epic of foundation and of Pantisocracy rewritten in essentially imperialist terms. In 1809 Southey completed another mythological romance, *The Curse of Kehama* (1810), this time on Hinduism, an extravagant story of a pariah of humble and patient merit and his persecution by, divinely assisted struggle against, and eventual victory over, a would-be cosmocrat who at last overreaches himself—a story clearly intended to allude to the struggle against Napoleon and one that later served as a model for Percy Bysshe Shelley's greater fable of nonviolent resistance against overwhelming odds, *Prometheus Unbound* (1820). A third and final epic, *Roderick, the Last of the Goths*, appeared in 1814, the year after Southey's appointment to the laureateship; it narrates the fall of the Visigothic kingdom to the Moors in 711 A.D. and the beginning of the Spanish *reconquista* and the Asturian monarchy. This poem, Southey's greatest epic success at the time, is even more pointedly directed at the Napoleonic Wars and the Peninsular War in particular. Now, however, the ruling sentiment is one of ferocious vindictiveness and religious bigotry that stands in striking contrast to the antiwar theme of *Joan of Arc* and even to the reluctant militancy of *Madoc* and to the doctrine of redemption through the patient suffering of *Kehama*.

Greta Hall, Keswick, where Southey lived from 1803 until his death forty years later

The arc from the pacifism of *Joan of Arc* to the crusading spirit and unvarnished jingoism of *Roderick* and the laureate and anti-Bonapartist verses of those years (such as *Carmen Triumphale*, 1814, and *The Poet's Pilgrimage to Waterloo*, 1816) circumscribes most of Southey's career as a poet, though there were some later efforts, such as the lugubrious *Tale of Paraguay* (1825), about a family of South American mission Indians, or the unfortunate *Vision of Judgement* (1821) in hexameters, about George III's ascent to Southey's now thoroughly Tory heaven, not to mention later laureate odes and occasional ballads and metrical tales. During the last thirty years of his life, Southey's principal literary pursuit was that of a scholar and essayist. The story of that pursuit, more clearly than that of the poet, records the emergence of a conservative out of the fervid republican of the early years.

Southey's early prose venture, *Letters Written During a Short Residence in Spain and Portugal*, uses the flexible and currently popular medium of epistolary journalism to combine travelogue, description, and anecdote with essays, translations, and original poems and to pepper picturesque and often vivid scenic prospects and local color with republican sarcasms about "the double despotism of Church and State"—about monasticism, Catholic superstitions and "miracle-mongering," and the spectacle of royal extravagance and oppression in the midst of endemic poverty, ignorance, licentiousness, and disease. Southey has an eye for curious, bizarre, or telling details, customs, and costumes, and for scenic settings and humorous incidents. *Letters Written During a Short Residence in Spain and Portugal* is an early example of Southey's tenacious hold on facts as well as of his tendency to tar all things with the same brush. The volume proved popular, and a second edition, somewhat less spontaneous, more cautious and controlled, appeared in 1799. The *Portuguese Journal* of 1800-1801 is even more vivid, and is less glibly judgmental, though here too Southey indulges an antiseptic obsession with "superstition," and with filth, stench, and vermin, along with his love of the Iberian landscape.

After his first return from abroad, Southey embarked upon his career as a professional reviewer, first with notices of Spanish and Portuguese literature for the *Monthly Magazine* and then, in 1798, with reviews for the *Critical Review*, for which he wrote, among other things, a glowing account of Walter Savage Landor's oriental poem *Gebir* (September 1799) and the rather unsympathetic critique of Wordsworth and Coleridge's *Lyrical Ballads* (October 1798) with its notorious dismissal of the *Rime of the Ancient Mariner* as a "Dutch attempt at German sublimity." In 1802

*Southey in his study at Greta Hall, 1804 (portrait by Henry Edridge; National Portrait Gallery, London)*

Southey also became a regular contributor to the newly founded *Annual Review,* for which he reviewed some 150 titles during the next six years, most of them ephemeral.

Like his travelogues, his reviews are essentially journalistic: largely synoptic and digestive, proceeding by summary paraphrase and direct quotation, and based in their judgment on common sense and personal taste rather than on theoretical principles like those informing Coleridge's criticism. Even so, Southey's reviews are of historical importance insofar as, at a time when reviewers still wrote anonymously and therefore could "tomahawk" with impunity, they helped to usher in a more considerate and sympathetic approach to what Southey himself termed the "ungentle craft." Literary jobbing of this sort was a fairly lucrative employment in that age of rapidly expanding book markets and remained throughout Southey's life a principal source of his income. Although largely hackwork, these reviews also laid the foundation for his later *Quarterly* essays and even an achievement such as *The Life of Nelson* (1813).

During these years Southey also established himself as a translator and textual editor. Between 1803 and 1808, he published prose adaptations of the three leading romances of chivalry of Iberian provenance, *Amadis of Gaul,* from a sixteenth-century Spanish version, *Palmerin of England,* essentially a modernization of Anthony Munday's seventeenth-century Englishing of a French variant of the romance, and *Chronicle of the Cid,* a translation of the early-sixteenth-century *Cronica del Cid,* supplemented by material derived from the earlier *Poema del Cid* and various popular ballads. Southey has the distinction of being the first to argue for the Portuguese origin of *Palmerin of England*—his claim of a like origin of *Amadis of Gaul* was based on a confusion of

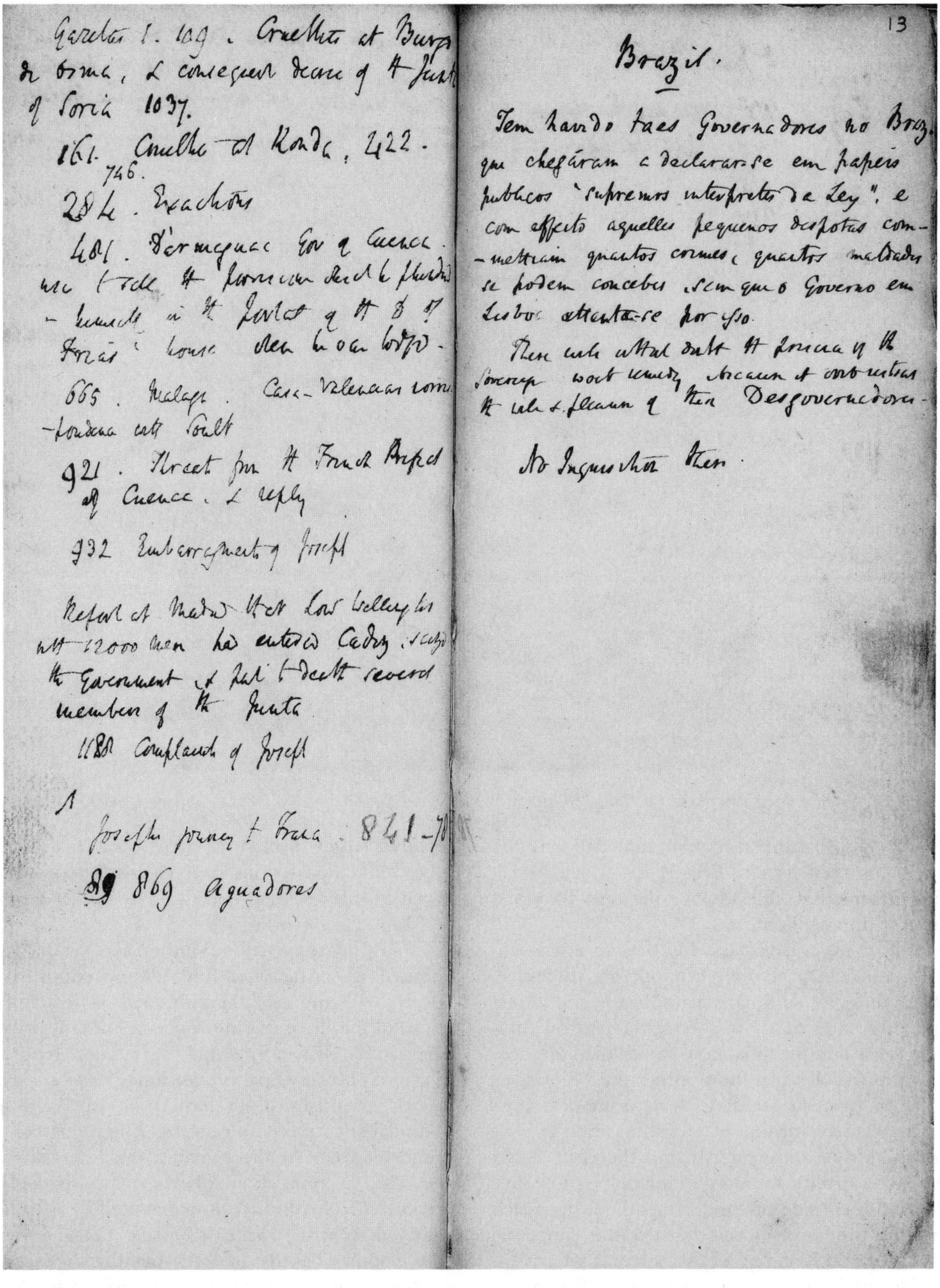

*Pages from a notebook Southey kept in 1808-1811 (HM 2635, vol. 3; Henry E. Huntington Library and Art Gallery)*

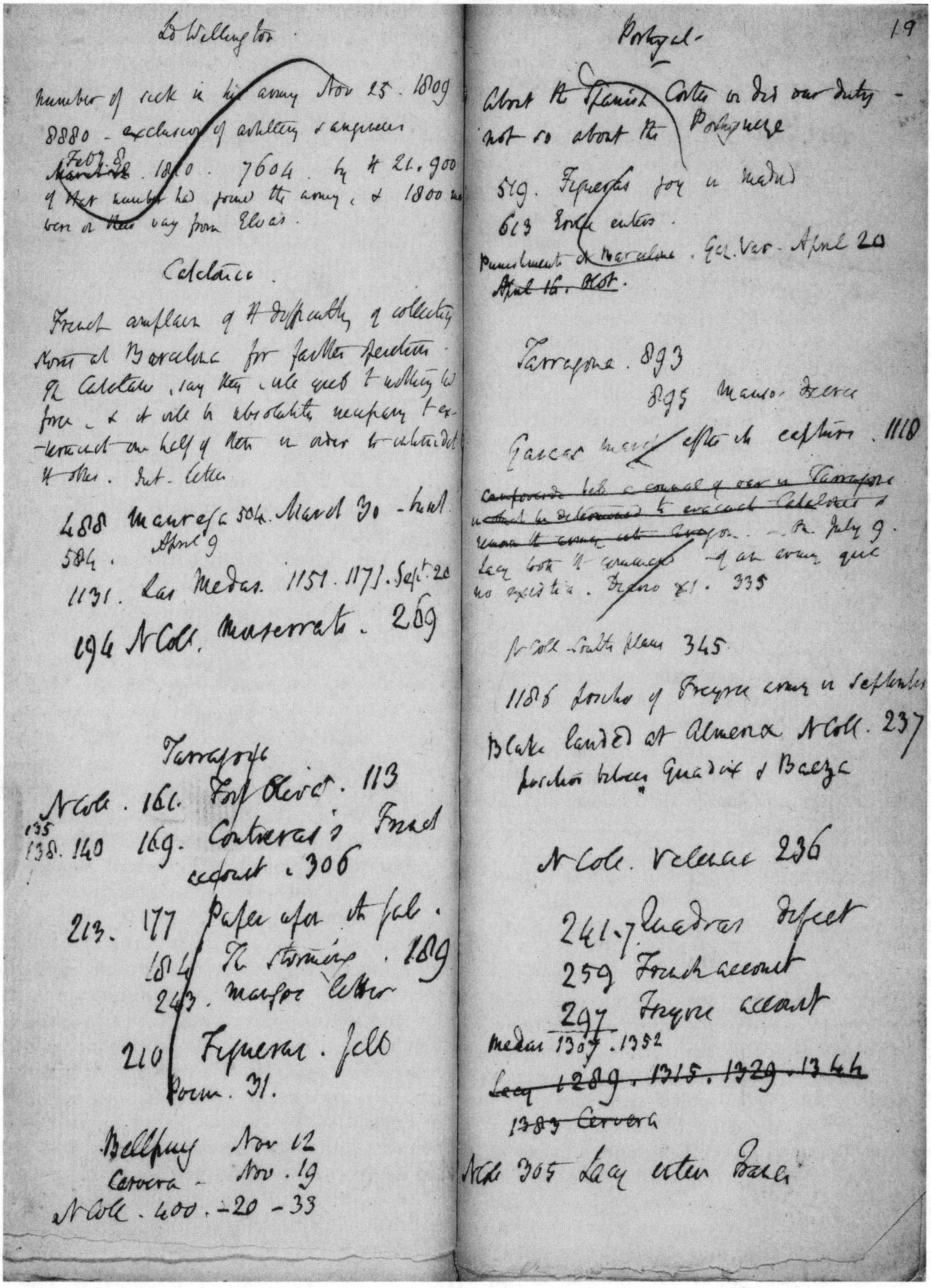
Ld Wellington.

number of sick in his army Nov 25. 1809
8880 – exclusive of artillery & engineers
~~March~~ Feb 8. 1810. 7604. by 4 21.900
of that number had joined the army, & 1800 were on their way from Elvas.

Catalonia.

French complain of the difficulty of collecting stores at Barcelona for farther expeditions. The Catalans, say they, [illegible] & it will be absolutely necessary to exterminate one half of them in order to subjugate the other. Int. letter

488 Manresa 504. March 30 – burnt.
504. April 9
1131. Las Medas. 1151. 1171. Sept. 20
194 N Coll. Monserrat. 269

Tarragona
N Coll. 161. Fort Olivo. 113
135
138. 140 169. Contreras's French account. 306
213. 177 Papers after the fall.
184 The storming. 189
243. Marshal's letter
210 Figueras. fell
Poem. 31.

Bellpuig Nov 12
Cervera – Nov. 19
N Coll. 400. –20 –33

Portugal. 19

About the Spanish Cortes we did our duty – not so about the Portuguese

579. Figueras joy in Madrid
613 Eroles enters.
Punishment at Barcelona. Gz. Var. April 20
~~April 16. 1811~~.

Tarragona. 893
895 Manso. Decree
Caceres [illegible] after the capture. 1110

~~Campoverde held a council of war in Tarragona [illegible] determined to evacuate Catalonia & [illegible] Aragon.~~ – The July 9. Lacy took the command of an army [illegible] no expedition. [illegible] 81. 335

N Coll. South [illegible] 345.

1186 Forces of Freyre army in September
Blake landed at Almeria N Coll. 237
position between Guadix & Baeza

N Coll. Valencia 236

241.7 Guadras defeat
259 French account
297 Freyre account
Medas 1307. 1352
~~Lacy 1289. 1315. 1329. 1344~~
~~1383 Cervera~~
N Coll 305 Lacy enters Baza

names and is no longer accepted. As renditions they are of limited value. *Amadis of Gaul* in particular is bowdlerized, purged of most of its amorous content in the name of a narrow moral and stylistic decorum that appealed to the taste of the time—the work sold well—but is obsolete today. More durable has been the third of these translations, *Chronicle of the Cid*, whose martial spirit unsullied by carnality was more congenial to Southey and enabled him to produce a comprehensive narrative of Spain's national hero in a homogeneous, slightly archaic, paratactic style modeled on Sir Thomas Malory and the Bible.

In his travelogues, reviews, and translations, Southey served as a kind of middleman of literature intent on advertising, condensing, packaging, and importing literary goods, new and old, for readier consumption. This spirit of literary merchandising is embodied also in Southey's various textual editions of these years, including the three-volume collections of the writings of his unhappy fellow Bristowans Thomas Chatterton (1803; coedited with Joseph Cottle) and Henry Kirke White (1807). The latter includes a biographical introduction of small critical value, and both were essentially charitable undertakings to aid the families and the memory of these inheritors of unfulfilled renown. *Specimens of the Later English Poets* (1807), a massive compilation of eighteenth-century verse, most of it quite negligible, similarly reveals Southey's literary scholarship to be more antiquarian than critical and his criteria to be moral and didactic rather than aesthetic and intellectual. Of his various later editorial works, perhaps only the late *Works of William Cowper* (1835-1837), also prefixed with a "Life," retains a firm place in the history of textual scholarship.

While much of the prose Southey produced during the years 1803-1808 is either ephemeral or an endeavor to rescue the transient from oblivion by means of editing, translation, or synopsis, one work, *Letters from England* (1807), transcends the bulk by turning journalism into fiction and thus into art. Modeled on Montesquieu's *Lettres persanes* (1721) and Oliver Goldsmith's *Citizen of the World* (1760-1761), *Letters from England: By Don Manuel Alvarez Espriella* uses the form of the pseudonymous epistle to combine travelogue, satire, and personal essay into a fictional variant of the sort of epistolary journalism found already in *Letters Written During a Short Residence in Spain and Portugal*. Planned as early as 1803 as an "omnium gatherum" of "all that I know and much of what I think" about his place and time, its uses and abuses, *Letters from England* mingles social and political commentary and economic and cultural analysis with anecdote and descriptions of landscapes and townscapes to convey a cross section of English life and "manners," fashions and foibles, while employing the travel motif to impose a semblance of unity upon farraginous variety. Moreover, the device of a narrative persona, chosen partly to throw hostile critics off the scent, creates a beneficial stretch of aesthetic distance between the author and his material. By making his mouthpiece not only a foreigner but a Spaniard and Catholic, Southey achieves the triple effect of modifying his personal bias through narrative perspective while playing his anti-Catholicism off against his critique of British society, particularly his nascent conservatism in politics and economics and his lifelong deistical contempt for sectarian fanaticism and all manner of "pseudodoxia epidemica."

The fictional method is not without flaws. Scenic descriptions are at times merely topographical inventories, even in the often vividly perspectival account of the Lake District, and the narrative voice tends to become Southey's own whenever he advances from relatively trivial matters to issues that engage his emotions. Analogously, Southey's social-economic criticism blends shrewdness with nostalgia and erects progressive proposals on obsolescent principles. He inveighs against William Pitt's repressive and reactionary policies in the name of liberty and equality and against the exploitation and social neglect produced by an unchecked industrialization in terms of an extreme antimaterialism. He calls for legal, parliamentary, and military reform, as well as for government regulation of industry and commerce. Yet his premises are moralistic and agrarian and are inspired as much by fear of revolution as by a desire for improvement. Even so, *Letters from England* is of lasting interest as a sweeping, kaleidoscopic, and often humorous depiction of England at the epochal beginning of the nineteenth century—the narrative is set in 1802, during the Peace of Amiens—and as an early and articulate appeal to the social conscience in the face of revolutionary change, particularly in the eloquent evocation of the inhuman plight of the new industrial laboring class in factory towns such as Manchester. The book was popular and sold well—at least until the identity of the book's author became known.

*Letters from England* may be usefully juxtaposed with a second, much later piece of fictionalized polemic, the notorious *Sir Thomas More: or, Colloquies on the Progress and Prospects of Society*, written between 1820 and 1829 and published in 1829, with a second edition in 1831. As the title indicates, the epistolary model has here been replaced by the dialogue, Southey choosing as his new literary model the *Consolation* of Boethius. But one of the fictional interlocutors is again a Catholic, albeit this time a historical one, while the other, Montesinos (perhaps with an allusion to Miguel de Cervantes's *Don Quixote*, 1605), represents Southey himself, the setting of the dialogues being in fact Southey's library at Greta Hall in the "mountainous" Lake Country. As Renaissance man and arch-utopian, More provides a dramatic perspective on Southey's own time of epochal change and his early utopianism, while at the same time serving as a kind of spiritual father figure, on whom Southey can foist his most alarmist and apocalyptic views so as to retain for his alter ego Montesinos a modicum of youthful optimism and belief in progress and political justice. At other times, however, the two disputants seem to be interchangeable in their outlook, as they bandy sermons and citations, making the colloquy less a sustained dramatic "imaginary conversation" à la Landor (who professed to have derived the concept from Southey) than a mere expository mechanism—an altercation between A and B, as Charles Lamb remarked. More's historical Catholicism, in fact, gets in the way—Southey turns him into an embryonic Protestant—and the fiction of a visitation by and dialogue with a ghost becomes bizarre after the first encounter and irritating after the second or third. The work has often been praised for its limpid prose style. But that style is generally at its best in the numerous descriptive and anecdotal digressions—about local scenery, local legends, or Southey's library holdings—interspersed with the more portentous dialogues, rather than in the dialogues themselves.

Ideologically, *Sir Thomas More* epitomizes the conservatism of Southey's later years—an outlook increasingly authoritarian, paternalistic, moralistic, and imperialistic. Southey's shift to the right dates roughly from, and was in response to, the years 1808-1813, the period of the critical phase in Britain's struggle against Napoleon (the Peninsular War), of the Luddite Riots (1811) and the assassination of prime minister Spencer Perceval (1812), and of Southey's own engagement in 1809 as a reviewer for the conservative *Quarterly Review* and subsequent appointment as poet laureate (1813). The shift is evident in the *Quarterly Review* essays' long, and often formless disquisitions, a selection of which reappeared, revised and condensed, as *Essays, Moral and Political* in 1832, on the eve of the first Reform Bill. In them Southey inveighs in often shrill tones against the evils of the day as he saw them: materialism (whether philosophical or commercial), immorality, infidelity, and sedition, pacifism, Methodism, Malthusianism, Catholic emancipation, and parliamentary reform. Some of his diagnoses are accurate enough and his proposed remedies salutary: universal education, legislation to regulate industry and provide social benefits, and the like. But his analyses of the causes of economic and social dislocation—and therefore also his solutions—are generally one part science and two parts moralism. His reply to the Malthusian specter of overpopulation is biblical authority, on the one hand, and a naively arrogant colonialism and imperialism, on the other: God wants England to be fruitful and multiply so as to replenish the earth and subdue it as the "hive of nations." The purpose of education is indoctrination rather than emancipation, and the guarantee of social well-being is an aristocratic and ecclesiastic Establishment rather than any utilitarian calculus determined through democratic processes.

*Sir Thomas More* caps this evolving paternalistic vision of contemporary history as an Armageddon between the forces of law and order and moral and religious absolutes and the forces of materialism and anarchy, between the principles of obedience and authority and the dissolving agents of pluralism and skepsis. On a less apocalyptic level, Southey continues his critique of the "manufacturing system"—the "dorsal spine" of *Sir Thomas More*, as Jean Raimond put it. If Southey's analysis of the evils under an unregulated laissez-faire capitalism—concentration of wealth, consequent wage slavery, exploitation, Gradgrind mechanization, alienation deracination, and overall dehumanization—is ahead of its time, his nostalgia for medieval feudalism and theocracy as guarantors of order, security, and social harmony is merely romantic and retrogressive bad faith—as Thomas Macaulay drove home in his famous review (*Edinburgh Review*, January 1830). Even so, Southey was also able to contemplate the socialism of Robert Owen as an alternative model—over the objections of his ghostly interlocutor to Owen's freethinking: the device of

*Southey in 1828 (engraving based on a portrait by Sir Thomas Lawrence)*

the colloquy generated at least a saving touch of dialectic.

For all the volume of Southey's journalism and polemical writing, his chief aspiration as a prosateur—not surprisingly considering his predilection as a poet for the epic—was to be a historian. His most ambitious, and nearly lifelong, project was the great "History of Portugal," a work that was to be both epic and encyclopedic in scope, combining fullness and variety of narrative and description with unity of idea and design, and that would do for the Portuguese empire what Edward Gibbon's *Decline and Fall* (1776-1788) had done for Rome. The main opus was to have been accompanied by subsidiary volumes on the Portuguese colonies in Asia and South America, on monasticism, on the Jesuit missions, and on Iberian literature. As was to be expected, even in a writer of Southey's fanatical industry and punctuality, the work was never completed, and what must have been a voluminous manuscript disappeared mysteriously after his death. The abortiveness of Southey's most cherished project dramatizes his tragic flaw as a historian—indeed as a writer: his inability to select and to synthesize, to make the part stand synecdochically or metonymically for the whole. His strength lies in his skill in assembling a maximum of information into a manageable space, distilling, as he himself put it, "wine into alcohol."

The proof of that alcohol can be gauged from the only major portion of the complete Portuguese scheme that did reach publication, the massive *History of Brazil*. Prompted by Britain's new economic and political interest in Brazil consequent upon the move of the Portuguese court to Rio de Janeiro in 1807, the *History* was published in three increasingly bulky volumes between

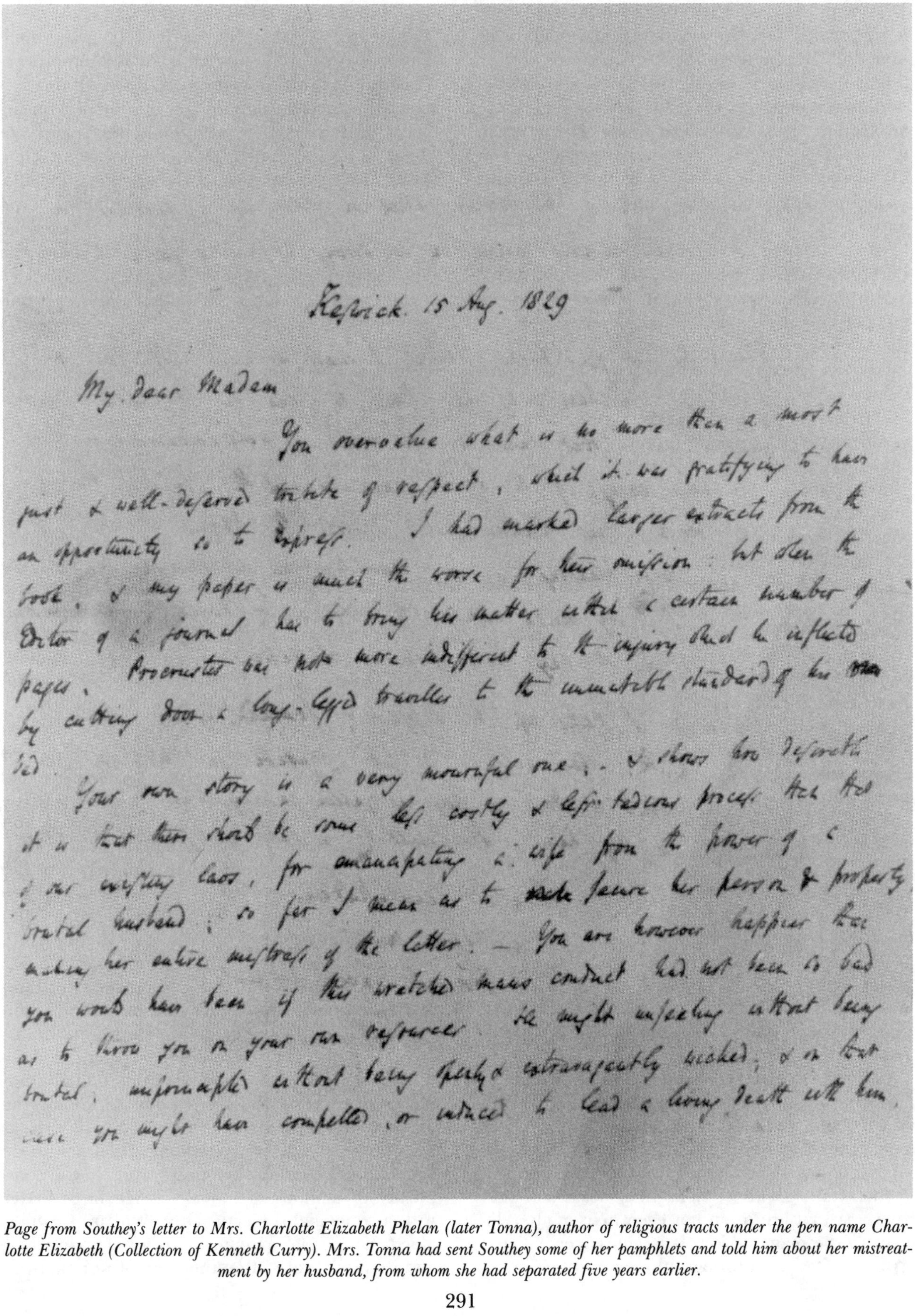

Keswick. 15 Aug. 1829

My dear Madam

You overvalue what is no more than a most just & well-deserved tribute of respect, which it was gratifying to have an opportunity so to express. I had marked larger extracts from the book, & my paper is much the worse for their omission: but often the Editor of a journal has to bring his matter within a certain number of pages. Procrustes was not more indifferent to the injury which he inflicted by cutting down a long-legged traveller to the immutable standard of his bed.

Your own story is a very mournful one; & shows how desirable it is that there should be some less costly & less tedious process than that of our existing laws, for emancipating a wife from the power of a brutal husband; so far I mean as to secure her person & property, making her entire mistress of the latter. — You are however happier than you would have been if this wretched man's conduct had not been so bad as to throw you on your own resources. He might unfeeling without being brutal, unprincipled without being openly & extravagantly wicked; & in that case you might have been compelled, or induced to lead a living death with him.

*Page from Southey's letter to Mrs. Charlotte Elizabeth Phelan (later Tonna), author of religious tracts under the pen name Charlotte Elizabeth (Collection of Kenneth Curry). Mrs. Tonna had sent Southey some of her pamphlets and told him about her mistreatment by her husband, from whom she had separated five years earlier.*

1810 and 1819. Southey soon came to disparage it in private, but he also hoped it would make him the "Herodotus of South America," and he doggedly pursued it—all twenty-three-hundred-odd pages of it—to the end. The first accurate and comprehensive Brazilian history ever written, it was based largely on an extensive collection of printed accounts and original documents brought from Portugal by Southey's uncle Hill and is still authoritative today—it has recently been translated for the second time into Portuguese—and is interesting especially for Southey's championship of the Jesuit missionaries, perhaps the single most prominent theme in the work. The writing is undeviatingly chronological in its breathless accumulation of historical details—from the discovery of the territory in 1500, through the period of the explorers and adventurers, the changing fortunes of the Jesuit missions, the rivalry between the Portuguese and the Dutch settlers, the eighteenth-century reforms and final expulsion of the Jesuits under the Marquês de Pombal, all the way to the arrival of the Portuguese court in 1808. It also dwells at length on the exotic appeal of local color, "manners," native customs (often lurid), reports about Amazons, and the savagery and cannibalism of the Indians, as well as their suffering from slavery and persecution. An inexhaustible source of information, the *History of Brazil* will produce fatigue or overload in the most determined reader. For Southeyan historical narrative at its best, that reader will do better to turn to a separately published subsidiary episode, *The Expedition of Orsua; and the Crimes of Aguirre* (1821; originally published in the *Edinburgh Annual Register for 1810* [1812]), a concise and engrossing narrative of an episode in the history of the search for El Dorado that explodes into mutiny, rebellion, and paranoid internecine terror and that, in its study of the corrupting effect of personal power in an exotic setting devoid of "Law and Order," was meant as an analogue of the French Revolution and in some ways anticipates Joseph Conrad's *Heart of Darkness* (1902).

There is little to recommend Southey's later historical works. The voluminous *History of the Peninsular War* (1823-1832), while containing dense and graphic episodes, such as the moving Siege of Saragossa, is crammed with verbatim documents and with digressions into local color and Iberiana that are often not even marginally relevant to the main subject. It is, moreover, vitiated as authoritative historiography by Southey's contemptuous disregard of the campaign accounts of Napoleon's Marshal Nicolas Jean de Dieu Soult and by Arthur Wellesley, Duke of Wellington's refusal to open his archives to Southey. It also suffers from overidealization of the Spanish insurgents and a corresponding underestimation of the role of the British in the war, that of Gen. John Moore in particular. It was thus speedily eclipsed by the authorized history published concurrently by Col. William Napier, who used all the available sources and had himself taken part in the campaign. Prejudice, partiality, and lack of synthesis also disfigure Southey's history of religion in England, the popular *Book of the Church* (1824), whose pervasive hostility toward Catholicism and Catholic emancipation perverts historiography to polemic—see also the *Vindiciæ Ecclesiæ Anglicanæ* (1826), Southey's rebuttal in the controversy that ensued.

As Southey's poetry, however fanciful, is essentially prosaic, so his prose, however factual, is inherently narrative and anecdotal rather than expository and analytical. It is thus in the genre of biography—one he himself deemed "the most useful of literary genres"—rather than in historiography proper that Southey's historical ambitions achieve their most lasting success. To be sure, prolixity and partiality are hazards in the biographies as well. The late *Lives of the British Admirals* (1833-1840), Southey's endeavor to write a naval history in biographical form, has been called the finest portrait gallery of Elizabethan naval heroes in existence and is notable for its pioneering use of Spanish and Portuguese sources. But the material adduced from these sources is often of doubtful relevance, and the volumes savor of task work and encyclopedic compilation. Similarly *The Life of Wesley* (1820) snowballs in Southey's hands into a massive chronicle of the Methodist movement, its antecedents, development, and architects—a movement to which Southey was not sympathetic and which he was not really competent to examine theologically. The story and portrait of John Wesley himself, to the extent to which it is not discolored by bias or obscured by insufficiently subordinated contexts, is faithful, vigorous, and admirable, and remains the most popular life of the founder of Methodism, although Southey lacks the empathy and the psychological acumen to do full justice, beyond praise and blame, to the complexity of a mind like Wesley's. He fares better with a congenial subject such as William Cowper, albeit here, too, circumstantiality, contingency, and digression are often the bane of portraiture.

*Cousins Sara Coleridge and Edith May Southey, daughters of Samuel Taylor Coleridge and Robert Southey, 1820 (portrait by Edward Nash; National Portrait Gallery, London)*

It is the rare coincidence of moral affinity and material restraint that accounts for the lasting popularity of Southey's first and finest biography, *The Life of Nelson* (1813). Essentially an expansion and elaboration of Southey's February 1809 review in the *Quarterly* of the "official" biography of Adm. Horatio Nelson by James Stanier Clarke and John M'Arthur (1806), Southey's *Life of Nelson* has in fact the synoptic character typical of contemporary reviewing and can be called a literary epitome of the earlier work, though it makes use of some additional sources. Southey's narrative is brisk, vivid, and for once almost undeviating. It has remained the classic portrayal of England's greatest naval hero.

Southey's account of Nelson is not one of mere hagiography. He sharply criticizes Nelson's obsequiousness to the repressive and degenerate court of Naples, especially in the bloody suppression of Adm. Francesco Carraciolo's rebellion, and of course, he condemns Nelson's adulterous relationship with Emma, Lady Hamilton, on whose "spell" he in fact blames all of Nelson's Neapolitan errors. On the other hand, however, he views Nelson's "infatuated attachment," as he primly calls it, as a fortuitous aberration and makes no attempt to *comprehend* Nelson's passion for Lady Hamilton and consequent separation from Lady Nelson—or, for that matter, his unimpaired friendship with Emma's husband, Sir William Hamilton. Though a full account of this side of Nelson's life was neither possible nor perhaps appropriate in an official biography, Southey's reticence on the matter strikes the modern reader as prudish and evasive.

Apart from his breach of domestic decorum and related indiscretions, however, Nelson was so thoroughly simpatico to Southey as to leave no need for a deeper, more dialectical empathy. His tactical genius and spectacular successes were the wonder of all, and his personal traits of kindliness mixed with pugnacity, humanity with combativeness, boyishness with devotion to duty, self-righteous contumacy with fanatical patriotism and royalism were so much Southey's own as to facilitate an apotheosis only less monumental than the one at London's Trafalgar Square. *The Life of Nelson* is in fact as much a prose epic, a kind of *Britannia Liberata*, as it is a work of historiography, and it remains Southey's one indubitable contribution to the English literary canon.

The year of the publication of *The Life of Nelson* was significantly the year of Southey's appointment as poet laureate, a title he kept until his death thirty years later. It was also the year in which Southey first conceived and began the odd farrago of narrative, anecdote, essay, reverie, humor, satire, plain nonsense, topography, "manners," genre painting, and "commonplace" entries called *The Doctor, &c.*, of which he finally published the first two volumes in 1834—again anonymously—and to which he was still adding when his mind began to fail four years later. Prompted by a jocose yarn Coleridge, and then Southey himself, used to spin about "Dr. Daniel Dove of Doncaster and his horse Nobs," whose "humour lay in making it as long-winded as possible" and each time telling it differently, *The Doctor, &c.* was modeled in part on François Rabelais and on Laurence Sterne's *Tristram Shandy* (1759-1767), in part on Montaigne, Richard Burton, and Thomas Browne, and was designed as an amphibious vehicle that would enable Southey to amuse and "play the fool," sound off on a variety of social, economic, and religious topics, and open a kind of old curiosity shop or intellectual flea market for his "multifarious collections" of reading notes, excerpts, and marginalia—the harvest of what he liked to compare to digging for pearls in a dunghill. More than in his epics with their voluminous notes, narrative here increasingly subserves a discursive and antiquarian purpose, to become at last a grotesque parody of Southeyan garrulousness and packrat mentality.

The narrative—what there is of it—projects essentially a nostalgic, agrarian idyll of the good old days before the eruption of revolutionary modernity. Dr. Daniel Dove, Shandean country physician and "flossofer," and represented as the mentor of the anonymous narrator's youth, is in fact an idealized self-portrait of "Dr. Southey" and mouthpiece for a Southeyan ideal of naive common sense, curious learning, domestic prudence, affection, and piety. He is surrounded by a cast of similarly innocuous characters. In some respects *The Doctor, &c.* not only echoes *Tristram Shandy* but anticipates both Thomas Carlyle's *Sartor Resartus* (1833-1834) and the comic genre painting of Dickens's *Pickwick Papers* (1836-1837). But it lacks the Faustian perplexity of the one and the Protean abundance of the other, as well as Sterne's Pyrrhonic wit. The book contains some true gems, including the famous story of "The Three Bears," which Southey seems to have derived in youth from his "half-saved" half uncle William Tyler (represented in *The Doctor, &c.* as Daniel's brother William Dove) and whose whimsical tone and spare, patterned folktalelike narration seem almost miraculous in the midst of so much logorrhea and have earned the tale a permanent place in the literature of the nursery. At their best the sketches and ruminations and "tattle-de-moys" of *The Doctor, &c.* have the unflagging curiosity, unbuttoned charm, and amiable chattiness of Southey's correspondence, which some critics value above his formal works. But too much in *The Doctor, &c.* is sentimental in its idylls, coy and feeble in its humor, commonplace and parochial in its conservatism, and obsessive in its frenetic wordplays and Burtonesque fascination with exploded opinions and bizarre trivia.

Southey has been called the architect and chief practitioner of a "Georgian style" in prose, a style that is pure and practical, in contrast to the ponderous and ornate solemnity of the likes of Samuel Johnson or Edward Gibbon or the rhetorical overkill of Edmund Burke. In trying to characterize Southey's style, one is apt to resort to negative terms: he does not have the intellectual substance and subtlety of Coleridge, or the mercurial wit and quaint charm of Charles Lamb, or the trenchancy and keen observation of William Hazlitt or Jane Austen, or the symphonic splendor of Thomas De Quincey, or the figurative force and transcendental extravagance of Thomas Carlyle, to mention only some chief contemporaries. His prose never becomes an aesthetic end in itself, and, when it does try to do so, as in portions of *The Doctor, &c.* it fails by straining too hard. Its closest antecedents and parallels are perhaps to be found in the unpretentious felicity of Joseph Addison and the workmanlike language of Walter Scott. To the least prepossessed

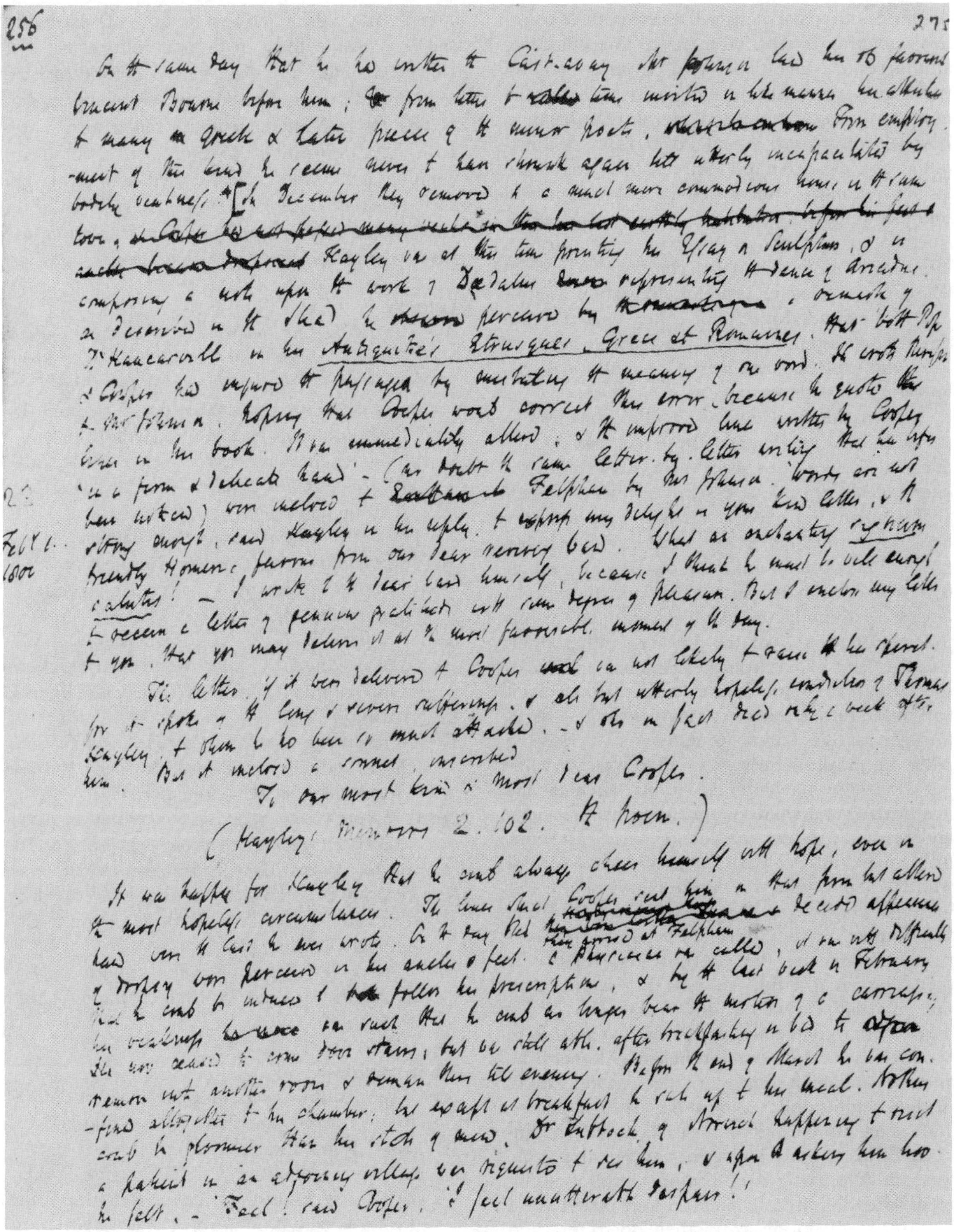

*Page from the manuscript for Southey's biography of William Cowper, published in volume 1 of Southey's edition of Cowper's works (1835-1837; MA 412, Pierpont Morgan Library)*

reader Southey's writing will often appear colorless and nondescript, poor in striking adjectives and arresting metaphors and given to passive verbs and constructions, and in its less guarded moments as loquacious and puerile. On balance, however, his prose is a model of transparent functionalism: clear, simple, direct, and vigorous; largely paratactic, but varied in its rhythms and sentence lengths; seemingly artless, yet taut, polished, and economical when time constraints did not promote makeshift; rhetorically forceful where appropriate in its use of alliteration, anaphora, and extended metaphor (often derived from the areas of warfare, travel, navigation, horticulture, and especially, medicine); and, above all, astonishing in its tireless abundance.

If in the final analysis Southey has less to say to today's reader than the other leading Romantics; if his causes seem dead, his ideas obsolete, his multitudinous researches inert; if with all his talent and energy, curiosity, and industry he is rarely touching or profound, it is largely because almost all his information and inspiration is only secondhand, derived from the books he read, accumulated, and worshipped in his fourteen-thousand-volume library, rather than also the fruit of hazardous experience and introspection. To be an author meant to transmit author-ity rather than to explore strange seas of thought as his fellow Romantics did. His life after the move to Keswick in 1803 was not without signal, even shattering events, such as the death of several children, including his first-born and his beloved first son and playmate, Herbert, or his many intense friendships, including several with women, one of whom, the minor poet Caroline Anne Bowles, he married on 4 June 1839—after twenty years of intimate correspondence—after the death in 1837 of the by then demented Edith Southey. But rather than opening his imagination fully to the force of the human condition, they caused him to retreat to the high ground of received beliefs. Although he always remained a somewhat truculent individualist, had doubts about some religious orthodoxies, and roamed to the ends of the earth and the beginnings of history in his reveries and researches, he was, after his early years, a staunch and even bigoted defender of both political and ecclesiastical hierarchies (if not always of their doctrines), and he turned down all job offers from newspapers, libraries, and universities that might have taken him away from the Lake District. He was endlessly curious about human nature but would not face it, whether in others or himself, except in the less volatile form of human culture, most of which he ended up despising as immoral or irrational, seditious or superstitious, dirty or even diabolical. His own mind eventually failed, after a lifetime of repressed passion and herculean compensatory labor, and he died of a stroke on the vernal equinox of 1843. He was buried in Crosthwaite Churchyard in Keswick, alongside his first wife and three of his children.

**Letters:**

*A Memoir of the Life and Writings of the Late William Taylor, of Norwich . . . (Containing his Correspondence with Robert Southey . . . and Other Eminent Literary Men)*, 2 volumes, edited by J. W. Robberds (London: Murray, 1843);

Joseph Cottle, *Reminiscences of Samuel Taylor Coleridge and Robert Southey* (London: Houlston & Stoneman, 1848);

*The Life and Correspondence of Robert Southey*, 6 volumes, edited by Charles Cuthbert Southey (London: Longman, Brown, Green & Longmans, 1849, 1850);

*Selections from the Letters of Robert Southey*, 4 volumes, edited by John Wood Warter (London: Longman, Brown, Green & Longmans, 1856);

*The Correspondence of Robert Southey with Caroline Bowles*, edited by Edward Dowden (Dublin: Hodges, Figgis / London: Longman, 1881);

*Letters of Robert Southey: A Selection*, edited by Maurice H. Fitzgerald (London, New York & Toronto: Oxford University Press, 1912);

*New Letters of Robert Southey*, 2 volumes, edited by Kenneth Curry (New York & London: Columbia University Press, 1965);

*The Letters of Robert Southey to John May, 1797-1838*, edited by Charles Ramos (Austin: Jenkins, 1976).

**Bibliographies:**

Ernest Bernbaum, *Guide through the Romantic Movement*, revised and enlarged edition (New York: Ronald Press, 1949);

Kenneth Curry, "Southey," in *The English Romantic Poets & Essayists: A Review of Research and Criticism*, edited by Carolyn Washburn Houtchens and Lawrence Huston Houtchens (New York: Published for the Modern Language Association by New York University Press, 1966), pp. 155-182;

*Caroline Ann Bowles, Southey's second wife (from Edward Dowden, ed.,* The Correspondence of Robert Southey with Caroline Bowles, *1881)*

Curry and Robert Dedmon, "Southey's Contributions to the *Quarterly Review," Wordsworth Circle*, 6 (Autumn 1975): 261-272;

Curry, *Robert Southey: A Reference Guide* (Boston: G. K. Hall, 1977);

Mary Ellen Priestley, "The Southey Collection in the Fitz Park Museum, Keswick, Cumbria," *Wordsworth Circle*, 11 (Winter 1980): 43-64.

**Biographies:**

Edward Dowden, *Robert Southey* (London: Macmillan, 1879);

William Haller, *The Early Life of Robert Southey* (New York: Columbia University Press, 1917);

Jack Simmons, *Southey* (London: Collins, 1945);

Malcolm Elwin, *The First Romantics* (New York: Longmans, Green, 1948).

**References:**

Ernest Bernhardt-Kabisch, *Robert Southey* (Boston: Twayne, 1977);

Marilyn Butler, "Revising the Canon," *Times Literary Supplement*, 4-10 December 1987, pp. 1349, 1359-1360;

Adolfo Cabral, *Southey e Portugal: 1774-1801* (Lisbon: Fernandez, 1959);

Geoffrey Carnall, *Robert Southey* (London & New York: Longmans, Green, 1964);

Carnall, *Robert Southey and His Age: The Development of a Conservative Mind* (Oxford: Clarendon Press, 1960);

Alfred Cobban, *Edmund Burke and the Revolt Against the Eighteenth Century: A Study of the Political and Social Thinking of Burke, Wordsworth, Coleridge, and Southey* (New York: Macmillan, 1929);

Kenneth Curry, *Southey* (London & Boston: Routledge & Kegan Paul, 1975);

Maria O. Da Silva Dias, *O Fardo Do Homem Branco: Southey, historiador do Brazil* (São Paulo: Companhia Editora Nacional, 1974);

Richard Hoffpauir, "The Thematic Structure of Southey's Epic Poetry," *Wordsworth Circle*, 6 (Autumn 1975): 240-249; 7 (Spring 1976): 109-116;

Kenneth Hopkins, *The Poets Laureate* (London: Bodley Head, 1954);

Mary Jacobus, "Southey's Debt to *Lyrical Ballads*," *Review of English Studies*, 22 (February 1971): 20-36;

Lionel Madden, ed., *Robert Southey: The Critical Heritage* (Boston: Routledge & Kegan Paul, 1972);

Edward W. Meachen, "From a Historical Religion to a Religion of History: Robert Southey and the Heroic in History," *Clio*, 9 (Winter 1980): 229-252;

Meachen, "History and Transcendence: Robert Southey's Epic Poems," *Studies in English Literature*, 19 (Autumn 1979): 589-608;

Warren U. Ober, "Lake Poet and Laureate: Southey's Significance to His Own Generation," Ph.D. dissertation, Indiana University, 1959;

Ludwig Pfandl, "Southey und Spanien," *Revue Hispanique*, 28 (March 1913): 1-315;

Jean Raimond, *Robert Southey: L'homme et son temps; L'oeuvre; Le role* (Paris: Didier, 1968);

Brian Wilkie, *Romantic Poets and Epic Tradition* (Madison: University of Wisconsin Press, 1965);

Herbert G. Wright, "Three Aspects of Southey," *Review of English Studies*, 9 (January 1933): 37-46.

**Papers:**

Major public collections of Southey's letters (of which some two thousand remain unpublished) and manuscripts are in the Berg Collection of the New York Public Library, the Bodleian Library, the British Library, the Fitz Park Museum in Keswick, the Huntingdon Library, the University of Rochester Library, the University of Kentucky Library, the National Library of Wales, and the Victoria and Albert Museum.

# Dorothy Wordsworth

*(25 December 1771 - 25 January 1855)*

Susan M. Levin
*Stevens Institute of Technology*

WORKS: "Address to a Child, During a Boisterous Winter," "The Mother's Return," and "The Cottager to her Infant," in *Poems By William Wordsworth, Including Lyrical Ballads, and the Miscellaneous Pieces of the Author*, 2 volumes (London: Printed for Longman, Hurst, Rees, Orme & Brown, 1815), I: 8-10, 11-13, 160;

*Recollections of a Tour Made in Scotland, A.D. 1803*, edited by J. C. Shairp (Edinburgh: Edmonston & Douglas, 1874; New York: Putnam's, 1874);

*Journals of Dorothy Wordsworth*, 2 volumes, edited by William Knight (London & New York: Macmillan, 1897); first complete edition, 2 volumes, edited by Ernest de Selincourt (London: Macmillan, 1941; New York: Macmillan, 1941);

*George & Sarah Green, A Narrative*, edited by Ernest de Selincourt (Oxford: Clarendon Press, 1936).

**Editions:** *Journals of Dorothy Wordsworth*, edited by Mary Moorman (London: Oxford University Press, 1971);

"The Collected Poems of Dorothy Wordsworth" and "Mary Jones and her Pet-lamb," edited by Susan M. Levin, in her *Dorothy Wordsworth and Romanticism* (New Brunswick, N.J.: Rutgers University Press, 1987);

*The Grasmere Journal*, edited by Pamela Woof, with an introduction by Jonathan Wordsworth (London: Joseph, 1989).

Dorothy Wordsworth wrote for nearly seventy years but published almost nothing. Her work, however, has been preserved, admired, and is finally achieving nearly complete publication. The issues her writing raises for the modern reader are significant. What constitutes a literary text? Can descriptions of baking gingerbread, washing one's hair, doing laundry, or looking at flowers be literature? Dorothy's preferred form of expression was the journal, and she characteristically wrote about the seeming trivia of everyday life. Reading Dorothy Wordsworth's journals, one inevitably feels in the presence of a "real author"; yet partly because of her own self-denigration she has often not been regarded as such.

For Dorothy Wordsworth, as for many women, the process of journal writing was the process of establishing an identity. As she describes a landscape, ironing shirts, or sitting with a child, she organizes her emotions. She also wrote stories, letters, and poems. All her works reveal a woman living and working at the center of a Romantic writing community in England, and they explore the possibilities and pressures of such a life. In her account of the domestic, she tells a woman's story of reading, writing, walking, and talking, a life in nature and in art. She records the land and the people of the Lake Country, as well as the evolving Wordsworthian art, her own and her brother's.

Born in Cockermouth in 1771, she was the only daughter among the five children of John and Ann Cookson Wordsworth. The family was prosperous, her father being in charge of the legal affairs of Sir James Lowther, a wealthy landowner. But in March 1778, when Dorothy was six, her mother died, and she was sent to live with a succession of relatives, who treated her sometimes as a loved guest, sometimes as a glorified servant. She was never permitted to return to her father's house, although her brothers gathered there, an exclusion that disturbed her greatly.

In 1781 Dorothy was sent to boarding school, but, after her father suddenly died on 30 December 1783, she was forced to leave for monetary reasons. She worried about money for most of her life. She was able to continue in a school near the home of her "Aunt" (her mother's cousin Elizabeth Threlkeld) until she was fifteen, but then she was sent to live with her maternal grandparents, Mr. and Mrs. William Cookson. An uncle, the Reverend William Cookson, agreed to tutor her, so she learned French, math,

*Dorothy Wordsworth circa 1806 (silhouette by an unknown artist; Wordsworth Trust, Dove Cottage, Grasmere)*

and geography. After he married in October 1788, she went to live with him and his wife, Dorothy Cowper Cookson, at Forncett. There Dorothy Wordsworth helped establish and run a small school for the local country girls.

Consistently she returned to one fantasy: setting up a household with her brother William. Despite the disapproval of their relatives, who predicted economic distress and social embarrassment, in 1795 William and Dorothy Wordsworth moved to Racedown, where William Wordsworth began his project of becoming one of England's greatest writers; Dorothy Wordsworth kept house, helped her brother with his work, wrote numerous letters, and cared for a three-year-old child, Basil Montague. Having formed a strong friendship with Samuel Taylor Coleridge, Dorothy and William moved to Alfoxden House in July 1797 to be near the Coleridge family. Here Dorothy began her Alfoxden notebook, recording her life with her brother.

Only about three and one-half months of these journal-type entries survive. Her concerns were the countryside around Alfoxden House and her presence in that natural world with her brother and Coleridge. Beginning with a description of the first signs of winter thaw, the notebook masses fragmented, often elliptical phrases. Her descriptions are compellingly precise. It is as if she defined the world and her place in it through piling up of detail. Her presence, however, is not aggressive. She seldom used the singular "I," preferring to portray herself as part of a larger "we." Yet, she was apart from the group, an isolated woman. Walking with Coleridge on 4 February 1798, she observed: "Midges or small flies spinning in the sunshine; the songs of the lark and redbreast; daisies upon the turf; the ha-

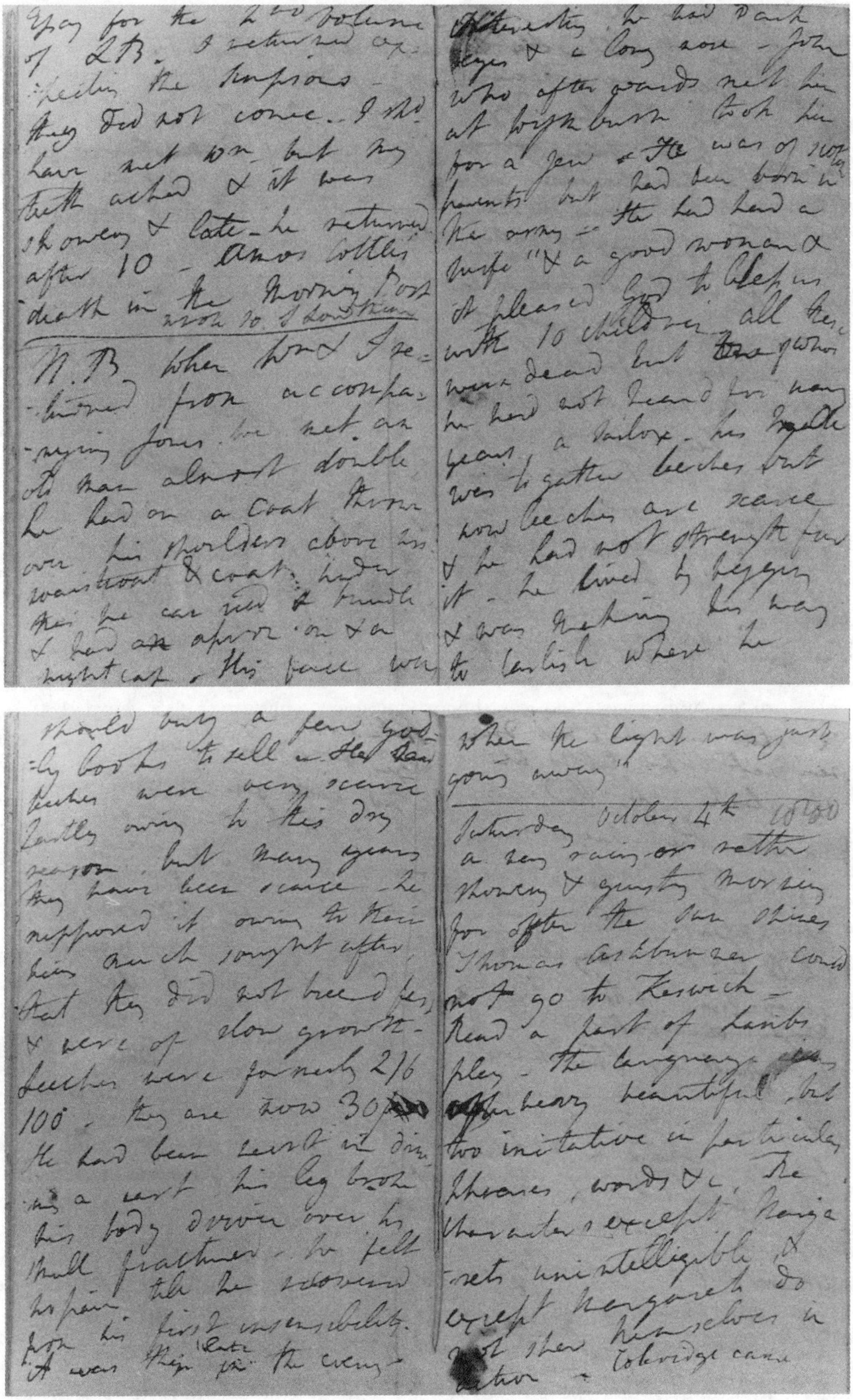

Essay for the 2nd volume of LB. I returned expecting the Simpsons — they did not come. I should have met W. but my teeth ached & it was showery & late — he returned after 10 — Amos Cottle's death in the Morning Post wrote to S Lowthian

N.B. When Wm & I returned from accompanying Jones we met an old man almost double he had on a coat thrown over his shoulders above his waistcoat & coat. Under this he carried a bundle & had an apron on & a night cap. His face was interesting. He had dark eyes & a long nose — John who afterwards met him at Wythburn took him for a Jew. He was of Scotch parents but had been born in the army. He had had a wife "& a good woman & it pleased God to bless us with 10 children" all these were dead but one of whom he had not heard for many years, a sailor. His trade was to gather leeches but now leeches are scarce & he had not strength for it. He lived by begging & was making his way to Carlisle where he should buy a few godly books to sell. He said leeches were very scarce partly owing to this dry season but many years they have been scarce. He supposed it owing to their being much sought after, that they did not breed fast, & were of slow growth. Leeches were formerly 2/6 100, they are now 30/. He had been hurt in driving a cart his leg broke his body driven over his skull fractured. He felt no pain till he recovered from his first insensibility. It was then late in the evening — when the light was just going away."

Saturday October 4th 1800. A very rainy or rather showery & gusty morning for often the sun shines. Thomas Ashburner could not go to Keswick — Read a part of Lamb's play. The language is often very beautiful, but too imitative in particular phrases, words &c. The characters except Margaret's unintelligible, & except Margaret's do not show themselves in action. Coleridge came

*Dorothy Wordsworth's journal entry for 3 October 1800, recording the meeting with a leech gatherer that was the inspiration for William Wordsworth's poem "Resolution and Independence" (Wordsworth Trust, Dove Cottage, Grasmere)*

zels in blossom; honeysuckles budding. I saw one solitary strawberry flower under a hedge. The furze gay with blossom." The singular object, the solitary strawberry blossom, is defined in part by its larger context. The terms of this description—community and that which is solitary in the group, unity and fragmentation—organize much of Dorothy Wordsworth's writing. At this time William began consulting his sister's journal to aid his own writing. Dorothy's language intermingles with her brother's. In her journal she wrote, "At once the clouds seemed to cleave asunder, and left her in the centre of a black-blue vault." William's "A Night-piece" reads: "—the clouds are split / Asunder,—and above his head he sees / The clear Moon, and the glory of the heavens." Coleridge too uses her words.

With her brother, Coleridge, and his student, John Chester, Dorothy went to Germany in 1798 and there recorded her impressions in her *Journal of Visit to Hamburgh and of Journey from Hamburgh to Goslar*, first published in its entirety in Ernest de Selincourt's edition of her *Journals* (1941). The extraordinary attention to detail seems meant to fix events for her companions as well as for her own remembrances. She was the group amanuensis. While the journal reveals her excitement at the trip, it also exhibits a kind of crankiness. The German winter proved long and somewhat disappointing. Dorothy and William finally returned home in December 1799 and settled at Dove Cottage in Grasmere.

Life with William at Dove Cottage provided Dorothy with the material for what is perhaps her finest work—the Grasmere journals. Kept from May 1800 into January 1803, her notebooks address literary, social, and political issues of early-nineteenth-century England by recording daily, domestic details. On 14 May 1800 she sat at home with a "head-ach," wishing for a letter from William, who was away, when a young woman came to beg at the door, destitute because it had cost so much to bury her husband and three children. Times were difficult in England; thrown off the land, people were moving to what would become the squalid slums of industrialized England. Dorothy recorded their passing through Grasmere, which was becoming increasingly gentrified. As a neighbor observed to Dorothy as they strolled around Rydale on 18 May, "in a short time there would be only two ranks of people, the very rich and the very poor, for those who have small estates says he are forced to sell and all the land goes into one hand." By recounting such details Dorothy gave an account of the world and her place in it. Her home with William stood steadfast against the dislocations she observed around her.

Always, there were her brother and her brother's poetry. "I baked pies and bread. William worked hard at the Pedlar and tired himself" (1 February 1802). Although she never wrote so, the fact that she helped make this poetry possible is intrinsic to the journal. It was she who organized the household and was responsible for the cooking and the cleaning. Her attentions to daily necessities allowed her brother the time to concentrate on his work.

Dorothy's writing in the Grasmere journals also provided William with language and images for his poetry. Before he wrote "I wandered lonely as a cloud," Dorothy described a walk on which they discovered "daffodils so beautiful they grew among the mossy stones about and about them, some rested their heads upon these stones as on a pillow for weariness and the rest tossed and reeled and danced and seemed as if they verily laughed with the wind that blew upon them over the lake, they looked so gay ever glancing ever changing" (15 April 1802). William's poem "Beggars" is "taken from a Woman whom I had seen in May—(now nearly 2 years ago) when John and he were at Gallow Hill" (13 March 1802). The Grasmere journals were an important source for William's verse, although sometimes her brother could not "escape from" her "very words and so he could not write the poem" (13 March 1802).

The Grasmere notebooks also reveal Dorothy's feelings about her brother's decision to take Mary Hutchinson as his wife. Although she wanted him to marry, Dorothy seemed filled with anxieties at having to share him with another. Certain image patterns through the journal pick up resonances as the work progresses. One such pattern is a series of references to different kinds of birds. Fixing on a family of swallows that must rebuild the nest that fell from outside her window (25 June 1802), she finds a natural object that figures her particular emotional concerns—her worries about her own domestic scene, her family, her nest at Grasmere and what the presence of William's wife would do to that life. Dorothy did not go to the church to witness the marriage on 4 October 1802. Rather, her journal tells of a private ceremony with William in which "I gave him the wedding ring—with how deep a blessing! I took it from my forefinger where I had worn it

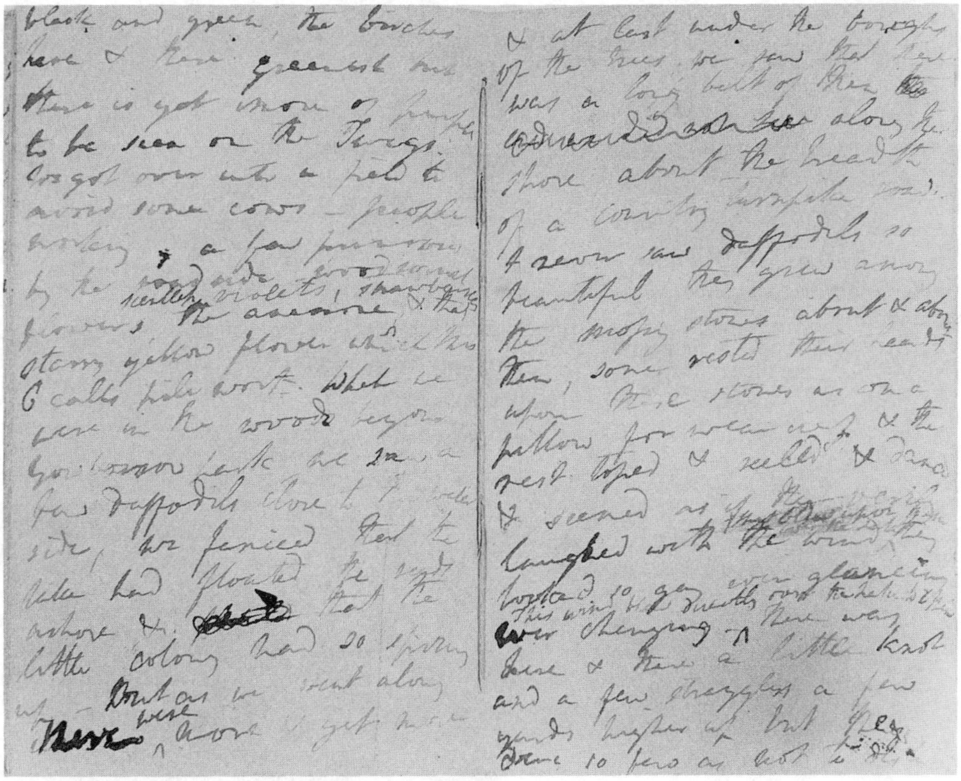

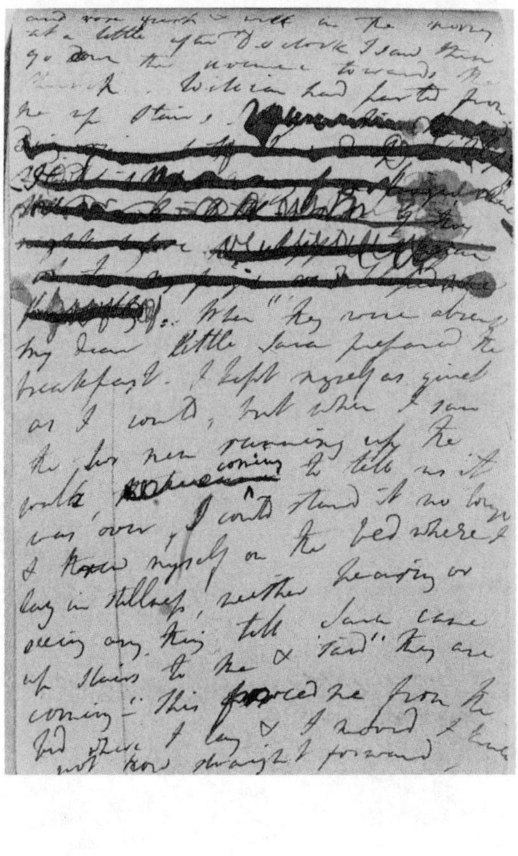

*Journal entry for 15 April 1802 (top), describing daffodils at Ullswater (the source for William Wordsworth's "Daffodils"), and the page with Dorothy Wordsworth's account of her brother's wedding day, 4 October 1802 (bottom), with deletions by an unknown censor (Wordsworth Trust, Dove Cottage, Grasmere)*

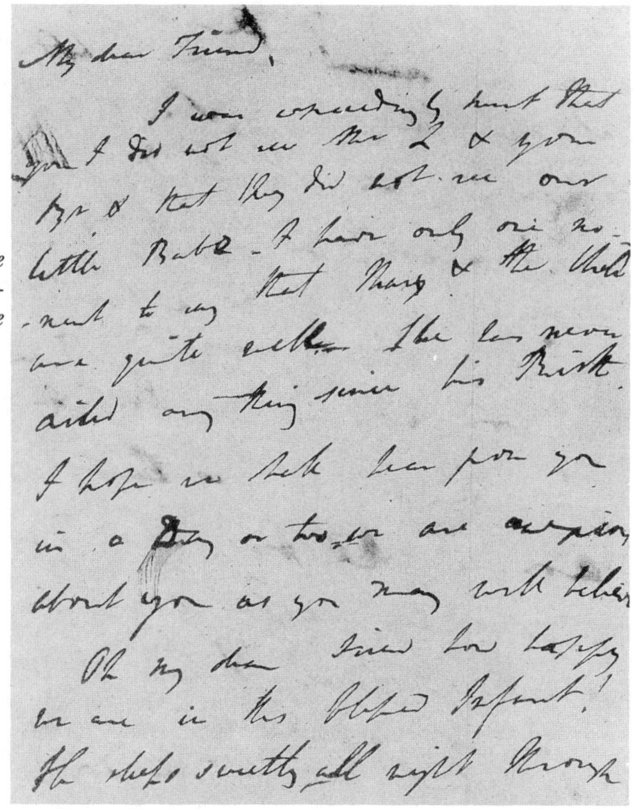

My dear Friend,

I was exceedingly hurt that you did not see the 2 & your eyes & that they did not see our little Babe – I have only one [illegible] to say that Mary & the Child [illegible] were quite well. She has never ailed any thing since his Birth. I hope we shall hear from you in a day or two we are anxious about you as you may well believe. Oh my dear friend how happy we are in this blessed Infant! He sleeps sweetly all night through

Dorothy Wordsworth's 29 June 1803 letter to Catherine Clarkson, describing her nephew John, born eleven days earlier to William and Mary Wordsworth (*from Ernest de Selincourt,* Dorothy Wordsworth: A Biography, *1965*)

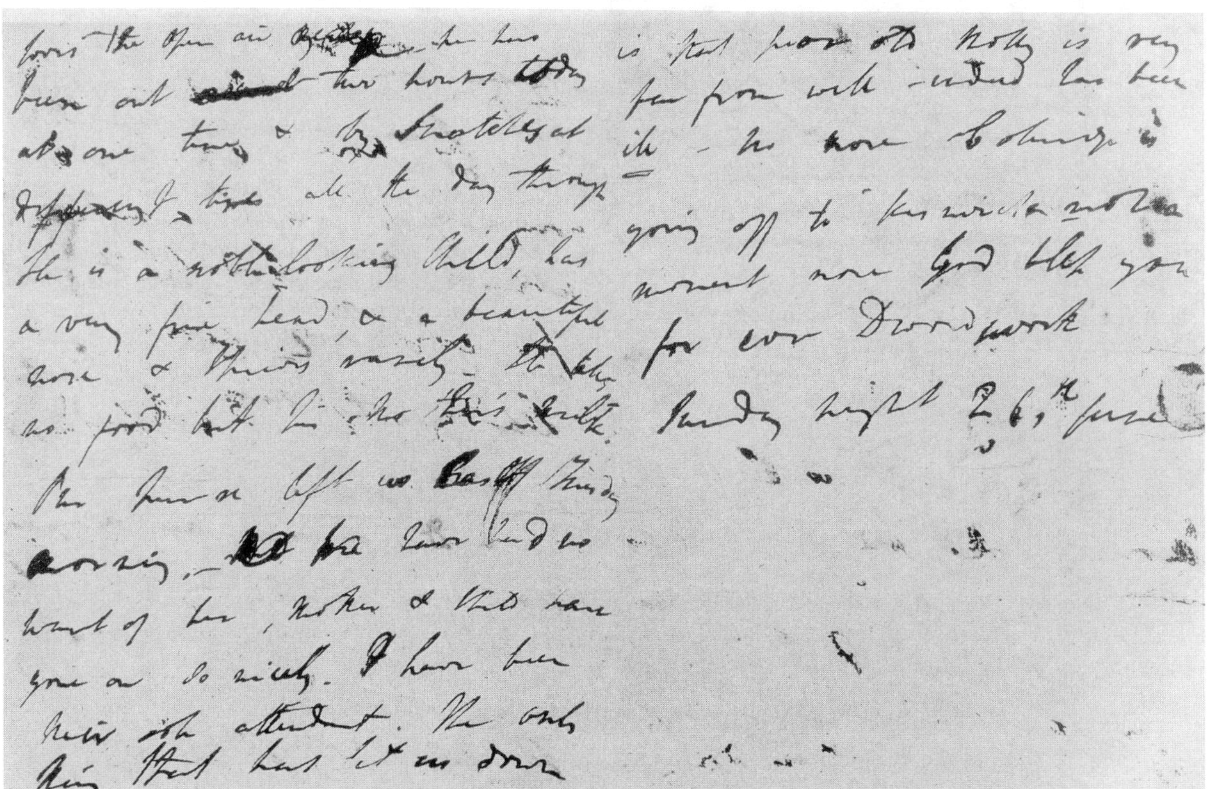

from the open air [illegible] he has been out two hours today at one time & by snatches at different times all the day through – He is a noble-looking Child, has a very fine head, & a beautiful nose & [illegible] [illegible] as good but [illegible] The [illegible] left us [illegible] Thursday morning – we have had no want of her, Mother & Child have gone on so nicely. I have been their sole attendant. The only thing that has let us down is that poor old Molly is very far from well – indeed has been ill – No more Coleridge is going off to Keswick not a moment more God bless you for ever D Wordsworth

Sunday night 26th June

the whole of the night before—he slipped it again onto my finger and blessed me fervently." She kept herself "quiet" at home until "I could stand it no longer and threw myself on the bed where I lay in stillness, neither hearing or seeing anything." This autistic moment on William's wedding day is a direct breakdown of community, a moment of selfhood that suggests the possible bankruptcy of her communal investment. It is interesting to note that the lines containing Dorothy's account of the wedding were covered over with thick, black ink. Somebody evidently found them embarrassing. In fact, some of the Grasmere journals have completely disappeared. Much speculation has occurred as to the contents of the missing pages. Dorothy's chronicling of various personal pains and ailments was bound to be offensive to relatives who controlled her manuscripts after her death. Not only are some manuscripts lost and some passages inked over, but also some passages have been covered with blank pieces of paper.

After the marriage, Dorothy lived with her brother and his wife, helping to care for their children and their house and assisting in William's career. Her journals provided much material for his poems; his home provided her with a domestic center and a life to write about. She adored her sister-in-law, nieces, and nephews. Yet the ambivalence of her emotions is palpable in Thomas De Quincey's "Literary Reminiscences," which record a visit to the Wordsworths in November 1807. He begins describing Mary and then turns to Dorothy.

> Immediately behind her moved a lady, shorter, slighter, and perhaps, in all other respects, as different from her in personal characteristics as could have been wished for the most effective contrast. "Her face was of Egyptian brown"; rarely in a woman of English birth, had I seen a more determinate gypsy tan. Her eyes were not soft, as Mrs. Wordsworth's, nor were they fierce or bold; but they were wild and startling, and hurried in their motion. Her manner was warm and even ardent; her sensibility seemed constitutionally deep; and some subtle fire of impassioned intellect apparently burned within her, which being alternately pushed forward into a conspicuous expression by the irrepressible instincts of her temperament, and then immediately checked, in obedience to the decorum of her sex and age, and her maidenly condition, gave to her whole demeanor, and to her conversation, an air of embarrassment, and even of self-conflict, that was almost distressing to witness.

The "self-conflict" and "impassioned intellect" manifest themselves in Dorothy's work during this period—in her journals, in a short story called "Mary Jones and her Pet-lamb," and in the poems she began to write. Life at Dove Cottage with William, Mary, and their babies could not have been easy; yet it provided Dorothy with a secure existence that held more possibilities than were offered to most women of her age. She was able to travel and to write.

William and Dorothy frequently left Mary and the children to make extended walking tours. In 1803 they went to Scotland with Coleridge for six weeks. Her *Recollections of a Tour Made in Scotland, A.D. 1803* is close to three hundred pages consisting of descriptions of events and considerations of the whole process of travel writing. At least five manuscript copies exist of the *Recollections*. The work was given to several friends, who found it so interesting that they persuaded her to prepare it for publication. She was never able to bring the project to completion, but a posthumous edition appeared in 1874.

Typically, Dorothy sees and describes with more precision than others as she records the landscapes and people they encounter on their progress through Scotland. She focuses on particular details. In contrast to her brother, who often describes to generalize, Dorothy allows what she includes and the arrangements of her descriptions simply to suggest larger connotations.

In the *Recollections* domestic scenes of women and their families occupy a great deal of her attention. Toward some of the women she appears disdainful, associating their poverty with slovenliness and stupidity. To those who strike her as exhibiting intelligence she is more responsive. The women whom she encounters allow her to discuss lives different from hers and provide both an affirmation of her choice to be the woman who can travel and write and an awareness of what she has sacrificed.

Her next record of a trip with William is the November 1805 "Excursion on the Banks of Ullswater," first published in its entirety in 1941. Although much more modest in scope than her record of her 1803 journey, it also juxtaposes, through massed detail, the adventurous life of a nineteenth-century traveler and the counterforce of her domestic scene. She concludes: "Reached home an hour before midnight. Found Mary and the children in bed—no fire—luckily Wm. was warm with walking, and I not cold, having wrapped myself most carefully, and the night

*Dorothy Wordsworth, 1833 (portrait by S. Crosthwaite; Collection of Richard Wordsworth and Mary Henderson)*

being mild. Went to bed immediately after supper."

Dorothy recorded her 1805 walks with William in a notebook that also contains a short story, "Mary Jones and her Pet-lamb," written to "amuse" her brother's children. While the story is a simple tale of a young girl whose father brings her a lamb to care for because its mother has died, it can also be read as a statement of basic childhood anxieties and fantasies, as well as a narrative of the way a young girl grows into a nurturing, caring woman.

The lamb runs away when the little girl is at church, and Mary sets out to find her. The girl becomes lost, and her frantic parents, having searched the night, find her asleep in the heather by the lamb's side. They carry her home where she and the lamb live happily ever after. The child is thus part of a secure family group that cherishes and protects her. She is attached to her mother but undergoes a process of separation, after which she returns with a new maturity that enables her to care for her parents. Both the natural world and parental presences are preserving forces in the story.

Perhaps because of her own early deprivation, perhaps because of her attachment to William's children, Dorothy wrote a great deal about caring for children. Child care is the subject of three early poems that she called "To my Niece Dorothy, a sleepless Baby," "An address to a Child in a high wind," and "The Mother's Return." While she was primarily a writer of prose, Dorothy did write some thirty poems. The three early pieces were published in William's *Poems* (1815) under somewhat different titles. In these poems, the speaker comforts or corrects a child about the ways of nature and grown-ups.

The peaceful days of poetry, children, laundry, baking, nature, and walking were shattered in 1805 by the drowning of Capt. John Wordsworth, Dorothy and William's much-loved brother. During the next years, Dorothy tried to deal with this loss as well as with the family's estrangement from Coleridge, which grew during their extended stay at Coleorton from October 1806 until July 1807. They returned to Grasmere and moved into Allan Bank, a place which rendered Dorothy's housekeeping tasks all the more difficult. The house was in poor shape, and the chimneys smoked, but it was the only available rental in Grasmere.

Dorothy's strong involvement in the life of Grasmere vale is evident in her writing about the deaths of George and Sarah Green. In 1808 the two perished in a snowstorm, leaving eight children, for whom the community organized care. Partly to help raise money, Dorothy composed an account of these events, *A Narrative Concerning George & Sarah Green of the Parish of Grasmere.* At least three authors produced versions of the tale: Dorothy, William, and Thomas De Quincey. Hers was generally considered the most compelling. Though a friend asked her to have it printed, she refused. It was first published in 1936, as *George & Sarah Green.*

Her narrative affirms a mode of social assistance in which groups work together to take care of their own. Dorothy's shaping of the story also relates it to primary concerns of her own emotional life. A mother is taken from her children, and Dorothy raises questions about the nature of this tragedy. Are there possible explanations for such a loss? Can responsibility be assigned? Can it rest with the natural world that generated the storm of death and destruction? Is the fault with the mother who did not stay at home, thus in a sense allowing herself to be trapped by the storm? Within a simple, straightforward account of events, Dorothy examines these issues. She seems especially interested in Jane, the eldest girl, who tries to act as a mother to her siblings. At the same time the story suggests that an eleven-year-old girl and a community can compensate for lost parents, *A Narrative Concerning George & Sarah Green* shows violent disruption and destruction that lead to an irrevocable loss.

Dorothy herself suffered two more such losses with the deaths of her niece Catherine in June 1812 and of her nephew Thomas six months later. Partly to remove themselves from overwhelmingly painful memories of the children, the family moved to Rydal Mount, where Dorothy lived until her death. She continued to record details of daily life, carried on a voluminous correspondence, kept a commonplace book in which she worked on her poems, and wrote journals of her travels.

By this time the family was more prosperous, so Dorothy was able to get away more. In *Journal of a Tour on the Continent 1820* she writes of a trip in July-October 1820 with William and Mary to many of the scenes described in *The Prelude.* It is finally her turn to cross the Alps, and her journal sets her version of such a journey against her brother's memories. She directs her view to experiences and places that she had known previously through his observations. She insists on the primacy of physical detail, unlike William, who at his first sight of Mont Blanc "grieved / To have a soulless image on the eye / Which had usurped upon a living thought / That never more could be." Dorothy's characteristic emphasis is on the reality that stimulates her imagination.

While rejoicing that she can finally make the journey, that she has the strength and energy to be "the first in the ascent," in the *Journal of a Tour on the Continent 1820* Dorothy also conveys the feeling of time lost, that somehow she is thirty years too late. The journal reveals certain contradictions of her life: her adoration of her brother and her resentment of him; her enjoyment at what she is doing and the sense that the world is passing by; her affirmation of her choice of life and her feeling that her potential has been wasted. The most complete edition of the journal was published in 1941.

Her visit to Scotland in 1822 also resulted in a journal that shows an older woman considering age and progress. First published in its entirety in 1941, *Journal of my Second Tour in Scotland* contrasts her 1822 trip with Joanna Hutchinson, a woman who was fragile and often ill, with the trip she had made twenty years earlier in the company of her brother and Coleridge. Although she was the stronger woman responsible for the arrangements of the trip, Dorothy was aware that she was no longer the adventurous person who visited Scotland in 1803. She was restricted by Joanna's condition and her own age. She also had to address the unpleasant situations that arise when two women travel alone. In 1828 she began her *Journal of a Tour in the Isle of Man* by writing that she did not even

*Dorothy Wordsworth in an invalid's chair, 1842 (sketch by J. Harden; Abbot Hall Art Gallery, Kendal)*

want to make the trip. This work, which focuses on death, destruction, and decay, remained unpublished until 1941.

Dorothy was rather more sanguine about visiting her nephew John, a curate at Whitwick, in November 1828. She stayed several months to keep house for him, but in April 1829 she became gravely ill. She recovered, but over the next ten years she suffered subsequent attacks and a general decline in health. Finally, she became fat, immobile, and mentally unstable. She seemed to slip in and out of sanity. Perhaps she had arteriosclerosis; perhaps she began living out some kind of repressed mental life. No longer able or possibly no longer willing to help her brother with his poetry, she fixed on her own verse. Some of her poems compellingly contrast days of youth and health with those of age and pain. The vocabulary of William's nature appears in Dorothy's poems as she engages his myths of time, memory, and the natural world. In "Tintern Abbey" William knows "Nature never did betray / The heart that loved her." The Dorothy who declaimed her poems while sitting in a wheelchair on the Rydal Mount terrace or who copied them over and over in an increasingly shaky hand may have been the object of nature's most grievous betrayal. She outlived her brother for five years, dying in 1855 at the age of eighty-three.

Dorothy Wordsworth refused to consider her writing worthy of attention or publication. Her own contemporaries, however, valued her work for its clarity, for its judiciousness, and for what they could take from it for their own endeavors. As more of her work has been recovered, twentieth-century readers have been able to appreciate it in terms of current modes of literary analysis and theories of women's particular emotional and psychological development. In the age of English Romanticism, which established the validity of taking the self as a literary topic, Dorothy Wordsworth told the story of a woman of genius within and against that great tradition.

**Letters:**

*The Letters of William and Dorothy Wordsworth*, 6 volumes, edited by Alan G. Hill, Mary Moorman, and Chester L. Shaver (Oxford: Clarendon Press, 1967-1982).

**Bibliography:**

Elizabeth Russell Taylor, "Dorothy Wordsworth: Primary and Secondary Sources," *Bulletin of Bibliography*, 40 (December 1983): 252-255.

**Biographies:**

Edmund Lee, *Dorothy Wordsworth: The Story of a Sister's Love* (London: J. Clarke, 1886);

Catherine Macdonald Maclean, *Dorothy Wordsworth: The Early Years* (New York: Viking, 1932);

Ernest de Selincourt, *Dorothy Wordsworth: A Biography* (Oxford: Clarendon Press, 1933);

Robert Gittings and Jo Manton, *Dorothy Wordsworth* (Oxford: Clarendon Press, 1985).

**References:**

Alec Bond, "Reconsidering Dorothy Wordsworth," *Charles Lamb Bulletin*, new series 47-48 ( July and October 1984): 194-207;

Elizabeth Hardwick, "Dorothy Wordsworth," in her *Seduction and Betrayal* (New York: Random House, 1975);

Kurt Heinzelman, "The Cult of Domesticity: Dorothy and William Wordsworth at Grasmere," in *Romanticism and Feminism*, edited by Anne K. Mellor (Bloomington: Indiana University Press, 1988), pp. 52-78;

Margaret Homans, *Bearing the Word: Language and Female Experience in Nineteenth-Century Women's Writing* (Chicago: University of Chicago Press, 1986);

Homans, *Women Writers and Poetic Identity* (Princeton: Princeton University Press, 1980);

Carl H. Ketcham, "Dorothy Wordsworth's Journals, 1824-1835," *Wordsworth Circle*, 9 (Winter 1978): 3-16;

Susan M. Levin, *Dorothy Wordsworth and Romanticism* (New Brunswick: Rutgers University Press, 1987);

Alan Liu, "On the Autobiographical Present: Dorothy Wordsworth's *Grasmere Journals*," *Criticism*, 26 (Spring 1984): 115-137;

James Holt McGavran, "Dorothy Wordsworth's Journals," in *The Private Self*, edited by Shari Benstock (Chapel Hill: University of North Carolina Press, 1988), pp. 230-253;

Susan J. Wolfson, "Individual in Community: Dorothy Wordsworth in Conversation with William," in *Romanticism and Feminism*, edited by Anne K. Mellor (Bloomington: Indiana University Press, 1988), pp. 139-166.

**Papers:**

Most of Dorothy Wordsworth's manuscripts are preserved at the Dove Cottage Library in Grasmere, England. The Cornell University Library holds photocopies of the Dove Cottage material as well as many other original manuscripts. Holographs may also be found at the Pierpont Morgan Library and in the Coleridge Collection of Toronto's Victoria University Library, the Ashley Collection in the British Museum, the Bristol Central Library in England, the Lilly Library at Indiana University, the Brown University Library, and the Swarthmore College Library.

# William Wordsworth

*(7 April 1770 - 23 April 1850)*

Joseph Duemer
*Clarkson University*

See also the Wordsworth entry in *DLB 93: British Romantic Poets, 1789-1832: First Series.*

BOOKS: *An Evening Walk. An Epistle; in verse. Addressed to a young Lady, from the Lakes of the North of England* (London: Printed for J. Johnson, 1793);

*Descriptive Sketches. In Verse. Taken during a Pedestrian Tour in the Italian, Grison, Swiss, and Savoyard Alps* (London: Printed for J. Johnson, 1793);

*Lyrical Ballads, with a few Other Poems*, by Wordsworth and Samuel Taylor Coleridge (Bristol: Printed by Biggs & Cottle for T. N. Longman, London, 1798; London: Printed for J. & A. Arch, 1798; revised and enlarged edition, 2 volumes, London: Printed for T. N. Longman & O. Rees by Biggs & Co., Bristol, 1800; revised again, London: T. N. Longman and O. Rees, 1802; Philadelphia: Printed & sold by James Humphreys, 1802);

*Poems, in two Volumes* (London: Printed for Longman, Hurst, Rees & Orme, 1807);

*Concerning The Relations of Great Britain, Spain, and Portugal to Each Other, and to the Common Enemy, at this Crisis; and Specifically as Affected by the Convention of Cintra* (London: Printed for Longman, Hurst, Rees & Orme, 1809);

*The Excursion, being a portion of The Recluse, a Poem* (London: Printed for Longman, Hurst, Rees, Orme & Brown, 1814; New York: C. & S. Francis, 1849);

*Poems By William Wordsworth, Including Lyrical Ballads, and the Miscellaneous Pieces of the Author*, 2 volumes (London: Printed for Longman, Hurst, Rees, Orme & Brown, 1815);

*The White Doe of Rylstone: or The Fate of the Nortons. A Poem* (London: Printed for Longman, Hurst, Rees, Orme & Brown by James Ballantyne, Edinburgh, 1815);

*Thanksgiving Ode, January 18, 1816. With Other Short Pieces, Chiefly referring to Recent Public Events* (London: Printed by Thomas Davison for Longman, Hurst, Rees, Orme & Brown, 1816);

*A Letter to A Friend of Robert Burns* (London: Printed for Longman, Hurst, Rees, Orme & Brown, 1816);

*Two Addresses to the Freeholders of Westmoreland* (Kendal: Printed by Airey & Bellingham, 1818);

*Peter Bell, A Tale in Verse* (London: Printed by Strahan & Spottiswoode for Longman, Hurst, Rees, Orme & Brown, 1819);

*The Waggoner, A Poem. To Which are added, Sonnets* (London: Printed by Strahan & Spottiswoode for Longman, Hurst, Rees, Orme & Brown, 1819);

*Miscellaneous Poems of William Wordsworth*, 4 volumes (London: Printed for Longman, Hurst, Rees, Orme & Brown, 1820);

*The River Duddon, A series of Sonnets: Vaudracour and Julia: and Other Poems. To which is annexed, A Topographical Description of the Country of the Lakes, in the North of England* (London: Printed for Longman, Hurst, Rees, Orme & Brown, 1820);

*A Description of the Scenery of the Lakes in The North of England. Third Edition, (Now first published separately)* (London: Printed for Longman, Hurst, Rees, Orme & Brown, 1822; revised and enlarged, 1823); revised and enlarged again as *A Guide through the District of the Lakes in The North of England* (Kendal: Published by Hudson & Nicholson / London: Longman & Co., Moxon, and Whitaker & Co., 1835);

*Memorials of a Tour on the Continent, 1820* (London: Printed for Longman, Hurst, Rees, Orme & Brown, 1822);

*Ecclesiastical Sketches* (London: Printed for Longman, Hurst, Rees, Orme & Brown, 1822);

*The Poetical Works of William Wordsworth*, 4 volumes (Boston: Published by Cummings & Hilliard, printed by Hilliard & Metcalf, 1824);

*The Poetical Works of William Wordsworth* (5 volumes, London: Printed for Longman, Rees,

*William Wordsworth, 1806 (portrait by Henry Edridge; Wordsworth Trust, Dove Cottage, Grasmere)*

Orme, Brown & Green, 1827; revised edition, 4 volumes, London: Printed for Longman, Rees, Orme, Brown, Green & Longman, 1832);

*The Poetical Works of William Wordsworth* [pirated edition] (Paris: A. & W. Galignani, 1828);

*Selections from the Poems of William Wordsworth, Esq. Chiefly for the Use of Schools and Young Persons*, edited by Joseph Hine (London: Moxon, 1831);

*Yarrow Revisited, And Other Poems* (London: Printed for Longman, Rees, Orme, Brown, Green & Longman and Edward Moxon, 1835; Boston: J. Monroe & Co, 1835; New York: R. Bartlett & S. Raynor, 1835);

*The Poetical Works of William Wordsworth* (6 volumes, London: Moxon, 1836, 1837; enlarged, 7 volumes, 1842; enlarged again, 8 volumes, 1851);

*The Complete Poetical Works of William Wordsworth*, edited by Henry Reed (Philadelphia: J. Kay, Jun., and Brother / Boston: J. Munroe, 1837);

*The Sonnets of William Wordsworth* (London: Edward Moxon, 1838);

*Poems, Chiefly of Early and Late Years; Including The Borderers, A Tragedy* (London: Edward Moxon, 1842);

*Kendal and Windermere Railway. Two Letters Reprinted from The Morning Post. Revised, with Additions* (Kendal: Printed by Branthwaite & Son, 1845; London: Whittaker & Co. and Edward Moxon / Kendal: R. Branthwaite & Son, 1845);

*The Poems of William Wordsworth, D.C.L., Poet Laureate* (London: Moxon, 1845);

Wordsworth, M. H. Abrams, and Stephen Gill (New York: Norton, 1979);

Wordsworth's birthplace, Cockermouth, Cumberland

*The Poetical Works of William Wordsworth, D.C.L., Poet Laureate*, 6 volumes (London: Moxon, 1849, 1850);

*The Prelude, Or Growth of a Poet's Mind, An Autobiographical Poem* (London: Moxon, 1850; New York: D. Appleton / Philadelphia: Geo. S. Appleton, 1850);

*The Prose Works of William Wordsworth*, edited by Reverend Alexander B. Grosart (London: Moxon, 1876; facsimile, New York: AMS Press, 1967);

*The Recluse* ["Home at Grasmere"] (London & New York: Macmillan, 1888).

**Editions:** *Poems of Wordsworth*, chosen and edited by Matthew Arnold (London & New York: Macmillan, 1879);

*Wordsworth's Literary Criticism*, edited by Nowell C. Smith (London: H. Frowde, 1905);

*The Poetical Works of William Wordsworth*, 5 volumes, edited by Ernest de Selincourt and Helen Darbishire (Oxford: Clarendon Press, 1940-1949; volumes 2 and 3 revised, 1952, 1954);

*A Guide Through the District of the Lakes in the North of England*, introduction by William Merchant (London: Hart-Davis, 1951);

*The Political Tracts of Wordsworth, Coleridge & Shelley*, edited by R. J. White (Cambridge: Cambridge University Press, 1953);

*William Wordsworth: Selected Poems and Prefaces*, edited by Jack Stillinger (Boston: Houghton Mifflin, 1965);

*Literary Criticism of William Wordsworth*, edited by Paul M. Zall (Lincoln: University of Nebraska Press, 1966);

*The Prose Works of William Wordsworth*, 3 volumes, edited by W. J. B. Owen and Jane Worthington Smyser (Oxford: Clarendon Press, 1974);

*The Cornell Wordsworth*, 14 volumes to date, general editor, Stephen M. Parrish (Ithaca, N.Y.: Cornell University Press, 1975- );

*The Prelude 1799, 1805, 1850*, edited by Jonathan

*Hawkshead Grammar School, where Wordsworth was a student from May 1779 until summer 1787*

*William Wordsworth: The Poems*, 2 volumes, edited by John O. Hayden (Harmondsworth: Penguin / New Haven: Yale University Press, 1981);

*The Poetical Works of Wordsworth*, edited by Paul D. Sheats (Boston: Houghton Mifflin, 1982) —revision of the 1904 Cambridge Wordsworth;

*William Wordsworth*, edited by Stephen Gill, Oxford Author Series (London: Oxford University Press, 1984).

OTHER: Joseph Wilkinson, *Select Views in Cumberland, Westmoreland, and Lancashire*, includes an introduction by Wordsworth (London: Published for Wilkinson by R. Ackermann, 1810).

Discussing prose written by poets, Joseph Brodsky has remarked, "the tradition of dividing literature into poetry and prose dates from the beginnings of prose, since it was only in prose that such a distinction could be made." This insight is worth bearing in mind when considering the various prose works of the *poet* William Wordsworth. For Wordsworth poetic composition was a primary mode of expression; prose was secondary. Wordsworth seems to have written prose mostly in order to find a structure for his poetic beliefs and political enthusiasms. Over the course of a prolific poetic career, in fact, Wordsworth produced little prose, though he did compose two works of lasting general interest, one on poetics—"Preface to Lyrical Ballads"—and the other on the landscape of his native region—his tourist handbook, *A Guide through the District of the Lakes*, which retains more than a local interest as geographical background to his poems and biography. Wordsworth is not, of course, remembered as a prose writer but as a poet of spiritual and epistemological speculation, a poet concerned with the human relationship to nature. Yet recently, certain critics, as part of a revisionist critique of older interpretations of Wordsworth's verse, have turned to his political essays for evidence, especially concerning the poet's rejection of his youthful radicalism. Wordsworth's political writings, especially "A Letter to the Bishop of Llandaff," *The*

*Convention of Cintra* (1809), and *Two Addresses to the Freeholders of Westmoreland* (1818), while historically significant, are of primary interest as background for the poetry: for Wordsworth, poetics always determined politics.

William Wordsworth, son of John and Ann Cookson Wordsworth, was born on 7 April 1770 in Cockermouth, Cumberland. The Wordsworth children—Richard, William, Dorothy, John, and Christopher—remained close throughout their lives, and the support Dorothy offered William during his long career has attained legendary status. John Wordsworth, William's father, was legal agent to Sir James Lowther, Baronet of Lowther (later Earl of Lonsdale), a political magnate and property owner. Wordsworth's deep love for the "beauteous forms" of the natural world was established early. The Wordsworth children seem to have lived in a sort of rural paradise along the Derwent River, which ran past the terraced garden below the ample house whose tenancy John Wordsworth had obtained from his employer before his marriage to Ann Cookson. William attended the grammar school near Cockermouth Church and Ann Birkett's school at Penrith, the home of his maternal grandparents. The intense lifelong friendship between Dorothy and William Wordsworth probably began when they, along with Mary Hutchinson, attended school at Penrith. Wordsworth's early childhood beside the Derwent and his schooling at Cockermouth are vividly recalled in various passages of *The Prelude* and in shorter poems such as the sonnet "Address from the Spirit of Cockermouth Castle." His experiences in and around Hawkshead, where William and Richard Wordsworth began attending school in 1779, would also provide the poet with a store of images and sensory experience that he would continue to draw on throughout his poetic career, but especially during the "great decade" of 1798 to 1808. This childhood idyll was not to continue, however. In March of 1778 Ann Wordsworth died while visiting a friend in London. In June 1778 Dorothy was sent to live in Halifax, Yorkshire, with her mother's cousin Elizabeth Threlkeld, and she lived with a succession of relatives thereafter. She did not see William again until 1787.

In December of 1783 John Wordsworth, returning home from a business trip, lost his way and was forced to spend a cold night in the open. Very ill when he reached home, he died 30 December. Though separated from their sister, all the boys eventually attended school together at Hawkshead, staying in the house of Ann Tyson. In 1787, despite poor finances caused by ongoing litigation over Lord Lowther's debt to John Wordsworth's estate, Wordsworth went up to Cambridge as a sizar in St. John's College. As he himself later noted, Wordsworth's undergraduate career was not distinguished by particular brilliance. In the third book of *The Prelude* Wordsworth recorded his reactions to life at Cambridge and his changing attitude toward his studies. During his last summer as an undergraduate, he and his college friend Robert Jones—much influenced by William Coxe's *Sketches of the Natural, Civil, and Political State of Swisserland* (1779)—decided to make a tour of the Alps, departing from Dover on 13 July 1790.

Though Wordsworth, encouraged by his headmaster William Taylor, had been composing verse since his days at Hawkshead Grammar School, his poetic career begins with this first trip to France and Switzerland. During this period he also formed his early political opinions—especially his hatred of tyranny. These opinions would be profoundly transformed over the coming years but never completely abandoned. Wordsworth was intoxicated by the combination of revolutionary fervor he found in France—he and Jones arrived on the first anniversary of the storming of the Bastille—and by the impressive natural beauty of the countryside and mountains. Returning to England in October, Wordsworth was awarded a pass degree from Cambridge in January 1791, spent several months in London, and then traveled to Jones's parents' home in North Wales. During 1791 Wordsworth's interest in both poetry and politics gained in sophistication, as natural sensitivity strengthened his perceptions of the natural and social scenes he encountered. In a letter to William Matthews, a Cambridge friend, he lamented his lack of Italian and weak Spanish—he would have liked to be reading modern poetry.

Wordsworth's passion for democracy, as is clear in his "Letter to the Bishop of Llandaff" (also called "Apology for the French Revolution"), is the result of his two youthful trips to France. In November 1791 Wordsworth returned to France, where he attended sessions of the National Assembly and the Jacobin Club. In December he met and fell in love with Annette Vallon, and at the beginning of 1792 he became the close friend of an intellectual and philosophical army officer, Michel Beaupuy, with whom he discussed politics. Wordsworth had been an instinc-

*Wordsworth in April 1798 (portrait by William Shuter; Cornell Wordsworth Collection, Cornell University Library)*

tive democrat since childhood, and his experiences in revolutionary France strengthened and developed his convictions. His sympathy for ordinary people would remain with Wordsworth even after his revolutionary fervor had been replaced with the "softened feudalism" he endorsed in his *Two Addresses to the Freeholders of Westmoreland* in 1818.

While still in France, Wordsworth began work on the first extended poetic efforts of his maturity, *Descriptive Sketches*, which was published in 1793, after the appearance of a poem written at Cambridge, *An Evening Walk* (1793). Having exhausted his money, he left France in early December 1792 before Annette Vallon gave birth to his child Caroline. Back in England, the young radical cast about for a suitable career. As a fervent democrat, he had serious reservations about "vegetating in a paltry curacy," though he had written to William Matthews from France in May 1792 that he intended to be ordained the following winter or spring. Perhaps this plan was why he was reading sermons early in 1793, when he came across a sermon by Richard Watson, Bishop of Llandaff, on "the Wisdom and Goodness of God" in making both rich and poor, with an appendix denouncing the French Revolution. His democratic sympathies aroused, he spent several weeks in February and March working on a reply.

By this time, his relationship with Annette Vallon had become known to his English relatives, and any further opportunity of entering the Church was foreclosed. In any case Wordsworth had been reading atheist William Godwin's recently published *Political Justice* (1793), and had come powerfully under its sway. "A Letter to the Bishop of Llandaff"—not published until 1876, when it was included in Alexander B. Grosart's edition of Wordsworth's prose—is the youthful poet and democrat's indignant reply to the forces of darkness, repression, and monarchy. Its prose shares something of the revolutionary clarity of Thomas Paine's. Wordsworth, in fact, quoted Paine in his refutation of Bishop Watson's appendix: "If you had looked in the articles of the rights of man, you would have found your efforts superseded. Equality, without which liberty cannot exist, is to be met with in perfection in that state in which no distinctions are admitted but such as have evidently for their object the general good." Just how radical Wordsworth's political beliefs were during this period can be judged from other passages in this "Letter": "At a period big with the fate of the human race, I am sorry that you attach so much importance to the personal sufferings of the late royal martyr.... You wish it to be supposed that you are one of those who are unpersuaded of the guilt of Louis XVI. If you had attended to the history of the French revolution as minutely as its importance demands, so far from stopping to bewail his death, you would rather have regretted that the blind fondness of his people had placed a human being in that monstrous situation...." Remarking upon the stripping of property from the French priesthood, Wordsworth asserted: "The assembly were true to justice and refused to compromise the interests of the Nation by accepting as a satisfaction the insidious offerings of compulsive charity. They enforced their right: they took from the clergy a considerable portion of their wealth, and applied it to the alleviation of the national misery."

"A Letter to the Bishop of Llandaff" is remarkable partly because Wordsworth seems to have begun relinquishing its tenets almost as soon as he had composed them. Though he remained for the time being a strong supporter of the French Revolution, the poetic side of Wordsworth's personality began asserting itself, causing the poet to reexamine, between 1793 and 1796, his adherence to Godwin's rationalistic model of human behavior, upon which Wordsworth's republicanism was largely founded. Whether "A Letter to Bishop the of Llandaff" remained unpublished through caution or circumstance is not clear. As Wordsworth turned his attention to poetry, he developed, through the process of poetic composition, his own theory of human nature, one that had very little to do with Godwin's rationalism. During this period Wordsworth met another radical young man with literary aspirations, Samuel Taylor Coleridge.

In 1794 and 1795 Wordsworth divided his time between London and the Lake Country, at one point telling William Matthews that he would rather be in London because cataracts and mountains were good occasionally but would not do for constant companions. Nevertheless, in September 1795 William and Dorothy Wordsworth settled at Racedown Lodge in Dorset, the first of their several Lake Country dwellings. In *The Prelude* Wordsworth wrote that his sister "Maintained a saving intercourse / With my true self," and "preserved me still / A poet." At Racedown Wordsworth composed *The Borderers*, a tragedy in which he came fully to terms with Godwin's philosophy, finally rejecting it as an insufficiently rich approach to life for a poet. Then Wordsworth for the first time found his mature poetic voice, writing *The Ruined Cottage*, which would be published in 1814 as part of *The Excursion*, itself conceived as one part of a masterwork, *The Recluse*, which was to worry Wordsworth throughout his life, a poem proposed to him by Coleridge and planned as a full statement of the two poets' emerging philosophy of life.

In 1797, to be closer to Coleridge, the Wordsworths moved to Alfoxden House, near the village of Nether Stowey. Because of the odd habits of the household—especially their walking over the countryside at all hours—the local population suspected that the Wordsworths and their visitors were French spies, and a government agent was actually dispatched to keep an eye on them. The years between 1797 and 1800 mark the period of Wordsworth and Coleridge's close collaboration, and also the beginning of Wordsworth's mature poetic career. Wordsworth wrote the poems that would go into the 1798 and 1800 editions of *Lyrical Ballads*—poems such as "Tintern Abbey," "Expostulation and Reply," "The Tables Turned," "Goody Blake and Harry Gill," and "Michael" (written, Wordsworth told James Fox, "to shew that men who did not wear fine clothes can feel deeply"). During 1798 Wordsworth also worked on a piece of prose setting out his evolving ideas on justice and morality. Called the "Essay on Morals" by later editors, it was set aside and never finished. Wordsworth seems to have been attempting to work out and justify his changing political and social ideas—ideas that had begun to develop intuitively during the process of poetic com-

*The cottage in Grasmere where the Wordsworths lived from December 1799 until May 1808 (drawing by Dora Wordsworth, circa 1826, based on a circa 1806 drawing by Amos Green; Wordsworth Trust, Dove Cottage, Grasmere). The house was later named Dove Cottage.*

position. The poet in Wordsworth was beginning to dominate the democrat, and the poet found a political philosophy based on power, violence, and reason anathema. In the "Essay on Morals" Wordsworth concerns himself with the relationship between writing and political justice, and, though he had explicitly rejected Edmund Burke's philosophy in his scorching "Letter to the Bishop of Llandaff," he seems to be developing a Burkean idea of community.

In September 1798 the Wordsworths set off for Germany with Coleridge, returning separately, after some disagreements, in May 1799. In Germany Wordsworth continued to write poems, and when he returned to England he began to prepare a new edition of *Lyrical Ballads.* The second edition—that of 1800—included an extended preface by Wordsworth, explaining his reasons for choosing to write as he had and setting out a personal poetics that has remained influential and controversial to the present day. For Victorian readers such as Matthew Arnold, who tended to venerate Wordsworth, the preface was a fount of wisdom; but the modernists were deeply suspicious of Wordsworth's reliance on *feeling*: poets such as T. S. Eliot and Ezra Pound, while they could accept the strictures on poetic diction, found the underlying theory unacceptable. Subsequent critics have focused on the literary and historical sources of Wordsworth's ideas, demonstrating that, while the poet certainly reinvented English poetic diction, his theories were deeply rooted in the practice of earlier poets, especially John Milton. This preface, Wordsworth's only extended statement of his poetics, has become the source of many of the commonplaces and controversies of poetic theory and criticism. For Wordsworth, poetry, which should be written in "the real language of men," is nevertheless "the spontaneous overflow of feelings: it takes its origin from emotion recollected in tranquility."

The "Preface to Lyrical Ballads" (revised and expanded many times for later editions) is not a systematic poetics, but a partly polemical, partly pedantic, and still problematic statement of Wordsworth's beliefs about poetry and poetic language. The preface in all its versions is highly discursive, the poet "thinking aloud" in an attempt to formulate ideas about poetry based on poems he has already written. It is important to remember when reading the preface that it both chronologically and logically follows the composition of most of the poems. The two central ideas of the preface are the need for reforming poetic diction—which, according to Wordsworth, had become far too artificial—and the role of the poet in society, which Wordsworth saw as having become too marginal. He had also come to the conclusion that the troubles of society were specifically urban in nature. This view finds eloquent expression in Wordsworth's most powerful early poem, "Tintern Abbey." Thinking of the way in which his memories of the Wye River valley had sustained him, Wordsworth wrote:

> Though absent long,
> These forms of beauty have not been to me,
> As is a landscape to a blind man's eye:
> But oft, in lonely rooms, and mid the din
> Of towns and cities, I have owed to them,
> In hours of weariness, sensations sweet [.]

The poem concludes with a meditation on the power of nature to prevail against the false and superficial "dreary intercourse of daily life" that Wordsworth associated with city life, especially literary life in London. In the preface, Wordsworth characterized those forces as acting against the elevation of mind in which the poet specializes, and he identified them with urban life:

> For a multitude of causes unknown to former times are now acting with combined force to blunt the discriminating powers of the mind, and unfitting it for all voluntary exertion to reduce it to a state of almost savage torpor. The most effective of these causes are the great national events which are daily taking place, and the encreasing accumulation of men in cities, where the uniformity of their occupations produces a craving for extraordinary incident which the rapid communication of intelligence hourly gratifies. To this tendency of life and manners the literature of theatrical exhibitions of the country have conformed themsellves. The invaluable works of our elder writers, I had almost said the works of Shakespear and Milton, are driven into neglect by frantic novels, sickly and stupid German Tragedies, and deluges of idle and extravagent stories in verse.

In a letter to Catherine Clarkson years later (4 June 1812), Wordsworth blamed not social institutions but people themselves for the ills of society: "As to public affairs; they are most alarming . . . The [Prince Regent] seems neither respected or beloved; and the lower orders have been for upwards of thirty years accumulating in pestilential masses of ignorant population; the effects now begin to show themselves. . . ." These words are remarkable in light of Wordsworth's early identification with just such "masses of population," though it is evident even in the preface that he had already begun to represent "the lower orders" as fundamentally removed from the affairs of both state and the arts. This belief is extraordinary considering the faith he had expressed in "the people" in "A Letter to the Bishop of Llandaff."

Even before the publication of the first edition in 1798, Wordsworth was certainly aware that the poems in *Lyrical Ballads* were different from the conventional verse of the day, and he knew that fashionable reviewers would probably dismiss them as insufficiently elevated in tone and subject matter. They did, with a vengeance, and a good part of Wordsworth's additions to the preface for the 1802 edition are attempts to answer his critics. But even in the 1800 version of the preface Wordsworth made an explicit connection between a plain poetic diction and a proper relationship to nature and society; that is, he makes the issue of poetic diction a moral one, and his critique of a sonnet by Thomas Gray is an ethical demonstration as well as an example of literary criticism directed by one generation against the preceding one. As Wordsworth revised the preface for later editions, the changes reflected Wordsworth's increasingly conservative and establishment views.

By December 1799 William and Dorothy Wordsworth were living in Dove Cottage, at Town End, Grasmere. In May 1802 Sir James Lowther, Earl of Lonsdale, died, and, though the litigation over his debt to the estate of Wordsworth's father had not been settled, his heir, Sir William Lowther, agreed to pay the Wordsworth children the entire sum. With financial prospects, Wordsworth married Mary Hutchinson on 2 October 1802. The settlement helped to support a growing family and also allowed the Wordsworths to continue their generosity to various friends and men of letters, many of whom came to stay at Dove Cottage, sometimes for months on end. The death of the earl of Lonsdale also marked the beginning of a close economic and political relationship between William Wordsworth and Sir William Lowther (who became earl of Lonsdale in 1807) that would have a significant effect on the poet's political philosophy in the years to come.

*Mary Hutchinson Wordsworth (silhouette by an unknown artist; Wordsworth Trust, Dove Cottage, Grasmere)*

Wordsworth continued to write poetry with energy and passion over the next several years, and while fashionable critics such as Francis Jeffrey continued to snipe, his reputation and finances slowly improved. During these years he composed "The Solitary Reaper," "Resolution and Independence," and "Ode: Intimations of Immortality," perhaps the greatest lyrics of his maturity. In these poems Wordsworth presents a fully developed, yet morally flexible, picture of the relationship between human beings and the natural world. Influenced by Neoplatonism, these poems also prepare the way for Wordsworth's return to conventional religious belief. In 1805 Wordsworth completed a massive revision of the "poem to Coleridge" that would be published, after undergoing periodic adjustment and revision, after the poet's death in 1850. Many critics believe that the "1805 Prelude," as it has come to be called, is Wordsworth's greatest poetic achievement.

In May 1808, his "great decade" behind him, Wordsworth moved with his family to Allan Bank, a larger house in Grasmere. Thomas De Quincy took over Dove Cottage. Evidence of a decisive turn in Wordsworth's social and political views—and, by extension, his poetical views as well—during this period is to be found in *The Convention of Cintra* (1809), an extended political tract concerning the British expedition to Portugal to fight against Napoleon's forces encamped on the Spanish peninsula. In 1793 Wordsworth had written in his "Letter to the Bishop of Llandaff," "In France royalty is no more." In 1808 he might have said "In William Wordsworth, Jacobinism is no more." In place of Wordsworth's early belief in equality, *The Convention of*

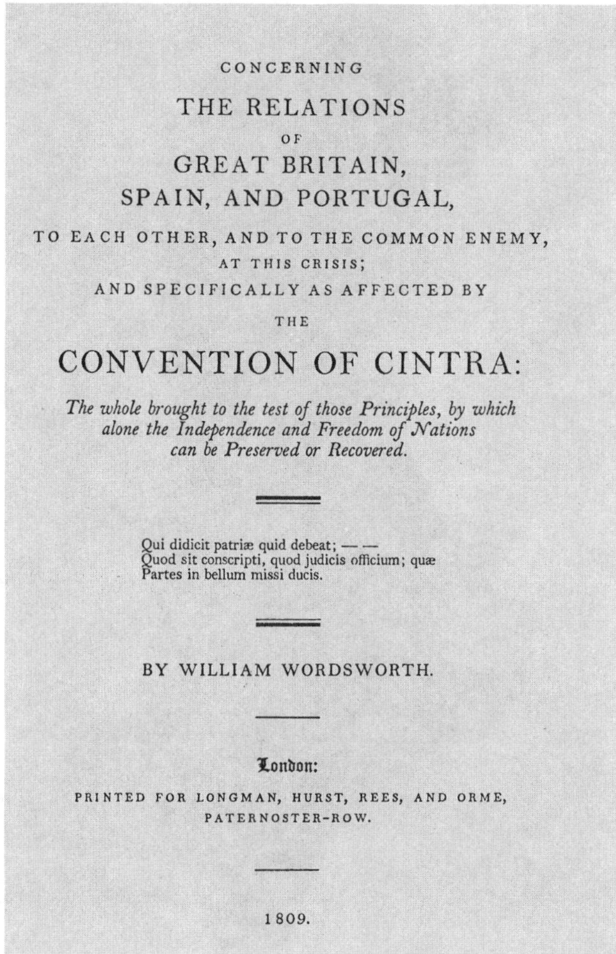

CONCERNING
THE RELATIONS
OF
GREAT BRITAIN,
SPAIN, AND PORTUGAL,
TO EACH OTHER, AND TO THE COMMON ENEMY,
AT THIS CRISIS;
AND SPECIFICALLY AS AFFECTED BY
THE
CONVENTION OF CINTRA:

*The whole brought to the test of those Principles, by which alone the Independence and Freedom of Nations can be Preserved or Recovered.*

Qui didicit patriæ quid debeat; — —
Quod sit conscripti, quod judicis officium; quæ
Partes in bellum missi ducis.

BY WILLIAM WORDSWORTH.

London:
PRINTED FOR LONGMAN, HURST, REES, AND ORME,
PATERNOSTER-ROW.

1809.

*Title page for the book that marks Wordsworth's turn away from the radical politics of his youth*

*Cintra* presents a narrowly patriotic and nationalist view of European politics and a profoundly reactionary political philosophy expressed in tortured rhetoric:

> But, from the moment of the rising of the people of the Pyrenean peninsula, there was a mighty change; we were instantaneously animated; and, from that moment, the contest assumed the dignity, which it is not in the power of any thing but hope to bestow; and, if I may dare to transfer language, prompted by a revelation of the state of being that admits not of decay or change, to the concerns and interests of our transitory planet, from that moment "this corruptible put on incorruption, and this mortal put on immortality."

The rest of Wordsworth's peroration is similarly tangled in syntax and thought. Furthermore, Wordsworth seems to have retreated into a form of rationalism he had rejected in order to become the great poet of 1797-1807:

> Never, indeed, was the fellowship of our sentient nature more intimately felt—never was the irresistible power of justice more gloriously displayed than when the British and Spanish Nations, with an impulse like that of two ancient heros throwing down their weapons and reconciled in the field, . . . embraced each other—to solemnize this conversion of love, not by festivities of peace, but by combating side by side through danger and under affliction in the devotedness of perfect brotherhood. This was a conjunction which excited hope as fervent as it was rational.

Throughout *The Convention of Cintra* Wordsworth seems to have given himself over to rigid abstractions such as Patriotism, Justice, and Power, and it is possible to argue that the diminution of Wordsworth's poetic power dates from this period. If "A Letter to the Bishop of Llandaff " was derivative of Godwin, *The Convention of Cintra* is certainly derivative of Edmund Burke. When Henry Crabb Robinson showed a copy of Wordsworth's pamphlet to Thomas Quayle, Quayle said that Wordsworth's style resembled the worst of Burke's. The radical republican of 1793 has by this point adopted not only Burke's style but the essence of his thought as well. The transformation of his ideas seems to have cost Wordsworth his clarity of language, so apparent in "A Letter to the Bishop of Llandaff," and even the "Preface to Lyrical Ballads," which, though structurally complicated, is never obscure in the way of *The Convention of Cintra*.

In spite of his claim that he wrote "so few letters, and employ my pen so little in any way," Wordsworth was a prolific correspondent throughout his life, and his letters provide a useful prose fabric upon which to trace the embroidery of the poems. One brief sequence of letters from 1811 and 1812 illustrates Wordsworth's range of tone and subject in this literary subgenre. Writing on 28 March 1811 to C. W. Pasley, who had sent Wordsworth a copy of his *Military Policy and Institutions of the British Empire* (1810), Wordsworth said how much he enjoyed the book, which he had "expected with great impatience," and remarked that having read it carefully, he considered himself "in a high degree instructed" by the volume. Then the theorist of *The Convention of Cintra* began a critique of Pasley's book, which according to Wordsworth is overly pessimistic about Britain's chances for defeating France and overly belligerent in suggesting that the English must launch an all-out war of conquest, beginning in Sicily, on the European continent, planting the seeds of justice wherever the armies are successful. Wordsworth, whose life had taught him to be economically astute, saw the folly of such an expedition, and told Pasley so, in exquisite detail. In fact, one is able to gain a clearer appreciation of Wordsworth's later political thinking from this and other letters of the period than from *The Convention of Cintra* with its overblown rhetoric. The letter to Pasley has the considerable virtue, for the sake of Wordsworth's prose, that it is rooted in the specifics of replying to an actual text. The letter to Pasley still, however, exhibits the poet's lamentable willingness to subscribe to the clichés of nationalism: "Was there ever an instance, since the world began, of the peaceful arts thriving under a despotism so oppressive as that of France is and must continue to be, and among a people so unsettled, so depraved, and so undisciplined in civil arts and habits as the French nation must now be?" In his youth, Wordsworth, while an enthusiast of the French Revolution, had the analytic ability of a historian; by 1811 he had only the empty categories of a pedant. His idealism, adopted for the purposes of poetic composition, led him to sweeping political conclusions unfounded in reality: "The *mind* of the Country [England] is so far before that of France, and that *that* mind has empowered the *hands* of the country to raise so much national wealth, that France must condescend to accept from us what she will be unable herself to produce" [emphasis in original]. Wordsworth argued that Pasley's scheme is unnecessary because the *mind* and *hands* of England would produce the economic defeat of the French. There is, as has been noted, considerable economic acumen in this letter, though the commonsense insights are continually undercut by the rhetoric in which they are couched.

Another side of Wordsworth is revealed in a 6 February 1812 letter to the earl of Lonsdale: "I regret that it is not in my power to wait upon you personally; as the experience which I have had of your Lordship's gracious manners would have rendered quite pleasing to me the delicate task, which, through the means of a Letter, I am undertaking not without some reluctance." Wordsworth's self-consciousness clings to every word, as well it might—he was asking that Lord Lonsdale consider appointing him to "any Office [that] should be at your Lordship's disposal (the duties of which would not call so largely upon my exertions as to prevent me from giving a considerable portion of my time to study). . . ." Though he had to wait more than a year, in 1813 Wordsworth was appointed, under Lonsdale's patronage, to the post of Distributor of Stamps for Westmorland and Penrith.

On Wednesday evening, 2 December 1812, William Wordsworth wrote to his friend Robert Southey about the death of Thomas Wordsworth, the poet's six-year-old son, the previous day. The simplicity and directness of this letter communicate Wordsworth's sorrow with great power and integrity:

> Symptoms of the measles appeared upon my Son Thomas last Thursday; he was most favorable held till tuesday, between ten and eleven at that hour was particularly lightsome and comfortable; without any assignable cause a sudden change took place, an inflammation had commenced on the lungs which it was impossible to

*William and Mary Wordsworth, 1839 (portrait by Margaret Gillies; Wordsworth Trust, Dove Cottage, Grasmere)*

> check and the sweet Innocent yielded up his soul to God before six in the evening. He did not appear to suffer much in body, but I fear something in mind as he was of an age to have thought much upon death a subject to which his mind was daily led by the grave of his Sister.

Thomas was the second child of William and Mary Wordsworth to die in childhood. Catherine had died the previous June, a few months before her fourth birthday.

In late 1812 Lord Lonsdale proposed that he provide one hundred pounds a year for the support of Wordsworth and his family until a salaried position became available. Wordsworth was at first somewhat reluctant to accept the patronage, but he accepted, and on 8 January 1813 he wrote to acknowledge receipt of payment. He was relieved when the post of Distributor of Stamps was offered to him a few months later. With this assurance of economic security, the Wordsworths moved to Rydal Mount, the poet's final home, in May 1813. Lonsdale's gift and patronage marked a deepening of the relations between the aristocratic earl and the formerly radical republican and supporter of revolution in France and democracy in England. Politically, Wordsworth had completely transformed himself; poetically, he repeated earlier formulas and began rearranging his poems in a seemingly infinite sequence of thematically organized volumes.

Other than letters and miscellaneous notes, Wordsworth's political prose writings conclude with *Two Addresses to the Freeholders of Westmoreland* (1818). These have been described by one critic as "nearly unreadable," but they are crucial to an understanding of Wordsworth's entanglement in local and national politics. As Distributor of Stamps, Wordsworth should not have engaged in electioneering, but his two addresses back the local nobility in no uncertain terms. By this time, Wordsworth had come to believe that the only way to preserve the virtues celebrated in "Michael" and other early poems was to maintain the traditional social orders of English society. Fully the Tory mouthpiece, Wordsworth argued that the Whigs had put too much faith in human nature, as they (and he) did at the commencement of the French Revolution. The *Two Addresses* praise Edmund Burke for just those values Wordsworth had earlier excoriated. By this time Wordsworth had fully incorporated Burke's system of beliefs into his own, and several passages of the 1850 *Prelude* are redolent with Burkean sentimental and political philosophy.

Wordsworth's last major work in prose represents a return to his earliest interest in the land and scenery of the English Lake District. In 1810 artist Joseph Wilkinson published *Select Views in Cumberland, Westmoreland, and Lancashire*, with an introduction by Wordsworth. In 1822 Wordsworth returned to his introduction, expanding it into a book most commonly known as *A Guide through the District of the Lakes*, which continues to be republished in a variety of editions. Wordsworth's love of his native region is evident in the *Guide*, which remains useful for the reader of Wordsworth's poetry as well as for the tourist of the Lake District.

Samuel Taylor Coleridge died in 1834, and, though the men had grown apart, Wordsworth continued to pay particular attention to Coleridge's erratic first son, Hartley, a minor poet and biographer who haunted the Lake District on "pot house wanderings," to use Wordsworth's memorable phrase. Hartley, the child addressed in Coleridge's "Frost at Midnight" and Wordsworth's "To H.C. Six Years Old," as well as the basis for the child represented in the Immortality Ode, was a feckless figure beloved by the local farmers, and Wordsworth took a special interest in seeing to his welfare. Hartley died in 1849, only a few months before Wordsworth, who instructed that his friend's son be buried in the Wordsworth plot in Grasmere Churchyard. "He would have wished it," said Wordsworth.

In 1843 Wordsworth was named poet laureate of England, though by this time he had for the most part quit composing verse. He revised and rearranged his poems, published various editions, and entertained literary guests and friends. When he died in 1850 he had for some years been venerated as a sage, his most ardent detractors glossing over the radical origins of his poetics and politics. Wordsworth's prose, while not extensive and often difficult, reveals the poet's historical context. A careful reading of Wordsworth's prose will lead, perhaps, to a clearer understanding of the path he traveled from the eighteenth century to the Victorian age, and modern readers will recognize the origins of their own literary and political culture.

**Letters:**

*The Early Letters of William and Dorothy Wordsworth, 1787-1805*, 1 volume, edited by Ernest de Selincourt (Oxford: Clarendon Press, 1935); *The Letters of William and Dorothy Wordsworth: The Middle Years*, 2 volumes, edited by de Selincourt (Oxford: Clarendon Press, 1937); *The Letters of William and Dorothy Wordsworth: The Later Years*, edited by de Selincourt (Oxford: Clarendon Press, 1939); revised and enlarged by Chester L. Shaver, Mary Moorman, and Alan G. Hill as *The Letters of William and Dorothy Wordsworth*, 5 volumes (Oxford: Clarendon Press, 1967-1988);

*The Love Letters of William and Mary Wordsworth*, edited by Beth Darlington (Ithaca, N.Y.: Cornell University Press, 1981);

*The Letters of William Wordsworth: A New Selection*, edited by Hill (New York: Oxford University Press, 1984).

**Bibliographies:**

Thomas J. Wise, *A Bibliography of the Writings in Prose and Verse of William Wordsworth* (London: Printed for private circulation by Richard Clay & Son, 1916; reprinted, Folkestone & London: Dawsons of Pall Mall, 1971);

Wise, *Two Lake Poets: A Catalogue of Printed Books, Manuscripts, and Autograph Letters by William Wordsworth and Samuel Taylor Coleridge* (London: Printed for private circulation, 1927; reprinted, London: Dawsons of Pall Mall, 1965);

James V. Logan, *Wordsworthian Criticism: A Guide and Bibliography* (Columbus: Ohio State University, 1947; reprinted, New York: Gordian, 1974);

Elton F. Henley and David H. Stam, *Wordsworthian Criticism 1945-64: An Annotated Bibliography* (New York: New York Public Library, 1965);

Mark L. Reed, *Wordsworth: The Chronology of the Early Years, 1770-1779* (Cambridge: Harvard University Press, 1967);

Stam, *Wordsworthian Criticism 1964-73: An Annotated Bibliography* (New York: New York Public Library, 1974);

Reed, *Wordsworth: The Chronology of the Middle Years, 1800-1815* (Cambridge: Harvard University Press, 1975);

N. S. Bauer, *William Wordsworth: A Reference Guide to British Criticism, 1793-1899* (London: Hall, 1978);

Karl Kroeber, "William Wordsworth," in *The English Romantic Poets: A Review of Research and Cricitism*, fourth edition, edited by Frank Jordan (New York: Modern Language Association, 1985);

Mark Jones and Kroeber, *Wordsworth Scholarship and Criticism, 1973-84, An Annotated Bibliography, with Selected Criticism, 1809-1972* (New York: Garland, 1985);

Jones, *Wordsworth Scholarship and Criticism, 1973-84, An Annotated Bibliography, with Selected Criticism, 1809-1972* (New York: Garland, 1985);

Jones, "Wordsworth Scholarship and Criticism, 1986 Update," *Wordsworth Circle*, 19 (Autumn 1988): 220-230.

**Biographies:**

Christopher Wordsworth, *Memoirs of William Wordsworth*, 2 volumes (London: Moxon, 1851);

Emile Legouis, *The Early Life of William Wordsworth, 1770-1798*, translated by J. W. Matthews (London: Dent, 1897);

George McLean Harper, *William Wordsworth, His Life, Works, and Influence*, 2 volumes (London: Murray, 1916);

Legouis, *William Wordsworth and Annette Vallon* (London & Toronto: Dent, 1922);

Edith Batho, *The Later Wordsworth* (Cambridge: Cambridge University Press, 1933);

Frederika Beatty, *William Wordsworth of Rydal Mount* (London: J. M. Dent, 1939);

Mary Moorman, *William Wordsworth: A Biography*, 2 volumes (Oxford: Clarendon Press, 1957, 1965; New York: Oxford University Press, 1957, 1965);

Ben Ross Schneider, Jr., *Wordsworth's Cambridge Education* (Cambridge: Cambridge University Press, 1957);

T. W. Thompson, *Wordsworth's Hawkshead*, edited by Robert Woof (New York: Oxford University Press, 1970);

Hunter Davies, *William Wordsworth: A Biography* (London: Weidenfeld & Nicolson, 1980; New York: Atheneum, 1980);

F. B. Pinion, *A Wordsworth Chronology* (Boston: G. K. Hall, 1988);

Stephen Gill, *William Wordsworth: A Life* (Oxford: Clarendon Press, 1989).

**References:**

M. H. Abrams, ed., *Wordsworth: A Collection of Critical Essays* (Englewood Cliffs, N.J.: Prentice-Hall, 1972);

F. W. Bateson, *Wordsworth: A Reinterpretation* (London: Longmans, Green, 1956);

Alan J. Bewell, *Wordsworth and the Enlightenment: Nature, Man, and Society in the Experimental Poetry* (New Haven: Yale University Press, 1989);

Don H. Bialostosky, *Making Tales: The Poetics of Wordsworth's Narrative Experiments* (Chicago: University of Chicago Press, 1984);

Frances Blanchard, *Portraits of Wordsworth* (London: Allen, 1959);

James K. Chandler, *Wordsworth's Second Nature: A Study of the Poetry and Politics* (Chicago: University of Chicago Press, 1984);

John Danby, *The Simple Wordsworth: Studies in the Poems 1797-1807* (London: Routledge & Kegan Paul, 1960);

Frances Ferguson, *Wordsworth: Language as Counter-Spirit* (New Haven: Yale University Press, 1977);

David Ferry, *The Limits of Mortality: An Essay on Wordsworth's Major Poems* (Middletown, Conn.: Wesleyan University Press, 1959);

William H. Galperin, *Revision and Authority in Wordsworth: The Interpretation of a Career* (Philadelphia: University of Pennsylvania Press, 1989);

Frederick Garber, *Wordsworth and the Poetry of Encounter* (Urbana: University of Illinois Press, 1971);

Spencer Hall, ed., with Jonathan Ramsey, *Approaches to Teaching Wordsworth's Poetry* (New York: Modern Language Association, 1986);

Geoffrey Hartman, *Wordsworth's Poetry: 1787-1814* (New Haven: Yale University Press, 1964);

Raymond Dexter Havens, *The Mind of A Poet: A Study of Wordsworth's Thought* (Baltimore: Johns Hopkins University Press, 1941);

Mary Jacobus, *Tradition and Experiment in Wordsworth's Lyrical Ballads (1798)* (Oxford: Clarendon Press, 1978);
Lee M. Johnson, *Wordsworth and the Sonnet*, Anglistica, 19 (Copenhagen: Rosenkilde & Bagger, 1973);
Kenneth R. Johnston, *Wordsworth and "The Recluse"* (New Haven: Yale University Press, 1984);
Johnston and Gene W. Ruoff, eds., *The Age of William Wordsworth* (New Brunswick, N.J.: Rutgers University Press, 1987);
John Jones, *The Egotistical Sublime: A Study of Wordsworth's Imagination* (London: Chatto & Windus, 1954);
John Jordan, *Why the Lyrical Ballads? The Background, Writing, and Character of Wordsworth's 1798 Lyrical Ballads* (Berkeley: University of California Press, 1974);
Thèresa M. Kelley, *Wordsworth's Revisionary Aesthetics* (Cambridge: Cambridge University Press, 1988);
Karl Kroeber, *Romantic Landscape Vision: Constable and Wordsworth* (Madison: University of Wisconsin Press, 1975);
Marjorie Levinson, *Wordsworth's Great Period Poems* (Cambridge: Cambridge University Press, 1986);
Herbert Lindenberger, *On Wordsworth's Prelude* (Princeton: Princeton University Press, 1963);
Alan Liu, *Wordsworth: The Sense of History* (Palo Alto, Cal.: Stanford University Press, 1989);
Peter J. Manning, "Wordsworth at St. Bees: Scandals, Sisterhoods, and Wordsworth's Later Poetry," *ELH*, 52 (Spring 1985): 33-58;
David McCracken, *Wordsworth and the Lake District: A Guide to the Poems and Their Places* (New York: Oxford University Press, 1984);
Richard Onorato, *The Character of the Poet: Wordsworth in The Prelude* (Princeton: Princeton University Press, 1971);
W. J. B. Owen, "Cost, Sales, and Profits of Longman's Editions of Wordsworth," *Library*, 12 (June 1957): 93-107;
Judith W. Page, " 'The Weight of Too Much Liberty': Genre and Gender in Wordsworth's Calais Sonnets," *Criticism*, 30 (Spring 1988): 189-203;
Reeve Parker, "Reading Wordsworth's Power: Narrative and Usurpation in *The Borderers*," *ELH*, 54 (Summer 1987): 299-331;
Stephen M. Parrish, *The Art of the Lyrical Ballads* (Cambridge: Harvard University Press, 1973);
Markham Peacock, Jr., ed., *The Critical Opinions of William Wordsworth* (Baltimore: Johns Hopkins University Press, 1950);
David Perkins, *Wordsworth and the Poetry of Sincerity* (Cambridge: Harvard University Press, 1964);
Donald H. Reiman, "The Poetry of Familiarity: Wordsworth, Dorothy, and Mary Hutchinson," in *The Evidence of Imagination*, edited by Reiman and others (New York: New York University Press, 1978), pp. 142-177;
Reiman, ed., *The Romantics Reviewed*, part A, volumes 1 and 2 (New York: Garland, 1972);
Nicholas Roe, *Wordsworth and Coleridge: The Radical Years* (Oxford: Oxford University Press, 1988);
Roger Sales, *English Literature in History 1780-1830—Pastoral and Politics* (New York: St. Martin's Press, 1983);
Paul D. Sheats, *The Making of Wordsworth's Poetry 1785-1798* (Cambridge: Harvard University Press, 1973);
David Simpson, *Wordsworth's Historical Imagination* (New York: Methuen, 1987);
Gayatri Chakravorty Spivak, "Sex and History in *The Prelude* (1805): Books Nine to Thirteen," *Texas Studies in Literature and Language*, 23 (Fall 1981): 324-360;
Edwin Stein, *Wordsworth's Art of Allusion* (University Park: Pennsylvania State University Press, 1988);
Susan J. Wolfson, *The Questioning Presence: Wordsworth, Keats, and the Interrogative Mode in Romantic Poetry* (Ithaca, N.Y.: Cornell University Press, 1986);
Carl Woodring, *Wordsworth* (Boston: Houghton Mifflin, 1965);
Jonathan Wordsworth, *The Music of Humanity* (London: Oxford University Press, 1969);
Wordsworth, ed., *Bicentenary Wordsworth Studies in Honor of John Alban Finch* (Ithaca, N.Y.: Cornell University Press, 1970).

**Papers:**

The main depository for manuscript and papers of Wordsworth and his close circle is the Wordsworth Library, Grasmere. In the United States the libraries at Cornell and Indiana universities have strong Wordsworth collections.

# Books for Further Reading

Abrams, M. H. *The Mirror and the Lamp; Romantic Theory and the Critical Tradition.* New York: Oxford University Press, 1953.

Abrams. *Natural Supernaturalism: Tradition and Revolution in Romantic Literature.* New York: Norton, 1971.

Abrams, ed. *English Romantic Poets: Modern Essays in Criticism.* New York: Oxford University Press, 1960; revised, 1975.

Aers, David, Jonathan Cook, and David Punter. *Romanticism and Ideology: Studies in English Writing 1765-1830.* London & Boston: Routledge & Kegan Paul, 1981.

Ball, Patricia M. *The Central Self: A Study in Romantic and Victorian Imagination.* London: Athlone Press, 1968.

Beaty, Frederick L. *Light from Heaven: Love in British Romantic Literature.* De Kalb: Northern Illinois University Press, 1971.

Bloom, Harold. *The Visionary Company: A Reading of English Romantic Poetry,* revised and enlarged edition. Ithaca, N.Y.: Cornell University Press, 1971.

Bloom, ed. *Romanticism and Consciousness: Essays in Criticism.* New York: Norton, 1970.

Bostetter, Edward E. *The Romantic Ventriloquists: Wordsworth, Coleridge, Keats, Shelley, Byron,* revised edition. Seattle: University of Washington Press, 1963.

Bowra, C. M. *The Romantic Imagination.* Cambridge, Mass.: Harvard University Press, 1950.

Brisman, Leslie. *Romantic Origins.* Ithaca, N.Y.: Cornell University Press, 1978.

Butler, Marilyn. *Romantics, Rebels, and Reactionaries: English Literature and its Background 1760-1830.* Oxford & New York: Oxford University Press, 1981.

Clubbe, John, and Ernest J. Lovell, Jr. *English Romanticism: The Grounds of Belief.* De Kalb: Northern Illinois University Press, 1983.

Cooper, Andrew M. *Doubt and Identity in Romantic Poetry.* New Haven: Yale University Press, 1988.

Curran, Stuart. *Poetic Form and British Romanticism.* New York & Oxford: Oxford University Press, 1986.

Eaves, Morris, and Michael Fischer, eds. *Romanticism and Contemporary Criticism.* Ithaca, N.Y.: Cornell University Press, 1986.

Ellison, Julie K. *Delicate Subjects: Romanticism, Gender, and the Ethics of Understanding.* Ithaca, N.Y.: Cornell University Press, 1990.

Enscoe, Gerald E. *Eros and the Romantics: Sexual Love as a Theme in Coleridge, Shelley and Keats.* The Hague: Mouton, 1967.

Ford, Boris, ed. *From Blake to Byron, New Pelican Guide to English Literature*, volume 5. Harmondsworth, U.K.: Penguin, 1962.

Frye, Northrop. *A Study of English Romanticism*. New York: Random House, 1968.

Frye, ed. *Romanticism Reconsidered: Selected Papers from the English Institute*. New York: Columbia University Press, 1963.

Gleckner, Robert F., and Gerald E. Enscoe. *Romanticism: Points of View*, second edition. Englewood Cliffs, N.J.: Prentice-Hall, 1970.

Harris, R. W. *Romanticism and the Social Order 1780-1830*. London: Blandford, 1969.

Hoeveler, Diane Long. *Romantic Androgyny: The Women Within*. University Park: Pennsylvania State University Press, 1990.

Jack, Ian. *English Literature 1815-1832*. Oxford: Clarendon Press, 1963.

Jackson, J. R. de J. *Poetry of the Romantic Period*. London & Boston: Routledge & Kegan Paul, 1980.

Jordon, Frank, ed. *The English Romantic Poets: A Review of Research and Criticism*, fourth edition. New York: Modern Language Association, 1985.

Kermode, Frank. *Romantic Image*. London: Routledge & Kegan Paul, 1957.

Klancher, Jon P. *The Making of English Reading Audiences, 1790-1832*. Madison: University of Wisconsin Press, 1987.

Knight, G. Wilson. *The Starlit Dome: Studies in the Poetry of Vision*. London & New York: Oxford University Press, 1941.

Kroeber, Karl. *Romantic Narrative Art*. Madison: University of Wisconsin Press, 1960.

Levinson, Marjorie. *The Romantic Fragment Poem: A Critique of a Form*. Chapel Hill: University of North Carolina Press, 1986.

Levinson and others. *Rethinking Historicism: Critical Readings in Romantic History*. Oxford & New York: Blackwell, 1989.

McFarland, Thomas. *Romantic Cruxes: The English Essayists and the Spirit of the Age*. Oxford & New York: Oxford University Press, 1987.

McFarland. *Romanticism and the Forms of Ruin: Wordsworth, Coleridge, and Modalities of Fragmentation*. Princeton: Princeton University Press, 1981.

McGann, Jerome J. *The Romantic Ideology: A Critical Investigation*. Chicago & London: University of Chicago Press, 1983.

Mellor, Anne K. *English Romantic Irony*. Cambridge, Mass.: Harvard University Press, 1980.

Mellor. *Romanticism and Feminism*. Bloomington: Indiana University Press, 1988.

Metzger, Lore. *One Foot in Eden: Modes of Pastoral in Romantic Poetry*. Chapel Hill: University of North Carolina Press, 1986.

Morse, David. *Romanticism: A Structural Analysis*. Totowa, N.J.: Barnes & Noble, 1982.

Porter, Roy, and Mikulas Teich, eds. *Romanticism in National Context*. Cambridge & New York: Cambridge University Press, 1988.

Prickett, Stephen, ed. *The Romantics*. New York: Holmes & Meier, 1981.

Redpath, Theodore, *The Young Romantics and Critical Opinion, 1807-1824: Poetry of Byron, Shelley, and Keats as Seen by Their Contemporary Critics*. London: Harrap, 1973.

Reed, Arden, ed. *Romanticism and Language*. Ithaca, N.Y.: Cornell University Press, 1984.

Reiman, Donald H. *English Romantic Poetry, 1800-1835: A Guide to Information Sources*. Detroit: Gale Research, 1979.

Reiman. *Intervals of Inspiration: The Skeptical Tradition and the Psychology of Romanticism*. Greenwood, Fla.: Penkevill, 1988.

Reiman. *Romantic Texts and Contexts*. Columbia: University of Missouri Press, 1987.

Reiman, ed. *The Romantics Reviewed: Contemporary Reviews of British Romantic Writers*, 9 volumes. New York & London: Garland, 1972.

Renwick, W. L. *English Literature 1789-1815*. Oxford: Clarendon Press, 1963.

Richardson, Alan. *A Mental Theater: Poetic Drama and Consciousness in the Romantic Age*. University Park: Pennsylvania State University Press, 1987.

Rodway, Allen. *The Romantic Conflict*. London: Chatto & Windus, 1963.

Simpson, David. *Irony and Authority in Romantic Poetry*. London: Macmillan, 1979.

Siskin, Clifford. *The Historicity of Romantic Discourse*. New York: Oxford University Press, 1988.

Sullivan, Alvin, ed. *British Literary Magazines*, 4 volumes. Westport, Conn.: Greenwood Press, 1983-1986.

Swingle, L. J. *The Obstinate Questionings of English Romanticism*. Baton Rouge: Louisiana State University Press, 1987.

Thorburn, David, and Geoffrey Hartman, eds. *Romanticism: Vistas, Instances, Continuities*. Ithaca, N.Y., & London: Cornell University Press, 1973.

Thorlby, Anthony, ed. *The Romantic Movement*. London: Longmans, 1966.

Watson, J. R. *English Poetry of the Romantic Period 1789-1830*. London & New York: Longmans, 1985.

Wilkie, Brian. *Romantic Poets and Epic Tradition*. Madison: University of Wisconsin Press, 1965.

Williams, Raymond. *Culture and Society, 1780-1950*. New York: Columbia University Press, 1958.

Woodring, Carl. *Politics in English Romantic Poetry*. Cambridge, Mass.: Harvard University Press, 1970.

Wordsworth, Jonathan, Michael C. Jaye, and Robert Woof, with the assistance of Peter Funnell. *William Wordsworth and the Age of English Romanticism*. New Brunswick & London: Rutgers University Press / Wordsworth Trust, 1987.

# Contributors


| | |
|---|---|
| Ernest Bernhardt-Kabisch | *Indiana University* |
| Martin A. Cavanaugh | *Washington University* |
| Gregory Claeys | *Washington University* |
| Natalie Bell Cole | *Oakland University* |
| Thomas L. Cooksey | *Armstrong State College* |
| Winifred F. Courtney | *Greenwood, S.C.* |
| Joseph Duemer | *Clarkson University* |
| Keith Hanley | *University of Lancaster* |
| Leslie Haynsworth | *Columbia, South Carolina* |
| John R. Holmes | *Franciscan University of Steubenville* |
| Ronald J. Hunt | *Ohio University* |
| Nicholas R. Jones | *Oberlin College* |
| Michael Laine | *Victoria College, University of Toronto* |
| Susan M. Levin | *Stevens Institute of Technology* |
| Richard D. McGhee | *Arkansas State University* |
| James C. McKusick | *University of Maryland, Baltimore County* |
| James Sambrook | *University of Southampton* |
| Elizabeth Thornton | *Columbia, S.C.* |
| Arthur E. Walzer | *University of Minnesota* |

# Cumulative Index

*Dictionary of Literary Biography,* Volumes 1-107
*Dictionary of Literary Biography Yearbook,* 1980-1990
*Dictionary of Literary Biography Documentary Series,* Volumes 1-8

# Cumulative Index

**DLB** before number: *Dictionary of Literary Biography,* Volumes 1-107
**Y** before number: *Dictionary of Literary Biography Yearbook,* 1980-1990
**DS** before number: *Dictionary of Literary Biography Documentary Series,* Volumes 1-8

## A

## B

## C

## D

## E

## F

## H

## K

## L

## M

## N

## O

## P

## S

## U



## V

## W

## Y



## Z

**(Continued from front endsheets)**

**80:** *Restoration and Eighteenth-Century Dramatists,* First Series, edited by Paula R. Backscheider (1989)

**81:** *Austrian Fiction Writers, 1875-1913,* edited by James Hardin and Donald G. Daviau (1989)

**82:** *Chicano Writers,* First Series, edited by Francisco A. Lomelí and Carl R. Shirley (1989)

**83:** *French Novelists Since 1960,* edited by Catharine Savage Brosman (1989)

**84:** *Restoration and Eighteenth-Century Dramatists,* Second Series, edited by Paula R. Backscheider (1989)

**85:** *Austrian Fiction Writers After 1914,* edited by James Hardin and Donald G. Daviau (1989)

**86:** *American Short-Story Writers, 1910-1945,* First Series, edited by Bobby Ellen Kimbel (1989)

**87:** *British Mystery and Thriller Writers Since 1940,* First Series, edited by Bernard Benstock and Thomas F. Staley (1989)

**88:** *Canadian Writers, 1920-1959,* Second Series, edited by W. H. New (1989)

**89:** *Restoration and Eighteenth-Century Dramatists,* Third Series, edited by Paula R. Backscheider (1989)

**90:** *German Writers in the Age of Goethe, 1789-1832,* edited by James Hardin and Christoph E. Schweitzer (1989)

**91:** *American Magazine Journalists, 1900-1960,* First Series, edited by Sam G. Riley (1990)

**92:** *Canadian Writers, 1890-1920,* edited by W. H. New (1990)

**93:** *British Romantic Poets, 1789-1832,* First Series, edited by John R. Greenfield (1990)

**94:** *German Writers in the Age of Goethe: Sturm und Drang to Classicism,* edited by James Hardin and Christoph E. Schweitzer (1990)

**95:** *Eighteenth-Century British Poets,* First Series, edited by John Sitter (1990)

**96:** *British Romantic Poets, 1789-1832,* Second Series, edited by John R. Greenfield (1990)

**97:** *German Writers from the Enlightenment to Sturm und Drang, 1720-1764,* edited by James Hardin and Christoph E. Schweitzer (1990)

**98:** *Modern British Essayists,* First Series, edited by Robert Beum (1990)

**99:** *Canadian Writers Before 1890,* edited by W. H. New (1990)

**100:** *Modern British Essayists,* Second Series, edited by Robert Beum (1990)

**101:** *British Prose Writers, 1660-1800,* First Series, edited by Donald T. Siebert (1991)

**102:** *American Short-Story Writers, 1910-1945,* Second Series, edited by Bobby Ellen Kimbel (1991)

**103:** *American Literary Biographers,* First Series, edited by Steven Serafin (1991)

**104:** *British Prose Writers, 1660-1800,* Second Series, edited by Donald T. Siebert (1991)

**105:** *American Poets Since World War II,* Second Series, edited by R. S. Gwynn (1991)

**106:** *British Literary Publishing Houses, 1820-1880,* edited by Patricia J. Anderson and Jonathan Rose (1991)

**107:** *British Romantic Prose Writers, 1789-1832,* First Series, edited by John R. Greenfield (1991)



## Documentary Series

**1:** *Sherwood Anderson, Willa Cather, John Dos Passos, Theodore Dreiser, F. Scott Fitzgerald, Ernest Hemingway, Sinclair Lewis,* edited by Margaret A. Van Antwerp (1982)

**2:** *James Gould Cozzens, James T. Farrell, William Faulkner, John O'Hara, John Steinbeck, Thomas Wolfe, Richard Wright,* edited by Margaret A. Van Antwerp (1982)

**3:** *Saul Bellow, Jack Kerouac, Norman Mailer, Vladimir Nabokov, John Updike, Kurt Vonnegut,* edited by Mary Bruccoli (1983)

**4:** *Tennessee Williams,* edited by Margaret A. Van Antwerp and Sally Johns (1984)

**5:** *American Transcendentalists,* edited by Joel Myerson (1988)

**6:** *Hardboiled Mystery Writers,* edited by Matthew J. Bruccoli and Richard Layman (1989)

**7:** *Modern American Poets,* edited by Karen L. Rood (1989)

**8:** *The Black Aesthetic Movement,* edited by Jeffrey Louis Decker (1991)